Unger's Concise Bible Dictionary

with

Complete Pronunciation Guide to Bible Names

Unger's Concise Bible Dictionary

Merrill F. Unger

with

Complete Pronunciation Guide to Bible Names

W. Murray Severance

BAKER BOOK HOUSE
Grand Rapids, Michigan 49506

First reprinted 1985 by Baker Books
a division of Baker Book House Company
P.O. Box 6287, Grand Rapids, MI 49516-6287

Seventeenth printing, July 2002

Printed in the United States of America

For current information about all releases from Baker Book
House, visit our web site:
http://www.bakerbooks.com

Bible Dictionary

Acknowledgments

Photograph sources are listed with each photo caption according to the following abbreviations:

HPS – Historical Pictures Service, Chicago
MPS – Matson Photo Service, Alhambra, Cal.
OI-UC – Oriental Institute, University of Chicago
RTHPL – Radio Times Hulton Picture Library, London
R.B. – Russ Busby, Billy Graham Evangelistic Association, Atlanta
UMP – University Museum, University of Pennsylvania, Philadelphia

AARON (ār'ŭn). The brother of Moses and Miriam and the first high priest of Israel. Although he had a sinful weakness common to fallen humanity (Exod. 32), in his high and holy calling he was a symbol of Christ, the Great High Priest. Both were divinely chosen. Aaron served as mediator between God and Israel. Christ is the only mediator between God and man (1 Tim. 2:5). Both had to be clean. As a sinner Aaron was purified through cleansing. As God incarnate Christ was intrinsically sinless. Both were perfectly clothed—Aaron with his coat, robe, and ephod and Christ in robes of glory and beauty. Both were crowned—Aaron with his miter and Christ with his many diadems (cf. Exod. 28:1-43). Both were consecrated and anointed—Aaron with oil and Christ with the Holy Spirit (cf. Lev. 8:22-30 with Matt. 3:16, 17 and John 17:16, 17). Both were blameless—Aaron outwardly and Christ totally. Christ is described as "holy, harmless, and undefiled" (Heb. 7:26). Like Moses, Aaron was excluded from the Promised Land (Num. 20:12) and died on Mount Hor in Edom (Num. 20:23-29).

ABANA, ABANAH (á-bá'ná). Named Chrysorrhoas ("Golden River") by the Greeks, Abana is one of the rivers of Syria mentioned by Naaman the leper (2 Kings 5:12). It is probably to be identified with the modern Barada, which has its source in the Antilebanon mountains 18 miles northwest of Damascus. After flowing through the city, the river loses itself in the marshy lake, Bahret el-Kibliyen, about 18 miles to the east. It waters fertile gardens and orchards.

ABARIM (ăb'á-rîm). The eastern highlands of Moab (Num. 27:12; 33:47). The word indicates the passageways that opened up the plains or grazing lands facing Jericho.

ABDON (ăb'dŏn). One of the judges of Israel (Judg. 12:13).

ABEDNEGO (á-bĕd'nė-gō). The Babylonian name given to Azariah, Daniel's companion in exile (Dan. 1:7). He and his companions were delivered from the fiery furnace (Dan. 3:8-30). The name is a dissimilation of *Abed-Nebo (Nabu)*, "servant of the god Nabu," to avoid giving a heathen name to a Jew.

ABEL (ā'bĕl). The second son of Adam and Eve. He was murdered by his brother Cain (Gen. 4:1-8; Matt. 23:35). Abel was the first human being to die, the first person on earth to be murdered, and the first man to be associated with Christ and to present an offering acceptable to God. Christ's blood is said to be better than Abel's because it cries out for mercy while Abel's cries out for vengeance (Heb. 12:24). Abel prefigures the spiritual man justified by faith in atoning blood and a divinely approved substitute (Heb. 9:22; 11:4).

ABI (ā'bî) (abbreviated from Abijah, "the Lord is a father"). The mother of Hezekiah, king of Judah. Although she was the wife of the faithless Ahaz, this queen mother must have been a godly woman. Following her name and that of her son occurs the following significant biblical phrase: "And he (Hezekiah) did that which was right in the sight of the Lord" (2 Kings 18:3). Though handicapped by the godless weakness of her husband, Abi faithfully and tenderly instructed her young son and future king of Judah in the ways of the Lord. When Hezekiah assumed office he rooted out idolatry and was able to stand against the power of Assyria, evidently because of the faith he received at his mother's knee (2 Kings 18:1 – 20:21).

ABIATHAR (à-bī′à-thär) ("father of excellence"). The son of Ahimelech the priest. He was a co-priest with his father at Nob. He alone escaped the massacre of Saul, later joining David at Keilah (1 Sam. 22:20-23; 23:6). He assisted David spiritually and helped take the ark to Jerusalem (1 Chron. 15:11; 27:34). He became one of David's counselors (2 Sam. 15:35-37; 17:15). He was deposed from office by Solomon for conspiracy (1 Kings 1, 2).

ABIGAIL (ăb′ĭ-gāl) (apparently "the father is rejoicing"). (1) The wife of Nabal. She was a woman of beauty, sagacity, and common sense, but was married to a sullen, foolish husband who took pains to insult David's kindness. On the death of Nabal (Hebrew, "fool"), she became one of David's wives (1 Sam. 25:3-44; 27:3; 2 Sam. 2:2). She was taken captive by the Amalekites when Ziklag was raided, but was rescued by David (1 Sam. 30:5, 18). She bore David a son named Chileab (2 Sam. 3:3) or Daniel (1 Chron. 3:1). (2) A half sister of David (1 Chron. 2:16). She was a daughter not of Jesse but of Nahash (cf. 2 Sam. 17:25). She was the mother of Amasa, at one time a commander in David's army (2 Sam. 19:13).

ABIHAIL (ăb′ĭ-hāl) ("the father is strength"). (1) The wife of Abishur in the line of Judah's descendants to David (1 Chron. 2:29). (2) A wife of King Rehoboam and a descendant of Eliab, David's brother (2 Chron. 11:18). However, some interpret the text to mean that Abihail was the mother of Rehoboam's wife, Mahalath.

ABIHU (à-bī′hū) ("my father is he," i.e. Jehovah). One of Aaron's sons. He saw God in his glory (Exod. 24:1, 9-11), yet dared to flout the ritual Law and was killed by holy fire (Lev. 10:1-7).

ABIJAH (à-bī′jà) ("my father is Jehovah"). (1) A son of Samuel (1 Sam. 8:2). (2) A priestly descendant of Eleazar (1 Chron. 24:4, 10; Luke 1:5). (3) A son of Jeroboam I (1 Kings 14:1-18). (4) A king of Judah, also called Abijam (2 Chron. 11: 20; 13:1; 1 Kings 14:31; 15:1). He was the son and successor of Rehoboam, censured for adherence to the corrupt religious policy of his father (1 Kings 15: 1-3). He won a great victory over the army of Jeroboam I (2 Chron. 13:1-19). His name also appears as Abijam, "father of sea (west)" in 1 Kings 14:31; 15:1. (5) Hezekiah's mother. See "Abi."

ABIMELECH (à-bĭm′ĕ-lĕk) ("the [divine] king is my father"). (1) A common surname of Philistine kings (Gen. 20:1-18; 21:22-32; 26:1-33). The titles "Pharaoh" among the Egyptians and "Agag" among the Amalekites offer parallels. (2) One of Gideon's sons. He massacred all his seventy brothers except Jotham. He reigned as king and died a violent death (Judg. 9: 1-57). (3) A priestly son of Abiathar (1 Chron. 18:16) according to the Massoretic Text, but perhaps a scribal error for Ahimelech (cf. 2 Sam. 8:17).

ABIRAM (à-bī′ràm) ("the exalted one is [my] father"). (1) One of the rebels who fomented an uprising against Moses (Num. 16:1-3). (2) The eldest son of Hiel of Bethel. He rebuilt Jericho about 870 B.C., thus incurring the curse of God pronounced by Joshua (Josh. 6:26). The foundations of the city were laid at the cost of Abiram's life (1 Kings 16:34).

ABISHAG (ăb′ĭ-shăg) (possibly "my father is a wanderer"). A very beautiful young woman called a "Shunamite," that is, a native of Shunem (1 Kings 1:3), a town near Jezreel and about five miles north of Mount Gilboa. She was brought to the aged David probably as a medical measure to restore the king's natural vigor (1 Kings 1:1-4, 15). Solomon regarded Abishag as David's wife and put Adonijah to death for treason when he requested her as his wife (1 Kings 2:13-25).

ABISHAI (à-bĭsh′à-ī) ("father of gift" or "my father is Jesse"). A high officer in

David's army and the brother of Joab and Asahel (2 Sam. 2:18; 23:18; 1 Chron. 11: 20, 21).

ABITAL (ăb′ĭ-tăl) ("the father is dew"). One of David's wives and the mother of Shephatiah, who was born at Hebron (2 Sam. 3:3-5; 1 Chron. 3:3).

ABNER (ăb′nēr) ("father is light"). A cousin of King Saul and captain of his army. At Saul's death he obtained for Ishbosheth (Saul's son) the allegiance of all the tribes except Judah (2 Sam. 2:8-10). Alienated by Ishbosheth, he defected to David's side (2 Sam. 3:7-10) but was treacherously murdered by Joab.

ABOMINATION. The rendering of the Hebrew word which refers to gross affront to God through idolatry — the violation of the first and second commandments of the Decalogue (Exod. 20:1-7). Thus Molech (Milcom), the national god of the Ammonites, is called "the abomination of the Ammonites" (1 Kings 11:5) and "Chemosh, the abomination of Moab" (1 Kings 11:7).

ABOMINATION OF DESOLATION. Daniel refers to this future event (Matt. 24:15) as the forcible interruption of the Jewish ritual of worship by the Roman prince (cf. Dan. 9:27). This wicked ruler will break his covenant with the Jews in the middle of Daniel's seventieth week and will introduce idolatrous "abominations" that will render the restored sanctuary in Jerusalem "desolate." This sacrilege is foreshadowed by the profanation of the Jewish Temple in the time of the Maccabees (Dan. 11:21-29) by Antiochus IV Epiphanes (175-164 B.C.).

ABRAHAM (ā′brȧ-hăm). The great representative of justification by faith (Gen. 15:6; Rom. 4:1-25). His original name, Abram ("high or exalted father," Gen. 11:27 — 17:5), was changed to Abraham ("father of a multitude") at the time of ratification of the Abrahamic Covenant and the promise of future progeny (Gen. 17:5). He was called out of Ur in southern Babylonia at about 2000 B.C. and lived in Haran in the Balikh-Habur region of Northern Mesopotamia until his father, Terah, died. Then he entered Canaan, which his ancestors through Isaac and Jacob were to inherit and through whom the promised Redeemer

was to come (Matt. 1:1). His faith and obedience as a "sojourner and pilgrim" and his offering of Isaac are portrayed as outstanding illustrations of justifying faith in action (Heb. 11:8-19; James 2:20-23).

ABSALOM (ăb′sȧ-lŏm) ("father of peace"). The third son of David by Maacah, daughter of the King of Geshur (2 Sam. 3:30). He murdered his older half brother, Amnon, and fled to Geshur (2 Sam. 13:1-39). After three years of exile and two years of banishment from the court, he was received back into favor. David was repaid by Absalom's plot against his throne (2 Sam. 15:1-15). The result was tragic civil war and the death of the usurper (2 Sam. 18:9-17).

ACACIA. A tree found in several species in Sinai. The most common is an evergreen, ten to eighteen feet tall and adorned with yellow flowers. The wood is hard and durable and was used in the Tabernacle for the ark, the altars and their staves, the table boards, and the bars and pillars (Exod. 25:10, 13, 23, 28; 26: 15, 26; 27:1, 6). Acacias flourished in the Jordan Valley at Beth-Shittah (House of Acacia) and Shittim (Acacias).

ACCAD (ăk′ăd). A city of the lower alluvial plain of Shinar in ancient Sumer. It is identified with Akkadian *Akkadu* and Sumerian *Agâde* of the cuneiform inscriptions. It formed the original kingdom of Nimrod (Gen. 10:10) and is listed with such other archeologically known cities as Erech (Uruk) and Babel (Bâb-il). It was the capital of Sargon's empire during the twenty-second and twenty-third centuries B.C. The city was destroyed with the fall of the Akkadian dynasty; its site still awaits discovery.

ACCO, ACRE (ăc′kō; ā′kêr). A harbor and city-state on the bay of Acre, north of Mount Carmel. The city is first named in Egyptian sources in the Execration Texts of the nineteenth century B.C. It is also referred to in the Amarna Letters (1370 B.C.) and other later sources. At the time of Israel's conquest of Canaan, the tribe of Asher pressed toward the coast but did not drive out the inhabitants of Acco (Judg. 1:31, 32). In 733 B.C. Acco came under Assyrian domination. It was renamed Ptolemais in Hellenistic times and came under Roman domination in 65 B.C. Paul landed there on his third voyage (Acts 21:7). The modern name is Acre.

ACHAEANS (á-kē'ăns). Also called Mycenaeans, this people inhabited Mycenae and environs (in northeastern Peloponnesos in Greece) from 1400 to 1100 B.C. The splendor of Mycenaean civilization was brought to light by Heinrich Schliemann in his excavations at Mycenae in 1874-1876 and by later excavators. At the height of their power the Mycenaeans were able to contend successfully with the Minoans of Crete for control of the Aegean Sea. Driven from their native home in Greece by the barbaric Dorians around 1200 B.C., they sought new homes on the mainland of Asia Minor. Failing this, they swept down the Eastern Mediterranean. Rameses III (1195-1175 B.C.) defeated them and turned them back to Palestine and the Phoenician Coast, where they established themselves and mingled with the Semitic Phoenicians. See also under "Philistines" and "Phoenicians."

ACHAIA (á-kā'ya). The Roman province which comprised most of ancient Greece south of Macedonia (Acts 18:12, 27; 19:21; Rom. 15:26; 1 Cor. 16:15; 2 Cor. 1:1; 9:2; 11:10; 1 Thess. 1:7, 8). The Achaian land appears in the Homeric poems as the home of the Achaians. At the time of Paul the proconsul of Achaia was Gallio (Acts 18:12) and the seat of administration was Corinth.

ACHAN (á'kăn). A man of Judah who violated the sacrificial ban in the assault of Jericho. He and his family were put to death in the valley of Achor ("trouble, distress"), south of Gilgal (Josh. 7:1-26).

ACHISH (á'kĭsh). A king of Gath in the time of David and Solomon. David resided incognito with him while fleeing Saul's anger (1 Sam. 21:10-15). Later Achish gave Ziklag to David (1 Sam. 21:1-12).

ACHSAH (äk'såh) ("an anklet"). A daughter of Caleb, who promised to give her in marriage to anyone who would capture Kiriath-Sepher (a city near Hebron). Othniel, Caleb's younger brother or half brother, captured the town and received the maiden as his wife. At Achsah's request her father gave her the upper and lower springs (Josh. 15:16-19), thus evidently sharing with her as he had with his three sons (named in 1 Chron. 4:15).

ACRE (ā'kêr). See "Acco."

ADAD. A Syrian deity whose death was associated with summer drought. His name is combined with Rammam, the storm god, as Hadad-Rimmon (Zech. 12:11).

ADAH (ā'dà) ("ornament" or perhaps "light"). (1) One of the two wives of Lamech and the first woman after Eve mentioned by name in the Bible. She was the mother of Jabal (whose descendants developed nomadic life) and of Jubal (who invented music – Gen. 4:19-22). As the two wives of Lamech, Adah and her sister Zillah are the first women in the Bible cited as being part of a polygamous household. They were in the godless line of Cain (Gen. 4:17-24). (2) One of the Canaanite wives of Esau and the daughter of Elon the Hittite (Gen. 36:2). She appears to be the same person as Bashemath (cf. Gen. 26:34). She and Esau's other wives were mothers of the Edomites, who subsequently migrated to Mount Seir (Gen. 36:8).

ADAM (ăd'əm). (1) The first human being created by God in his own image (Gen. 1:27; 2:7). Through the creation of woman from man and procreation through the two sexes, mankind was created in Adam. In addition to being a proper name, the term denotes mankind as a whole. Adam was created innocent but fell into sin by disobedience, bringing physical, spiritual, and eternal death upon mankind (Gen. 2:17 – 3:24). God's plan of redemption centers in Christ, the last "Adam," who delivers fallen humanity from threefold death and bestows upon believers threefold life – physical, spiritual, and eternal (John 3:16; 1 Cor. 15:45; Rom. 5:17). (2) A town east of the Jordan where the waters of the Jordan were dammed so that the Israelites could pass over (Josh. 3:9-17). The site is Tell ed-Damiyeh, located in the delta of the Jabbok shortly before it empties into the Jordan.

ADDER. In the King James Version this word is used to translate four Hebrew words that apparently refer to various species of venomous snakes. The *pethen* is the so-called "deaf adder" (because it is impervious to the voice of the snake-charmer — Psa. 58:4, 5). It is extremely venomous (Psa. 91:13) and seems identifiable with the *naja haje* of Egypt (Deut. 32:33; Job 20:14, 16; Isa. 11:8). The *akshūb* (Psa. 140:3; Rom. 3:13) is either a viper or an asp. The *siphōni* (Isa. 11:8; 14:29; 59:5) is perhaps the Great Viper, translated in the King James Version as "cockatrice." The *shephiphon* is the horned cerastes, a poisonous viper of Arabia and Egypt which reaches a length of three to six feet. It was worshiped at Thebes. It is mentioned in Genesis 49:17.

ADON, ADONAI (ä′dō-nī). Two closely related Hebrew words meaning "lord," "my lord," or "lordship." The primary designation of this name of Deity is *master;* it defines the relation of the Lord to the believer as a servant. The divine Lord and Master has a right to implicit obedience (Luke 6:46; John 13:13, 14). The servant has the right to divine direction in service (Isa. 6:8-12; cf. Exod. 4:10-12; Josh. 7:8-11).

ADONAI JEHOVAH (ä′dō-nī ji-hō′və). This compound name of Deity, translated "Lord God" in the King James Version, combines the Adonai character (see above) with the Jehovah meaning (see "Jehovah, Yahweh"). The prime emphasis is on the "Adonai" meaning (cf. Gen. 15:8; Deut. 3:24; 9:26; Josh. 7:7; 1 Kings 2:26; Isa. 7:7).

ADONIJAH (ă-dō-nī′jäh) ("my lord is Jehovah"). David's fourth son, who lost the succession of the throne to Solomon (1 Kings 1:5-53). Solomon executed him when his request for David's concubine, Abishag, was construed as a renewed attempt to claim the throne (1 Kings 2:13-25).

ADONIRAM (ă-dō-nī′räm) ("my lord is exalted"). An official in charge of forced labor under Solomon (1 Kings 4:6). He was stoned to death by the rebellious people, precipitating the division of the kingdom under Rehoboam. (cf. 1 Kings 12:18). He is evidently the same person as Adoram.

ADONIS (ə-dō′nis). The Greek representation of Tammuz. The death of this deity was associated with summer drought and the parching of vegetation.

ADONI-ZEDEK (ă-dō′nī-zĕ′dĕk) ("my lord is righteous"). An Amorite king of Jerusalem who joined a coalition of four other Canaanite kings against the Israelites and their allies at Gibeon. Joshua put these kings to death and buried them in a cave at Makkedah, where they had fled (Josh. 10:1-27).

ADOPTION. In regeneration a believer receives the nature of a child of God. By adoption (Greek *huiothesia*, "placing as a son") he receives the position of an adult son (Eph. 1:5; Gal. 3:23 – 4:7; 1 John 3:1, 2). The indwelling Spirit imparts the realization of sonship in the believer's present experience (Gal. 4:6). However, the full manifestation of sonship will not be witnessed till the resurrection, called "the redemption of the body" (Rom. 8:23; Eph. 1:14).

ADRAMMELECH (ă-drăm′mĕl-ĕk). (1) One of the sons of Sennacherib. He and his brother Sharezer murdered their father in 681 B.C. (2 Kings 19:37; Isa. 37:38). This event is also cataloged in the Babylonian Chronicle. (2) A pagan divinity imported from Sepharvaim to Samaria (2 Kings 17:31).

ADRAMYTTIUM (ă-dră-mĭt′tĭ-ŭm). A seaport in Mysia in the northwest part of the Roman province of Asia where Paul boarded "an Adramyttian ship" (Acts 27:2).

ADRIA, ADRIATIC (ä′drĭ-à). Originally the gulf into which the Po River of Northern Italy emptied. It was apparently named from the town of Adria located on this river. The name was later extended to include the entire body of water between the eastern shore of Italy and Illyricum, Dalmatia, Macedonia, and Achaia (Greece). In New Testament times it included the central Mediterranean Sea between Crete and Melita (Malta), where Paul was storm-tossed and shipwrecked.

ADULLAM (à-dŭl′lăm). A cave in which David hid from the murderous hate of Saul (1 Sam. 22:1). Nearby had existed a Canaanite city (Gen. 38:1, 2). Adullam was located in the territory of Judah (Josh. 12:15). It is mentioned by Micah (Mic. 1:15) and was inhabited after the exile (Neh. 11:30). It is identified with present-day Tell esh-Sheikh Madkhur, halfway between Jerusalem and Lachish.

ADUMMIM (à-dŭm'ĭm). A steep pass on the boundary between Judah and Benjamin (Josh. 15:7; 18:17) in the road from Jericho to Jerusalem. It is the traditional scene of the parable of the good Samaritan (Luke 10:25-37).

ADVENTS OF CHRIST. The two advents of the Messiah were foreseen in two aspects in the Old Testament—that of rejection and suffering (Isa. 53:1-9; Psa. 22:1-21) and that of earthly power and glory (Isa. 11:1-10; Jer. 23:5-8; Ezek. 37:20-28). These two aspects frequently blended together into one picture. The prophets themselves were puzzled by this apparent contradiction (1 Pet. 1:10-12). It was solved by partial fulfillment. Christ was born at Bethlehem (Mic. 5:2) of a virgin (Isa. 7:14), and at the beginning of his public ministry announced that the predicted kingdom was "at hand" (Matt. 4:17). The rejection, crucifixion, death, burial, and resurrection of the King followed in due course. Both before his death and after his resurrection the King repeatedly announced his second advent in power and glory.

The second advent bears a threefold relationship—to the church, to the nation Israel, and to the Gentile nations. To the church it will mean the descent of the Lord into the air to raise believers who have died and to translate believers who are still living (1 Thess. 4:13-18; 1 Cor. 15:51, 52; Phil. 3:20, 21). This is a constant expectation and happy hope (John 14:1-3; Tit. 2:13). To Israel the Lord's return will mean national regathering, conversion, and establishment in kingdom blessing (2 Sam. 7:16; Zech. 14:1-9). To the Gentile nations Christ's advent will bring judgment and destruction of the present political world-system (Matt. 25:31-46). This will be followed by worldwide Gentile conversion and participation in kingdom blessing (Isa. 2:2-4; 11:10).

ADVOCACY OF CHRIST. This activity of the glorified Savior in heaven is carried on in behalf of sinning saints (1 John 2:1) in the presence of the Father. By virtue of the eternal efficacy of his sacrifice, the divine Advocate restores his erring ones to fellowship (John 9:10; Psa. 23:3).

AEGEAN SEA (ė-jē'ăn). This body of water is not specifically named in Scripture but is included in the reference to "islands of the sea" in Isaiah 11:11. It is directly connected with many places which Paul visited (e.g. Acts 20:13-16; 21:1, 2). This beautiful, island-dotted body of water was bounded by Macedonia on the north, the island of Crete on the south, Greece on the west, and Asia Minor on the east. Its name probably came from Aegeus, the father of Theseus, who drowned himself there.

AGABUS (ăg'à-bŭs). A prophet of Jerusalem who predicted a great famine, which took place in the reign of Emperor Claudius (A.D. 41-54). At Caesarea he dramatized a prediction of Paul's fate at Jerusalem (Acts 21:10, 11).

AGAG (ā'găg). Apparently the common title of the kings of the Amalekites (Num. 24:7). The name is specifically used of the king of the Amalekites spared by Saul in disobedience to God's command (1 Sam. 15:1-35).

AGAR (ā'gàr). The Greek form of Hagar.

AGE. An age is a period of time (Greek *aion*) in which God accomplishes certain purposes. Through Christ God programmed or arranged the successive ages of time (Heb. 1:2). Prominent in these time periods is the Mosaic age, extending from the giving of the Law at Sinai to the death of Christ. Concurrent with part of the Mosaic age is the era covered by "the times of the Gentiles," extending from the captivity of the Jews in 605 B.C. to the second advent of Christ. Following the Mosaic age is the church age, extending from Pentecost to the rapture. After this period the Tribulation and the second advent will witness the renewed divine dealing with Israel preparatory to the kingdom age. The latter will be inaugurated by the second advent of Christ and will end "the times of the Gentiles."

AGRICULTURALIST. The farmer was one of the oldest types of workers in Palestine. Good farming can be traced back to 7500 B.C. in the vicinity of Jericho, where irrigation was prominent. On the tributaries of the Jordan River irrigation cultures were common in the prehistoric period. But from the earliest times most of Palestine's farmers depended on rain. The long drought from June till October

A sower spreads seed in the stony Kidron Valley east of Jerusalem. (© *MPS*)

was broken by the "early rains." By November or early December the moistened earth was ready for plowing and sowing. The copious winter showers gave the crops their major moisture, but they were brought to maturity by the "latter rains" of March and April.

Wheat and barley constituted the chief grains. Various legumes, such as lentils, peas, and beans formed a second crop. Vegetables were also grown with onions and garlic. Various herbs and seeds furnished condiments. Farmers were busy harvesting the barley crop in April and May, and it preceded the wheat harvest by several weeks or sometimes a month. By that time a summer crop of millet had been sown on land left fallow through the winter. Sickles were used by the reapers.

AGRIPPA (à-grĭp′à). (1) "Herod the King" (Acts 12:1), the grandson of Herod the Great. He is known as Herod Agrippa I. He received from Emperor Caligula both his title and his territory (the regions northeast of Palestine). Galilee and Peraea were added to his territory in A.D. 39 and Judea and Samaria in A.D. 41. His sudden death at the age of 54 (A.D. 44) is narrated in Acts 12:20-23 and is corroborated by Josephus (*Antiquities* XIX: 8,2). (2) The son of Herod Agrippa I, known as Herod Agrippa II. He is best known to Bible readers for his encounter with Paul at Caesarea (Acts 25:13—26: 32), whom he banteringly charged with

trying to make a Christian of him (Acts 26:28).

AHASUERUS (à-hăz-u-ē′rŭs). (1) Xerxes I, King of Persia during 485-465 B.C. and the husband of Esther (Esth. 1:2; 2:16, 17). (2) The father of Darius the Mede (Dan. 9:1).

AHAZ (ā′hăz). A wicked, idolatrous king of Judah (732-716 B.C.). His name means "he has grasped" and is an abbreviation of Jehoahaz. He refused to join an anti-Assyrian coalition with Pekah of Israel and Rezin of Damascus. The result was an invasion of Judah by these two powers (2 Kings 16:5; Isa. 7:1-9). Ahaz' trust in Assyria cost Judah a century-and-a-half of vassalage and financial drain.

AHAZIAH (ā-hà-zī′à) ("the Lord has laid hold of"). (1) A king of Israel and the son and successor of Ahab. He ruled during 853-852 B.C. (1 Kings 22:51—2 Kings 1: 18). He was a weak ruler dominated by an idolatrous mother. During his brief reign Moab revolted (2 Kings 1:1) and Ahaziah's maritime venture with Jehoshaphat of Judah ended in disaster (2 Chron. 20:35-37). (2) A king of Judah and the youngest son of Jehoram (2 Chron. 22:1). He reigned barely a year, being slain by Jehu (2 Kings 9:16-28; 2 Chron. 22:6-9).

AHIJAH (à-hī′jäh). A prophet from Shiloh. He protested Solomon's idolatry and symbolically predicted the breakup of the kingdom (1 Kings 11:28-40). He also denounced Jeroboam's idolatry and foretold the extinction of his house and the eventual downfall of Israel (1 Kings 14: 1-16).

AHIKAM (à-hī′kăm) ("my brother has arisen"). A member of Josiah's deputation to the prophetess Huldah (2 Kings 22:12-14; 2 Chron. 34:20, 21). He became Jeremiah's benefactor (Jer. 26:24) and was the father of Gedaliah, the governor appointed by Nebuchadnezzar (2 Kings 25:22; Jer. 39:14).

AHIMAAZ (à-hĭm′à-ăz) ("my brother is wrath"). A son of Zadok and a helper of David during Absalom's revolt (2 Sam. 15:27, 36; 17:17-22). He was one of the messengers who brought news of Absalom's defeat (2 Sam. 18:19-32).

AHIMELECH (à-hĭm′é-lĕk) ("brother of a king"). The priest at Nob who was slain by Saul for giving David showbread and

Goliath's sword (1 Sam. 21:1 – 22:23).

AHINOAM (a-hĭn'ō-ăm) ("the brother is delight"). (1) Saul's wife, a daughter of Ahimaaz, and the first queen of Israel (1 Sam. 14:50). She presided over Saul's rustic palace-fort at Gibeah and suffered under her royal spouse when he became mentally unbalanced and spiritually oppressed by demon power. She had great consolation in her noble son, Jonathan (cf. 2 Sam. 1:26), who may have inherited her qualities. Ahinoam was also the mother of two other sons, Ishui and Melchisua, and two daughters, Merab and Michal (the latter becoming David's first wife). (2) One of David's eight wives. She was a native of Jezreel, a town at the head of the Valley of Jezreel (present-day Zerein), although Jezreel in Judah (Josh. 15: 56; 1 Sam. 25:43) may be meant. Ahinoam and Abigail were taken captive by the Amalekites at Ziklag, but David and his 600 followers rescued them. After Saul's death David took Ahinoam and Abigail to reside at Hebron. Both undoubtedly witnessed David's anointing as king. Ahinoam bore Amnon, who was murdered by Absalom for dishonoring Tamar.

AHITHOPHEL (a-hĭth'ŏ-fĕl). One of David's advisors who defected to Absalom (2 Sam. 16:23; 15:12, 31).

AHITUB (a-hĭ'tŭb) ("brother of good"). A son of Phinehas, grandson of Eli (1 Sam. 14:3), and father of Ahimelech the priest (1 Sam. 22:9).

AHOLAH, OHOLAH (a-hō'läh) ("her tent"). A feminine name employed by Ezekiel to personify Samaria and the kingdom of Israel as a woman of loose character, unfaithful to the Lord (Ezek. 23:1-49). She is designated as the elder sister of Aholibah (representing Jerusalem and the Southern Kingdom), because the Northern Kingdom was the larger.

AHOLIBAH, OHOLIBAH (a-hōl'ĭ-bäh) ("my tent is in her"). See "Aholah."

AHOLIBAMAH, OHOLIBAMAH (a-hōl-ĭ-bä'mäh) ("my tent is a high place"). A wife of Esau and daughter of Anah the Hivite (Gen. 36:2). She is also called Judith ("praiseworthy") in Genesis 26:34.

AI (ā'ī). A Canaanite city near Bethel (Gen. 12:8) which was destroyed by Joshua (Josh. 7, 8). The site presently held to be Ai is et-Tell, located two miles east-southeast of Bethel and identified as modern Beitin. However, excavations at et-Tell yield confusing evidence that proves it is not the Ai of Scripture. Further archeological research will one day probably locate the true Ai.

AIJALON, PLAIN OF (ā'ja-lŏn). See under "Plains of Scripture."

AKKADIANS (ɔ-kā'dē-ɔns). The Semitic Akkadians settled in Northern Babylonia about 3000 B.C. and gradually began to supersede the earlier non-Semitic Sumerians until they became dominant in both northern Babylonia (Akkad) and southern Babylonia (Sumer). This took place in the first Akkadian state under Sargon I and his successors (2371-2191 B.C.). The founding of Akkad (Agade) is attributed to Nimrod (Gen. 10:10). For a period the revival of Sumerian power threatened to put a stop to Akkadian expansion. About 2000 B.C., however, new Semitic invasions helped to drive the Sumerian culture out of existence. Akkadian became the official language of all Mesopotamia and, in succeeding centuries, the lingua franca of the ancient world. Early literary remains of the Sumerians, such as the Epic of Gilgamesh, were inscribed in Akkadian and preserved for posterity in cuneiform on clay tablets.

ALEXANDER (ăl-ĕx-ăn'dēr). (1) A common Hellenistic name (cf. Acts 4:6; 19: 33). (2) A pernicious false teacher mentioned in 1 Timothy 1:20. (3) A coppersmith or metalworker who was a bitter enemy of Paul (2 Tim. 4:14).

Young Alexander the Great founded the Macedonian (Grecian) Empire. (© *RTHPL*)

ALEXANDER THE GREAT (ăl-ĕx-ăn'

dēr). Destroyer of the Persian Empire. From 336 B.C. till his death in 323 B.C. he conquered the civilized world of the time. His generals founded a number of Hellenistic kingdoms out of his conquests. The Herods of the New Testament era constitute the epilogue to this era. Their Hellenizing influence produced the agonies of the Jews in the Maccabean age and resulted in the tensions that surrounded the Cross.

ALEXANDRIA (ăl-ĕg-zăn′drĭ-á). The cosmopolitan city founded by Alexander the Great in 331 B.C. about 14 miles from the westernmost mouth of the Nile. It was the capital of Egypt during the Hellenistic and Roman periods. It ranked with Rome as one of the most important cities of the Greco-Roman world. Its lighthouse (Pharos) was one of the seven wonders of the ancient world. Its great library was world-famous.

ALGUM (perhaps a variant form of Almug). A timber imported by Solomon from Ophir and Lebanon (1 Kings 10:11, 12). Its identity is uncertain. It is thought to be red sandalwood, native to India and Ceylon.

ALMOND. An early-blossoming nut tree of Palestine. It is called in Hebrew shāqēd, "the awakening one." Two varieties are common — the bitter, with gorgeous white blossoms, and the sweet, with roseate blossoms. Almonds were sent by Jacob to the Egyptian dignitary (Gen. 43:11). Aaron's rod budded with almond blossoms (Num. 17:8). The cups of the branches of the golden candlestick were in the form of almond blossoms (Exod. 25:33, 34). Jeremiah envisioned the rod of an almond tree, symbolizing the Lord's wakefulness (Jer. 1:11, 12).

ALMS. The Mosaic Law encouraged benevolence to the needy (Deut. 15:7-11; 24:19-22; Lev. 19:9, 10). Our Lord also commended true almsgiving (Matt. 19:21; Luke 11:41; 12:33). He directed that it be done discreetly and sacrificially (Matt. 6:2-4; Luke 12:33, 34). He and his disciples practiced it (John 13:29). Paul encouraged cheerful giving (2 Cor. 9:6, 7; cf. Heb. 13:16). Paul was diligent in collecting for the poor of Jerusalem and Judea (Rom. 15:25-28; 1 Cor. 16:1; Gal. 2:10).

ALOES. The species *Aquilaria agallocha* or eaglewood, a tropical tree native to Southern Asia. It has fragrant wood and clustered flowers. It is used as an incense and spice ingredient, as well as in medicine and perfumery (Psa. 45:8; Prov. 7:17; Song 4:14; John 19:39). Lign-aloes is probably referred to in Numbers 24:6.

ALPHA AND OMEGA (Grk. ′alpha; ōmega). The first and last letters of the Greek alphabet. The expression "alpha and omega" frequently refers to Christ as "the first and the last," the eternal God. See Revelation 1:8; 21:6; 22:13.

ALPHAEUS (ăl-fē′ŭs). (1) The father of Levi the tax collector (Mark 2:14). He is generally identified with Matthew the Apostle. (2) The father of the apostle James (Matt. 10:3; Mark 3:18; Luke 6:15; Acts 1:13).

ALTAR. A raised mound of earth or stone or other type of platform on which sacrifices were made (Exod. 20:24; 1 Sam. 14:33-35; cf. Judg. 6:19-21; 13:19, 20). Indoor altars were fashioned of wood or metal, and horns were often added. Anyone who grasped these horns obtained divine protection (1 Kings 1:50; 2:28).

ALTAR OF BURNT OFFERING. The brass or bronze altar was situated at the threshold of the Tabernacle. It symbolized the fact that the shedding of blood is basic to man's access to God. It prefigures Christ as our burnt sacrifice, offering himself without spot to God (Exod. 27:1-8; Heb. 9:14). The bronze signifies divine judgment in action (Num. 21:9; John 3:14).

ALTAR OF INCENSE. Situated in the holy place in front of the veil, the altar of incense portrays Christ as the believer's intercessor (John 17:1-26; Heb. 7:25), through whom the believer's praise and prayer rise up to God (Heb. 13:15). The incense, offered twice daily, symbolizes prayer, which rises fragrantly and acceptably to heaven (Rev. 5:8; 8:3). The acacia wood overlaid with gold speaks of Christ's humanity united to deity (Exod. 30:1-5).

AMALEK, AMALEKITES (ăm′á-lĕk; ăm′á-lĕk-īts). Nomadic desert people who were descendants of Esau (Gen. 36:12). At the time of the Exodus they were concentrated about Kadesh-barnea, southwest of the Dead Sea and west of Edom (Num. 13:29; 14:25). They clashed with Israel at Rephidim and were defeated (Exod. 17:8-13). Israel's foolhardy attempt to enter Palestine in self-will after their failure at Kadesh-barnea resulted in defeat by the Amalekites at Hormah (Num. 14:40-45). During the period of the Judges the Amalekites assisted the Moabites and the Midianites in their attempt to occupy and raid Israelite territory (Judg. 3:12-14; 6:1-6). Saul and David fought them (1 Sam. 15:1-33; 30:1-20). They were not completely defeated until Hezekiah's day (1 Chron. 4:43).

AMASA (ăm′á-sä). Commander of Absalom's rebel army (2 Sam. 17:25). He was defeated by Joab (2 Sam. 18:6-8) and pardoned by David. He replaced Joab as David's army commander (2 Sam. 19:13) but was treacherously murdered by Joab (2 Sam. 20:9-12).

AMAZIAH (ăm-á-zī′á) ("the Lord is mighty"). (1) A king of Judah (2 Kings 14:1-20) and a son of Joash (2 Chron. 24:27). He defeated the Edomites but was defeated by Israel. He fled to Lachish when a conspiracy was formed against him, and was murdered there (2 Chron. 25:1-28).

AMMINADAB (ăm-mĭn′á-dăb). Father-in-law of Aaron (Exod. 6:23) and an ancestor of David (Ruth 4:19; Matt. 1:4; Luke 3:33).

AMMONITES (ăm′mŏn-īts). Descendants of Lot (Gen. 19:38). They occupied Transjordan from the River Arnon on the south to the River Jabbok on the north. Their capital was at Rabbath-Ammon (present-day Amman, capital of Jordan). They were related to Israel but were in frequent conflict with the twelve tribes. They joined the Moabites in hiring Balaam to curse Israel (Deut. 23:3-6). Periodically they oppressed Israel (Judg. 3:13; 10:6-9) and were subdued by David (2 Sam. 11, 12). The Ammonites invaded Judah in Jehoshaphat's reign, but were defeated (2 Chron. 20:1-30). They paid tribute to Uzziah and Jotham (2 Chron. 26:8; 27:5). After the fall of Jerusalem they frustrated the attempt of the Jews to form a new community (2 Kings 25:25; Neh. 4:3, 7, 8). They were denounced as enemies of Israel by the prophets (Jer. 49:

1-6; Ezek. 25:1-7; Amos 1:13-15; Zeph. 2:8-11).

AMNON (ăm′nŏn) ("faithful"). David's firstborn son. He was murdered by Absalom for defiling the latter's sister Tamar (2 Sam. 13:1-29).

AMON, AMUN (ā′mŏn). (1) A king of Judah and son of Manasseh (2 Kings 21:19-26). His two-year reign was terminated by his assassination, probably as a victim of court intrigue. He followed the gross idolatry of his father. (2) A local god of Thebes (No). Through union with the sun-god, Amun became the chief Egyptian deity under the eighteenth dynasty (cf. Jer. 46:25; Nah. 3:8, RSV margin).

AMORITES (ăm′ŏ-rīts). A people of Canaan (Gen. 10:16) often listed with the Hittites, Perizzites, etc. as enemies of Israel (Exod. 33:2). They were dispersed throughout the central highland ridge and in the hill country east of Jordan. The name became a general designation for the inhabitants of Canaan (Gen. 48:22; Josh. 24:15). At the time of Israel's conquest of the land Amorite kings ruled most of East Jordan and had to be conquered (Josh. 12:1-6; Judg. 1:36).

From about 2500 B.C. Sumerian and Akkadian inscriptions refer to the Amorites as desert people unacquainted with civilized life. Their center of population was in the mountains of Basar (probably Jebel Bishri, north of Palmyra). About 2000 B.C. the Amorites moved into Babylonia in force. They were in part responsible for the fall of the powerful third dynasty of Ur, and took over the rule of several towns, including Larsa. They established a dynasty at Babylon. Under the great king Hammurabi they conquered the two other important Amorite states of Ashur and Mari (1750 B.C.).

Another Amorite group had settled in the Lebanon district and were engaged in horse trading. This Amorite kingdom flourished into the Amarna Period and the nineteenth dynasty in Egypt, when tribute was recorded from the state of Amor. The port of Amur apparently was Sumur (present-day Tell Simiriyan, south of Arvad; cf. Josh. 13:4). Other Amorite infiltrations into Syrian Palestine resulted in the numerous Amorite kingdoms that withstood Israel's conquest of Palestine (1400-1375 B.C.).

AMOS (ā'mŏs) ("burden"). A prophet who was a native of Tekoa in Judah, about six miles south of Bethlehem (Amos 1:1). He was a humble shepherd and dresser of sycamore trees (7:14, 15). He prophesied to the Northern Kingdom and clashed with the worldly, compromising high priest, Amaziah, at Bethel (765-750 B.C. — Amos 7:10-17).

AMPHIPOLIS (ăm-fĭp'ō-lĭs). The capital city of the first district of Macedonia. It was located about 30 miles southwest of Philippi on the Via Egnatia. Paul passed through this important city on his way to Thessalonica (Acts 17:1).

AMULET. An ornament or charm worn partly for adornment and partly as protection against evil spirits. While the wood amulet actually appears only once in the Bible (Isa. 3:20) in a list of feminine adornments, the earrings which Jacob buried at Shechem (Gen. 35:4) and the crescents which were hung from the necks of Midianite camels (Judg. 8:21) were also apparently amulets. Various kinds of amulets have been found in Palestinian excavations.

ANAH (ā'näh) (perhaps "listening to"). The mother of Esau's wife, Oholibamah, and grandmother of Esau's children (Gen. 36:2, 14, 18, 25). She was apparently contemporary with Isaac's wife, Rebekah, who opposed her son's marriage with the Hittite line because it was descended from Hagar (Gen. 26:34, 35).

ANANIAS (ăn-à-nī'ăs) (The Greek form of Hananiah). (1) An early Christian who, with his wife Sapphira, sinned the sin that resulted in physical death (1 John 5:16) by lying to the Holy Spirit (Acts 5:1-11). (2) A Christian at Damascus who was sent to restore sight to Saul of Tarsus after his conversion and to admit him to fellowship by baptism (Acts 9:10-18). (3) A high priest prominent in the political intrigues in Jerusalem from A.D. 48 to his assassination in A.D. 67.

ANATHEMA (à-năth'ē-mà). When a person, animal, or inanimate object was put under a ban or curse (Hebrew *ḥerem*) because of connection with idolatry (Exod. 22:20), it was said to be devoted to destruction or accursed (Lev. 27:28, 29).

In the case of a person or animal it was unredeemable and was to be put to death. In the case of an inanimate object indestructible by fire (such as silver or gold) it was to be put in the Lord's treasury. In the New Testament the ban or curse acquired a more generalized sense. It became expressive of very strong feeling (Rom. 9:3) or of reprehension or severe condemnation (1 Cor. 12:3; 16:22; Gal. 1:9).

ANATHOTH (ăn'à-thŏth). A priestly city in Benjamin, the birthplace of Jeremiah (Jer. 1:1). The name has been preserved in Anata, three miles north of Jerusalem. The original town, however, was situated at the ruin of Ras el-Karrubeh, about a half-mile to the southwest.

ANDREW (Greek *Andreas*, "manly"). The fisherman brother of Simon Peter (John 1:44; Matt. 4:18; Mark 1:16-18; Luke 6:14).

ANGEL OF THE LORD. This expression in the Old Testament usually indicates the presence of God in angelic form (Gen. 16:7-14; 22:10-18; Exod. 3:1-6; Judg. 2:1-5; 6:11-24; 13:1-23).

ANGELS. Angels are a special order of created beings. Unlike humans, they are purely spirit beings (Psa. 104:4; Heb. 1:14). However, they have power to become visible in the semblance of human form (Gen. 19:1-22; 1 Kings 19:5-8; 2 Kings 1:3, 15; Acts 12:7-9). Wisdom and strength are chief attributes of the angelic order (2 Sam. 14:20; Psa. 103:20). They belong to the realm of the spiritual and supernatural and are very numerous (Psa. 68:17; Matt. 26:53; Heb. 12:22; Rev. 5:11). They are sometimes called "sons of God" (Gen. 6:2; Job 1:6; 2:1).

Angels are either fallen or unfallen. The host of fallen angels are apparently the demons. They followed Satan in the primeval revolt (Isa. 14:12-14; Ezek. 28:11-19). Some of them are unbound and are free to do Satan's bidding. Others are chained in darkness, awaiting judgment (2 Pet. 2:4). Certain imprisoned demons will be let loose during the Great Tribulation (Rev. 16:12-14).

Unfallen angels function as "ministering spirits" to believers (Heb. 1:14). This ministry apparently begins in infancy and continues throughout our earthly life (Matt. 18:10; cf. Psa. 91:11). It particularly concerns physical safety and the well-being of God's children (1 Kings 19:5; Psa. 34:7; 91:11; Dan. 6:22; Matt. 2:13, 19; 4:11; Acts 5:19; 12:7-10). See also "Archangels" and "Cherubim and Seraphim."

ANIMALS. Ever since the fall of man, domestic animals have held an important place in the history of God's people. The shedding of sacrificial blood (typifying fallen man's need of a Redeemer) has always been the only way of access to God (Gen. 3:21; 4:1-7). Israelite religion streamed with the blood of sacrifices, for without the shedding of blood there is "no remission" (Heb. 9:7, 22; cf. Exod. 12:13; 29:16; 30:10; Lev. 1:5; Eph. 1:7; Col. 1:20; 1 Pet. 1:2; Rev. 1:5).

Domesticated animals also played a very important role in the daily lives of people in Bible lands. Oxen, sheep, and goats constituted the ordinary man's wealth, and a common word for cattle was *miqneh*, denoting "property." The patient ox served as a beast of burden and pulled the plowshare that tilled the earth. Sheep furnished wool for clothing. Goats furnished milk from which various dairy products were made. All of these animals furnished meat. But only those animals that chewed the cud and had split hoofs (such as the above) were clean and fit for food under the Mosaic Law (Lev. 11:1-8; Deut. 14:4-8). The ass was also a common beast of burden, but could not be yoked with an ox (Deut. 22:10). Crossbreeding was not allowed; hence mules had to be imported into Israel. Lambs and kids served as pets. Dogs in Israel were considered unclean and were rarely domesticated as household pets. In the Roman Empire, however, both dogs and cats were used as pets. The cat is not mentioned in the Bible.

ANISE (ăn'ĭs). A flavoring and condiment, the correct rendering in Matthew 23:23 being "dill." Dill (*Anethum gaveolens*) is of the same order as anise, resembling it in appearance and properties but being much more commonly grown. Anise (*Pimpinella anisum*), resembling caraway, was only occasionally cultivated in the East for use as a seasoning and a medicine. Dill is used in flavoring pickles and yields an oil used in medicine.

ANKLET. "Bangles" or "anklets" are rendered "tinkling ornaments about their feet" (Isa. 3:18), from the Hebrew root meaning "rattle" or "tinkle." They appear in Isaiah's description of the luxurious articles of the daughters of Zion. Numerous ankle bracelets have been recovered by archeological excavations all over Palestine. Most of them are of bronze. At Lachish they are found in position in graves.

ANNA (ăn'à) (Greek form of Hebrew *Hannah*, "grace"). The first woman to acclaim Christ as the Messiah (Luke 2: 36-38). She was a widow, the daughter of Phanuel of the tribe of Asher. At the age of 84 she visited the Temple daily; she was there when the infant Jesus was brought in to be dedicated. As a prophetess she recognized him and proclaimed him as the long-promised Messiah.

ANNAS (ăn'às) (Greek for *Hanan*, contraction of *Hananiah*, "Jehovah is gracious"). A high priest at Jerusalem when John the Baptist began his ministry (Luke 3:2). He was deposed as high priest by the Roman procurator Valerius Gratus about A.D. 15. Although no longer officiating when Jesus was arrested, he still bore the honorary title (Luke 3:2; Acts 4:6; cf. John 18:13, 24).

ANNIHILATION. The erroneous belief that the wicked will be wholly destroyed and blotted out of conscious existence in eternity. Scripture shows the falsity of this notion (Jude v. 13; Rev. 14:9-11).

ANOINT, ANOINTING. Anointing with oil was a common custom in Bible lands (Deut. 28:40; Ruth 3:3; Mic. 6:15). Such anointing was a mark of respect which a host often paid his guests (Psa. 23:5; Luke 7:46). Anointing with oil was also a rite by which prophets (1 Kings 19:16; Psa. 105:15), priests (Exod. 40:15; Num. 3:3; Exod. 29:29; Lev. 16:32), and kings (1 Sam. 9:16; 10:1; 1 Kings 1:34) were officially inaugurated into their office. Under the Jewish economy the sick were also anointed with oil (Mark 6:13; James 5:14).

The Messiah was the "Anointed One" par excellence (Psa. 2:2; Isa. 61:1; Luke 4:18). Christians are also anointed with the Holy Spirit by God (2 Cor. 1:21).

ANT. Any of a group of black or red insects, generally wingless, that live in colonies. The ant furnishes an example of industry and forethought. That the ant of Palestine stores food on which to live in winter is intimated in the Bible (Prov. 6: 6-8; 30:24, 25) and clearly asserted in similar Arabic maxims.

ANTELOPE. A ceremonially clean animal fit for food and captured in nets. It is clear that the gazelle, a species of antelope, was found in biblical Palestine. But it is not certain that other antelopes had their habitat there. Some take the animal to be one of the hollow-horned mammals (*Bovidae*) generally classified as antelopes.

ANTICHRIST. The Antichrist of the last days is "the man of sin," "the son of perdition" (2 Thess. 2:3), the devil-indwelt opposer of Christ (Rev. 13:1-10). "Many antichrists" (1 John 2:18) and those who have the "spirit of antichrist" (1 John 4: 3) precede and prepare the way for the final Antichrist, the "vile person" of Daniel 11:21. The denial of the incarnation of the eternal Word (John 1:14) is the supreme mark of all antichrists.

ANTIOCH (ăn′tĭ-ŏk). (1) A great Hellenistic city in northwest Syria (modern Antakya, Turkey). It ranked with Rome and Alexandria as one of the three greatest cities of the Greco-Roman world. Through its seaport, Seleucia Pieria, it was a great commercial emporium connecting land and sea routes east and west. It was also a great cultural center and the metropolis from which early Christianity spread to Asia Minor and Europe. The church there (Acts 13:1) fostered Paul's great missionary tours (Acts 13:2−20: 38). (2) A Hellenistic city founded by Seleucus I (300 B.C.) in the lake district of southwest Asia Minor. In 188 B.C. the city was declared free after the defeat of Antiochus III by the Romans. Antony made it a part of the domain of the Galatian king Amyntas in 36 B.C. After Amyntas' death the city was incorporated in the Roman province of Galatia (25 B.C.). Paul preached in the synagogue to a congregation of Jews who had settled there in Seleucid days and to Greek-speaking Gentiles (Acts 13:14-43). The ancient site has been found two miles to the east of modern Yalvac; some of its ancient splendor has been unearthed.

ANTIOCHUS THE GREAT (ăn-tī′ŏ-kŭs) (Greek, "withstander"). Antiochus III (223-187 B.C.), king of Syria, sixth ruler of the dynasty of the Seleucidae. He won a great victory at Paneas in 198 B.C., thereby gaining a dominant position in the East. He was defeated by Rome at Magnesia in 190 B.C.

ANTIOCHUS EPIPHANES (ăn-tī′ŏ-kŭs e-pĭf′ȯ-nēz). The eighth ruler of the house of Seleucidae during 175-163 B.C. (1 Macc. 1:10; 6:16). A fanatical Hellenizer, he clashed with the Jews and persecuted them insanely. He robbed and desecrated the Temple, commanded the sacrifice of swine, destroyed the sacred Hebrew books, and forbade circumcision. His outrages precipitated the Maccabean revolt (1 Macc. 1:41-53). He died shortly after receiving news of the Jewish uprising (1 Macc. 6:1-16).

ANTIPAS (ăn′tĭ-pȧs) (a shortened form of Antipater). A son of Herod the Great, he inherited the Galilean and Perean portions of his father's kingdom. He imprisoned and executed John the Baptist (Mark 6:14-28) and had a brief encounter with Jesus when the latter was sent to him by Pilate for judgment (Luke 23:7, 15). Our Lord called him "that fox" (Luke 13:31, 32). In A.D. 39 he was deposed by the Emperor Caligula, and ended his days in exile.

ANTONIA, TOWER OF (ăn-tō′nĭ-ȧ). A palatial guard tower rebuilt by Herod the Great at the northwest corner of the Temple court at Jerusalem. It served as a royal residence as well as soldiers' quarters. The fortress is not explicitly named in Scripture. It is, however, alluded to as "barracks" (AV "castle") in Acts 21:34-37; 22:24; 23:10, 16, 32.

APE (Hebrew *qōph*, a loan word from Egyptian *gwf*, "monkey"). It is impossible to identify with exactness the "apes" which Solomon's Red Sea Tarshish fleet (1 Kings 10:22) brought back from Ophir (apparently located in Somaliland, Africa). It is likely that these animals were not apes at all (tailless) but were instead monkeys (having tails) or baboons. These were well-known in Egypt, where the god Thoth was frequently represented by a baboon. The commonest baboon in this area is the Arabian species (*papio hamadyas*) found in Arabia, Abyssinia, and the Sudan.

APHRODITE (ăf-rə-dī'tē). A goddess identified with the Semitic Ashtoreth (Astarte), who mourned the dead Adonis. Sacred prostitution of the Fertility Cult was associated with this polluted deity. See "Ashtoreth."

APOLLONIA (ăp-ŏ-lō'nĭ-à). A Greek city in Macedonia through which Paul and Silas passed on the way to Thessalonica (Acts 17:1). The city was situated on the Via Egnatia, 30 miles from Amphipolis and 38 miles from Thessalonica.

APOLLONIUS (ăp'ŏ-lō'nĭ-ŭs). An official under Antiochus Epiphanes who persecuted the Jews (1 Macc. 1:29-32; 2 Macc. 5:24-26). He was defeated and slain by Judas Maccabeus (1 Macc. 3:10).

APOLLOS (à-pŏl'lŏs). An Alexandrian Jew and disciple of John the Baptist (Acts 18:24-28). He knew only John's preparatory baptism, but was taught the truth of the Spirit's baptism and the Christian message by Priscilla and Aquila. Under Paul's ministry Apollos' disciples received the Holy Spirit (Acts 19:1-7), for which John's baptism prepared the way.

APOSTASY. A doctrinal departure by professed believers who have never been regenerated and who deliberately reject the cardinal Christian truths of Christ's deity and redemptive sacrifice (1 John 4: 1-3; 2 Pet. 2:1). Apostasy differs from error and heresy, which are consonant with saving faith. Apostasy is irremediable, and awaits divine judgment (2 Pet. 2:1-3).

APOSTLE. The word denotes a "messenger," a "delegate," one "dispatched with orders." Apostles were chosen by the Lord himself and were endued with sign-gifts and miraculous powers attesting their office (Matt. 10:1; Acts 5:15, 16; 16: 16-18). An apostle was also an eyewitness of the resurrected Christ (Acts 1:22; 1 Cor. 9:1). Except in the general sense of a "messenger for Christ," apostles have not existed since the early days of the Church.

APOTHECARY. The King James Version's rendering for a perfumer (one who prepared cosmetics and mixed fragrant unguents). A typical king is pictured in 1 Samuel 8:13 as requiring the services of "perfumers" (RV margin, RSV) as well as "cooks and bakers." Archeology illustrates the reference. The great palace at Mari on the middle Euphrates had its own perfumery in the eighteenth century B.C. It supplied large quantities of various ointments for the royal officials, for personal use, and for ritual festivals and banquets.

APPHIA (ăf'ĭ-à). A Christian woman at Colosse or Laodicea mentioned by Paul in his letter to Philemon (verse 2). She may have been Philemon's wife.

APPLE (Hebrew *tappuah*, Arabic *tuffakh*). A tree and its fruit probably to be identified with our apple tree (*Pyrus malus*). Some scholars try to identify it as the apricot, the citron, or the quince, but serious objections exist against these identifications. The apple tree was well known and extensively cultivated in ancient times. Parts of Palestine are suitable for the cultivation of this tree.

APRICOT. It is questionable that the apricot was established in Palestine in biblical times. See under "Apple." "Apples of gold" (Prov. 25:11) are evidently not apricots.

AQABA, GULF OF. (ä'kà-bä). Although not named in Scripture, this body of water is suggested in the biblical allusion to Solomon's copper fleet which sailed from Elath and Ezion-Geber (1 Kings 9:26, 27). It constitutes the eastern arm of the Red Sea, which today gives Israel access to the sea on the south. The Sinai Peninsula separates it from the western arm of the Red Sea (the Gulf of Suez).

ARABAH (ăr'à-bäh). See under "Valleys of Scripture" and "Wilderness."

ARABIANS. A general term for the inhabitants of the huge peninsula of Arabia. It is bordered by the Fertile Crescent on the north, the Red Sea and the Gulf of Aqabah on the west, the Indian Ocean on the south, and the Persian Gulf and Gulf of Oman on the east. Its area is about one-third that of the United States. The interior is largely desert, but important kingdoms flourished on the southwestern coasts. The main reason for the prosperity of these kingdoms was their location on the incense trade routes from the countries of the south coast and Ethiopia.

The "table of the nations" in Genesis 10 lists a number of South Arabian peoples as the descendants of Joktan, a son of Eber of the family of Shem. He is listed as the progenitor of Almodad, Sheleph, Hazarmaveth, Jerah, Hadoram, Uzal, Diklah, Obal, Abimael, Sheba, Ophir, Havelah, and Jobab (Gen. 10:25-29). Modern tribes in south and southwest Arabia claim that pure Arabs are descended from Joktan.

A number of north Arabian tribes are listed as springing from Abraham through Keturah and Hagar (Gen. 25:1-4, 12-16). Among Esau's descendants a number of Arabian peoples are mentioned (Gen. 36:1-18). At the time of Jacob two groups of Abraham's descendants appear as caravan traders — the Ishmaelites and the Midianites (Gen. 37:25-36). In Solomon's reign contacts with Arabia became prominent after the famous visit of the Queen of Sheba (1 Kings 10:1-13) and the tribute received from "the kings of Arabia" (2 Chron. 9:14) and the "steppe dwellers" ("children of the East"). (These were the people occupying the semi-desert regions to the east and south of Palestine.) In the ninth century Jehoshaphat received tribute from the Arabians (2 Chron. 17:11). In Hezekiah's time the Arabs were very familiar to the Jews; some were even hired to defend Jerusalem against Sennacherib. Arabians were coming into prominence as traders in the closing years of the kingdoms of Judah (Jer. 25:23, 24; Ezek. 27:21, 22).

ARAD (ā'răd). A Canaanite city of the Negeb in the Mosaic era (Num. 21:1-3). The city was destroyed later by the Israelites, and its site was occupied by the nomadic Kenites (Judg. 1:16). The modern site is about 16 miles south of Hebron.

ARAMEANS (ăr'à-mē'ăns). A Semitic people named with Elam and Assyria in Genesis 10:22, 23 and 1 Chronicles 1:17. The Arameans infiltrated Mesopotamia and Syria from the Arabian desert fringes from the third millennium onward. By Abraham's time (2000 B.C.) numbers of them were settled in the Balikh-Habur region (near Haran), called Aram-Naharaim or Paddan-aram (Gen. 28:5). Contact between the Hebrews and Arameans goes back to patriarchal times (Deut. 26:5). The maternal ancestry of Jacob's children is Aramaic.

By the middle of the eleventh century B.C. Aramaic states began to appear north and east of Canaan. Aram-Zobah rose to power on the eve of the Hebrew monarchy (1 Sam. 14:47; 2 Sam. 8:3; 10:6). It lay north of Damascus and its power extended to Hamath on the northwest. It had to be subdued by David, who laid the foundation of Solomon's empire (2 Sam. 8:3-11). Aram-Damascus rose to power toward the end of Solomon's reign and waged intermittent war with the Northern Kingdom during most of its national existence. The Aramean power which was centered in Damascus was crushed only a decade before the fall of Israel in 722 B.C.

Aram-maacah was another Aramaic principality. It was situated east of the Jordan near Mount Hermon (Josh. 12:5; 13:11). Geshur was still another Aramaic kingdom near Maacah and Dan (Judg. 18:29). The Arameans exerted a powerful influence in the ancient Near East. Their language became the lingua franca of the Bible world by the time of Jesus.

Mount Ararat, viewed from the village of Kinakin, as engraved by T. Fielding in early 1800s (© *RTHPL*)

ARARAT (ăr'a-răt). A country in Armenia in the vicinity of Lake Van (Assyrian *Urartu*). The mountains of this region were the resting place of the ark after the deluge (Gen. 8:4). The murderers of Sennacherib fled to "the land of Ararat" (2 Kings 19:37; Isa. 37:38). This event is substantiated by the *Babylonian Chronicle* (III:34-38) for the year 681 B.C.

ARAUNAH (à-rä'nà). A Jebusite from whom David purchased a threshing floor on Mount Moriah in order to construct an altar to the Lord (2 Sam. 24:18-25). The place afterward became the site of Solomon's Temple (2 Chron. 3:1). Araunah is called Ornan in Chronicles and Ornah in the Hebrew text of 2 Sam. 24:16.

ARCHANGELS. Michael and Gabriel are mentioned by name in Scripture (Dan. 8:16; 10:13; Luke 1:19; Jude 1:9; Rev. 12:7). The noncanonical book of Enoch also mentions Uriel, Raphael, Raquel, Saraqael, and Remiel. The archangel Michael sustains a particular relation to Israel and to the resurrections (Dan. 10:13, 21; 12:1, 2; 1 Thess. 4:16; Jude 1:9). Gabriel is employed in the most distinguished services (Dan. 8:16; 9:21; Luke 1:19, 26).

ARCHELAUS (är-kė-lā′ŭs) ("leader of people, chief"). A son of Herod the Great and brother of Herod Antipas. He ruled Judea as an ethnarch when Joseph and Mary returned from Egypt (Matt. 2:22). He was deposed and banished to Gaul for his cruelty about A.D. 6.

ARCHEOLOGY. Palestinian archeology is the handmaid of Bible history. This rapidly developing science illustrates and expands biblical backgrounds. It selects those material remains of Palestine and its adjacent countries which relate to the biblical period and narrative. The basic method of this science is to dig into the successive occupational layers of so-called "tells" or mounds which have accumulated over ancient towns. The

CLASSIFICATION OF ARCHEOLOGICAL PERIODS (ISRAEL)

Stone Age	
Palaeolithic (Use of flint and stone tools only)	Before 10,000 B.C.
Mesolithic	10,000
Neolithic	7000-5000
Pre-pottery	7000
Pottery	5000
Chalcolithic Age	4000-3200
Early (Transition from stone to bronze artifacts)	4000-3800
Middle	3800-3600
Late	3600-3200
Bronze Age	
Early Bronze (EB) = Early Canaanite (EC) I	3200-2900
Early Bronze (EB) = Early Canaanite (EC) II	2900-2600
Early Bronze (EB) = Early Canaanite (EC) III, IV	2600-2200
Intermediate Bronze = Middle Canaanite (MC)	2200-1950
Middle Bronze (MB) = Middle Canaanite (MC) I	1950-1750
Middle Bronze (MB) = Middle Canaanite (MC) II	1750-1550
Late Bronze (LB) = Late Canaanite (LC) I	1550-1400
Late Bronze (LB) = Late Canaanite (LC) IIa	1400-1300
Late Bronze (LB) = Late Canaanite (LC) IIb	1300-1200
Iron Age	
Iron Age (IA) I = Early Israelite I	1200-1050
Early Israelite II	1050-970
Iron Age (IA) II = Middle Israelite II	970-840
Middle Israelite III	840-580
Iron Age (IA) III = Late Israelite III	
Late Israelite IV	580-330
Hellenistic Period	
Hellenistic Age I	330-165
Hellenistic Age II = Maccabean	165-63
Hellenistic Roman Period	63 B.C. — A.D. 70
Roman Period	A.D. 70-330

farther down the archeologist digs, the older are the remains uncovered. Each layer or stratum has come to be dated by the artifacts and pottery it yields. As a result, definite archeological periods can be outlined and described.

ARCHER. Whether on foot or on horseback, archers constituted an important part of ancient armies. The bow and arrow as weapons figure prominently in the wars of Israel. The bow was normally made of seasoned wood. The bowstring was commonly ox-gut. Arrows were made of reeds or light wood and were tipped with metal. The bow varied in length. The battle bow (Zech. 9:10) was sometimes as much as five feet in length. To string a battle bow the lower end had to be held down by the foot to fasten the string in a notch. For this reason archers were called "bow treaders" in Hebrew. Certain tribes of Israel became famous for their bowmen (cf. 1 Chron. 5:18; 12: 2; 2 Chron. 14:8).

ARCHITECT. Before the period of the monarchy in Israel the architect did not figure prominently. But with the advent of the monarchy his skills became necessary in order to build the walled town and the higher area which formed a "fort within a fort." During the prosperous united monarchy the architect came into prominence as public buildings and private homes became more pretentious and demanded more skill in planning.

The Phoenicians were famous as architects and craftsmen. Hiram of Tyre (979-944 B.C.) supplied both David and Solomon with the architectural skill and artisans necessary to build royal residences and the famed Temple in Jerusalem (cf. 2 Sam. 5:11; 2 Chron. 2:13, 14; 4:11-16). See also "Builder."

AREOPAGITE (ăr-ė-ŏp′ȧ-gīt). A member of the venerated council of the Areopagus, so called because it convened on the Hill of the Areopagus at Athens (Acts 17: 19, 22). In New Testament times it still retained great prestige despite curtailment of many of its ancient powers. For example, it still retained special jurisdiction in matters of morals and religion. It was therefore quite natural that Paul, considered a "setter forth of strange gods," should be subjected to its adjudi-

cation (Acts 17:18).

ARISTARCHUS (ă-rĭs-tär′kŭs) (Greek, "best ruling"). A Macedonian of Thessalonica who accompanied Paul at Ephesus (Acts 19:29), traveled with him to Troas (Acts 20:4, 6), and sailed with him to Rome (Acts 27:2). He was also at one time a fellow-prisoner of Paul (Col. 4:10).

ARK OF THE COVENANT (Exod. 25: 10-22). A sacred container made of acacia wood (symbolizing Christ's humanity) and overlaid with pure gold (denoting Christ's deity). The ark represents Christ as possessing God's law in his heart, since it held the Decalogue (Exod. 25:21, 22). It also held a pot of manna, illustrating Christ as Life-sustainer. Later it also held Aaron's rod that budded (Num. 17: 10), portraying Christ in resurrection.

The mercy-seat was the gold top or lid of the ark. It illustrates how the divine throne was transformed from a throne of judgment into a throne of grace by the atoning blood sprinkled upon it. The two cherubim above the mercy-seat guarded the holiness of God's throne, symbolized by the Shekinah glory enthroned above it.

ARK OF NOAH. The ship which Noah was told to build (Gen. 6:14-16) is typical of Christ as the preserver of his people from judgment (Heb. 11:7). This preservation specifically embraces the remnant of Israel who will turn to the Lord during the Great Tribulation (Isa. 2:10, 11; 26: 20, 21). The "pitch" (Gen. 6:14) speaks of Christ's atoning work which keeps out the waters of judgment. The word rendered "pitch" (*kopher*) is the same root which is elsewhere rendered "atonement" (Lev. 17:11, etc.).

ARMAGEDDON (är-mȧ-gĕd′ŏn). The Mount of Megiddo is the ancient hill which the fortress of Megiddo overlooked (Rev. 16:16). It will be the focal point of the great advance of the armies of the Beast and False Prophet as they attempt to annihilate the Jews and banish the name of Christ from the earth. Here the demon-driven armies of the nations (Rev. 16:13, 14) will be destroyed by the return of Christ in glory in fulfillment of the "smiting stone" prophecy of Daniel 2:35.

ARMLET. A band or bracelet clasping the upper arm. King Saul wore one (2 Sam.

1:10). Israelite men wore such armlets in the desert (Num. 31:50). Closely allied to the male armlet was the feminine bracelet, to which Isaiah makes reference as an item of luxurious adornment (Isa. 3:20). Excavations of Palestinian tombs indicate that both armlets and bracelets bound on the wrist were common (Gen. 24:22, 30, 47; Num. 31:50; Ezek. 16:11; 23:42).

Bronze armor of Roman officers in first centuries of Christian era, as seen in Naples museum (*HPS photo*)

ARMOR. Both defensive and offensive armor and weapons of war are summarized in the Hebrew term *kēlim* (Gen. 27: 3; 1 Sam. 17:54) and the Greek term *hopla* (2 Cor. 10:4). The Hebrew term *nesheq*, "weapons," is also sometimes employed (2 Kings 10:2).

ARMY, ISRAELITE. No regular army existed in Israel previous to the reign of Saul. In premonarchical times the nation depended on divinely prepared military leaders in a time of crisis. Such a leader would often perform a heroic deed (Judg. 6:11 – 8:3). As a consequence, all able-bodied men would rally to his call. Sometimes, however, the response would not be complete (Judg. 5:16, 17).

After the establishment of the kingdom, a strong army became imperative not only for defense against hostile neighbors but also for offensive action to increase the borders of the realm. The nucleus of Saul's army was formed from permanent warriors selected by the king. David followed Saul's general military policy but greatly augmented the nation's military force (2 Sam. 15:18). Because of his efficient army David was able not only to defend the realm he had, but also to subdue neighboring peoples who proved hostile to his growing power. As a result he was able to carve out the empire which his son Solomon inherited.

From Solomon's time onward the army became an important institution in Israel. After the division of the kingdom both Israel and Judah had to support large armies. They frequently faced each other as foes, as well as hostile neighboring states. This situation made military strength imperative.

The Composition of the Israelite Army. The general levy of nonprofessional soldiers was divided into thousands, hundreds, fifties, and tens, each section with its own commander. This system seems to have come down from the Mosaic period (Exod. 18:24-26). The national army was supported by roving bands of marauders (Judg. 11:3). The backbone of the military, however, was the infantry. Cavalry did not play a prominent role until the reign of Solomon. This monarch introduced horses and chariots on a large scale (1 Kings 10:26; cf. 1 Kings 9: 22), despite the prohibitions of the Law (Deut. 17:16; 20:1). The stables uncovered at Megiddo reveal that there was space for 450 horses (1 Kings 4:26; cf. 1 Kings 9:15, 19).

The archer was a very necessary part of the army. The bow and arrow figure prominently on Assyrian and Egyptian reliefs (Gen. 21:20; 48:22; 2 Sam. 1:18; 2 Chron. 35:23). In early Israel soldiers were maintained by booty (unless the booty was under the "ban" – 1 Sam. 30: 24) or by the produce of the land around their encampment. Later, under the monarchy, soldiers received regular pay (1 Kings 4:27).

The Israelite Military Camp. Guarding the central military base *(mahaneh)* was of the utmost importance (Judg. 7:19). Soldiers slept in tents or brush arbors (2 Sam. 11:11). The whole camp was deployed in a circle or square (Num. 2) and was surrounded by a "barricade." A force always remained behind in battle to guard the camp (1 Sam. 25:13).

ARMY, ROMAN. In the New Testament era Rome ruled Palestine and the then-known world. The basic unit was the "century"—one hundred men commanded by a "centurion." The legion, 6000 men, was divided into ten cohorts. Sometimes a small cavalry division was attached. The auxiliary cohorts were customarily named with particular titles, such as "the Italian band" (Acts 10:1) or "the Augustan band" (Acts 27:1), and were frequently divided into ten centuries.

ARNON (är'nŏn). The river flowing into the Dead Sea opposite En-gedi. It marked the boundary between Moab to the south and Ammon to the north (Judg. 11:18). It formed the southern border of Reubenite territory at the time of the conquest (Deut. 3:12, 16). Arnon is sometimes known as the "Wadi Mojib."

ARTAXERXES (är-tȧ-zĕrk'sēz). The third son of Xerxes and his successor to the throne of Persia (465-424 B.C.). In the seventh year of his reign (458 B.C.) he permitted Ezra to conduct a group of exiles back to Jerusalem (Ezra 7:1-10). Later he permitted Nehemiah to return and build the walls of Jerusalem (Neh. 13:6).

ARTEMIS (är'tĕ-mĭs). See "Diana."

ARTISAN. Skilled workers in metal, wood, or stone were present among the Hebrews (Exod. 38:23; 2 Sam. 5:11). Although not themselves distinguished by unusual inventiveness or artistry, the Hebrews nevertheless appreciated and even imported extraordinary talent for special projects like Solomon's Temple. Bezaleel of Judah was divinely gifted for artistic work on the Tabernacle (Exod. 31:1-11; 35:30-35). Ironworking was learned from the Philistines (1 Sam. 13:19-21). The secrets of dyeing were acquired from the Phoenicians (2 Chron. 2:7). The Hebrew word for artisan (*ḥārāsh*) signifies "one who cuts in" to "carve" or "devise" something artistic and useful (Exod. 38:23; 2 Sam. 5:11; 2 Chron. 24:12).

ARVAD (är'văd). The northernmost of the Phoenician cities (Ezek. 27:8, 11). It is an island (1 Macc. 15:23) about two miles from the mainland and 125 miles north of Tyre (cf. Gen. 10:18). Arvad is present-day Ruwad.

ASA (ā'sȧ) ("physician" or perhaps a shortened name for "the Lord has healed"). A king of Judah from 911 to 870 B.C. He was a reformer (1 Kings 15:9-15; 2 Chron. 14:1-5; 15:16). He defeated an invasion of Ethiopians (2 Chron. 14:9-15) and thwarted Baasha's attempt to fortify Ramah. The king became diseased in his feet (1 Kings 15:23; 2 Chron. 16:12).

ASAHEL (ăs'ȧ-hĕl) ("God has made"). A nephew of David who served in David's army. He was famous for his valor and fleetness (2 Sam. 2:18). He was slain by Abner (2 Sam. 2:18-23).

ASAPH (ā'săf) ("collector"). A Levite (1 Chron. 6:39, 43) charged with the sacred music and song of the Tabernacle and whose descendants carried on the art (1 Chron. 25:1-7). Twelve Psalms (50 and 73–83) are attributed to the family of Asaph.

ASENATH (ăs'ĕ-năth) (Egyptian, "belonging to the goddess Neith"). The daughter of Potiphera, priest of the great national temple of the sun at On (Heliopolis), seven miles northeast of modern Cairo. She became Joseph's wife and bore him two sons, Manasseh and Ephraim, who were adopted by her father-in-law, Jacob (Gen. 41:45, 50-52; 46:20).

ASH. A Palestinian tree formerly of uncertain identification but now established as the laurel. It flourishes on the central highland ridge as far south as Hebron.

ASHDOD (ăsh'dŏd). A city of the Philistine Pentapolis, seat of the worship of Dagon (Josh. 13:3; 1 Sam. 5:1-8; 6:17). It is called Azotus in the New Testament (Acts 8:40).

ASHER (ăsh'ēr) ("happy"). The eighth son of Jacob (Gen. 30:12, 13), the progenitor of the tribe that bore his name.

ASHERAH (ȧ-shē'rȧ). The Hebrew form of the name of a Canaanite goddess. She appears in the Amarna Letters as Ashirtu (Ashratu). In the Ras Shamra literature from Ugarit in north Syria she is known as "Asherat, Lady of the Sea" and as the Mistress of the Gods. In the Old Testament she is associated with Baal (Judg. 3:7).

In addition to referring to the goddess

personally, the name "Asherah" also refers to the image of the goddess. The Israelites were ordered to cut down and burn the Asherim of the Canaanites (Exod. 34:13; Deut. 12:3) and were forbidden to harbor the idol beside God's altar (Deut. 16:21). See also "Grove."

ASHKELON, ASKELON (ăsh'kĕ-lŏn). A seacoast city of the Philistine Pentapolis. It is situated 12 miles north of Gaza in a valley on the Mediterranean coast (2 Sam. 1:20; Jer. 47:5-7; Amos 1:8; Zeph. 2:4; cf. Zech. 9:5).

ASHTORETH (ăsh'tṓ-rĕth). The "mother goddess," occupying a central place in the Fertility Cult and the groves or tree plantations dedicated to her (Isa. 1:29; Hos. 4:13). She corresponds to Ishtar of the Babylonians, Isis of the Egyptians, and Astarte of the Greeks. She was called "Queen of Heaven" (Jer. 44:19).

ASIARCHS. The administrators of the league of cities of the Roman province of Asia. The asiarchs were elected annually and were drawn from the wealthiest and most aristocratic citizens. From their ranks came the honorary high priests of the provincial cult of "Rome and the Emperor," established by the league in 29 B.C. Its headquarters were in the city of Pergamum. These chiefs of Asia (Acts 19:31) were patrons of the festivals and games at Ephesus. They were friendly to Paul.

ASP. See *pethen* under "Adder." The asp is of the same genus as the deadly cobra. It has a hood which it dilates when it is about to strike its victim.

ASS. (1) The wild ass (Hebrew ᶜarōd and pere'). It belongs to the genus *Asinus*, which contains several species of asses, both wild and domesticated. The ass genus belongs to the family of horses (*Equidae*). The wild ass is poetically described in Job 39:5-8. This species is known today as the onager (*Equus onager*), which is still extant in parts of Western and Central Asia. The wild ass of Syria (*Asinus hemippus*) is somewhat smaller than the onager (Job 24:5; 39:5; Psa. 104:11). The domestic ass is descended from the onager. It was domesticated probably as early as Neolithic times. (2) The domestic ass (Hebrew *ḥamōr*). It is a subspecies descended from

the onager. Tamed onagers appear in Mesopotamia in the third millennium B.C.. As a work animal the ass was used for carrying loads (Gen. 42:26; 1 Sam. 16:20; 25:18) and for agricultural work (Isa. 30:24). As a riding animal it was used before the horse became common (Num. 22:21; 2 Sam. 17:23; 2 Kings 4:24), even by people of position (Judg. 10:4; cf. Zech. 9:9; Matt. 21:1-7; John 12:14, 15). The meat of the animal was commonly eaten among the nations, as Xenophen and Pliny attest. But it was prohibited to Israelites by the Mosaic dietary laws (Lev. 11:1-8; Deut. 14:3-8; cf. 2 Kings 6:25). As an economic asset in an agricultural economy, the possession of an ass was a bare minimum for existence (Job 24:3).

ASSARION. See "Coins and Money."

ASSHUR (ăsh'ŭr). A city of Assyria situated on the Tigris River in Northern Iraq. The modern site has been excavated and has yielded many important texts and monuments. Asshur was the core of Assyria and its early capital. Asshur was also the chief god of the Assyrian pantheon, and was worshiped there from about 3000 B.C. Other capital cities at different periods were Calah, Nineveh, and Dur-Sharrukin.

ASSOS (ăs'ŏs). A seaport of Mysia in the Roman province of Asia (Acts 20:13, 14). At Troas Paul sent his associates around Cape Lectum by ship while he made the twenty-mile journey to Assos by land.

ASSURANCE-SECURITY. The believer's *security* rests in his position of union with Christ as a result of his faith in the complete efficacy of Christ's redemptive death and resurrection. The believer's *assurance* is realized when he rests confidently in his position in Christ as described by the written Word of God (John 3:14-18, 36; 5:24; 10:27-29; Rom. 3:21-23; 4:5; 5:1, 2; 6:23; 1 John 5:10-13). Assurance is the believer's full conviction that he possesses a salvation in which he will be kept eternally by God through Christ's fully efficacious redemption (2 Tim. 1:12).

ASSYRIANS (ă-sĭr'ĭ-ăns). A semitic people whose center of power was located at Asshur on the upper Tigris River (cf. Gen. 10:10, 11) and whose capital in the heyday of imperial power was Nineveh. Called "the giant of the Semites," Assyria under ruthless conquerors from Ashurnasirpal II (884-859 B.C.) to Ashurbanipal (668-630 B.C.) became a scourge to the Near East and particularly to the Kingdom of Israel. Israel fell to Shalmaneser V in 722 B.C., and Judah almost succumbed to Sennacherib in 701 B.C. Assyria was finally defeated by the combined forces of the Babylonians, Medes, and Scythians. Nineveh was destroyed in 612 B.C. (Nah. 3:1-3) and the last vestiges of Assyrian power were wiped out at Haran shortly afterward.

ASTROLOGY. An ancient pseudo-science that claims to predict human destiny by studying the supposed influence of the relative positions of the sun, moon, and stars. Horoscopes are formulated for individuals on the basis of the relative positions of the heavenly bodies at the moment of the person's birth. These charts of the signs of the Zodiac and the positions of the planets claim to point out important guidelines for a person's future. As a form of fortune-telling and occultism, astrology is strictly forbidden by Scripture (Deut. 17:2-5; Isa. 47:13, 14; Dan. 2:27, 28; 4:7) Through its origin in ancient star worship it violates the first commandment of the moral law (Exod. 20:1-6). Astrology is experiencing a modern-day revival, along with spiritism, magic, card laying, palmistry, psychometry, and other occult phenomena.

ASYLUM. In ancient Israel any homicide, even an accidental one, initiated the action of the "avenger of blood" (*goel*). The nearest relative of the victim was responsible for putting the killer to death. However, the law acted to protect the unintentional killer. It provided safety at any shrine or altar whose horns he was quick to grasp (1 Kings 1:50; 2:28). Six cities, easily accessible, were appointed as places of refuge from the avenger of blood (Deut. 19:1-10). Intentional killers could be dragged from the altar and the city of refuge and executed by the *goel* (Exod. 21:12-14; Deut. 19:11-13). If a killing was proved unintentional, the acquitted had to settle in the city of refuge to avoid the avenger of blood. After the Exile an amnesty was declared for

unintentional killers so that they could return home without fear. See also "Cities of Refuge."

ATHALIAH (ă-thá-li'áh) ("the Lord is exalted"). The daughter of Ahab and Jezebel (2 Kings 8:18, 26; 2 Chron. 21:6; 22:2). She was married to Jehoram, king of Judah. As his queen (2 Kings 8:18; 2 Chron. 21:6) and as queen of the land for six years (841-835 B.C.), Athaliah was a proponent of Baal-Melkart. She was the only ruling queen of Judah, and represents a northern intrusion into the otherwise uninterrupted Davidic dynasty in Judah. She possessed all the cunning craftiness and idolatrous wickedness of her infamous mother, Jezebel. Also like Jezebel, Athaliah met a violent death.

ATHENS (ăth'ĕnz). The chief city of Attica and the capital of modern Greece. It was the intellectual and artistic center of the Greco-Roman world. It was visited by Paul (Acts 17:15 – 18:1). The name of the city was apparently derived from the goddess Athena.

ATONEMENT. The doctrine of forgiveness of sins by means of Christ's expiatory sacrifice. According to Scripture the sacrifice of the Old Testament only "covered" the offerer's sin (cf. Heb. 10:1-4). But since the Israelite's offering implied the obedience of faith in recognition of the future redemptive provision, God suspended judgment of the sin in anticipation of Christ's sacrifice (Rom. 3:25). Christ's death finally "put away" the sins committed previously "in the forbearance of God." The New Testament form of the doctrine thus regards the crucifixion of Jesus Christ as an act of atonement for the sins of the world (John 1:29). By Christ's death sinners are rendered salvable. However, only those who actually trust in God's provision are actually saved. The New Testament word translated "atonement" really means "reconciliation." "Not only so, but we also joy in God through our Lord Jesus Christ, by whom we have now received the reconciliation" (Rom. 5:11, *New Scofield Bible*).

ATONEMENT, DAY OF. *Yom Kippur* (the tenth day of the seventh month in the Hebrew calendar) marked the climax of access to God within the limits of the Old

Testament doctrine of atonement. On that most solemn occasion the high priest (a figure of Christ) entered the Most Holy Place to make annual atonement for the nation (Lev. 16:1-34). The expiation was only for a year but envisioned the once-for-all removal of sin by Christ's death (Exod. 30:10; Heb. 9:7, 8; 10:19).

In contrast to the sinless Christ, the high priest had to offer for himself as well as for the people (cf. Heb. 7:26, 27 with Lev. 16:6).

The high priest selected two goats and cast lots concerning their role in the sacrifice. The one on which "the Lord's lot" fell was slain, portraying Christ's vindication through death of the divine holiness expressed in the Law (Lev. 16:8-10, 15-17; Rom. 3:24-26). The other goat was sent forth into the wilderness as a "scapegoat," portraying Christ's expiation of our sin from the presence of God (Lev. 16:20-22; Rom. 8:33, 34; Heb. 9:26). The high priest's entrance into the Most Holy Place prefigures Christ's entrance into heaven itself (Heb. 9:24) to present the infinite merits of his shed blood before God's throne. See "Azazel."

ATTALIA (ăt-à-lī′à). A harbor city on the southwest coast of Asia Minor from which Paul and Barnabas sailed back to Syrian Antioch (Acts 14:25). It was founded by Attalus II of Pergamum (159-138 B.C.). The town still exists as present-day Antalya.

ATTALUS (ăt′ə-ləs). The King of Pergamos, either Attalus II Philadelphus or his nephew, Attalus III Philometor (138-133 B.C.) (1 Macc. 15:22).

AUGUSTUS (à-gŭs′tŭs). An honorific title of the Roman Emperors meaning "revered" or "reverend." When rendered in Greek (sebastos), it bore implications of divinity. In 27 B.C. the title was bestowed upon the founder of the Empire, who was its ruler at the time of Jesus' birth (Luke 2:1). His full name was Gaius Julius Caesar Octavianus. Used as a name by itself, Augustus refers to "Caesar Augustus" or Octavian (27 B.C. — A.D. 14), its most illustrious bearer. The title was borne by later Roman emperors and in its feminine form (Augusta) by empresses. See also "Caesar."

AUREUS. Called also "golden denarius" (denarius aureus), this gold coin was introduced by Julius Caesar in his financial reforms of 49 B.C. It is referred to by Josephus (Antiquities XIV: 8, 5) but is not mentioned in the Bible.

AUROCHS. The wild ox (Bos primigenius). Tiglathpileser I (1115-1102 B.C.) is pictured on Assyrian reliefs hunting this animal in the Lebanon region. In later centuries the aurochs became extinct; however, it is survived by its descendant, the domesticated ox. The wild species was distinguished from the domesticated animal in that it had a flatter forehead and large horns with double curvature.

AXE. See "Battle-Axe."

AZARIAH (ăz-à-rī′à) ("the Lord has aided"). A king of Judah from 767 to 740 B.C. He was more commonly known as Uzziah (cf. 2 Kings 15:1-7; 2 Chron. 26:1-23). "Azariah" was also the name of at least a score of other less prominent people in the Old Testament.

AZAZEL (à-zā′zĕl). The word occurs only in the ritual of the Day of Atonement (Lev. 16:8, 10, 26). It apparently indicates "dismissal" or complete removal of sin from the camp of God's people. The word is used as an infinitive, "in order to remove." Some scholars interpret it as denoting the "scapegoat," the "goat that goes away." Others take it to denote a desolate region (cf. Lev. 16:22).

AZEKAH (à-zē′kä). A fortress city south of the Valley of Aijalon (Tell ez-Zakariyeh) and nine miles north of Beit Jibrin (Josh. 10:10, 11; 15:35; 1 Sam. 17:1). Rehoboam strengthened its fortifications about 918 B.C. (2 Chron. 11:5, 9). Mentioned in the fourth Lachish Letter, it was one of the last of Judah's fortified cities to fall to the Chaldeans in 588 B.C. (Jer. 34:7).

AZOTUS (à-zō′tŭs). The New Testament form of Ashdod.

AZUBAH (à-zū′bàh) ("forsaken"). (1) The wife of Caleb, one of Judah's descendants. By him she had three sons (1 Chron. 2:18, 19). (2) The daughter of Shilhi, wife of King Asa of Judah. She was the mother of King Jehoshaphat of Judah, who reigned during 870-848 B.C. She was evidently a very godly woman, belonging to that group of queen mothers in Kings and Chronicles whose biographies begin, "And his mother's name was" and "he did that which was right in the sight of the Lord" (2 Chron. 20:31,

32). Her husband was a godly man and her son Jehoshaphat became a godly king.

B

BAAL (bā'ăl). The great fertility god of the Canaanites. The Hebrew name means "master," "husband," or "lord." Baal was the son of El in the Ugaritic literature. Female deities associated with these male gods were Anath and Asherah. This fertility cult was extremely debased and presented a continual peril to Israelite worship of the one true God. Besides being grossly immoral, the Baal cults practiced child sacrifice (cf. Jer. 19:5).

Ruins of the Temple of Jupiter in Baalbek, Lebanon (© *MPS*)

BAALBEK (ba'ăl-bek). A town in modern Lebanon famous for its ancient pagan ruins and temples.

BAASHA (bā'ȧ-shȧ). The exterminator of the house of Jeroboam I and founder of the second brief dynasty of the Northern Kingdom (909-886 B.C.), fulfilling the prophecy of Ahijah (1 Kings 15:25-33). He continued the apostate religious policy of Jeroboam and thereby earned stern prophetic rebuke (1 Kings 15:34 — 16:6).

BABYLON (băb'ĭ-lŏn). A great city of antiquity whose ruins are located on a branch of the Euphrates River near the modern town of Hilla, southwest of Bagdad. Its history goes back to dim antiquity (cf. Gen. 11:1-9). The city boasted a great temple tower or "ziggurat." The city reached its pinnacle of glory under Nebuchadnezzar II (605-562 B.C.). Its walls, gates, temple tower, and other buildings made it famous (cf. Dan. 4:30).

BABYLONIANS. The people who occupied the eastern end of the Fertile Crescent from Hit on the Euphrates to the Persian Gulf. The heart of Babylonia was the fertile alluvial plain of Shinar (Gen. 11:2) between the Euphrates and the Tigris in the last two hundred miles of the course of these two great rivers as they flowed to the sea. The Babylonians in the course of centuries became a blend of original non-Semitic Sumerians, Semitic Akkadians, Amorites, and later Hurrian and Kassite stock. The Semitic strain predominated.

The Early Dynastic Period (2800-2500 B.C.) saw the advent of kingship and the powerful city-states of Eridu, Batibirra, Larak, Sippar, Shuruppak, Kish, and Uruk (Erech). The Sargonid Semitic dynasty followed (2371-2191 B.C.). See "Akkadians." This Semitic state conquered the various city-states and extended its power to the Mediterranean region. Gudea of Lagash (2150 B.C.), however, staged a Sumerian revival and dominated Ur and the southern cities toward the end of this period.

The powerful Third Dynasty of Ur (2113-2006 B.C.) evidently witnessed Terah and Abraham's migration (Gen. 11:31). With the fall of Ur the Amorites took control (1894-1595 B.C.) under a vigorous dynasty in which Hammurabi (1792-1750 B.C.) ruled over an empire, as the Mari Letters show. This period was followed by the rule of the Kassites (1595-1174 B.C.), who invaded Babylonia from the eastern hills and gradually took over the country.

After this period Assyria began to dominate this region and held it in complete control from 745 to 626 B.C. The Neo-Babylonian or Chaldean Empire (626-539 B.C.) witnessed the exile of Judah under Nebuchadnezzar II (605-562 B.C.), Amel-Marduk or Evil Merodach (562-560 B.C.), Neriglissar (560-556 B.C.), Labashi-Marduk (556 B.C.), and Nabonidus, assisted by his son Belshazzar (556-539 B.C.).

Cyrus the Great took possession of Babylon on October 16, 539 B.C., and encouraged the return of the Jews to Palestine (Ezra 1:1-11). From 539 to 332 B.C. the Achaemenid line of Persian kings ruled Babylonia as part of their far-flung empire. Alexander the Great captured Babylon in 331 B.C. and ruled the region as part of his extensive realm until his death in 323 B.C. A Hellenistic line ruled until 312 B.C. From then until 64 B.C. the country passed into the hands of the Seleucids. From 64 B.C. it passed to the Parthians, until it was conquered by the Arabs in A.D. 641.

BADGER. A burrowing animal with thick, short legs and long-clawed forefeet. It existed in Bible lands. However, the Hebrew *tahash* (Exod. 26:14; 35:7; Num. 4:25; Ezek. 16:10), whose skin was used for the outer covering of the Tabernacle and for sandals, was not the badger but the seal, especially the dugong (*Halicore hemprichii*). It has a round head and fish-like tail and exists in large numbers in the Red Sea.

BAKER. Bread made principally of barley or wheat was the basic food of the ancient world and was considered the staff of life (cf. Lev. 26:26). From earliest times the word "bread" was used for food in general (Gen. 3:19; Prov. 6:8, Hebrew). Those who prepared it, whether humble peasant housewife or chief baker in a palace (cf. Gen. 40:1), had an honorable task.

Flour mixed with water and seasoned with salt was kneaded in a special trough. To this was added leaven in the form of a small bit of fermented dough until the whole batch was leavened and ready for baking. Unleavened bread was baked for special occasions. The baking was done over a fire, on heated stones, on a griddle, or in an oven. The oven baking usually produced the best results.

BALAAM (bā'làm) ("swallower or conqueror of the nation"). A diviner-prophet (Josh. 13:22; cf. Num. 22:1 – 24:25) who was hired by the King of Moab to curse Israel, but was instead compelled by God to bless his people. As a typical mercenary prophet (2 Pet. 2:15), he erred in reasoning from natural morality that God must curse Israel because of her evil. He forgot the higher morality of the Cross, by which God can redeem the believing sinner without sacrificing his own justice (Rom. 3:26). Balaam's doctrine (Rev. 2:14) was his advice to corrupt the people who could not be cursed (Num. 31:15, 16; 23:8).

BALM, BALM OF GILEAD (gĭl'e-ăd). A resin apparently obtained in Gilead (Gen. 37:25; Jer. 8:22; 46:11) and exported from Palestine (Gen. 37:25; Ezek. 27:17). It was used as a healing ointment (Jer. 51:8). The balm cannot now be identified with any plant in Gilead. It has been claimed to be mastich, a product of the mastich tree (*Pistacia lentiscus*), common in Palestine. It is a bushy evergreen whose pale yellow gum was used for incense and as an ointment. Its leaves and berries and the oil from its bark were used as medicine. Classical authors have associated biblical "balm" with Mecca balsam (still imported into Egypt from Arabia).

BAPTISM. Ritual washing for purification from uncleanness of various sorts was common in the Old Testament (cf. Heb. 6:2; 9:10). Uncleanness was associated with childbirth, menstruation, contact with a corpse, certain diseases, idolatry, etc. Converts from heathenism were baptized. The Essenes baptized. John the Baptist employed the rite to signify repentance from sin. John's baptism was preparatory and introductory to Christ's spiritual baptism (Matt. 3:11; Mark 1:8; Luke 3:16; John 1:33; Acts 1:5; 11:15, 16).

Christ "baptized with the Holy Spirit" in the primary sense of providing "so great salvation" (Heb. 2:3). After his ascension the Holy Spirit came and "baptized" believers into union with the glorified Christ (1 Cor. 12:12, 13; Rom. 6:3, 4; Gal. 3:27).

BARABBAS (bär-ăb'as) ("son of Abba"). A bandit (John 18:40) arrested for political violence (Mark 15:7). Pilate offered to release either him or Jesus. The crowd chose Barabbas.

BAR-JESUS (bär-jē'sŭs) ("son of Joshua"). A magician and false prophet. Under demonic power he tried to dissuade Sergius Paulus, the proconsul of Cyprus, from accepting the gospel (Acts 13:6-12).

BAR-KOCHBA (bär-kôkh'bä). The leader of the second Jewish revolt against the Romans (A.D. 132-135). He was hailed as "Messiah, the Son of a Star," the *bar kochba* of Numbers 24:17.

BARLEY. One of the most ancient of cereals. In Palestine it is commonly cultivated in winter and harvested in May (Ruth 1:22). Several varieties belong to the genus *Hordeum*. It formed one of the essential staple foods of ancient Bible lands.

BARNABAS (bär'na-bas) ("son of prophetic consolation"). A companion of Paul on his first missionary tour (Acts 13:1–15:39).

BARTHOLOMEW (bär-thŏl'ŏ-mū). One of the Twelve Apostles. His first name was apparently Nathanael (John 1:45; cf.

Matt. 10:3; Mark 3:18; Luke 6:14; Acts 1:13).

BARUCH (bä'rŭk) ("blessed"). Jeremiah's friend and scribe (Jer. 36:1-32). The prophet placed the deed for some property in Baruch's hands (Jer. 32:6-16). He was taken to Egypt with Jeremiah (Jer. 43:1-7).

BARZILLAI (bär-zĭl'ā-i) ("made of iron"). A wealthy Gileadite who befriended David during Absalom's rebellion (2 Sam. 17:27-29). David later rewarded him (2 Sam. 19:31-40).

BASEMATH (băs'ĕ-măth). (1) One of Esau's wives, the daughter of Elon the Hittite (Gen. 26:34). (2) Another of Esau's wives, a daughter of Ishmael (Gen. 36:3, 13, 17). She was also called Makalath (Gen. 28:9). (3) A daughter of Solomon who was married to one of his twelve tax collectors (1 Kings 4:15).

BASHAN (bā'shăn). A mountainous region (cf. Psa. 68:15) east of Lake Huleh and the Lake of Galilee with elevated peaks reaching 2320 feet. Bashan was noted for its superior livestock (Deut. 32: 14; Ezek. 39:18).

BAT (Hebrew ʿaṭallēph). Under Mosaic Law the bat was classed with fowls and was ceremonially unclean (Lev. 11:13, 19; Deut. 14:11, 12, 18). Strictly speaking, the bat is a quadruped rather than a bird, and as such has teeth rather than a bill and is covered with hair instead of feathers. Its "wing" is really a featherless membrane connecting its front and rear legs.

BATHSHEBA (băth-shē'ba) ("daughter of the oath or seventh day"). The wife of Uriah the Hittite. King David committed adultery with her and plotted her husband's death in battle. Then David married her. After the death of the illicit child, Bathsheba gave birth to Solomon. The sordid tale is told in 2 Samuel 11.

BATTERING-RAM. A military machine used by Assyrians, Babylonians, and other ancient peoples to beat down the walls of besieged cities. It was generally a large beam with a head of iron somewhat resembling the head of a ram.

BATTLE-AXE. A military weapon with a wood handle and a metallic axe-head. It was commonly used in battle by the Hittites, Assyrians, Babylonians, and Elamites. The "battle-axe" of Jeremiah 51:20 (Hebrew *mēphiṣ*, "scatterer") is really a club, doubtlessly imbedded with iron nails. Herodotus mentions such a weapon carried by Assyrian troops in Xerxes' army.

BEANS. The common broad bean (*Vicia faba*) is well known in Palestine. With wheat, emmer, barley, and millet it furnished the basic diet of the population as a whole in Bible times.

BEAR. In Bible times bears roamed in forests over Palestine. The Syrian form of the brown bear is still found in parts of the Middle East, including Lebanon (though not in Palestine proper). David killed a bear near Bethlehem (1 Sam. 17:34-37). Near Bethel two female bears mauled a group of children who had mocked Elisha (2 Kings 2:23, 24). The bear figures prominently in Daniel's vision of the end of Gentile world power (Dan. 7:5).

BEAST, THE. A prophetic term denoting the great tyrant of the last days of world history. He will be Satan's agent of wrath against God and his Tribulation saints. The beast is described by several other biblical titles. In Daniel 7:8 he is called the "little horn"; in Daniel 9:27 and Matthew 24:15 he is seen as a desolator; in 2 Thessalonians 2:3 he is termed the "man of sin"; and in Revelation 13:1 he is described as a "beast out of the sea."

BEE. The name is correctly applied to several families of the order *Hymenoptera*, including solitary bees and bumblebees as well as honey bees (Hebrew *deborāh*). The honey bee is clearly referred to in Judges 14:8, Deuteronomy 1:44, and Psalm 118:12. In Isaiah 7:18 the prophet illustrates the Palestinian custom of calling honey bees by whistling for them: "The Lord shall hiss (whistle) for the bee that is in the land of Assyria."

"Abraham's Well" at Beersheba, today covered by a pumping station (© MPS)

BEERSHEBA (bē'ĕr-shē'bȧ). The chief city of the Negeb, famous from patriarchal times (Gen. 21:25-31; 26:32, 33). It was a religious sanctuary (Gen. 46:1-5). It marked the southernmost boundary of Israelite population (Judg. 20:1; 1 Chron. 21:2). See also under "Springs, Wells, and Pools."

BEETLE. The King James Version's rendering (Lev. 11:22) of a particular kind of leaping insect (Hebrew *hargōl*). It is not a beetle as defined in today's English, but is instead some type of grasshopper, locust, or cricket.

BEHEMOTH (bĕ-hē'mŏth) (plural of Hebrew *behēmāh*, "beast," an intensive plural denoting a large beast). A quadruped commonly taken as the hippopotamus of the Nile (*Hippopotamus amphibious*). Job pictures it eating grass like an ox and frequenting streams and rivers (Job 40:15-24). The hippopotamus is a large, amphibious animal with a huge tusk and short, stout legs. Its strength is incredible. Today these great beasts are only found far in the interior of Africa on the Upper Nile.

BELIAL (bē'lĭ-ȧl) ("worthless, destructive, wicked"). A Hebrew word used in expressions of contempt, as in Judges 19:22 and 1 Samuel 25:17, 25. In later times Belial became a designation of Satan, the Evil One (2 Cor. 6:15).

BELIEF. To "believe" in the biblical sense involves more than mere intellectual assent to a fact. The New Testament concept of believing (*pisteuo*) means *to trust in, to have faith in, to repose upon, to commit oneself to* (a person or an object). To truly believe therefore includes not only the passive assent of the mind but also the action of the will. "Whosoever believeth in him" (John 3:16) means *whoever trusts in God's Son so as to become united to him in life and destiny.* See also "Faith."

BELIEVER. A person who has exercised saving faith in Christ (1 Tim. 4:12). Compare Acts 2:44; 11:17; 13:48; Ephesians 1:13. All such are permanently sanctified in their position "in Christ" and are thus saints by calling (Rom. 1:7; 8:27; 1 Cor. 1:2). See also "Saint."

BELSHAZZAR (bĕl-shăz'ẽr) ("Bel has protected his kingship"). A regent of

Babylon during the reign of his father, Nabonidus (553-539 B.C.). He was warned of the approaching doom of the Neo-Babylonian Empire by the aged Daniel (Dan. 5:1-31) and was slain when the Persian troops gained access to the city through the dry riverbed of the diverted Euphrates.

BENAIAH (bĕ-nā'yà). A valiant man under David (2 Sam. 23:20-22) who supervised David's bodyguard (2 Sam. 8:18). He remained faithful to David during Absalom's rebellion (2 Sam. 20:23) and escorted Solomon to Gihon to be anointed as king (1 Kings 1:38).

BENEDICTIONS. In ancient Israel priests were charged with blessing people in God's name (Num. 6:23-27). In postexilic Judaism it became a custom to invoke blessings as additions to prayers in doxologies. The practice was followed in Christian doxologies (cf. Heb. 13:20, 21; Jude 1:24, 25).

BENHADAD (bĕn-hā'dăd) ("son of the god Hadad"). The name of several Aramaean kings at Damascus (890-770 B.C.). At least two of these are mentioned in Scripture: Benhadad I (1 Kings 15:18), possibly the same person as Benhadad II, foe of Ahab (874-853 B.C.); Benhadad III or II (796-770 B.C.), the son of Hazael (2 Kings 13:22-25), mentioned also in the stele of Zakir, king of Hamath.

BENJAMIN (bĕn'jà-mĭn) ("son of the right hand"). Jacob's youngest son by Rachel (Gen. 35:16-20). He was the progenitor of one of the twelve tribes of Israel.

BERNICE (bĕr-nī'sē) ("victorious"). The eldest daughter of Herod Agrippa I, king of Judea (A.D. 41-44). She was married to Herod, King of Chalcis, who died in A.D. 48. She accompanied her brother, Herod Agrippa II, so constantly that scandal arose. She was with him when Paul made his defense (Acts 25:23; 26: 30). Her loose character appears in the fact that she afterward became the mistress first of Vespasian and then of Titus.

BESOR (bē'sŏr). A brook (Wadi Ghazzeh) which flows into the Mediterranean Sea about five miles south of Gaza. Two hundred of David's men remained here while 400 others pursued the Amalekites (1 Sam. 30:9, 10).

BETHANY (bĕth'à-nĭ). A small village about a mile-and-a-half east of Jerusalem on the eastern slope of the Mount of Olives. It was the home of Mary, Martha, and Lazarus (John 11:1) and the site of Christ's Ascension (Luke 24:50, 51).

BETH-AVEN (bĕth-ā'vĕn). A wilderness region located east of Bethel and near Ai (Josh. 7:2; 18:12). The site served as a boundary mark for Benjamin's apportionment (Josh. 18:12).

BETHEL (bĕth'ĕl). (1) A city about twelve miles north of Jerusalem on the main north-south ridge road. Although it is identified with present-day Beitin, there are difficulties in relating it to its environment, and some nearby location may yet prove to be the ancient site. The original city, Luz, was built before the time of Abraham (Gen. 12:8). It was Jacob who named it Bethel (Gen. 28:16-19). Jeroboam I lifted Bethel to new prominence when he made it the Northern Kingdom's chief sanctuary and the rival of Jerusalem (1 Kings 12:25-33). (2) An eminence or "mountain" (Josh. 16:1; 1 Sam. 13:2; etc.) on the watershed near the city of Bethel.

BETHESDA (bĕ-thĕz'dà). See under "Springs, Wells, and Pools."

BETH-HORON (bĕth-hō'rŏn). A town near the border of Benjamin (Josh. 18:14), a Levitical city (Josh. 21:20, 22). It consisted of a lower city (Josh. 16:3; 18:13) fortified by Solomon (1 Kings 9:17), as well as an upper town (Josh. 16:5; 2 Chron. 8:5).

Bethlehem today, looking from the west (© MPS)

BETHLEHEM (bĕth'lė-hĕm). A town in Judah which was the birthplace of Christ (Matt. 2:1, 5, 6), the home of David (1 Sam. 17:15; 20:6), and the adopted home of Ruth (Ruth 1:19-22). There was also a Bethlehem in Galilee (Josh. 19:15).

BETH-PEOR, BAAL-PEOR (bĕth-pē'ŏr;

bā'ăl-pē'ŏr). A place about five miles northeast of the upper extremity of the Dead Sea in Transjordan. Moses was buried near this location (Deut. 34:6).

BETH-REHOB (běth-rē'hŏb). A town and region in the vicinity of Dan. It comprised the territory between Mount Lebanon and Mount Hermon (Judg. 18:28). It was occupied by the Arameans (2 Sam. 10:6).

BETHSAIDA-JULIAS (běth-sā'ĭ-då). A fishing village on the Sea of Galilee during the Roman period (Matt. 11:21; Mark 6:45; John 1:44). A new city was constructed by Philip the tetrarch and named Julias in honor of the Roman imperial family.

BETHSHAN, BETHSHEAN (běth-shē'ăn). A Bronze Age fortress city which guarded the entrance of the Valley of Jezreel from the east. In later years it was renamed Scythopolis. Its present-day remains are identified with Tell el-Husn near Beisan. Excavation of the city has yielded important archeological remains. During biblical times the city changed hands several times (cf. Josh. 17:11-18; Judg. 1:27, 28; 1 Sam. 31:7-12; 1 Kings 4:7, 12).

BETH-SHEMESH (běth-shē'měsh). A town on the border of Judah (Josh. 15:10) and a Levitical city (Josh. 21:13, 16). It was placed in Solomon's second district (1 Kings 4:7-9). It is identified with Tell er-Rumeileh, about fifteen miles west-southwest of Jerusalem. There was also a Beth-shemesh in Issachar (Josh. 19:22) and one in Naphtali (Josh. 19:38).

BEZALEL (běz'å-lĕl) ("in the shadow of God's protection"). A craftsman who fashioned much of the ornamental work of the Tabernacle in the desert (Exod. 31:1-11; 35:30-35).

BILDAD (bĭl'dăd) ("Bel has loved"). One of Job's friends and would-be comforters (Job 2:11; cf. Chaps. 8, 18, 25).

BILHAH (bĭl'hà) ("foolish, stupid"). Rachel's handmaid, given to her by her father, Laban, at the time of her marriage with Jacob. At her mistress' request she became one of Jacob's secondary wives and thereby the mother of Dan and Naphtali (Gen. 30:1-8). Later she committed adultery with Reuben (Gen. 35:22).

BINDING AND LOOSING. Power claimed by Jewish religious authorities to forbid or permit practices covered directly or indirectly by the Law of Moses. The Pharisees of Jesus' day claimed such power. On the basis of his full confession of the deity of Christ, Peter was given this power (Matt. 16:13-19). It was also shared by the other apostles (Matt. 18:18). Peter's use of this authority in declaring the gospel of forgiveness (John 20:23) is illustrated in Acts 10:44-48. Paul also used it (Acts 13:38, 39). The power is resident not in the preacher personally but in the gospel which he proclaims and the Savior which he presents under the authority of the Holy Spirit. See "Keys of the Kingdom of Heaven."

BISHOP. See "Elder."

BITHIAH (bĭ-thī'à) ("daughter of the Lord"). A daughter of Pharaoh and wife of a Judahite named Mered (1 Chron. 4:17). Her name apparently indicates that she became a convert to the worship of Israel's God.

BITTER HERBS. Herbs eaten with the Paschal lamb during the Passover (Exod. 12:8; Num. 9:11). They were symbolic of the bitter experiences of the enslaved Hebrews in Egypt prior to the Exodus. The herbs may refer to endives, chicory, lettuce, watercress, or "star thistles." Horseradish is now commonly used in Europe and America as "bitter herbs" with the Paschal lamb, but it was not known in Bible times.

BITTERN (Hebrew *qippōd*). Possibly a marsh bird. Such a bird by the name of bittern is common today around Lake Huleh, north of the Sea of Galilee. But many scholars categorize the biblical bittern not as a bird at all but rather a porcupine or lizard.

BLACKSMITH. See "Smith."

BLASPHEMY. Blasphemy refers principally to reviling God by word or action (Num. 15:30; Isa. 37:6) or directly cursing him (Lev. 24:11; Rev. 16:9). Notorious enemies of God are full of blasphemies (Rev. 13:1, 5, 6; 17:3). The Jews accused Jesus of this crime because he claimed to forgive sins (Matt. 9:3; Mark 2:7; Luke 5:21) and to be Christ the Son of God (Matt. 26:63-65; Mark 14:61-64; John 10:30-33). Those who oppose the gospel commit blasphemy (1 Tim. 1:13) and bring discredit on Christ by their actions (Rom. 2:24; James 2:7).

The reviling of human authority is dangerously similar to blaspheming God himself, since all authority is granted by God (Acts 13:45; 18:6; Jude 1:8-10). In its weaker sense blasphemy may denote slander of any person (1 Cor. 4:13; 1 Pet. 4:4). Blasphemy against the Holy Spirit is apparently attributing Christ's works to Satan (Matt. 12:31, 32; Mark 3:28-30; Luke 12:10).

BLESSINGS AND CURSINGS. Power-laden words for good or ill, spoken on the occasion of religious celebrations or other special occasions and often accompanied by gestures and symbolic actions. In the patriarchal period the blessing of a dying father was transmitted to his heir (Gen. 27:1-29). Such blessings were irrevocable (Gen. 27:30-40). In early premonarchic Israel blessings and cursings were apparently a customary part of the festival of covenant renewal (Deut. 11: 26-32).

Blessing formulas are found in the New Testament also, such as the Beatitudes (Matt. 5:3-12) and the benedictions found in the introductions and concluding portions of the Pauline letters. Curses appear seldom (cf. Mark 11:12-14), although the Book of Revelation contains both benedictions and woes (1:3; 8:13; 11:18; 14:13; 19:9; 22:7, 14, 18, 19). The ultimate blessing has been bestowed upon mankind through Christ Jesus.

BLOOD. Blood was regarded as the vehicle of life. Eating of flesh with the blood in it was accordingly forbidden among the Hebrews and early Christians (Acts 15:20).

BLOOD OF CHRIST. The blood of Christ was of infinite value (Rom. 5:9; Eph. 1:7; 2:13; Col. 1:14) because it represented his sinless life and vicarious death. "For the life of the flesh is in the blood" (Lev. 17:11). It was not the blood in the veins of the sacrifice but the blood of the slain victim upon the altar which was efficacious. "And I have given it (the blood) to you upon the altar to make an atonement for your souls; for it is the blood that maketh an atonement for the soul" (Lev. 17:11). Salvation by the mere imitation or influence of Christ's life is unknown in Scripture. It is the *death* of Christ that saves. His life is to be imitated only after the benefits of his death have been appropriated.

BLUE. The cord of blue upon the borders of the priests' garments (Num. 15:38) denotes the fact that the servants of God were to be heavenly in obedience and character. As the heavenly color, blue signified separation from earthly ambitions and desires.

BOAR. The wild swine, especially the male of the species (Psa. 80:13). The wild boar is three or more feet long. It has teeth projecting beyond the upper lip, constituting formidable tusks with which the boar rips open its enemies. The animal is still extant in the ravines east of the Jordan, in the swamps of the waters of Merom, in Lebanon, and in the Plain of Sharon.

BOAZ (bō′ăz) (probably "in him is strength"). Kinsman and husband of Ruth and ancestor of David and Christ (Ruth 2:1 – 4:22; Matt. 1:5).

BOGAZKÖY. The ancient capital of the Hittite Empire. Its present name is Hattusa. Here thousands of cuneiform tablets were unearthed in the archeological resurrection of the long-lost Hittites. The ruin is located in the great bend of the Halys River in Asia Minor (Anatolia).

BOHAN, STONE OF (bō′hăn). A landmark on the border between Judah and Benjamin (Josh. 15:6). It was in the wilderness region southwest of Jericho and not far from the Jordan River. It was known as "the Reubenite's thumb" (from *bohen*, "thumb").

BOOK. Books in Bible times were actually scrolls. These were documents written on strips of leather or papyrus. The scrolls were rolled up (Isa. 34:4) and often sealed (Rev. 5:1). Certain scrolls are mentioned by name in the Old Testament, such as the Book of the Covenant (Exod. 24:7), the Book of the Law (2 Kings 22:8), the Book of the Wars of the Lord (Num. 21:14), and the Book of Jasher (Josh. 10:13).

BOOK OF LIFE. In the Old Testament the term refers to physical life. "Let them be blotted out of the book of the living" (Psa. 69:28) means "let them die physically." Such is also the case in Exodus

32:32, 33, where Moses prays to be blotted out of God's book, and in Daniel 12:1, where all who "shall be found written in the book" will survive the Great Tribulation. Isaiah's reference to "everyone that is written among the living in Jerusalem" (Isa. 4:3) also embraces the *physically* living.

In the New Testament the book of life has reference to *eternal* life and the roster of believers (Phil. 4:3; Rev. 3:5; 22:19). At the Great White Throne judgment everyone not enrolled in the book of life is consigned to Gehenna (Rev. 20:12-15). This is the book of life of the slain Lamb, in which the names of the elect are recorded (Rev. 13:8; 21:27). The same idea occurs in Luke 10:20 and Acts 13:48.

BOOTHS, FEAST OF. Sometimes called the "Feast of Tabernacles," this Jewish event was one of three great annual festivals celebrated in the autumn at the end of the agricultural year (Lev. 23:34; Deut. 16:13). The pilgrims were to live in arbor shelters, reminiscent of Israel's wanderings.

BOTTLE-MAKER. Biblical "bottles" were usually tanned and sewn skins of animals. They were serviceable, but were subject to wear and tear (Josh. 9:4; Matt. 9:17).

BOW AND ARROW. See under "Archer."

BOX TREE. The *Boxus longifolia*, a small tree up to twenty feet high with small evergreen leaves and hard, fine-grained wood. The box, fir, and pine were the glory of Lebanon.

BOZEZ (bŏz'ĕs). One of two crags near Gibeah, in the mountain pass through which Jonathan attempted to surprise the Philistine garrison (1 Sam. 14:4-6).

BOZRAH (bŏz'rä). A town in Edom mentioned in Genesis 36:33, Isaiah 34:6, Jeremiah 49:13, and Amos 1:12. It was on the King's Highway, which ran through Transjordan to Ezion-geber on the Gulf of Aqabah. It was situated about 50 miles south-southeast of the southern extremity of the Dead Sea.

BRACELET. See "Armlet."

BRAMBLE, BRIER. Apparently a variety of *Rhamnus*, quite common in the Dead Sea area, the Jordan Valley, and at Jerusalem. Thorn bushes and brambles were often used as fences to protect vineyards and other cultivated areas (cf. Isa. 5:5; Song 2:15). The term "brier" is the rendering of no less than six Hebrew words referring to various types of burrs, thistles, and other prickly plants and shrubs (Judg. 8:7, 16; Isa. 9:18; 10:17; 55:13; Ezek. 2:6; 28:24; Mic. 7:4). The Greek word *tribolos* (caltrop, burr, thistle) occurs in Matthew 7:16 and Hebrew 6:8.

BRASS. See "Bronze."

BREASTPLATE. The breastpiece was fastened by gold chains to the shoulder-pieces of the priest's ephod. It consisted of a square pouch that was a repository for the Urim and Thummim and an oblong gold setting containing twelve precious stones engraved with the names of the Israelite tribes, one on each stone (Exod. 28:15-21, 29, 30). This foreshadows Christ as our Great High Priest (Heb. 3:1; 7:26; 9:11). He now represents us before God (Rom. 8:33, 34; Heb. 7:25; 9:24), bearing our names before him much as the High Priest of Israel carried the names of the tribes of Israel on his shoulders and on his breast (cf. Isa. 49:16).

BRICKMAKER. Brickmaking was the labor of peasants and the enslaved Israelites in Egypt. The craft as practiced in Egypt is graphically and accurately described in Exodus 5:6-19. Archeology reveals that straw and stubble were regularly used during this period. The chemical decay of the straw in the bricks increased the plasticity and strength of the clay.

In Egypt and Mesopotamia sun-dried bricks were common. Kiln-baked bricks were used for facings and pavement construction. In Palestine sun-dried bricks were the norm. House walls were frequently of brick construction on a stone foundation. Bricks in Mesopotamia and Egypt were often impressed with the ruler's name. Nebuchadnezzar II (605-562 B.C.) used at least five different stamps.

BRIDE. See under "Engagement" and "Marriage, Jewish."

BRIDE OF CHRIST. The Church is now viewed as a "chaste virgin" espoused or betrothed to Christ (cf. 2 Cor. 11:2) and still unmarried. The betrothal is legally binding and represents the individual members of the body of Christ. The Rapture represents the coming of the Bridegroom for his bride (1 Thess. 4:13-18). This event heralds the approaching marriage, when the bride becomes "the Lamb's wife," a figure of glorification and association with Christ in rule and destiny. The Marriage Supper of the Lamb in heaven (Rev. 19:7-9) is celebrated just prior to the Second Coming of Christ to the earth to set up his kingdom rule in association with the glorified Church and resurrected Old Testament saints.

The marriage of the Lamb is the consummation of the union of Christ and the Church as his bride. The figure is in keeping with the oriental custom of marriage, which consisted of the betrothal, the marriage, and the marriage supper. The subsequent marriage feast (Matt. 25: 1-13) with the ten virgins represents Israel at the end of the Tribulation. The five wise virgins prefigure the saved remnant, while the five foolish ones prefigure the professing but unbelieving part of the nation. Only those who possess the "oil" of the Holy Spirit (i.e., only true believers—cf. Rom. 8:9) can enter the kingdom. All others are excluded.

BRIER. See "Bramble, Brier."

BRONZE. In Scripture symbolism bronze represents divine judgment, as in the bronze altar and the bronze serpent (portraying God's judgment of sin) and in the bronze laver (symbolizing self-judgment of sin).

BRONZE SEA. A large vessel of cast bronze made by Hiram of Tyre for Solomon's Temple (1 Kings 7:23-26; 2 Chron. 4:2-5). It doubtless corresponded in use to the bronze laver of the Tabernacle. The molten sea was a copper bowl 15 feet in diameter and 7½ feet high. It rested on twelve oxen. When the Temple was plundered by the Babylonians the bronze sea was broken up and carried to Babylonia (2 Kings 25:13).

BROOM. A twiggy, nearly leafless bush which bears clusters of pink-white flowers. It grows in the Jordan Valley, Arabia, and the Peninsula of Sinai. The large stalk of the broom was used as fuel (Job 30:4) and made into charcoal (Psa. 120:4).

BUCKLER. A type of small shield (2 Chron. 14:8). It was a piece of defensive armor worn on the left arm. In early times bucklers were either of wood or wicker or else of wood covered with leather and sometimes ornamented with metal plates. The leather was oiled before battle to preserve it and make it glisten (Isa. 21:5). Smaller than the shield proper, the buckler was convenient for intercepting quick thrusts of the sword (Judg. 5:8; 2 Kings 19:32; Isa. 37:33). See also "Shield."

BUILDER. A builder was either a skilled or an unskilled workman (2 Chron. 34: 11). The humble peasant was a builder in the sense that he constantly had to repair his thatched roof and mend his house with sundried clay or bricks. Large projects required skilled stonemasons and carpenters as well as porters and untrained workers. Important edifices were planned and constructed under the close supervision of a "masterbuilder" or architect (Greek *architectōn*—1 Cor. 3:10). The chief builder checked the progress of the building with a "plumb line," a cord weighted with a heavy object (cf. Amos 7: 7, 8; Zech. 4:10; 2 Kings 21:13).

BULRUSH. See "Papyrus."

BURIAL. Under Mosaic Law (Deut. 21: 23) a corpse was to be buried on the day of death. The relatives of the deceased prepared the body for interment. Christ brought the hope of the resurrection of the body into clear focus (John 11:1-45). The rite of water baptism symbolizes the believer's identification with Christ in his death, burial, and resurrection (Rom. 6:3-6; Col. 2:12). See also under "Funerals, Jewish."

BURNING BUSH. A thorny bush (Hebrew *seneh*, Greek *batos*) which Moses saw aflame and from which the Lord spoke (Exod. 3:2-4; Mark 12:26). It was probably a form of the acacia (*Acacia vera* or *nilotica*), the Egyptian thorn, common in the Sinai Peninsula.

BUTCHER. The country farmer or shepherd served as his own butcher. In the walled cities, however, the occupation of butcher and meat salesman became a trade. Cattle had to be slaughtered, cleaned, and prepared for market. In the absence of refrigeration this was a daily occupation. At kings' courts or in the case of important people, servants were charged with this duty, which was included in the functions of a cook (cf. 1 Sam. 9:23). The Talmud speaks of a "street of the butchers" in Jerusalem.

BUTLER (Hebrew *mashqeh,* "one giving drink"). A court servant who tasted the king's wine. Butlers or cupbearers were often foreigners who became confidants of the king. A cupbearer at a Palestinian court is pictured on an ivory from Megiddo. Nehemiah was the cupbearer to Artaxerxes I of Persia (464-423 B.C.). The "butler" of the Pharaoh at the time of Joseph (Gen. 40:1-23) was the royal cupbearer. Cupbearers were part of Solomon's glittering court (1 Kings 10:5; 2 Chron. 9:4).

BYBLOS, BYBLUS. See "Gebal."

BYZANTIUM (bĭ-zăn'shĭ-ŭm). Constantinople or Istanbul, a Greek city. In the fourth century A.D. it was made the capital of the Roman Empire.

CABUL (kā'bŭl). A town in Asher (Josh. 19:27) ceded by Solomon to Hiram, King of Tyre (1 Kings 9:10-13).

CAESAR (sē'zēr). The designation of the Roman Emperors after Julius Caesar. The name was used by Julius' adopted son, Augustus, the first Roman Emperor (27 B.C.-A.D. 14; see Luke 2:1). Afterward it was assumed in turn by each of his successors, so that it became a title. References to various Caesars occur in 28 places in the New Testament. Tiberius Caesar (A.D. 14-37) is mentioned in Luke 3:1 and 23:2, Mark 12:14-17, and John 19:12-15. Claudius Caesar (A.D. 41-54) is referred to in Acts 11:28, 17:7, and 18:2. Nero (A.D. 54-68) is apparently intended in Acts 25:8, 26:32, 27:24, and 28:19 and Philippians 4:22.

Other Caesars living during the New Testament period but not mentioned in the Bible include Caligula (A.D. 37-41), Galba (A.D. 68-69), Otho (A.D. 69), Vitellius (A.D. 69), Vespasian (A.D. 69-79), Titus (A.D. 79-81), Domitian (A.D. 81-96), Nerva (A.D. 96-98), and Trojan (A.D. 98-117).

CAESAREA (in Palestine) (sĕs-à-rē'à). A city established by Herod the Great on the site of a former coastal station called Strato's Tower (Acts 8:40; 10:1; 18:22; 23:33; 25:6). It was a brilliant Hellenistic city with both a harbor and an amphitheater. It was the administrative center of the Roman government in Palestine.

Lofty source of the Jordan River, near Mount Hermon and Caesarea Philippi (© *MPS*)

CAESAREA PHILIPPI (sĕs-à-rē'à fĭ-lĭp'ĭ). A capital city founded by Philip the tetrarch, son of Herod the Great (Matt. 16: 13; Mark 8:27). It was located at the pagan cult center of Panias (Banias) near the headwaters of the Jordan River.

CAIAPHAS (kā′ya-făs). Joseph Caiaphas officiated as the Jewish high priest from about A.D. 18 to 36, when he was deposed by Vitellius, the governor of Syria. Caiaphas is mentioned in the biblical account of the raising of Lazarus (John 11:47-53), the trial of Jesus (Matt. 26:57; John 18: 24), and the trial of Peter and John (Acts 4:6-22).

CAIN (kān) ("acquisition"). The firstborn son of Adam and Eve. He became the world's first murderer (Gen. 4:1-8). Cain pictures man in his natural condition— lost and in desperate need of divine grace and atonement by shed blood (Eph. 1:7; Col. 1:14).

CALAMUS (Greek *kalamos*, "a reed"; Hebrew *keneh bosēm*, "reed of fragrance," and *kāneh*, "cane, reed"). An ingredient of the holy anointing oil (Exod. 30:23) and apparently also of certain sacrifices (Isa. 43:24; Jer. 6:20). It was imported (Jer. 6:20; Ezek. 27:19) from Europe and India. The calamus from Europe was evidently the *Acorus calamus*, common sweet sedge.

CALEB (kā′lĕb) ("dog"). One of the twelve scouts who explored Canaan (Num. 13). Through faith in God he was ready to enter the land immediately (Num. 13:30). Later he exercised the faith necessary to claim his inheritance (Josh. 14:6-14).

CALENDAR, HEBREW. Although the Old Testament gives clear evidence that the ancient Hebrews possessed a roughly calculated calendar, they have nowhere given a complete account of their system. The precise determination of this system still remains a problem of biblical research. The Hebrews probably always had a lunar-solar calendar. Such calendars were widely used throughout the ancient Near East from very early times.

1. *The Year.* The Hebrew word for "year" (*shanāh*, from the root "to change") is so named from the succession of the seasons. In Jewish civil time-reckoning the year began with the autumn equinox in the seventh month of Tishri (Exod. 23:16; 34:22). The Jewish religious year, however, began in the

spring (Exod. 12:2; Deut. 16:1, 6). This was the "beginning of months" to the Jews in commemoration of their joyous departure from the bondage of Egypt.

2. *The Months.* The Hebrew calendar year consisted of lunar months. The primitive Hebrew word for "month" (*yerah*), like cognates in other Semitic languages, was related to the word for "moon" (*yareah*). Each month was calculated to consist of 29 or 30 days. Since the lunar year was about 11 days less than the solar year, some method of correction was necessary. However, precisely how the Hebrews adjusted the lunar year to the solar year is not known. Possibly they inserted a second Adar (twelfth month) or second Elul (sixth month) within the lunar cycle of 3, 6, 11, 14, 17, or 19 years.

Important for controlling the calendar was the observation of the autumnal equinox, "the going out of the year" (Exod. 23:16), and the spring equinox, "the return of the year" (1 Kings 20:26; 2 Chron. 36:10). The lunar year began when the thin crescent of the new moon was first visible nearest the spring equinox while the sun was in Aries (Josephus, *Antiquities* III: 8, 4). Then the Passover on the fourteenth day of Nisan coincided with the first full moon (Exod. 12:2-6).

The months were usually designated numerically in all periods, although other names were sometimes used. Each month had connections with the seasons of the year and the annual festivals.

The early (pre-exilic) names of the months, now identifiable only for the first, second, seventh, and eighth months, are probably local descriptive names of the Palestinian seasons. This is known to be true of Abib; it means "the ripening of grain" (Exod. 13:4). The names of Ziw (1 Kings 6:1, 37), Ethanim (1 Kings 8:2), and Bul (1 Kings 6:38) are now uncertain in meaning. In the post-exilic period the names of the Babylonian calendar were adopted.

3. *The Seasons.* Despite the fact that the Hebrews employed a calendar based on lunar months, as farmers they frequently indicated the time of the year by reference to the seasons. The agricultural calendar followed well-defined periods—the

dry season (April – September) and the rainy season (October – March). The latter was again subdivided into "seed-time" (November – December) and "harvest" (April – June; cf. Gen. 8:22).

4. *The Gezer Calendar.* This calendar was discovered in the city of Gezer in 1908. It is an agricultural calendar roughly inscribed in stone, apparently by a schoolboy of the tenth century B.C. It

THE HEBREW CALENDAR YEAR						
Month	Pre-exilic Name	Post-exilic Name	Bible Reference	Present-day Equivalent	Season	Festival
1	Abib	Nisan	Exod. 12:2 Neh. 2:1	March-April	Spring Latter Rains Barley Harvest Flax Harvest	14, Passover 15-21, Un-leavened Bread 16, First-fruits
2	Ziw	Iyyar	1 Kings 6:1, 37	April-May	Dry Season Begins	
3		Siwan	Esth. 8:9	May-June	Early Figs	6, Pentecost, Feast of Weeks
4		Tammuz	Ezek. 8:14	June-July	Grape Harvest	
5		Ab		July-August	Olive Harvest	
6		Elul	Neh. 6:15	August-September	Dates, Summer Figs	
7	Ethanim	Tishri	1 Kings 8:2	September-October	Early Rains	1, Trumpets 10, Atonement 15-21, Taber-nacles 22, Solemn Assembly
8	Bul	Marheshwan	1 Kings 6:38	October-November	Plowing	
9		Kislev	Neh. 1:1	November-December	Sowing	25, Dedica-tion
10		Tebet	Esth. 2:16	November-December	Rains	
11		Shebat	Zech. 1:7	January-February	Almond Blossoms	
12		Adar	Ezra 6:15	February-March	Citrus Fruit Harvest	13, Purim (Lots)

lists the farming operations for the year: two months of storage, two months of planting grain, two months of spring growth, one month of hoeing up flax, one month of barley harvest, one month of harvesting everything else, two months of vine pruning, and one month of summer fruit.

5. *Other Methods of Calculating Time.* Historical events in the monarchical pe-

riod are commonly dated by the reigning years of rulers (2 Kings 3:1, 8:16; 12:1). Sometimes a memorable event is used in dating, such as the Exodus (1 Kings 6:1), the sojourn in Egypt (Exod. 12:40), the seventy-year exile in Babylon (Ezek. 33: 21), or the earthquake during Uzziah's reign (Amos 1:1; Zech. 14:5). In the post-exilic books of Haggai and Zechariah the datings are by the reign of the Persian kings (Hag. 1:1; Zech. 1:1, 6; etc.).

6. *Time Reckoning in the New Testament.* The New Testament writers usually referred to time in terms of the current Jewish calendar. Among the days of the week the Sabbath is frequently cited. Also mentioned is "the preparation," that is, the day before the Sabbath (Mark 15: 42; cf. John 19:31). Friday of the Passover week is referred to as "the preparation of the Passover" (John 19:14). The "first day of the week" (literally "one day after the Sabbath") received a new meaning after Christ's resurrection from the dead on that day (Acts 20:7; 1 Cor. 16:2).

Numerous references to the various Jewish festivals are found in the New Testament, especially in the Gospel of John (cf. John 2:13, 23; 5:1; 6:4; 7:2, 37; 10:22; 11:55, 56). References are also found in Matthew 26:2; Mark 14:1; Luke 22:1; Acts 2:1; 12:3, 4; 18:21; 20:6; 20: 16; 27:9; 1 Corinthians 16:8.

As in the post-exilic books of Haggai and Zechariah, dates in the New Testament are sometimes reckoned by reference to Gentile rulers. An elaborate reference is given in Luke 3:1, 2, where secular as well as religious authorities are named. Elsewhere in the New Testament Herod the Great is referred to (Matt. 2:1; Luke 1:5), as well as provincial governors Quirinius (Luke 2:2) and Gallio (Acts 18:12) and Roman Emperors Augustus (Luke 2:1), Tiberius (Luke 3:1), and Claudius (Acts 11:28).

7. *The Sectarian Calendar.* Minor calendar differences existed between the Sadducees and the Pharisees. Far more significant, however, is the cleavage between those in Judaism who subscribed to the sectarian calendar (known from the Book of Jubilees and now also from the Qumran Literature) and those who followed the traditional Jewish calendar.

Jesus and his disciples may have followed the sectarian calendar, thus possibly clarifying why they kept the Passover before his arrest while the chief priests and their aides did not keep it until after his crucifixion (cf. John 18:28).

CALF, GOLDEN. At Mount Sinai the Israelites turned to the worship of a golden bull (Exod. 32). Similar idolatrous representations were erected by Jeroboam I at the cult centers of Bethel and Dan (1 Kings 12:28, 29). They were doubtless similar to representations of the Egyptian deity Apis, even though the invisible God of Israel was regarded as enthroned above the bulls. In any case the statues were a dangerous innovation and a temptation to idolatry because of the pronounced bull affiliations of Baal, the great Canaanite deity.

CAMEL (Hebrew *gāmāl*, Greek *kamelos*). Most of the Bible references are to the one-humped *Camelus dromedarius* or Arabian camel. The species has two main types, the slow, burden-bearing camel (Gen. 37:25) and the swift dromedary (1 Sam. 30:17). A camel is an excellent beast of burden (Gen. 37:25; 1 Kings 10:2; Isa. 60:6); it can carry 450 to 550 pounds. A riding camel can cover between 65 and 75 miles in a day and is admirably adapted to desert or semi-desert areas. It eats desert plants and can go for several days without water. Its flat feet enable it to walk on the sand without sinking. Camel's hair was woven into cloth (Matt. 3:4).

Ageless vehicle of the Middle East may outlast the pyramids. (*Russ Busby photo*)

CAMEL DRIVER. Domesticated camels were employed to a limited degree beginning with the patriarchal period (from 2000 B.C.; cf. Gen. 12:16; 24:35; 30:43; 32:7; Job 1:3, 17; 42:12). In the thirteenth century the camel became widely used in caravan trade, superseding the earlier horse and the still earlier ass as a beast of burden. Men often conducted trade caravans as a permanent occupation, much as truckers today.

CAMPHIRE. See "Henna."

CANA (kā′nà). A town in Galilee (present-day Khirbet Qana) about eight miles north of Nazareth. It was here that Jesus changed water into wine (John 2:1-11; 4:46). Nathanael was a native of this town (John 21:2).

CANAANITES (kā′nà-nīts). The inhabitants of Canaan (the more ancient name of Palestine). As a geographical place name Canaan is apparently derived from "Hurrian," meaning "belonging to the land of red purple." This colorful designation derives from the commercial dye obtained from murex shells found on the Mediterranean coast and constituting an important item of trade of the seafaring Phoenicians. By the time of the Conquest the term "Canaan" designated Palestine in general. The term "Palestine" is of later Greek derivation and refers to Philistia, where the Philistines (Peleste) settled in large numbers in the twelfth century B.C.

The Canaanites inhabited the Syro-Palestinian coastland, particularly Phoenicia proper (Gen. 10:15-19; 12:5; 13:12; Num. 13:17-25). They were merchants and traders, specializing in the commerce of purple dye.

The Canaanites were mixed in race though predominantly Semitic. Fertility rites were prominent in their religion. Their pantheon and ritual are now well-known from the Ugaritic literature of the fourteenth century B.C. See also "Phoenicians."

CANDACE (kăn′dà-sē). A term applied to the reigning queens of the Ethiopian kingdom of Meroe in what is today the Sudan. Candace was a title roughly equivalent to "queen." The Candace whose treasurer Philip baptized was apparently the reigning queen mother not long after A.D. 30. The title was well known to ancient historians.

CANKERWORM (Hebrew *yelek,* "licker"). Undoubtedly the locust in the larva stage of its development. Joel 1:4 is probably intended to describe the various destructive stages of the locust as it grows to maturity rather than four separate animals, as in the King James Version.

CAPERNAUM (kà-pēr′na-ŭm). A town on the northwestern shore of the Lake of Galilee at the borders of Zebulun and Naphtali. There Jesus began his public ministry (Matt. 4:12-16; cf. Mark 1:21; Luke 4:31; John 2:12). The site is present-day Tell Hum (Hebrew Kefar Nahum); it is mentioned in Jewish sources. Its most prominent ruin is a synagogue built about A.D. 200.

CAPHTOR (käf′tŏr). An ancient name of Crete. It was the home of the Caphtorim (Deut. 2:23), one of the Hamitic peoples listed in the Table of the Nations as descended from Mizraim or Egypt (Gen. 10:14; 1 Chron. 1:12). Caphtor is the land from which the Philistines came (Jer. 47:4; Amos 9:7); they are thus presumably the same people as the Caphtorim (Deut. 2:23).

CAPPADOCIA (kăp-à-dō′shĭ-à). A region of Asia Minor north of Cilicia and south of Pontus. The Old Persian name was *Katpatuka* (Greek *Kappadokia,* Latin *Cappadocia*). After being a part of the Persian Empire, it became an independent kingdom about 255 B.C. In A.D. 17 it became a Roman province (Acts 2:9; 1 Pet. 1:1).

CAPTAIN. This term is used in English versions to render several Hebrew words, mainly because little is known of army ranks in Bible times. Three of the more common Hebrew words so rendered are *rab, sar,* and *pehah. Rab* means literally "one who is great" or "chief." It is employed principally of Assyrian and Babylonian officers, for example *rab tabbahim,* "captain of the guard" (2 Kings 25:8-21; Jer. 39:9–52:30), Rabshakeh, and Rabsaris (2 Kings 18:17). *Sar* literally means "prince" and *pehah* means "governor, commander" (1 Kings 20:24; 2 Kings 18:24; Isa. 36:9).

CARCHEMISH (kär′kė-mĭsh). The Syro-Hittite capital located on the great bend of the upper Euphrates River. It was captured by the Assyrians (Isa. 10:9). It was the place where the battle between Necho of Egypt and Nebuchadnezzar of Babylon was fought in 605 B.C. (2 Chron. 35:20; Jer. 46:2).

CARMEL, MOUNT (kär'mĕl). The promontory overlooking the bay of Haifa. There Elijah contended with the priests of Baal (1 Kings 18:19). Carmel (Hebrew *karmel*, "garden land") is actually a range of hills some 30 miles long, extending from the northwest to the southeast, from the south shore of the bay of Acre to the plain of Dothan. Mount Carmel proper is the main ridge at the northwest end.

CARPENTER. Both Joseph (Matt. 13:55) and Jesus (Mark 6:3) pursued the ancient trade of carpentry (Greek *tektōn*). In Old Testament times the "worker in wood" (Hebrew *harāsh cesim*) performed the various tasks required in the construction of wood buildings and furniture. He even made such agricultural implements as yokes, plows, and threshing instruments (2 Sam. 24:22; Isa. 28:27, 28). Carpenters also made carts, chariots (Song 3:9), and idols (Isa. 44:13-17). Phoenician craftsmen built ships (Ezek. 27:5, 6) and supplied the skill for erecting public buildings in the Davidic-Solomonic era (2 Sam. 5:11; 1 Kings 5:18).

CARTHAGE (kär'thĭj). The chief Punic city of North Africa, originally a Tyrian colony. It was the historic rival of Rome until destroyed in 146 B.C.

CASSIA (kăsh'ĭ-à) (Hebrew *ḳiddāh*). An aromatic wood and an ingredient of the holy anointing oil (Exod. 30:24). Cassia is derived from the bark of a species of the cinnamon tree (cf. Psa. 45:8).

CAT. There is no reference to the cat in the Bible. This seems to indicate that the animal was not commonly known or kept as a pet in Western Asia during the biblical period. Greek zoologists knew the cat, which was probably domesticated in Egypt. Bastet, a cat goddess, was the guardian deity of Bubastis. The cat was also closely connected with the sun-god, Re.

CATAPULT. A military machine employed by the Greeks and Romans for hurling stones against the parapets of walled towns. King Uzziah's "slings to cast stones" were giant catapults (2 Chron. 26:14).

CATERPILLAR. See "Locust."

CAUDA (kow'dà). A small island about 23 miles off the southeastern coast of Crete. Paul's ship ran under its lee when caught in the violent storm off Crete (Acts 27:16). Some ancient authorities call it Clauda (as in the King James Version). It is modern Gavdho.

CAVE. Caves are numerous in a limestone country like Palestine. In biblical times they were sometimes used as temporary homes (cf. Gen. 19:30; 1 Kings 19:9). They were natural tombs (Gen. 49:29-32; John 11:38). In periods of war and oppression they were ideal as places of refuge (Judg. 6:2; 1 Sam. 13:6; 24:3); the most notable cases were the caves at Makkedah (Josh. 10:16-27) and Adullam (1 Sam. 22:1; 2 Sam. 23:13). Sometimes caves were converted into storehouses or cisterns. See also under specific cave.

CEDAR, CEDAR OF LEBANON (Latin *Cedrus libani*, Hebrew *'erez*). One of the most famous trees of antiquity (1 Kings 5:6), reaching a height of 100 feet or more and a trunk diameter of 6 to 10 feet (Isa. 2:13; Ezek. 17:22; 31:3). Its fine timber was sought for the construction of palaces and temples (2 Sam. 5:11; 1 Kings 5:5, 6; 7:1-12; Ezra 3:7) and ships' masts (Ezek. 27:5). It was fragrant (Song 4:11) and was employed in ceremonial purification (Lev. 14:4; Num. 19:6). This noble tree still survives in the mountains of Syria and flourishes in the Taurus mountains of Asia Minor.

CELIBACY. The practice of remaining unmarried. Celibacy is nowhere commanded in Scripture, although the Apostle Paul describes circumstances under which it could be wise for an individual to abstain from marrying (1 Cor. 7:7-9, 25-40).

CENCHREA (sĕn'krē-à). The seaport of Corinth. It connected Corinth by sea to the East, as Lechaeum connected it with the West.

CENSER. A shallow, open-topped pan of bronze or gold (Exod. 27:3; 1 Kings 7:50) used for carrying live embers from the altar. When incense was placed on the sacred fire in these pans, they functioned as censers (Lev. 10:1; Num. 16:6; Rev. 8:3-5). The right to use the censer in the Temple worship was a God-ordained prerogative of the Aaronic priesthood (Num. 16:1-35; 2 Chron. 26:16-21).

CENTIPEDE. A general name for any

small, crawling animal with many feet. All such were declared unclean and were not to be eaten (Lev. 11:41, 42).

CENTURION. A Roman army officer who commanded a century (100 men). There were ten centurions in a cohort and sixty in a legion. The centurions were subordinate to the six tribunes of each legion and often deferred to them (Acts 22:26). However, the centurions were the backbone of the Roman army and controlled the discipline and efficiency of the legion as a military unit.

The importance of centurions in the Roman army and in the life of the empire is reflected in their prominence in the New Testament. The first Gentile to confront Jesus was a centurion (cf. Matt. 8:5-13; Luke 7:2-10). The first Gentile to confess that Jesus was the Son of God was also a centurion (Matt. 27:54; Mark 15:39). The first Gentile to be introduced to the gospel of grace was Cornelius the centurion (Acts 10:1-48). Paul was delivered to a Roman centurion for safe conduct to Rome (Acts 27:1).

CEPHAS (sē'fàs) (Greek *kēphas*, from Aramaic *kepha*, "stone or rock"). The Aramaic equivalent of "Peter" (Greek *petros*, "a stone"). The name given to Simon by Christ (John 1:42). See "Peter."

CHALDEANS (kāl-dē'ăns). Originally a semi-nomadic tribe which occupied the desert between North Arabia and the Persian Gulf (cf. Job 1:17). They settled in southern Babylonia around Ur (cf. Gen. 11:28; Acts 7:4). They were distinct from the Aramaeans. In the eighth century B.C. Chaldean power increased and Marduk-apla-iddina II, chief of the Chaldean district of Bit-Yakin, seized the throne of Babylon in 721-710 B.C. and again in 703-702 B.C., when he sought help from the West. He is the Merodach-Baladan of the Bible (2 Kings 20:12-19; Isa. 39:1).

In 626 B.C. a native Chaldean governor by the name of Nabopolasser came to the Babylonian throne. He founded a dynasty which ruled over a great empire. Among his successors were Nebuchadnezzar II (605-562 B.C.), Amel-Marduk or Evil-Merodach (562-560 B.C.), Nabonidus, and Belshazzar (556-539 B.C.). In Daniel's time the name Chaldea designated Babylonia as a whole (Dan. 1:1-4). The Chaldeans were prominent as a priestly class and were schooled in traditional astrology and philosophy (Dan. 1:17-20).

CHAMBERLAIN. The Hebrew word *saris* denotes a eunuch, an official in charge of the private quarters of a king or noble. As in the case of the cupbearer, the chamberlain had opportunity to gain the personal favor and confidence of his sovereign. Such an example was Nathan-meleck in the reign of Josiah (2 Kings 23:11). These officials were originally and customarily eunuchs, since they had access to the bedrooms of the palace women.

Chameleon—the animal that can "change its spots" (© *MPS*)

CHAMELEON. One of the numerous reptiles of the lizard family (Lev. 11:30). This particular lizard has the faculty of changing its color to blend with the objects surrounding it when in danger. This ability is due to the presence of both clear and pigment-bearing cells in its skin. See also "Lizard."

CHAMOIS (Hebrew *zemer*). A cloven-hoofed ruminant (Deut. 14:5) formerly thought to be the chamois, an alpine species never found near Palestine. More correct is "mountain sheep," commonly called "Barbary sheep," *Ammotragus lervia*. The mouflon (*Ovis musimon*) may also have been included.

CHANCELLOR. A Persian commanding official in the court of Artaxerxes (464-423 B.C.). The title probably denoted the office of Intelligence. See Ezra 4:8, 9, 17.

CHARIOT. Heavy, two-wheeled vehicles

drawn by asses and employed for war and peace in the third millennium B.C. in southern Babylonia (as demonstrated by discoveries at Ur and Kish). The true chariot, of lighter construction and drawn by the fleeter horse, did not come into use in Bible lands until the middle of the second millennium B.C. The Hittites and Egyptians adopted the horse-drawn chariot, as did many of the small city-states of Syria-Palestine (Gen. 41:43; 46: 29; 50:9). The Egyptian chariotry pursued Israel (Exod. 14:5-9, 23-28). The chariot became common in Israel during and after the time of David and Solomon (2 Sam. 8:4; 1 Kings 9:17-19; 10:28, 29). Ahab had a large chariotry, bringing 2000 chariots to the battle of Qarqar in 853 B.C. During the divided kingdom of Israel the chariot-driver was an important person in times of both war and peace in both Judah and Israel.

CHARM. See "Amulet."

CHEBAR RIVER (kē′bär). The Kabari Canal at Nippur in Babylonia (running east of the city). There Ezekiel saw his visions (Ezek. 3:15-22; 10:15).

CHEDORLAOMER (kĕd-ŏr-lå-ō′mēr). An Elamite king (unidentified) who led a coalition that invaded the Jordan Valley in the time of Abraham (about 2000 B.C.).

CHEESE. In a pastoral country like Syria-Palestine milk and its by-products of butter and cheese were important staple items of diet. Cheese was frequently presented as a gift (1 Sam. 17:18; 2 Sam. 17: 29). In time, cheesemaking became an important trade. The Tyropean Valley west of the city of David was the "Valley of the Cheese-Makers."

CHEMOSH (kē′mŏsh). The chief deity of the Moabites (Num. 21:29; Jer. 48:46). Solomon built a sanctuary to this deity at Jerusalem (1 Kings 11:7). It was later destroyed by Josiah (2 Kings 23:13). Chemosh is prominent in the Mesha Stone and is compounded with Athtar, the Venus Star. This indicates that Chemosh may have been the manifestation of this astral deity.

CHERITH (kē′rĭth). A brook or wadi in Transjordan where Elijah took refuge from Jezebel at God's direction (1 Kings 17:3-5). It was apparently in Gilead, but the precise location is uncertain.

CHERUBIM AND SERAPHIM (chĕr′ ŭb-ĭm; sĕr′ă-phĭm). The cherubim are celestial beings of the angelic order, evidently guardians of God's holiness (Gen. 3:24; Exod. 25:18-22). In Ezekiel 10 the chariot-throne of God, still upborne by cherubim, becomes mobile. Representations of cherubim from Samaria and Gebal (Byblos) depict a composite figure with a human face, an animal body with four legs, and two large wings.

The seraphim are mentioned only in Isaiah's vision (Isa. 6:1-13). They were human in form but had six wings. Like the cherubim, they seem to be an order of angelic beings responsible for certain functions of guardianship and worship. See also "Angels."

CHIEF PRIEST. See "High Priest."

CHILIARCH. A Roman commander of one thousand men. The word is usually translated "chief captain" in the King James Version. See also "Centurion."

CHINNERETH, CHINNEROTH (kĭn′ ĕ-rĕth; kĭn′ĕ-rŏth). The Old Testament name of the Sea of Galilee (Josh. 12:3). Some scholars think the name is derived from *kinnor*, the Hebrew word for "harp," since the lake is somewhat harp-shaped.

CHIOS (kī′os). One of the larger islands in the Greek Archipelago off the coast of Asia Minor in the Aegean Sea. It lies south of Lesbos at the entrance of the Gulf of Smyrna. Paul's ship passed by it on his last voyage to Palestine (Acts 20: 15).

CHITTIM, KITTIM (kĭt′ĭm). The island of Cyprus. Kittim denotes the Kitians, the people of Kit or Kiti (the ancient town of Kition located on the southern coast of Cyprus). Chittim is present-day Larnaka. The name Kition was extended not only to the entire island (Isa. 23:1, 12) but to the coastlands of the Eastern Mediterranean as well (Jer. 2:10; Ezek. 27:6; Dan. 11:30). The broader use is seen in the Apocrypha (1 Macc. 1:1; 8: 5) and in the Dead Sea Scrolls (the *Habbakuk Commentary*).

CHLOE (klō′ĕ) ("the verdant"). A woman whose household informed Paul at Ephesus that there were divisions among the Corinthian Christians (1 Cor. 1:11). She must have been well known to Paul and the Corinthian church in order to be able to vouch for the reliability of Paul's informants.

CHORAZIN (kó-rā′zĭn). A town of Galilee which lay north-northwest of Capernaum (Matt. 14:21; Luke 10:13).

CHOSEN PEOPLE. The Jewish people, selected by God to be separate from the other nations and to enjoy his special blessings (Deut. 7:6). This selection had a fourfold purpose: 1) to furnish mankind with a witness of the unity of God amid universal idolatry (Deut. 6:1-5; Isa. 43: 10-12); 2) to demonstrate to the Gentiles the blessedness of serving the true and only God (Deut. 33:26-29); 3) to receive, preserve, and transmit the written Word of God (Deut. 4:5-8; Rom. 3:1, 2); and 4) to be the human vehicle for the Messiah, the world's Savior (Gen. 3:15; 12:3; 22: 18; 28:10-14; 49:10; Isa. 7:14; Mat. 1:1; Rom. 1:3). Israel is now temporarily set aside in her national election (Rom. 11:1-25). She will be regathered and restored to national favor at the second advent of Messiah (Zech. 12:1 – 14:21; Luke 1:31-33). See also "Jews" and "Israelites."

CHRIST. See "Jesus Christ."

CHURCH, TRUE. The aggregate of all regenerated believers who have lived at any time during the period between Pentecost and the Rapture. All such are united to Christ and to one another by the baptism of the Spirit (1 Cor. 12:12, 13; Rom. 6:3, 4; Col. 2:12; Gal. 3:27). The Church is also pictured as Christ's "body," with Christ personally as the "head" (Eph. 1:22, 23). It is also described as a holy "temple" for God to live in by the Spirit (Eph. 2:21, 22). The Church is also seen espoused to Christ as a pure virgin to one husband (2 Cor. 11:2); she will be glorified at Christ's return in the air.

The Church is being formed by the crucified, risen, and ascended Lord Jesus Christ. He is exalted at God's right hand and is made "head over all things to the church" (Eph. 1:20-23). The new age of the Church was foretold by our Lord himself (Matt. 16:18) and was ushered in at Pentecost, when the Holy Spirit was given, received, and deposited in the new people of God (Acts 2:1-47; cf. John 14: 16, 26; 16:12-15). The age will end when the Church is completed at the Rapture (1 Thess. 4:13-18; 1 Cor. 15:53, 54). See also "Bride of Christ."

CILICIA (sĭ-lĭsh′ĭ-à). A region in southeastern Asia Minor known as "Kizzuwatna" to the Hittites, "Khillaku" to the Assyrians, and "Kilikia" to the Greeks. It is called Kue in the Old Testament (1 Kings 10:28 RSV; 2 Chron. 1:16 RSV). It was the fourth satrapy of the Persian Empire. Cilicia Pedias ("lowland"), in which Tarsus was located, was distinguished from Cilicia Trachea ("rugged"), the mountainous western part.

CILICIAN GATES (sĭ-lĭsh′ĭ-àn). A narrow pass from Syria-Cilicia which gives access to the interior of Asia Minor through the Taurus Mountains.

CINNAMON. A fragrant wood (Song 4:14; Rev. 18:13) used as an ingredient in the holy anointing oil (Exod. 30:23) and to perfume beds (Prov. 7:17) and other articles of furnishing or dress. The cinnamon tree is native to Ceylon and belongs to the laurel family. The bark yields a fragrant, yellow oil employed in perfumery.

CIRCUMCISION. God initiated this rite as the sign of the Abrahamic Covenant and a token of justifying faith in divine grace on the part of the circumcised (Gen. 17:10-14; Rom. 4:11, 12). Abraham was justified before God by faith *before* he was circumcised (Gen. 15:6). But his willing submission to the rite was a token of his faith in God's Word and his assent to the gospel of salvation by grace through faith, totally apart from works.

The Jewish generation newly departed from Egypt was circumcised at Gilgal (Josh. 5:2-9). The "reproach of Egypt" (bondage to Pharaoh) was "rolled away" at that time. Circumcision became a reminder that the Israelites were saved by God's grace and delivered from slavery to sin and Satan. Old Testament circumcision is analogous to New Testament water baptism, in which the believer identifies himself with Christ in death and resurrection (Rom. 6:1-11; Col. 2:11, 12). *Spiritual* circumcision is appropriating what Christ has provided for us and enjoying the new life of victory (Rom. 2: 28, 29; Phil. 3:3).

CITIES OF REFUGE. The six cities of

refuge, three on each side of the Jordan (Num. 35:6-34; Deut. 4:41-43; 19:1-13), illustrate Christ as the sinner's shelter from judgment (Rom. 8:1, 33, 34; Heb. 6: 17-20; cf. Psa. 46:1; 142:5). The refugee had to remain in the city of refuge until the death of the contemporary high priest. Then he was free to leave with impunity. Likewise the death of Christ, the Great High Priest, sets the sinner free. See "Asylum."

CLAUDA (klô'dà). See "Cauda."

CLAUDIA (klô'dĭ-à) (probably from Latin *claudos*, "lame"). A Christian woman, probably a Roman, who sent greetings to Timothy (2 Tim. 4:21). She is mentioned as the mother (or wife) of Linus, the first bishop of Rome, in the *Apostolic Constitutions* VII:46.

CLAUDIUS (klô'dĭ-ūs). The fourth Roman Emperor (A.D. 41-54), a nephew of Tiberius. He banished all Jews from Rome (Acts 18:2).

CLEANSING. Scripture describes the fallen race in Adam as unclean and unfit for God's presence or fellowship. The once-for-all bath of regeneration cleanses not only from "dead works," which are powerless to save, but from the sins that are powerful to condemn (Rev. 1:5; 1 Cor. 6:11; 1 John 1:7). Although the believer is cleansed permanently from all guilt of the Law (Heb. 10:1-14), he incurs daily defilement in his earthly pilgrimage. His daily sins must be confessed so that unbroken fellowship with the Father and the Son may be maintained (1 John 1:8-10). This cleansing is illustrated by Jesus' washing of his disciples' feet (John 13:1-17) and by the cleansing of the laver in the Old Testament. The ceremonial approach to God involved first the bronze altar of sacrifice (symbolizing the Cross) and then the laver of cleansing (symbolizing cleansing from daily defilement). See Exodus 40:6, 7.

CLEMENT (klĕm'ĕnt) ("kind, merciful"). A Christian at Philippi who assisted Paul (Phil. 4:3).

CLEOPAS (klē'ō-pàs). One of two disciples who conversed with the risen Christ on the Emmaus Road (Luke 24:18).

CLEOPATRA (klē-ō-păt'rà). The Queen of Egypt from 52 to 30 B.C. Through her relations with Mark Antony she ob-

tained part of the coast of Palestine and the revenue of Jericho. She ruled as coregent with her son by Julius Caesar. Octavian's victory at Actium precipitated her downfall. She thereupon committed suicide, and Egypt became a Roman Province.

CLOTHING AND DRESS. The Bible does not present a detailed description of the various kinds of clothing which were worn in Palestine, except in the case of the Mosaic priesthood. However, a fair idea of the general dress may be formed by piecing together scattered biblical references. This is adequately supplemented by references in extra-biblical written records from Egypt, Asia Minor, Mesopotamia, and Syria-Palestine and from tomb paintings, seal impressions, and other archeological sources. For example, the tomb of Khnumhotep at Benihasan in Egypt displays a group of Asiatics arriving in Egypt with eyepaint. Their clothing is vividly colored and furnishes information about the clothing of the Hebrew patriarchs and other nomadic peoples during the twelfth Egyptian Dynasty (about 1870 B.C.).

Materials for Clothing. Skins of animals, wool, linen, and goat's hair were the common materials available in Palestine. The most widely used material was wool spun from the fleece of sheep. When spun from goat's hair it supplied a cheap material for the poor as well as the coarse sackcloth worn by mourners (1 Kings 21: 27; Job 16:15; Jonah 3:6). Cotton was woven from the fibers of a plant (*Gossypium herbaceum*) evidently introduced from India by Persian times (Esth. 1:6; 8:15). It was not generally available in Palestine during the Old Testament period.

Mosaic law prohibited the wearing of mixed materials, such as wool and linen (Lev. 19:19; Deut. 22:11). The regulation reminded Israelites of their separation to God and their responsibility to observe God's ordained order. For the same reason one sex was not to wear clothes of the opposite sex (Deut. 22:5).

Dyes and Colors. White was the commonly preferred color of the Hebrews, the art of bleaching being known in early times (2 Kings 18:17; Isa. 7:3; Mal. 3:2; Mark

9:3). Scarlet was obtained from the juices of crushed cochineal insects found in oak trees. Black-purple or red-violet ("Tyrian" or "imperial" dye) was made from the mollusks *pupura* and *murex*, native to the Eastern Mediterranean coast. These dyes were used mainly for coloring expensive garments for royalty and nobility (Judg. 8:26; Prov. 31:22; Luke 16:19; Rev. 18:12, 16). They were also used in the Tabernacle fabric (Exod. 26:31). The "blue, purple, and crimson" were variations of these dyes (2 Chron. 3: 14; cf. John 19:2, 5).

In Palestine yellow dyes were made from ground pomegranate rind. The Phoenicians used safflower and turmeric. Blue was secured from the indigo plant imported from Syria or Egypt, where it had previously been transplanted from India.

Distinction between Male and Female Clothing. There was a general resemblance between the dress of men and women in biblical antiquity, the distinctions being far less marked than in western lands. But the differences were sufficiently obvious, for men and women were strictly prohibited from wearing one another's clothing (Deut. 22:5). Women wore finer materials with greater color and ornamentation, as well as veils and headcloths.

The most common items of dress were the shirt-tunic and the robe, comprising the basic inner and outer garments of both sexes. Women wore fine underwear (*sadin*) in addition (Prov. 31:24; Isa. 3: 23). See also specific item of clothing.

COAT OF MAIL (Hebrew *shiryon*). Armor which protected the torso and was made of scale-like plates of bronze (1 Sam. 17:5, 38). In Israelite times the coat of mail or cuirass was made of leather for the soldier and of bronze for the commander or general. Goliath had metal armor composed of bronze scales because he was the champion of the Philistines (1 Sam. 17:5). Ahab wore a cuirass when he was struck with an arrow "between the scale armor and the breastplate" (1 Kings , 22:34 RSV), that is, between the leather flaps of the cuirass at the waistline. Jeremiah 46:4 and 51:3 refer to the cuirass as an exceptionally light-armored coat con-

sisting of tiny iron plates fastened to a leather coat.

Such coats of metal date at least as early as the fifteenth century B.C., as is attested by discoveries at Ras Shamra, Boghazkeui, Nuzi, and Alalah. The later Greek equivalent of the metal cuirass was the *thorax*—armor used to protect war elephants (1 Macc. 6:43). Compare Paul's reference to "the breastplate of righteousness" in Ephesians 6:14.

COCKATRICE. See "Adder."

Pieces of silver—the price of infamous betrayal (© MPS)

COINS AND MONEY.

1. *The Pre-Coinage Period.* Prior to the introduction of coinage in the eighth century B.C., farm produce that could be bartered was the common medium of exchange. This consisted of such perishable commodities as wool, wheat, barley, and dates, and such non-perishable items as metals, timber, wine, honey, and livestock.

Metals as an exchange commodity were also used in commercial transactions. The most common of these in the ancient Near East was silver (cf. Gen. 13:2). Silver became so popular as a commodity that the Hebrew word for it became practically synonymous with the idea of money (cf. Gen. 17:13). Solomon bought chariots at 600 shekel-weight of silver and horses at 150 (1 Kings 10:29; cf. Lev. 5:15). Until the post-exilic era the *shekel* retained its literal meaning of a weight rather than a coin. The less-common gold was often listed following the silver (Gen. 13:2; 2 Kings 18:14).

Metal used for currency was circulated in the form of jewelry, objects in everyday use, or in various shapes (Gen. 24:22; Josh. 7:21; Isa. 13:12). Gold and silver were also circulated in the form of ingots, vessels, or dust. Bags or pouches were used to carry currency (Gen. 42:35; 2

Kings 5:23; Prov. 7:20; Hag. 1:6). Copper was often transported in the form of flat, circular disks.

Metals employed as currency had to be weighed out (Hebrew *shaqal*, "to weigh," hence *shekel*). The weighing was performed by the purchaser and verified by the seller in the presence of witnesses (Gen. 23:9; Jer. 32:9, 10). Standards varied from locality to locality; hence the expression "the silver current with the merchant" (Gen. 23:16, literal translation). Metals were also stamped with the place of origin (such as Ophir, 1 Kings 10:11, or Parvaim, 2 Chron. 3:6) or classified with respect to their refinement.

2. *The Period of Coined Money.* A coin is a piece of metal impressed with a seal attesting its title and weight so that it is acceptable on sight. Coinage first appeared in Asia Minor in the late eighth century B.C., when early silver specimens were recovered at Aegina. The first *staters* appeared when the proverbially rich Croesus (561-546 B.C.) minted *staters* in electrum (an alloy of gold and silver); his coins became dubbed "Croesides."

Coins were apparently introduced into the Persian Empire by Darius I (521-486 B.C.) after the conquest of Lydia. He gave his name to the thick gold *daric*, a 130-gram coin. It was familiar to the Jews in exile (Ezra 2:69 RSV; Neh. 7:70, 71 RSV).

The spread of coinage into Judah was apparently slow, possibly because of the images impressed into the coins. For example, the silver *shekels* of Nehemiah 5:15 and 10:32 may have been weights rather than coins. But the popularization of coins by Phoenician traders in the fifth and fourth centuries eventually began to have its effect on Judah. By the second century B.C., Syria and Palestine were under strong Hellenizing influence and the Greek *talent* and *drachma* began to be used widely. Their use continued well into New Testament times.

Although there is archeological evidence that the Jews attempted to mint their own coins in the fourth century B.C., it was not until the era of the Maccabees that they were successful in doing so. In 141 or 140 B.C. Antiochus VII granted permission to Simon Maccabeus to issue native coinage (1 Macc. 15:6), which appeared in circulation from that time on.

Money from a total of three different sources circulated in Palestine during this era. First was the official imperial coinage of Rome. Second was the provincial coinage minted at Antioch and Tyre; it was essentially Greek. Third was the local Jewish money, probably coined at Caesarea. Certain cities and client kings were also accorded the right to mint their own bronze coins.

Along with such a variety of coinage in circulation came an obvious need for money-changers. This was especially true at the Jewish feasts, when Jews from various parts of the Empire came to pay their poll tax to the Temple treasury (cf. Matt. 21:12; Mark 11:15; Luke 19:45, 46; John 2:13-17).

Coins commonly used during the New Testament era are described below.

Assarion (Greek *assarion*). A Roman copper coin translated "farthing" in the King James Version of Matthew 10:29 and Luke 12:6. It was worth a quarter of the bronze *sestertius* and one-sixteenth of the silver *denarius*. It was equal to roughly one cent in American money.

Denarius (Greek *denarion*). This standard Roman silver coin was equal to the Greek *drachma* and was equivalent to about 16 cents in today's money. Twenty-five *denarii* constituted the gold *aureus*. It is translated "penny" in the King James Version of Matthew 22:19. It was the average day's pay for a farm laborer in Palestine (Matt. 20:1-16).

Drachma (Greek *drachmē*). The silver *drachma* was the basic Greek coin while the silver *denarius* was the basic Roman coin. The two coins were roughly equal in value, each being worth about 16 cents. There were 100 *drachmai* to the *mina* and 6000 to the *talent*. It is the piece of silver referred to in Luke 15:8-10. The *didrachmon* or *double drachmon* was substituted for the *half-shekel* required for the annual Temple tax. The *tetradrachma* (*quadruple drachma* or *stater*) equaled one shekel, the tax for two people.

Lepton (Greek *leptos*). This is the famous "widow's mite" (Mark 12:42; Luke 21:2); the term denoted the smallest piece of money imaginable. It is the only Jewish coin alluded to in the New Testament. The *leptos* was bronze and was equal in value to one-half the Roman *quadrans* or one-eighth the *assarion*.

Mina (Greek *mna*). The "pound" of Luke 19:12-26. It is equivalent to one hundred denarii (about 16 dollars in present American currency).

Quadrans (Greek *kodrantēs*). The smallest Roman coin, equivalent in value to one-quarter of the copper *assarion*. It could be paraphrased "the last penny" in Matthew 5:26. (The coin is equivalent in value to about one-quarter of an American penny).

Sestertius. A Roman coin equivalent to one-quarter of a *denarius*. It is not referred to in the Bible.

Shekel. During the first revolt (A.D. 66-70) the Jews proudly coined their own silver for the first time, issuing shekels, half-shekels, and quarter-shekels.

Stater. The *tetradrachma*. See under "Drachma."

Talent. A unit of monetary reckoning rather than an actual coin. The Roman-Attic talent was equivalent to 240 *aurei*, roughly 960 American dollars. In Matthew 18:24, ten thousand talents signifies a very large sum of money. In Matthew 25:15-28 the silver talent is probably intended.

COLORS. Blue, purple, scarlet, fine-twined linen, and gold were prominent in the Tabernacle and priesthood, picturing various aspects of the person and work of Christ (cf. Exod. 26:31, 32, 36, 37, etc.). Blue, the color of the heaven, speaks of separation from evil and a heavenly walk. Purple, the color of royalty, portrays Christ's kingly role. Scarlet, the color of blood, speaks of Christ's atoning work. White, the color of purity, suggests Christ's sinlessness. Gold bespeaks Christ's deity.

COLOSSE (kȯ-lŏs′ė). A city in the Roman province of Asia in the western part of what is now Turkey. It was situated 10 miles up the Lycus Valley from Laodicea on the main road from Ephesus to the east. Paul wrote his "Epistle to the Colossians" to the church in this city. The modern site (near Khonai) is not inhabited.

COMMANDMENTS. Commandments are principles of action which the Creator requires of all his creatures. They derive from the moral law of God, which is as eternal as God himself because it is a reflection of his eternally holy character and being. The commandments are summarized in the law of love—love of the creature for the Creator and love of the creature for his fellow-creatures (cf. Deut. 6:5; 10:12; Matt. 22:37-40). Sin entered the universe when Lucifer and a host of other angels broke the moral law of God. Human beings sinned for the same reason. Yet both fallen angels and fallen men will continue to be judged for their response to the eternal moral law, since God did not change when his creatures sinned.

Since fallen angels and unsaved men will be judged according to their works (their reaction to the moral law of God— Rev. 20:11-15), there will be degrees of punishment in Gehenna. Unfallen angels and redeemed men will also be judged according to their reaction to the moral law of God. This necessitates degrees of reward in heaven and the sin-cleansed universe (Rom. 14:10; Gal. 6:7; 1 Cor. 3:11-15; 2 Cor. 5:10; Eph. 6:8; Col. 3:24, 25).

The Ten Commandments from Sinai (Exod. 20:1-17) are an adaptation of the eternal moral law of God to the exigencies of the Mosaic Covenant made with the elect nation Israel. God imposed his moral law directly and dramatically upon Israel in order to display his covenant grace through them and to demonstrate to all the world the benefits of serving the one true God. This does not mean that non-Jews are free to ignore God's eternal moral law. All men are obligated to keep the law in its eternal features by virtue of their creaturehood.

The Mosaic Decalogue contains one commandment—that of Sabbath observance—which is unique to the Jewish people and which was never imposed on any other nation (Exod. 20:8-11). Observance of the Sabbath was a strict moral obligation of the covenant people. Breaking it was punishable by death (Exod. 31:14; Num. 15:32-36).

All the other commandments of the Decalogue are universally binding upon all mankind in every age and are set forth in the New Testament under grace. No fallen man can keep these commandments to merit salvation before God. However, all men are to keep them outwardly as the basis of human law and are required to do so. For this they will give account both to God in the final judgment and to their fellow men in this life. See under "Decalogue."

CONCUBINE. A woman in biblical times who sustained a semi-married relationship with a man. She was less privileged than a wife but more privileged than a mistress in the modern sense. In biblical times the wife was on an equal social basis with her husband while the concubine was a bondmaid, quite frequently the servant of the wife (Gen. 29:24, 29) and often a captive taken in war (Deut. 21:10-14). A Hebrew woman might become a concubine by first falling into the condition of servitude. However, her position and treatment came under special restrictive legislation (Exod. 21:7-11).

The concubine's children were not accounted illegitimate, but constituted a kind of supplementary family. Their names frequently occur in the patriarchal narratives (Gen. 22:24). Their position and inheritance depended on the desire of the father (Gen. 25:6). Unlike a wife, a concubine could be rejected without a bill of divorce.

The whole system of concubinage, like polygamy, was clearly a perversion of the divine order of the sexes (Gen. 2:24). God permitted it to exist temporarily, but under limitations unheard of among neighboring pagan peoples. Scripture does not attempt to minimize the sad consequences resulting from the practice of polygamy and concubinage, even when it occurred among Bible heroes (Gen. 16:1-16).

CONEY (Hebrew *shaphan*). Not the English coney (the rabbit) but the rock badger, the *Hyrax syriacus*. It looks like a rabbit, even moving its jaws as if it were chewing the cud like the rabbit, but it does not actually ruminate. The rock badger lives among the rocks (Psa. 104:18; Prov. 30:26). It is found in sections of Palestine and the Sinai Peninsula.

CONFESSION. Confession of Christ as Savior is that heart-response to God by which faith in Christ as one's Sin-Bearer is sealed (cf. Rom. 10:9, 10; 1 John 4:2, 3, 15). Confession as an act of a sinning saint involves not salvation but fellowship. The sinning Christian turns to the Father in full acknowledgement of his sin and accepts God's estimate of it. On the divine side, cleansing and forgiveness are provided in the faithfulness of God, since Christ has borne the sin in question (1 John 1:9).

CONSCIENCE. An inborn moral monitor found in every man. Conscience lifts man above the animal level. Rejection of God's revelation of himself in nature and in Scripture results in demonic delusion, idolatry, and a desensitized conscience (1 Tim. 4:1, 2).

CONSUL. The title of the two chief military and political magistrates in the Roman Republic. Although they are not mentioned in the Bible, a certain consul named Lucius is mentioned in 1 Maccabees 15:16.

CORBAN. An offering or oblation (Mark 7:11). The term in post-exilic Judaism refers to a gift consecrated to God for religious purposes. The Mishna declares that anything set apart by the use of the term, even rashly, could not thereafter be used for any other purpose. Christ refers to this special use of the word in Mark 7:11.

CORIANDER (Hebrew *gad*). A plant bearing pink and white blossoms and yielding white seeds and small globular fruit used as a condiment. Manna resembled coriander seed (Exod. 16:31; Num. 11:7).

CORINTH (kōr'ĭnth). A commercial metropolis at the western end of the isthmus between central Greece and the Peloponnesus. It controlled trade routes across the isthmus through its western port, Lechaeum, and its eastern outlet at Cenchrea. Augustus made it the capital of the province of Achaia; it was ruled by a proconsul. Paul stayed eighteen months in Corinth on his second tour

(Acts 18:1-18). To the church there he penned 1 and 2 Corinthians.

CORMORANT (Hebrew *shālāk*). A ceremonially unclean bird (Lev. 11:13, 17; Deut. 14:12, 17). It is apparently the common cormorant (*Phalacrocorax carbo*), a large water bird of the pelican family. The bird is found in Palestine along the Maritime Coast and on the Sea of Galilee. Another species, the pygmy cormorant, is sometimes found along the streams of Palestine which empty into the Mediterranean.

CORN. The term "corn" is an archaic generic designation for the staple cereals cultivated in Palestine. So truly are these grains the staff of life that the term "corn and wine" figuratively comprehends the entire vegetable produce of the field (Gen. 27:28; Deut. 7:13). The chief cereals were wheat, emmer, barley, and millet. Certain legumes, such as beans and lentils, were also basic staples.

CORNELIUS (kôr-nē'li-ŭs). A Roman centurion who became the first Gentile to receive the gospel of Christ and the great salvation ministered by the outpoured Spirit (Acts 10:1-48).

COS, COOS (kŏs; kō'ŏs). An island of the Aegean Sea off the coast of Caria in Asia Minor. It lay about a day's sail between Miletus and Rhodes (Acts 21:1). The island is famous as the birthplace of Hippocrates and the site of the medical school which he founded there in the fifth century B.C.

COUNSELOR. In Old Testament times counselors were members of the king's court (2 Chron. 25:16; Isa. 1:26; 3:3). In some instances the counselor was apparently next in power to the king himself (Mic. 4:9; cf. Job 3:14; 12:17). In New Testament times counselors were members of advisory or legislative bodies.

The Greek word *bouleutēs* denotes a "decider" or "deliberator." Joseph of Arimathea, a member of the Sanhedrin or Jewish supreme court, was such an official (Mark 15:43; Luke 23:50). See also "Chancellor."

COW (Hebrew *ʿeglah*). Cows were domesticated early in human history. Abraham and other patriarchs herded cows (Gen. 13:2; 32:15). Egypt and Palestine afforded excellent pasturage (Gen. 41:2; Deut.

7:13; 1 Sam. 6:7). Cows' milk served as food (2 Sam. 17:29), together with the milk of camels and goats (Gen. 32:15; Prov. 27:27).

COZBI (kŏz'bĭ) (Akkadian *kuzbu*, "voluptuousness"). A Midianite woman slain at Shittim by Phinehas, grandson of Aaron (Num. 25:6-8, 14, 15; cf. Psa. 106:30, 31). The woman was a seducer and was guilty of immorality and complicity with Baal worship. As a princess (daughter of Zur, head of a chief tribe in Midian), her influence for evil was great. She beguiled Zimri, prince of a chief house of Simeon. Phinehas slew both Zimri and Cozbi with a javelin to cleanse Israel and stay a plague caused by complicity with idolatry (Num. 25:6-8, 14, 15).

CRAFTSMAN. See "Artisan."

CRANE (Hebrew *āgūr*). A large, elegant migrating bird that emits a chattering sound (Isa. 38:14). It is a long-legged wading bird, migrating south from Europe and Asia at the approach of winter.

CREATION. The account of the origin of the earth and the universe as contained in the Word of God. It is the authoritative answer to the fiction of evolution. The choice in the matter is to believe either God's revelation or man's theorizing. Direct creation by God answers the basic problem. The theory of evolution merely drives the idea of origin back into oblivion, leaving the central problem of a first cause no nearer solution. Moreover, it ignores the marvelous design and purpose manifested everywhere in the natural world.

The Bible account of creation is simple and elevated in tone, in contrast to the crass polytheistic concepts of the ancient world. But the creation of the world out of nothing makes sense only to those who have faith in the God of revelation, infinite in power and wisdom (Heb. 11:3). The visible universe is then understood to proceed from the invisible God. On earth man is made in God's image as the mysterious projection of the unseen into the seen. Christ is both the perfect projection and the Author of creation (John 1:1-3; Col. 1:15-17).

CRETE (krēt). A mountainous island about 156 miles long and 7 to 35 miles broad which is situated at the southern extremity of the Aegean Sea. It is evidently referred to as "Caphtor" in the Old Testament (Jer. 47:4; Amos 9:7). In the New Testament, Cretans are mentioned among those present at Pentecost (Acts 2:11). The island figures prominently in the account of Paul's journey to Rome (Acts 27:7-22). His vessel sailed past Salmone at the eastern end and put in at a port called Fair Havens (near Lasea in the center of the south coast). The ship missed the better wintering berth at Phenice in the southwest and was plunged into the terrible storm recounted in Acts 27. After his imprisonment Paul apparently revisited Crete, where he left Titus to carry on the work. The heyday of Cretan civilization was reached about 1750-1400 B.C.

CRETANS (krē'táns). The inhabitants of the island of Crete (Caphtor). Their culture flourished under Minoan civilization of the second millennium B.C. and was centered at their capital of Knossos on the north-central coast of the island, facing the Aegean Sea. Crete became part of the Hellenic world when their domination of the Aegean Sea was brought to an end by the Achaeans. The Philistines came from Caphtor or Crete (Jer. 47:4; Amos 9:7) and were the "Cherethites and Pelethites" of David's bodyguard (2 Sam. 8:18). Jews came from Crete to celebrate Pentecost at Jerusalem (Acts 2:11). Paul sailed along the coast of Crete on his voyage to Rome (Acts 27:7-22). Christianity was planted in the island and Titus was appointed as overseer of the churches (Tit. 1:5).

CROCODILE. The word "crocodile" does not occur in the King James Version but is thought to be the reptile described as "leviathan" in Job 41. Egypt was the habitat of the crocodile.

CROSS. The framework of wood on which Christ was nailed. Theologically the word denotes the central meaning of Christ's sufferings and redemptive death on that instrument of torture (Gal. 6:14). The Cross reveals what the world is and judges it in the light of divine holiness and grace (John 12:31-33). See also "Crucifixion."

CROWN. A reward to be bestowed on believers at the judgment seat of Christ for faithful service to the Savior (1 Cor. 3:12-14; 2 Cor. 5:10). Several crowns are described in Scripture: *the incorruptible crown,* a reward for those who discipline bodily appetites (1 Cor. 9:24, 25); *a crown of life* for those who successfully endure testings (James 1:12); *the victor's crown* (2 Tim. 4:8) for those who finish their course and love Christ's appearing; *the faithful pastor's crown* (1 Pet. 5:4) for those who diligently shepherd God's flock; and *the martyr's crown* for those who are "faithful to death" (Rev. 2:10).

CRUCIFIXION. Oriental in origin, the inhuman practice of nailing a criminal to a wooden cross was adopted by the Romans as a punishment for especially loathsome criminals. Crucifixion was considered a dishonorable death, and was not inflicted on Roman citizens except for treason against the state. Usually the victim was scourged first and then compelled to carry the transverse beam of the cross to the place of execution. His crime was written on a placard and hung around his neck or carried ahead of him. The placard was then fastened to the cross as a warning to others. This is why the crosses, although erected outside city walls (cf. Heb. 13:12), were placed near busy highways and heavily frequented sites (cf. Matt. 27:36, 39, 55; Mark 15:29, 35, 40; Luke 23:35, 48, 49).

CUBIT. See under "Weights and Measures."

CUCUMBER. The *Cucumis chate,* very common in Egypt, was somewhat sweeter than the common cucumber, *Cucumis sativus.* The Israelites longed for it in the desert, together with the leeks and onions of Egypt (Num. 11:5). The cucumber was cultivated in Palestine with other similar vegetables and melons (Isa. 1:8).

CUMMIN. A fennel-like plant yielding white flowers and seeds which were eaten with food as a spice or relish (Isa. 28:25, 27). The Pharisees were meticulous about tithing it (Matt. 23:23). Caraway seeds have largely supplanted cummin as a condiment, being more tasty and nutritious.

CURSE. The entrance of sin into the human family brought with it the curse (Gen. 3:7-19). This involved the shame caused by sin (Gen. 3:7), estrangement from God (3:8, 9), fear (3:10), degradation of the serpent (3:14), a struggle between Satan's people and God's people (3:15), female childbirth problems and female subordination to man (3:16), a hostile, thorn-producing earth which required laborious cultivation (3:17-19), and threefold death — spiritual, physical, and eternal. The Old Testament ends with the curse still in effect (Mal. 4:6). The New Testament begins (Matt. 1:1) with Christ, who came to remove the curse by becoming a curse for us on the Cross (Gal. 3:13; Rev. 21:3, 4; 22:3).

The curse as an uttered imprecation was forbidden against 1) a leader of the people, as a representative of God (Exod. 22:28); 2) a deaf person (Lev. 19:14); 3) one's parents, as representatives of the Lord (Exod. 21:17; Lev. 20:9; Matt. 15:4; Mark 7:10); and 4) most important of all, God himself (Lev. 24:10-16). See also "Blessings and Cursings."

CUSH (kŭsh). (1) A son of Ham and the progenitor of the Arabian tribes of Seba, Havilah, Sabtah, Raamah, and Sabteca (Gen. 10:6-8). (2) The territory south of Egypt. It was the "Ethiopia" of classical writers and is present-day Northern Sudan. Syene or Seveneh (modern Aswan) was the frontier between Egypt and Ethiopia in the first millennium B.C. (Ezek. 29:10, RSV; cf. Psa. 68:31; 87:4; Zeph. 2:12; 3:10; Esth. 1:1). The Ethiopians (Nubians) were dark-skinned (Jer. 13:23). The runner who bore news of Absalom's death to David was a Cushite (2 Sam. 18:21, 23), as was Ebed-Melek of Jeremiah's day (Jer. 38:7) and Queen Candace's minister (Acts 8:27).

CUTHAH (kū'thȧ). A Mesopotamian city north of Babylon. From Cuthah the Assyrians deported people to Samaria (2 Kings 17:24). It is modern Tell Ibrahim.

CYPRESS (Hebrew *te ʿashur*). The cypress tree is native to Palestine and has recently been found growing wild in Gilead and Edom. It is cultivated widely in Palestine. The tree grows to forty or more feet in height and has globular, seed-bearing cones.

CYPRIOTS (sĭp'rĭ-ŏts). Inhabitants of the island of Cyprus in the Eastern Mediterranean. Its people were anciently called Kittim and were descendants of Javan (Gen. 10:4). A seafaring people, they gave the name "Kittim" or "Chittim" not only to the entire island of Cyprus but also to the coastlands of the eastern Mediterranean (Isa. 23:1, 12; Jer. 2:10; Ezek. 27:6).

CYPRUS (sī'prŭs) (Latin *cyprium*, "copper"). An Eastern Mediterranean island about 60 miles west of the coast of Syria and about the same distance south of the coast of Asia Minor. It is about 140 miles long and 60 miles wide at its broadest point. Its ancient name was Kittim or Chittim. The island was famous for its copper mines. Cyprus came under the government of Rome in 58 B.C. It was first an imperial province (27-22 B.C.) but later became a senatorial province under a pro-consul. This was its government when it was visited by Barnabas and Paul (Acts 13:4) and later by Barnabas and Mark (Acts 15:9). Paul sailed by it at least twice without landing (Acts 21:3; 27:4).

CYRENE, CIRENE (sī-rē'nė). A Greek colony founded in the seventh century B.C. In Roman times it formed a province with Crete, and the general area of Libya west of Egypt was called Cyrenaica (Matt. 27:32; Mark 15:21; Luke 23:26; Acts 2:10; 11:20; 13:1).

CYRUS (sī'rŭs). Cyrus II the Great, founder of the Persian Empire (559-530 B.C.). He is mentioned in the Book of Isaiah (44:28; 45:1-14). He conquered Babylon and repatriated the Jews (cf. Ezra 1:1-4).

D

DAGGER (Hebrew *hereb*). An easily handled, short sword used for stabbing. In the King James Version the word is translated "dagger" only in the Ehud story (Judg. 3:15-23). Weapons less than 16 inches in length are normally called daggers by archeologists. The Hebrews, however, apparently made no such distinction. Since Ehud's weapon was a cubit in length (about 17.5 inches), it could properly be translated "sword." Numerous daggers have been found in Bronze and Iron Age archeological sites throughout Egypt, Palestine, and Mesopotamia. The dagger was normally worn in a small sheath.

DALMANUTHA (dăl-mȧ-nū'thȧ). A district and town on the western shore of the Lake of Galilee (Mark 8:10). It is apparently the same place as Meijdel, Taricheae, Magadan, and Magdala (Matt. 15: 39).

DALMATIA (dăl-mā'shĭ-ȧ). A Roman province roughly equivalent in territory to Illyricum. It was bound on the north by Pannonia, on the east by Moesia, on the south by Macedonia, and on the west by the Adriatic Sea (cf. 2 Tim. 4:10).

DAMARIS (dăm'ȧ-rĭs). An Athenian woman who believed the message of Paul when he preached before the Areopagus (Acts 17:34). The name, mentioned only here in Scripture, may be a variant of "Damalis" ("heifer"), a fairly common name in biblical times.

DAMASCUS (dȧ-măs'kŭs). An important trade city located east of the Anti-Lebanon Mountains in a well-watered plain of gardens and orchards. It was associated with Abraham (Gen. 14:15; 15:2). From about 931 to 732 B.C. it was the center of Aramean power in Syria, and its inhabitants frequently warred with Israel (1 Kings 11:24; 22:1-40). It was conquered by Assyria in 732 B.C. (2 Kings 16:9). Christianity made early converts there (Acts 9:10, 19). Although Damascus was actually located in the Roman province of Syria, it was regarded as part of Decapolis. An officer of the Nabataean king Aretas had authority there (2 Cor. 11:32).

DAN. (1) A town and cult center at the headwaters of the Jordan River southwest of Mount Hermon. It was the northernmost town of Israel (Deut. 34:1; 1 Kings 4:25). Formerly called Laish, it was renamed by the tribe of Dan (Judg. 18:29). Jeroboam I made it one of his centers of worship (1 Kings 12:28, 29). It was denounced by the prophets (Amos 8:14). The modern site is Tell el-Qadi. Caesarea Philippi was located in this general region. (2) Jacob's son by Bilhah (Gen. 30:5, 6). His future was predicted in Genesis 49:16, 17.

DANCING. Both secular and religious dancing were common among the Israelites, as among other peoples of antiquity. The dance stressed the happy events of life (Jer. 31:4, 13), such as victories (1 Sam. 18:6; 21:11; 29:5; 30:16), weddings and festal occasions (Matt. 14:6; Mark 6: 22), and the wine harvest (Judg. 9:27). Music and dancing provided part of the prodigal son's homecoming festivities (Luke 15:25).

Dancing was also a religious practice among Israel's neighbors. The priests of Baal danced around altars (1 Kings 18:26) and the Phoenicians danced to Baal Melcarth. Israelites also sometimes danced as an act of worshipful joy to the Lord (2 Sam. 6:14; cf. Psa. 68:25).

DANIEL (dăn'yĕl) ("God has judged"). The great Old Testament prophet of the "times of the Gentiles" (605 B.C. to the second advent of Christ). His prophecies form the foundation of the prophetic disclosures of the entire Book of Revelation, especially as these predictions relate to the Great Tribulation and the reinstatement of the nation Israel at the second advent (Dan. 2:31-45; 9:24-27; 12:1-13; cf. Rev. 6:1 – 19:16; 20:1-9).

DARIUS (dà-rī'ŭs). Darius I the Great (522-486 B.C.), the Persian monarch of the Behistun Inscription and the benefactor of the Jews during the building of the Temple and the ministry of Haggai and Zechariah (520-515 B.C.).

King Darius and his crown prince, Xerxes, greet subjects in this bas-relief in Persepolis, Iran. *(OI-UC photo)*

DARIUS THE MEDE (dà-rī'ŭs; mēd). The son of Ahasuerus or Xerxes, who ruled Babylon on the death of Belshazzar (Dan. 9:1; cf. 5:30, 31; 6:1). Some scholars identify him with Gubaru, governor of Babylon and the region beyond the Euphrates River. Others identify him with Cyrus the Great.

DATHAN (dā'thăn). One of the men who rebelled against Moses' leadership (Num. 16:1-35; Psa. 106:17).

DAUGHTER. The word "daughter" occurs in the Scriptures more than 200 times. Daughters are mentioned by name less frequently than sons, since the family lineage and name ran in the line of the son. Hence fathers frequently regarded their daughters less highly than their sons. A father might even sell his daughter as a bondwoman (Exod. 21:7), though not to a foreigner (Exod. 21:8).

In addition to the many daughters mentioned by name in Scripture, dozens are cited by reference to their fathers or other people. A few of the more significant unnamed daughters of Scripture are described below.

1. *Adam's Daughters.* Adam lived for a total of 930 years (Gen. 5:5). He had sons and daughters for 800 years after he begot Seth, who was born when Adam was 130 years old (Gen. 5:3, 4). Doubtless Adam also had sons and daughters before Seth was born. The reason these are not mentioned in the genealogy of Genesis 5:3-5 is that among all of Adam's children only Seth was in the messianic line (Gen. 4:25). (In the table from Adam to Noah only the messianic links are given.) There is every reason to believe that Adam had many sons and daughters both before and after Seth's birth. It is inconceivable that he would postpone obeying God's command to "be fruitful and multiply and fill the earth" (Gen. 1:28) for well over a century!

It is also inconceivable that Eve (whose conception of children was greatly increased as a result of the fall – Gen. 3:16) would have had no progeny in the 120 or so years intervening between Abel and Seth, especially since she and Adam were fully mature and capable of bearing children from the day of their creation.

Adam's sons and daughters therefore undoubtedly constituted a multitude of people – perhaps hundreds – by the time Seth was born into the messianic line. By the time of his death Adam may well have had thousands of children.

2. *Daughters of Men.* Some scholars interpret the "daughters of men" of Genesis 6:2, 4 as women from the unrighteous line of Cain, and the "sons of God" mentioned in these verses as the more upright line of Seth. However, this interpretation scarcely comes to grip with the scope of the passage.

The "daughters of men" are simply mortal women (Gen. 6:1-6). The "sons of God" are angels (Job 1:6; 2:1) or evil spirit beings that had illicit experiences with the human race. The occasion was a terrifying outburst of occultism that threatened the breakdown of God's ordained human and angelic orders in creation (Jude 1:6, 7). The impending catastrophe necessitated the destruction of the race by a flood. The "Nephilim" or "giants" of Genesis 6:4 were the monstrous offspring of this wicked intercourse between fallen angels and the human race.

3. *Daughters of the Philistines.* Philistine women whom Israelite men were not to marry (2 Sam. 1:20). They are also called "the daughters of the uncircumcised," since they had no part with God's covenant people (cf. Gen. 17:9-14).

4. *Daughters of Zion.* A figurative expression for the worldly-minded women of Jerusalem (Isa. 3:16). The prophet Isaiah denounced their vanity (Isa. 3:16-26).

5. *Jephthah's Daughter.* The only child of Jephthah, the ninth judge of Israel. When war broke out between Israel and the Ammonites, Jephthah (who had been cast out of his father's house by his brothers as illegitimate) was recalled out of the land of Tob to raise an army to fight the Ammonites (Judg. 11:1-29). It was then that Jephthah made a tragic vow to devote to the Lord as a burnt offering whatever came forth from the doors of his house to meet him (Judg. 11:30, 31).

Jephthah won a great victory. But upon his return to his home in Mizpeh he was greeted first by his only daughter. As a result Jephthah felt bound by his vow to devote his daughter to the Lord as a burnt offering. It is not certain whether she was actually offered as a human sacrifice or whether she was devoted to celibacy in the service of the Lord's Tabernacle. Whatever the vow entailed, it at least meant that she could not marry or bear children (Judg. 11:37-40).

6. *King's Daughter.* "The king's daughter" (Psa. 45:13) is a foreign princess about to be wed to a king of Israel. The whole Psalm is messianic. Portrayed are the supreme beauty of the King (Psa. 45:1, 2), his coming in glory (Psa. 45:3-5; Rev. 19:11-16), and his deity and reign (Psa. 45:6, 7; Isa. 11:1-5; Heb. 1:8, 9). The King's daughter is associated with him in earthly rule as queen (the glorified Church—Psa. 45:9-13). The virgin companions of the queen (Psa. 45:14, 15) would seem to be the Jewish remnant (Rom. 11:5; Rev. 14:1-5). The Psalm closes with a description of the earthly fame of the King (Psa. 45:16, 17).

7. *Lot's Daughters.* Lot's two daughters became guilty of shameful incest with their father. Through this act the elder daughter became the ancestress of the Moabites and the younger one became the ancestress of the Ammonites (Gen. 19:30-38). Lot had been warned by angels to leave the wicked city with his wife and two daughters (Gen. 19:12-16). Lot's worldly wife met judgment when she turned back. She left her carnal stamp on her two daughters and husband, whose careers ended in shame.

8. *Pharaoh's Daughter.* An Egyptian princess who saved the life of the baby Moses (Exod. 2:5-10). She was thus unwittingly preparing Israel's great deliverer and lawgiver (Acts 7:20-22). Under the cruel decree of her father, one of the Pharaohs of Egypt (probably Thutmose III, about 1490-1450 B.C.), the child would otherwise have been doomed to die, since all male children had been ordered slain in order to curb the rapid increase of the Hebrews.

Moses' mother tried to hide her baby. When she could no longer do this, she placed him in a little basket-boat she had made and set him afloat among the reeds of the Nile where the princess came to bathe. The bold plan of faith worked. Pharaoh's daughter saw the child, took him to her heart, and adopted him as her own. Moses was educated in the highest Egyptian circles and was prepared by God for his great life's work. God used the gentleness of a great princess to work out his divine plan.

9. *Philip's Daughters.* Four unmarried women of New Testament times who had the gift of prophecy (Acts 21:9). Their father, Philip, was an evangelist (Acts 21:8). He evangelized Samaria (Acts 8:5-8), preached to and baptized the Ethiopian eunuch (Acts 8:26-40), and was a church deacon (Acts 6:5).

10. *Priest's Daughter.* The daughter of a Jewish priest was strictly forbidden to have illicit sexual relations (Lev. 21:9). Such a sin would profane the holy calling of her father, from whose family a high degree of purity was expected. The penal-

ty for harlotry in such a case was burning with fire, so serious was such a crime considered.

11. *Seth's Daughters.* Like his father, Adam, Seth had many sons and daughters both before and after the birth of the messianic heir. Enosh was born when Seth was 105 years old. Enosh alone is mentioned by name because, like his father, Seth, he was in the messianic line. Seth's daughters were granddaughters of Adam. However, Adam also had a multitude of great-grandchildren, great-great-grandchildren, etc. by the time Seth was born. In fact, by the time of Seth's birth the population of the earth was substantial. By Enosh's time men were extremely numerous on the earth.

12. *Shem's Daughters.* The genealogy of Genesis 11:10-32 lists the Semitic line from the Flood to Abraham. Those in the line of Messiah who begot sons and daughters were Shem, Arpachshad, Salah, Eber, Peleg, Reu, Serug, Nahor, Terah, and Abraham. These constitute ten messianic links in the line from Adam to Noah and ten from Noah to Abraham.

Shem's generations (Gen. 11:10-32) mark an important turning point in God's dealings with men. Until this point God had dealt with the whole Adamic race. Now he concentrated in the Semitic line, from which the Redeemer was to come.

DAVID (perhaps "beloved" or possibly from Babylonian *dawidum*, "chief"). Israel's second and most beloved king, founder of the Davidic dynasty, which lasted till the Babylonian exile. He is famous as the ancestor, forerunner, and foreshadower of the Lord Jesus Christ, David's "son" and Lord (Psa. 110:1; Rev. 22:16). His brilliant career is outlined from 1 Samuel 16:1 to 1 Kings 2:11.

DAVID, CITY OF. The original Jebusite stronghold on the southeastern side of the city of Jerusalem. It was taken by David and made the capital of the kingdom of the twelve tribes (2 Sam. 5:6-9).

DAY. (1) That part of the solar day which is light (Gen. 1:5, 14; John 11:9). (2) A period of 24 hours (Matt. 17:1; Luke 24: 21). (3) A period set aside for some special purpose, as "the day of atonement"

(Lev. 23:27). (4) An extended period of time during which certain revealed purposes of God are to be worked out (Gen. 2:4; 2 Pet. 3:10).

DAY OF CHRIST. In all New Testament references, the day of Christ is related to the Rapture of the church and the judgment seat of Christ (1 Cor. 1:8; 5:5; 2 Cor. 1:14; Phil. 1:6, 10; 2:16; 2 Thess. 2:2).

DAY OF THE LORD. In contrast to the day of Christ, which involves blessing and reward for saints in heaven, the day of the Lord involves judgment on unbelieving Jews and Gentiles during the Tribulation (Isa. 2:12; Joel 1:15; Mal. 4: 5, 6). The day of the Lord encompasses a prolonged period when God openly intervenes in human affairs. The period extends from the Rapture of the church until the dawn of the eternal state, with the end of the period merging into the "day of God" (2 Pet. 3:10-12).

DAYSMAN. A mediator (Job 9:33; 1 Tim. 2:5). Job longed for someone who understood both God and man and was able to draw both of them together (Job 9:32, 33; 16:21; 23:3, 4). Job's longing has been thoroughly fulfilled in our Lord Jesus Christ. In him God became man in order to bring man to God (1 Tim. 2:5). See also "Mediation."

DEACON. The basic meaning of deacon (Greek *diakonos*) is "servant" (Matt. 20: 26; 23:11; Mark 10:43; etc.) or "helper" (1 Thess. 3:2). The term is employed of a church official dedicated to the service of God and man (Phil. 1:1; 1 Tim. 3:8).

DEACONESS. A Christian woman who served the church (Rom. 16:1).

Mineral riches—potassium and magnesium—are dug at the south end of the Dead Sea. (© *MPS*)

DEAD SEA. The highly saline body of water which forms the terminus of the Jordan River. It is about 48 miles long, 6 to 9 miles wide, 1300 feet deep in spots, and 1280 feet below sea level. Masada, the famous fortress of the Maccabees and Herod the Great, once guarded a Roman road that passed through the shallow waters of the southern end. The earthquake-ridden cities of Sodom and Gomorrah also lie beneath these shallow southern waters. The Dead Sea is called the "Salt Sea" in Genesis 14:3, the "Eastern Sea" in Ezekiel 47:18, and the "Sea of Arabah" in Deuteronomy 4:49 RSV.

DEATH. Threefold death—spiritual, physical, and eternal—is the result of the fall of man and the curse of sin that followed (Gen. 2:17). Spiritual death (separation from the life of God and fellowship with God) came upon all who are "in Adam," that is, the entire human race. Both eternal death (everlasting separation from God in Gehenna) and physical death also eventually overtake all who are "in Adam." But all who have been regenerated are "in Christ" and are blessed with threefold life—spiritual life, eventual triumph over physical death in glorification of the body, and eternal life that delivers from eternal death.

DEBIR (dē'bĭr). (1) A Canaanite city taken by Israel (Josh. 10:38, 39; 15:15; Judg. 1: 11). It became a Levitical city in Judah (Josh. 21:15; 1 Chron. 6:58). It is identified with present-day Tell Beit Mirsim and has been excavated. (2) A town on the border of Gad (Josh. 13:26). It is also called Lo-debar (2 Sam. 9:4; 17:27). The town is modern Umm ed-Dabar.

DEBORAH (dĕb'ō-rà) ("a bee"). (1) Rebekah's nurse, who came with her from Mesopotamia to Canaan. She was highly esteemed by Jacob's family. When she died she was buried with much sorrow under an oak below Bethel, the place being named "Allon-bacuth" (RSV) or "oak of weeping" (Gen. 35:8). Rachel's death in childbirth shortly afterward has been tied to the death of Deborah and the absence of her professional skill to aid her mistress (Gen. 35:19). (2) A prophetess and judge. She summoned Barak to fight against Sisera and went with him to battle (Judg. 4:4-24). After a great victory with the Lord's help, she composed a song of triumph (Judg. 5:1-31). She was a gifted administrator and judge as well as an intrepid leader. She judged Israel between Ramah and Bethel under a palm tree named in her honor (Judg. 4:4, 5). Deborah ranks among the great heroines of the Bible.

DECALOGUE. See "Commandments."

DECAPOLIS (dē-kăp'ō-lĭs). The Greek name for a league of approximately ten Hellenistic or Hellenized cities and accompanying territories in the Roman period. The cities included Scythopolis (west of the Jordan), certain cities east of Perea, and Dion, Abila, and Damascus. In the New Testament, Decapolis appears as the Gentile territory bordering on Galilee and Perea (Matt. 4:25; Mark 5:20; 7:31).

DEDICATION, FEAST OF. Held on 25 Kislew (our November or December), this Jewish celebration lasted eight days. It commemorated the cleansing of the Temple and altar by Judas Maccabeus in 165 B.C. (John 10:22; 1 Macc. 4:47-59). The prominence of lamps and lighting in the Feast gave rise to its popular name of "Feast of Lights."

DEITY. See "God."

DELILAH (de-lī'là). A seductive woman of Sorek (apparently a Philistine) with whom Samson was infatuated (Judg. 16: 4). When Samson, the hero of the tribe of Dan, had humiliated the Philistines on repeated occasions, they bribed Delilah to find out the secret of his great strength (Judg. 16:5). After resisting her wiles three times, Samson finally succumbed and told her the secret of his power—his uncut hair, the symbol of his dedication to the Lord (Judg. 16:7-20; cf. 13:2-5). She then turned him over to the Philistines, who imprisoned him (Judg. 16:21). Delilah represents the worldly seductress who lures a man of God to ruin by compromise with sin.

DEMAS (dē'màs). Paul's fellow-laborer (Col. 4:14; Philem. 1:24). He later deserted the Apostle for worldly reasons (2 Tim. 4:10).

DEMETRIUS I SOTER (dē-mē'trĭ-ūs, sō'tⱥr) ("belonging to Demeter," the goddess of agriculture). The King of Syria from 162 to 150 B.C. (1 Macc. 7:1-4). It was in battle with him that Judas Maccabeus lost his life (1 Macc. 9:1-19).

DEMONS. Evil spirits (Matt. 12:43-45) who are probably fallen angels. They are Satan's agents (Matt. 12:26, 27) and, like him, oppose the Word and will of God. As invisible spirits they can enter and control the body of both human beings and animals (Mark 5:2-13). All demons are evil in that they oppose God. Many are openly unclean and vicious (Matt. 8:28; 9:33; 10:1; Mark 1:23; 5:2-13; 9:17-27; Luke 6:18). Others, however, are deceptively "good," educated, refined, and religious (1 Tim. 4:1, 2; 1 John 4:1-3). These are the most dangerous because they impose themselves on undiscerning people as spirits from God, thereby deluding the unwary into error, false religions, and erratic conduct. Like their leader, Satan, they often masquerade as "angels of light" (2 Cor. 11:14).

Evil spirits may exercise a varying degree of control over both saved and unsaved people. They may simply harass their victim from without or, if the victim permits entry by seriously violating God's moral law, they may enter in and inhabit the person's body. A person becomes especially vulnerable to demon influence or possession if he dabbles in occultism, in which he violates the first two commandments of the Decalogue and insults God's deity. Such inhabiting demons may inflict certain physical maladies (Matt. 12:22; 17:14-18; Luke 13:16) as well as certain mental and spiritual disorders. (However, it is essential that demon-inflicted maladies be distinguished from other disorders to which men are subject. For example, some mental problems are the legitimate domain of psychologists and psychiatrists, whereas other disorders can be corrected only by expulsion of the demon or demons through the ministry of a Spirit-filled servant of God.)

DEPRAVITY. A theological term which describes what the infinitely holy God sees as he looks on unsaved men. This depravity contrasts sharply with what *man* sees when he looks at himself or his fellow men. The phrase "total depravity" does not imply that there is no good of any kind in unsaved people but rather that the unsaved are totally unqualified to enter heaven on the basis of their own merit (Rom. 3:10-18; 5:12; Eph. 2:1-3). They are all "in Adam" and "under sin" and are therefore confined to faith in Christ, God's gracious gift, as their only means of salvation (John 3:18; Eph. 2:8, 9).

DERBE (dẽr'bē). A town of the Lycaonian district of Roman Galatia. It was the most easterly place visited by Paul and Barnabas (Acts 14:6, 7). Beyond lay the client kingdom of Antiochus. The site has been identified as modern Kerti Huyuk, 13 miles north-northeast of Karaman and 60 miles southeast of Lystra.

DESERT. See "Wilderness."

DEVIL (Greek *diabolos*, "slanderer"). Satan, the great fallen angel and the accuser of God's people (Rev. 12:9, 10). He seeks to "devour them as a lion" (1 Pet. 5:8) and to delude them as an "angel of light" (2 Cor. 11:14). He is called "Belial" ("worthless and no good" — 2 Cor. 6:15), "Satan" ("adversary" — Job 2:1), and "that old Serpent" (Rev. 12:9).

DEVILS. See "Demons." ("Devils" in the King James Version always refers to demons. There is only one "devil" — Satan himself.)

DIANA (dī-ă'nà). The Latin name for Artemis, the Greek goddess of the moon and the hunt. Her temple at Ephesus was one of the seven wonders of the ancient world (Acts 19:27). The local silversmiths, who made small votary shrines for Artemis, instigated a riot when Paul's powerful ministry cut into their lucrative trade (Acts 19:23-41). Inscriptions from Ephesus label this deity "Artemis the Great" (cf. Acts 19:27, 28, 34).

DIBON (dī'bŏn). An important Moabite city where the Mesha Stone was found (Num. 21:30; 32:3). It was claimed by the Israelites (Num. 32:34; Josh. 13:9) as a Moabite city (cf. Isa. 15:2; Jer. 48:18).

DIETARY LAWS. Israel was called to be a holy nation. The Mosaic Code distinguished between clean and unclean animals (Lev. 11:1-47). Only clean animals were to be eaten by a holy people. This regulation served a hygienic purpose and was also intended as a guard against idolatrous practices. In keeping with this concept, the Jews washed their hands before touching food and practiced meticulous ceremonial cleanliness (Mark 7:4).

DINAH (dī'nà) (perhaps "judgment"). A daughter of Jacob by his concubine Leah (Gen. 30:21). She was either seduced or raped by the young Hivite prince Shechem, the son of Hamor (Gen. 34:1, 2). Shechem afterward wished to take her in honorable marriage (Gen. 34:3, 4). Her brothers outwardly agreed, on condition that the Hivites be circumcised (Gen. 34:7-17). But while the males were recovering, Simeon and Levi, two of Dinah's full brothers, killed all the males of the place, including Hamor and Shechem (Gen. 34:24-29). Jacob was horrified at the slaughter and denounced it on his deathbed (Gen. 49:5-7). By this outrageous crime the district of Shechem fell to Jacob as tribal chief. However, he bequeathed it not to those responsible for the crime but to Joseph (Gen. 48:22).

DIOTREPHES (dī-ŏt're-fēz). ("nurtured by Zeus"). The professed disciple who refused to recognize the authority of the Apostle John. He domineeringly sought the preeminence (3 John 1:9) to the dethronement of Christ (cf. Col. 1:18). He illustrates church dictators who substitute self for Christ.

DISCIPLE. Christ enunciated stringent requirements for being his disciple. A true disciple must "hate" his life (Luke 14:26), "bear his cross" (Luke 14:27), and forsake everything (Luke 14:33). If taken at face value Christ's terms of discipleship are met by very few believers today.

DISPERSIONS OF ISRAEL. On the basis of her unchangeable covenants Israel is guaranteed ultimate possession of the land of promise (Deut. 30:1-8). Clearly predicted were three dispersions and three regatherings. The three dispersions have already occurred: that into Egypt (Gen. 15:13-16), that of the captivities (Israel in 722 B.C. and Judah in 586 B.C.—cf. Jer. 25:11, 12; Dan. 9:1, 2), and the present dispersion (having begun with the destruction of Jerusalem in A.D. 70 and continuing until Christ's second advent). It is at the second advent that Israel will be regathered for the last time (Deut. 30:1-3; Ezek. 37:21-28).

DIVINATION. The pagan and occult counterpart of biblical prophecy. It involves consultation of heathen gods for guidance with respect to the future. Divinatory methods embrace astrology, necromancy, spiritism, interpretation of dreams, and occult visions. Less familiar methods entail the use of arrows and the examination of animal livers (Ezek. 21:21). Divination by rods (Hos. 4:12) and by psychic clairvoyance (Acts 16:16-18) was also practiced in the ancient world. Divination was forbidden in Israel because of its demonic implications (Deut. 18:9-12).

DIVINITY OF KINGS. In ancient times kings, like priests, were frequently anointed as sacred persons. Among the pagans the king was regarded as the visible representative of the national deity and was accorded divine honors.

DIVORCE. The original creatorial relationship which God established between the sexes was strict monogamy. A man was to leave his parents and be joined to his wife, thereby entering a permanent and unbreakable union in which the two parties became "one flesh" (Gen. 2:24; Matt. 19:4-6; Mark 10:6-9). The earliest fragments of sacred history and the earliest laws evidence the radical perversion of the original divine order (Gen. 4:23; 16:1, 2; Exod. 20:17). The Mosaic Law attempted only to curb these perversions by imposing restraints on what by that time had become established custom. Our Lord reminded the Pharisees of this fact by showing them that divorce under the Law was a concession to the hardness of the human heart (cf. Deut. 24:1-4) and that "from the beginning it was not so" (Matt. 19:7, 8; Mark 10:2-12).

The Mosaic statute, although a concession to human weakness, was evidently aimed at encouraging reconciliation and thus preserving the original covenant of Genesis 2:24. Such a divorce proceeding would take time, invite reflection, and enlist the unbiased counsel of magistrate and priest. It would thus tend to effect a reconciliation. The Mosaic statute was certainly not slanted to ignore God's hatred of marital infidelity and the breaking of the marriage tie (Mal. 2:14-16).

Christ's teaching on divorce and remarriage is based strictly on the original relationship which the Creator established between the sexes (Gen. 2:24). He does not concede to custom or accommodate human weakness, as does the Law of Moses. He forbids divorce and remarriage completely, with only one exception — the crime of adultery (Matt. 5:32; 19:9). He even declares that the union of a divorced woman with another man is adulterous, both for herself and for her husband. (In stating this, Christ evidently puts the woman on the same plane as the man. This is in contrast to the Mosaic Code, which did not permit a woman to separate from her husband for any reason.)

The Apostle Paul supplements but does not alter the teaching of our Lord. If a rift develops between a Christian couple they must be reconciled if possible. If this is not possible they may separate but must not remarry (1 Cor. 7:10, 11). If one party of an unsaved couple becomes converted he or she is to attempt to win his or her mate to the Lord (1 Cor. 7:13, 14, 16). If the unsaved partner finds the new faith intolerable, the believer is not to prevent him (or her) from leaving (1 Cor. 7:15). Believers must never marry unbelievers (2 Cor. 6:14).

DOEG (dō'ĕg) ("fearful, timid"). An Edomite and the chief of King Saul's herdsmen. It was he who informed Saul of Ahimelech's aid to David. As a result of Doeg's deceit Ahimelech and the priests at Nob were massacred by Saul (1 Sam. 22:6-19).

DOG. Dogs were domesticated long before Israel's history began. But in the Bible dogs appear mainly as scavengers, haunting the streets and refuse dumps of the city. They were considered unclean and vicious (Psa. 59:6, 14; Exod. 22:31; 1 Kings 14:11; 16:4; cf. Psa. 22:16, 20). However, shepherd dogs are mentioned (Job 30:1). In the New Testament the dog apparently appears as a pet (Matt. 15: 26, 27; Mark 7:27, 28).

DOLMEN. A sepulchral monument consisting of a large slab of stone placed on other unhewn stones. Some think these stone arrangements found throughout Palestine were erected as primitive altars and offering tables for the dead.

DOMITIAN (dȯ-mĭsh'ȧn). The Roman emperor from A.D 81 to 96. It was he who banished the Apostle John to the Island of Patmos.

DONKEY. See "Ass."

DOR (dōr). A town on the Mediterranean Coast south of Mount Carmel and north of Tantura. A Canaanite town, it was allotted to Manasseh even though it was in Asher (Josh. 17:11; cf. Judg. 1:27). It was later reckoned to Ephraim. It was a harbor town in the Hellenistic and Roman era.

DORCAS (dôr'kăs) ("gazelle"). A Christian woman of good works who was also called Tabitha. She was a friend and helper of the poor who lived in Joppa. When she died, Peter was summoned; he called her back to life. The incident caused many to believe on the Lord Jesus Christ (Acts 9:36-43). Dorcas is famous as a woman who unselfishly gave herself to help the needy and poor.

DOTHAN (dō'thȧn). A town in the fertile plains of the hill country about a dozen miles north of Shechem (Gen. 37:17; 2 Kings 6:13). Excavations reveal that the site, Tell Dotha, was occupied from the Early Bronze Age to the Assyrian invasions of the eighth century.

DOVE. A name for various species of pigeons. They constitute a family called *Columbidae.* Four species abound in Palestine — the ringdove or wood pigeon, the stock dove, the rock dove, and the ash-rumped rock dove. The dove is described as having a plaintive voice (Isa. 38:14) and as being gentle and affectionate (Song 2:14; 5:2) but not particularly sagacious (Hos. 7:11). It was used in Temple sacrifices (Matt. 21:12; Luke 2: 24). Its gentle, harmless nature (Matt. 10: 16) makes it a fit symbol of the Holy Spirit (Luke 3:22). See also "Pigeon."

DRAGON. A mythological monster conceived as a huge serpent with wings and claws. This may be the implication of some of the Old Testament allusions. In the New Testament the dragon (Greek *drakōn*) is an apocalyptic figure of Satan, that "old serpent the devil" (Rev. 12:3, 4; 13:2; 16:13; 20:1-3). In some of the Old Testament passages the dragon seems to refer to the crocodile ("leviathan" — Isa. 27:1; 51:9). The association with Egypt, the habitat of the crocodile, suggests the same possibility in Ezekiel 29:3 (compare Jeremiah 51:34).

DRAWER OF WATER. In Bible lands water had to be carried from cisterns and springs, which were sometimes quite a distance away. Those who carried the water often had an assigned daily responsibility. An illustration of this is furnished by the Gibeonites, who were assigned to draw water and cut wood for the Tabernacle and the priests and Levites (Josh. 9:21, 23, 27).

DRESSER OF SYCAMORE FRUIT. The original text of Amos 7:14 indicates that Amos was a dresser or tender of sycamore fruit. This involved slitting the top of each fig to guarantee its ripening. The sycamore-fig *(Ficus sycmorus)* has evergreen leaves and yields an edible fruit. King David appointed an overseer to superintend the olive and sycamore trees (1 Chron. 27:28; cf. Psa. 78:47). Zacchaeus climbed such a tree to see Jesus (Luke 19:4).

DROMEDARY. See "Camel."

DRUSILLA. (drū-sĭl′á). The third and youngest daughter of Agrippa I, King of Judea. Her brother, Agrippa II, had her married to Azizus, king of Emesa. When Felix was procurator of Judea (A.D. 52-60), he fell in love with Drusilla. Goaded on by the petty tyranny of her sister, Bernice, Drusilla defied the Jewish law, left her husband, and married Felix, a Gentile and an idolater. It is understandable why Felix trembled when Paul, then a prisoner, reasoned before him and Drusilla of righteousness, temperance, and judgment to come (Acts 24:24, 25).

DUGONG. See under "Badger."

DUMAH (dū′má). A town of Arabia (Gen. 25:14; 1 Chron. 1:30; Isa. 21:11) located about halfway across the Peninsula between Palestine and Southern Babylonia.

DYES AND COLORS. See under "Clothing and Dress."

EAGLE. The Hebrew word *nesher* is undoubtedly as much a generic term as the English word "eagle," including besides the true eagle (of the family *Accipitridae* of the genus *Aquila*) other large birds of prey, particularly the griffon vulture (Mic. 1:16; Matt. 24:28). The eagle was classified as unclean (Lev. 11:13). It was the monarch of the birds and the largest flying creature to be found in Bible lands. It had a majestic sweep in flight (Prov. 23:5; Isa. 40:31; Obad. 1:4). It swooped down on its prey (Job 9:26) and nested in inaccessible places (Job 39:27; Jer. 49:16). However, the eagle showed great solicitude for its young (Deut. 32:11). The allusion to the renewal of its youth (Psa. 103:5) doubtless refers poetically to its very long life. Ancient naturalists knew the difference between the eagle and the vulture. The vulture is generally a car-

rion-eating bird (cf. Matt. 24:28) with an unfeathered neck and head, and is a somewhat more social creature than the eagle.

EARRING. An ornament of both men and women, the earring was a ring *(nezem)* worn in the earlobes (Gen. 35:4; Exod. 32:2, 3; 35:22; Prov. 25:12; Job 42:11). The earring was the characteristic ornament of the Ishmaelites (Judg. 8:24-26). Their kings were also adorned with crescent-shaped amulets and eardrops (Judg. 8:26).

EBAL (ē′bál). A 3085-foot-high mountain peak in the central highland ridge northeast of Mount Gerizim. Both Mount Ebal and Mount Gerizim overshadow Shechem (modern Nablus). The natural amphitheater between these two peaks has wonderful acoustical properties. It was from these two mountains that the Mosaic blessings and curses were intoned upon the Jewish people (Deut. 11:26-30; 27:11 – 29:1).

EBED-MELECH (ē'bĕd-mē'lĕk) ("king's servant"). An Ethiopian palace eunuch in Zedekiah's time (597-586 B.C.). He was a credit to his race, assisting Jeremiah in his release from prison (Jer. 38:7-13).

EBER (ē'bēr) ("other side, region beyond"). A descendant of Shem and progenitor of the Hebrews (Gen. 10:22, 24; 11:16-26), of various Arabian tribes (Gen. 10:25-30), and of certain Aramaean tribes descended from Nahor (Gen. 11:29; 22:20-24). Eber originally belonged to the region beyond the Euphrates; it was from this locale that his name was probably derived.

EBONY. A hard, black wood used for inlaying. It was apparently obtained from India or Ceylon (Ezek. 27:15). Merchants of Dedan traded with it in the markets of Tyre. The Greeks were familiar with a black ebony from Ethiopia and a variegated species from India.

ECBATANA (ĕk-băt'ă-nà). The capital of ancient Media. It lay southwest of the Caspian Sea and was a royal city of Persia (Ezra 6:2; 2 Macc. 9:3). The city is modern Hamadan.

EDEN (ē'dĕn). (1) The original habitation of man. It was located somewhere in lower Babylonia in the Tigris-Euphrates country (Gen. 2:10-14). The Pishon and Gihon were probably canals that connected the Tigris and Euphrates as ancient riverbeds. (2) The land conquered by the Assyrians. It is the same as Bit-Adini or Beth-eden in the Balikh-Habur region of northwest Mesopotamia (Ezek. 27:23; Amos 1:5; Isa. 37:12).

EDOM (ē'dŏm) ("red"). A name of Esau, the older son of Isaac (Gen. 25:30; 36:1, 8, 19).

EDOMITES (ē'dŏ-mīts). A people descended from the Hebrews through Esau, the brother of Jacob and the grandson of Abraham (Gen. 36:9). They occupied the area south of the Dead Sea from the Wadi Zered to the Gulf of Aqabah, a 100-mile-long depression (Deut. 2:12; Judg. 11:18). The rugged terrain has peaks rising to 3500 feet. While not a fertile land, good arable areas are found (Num. 20:17, 19). The capital was Sela, situated on a small plateau behind Petra. Other important towns were Bozrah and Teman. In Bible times the King's Highway passed along the eastern plateau (Num. 20:17). Israel was refused passage over this road during the Exodus (Num. 20:14-21). Despite this discourtesy the Israelites were forbidden to hate their Edomite relatives (Deut. 23:7, 8). However, the contacts of Israel with Edom were fraught with bitter wars and lingering animosities.

Saul fought with the Edomites (1 Sam. 14:47). David conquered them (2 Sam. 8: 13, 14), enabling Solomon to build a port at Ezion-Geber (1 Kings 9:26-28) and to exploit the copper mines of the region, as attested by archeology. Later kings of Judah also warred with Edom. Uzziah dominated the country and restored the port at Elath (2 Kings 14:22). Ahaz lost control of Edom and it became a vassal state of Assyria after about 736 B.C. See also "Idumeans."

EGLAH (ĕg'là) ("heifer"). One of David's eight wives, probably the least known. She was the mother of Ithream (2 Sam. 3: 5; 1 Chron. 3:3).

EGYPT, RIVER OF (ē'jĭpt). Modern Rhinocorura (Wadi el Arish), 45 miles southwest of Gaza on the borders of Egypt (Gen. 15:18; Num. 34:5).

The Sphinx and Pyramids of Gizeh, Egypt, near Cairo, mark the tombs of royalty. (© *MPS*)

EGYPTIANS (ė-jĭp'shăns). According to the Table of the Nations, Mizraim (Egypt) was the son of Ham and the brother of Canaan, Put, and Cush (Gen. 10:6). Ancient Egyptians were Hamites and belonged to the white race, which in prehistoric times migrated in successive waves into the country of Egypt. In later times other migrations from Babylonia (largely Semitic) left their influence upon the people and their language. In the course of history a Nubian element was also injected into the Egyptian mixture. This remarkable people occupied the fertile ribbon of the Nile Valley from the second cataract in Semneh (present-day Aswan) to the Mediterranean Sea, a distance of some 800 miles.

The Egyptians had from prehistoric times organized their country under two divisions, Upper and Lower Egypt (giving rise to the dual form of the Hebrew name "Mizraim"). At about 2900 B.C. the country was united under Menes. Manetho, a priest of the third century B.C., wrote a history of Egypt which divided the period 2900-332 B.C. into 30 royal dynasties. During this period the marvelous civilization of the Nile Valley was developed. This information has been brought to light by archeological research from about A.D. 1800 to the present. Because Egypt figures so prominently in the pages of the Bible, these archeological findings have shed great light on much of the Old Testament.

EHUD (ē'hŭd) (probably shortened from "Abihud"). The second judge of Israel. He slew Eglon of Moab and delivered and judged Israel (Judg. 3:15–4:1).

EKRON (ĕk'rŏn). One of the five principal Philistine cities (Josh. 15:45, 46). It has recently been identified with Khirbet al-Muqannac, about 25 miles west of Jerusalem. The ark was taken there after it had been removed from Gath (1 Sam. 5:10-12). The city is prominent in the records of the Assyrian Kings Sennacherib and Esarhaddon.

EL (ĕl). See "Elohim."

ELAM (ē'lăm) (probably from Akkadian *elamtu*, "highland"). A son of Shem and progenitor of the Elamites.

ELAMITES (ē'lȧ-mīts). The inhabitants of the highland region beyond the Tigris River and east of Babylonia. Their capital was at Susa. They are listed among the sons of Shem (Gen. 10:22), probably because of their periodic invasions into Babylonia and their amalgamation with the Semites who had been exiled there. Sargon of Akkac conquered Elam around 2150 B.C. Ur was destroyed by the Elamites at about 2000 B.C., not long after Abraham and Terah had left the cities. In the eighteenth century B.C. Elam's expansionist aspirations were thwarted by Hammurabi. During the Kassite period Elam seems to have held the position of a province, having been conquered by Kurigalzu II about the middle of the fourteenth century. Elamite power revived intermittently thereafter. Shutruk-Nahunte (1200 B.C.) was able to raid Babylon and carry off the famous Law Code of Hammurabi, rediscovered in A.D. 1902 at Susa. By 1130 B.C. Nebuchadnezzar I had conquered Elam so thoroughly that it remained in comparative eclipse for three centuries.

In the eighth century B.C. Elam allied itself with Babylonia against Assyrian aggression. The struggle ended with the complete destruction of Elam's power by Ashurbanipal in about 645 B.C. In the Chaldean and Persian periods Elam held a subordinate position.

ELATH, ELOTH (ē'lăth; ē'lŏth). Sometimes called Ezion-Geber, Elath was a settlement at the north end of the Gulf of Aqabah. It is first mentioned as a stopping place for Israel during her exodus from Egypt (Num. 23:35, 36; Deut. 2:8). In about 955 B.C. Solomon developed copper and iron mining and smelting in the Arabah north of Ezion-geber (at the site of modern Tell el-Kheleifeh, two-and-a-half miles west of Aqabah). Old Elath (Ezion-geber-Elath) served as the terminal point for Solomon's trading fleet to Ophir and Arabia. The Edomites intermittently controlled this region (2 Kings 14:22).

ELDAD (ĕl'dăd) ("God has loved"). An elder who (with Medad) assisted Moses in governing Israel (Num. 11:24-30).

ELDER. A person of age and experience who was considered well qualified to rule. The Jews (Exod. 3:16; Num. 11:25) as well as the Egyptians (Gen. 50:7), the Moabites, and the Midianites (Num. 22:7), had elders. They acted as judges and filled various civil capacities (Deut. 21:1-9; Josh. 20:1-6) throughout the entire period of Old Testament history (2 Sam. 5:3; 1 Kings 8:1-3; 20:7; 2 Kings 19:1, 2; Ezek. 8:1). In the Hellenistic period Jewish synagogues were normally governed by a council of elders under the chairmanship of a "ruler of the synagogue." In religious matters all Jews were subject to the 71-member Sanhedrin. During the New Testament period the high priest was chairman *ex officio* of this august body.

The Christian church also followed the practice of employing men of age and experience in matters of ruling. The elder *(zaqen)* of the Old Testament became the presbyter *(presbuteros)* of the New Testament. Paul and Barnabas ordained elders in all the Gentile churches (Acts 14:23). The Apostle directed Titus to do the same in Crete (Tit. 1:5).

The elders at Ephesus (Acts 20:17-35) are also called "overseers" or "bishops" (Greek *episcopoi*—Acts 20:28), suggesting that the terms "presbyter" and "bishop" are interchangeable in New Testament usage. All elders were of equal rank; the eldership acted in a corporate capacity. The term "presbytery" *(presbuterion)* is employed to describe the body of elders that ordained Timothy (1 Tim. 4:14).

Duties of elders or presbyters included visitation of the sick (James 5:14), preaching and teaching (1 Tim. 5:17), general oversight of the local congregation (1 Pet. 5:1-4), receiving and dispensing gifts (Acts 11:29, 30), and rendering decisions on problems (Acts 15:1-6; 16:1-4).

ELEAZAR (ĕ-lē-ā′zàr) ("God has helped"). A priest, the third son of Aaron and the father of Phinehas (Exod. 6:23, 25; 28:1). He became chief of the Levites when his brothers Nadab and Abihu were killed for failing to offer sacrifices in the manner God had prescribed (Lev. 10:1-7; Num. 3: 4, 32). He succeeded Aaron upon the latter's death (Num. 20:22-29; Deut. 10:6).

ELECTION. The sovereign right of God to choose who from among his created beings shall be granted a position of special favor. Scripture reveals two major elections: 1) the nation Israel (Matt. 24: 1−25:46; Rom. 9:1-18; 11:1-36) and 2) the church of Christ (John 17:1-26; Rom. 8:28-39; Eph. 1:4-6). These two entities of God's people must be differentiated if Bible truth is to be understood.

Election is based on five divine decrees:

1) the decree to create; 2) the decree to permit the fall of man; 3) the decree to elect some to salvation; 4) the decree to provide a Savior; and 5) the decree to save the elect. The theological questions involved have divided believers into two main categories—Calvinists and Arminians.

The five points of Calvinism are 1) total depravity (utter inability of fallen man to redeem himself); 2) unconditional election; 3) a limited redemption; 4) efficacious grace; and 5) perserverance of the saints.

The opposing five points of Arminianism are 1) conditional election according to divine foreknowledge; 2) a universal redemption (although only those who believe are actually saved); 3) salvation by grace bestowed at birth; 4) resistible grace; and 5) possible falling from grace.

Israel's election guarantees 1) an everlasting nation; 2) an everlasting possession of their land; 3) an everlasting throne; 4) an everlasting king; and 5) an everlasting kingdom (2 Sam. 7:4-17; 1 Chron. 17:3-15).

ELEPHANT. A genus of large animals with ivory tusks native to Asia and Africa. This huge animal was used in wars (1 Macc. 1:17; 3:34; 6:37; 2 Macc. 14:12) during the time of the Seleucid kings. Maccabean coins depict the elephant.

ELEPHANTINE (ĕl′-ĕ-făn-tĭ-nĕ). The site of a Jewish military colony adjacent to Syene (modern Aswan) in the sixth and fifth centuries B.C. From this place came the important Aramaic documents known as the Elephantine Papyri.

ELI (ē′lī) ("high," possibly a contraction for "God is high"). A high priest and judge of Israel for forty years (1 Sam. 1: 1−4:18). Eli was a godly man but failed to exercise parental authority. As a result his two sons disgraced the priesthood and brought judgment upon both the house of Eli and the nation of Israel.

ELIAKIM (ĕ-lī′à-kĭm). A high official of Hezekiah's court who conferred with the Assyrians (2 Kings 18:18-37; Isa. 36:3-22; cf. 2 Kings 19:2; Isa. 37:2). Isaiah commended Eliakim and promised him such exalted blessings from God that he must be regarded as a messianic type (Isa. 22:20-25).

ELIEZER (ĕl-ĭ-ē'zēr) ("God is a helper"). A citizen of Damascus and Abraham's steward (Gen. 15:2; cf. 24:2).

ELIHU (e-lī'hū) ("God is He" or "He is God"). One of Job's friends who gave counsel during Job's sufferings (Job Chaps. 32 – 37).

ELIHU (é-lī'hū) ("God is he" or "He is "the Lord is God"). A great prophet of the ninth century B.C. who fought Baal worship (1 Kings 18:17 – 19:18). He rebuked kings (1 Kings 21:20-22; 2 Kings 1:16). He was a mighty intercessor (1 Kings 17:20-22; 18:36-40; James 5:17) and performer of miracles (1 Kings 17: 10-24) but was prone to discouragement (1 Kings 19:4) and was fallible in judgment (1 Kings 19:14, 18). He was divinely and signally honored (2 Kings 2:11; Matt. 17:3).

ELIPHAZ (ĕl'ĭ-făz) (possibly "God is fine gold"). One of Job's friends from Teman in Arabia (Job 2:11; 4:1; 15:1; 22:1; 42:7, 9). He was a religious dogmatist who gloried in his wisdom and tried to press Job into the mold of his own experience.

ELISABETH (é-lĭz'à-bĕth) ("God is an oath," i.e., the absolutely faithful One). The wife of the priest Zacharias and the mother of John the Baptist. She was of the house of Aaron and bore the Greek equivalent of the name of Aaron's wife, Elisheba. She was a relative of Mary of Nazareth. Inspired by the Holy Spirit, Elisabeth welcomed Mary as the mother of the promised Messiah (Luke 1:41-45).

ELISHA (é-lī'shà) ("God is salvation"). (1) Elijah's successor in prophetic ministry in the Northern Kingdom (1 Kings 19:16-21). He witnessed Elijah's translation and received a double portion of his spirit in order to conduct a miracle-filled ministry to offset the apostasy and inroads of Baalism (2 Kings Chaps. 2 – 13). He became a model spiritual leader, characterized by mercy (2 Kings 2:19-22), unselfishness (2 Kings 5:8-10, 15, 16, 25, 26), and patient endurance (2 Kings 5:17-19). (2) Apparently Kittim or Cyprus, the "Alashia" of the Amarna Letters and the Egyptian and cuneiform sources. These texts indicate that Alashia exported copper from the east coast of Cyprus. Elishah was the eldest son of Javan (Gen. 10:4).

ELISHEBA (é-lĭsh'é-bà). The wife of Aaron and the ancestress of the entire Levitical line. She bore Aaron four sons: Nadab, Abihu, Eleazar, and Ithamar (Exod. 6:23). From these last two sons descended the long line of priests who ministered in the sanctuary and taught God's Law.

ELKANAH (ĕl-kā'nà) ("God has created"). The father of Samuel (1 Sam. 1:19, 20). He was a Levitical descendant (1 Sam. 1: 1).

ELM. See "Terebinth."

ELOHIM (ĕ-lō'hīm). The primary word for God in the Old Testament, occurring in hundreds of passages. The noun is plural in form but singular in meaning when referring to God. The triunity of God is intimated in the Old Testament and clearly revealed in the New Testament. The singular form of the word, "El," denotes either "God" or "a god." (In the Ugaritic literature El refers to the chief god of the Canaanite pantheon, the father of Baal). In Scripture the singular form usually occurs in compound names such as 1) *El Olam*, "the everlasting God," expressing the eternity of the divine Being (Gen. 21:33); 2) *El Elyon*, "God the Highest" and "the Possessor of heaven and earth" (Gen. 14:18, 22); 3) *El Gibbor*, "Mighty God" (Isa. 9:6); and 4) *El Shaddai*, "Almighty or all-sufficient God" (Gen. 17:1), the name by which he revealed himself to the patriarchs prior to Israel's redemption out of Egypt (Gen. 28:3; 35:11; 48:3). See also "Adonai," "Adonai Jehovah" and "Jehovah."

ELYMAS (ĕl'ĭ-màs). A magician and false prophet who through demonic power opposed Paul and Barnabas at Paphos in Cyprus (Acts 13:8-11).

EMBALMING. Out of religious motives the Egyptians attempted to preserve the bodies of their dead for the longest possible time. They thus developed the complicated art of embalming and mummification. The burial of Jacob and Joseph followed this custom (Gen. 50:1-3, 26), though the Israelites did not practice embalming themselves.

EMBROIDERING. The Israelites knew the art of embroidery (cf. Exod. Chaps. 27, 28, 35, 36, 38, 39). They probably learned it from the Egyptians, who also practiced it (Ezek. 27:7). The Jews employed embroidery freely in making the priestly vestments and materials of the Tabernacle. The robes of Assyrian and Babylonian kings were also richly embroidered, as the monuments attest.

EMMAUS (ĕ-mā′ŭs). A village near Jerusalem where Jesus appeared to two disciples after his resurrection (Luke 24:13). The town is possibly to be identified with present-day Colonia Amasa, about seven miles from Jerusalem.

EMMER. A kind of inferior wheat with more modest growth characteristics than durum wheat (Exod. 9:32; Isa. 28:25; Ezek. 4:9). This plant, called "rye" or "fitches" in the King James Version, is *Triticum dioccum.* No evidence exists that rye, fitches, or spelt were grown in biblical times in Palestine. Emmer, however, has been found in old Egyptian tombs, indicating that it was almost certainly grown in the Near East.

EMPEROR. A title of the ruler of the Roman Empire. It is derived from the Latin *imperator,* which was originally bestowed temporarily on a general who had been victorious in battle. Julius Caesar, however, retained the title permanently. Through his example it came to signify supreme military authority. It was employed by Augustus and his successors in this sense. Peter uses the term "king" *(basileus)* to refer to the Emperor (1 Pet. 2:13, 17). The title "Augustus" (the rendering of the Greek word *sebastos,* "revered, reverend") as well as the title "Caesar" occur in Acts 25:21, 25. Ideally the emperor ruled as *princeps* or "head of state." But corruption and abuse of power led to military autocracy, with the Emperor ruling his people as an imperator ruled his troops. Worse still, the title "Augustus" led to emperor worship. See "Emperor Cult" below.

EMPEROR CULT. From the time of Augustus (31 B.C. – A.D. 14) Roman emperors accepted the eastern belief in the divinity of kings. As a result they bore divine titles and were worshiped as Jupiter incarnate. Temples to the god Augustus and the goddess Roma were established throughout the Empire. Belief in imperial divinity was used as a means of keeping subject peoples loyal to Rome. Although the Jews were exempted from emperor worship, the Christians were not. They were looked upon as subversives and frequently suffered martyrdom for refusing to offer sacrifice and burn incense before the Emperor's image.

ENCHANTMENT. This term denotes the practice of the occult arts, notably magic and sorcery (Exod. 7:11, 22; 8:7). Magicians used various bizarre rituals and mutterings to enlist demonic powers (Isa. 8:19). Any resort to these methods of imposture was strictly prohibited by the Mosaic Law (Lev. 19:26). But occultism flourished in idolatrous pagan religions (2 Kings 17:17), even in the Christian era (Acts 13:6-8). See also "Demons," "Divination," and "Magic."

EN-DOR (ĕn′dôr). A village about four miles south of Mount Tabor (Josh. 17:11, 12). It was the home of the spirit medium whom King Saul consulted (1 Sam. 28:7).

ENGAGEMENT (Betrothal). In ancient Israel marriage was preceded by a period of betrothal. In earliest times the betrothal was largely a matter of business, and concerned chiefly the parents and near family friends (Gen. 21:21; 24:3). Distinction was clearly made between the betrothed and the married (Deut. 20:7). Later, under the second Jewish commonwealth, a legal ceremony for the betrothal was established by the rabbinical law. But at all periods of Israelite history betrothal was regarded as more than merely a promise to marry. It was considered the initial act of marriage and, like marriage itself, was dissoluble only by death or divorce.

Faithlessness to the betrothal vow was regarded as adultery and was punished as such (Lev. 19:20; Deut. 22:23-27). This is why Joseph was contemplating divorcing his betrothed wife, Mary, until he was apprised by the angel that her child was supernaturally conceived by the Holy Spirit (Matt. 1:18-25). After the betrothal a period of time (longer or shorter according to circumstances) was allowed to elapse before the nuptials (Gen. 24:55, 67; Deut. 20:7; Judg. 14:1-3, 7, 8). Later this period of time became established by talmudic law as a month for widows and a full year for virgins.

Between betrothal and marriage no sexual intercourse was allowed between the betrothed (Matt. 1:18). The ceremony of betrothal consisted of the simple act of the bridegroom handing to the bride or her representative a written engagement or a token of money. This was done in the presence of witnesses and was accompanied with the words "Be thou consecrated (wedded) to me." Since medieval times a ring has taken the place of the coin as the customary sign of betrothal.

Before the betrothal actually took place it was customary to agree upon a dowry. Customarily this was presented to the bride's parents (Exod. 22:16, 17; 1 Sam. 18:25), though sometimes it was given to an older brother (Gen. 24:53; 34:12). The dowry was considered a present to the bride or her parents for the purpose of sealing the engagement or enabling the bride to assume a worthy place in her future home (cf. Gen. 31:15). In rabbinical law, established at least by 100 B.C., the dowry was defined as a settlement upon the wife and was made as indispensable as is the marriage license today.

The dowry varied according to the circumstances of those concerned. Ordinarily it ranged from 30 to 50 shekels (approximately 20 to 30 dollars in terms of today's money). Other types of dowries were sometimes agreed upon (Gen. 29: 18; Josh. 15:16). Sometimes parents themselves bestowed presents on their daughters at the time of their betrothal (Gen. 29:24, 29; Tobit 10:11).

ENGRAVING. Engraving on ivory, bone, and precious stones was a skilled art in ancient Bible lands. Examples of Canaanite ivories come from Lachish (fourteenth century B.C.), Hagor (thirteenth century B.C.), and Tell Beit Mirsim. Ivories from Megiddo (twelfth century B.C.) and Samaria in Ahab's time (ninth century B.C.) are very similar to contemporary ivories from Arslan Tash (Syria) and Nimrud (Iraq). Some of the ivories are inlaid with gold, lapis-lazuli, colored stones, and glass.

Precious and semi-precious stones were also cut and carved. Inscribed seals have been recovered in jasper, agate, onyx, jade. opal, amethyst, and chalcedony. The modern method of facet cutting was not used. Instead, the stones were rounded and polished. Frequently they were also engraved and sculptured.

ENOCH (ē'nŭk) ("dedicated"). A pre-flood patriarch who lived a godly life and was translated to heaven at the age of 365 years (Gen. 5:18-24; Heb. 11:5). Jude refers to a prophecy of Enoch (Jude 1:14, 15), which is also recorded in the Book of Enoch.

EPAPHRAS (ĕp'á-frăs). A fellow-laborer of Paul who excelled in intercessory prayers (Col. 4:12).

EPAPHRODITUS (ė-păf-rŏ-dī'tŭs) ("lovely, charming"). A trusted messenger between Paul and the churches (Phil. 2:25; 4:18).

EPHAH (ē'fá). See under "Weights and Measures."

EPHESUS (ĕf'ė-sŭs). The principal city of the Roman province of Asia on the west coast of what is now Asiatic Turkey. The city was located at the mouth of the Cayster River between the mountain ranges of Koressos and the sea. It has been extensively excavated. The Temple of Diana was uncovered about a mile to the northeast. Christianity may well have been introduced to Ephesus by Paul's friends Aquila and Priscilla. Paul made a short visit there himself on his second missionary tour (Acts 18:18, 19). On his third tour he ministered there for over two years (Acts 19:8-10).

EPHOD (ē'fŏd). The linen ephod was apparently a simple, kimono-type article of priestly dress worn by the priests of Nob (1 Sam. 22:18), by Samuel (1 Sam. 2:18), and by David (2 Sam. 6:14). This ordinary ephod is to be distinguished from the high priest's ephod of costly material inwrought with gold, purple, and scarlet (Exod. Chaps. 28, 39). This latter garment reached from the chest to the hips. A special ephod was also used for oracular purposes (1 Sam. 21:9).

EPHRAIM (ē'frá-ĭm) ("doubly fruitful"). (1) The second son of Joseph by Asenath and the progenitor of a tribal family (Gen. 41:52; Num. 1:10). (2) The hill country of Central Palestine, extending from Bethel (12 miles north of Jerusalem) to the plain of Shechem (Josh. 17:15).

EPHRATHAH, EPHRATH (ĕf'rá-tá; ĕf'rāth) ("fruitfulness"). One of the wives of Caleb and the mother of Hur (1 Chron. 2:19).

EPHRON (ē'frôn). A hill or mountainous area between Nephtoah and Kiriath-Jearim (northwest of Jerusalem). The region defined part of the border of Judah (Josh. 15:9).

EPICUREANS (ĕp-ĭ-kŭ-rē'ānz). The founder of this philosophic school, Epicurus (341-270 B.C.), taught that happiness is to be attained by serene detachment which banishes all fear of divine intervention in life or of punishment after death. He conceived the gods as following to perfection the life of serene detachment (including detachment from human beings). Death, according to Epicurus, brings a dispersion to our constituent atoms. Paul encountered devotees of this school at Athens (Acts 17:18-20). It is not surprising that they found Paul's doctrine of the resurrection both strange and unpalatable. A later perversion of the original Epicurean philosophy has given the term "epicure" its modern connotation. (The original Epicureans did not advocate the pursuit of extravagant or illicit pleasure.)

ERASTUS (ė-răs'tŭs) ("beloved"). An assistant whom Paul sent to Macedonia (Acts 19:22; 2 Tim. 4:20). The official at Corinth, a convert of Paul, may be the same person (Rom. 16:23).

ERECH, URUK (ē'rĕk; ōō'rŏŏk). Modern Warka. It was founded around 4000 B.C. and was the leading city of Sumer and Babylonia. Its archeological finds include ziggurats and early pictograph tablets.

ERIDU (ā'ri-dōō). A city of Sumer and Babylonia. In the Sumerian king list it appears as the oldest city of Sumer. Found in this city (present-day Abu Shahrein) were the earliest writings on clay tablets.

ESARHADDON (ė-sär-hăd'ŏn) ("Asshur has given a brother"). Sennacherib's son and successor on the throne of Assyria, reigning from 680 to 668 B.C. He subdued Egypt and lifted Assyria to the zenith of power.

ESAU (ē'sô) ("hairy"). The elder son of Isaac and the twin brother of Jacob by Rebekah (Gen. 25:21-26). He was a skillful hunter but a secular-minded man, trading his birthright for a fleshly craving (Gen. 25:29-34; Heb. 12:16).

ESDRAELON, PLAIN OF (ĕs-drȧ-ē'lŏn). See under "Plains."

ESHCOL, BROOK OF (ĕsh'kŏl). A stream and wadi near Hebron where the Hebrew scouts cut down a cluster of grapes (Num. 13:23).

ESSENES (ĕs-sēnz'). A monastic religious order from about the time of Christ. The Essenes were a small sect rather than an influential party like the Pharisees or Sadducees. Philo, Josephus, and Pliny furnished the only sources of information on this reformation group in Judaism until the discovery of the Dead Sea Scrolls in 1947. This group or a similar one is now well-known as the result of the excavations of their headquarters at Qumran (on the northwest shore of the Dead Sea). The recovery of their Book of Discipline has substantiated ancient sources. They retired from society to pursue prayer and the practice of God's laws in order to offset the darkness and evil work in the world.

ESTHER (ĕs'tēr) (Akkadian *ishtar* or Persian *stara*, "star"). A beautiful Jewish maiden who became queen of Persia and thereby saved the Jews in the Empire from destruction. Esther's cousin and former guardian, Mordecai, had aroused the enmity of Haman, the prime minister. Haman goaded the king to authorize the massacre of all Jews in the Empire (Esth. 3:8-15). Mordecai informed Esther of the diabolical plot and urged her to appeal to the king. At the risk of her life Esther interceded (Esth. 4:15-5:4), telling the king that the edict would mean the destruction of her and her people. She persuaded her royal husband to issue a new decree which permitted the Jews to take vengeance on their enemies. Meanwhile Haman's wickedness was exposed and he was executed on the gallows which he had prepared for Mordecai. The Jews annihilated their foes and Mordecai became the new prime minister. Then Mordecai and Esther instituted the annual fest of Purim to commemorate Jewish deliverance from destruction (Esth. 9: 20-32).

ETAM (ē'tăm). A rock where Samson hid after slaughtering a number of the Philistines (Judg. 15:8). It is somewhere in the vicinity of Zorah.

ETERNAL LIFE. When Adam sinned, the human race incurred threefold death — spiritual, physical, and eternal (Gen. 2:17). In Adam "all die" (1 Cor. 15:22) in this threefold sense. Unregenerate man is dead spiritually (Eph. 2:1), without contact or fellowship with God. He must also die physically and be eternally separated from God (Rev. 20:11-15). Eternal life "in Christ" abrogates this three-fold death. Spiritual death gives way to spiritual life as a present possession (Rom. 6:23; 1 John 3:14). Physical death is conquered in the resurrection and glorification of the body (1 Cor. 15:50-54) or in the translation of the living at the Lord's coming (1 Thess. 4:13-18). Eternal death is cancelled by eternal life. No one possessing eternal life will ever be cast into eternal hell (Gehenna). Eternal life is as eternal as Christ himself and is imparted to the believer at the new birth (John 3:3-17).

ETHBAAL (ĕth′bȧ-ăl) ("with him is Baal"). A Phoenician king and father of the infamous Queen Jezebel (1 Kings 16:31).

ETHIOPIA (ė-thĭ-ō′pĭ-à). See "Cush."

ETHNARCH. A Greek term meaning "ruler of the people." It was a title of royalty bestowed upon a client king. It was higher than "tetrarch" but lower than "king" (1 Macc. 14:47). Archelaus, son of Herod the Great, "king" of Judea, was not deemed worthy of the title that his father bore but was appointed merely as an "ethnarch" (Josephus, *Antiquities* XVII: 11,4). Josephus and Matthew used popular terminology in referring to Archelaus as "king" (*Antiquities* XVIII:4,3).

The only actual use of the term "ethnarch" occurs in 2 Corinthians 11:32. This ruler was probably the appointed representative of the Nabatean king Aretas (9 B.C.-A.D. 39), who controlled Damascus. However, if the city was Roman-controlled, the ethnarch was a Nabatean with functions similar to the Jewish ethnarch in Jerusalem.

EUNICE (û-nī′sḕ) ("blessed with victory"). A pious Jewess and the mother of Timothy (2 Tim. 1:5). Godly training by Timothy's mother (and grandmother, Lois) contributed to the stalwart Christian character of the young pastor, whom Paul commended as "my dearly beloved son" (2 Tim. 1:2).

EUODIA (û-ō′dĭ-ä) ("good journey, success"). A Christian woman in the church at Philippi. She and Syntyche were advised by Paul to resolve their difficulties and to get along with each other amicably (Phil. 4:2).

EUPHRATES (û-frā′tēz) (Hebrew *Perath*). The largest river in West Asia. It is called "the river" (Deut. 11:24) and flows for 1200 miles to the Persian Gulf from its two main effluents in East Turkey. Along with the Tigris, it has formed the rich alluvial plain of lower Babylonia. Many important cities of antiquity, including Babylon, were situated on its banks in the southern plain, which was the cradle of civilization (cf. Gen. 2:14).

EUTYCHUS (û′tĭ-kŭs) ("happy, fortunate"). A young man of Troas who fell asleep during Paul's long sermon and fell to his death from a window. He was miraculously revived by Paul (Acts 20:7-12).

EVE (ēv) (Hebrew *Hawwah*, "life"). The first woman, named "life" because she was to become the mother of the entire subsequent human race (Gen. 3:20). She was created from man (Gen. 2:21, 22) in order to be "a helper fit for him" (Gen. 2:18, RSV).

EVERLASTING FATHER. An honorific messianic title or appellative. It is literally "Father of Eternity," meaning "the Eternally Existing One" (Isa. 9:6). Eastern kings were also honorifically described as living forever (Dan. 2:4).

EVIL-MERODACH (ē′vĭl-mḕ-rô′dăk) (Akkadian *Amel-Marduk*, "man of Marduk"). Nebuchadnezzar's son and successor (562-560 B.C.). He released Jehoiachin of Judah from a 37-year imprisonment (2 Kings 25:27-30; Jer. 52:31-34). This event is corroborated by cuneiform records of the era. Evil-Merodach was slain in a palace coup and was succeeded in the throne by Neriglissar, the chief conspirator.

EXORCISM. Expulsion of demons by the power of God through the name of Christ can be Satanically imitated by its occult counterpart, called exorcism. The exorcist (Matt. 12:27; Acts 19:13) casts out demons by magical conjurations, incantations, and occult rigmaroles. The dispossessions are not genuine; Satan does not actually cast out his own demons (cf. Matt. 12:22-30) but simply relocates and regroups them for further attacks. But Christ practiced genuine demon expulsion (Mark 5:1-13), as did the Apostles and other early Christians.

EZEKIEL (ê-zēk′yēl) ("God strengthens"). One of the major prophets of the Old Testament. Ezekiel prophesied in Babylonian exile, about 593 to 571 B.C. (Ezek. 1:1-3). Before the fall of Jerusalem he predicted the same fate for the wicked city as had Jeremiah (Ezek. Chaps. 1-24). He stressed the Lord's justification in sending his people into exile (cf. Ezek. 18:25-30; 33:17-20). His great prophecies center in hopeful predictions, and include a full vision of the final restoration of Israel (Ezek. Chaps. 33-48).

EZION-GEBER (ē′zĭ-ŏn-gē′bēr). See "Elath."

EZRA (ĕz′rà) ("help"). A learned scribe of priestly descent who led one of the contingents of Jews returning from exile in about 458 B.C. (before Nehemiah rebuilt the walls in 445 B.C.). He labored to eliminate all paganistic influences from Jewish life (see books of Ezra and Nehemiah). Ezra is credited with important influence in determining the canonicity of certain Old Testament books.

FADUS, CUSPIUS. The Roman procurator of Judea after the death of Agrippa I in A.D. 44. He ruthlessly suppressed patriotic outbreaks.

FAIR HAVENS. A small bay situated on the south coast of Crete a few miles east of Cape Matala (Acts 27:8). It was the last place Paul's ship could stay in order to avoid the northwest wind.

FAITH. In its simplest concept faith is personal confidence in God. It brings with it the blessing of honoring God. Faith can be exercised in several important ways. 1) *Saving faith* is the Spirit-induced confidence which causes a person to trust Christ as his sin-bearer (Acts 16:31; Eph. 2:8, 9). 2) *Serving faith* is the confidence in God which prompts a believer to yield his redeemed life to God's will (Rom. 12:1, 2). 3) *Sanctifying faith* denotes the believer's confidence in Christ as his source of sustaining grace and divine power (Rom. 6:11). 4) *Responsive faith* is a working belief which produces the fruit of the Spirit (Gal. 5:22, 23). 5) *Creedal or doctrinal faith* is trust in the body of revealed truth (1 Cor. 16: 13; Col. 1:23; 2:7; Jude 1:3). Faith pleases God and frees him to act on behalf of those who honor him by believing his Word (Heb. 11:6). See also "Belief."

FALL OF MAN. By disobeying God mankind fell from a state of innocence and incurred threefold death — immediate spiritual death, gradual physical death, and eventual eternal death (Gen. 2:17; 3: 1-15; 5:5; Rev. 19:20; 20:10, 14, 15). By Adam's sin all mankind came under the power of sin and death (Rom. 5:12; 1 Cor. 15:21, 22). Men can be released from this state of alienation and condemnation only by faith in Christ's atoning death on

"Adam and Eve Seal" found near Nineveh—dated by A.E. Speiser at about 3500 B.C. *(UMP photo)*

the cross (Rom. 5:13-21). See also "A-tonement" and "Redemption."

FALLOW DEER (Hebrew *yaḥmūr,* "brown goat"). In North Galilee the name *yaḥmūr* is still given to the roebuck (*Capreolus capraea* or *Cervus capreolus*). It is a dark reddish-brown in summer and a yellowish-gray in winter, with a large patch of white on the rump. It has antlers with three points and casts its horns every year. It is common in Europe and Asia. It was a ceremonially clean animal and was used for food (Deut. 14:5; 1 Kings 4:23). Some scholars identify the *yaḥmūr* with the bubale, a bovine antelope whose flesh is a delicacy.

FAMILY, JEWISH. As a result of common descent from Abraham and close tribal and inter-tribal unity, the family unit was viewed by the ancient Hebrews as the compact and basic institution of their society. The Hebrew concept of a house always included the thought of a family. A single word was used to designate both the dwelling and its inhabitants (see Genesis 46:31). In its original connotation the word embraced the concept of something built up or built together, each member being considered a vital and inseparable part of the structure (Gen. 16:2; 30:3; Deut. 25:9). The structure was in turn considered an inseparable part of the larger family unit, the clan and the tribe.

In harmony with their high view of the family, the Hebrews regarded children as one of life's greatest blessings (Psa. 113:9; 127:3-5). They were earnestly prayed for when not given, and their birth occasioned a time of great rejoicing (Gen. 15:2-5; 1 Sam. 1; Ruth 4:11). The hope of Israel lay in the birth of a future child who would be the Savior, the promised "Seed of the woman" (Gen. 3:15; Isa. 9:6,7).

The consideration which the Bible gives to children and childhood is both significant and delightful. It shows up conspicuously against the dark background of compassionless paganism, where children were often exposed or killed, frequently in the name of religion. Parental love toward offspring gilds the pages of Scripture (Gen. 37:34, 35; 2 Sam. 19:4; cf. Psa. 103:13). But this affection was not a weak indulgence. Rigorous discipline and training were part and parcel of it (Prov. 10:1; 13:24; 23:14; 29:15) on the part of both the parents and the state (Exod. 13:8; Deut. 4:9; 6:7; 11:19; 31:13). The fundamental philosophy of education was that "the fear of the Lord is the beginning of wisdom" (Prov. 1:7; 9:10). The mother and grandmother were featured in this godly training (cf. 2 Tim. 1:5; 3:15).

The Jewish firstborn son had a privileged position, even during the father's lifetime (Gen. 43:33). At his father's death he received twice as much of the father's estate as any other child (Deut. 21:17). He also assumed the position of father and head of family. Along with these rights went the duty of providing for the mother, if living, as well as other dependent members of the household. When the father acted as family priest the firstborn also inherited this function (Gen. 27:29; Deut. 21:17; cf. Num. 3:41).

The firstborn son might sell his birthright if he desired (Gen. 25:29-34; Heb. 12:16, 17). In such a case the father would direct how his property was to be distributed after his decease. The idea of a will in a technical sense is not mentioned until the Epistle to the Galatians (Gal. 3:15).

Ordinarily daughters did not inherit property. It was expected that they would be provided for by the eldest brother or by a husband (Gen. 31:14, 15). When there were no male children, daughters became joint-heirs of their father's estate if they did not marry outside the family line.

Even then they could sometimes claim their portion if the husband assumed the family name of his wife. When a family consisted only of unmarried daughters their names were entered in the registers of families as representatives of the father's house (Num. 27:1-11).

FARMER. See "Agriculturalist."

FATHERHOOD OF GOD. God is the Father of our Lord Jesus Christ (2 Cor. 1: 3) in the sense that Christ is the eternal Son of the Father with respect to his deity. He is said to be "the God . . . of our Lord Jesus Christ" (John 20:17; 2 Cor. 11:31; Eph. 1:3; 1 Pet. 1:3). God is also the Father of all men in the restricted sense of being their Creator (Luke 3:38; Acts 17:28). Spiritually the unsaved are "children of the devil" (John 8:44). God's covenant relation to the elect nation Israel is prefigured in a Father-son relationship (Exod. 4:22; Deut. 32:6; Isa. 63:16; 64:8).

FATHOM. See under "Weights and Measures."

FEAST OF TABERNACLES. See "Booths, Feast of."

FELIX, ANTONIUS (fē'lĭx). The Roman procurator of Judea from A.D. 52 to 59. He married Drusilla, Herod Agrippa I's daughter. Nero recalled him because of his greed and cruelty. He kept Paul in prison at Caesarea because no bribe was offered (Acts 23, 24).

FESTUS, PORCIUS (fĕs'tŭs, pôr'shĭ-ŭs). The Roman procurator of Judea from A.D. 60 to 62. Paul refused his proposal to be tried at Jerusalem and instead appealed to Caesar (Acts 25). Festus was one of the better governors.

FIG TREE. One of the most popular trees because of its delicious fruit and heavy shade. The common species (*Ficus carica*, Num. 13:23; 20:5; Matt. 7:16) was extensively cultivated in Palestine in biblical times. To "sit under one's vine and fig tree" symbolized prosperity and security (1 Kings 4:25; Mic. 4:4; Zech. 3:10). The tree bears successively three kinds of fruit: 1) the late (autumn) figs (Jer. 8:13; 29:17), the main crop from August until winter; 2) the green or winter figs (Song 2:13; Rev. 6:13), which, in the absence of ripening weather, spend the winter on the branches and ripen in the spring; and

Fig tree with its first fruit (© *MPS*)

3) the first-ripe figs (Isa. 28:4; Jer. 24:2; Hos. 9:10; Mic. 7:1; Nah. 3:12), the most delicious figs, those that cling to the tree and ripen in the summer from June onward. Apparently a healthy tree had fruit on it for about ten months. Jesus evidently expected green figs on the tree he cursed (Matt. 21:18, 19).

FINGER RING. This was properly the signet-ring of a king, taken from the hand and given as a token of authority (Gen. 41:42; Esth. 3:10; 8:2). It was frequently employed in the sealing of official documents and messages (Esth. 3:12; 8:8, 10). Closely related to it was the seal ring, *hotham*, which bore the name of the wearer and was usually carried on a cord around the neck (Gen. 38:18). It was sometimes also worn on the hand (Jer. 22:24). This was the *sphragis* of the New Testament (Rom. 4:11; 1 Cor. 9:2; 2 Tim. 2:19; Rev. 5:1, 2; 6:1-12; 7:2; 8:1; 9:4).

FIR TREE (Hebrew *berosh*, botanically in the genus *Pinus*). Two varieties of these evergreen, cone-bearing trees are native to the hills of Palestine and Lebanon — *Pinus brutia* and *Pinus halepensis*. The latter is called the Syrian or Aleppo pine (Isa. 41:19; 55:13). In Gilead there are extensive forests of *Pinus carica* on the higher elevations. The stone pine (*Pinus maratima*) grows on the coast and in sandy plains and has edible seeds. This is probably the tree referred to in Hosea 14: 8. The true fir of the region is *Abies cili-*

cica, growing in the higher heights of Lebanon (2 Sam. 6:5; Song 1:17; 1 Kings 5:8; Isa. 14:8; Zech. 11:2). It was used (along with cedar) in Solomon's Temple (1 Kings 5:8), for ship planks (Ezek. 27:5), and for musical instruments (2 Sam. 6:5).

FISH. Fish constituted an important part of the diet of the people of Bible lands. While in Egypt Israel ate fish freely (Num. 11:5). The Nile and its several branches in the Delta yielded a variety of fish (Isa. 19:8). Fishing also constituted an important industry in the Mediterranean, though it was largely in the hands of the Phoenicians in the north (Neh. 13: 16) and the Philistines in the south. The fishing industry of Palestine centered in the Sea of Galilee, which swarmed with many varieties of fish. Fish were sold at Jerusalem (Neh. 13:16) and elsewhere. Fishing figures prominently in the life of our Lord and his disciples (Mark 1:16-20; Luke 5:4-7; John 21:1-14).

FISHERMAN. Fish abounded in Egypt (Num. 11:5). A tomb painting from Thebes from the fifteenth century B.C. shows an Egyptian dignitary spearing fish in the marshes with a two-pronged lance from a papyrus skiff. The Sea of Galilee swarmed with fish (Luke 5:6). Even today 24 species abound.

At least seven of Jesus' disciples were fishermen (Matt. 4:18, 21; John 1:44; 21:2). On the Sea of Galilee they used small boats propelled by oars (John 6:19) and probably sails as well. Night fishing was common (Luke 5:5; John 21:3). Nets were frequently used (Matt. 4:18; Luke 5: 4). Sometimes nets were dragged to the shore (Matt. 13:48; John 21:8). The fish were then sorted and the unwanted ones thrown away (Matt. 13:48).

FISH MERCHANT. The fisherman sold his catch to a trader. At Jerusalem there was a Fish Gate, through which traders brought their fish to sell to the people (Zeph. 1:10). Fish also abounded at Tyre, and Tyrian fish merchants lived in Jerusalem in post-exilic times (Neh. 13:16). Often the fish were sold roasted rather than fresh. The salting and drying of fish in preparation for shipment to distant places became a flourishing industry, employing many workers. The fish which the Tyrians sold in Jerusalem and the fish from the Lake of Galilee were in all probability prepared in this way. The fish used to feed the five thousand and the four thousand (Matt. 14:15-21; 15:32-38) were probably the dried and salted variety.

FLAGS. Reeds growing by the brink of the Nile River (Hebrew *suph*, Exod. 2:3, 5; Isa. 19:6). The word denotes aquatic vegetation, whether seaweeds (Jonah 2:5) or freshwater reeds. Moses' mother made the tiny boat for her son out of "bulrushes" or papyrus. The Red Sea in Hebrew is *yam suph*, "Sea of Reeds." Another Hebrew word is used in Job 8:11 to denote flags or reeds, and probably also aquatic vegetation in a general sense. See also "Papyrus."

FLAX. A small plant cultivated for its bark (which furnishes the fiber out of which linen is woven) and for its seeds (out of which linseed oil is extracted — Isa. 42:3; Matt. 12:20). The flax plant was grown in Egypt and elsewhere (Exod. 9:31). Its fine fibers were woven like wool (Isa. 19: 9; Prov. 31:13; Hos. 2:5). Its stalks were spread on rooftops to dry in the sun (Josh. 2:6).

FLEA. A small flying insect mentioned in 1 Samuel 24:14 and 26:20. The flea is parasitic on man and beast and is an aggravating pest in Palestine.

FLESH. The word "flesh" has two general meanings in Scripture. It sometimes refers simply to the human body (John 3:6; 6:51; 1 Cor. 15:39; Eph. 5:31). Frequently, however, it refers to the sin nature acting within the human body. At conversion the believer receives a new nature, but the old nature is never eradicated. However, as the Christian yields to the indwelling Holy Spirit the fruit of the Spirit is produced in his life, thereby displacing the strong sinful desires of the old Adamic nature (Gal. 5:16-26).

FLORUS, GESSIUS. The Roman procurator from A.D. 64 to 66. His unprincipled conduct precipitated open revolt against Roman rule.

FLY. A two-winged insect of the order *Diptera*, especially the domestic fly, *Musca domestica*. The fly was so annoying that the people of Ekron worshiped a deity which they called Baal-zebub or "lord of flies" because he was considered able to ward them off (2 Kings 1:2). The dog-fly, a voracious biting insect of Egypt, is mentioned in Exodus 8:21 and Psalm 105:31.

FOREKNOWLEDGE. God's prior, determinative knowledge of all future events. The biblical concept of foreknowledge emphasizes God's own plan for man's future rather than God's prior knowledge of man's free choices (cf. Job 23:13, 14; Psa. 139:1-24; Jer. 1:5; Acts 2:23; 15:18; Rom. 8:28, 29; 1 Pet. 1:2).

FOREST. During the Middle Bronze Age (2000-1500 B.C.) the hill country of Palestine was covered with forests. In later centuries of Israelite occupation some of this forest land was cleared for settlements and farming. Still, considerable areas of woodland remained intact. One wooded area stretched from the Mediterranean Sea to the hill country of Ephraim (Josh. 17:15, 18). Another was located in Judah (1 Sam. 22:5). "The Forest of Ephraim" is specifically named (2 Sam. 18:6) and is generally supposed to have been in Transjordan near Mahanaim. The most famous forests were in Lebanon, whose renowned firs and cedars supplied woods for temples and kings' palaces (1 Kings 7:2). Part of the Jordan Valley was a luxuriant jungle with abundant wildlife. Some of the more significant forests of Scripture are described below.

Arabia, Forest in (Isa. 21:13). In this huge peninsula rainfall was scarce; even in the southwest, with its higher rainfall, forests were rare, being replaced by thickets of scrub and small trees. Arabia consists of the huge area bounded by the Fertile Crescent on the north, the Indian Ocean on the south, the Red Sea on the west, and the Persian Gulf and the Gulf of Oman on the east.

Beth-aven, Wood near (1 Sam. 14:25). A place where the Israelites collected honey. Beth-aven ("house of nothingness or idolatry") was located in the territory of Benjamin, near Ali, east of Bethel (Josh. 7:2), and west of Michmash (1 Sam. 13:5; cf. 14:23). It lay on the border of the wilderness (Josh. 18:12), which consisted of a heavily wooded area. This was possibly near the forest between Jericho and Beth-

el, where bears attacked the children who taunted the prophet Elisha (2 Kings 2:24).

Carmel, Forest of (2 Kings 19:23). Mount Carmel is the 1740-foot-high main ridge at the northwest end of a range of hills which extends southeast from the Bay of Acre to the plain of Dothan. Anciently it was densely vegetated, with its luxuriant growth reflected in Amos 1:2 and 9:3, Micah 7:14, and Nahum 1:4. In Song of Solomon 7:5 "the forest of Carmel" is an apt figure for thick, bushy hair. Parts of the forest were apparently cultivated to the summit with fruit trees and orchards (Isa. 33:9; 35:2; Jer. 50:19). The forest probably consisted chiefly of fruit trees (Mic. 7:14), although thickets of prickly oak and juniper covered the hills of the Carmel range.

Ephraim, Wood of (2 Sam. 18:6). The site of the battle between King David's men and Absalom's rebels. It was evidently located in Transjordan in the general vicinity of Mahanaim of Gilead (2 Sam. 17:24).

Forest of the South (Ezek. 20:45-49). The forest land of Judah, in which the Lord promised to kindle a fire to devour "every green tree and every dry tree" (the trees representing people). These forests in the mountains of Judah are referred to in 2 Chronicles 27:4 as the place where King Jotham built forts.

Lebanon, Forest of (2 Kings 19:23). The Lebanon mountains consist of two ranges running north and south, and are most famous for their forests of gigantic cedars. Fir trees and cypresses also abounded here (1 Kings 5:6-10; 2 Kings 19:23; Isa. 60:13; Zech. 11:1). Lebanon supplied timber for kings' palaces, temples, and masts for Phoenician ships. Lebanon formed the northwest boundary of the Promised Land (Deut. 1:7).

FORGIVENESS. During the Old Testament period sins were "covered" in anticipation of Christ's coming sacrifice (Acts 17:30; Rom. 3:25). Christ's great work of atonement was prefigured by the animal sacrifices (Heb. 9:13, 14). In this New Testament era the believer enjoys full forgiveness the moment he places his faith in Christ (Acts 13:38, 39). The believer never faces condemnation, for all his trespasses — past, present, and future — have been forgiven (John 3:18; 5:24; Col. 2:13). However, when a believer sins he forfeits *fellowship* with the Father and the Son. He must accordingly confess his sin and claim the forgiveness which the Father extends (1 John 1:9 — 2:2).

If a believer persists in unconfessed sin he will be chastised by the Father, though not condemned with the world (1 Cor. 11:31, 32). The ultimate in God's chastening is "the sin unto (physical) death" (1 John 5:16; cf. John 15:2; 1 Cor. 11:30). In this case God removes the severely sinning saint from this life so that he will not be "condemned with the world" (1 Cor. 11:31, 32).

The unpardonable sin was attributing to Satan the power of the Holy Spirit in the earthly ministry of Christ (Matt. 12:22-32). This sin is not possible now and is inconsonant with the gospel of "whosoever will." Rejecting Christ as Savior is the nearest present-day equivalent.

FOX. Several species of foxes and the closely-related jackal are found in Palestine. They are members of the *Canidae* or dog family. Foxes usually remain solitary, while jackals run in packs. The Hebrew term *shucal* and the Greek term *alōpēx* apparently include both of these species. These animals eat fruit and vegetables, notably grapes (Song 2:15). It is probable that the 300 animals caught by Samson were jackals (Judg. 15:4), since foxes are extremely difficult to catch. The jackal devours carrion (Psa. 63:10), which the fox is loathe to do. See also "Jackal."

FRANKINCENSE. A white, aromatic gum resin with an odor similar to that of balsam, especially when burnt. The frankincense tree consists of a number of species, several native to India and others coming from the Somali coast of Africa and South Arabia. It was an ingredient in the holy anointing oil (Exod. 30:34) and the meal offerings (Lev. 2:1, 2). Pure frankincense was poured on the showbread (Lev. 24:7; 1 Chron. 9:29). Frankincense was imported to Palestine from Arabia (Isa. 60:6; Jer. 6:20).

FRINGED GARMENT. The common robe of the ancient East had a fringed edge, in which the Israelites were required to insert a blue thread to remind them that they were God's people. The Pharisees ceremoniously enlarged these fringes (Matt. 23:5).

FROG. An amphibious animal (Exod. 8:3). The frog of the Old Testament is probably *Rana punctata*, the spotted frog of Egypt. In Revelation 16:13, 14 the noisy, croaking frogs represent demonic agencies that stir up wicked men to fight against God at Armageddon.

FRUITBEARING. Fruitfulness is the result of union with Christ (John 15:1-5). This union is symbolized by the vine and the branches. The believer is "in Christ" much as a branch is in the vine. Three conditions of fruitbearing are indicated: 1) cleansing or pruning (John 15:2, 3); 2) abiding (John 15:4), that is, relying on Christ. In this condition the life of Christ flows through the believer much as the life of the vine enters the branches; and 3) obedience to Christ's commandments (John 15:10, 12, 14).

FULLER. Before fabrics were dyed it was necessary to cleanse their fibers of natural oils or gums. This cleansing and bleaching process was the duty of the fuller. He worked near a supply of water so that fabrics could be cleansed by treading them on stones submerged in water. For this reason the fuller was called a "trampler" (Hebrew *kabas*). Several references to the "fuller's field" at Jerusalem occur in the Bible (2 Kings 18:17; Isa. 7:3; 36:2).

For cleansing, natron or niter was sometimes imported from Egypt. It was mixed with white clay and used as soap (Prov. 25:20; Jer. 2:22). Alkali was supplied by burning the soda plant (*Salsola kali*). Malachi refers to "fuller's soap" (Mal. 3:2; cf. Mark 9:3).

FUNERALS, JEWISH. It was customary for Hebrews to take formal and affectionate leave of those about to die (Gen. 49). The lifeless body was then washed and wrapped in a linen cloth (Matt. 27:59; John 11:44). Sweet-smelling spices were laid in the folds of the enveloping shroud. This was intended to offset any odor produced by rapid decay of the unembalmed body. It also served as a medium for the expression of love and respect, much as flowers do today.

Embalming was not ordinarily practiced among the Hebrews (Gen. 50:2, 26). Burial in the ground or, if possible, in a rock tomb usually took place on the same day as death. This was necessitated by the rapid deterioration of the unembalmed corpse and the fact that the dead body was ceremonially defiling (Num. 19:11-16). The corpse was usually carried to its place of interment on a bier attended by a procession in which hired mourners took part.

The Israelites, in contrast to the Greeks and Romans, did not practice cremation. They interred but did not burn their dead, in harmony with the Egyptians and with other Semites. The bones of Saul and his sons were burned only to preserve their bodies from insult. After being reduced to ashes they were respectfully buried (1 Sam. 31:8-13). Exposing corpses to birds of prey was regarded as the acme of indignity (1 Kings 14:11; Jer. 16:4). Rizpah, Saul's concubine, watched the bodies of his seven sons in order to prevent this disgrace from befalling them (2 Sam. 21:10).

The Hebrews often buried entire families in the same tomb (Gen. 47:29, 30; Judg. 8:32; 16:31; Ruth 1:17). Thus Joseph of Arimathaea underwent a significant sacrifice in offering his family sepulchre as a place of interment for the body of Jesus (Matt. 27:57-60). The Hebrews distinguished clearly between the tomb of the body and the spirit world where the soul went (Gen. 25:8). Rock tombs were sealed with huge stones (Mark 16:1-4; John 20:1).

Lamentation for the dead began at the moment of death and continued unabated until after the burial or entombment. Hired professional mourners, generally women, joined their lamentations with the family and friends (Mark 5:38, 39). They wept, uttered cries of grief, beat their bodies, pulled out their hair, threw dust on their heads, tore their garments, put on sackcloth, and fasted (Gen. 37:34; 2 Sam. 13:31; 19:4).

Expressly forbidden to both priests (Lev. 21:5) and the people at large (Lev. 19:27, 28; Deut. 14:1) were bodily lacerations, ritualistically trimmed beards, baldness between the eyes, and "rounded" (mutilated) corners of the head.

The usual period of mourning lasted seven days (Gen. 50:10), although in unusual cases it might be as long as thirty days, as in the death of Aaron (Num. 20:28, 29) and Moses (Deut. 34:5-8). The custom of making an offering for the dead appears first in an apocryphal book in the second century B.C. (2 Macc. 12: 43).

FURLONG. See under "Weights and Measures."

GAASH, BROOKS OF (gā'āsh). Seasonal streams apparently issuing from Mount Gaash near Timnath-Serah in the mountains of Ephraim. One of David's heroes came from this region (2 Sam. 23:30).

GABBATHA (gāb'ȧ-thȧ). A place in Jerusalem called "the Pavement" (Greek *lithostrotos* — John 19:13). It was located at or near the Tower of Antonia, north-west of the Temple area. It is buried beneath the present-day Church of the Daughters of Zion.

GAD (găd). Jacob's seventh son and a progenitor of one of the tribes of Israel (Gen. 30:10, 11; 46:16; 49:19).

GADARA (găd'ȧ-rȧ). A locality near the southeast shore of the Lake of Galilee in the district of Gadara. It lay six miles southeast of the Lake near the gorge of the Yarmuk. It was in this town that Jesus healed two demon-possessed men (Matt. 8:28-34; Mark 5:1-17; Luke 8:26-37).

GAIUS CALIGULA (gā'yŭs kȧ-lĭg'ù-lȧ). The Roman Emperor from A.D. 37 to 41. He was an eccentric, impious ruler who claimed to be divine and foolishly attempted to have his statue erected in the Jewish Temple at Jerusalem. His career came to an early end by assassination.

GALATIANS (gȧ-lā'shĭ-ȧns). A Celtic tribe that invaded Asia Minor in the third century B.C. Called Gauls, these Indo-European people gradually settled in the territory in which were located the old Phrygian cities of Pessinus and Tavium. Ancyra (modern Ankara) became their capital. Under Roman rule the Galatians were given autonomy. During the reign of their last king, Amyntas (25 B.C.), their territory was greatly enlarged on the south to include part of Phrygia, Pisidea, Lycaonia and Isauria. After the death of Amyntas this enlarged region was made a Roman province. In 7 B.C. still other additions were made. In Paul's day the term "Galatia" referred to both the original Galatic region and the larger territory of the Roman Province.

GALBANUM (găl'bȧ-nŭm). A fragrant spice which constituted one of the four ingredients of the holy incense (Exod. 30:34). It was made from the gum of two umbelliferous plants native to Persia.

GALILEE, SEA OF (găl'ĭ-lē). Palestine's largest lake, located near the northeast corner of the country along the Jordan River. It is also called "the lake of Gennesaret" (Luke 5:1) and "the sea of Tiberias" (John 21:1). This latter name was derived from the city of Tiberias, which had been founded by Herod Antipas on

Calm moments on the Sea of Galilee (© *MPS*)

the western shore of the lake about A.D. 20. In Old Testament times the lake was named "the sea of Chinneroth." The lake is about 13 miles long, 7 miles across at its widest point, and 695 feet below sea level. It is mentioned a number of times in the Gospels in connection with the activities of Christ and his disciples. See also "Chinneroth."

GALL (Hebrew *rōsh*, Greek *cholē*). A bitter, poisonous herb (Deut. 29:18; 32:32) that grew commonly in the fields (Hos. 10:4). A drink of gall water is compared to a severe punishment (Jer. 8:14; 9:15; 23:15). While hanging on the Cross, Christ was offered sour wine mixed with gall (Matt. 27:34; Mark 15:36; Luke 23:36; John 19:29, 30; cf. Psa. 69:21).

GALLIO (găl'ĭ-ō). The Roman proconsul of Achaia at the time of Paul's first visit to Corinth (A.D. 51-52). Paul was accused before him but was acquitted. Gallio exhibited indifference regarding the Jews' hatred of the Apostle (Acts 18:12-17).

GAMALIEL (gȧ-mā'lĭ-ĕl) ("God has rewarded"). A renowned doctor of Jewish law (Acts 5:34) who had instructed Saul of Tarsus (Acts 22:3). He showed great wisdom and moderation in opposing persecution of the apostles. If their work were simply man's, he counseled, it would fail. If it were from God, opposition to it would be vain and wicked (Acts 5:34-40). It is possible that he was a secret believer in Christ (cf. John 12:42, 43).

GAMES, JEWISH. There is little indication that the Hebrews indulged to any great extent in diversion for its own sake. As a God-fearing and largely pastoral and agricultural people, they had little time or money during most of their history to engage in those pastimes that have corrupted more affluent pagan societies. What leisure the Israelites enjoyed was to a large extent expended on their religious activities and sacred festivals. Their social life was distinctly home- and God-centered, in line with their divine calling and mission.

Simple home pleasures included riddle-telling and witty repartee. Ballplaying and other games known to have been played in Egypt must at least occasionally have been enjoyed in Israel (cf. Isa. 22: 18). Jewish children played various youthful games (Zech. 8:5; Matt. 11:16, 17; Luke 7:31, 32). In David's time archery was a pastime for royal youths and others (1 Sam. 20:20; Job 16:12, 13).

Public games, on the other hand, were not welcomed by the Jews. The introduction of Greek sports and the gymnasium during the Maccabean era was resisted as an insult to the faith of their fathers (1 Macc. 1:14; 2 Macc. 4:12-14). The Apostle Paul refers to the Greek games for purposes of illustration, especially boxing and the foot race (1 Cor. 9:24-27; Phil. 3:14; 2 Tim. 2:5; 4:7, 8). He also makes reference to the gladiatorial contests, which were a common diversion of the debauched pagan society of the first century A.D.

GARDENER. Kings, courtiers, and people of nobility had palaces and estates that called for large numbers of workers skilled in all phases of horticulture. Spices and choice plants graced the gardens of the wealthy (Song 5:1; 6:2, 11), which were customarily walled (Song 4: 12) and often graced by a summerhouse (2 Kings 9:27). The palace at Jerusalem had the well-known "king's garden" (2 Kings 25:4; Jer. 39:4; 52:7; Neh. 3:15). Sumptuous pleasure gardens surrounded the Persian royal palaces (Esth. 1:5; 7:7, 8).

Fruit orchards, vegetable gardens, vineyards, and olive yards were often included in a pleasure garden (1 Kings 21:2; Amos 4:9; 9:14; Song 4:16; Eccl. 2:5). Even private citizens often had well-landscaped estates. Egyptian and Mesopotamian kings had splendid yards. The Canaanite kings of Ugarit had a fine garden gracing an inner court of the palace in the fourteenth and thirteenth centuries B.C.

GARLIC. A bulbous, onion-like plant which was popular in Egypt (Num. 11:5). It belongs to the onion family but has a stronger scent and flavor than the onion. It was eaten by the poor as a relish.

GATH (găth). One of the five Philistine cities (Josh. 13:3; 1 Sam. 17:4; 21:10; 2 Sam. 1:20; 2 Kings 12:17; Mic. 1:10). It was probably northwest of Lachish.

GAZA (gā′zà). One of the five Philistine cities (Gen. 10:19; Josh. 11:22; 13:3). Although it had been reckoned to Judah (Josh. 15:47), it was in Philistine hands again by the time of the Judges (Judg. 16: 21; 1 Sam. 6:17). In New Testament times it was an independent city (Acts 8: 26). It is present-day el-Gazzeh.

GAZELLE. A small antelope, the *Gazella dorcas*. It was ceremonially clean (Deut. 12:22; 14:5), was hunted (Prov. 6:5; Isa. 13:14), and was extremely fleet-footed (2 Sam. 2:18). It possessed great beauty and grace (Song 2:9; 8:14) and was very timid. It is found in Syria, Egypt, and Arabia.

GEBAL (gē′băl). A Phoenician seaport on a bluff overlooking the Mediterranean Sea north of Sidon. It adjoins the Lebanese village of Jebeil. The Greeks named the city Byblus ("papyrus"), for here they saw scrolls made from imported Egyptian papyrus reeds. The territory of the Gebalites is mentioned in Joshua 13: 5. Its stonemasons were employed by Solomon (1 Kings 5:18, RSV). Their shipbuilders were skillful in caulking (Ezek. 27:9).

GEDALIAH (gĕd-à-lī′à) ("the Lord is great"). The appointed governor of Judah after the fall of Jerusalem. He resided at Mizpah, where he was treacherously assassinated (2 Kings 25:22-26).

GEHAZI (gē-hā′zī) ("valley of vision"). Elisha's servant, who proved to be unholy and avaricious (2 Kings 5:20-27), in contrast to his master, who was dedicated and holy.

GEHENNA (gĕ-hĕn′à). The Aramaic form of the Hebrew word *Gehinnom*, "the Valley of Hinnom" (also called *Tophet*). This valley lay southwest of Jerusalem and was notorious as a place where children had been burned as sacrifices to

Moloch. Later the place was made a dumping ground for offal and a burning ground for garbage (cf. Mark 9:44, 46, 48). The valley came to symbolize the place of eternal punishment for the wicked. Theologically, "Gehenna" is identical in meaning with "the lake of fire," the eternal prison of the wicked (Rev. 19:20; 20:10, 14, 15).

GENTILES. A biblical term which refers to non-Jewish nations and individuals. God's purpose in this age is to "visit the Gentiles to take out of them a people for his name" (Acts 15:14). These, together with converted Jews, form the Church, the "body of Christ." The "fullness of the Gentiles" is the completion of this purpose — the time when the last member of the true church will have been called out (Rom. 11:25; 1 Cor. 12:12, 13; Eph. 4:11-13). The "times of the Gentiles" (Luke 21:24) covers the extended period from Judah's captivity (to Nebuchadnezzar in 605 B.C.) until the second advent of Christ and the inauguration of the kingdom age. The judgment of individual Gentiles will take place at Christ's return to establish his kingdom over Israel (Matt. 25:31-46).

GERAR (gē'rär). An ancient town south of Gaza (Gen. 10:19) where Abraham and Isaac lived (Gen. Chaps. 20, 21, 26). The site is identified with present-day Tell Jemmeh, eight miles south of Gaza.

Mount Gerizim towers over ruins of Shechem. (© MPS)

GERIZIM (gĕr'ĭ-zĭm). The mountain which forms the south boundary of the valley in which Nablus (ancient Shechem) lies. Mount Gerizim and the more elevated Mount Ebal face each other. When the Israelites conquered Central Palestine, Joshua carried out the directions of Moses, placing half of the tribes in front of Mount Gerizim in order to pronounce blessings and the other half in front of Mount Ebal in order to pronounce curses (Deut. 11:29, 30; 27:11-26). The erection of a Temple there in the fourth century B.C. made Gerizim a holy mountain of the Samaritans.

GEZER (gēz'ẽr). A Canaanite city (Josh. 10:33) in Ephraim (Josh. 16:10). It was captured by the Egyptians and presented to Solomon (1 Kings 9:15-17). It is present-day Tell Jezer, which has been excavated. It lies 23 miles west-northwest of Jerusalem in the low country just east of Gibbethon. Excavations have uncovered levels from Chalcolithic to Maccabean times. The Greek form of the name is Gazara (1 Macc. 4:15).

GIBBETHON (gĭb'ē-thŏn). A town in the original territory of Dan (Josh. 19:44). It was a Levitical city (Josh. 21:23). It later fell into Philistine hands (1 Kings 15:27; 16:15, 17).

GIBEAH (gĭb'ē-à). The capital of Saul's kingdom (1 Sam. 10:26; 15:34). Excavations reveal that the town which existed during the period of the Judges was destroyed about 1100 B.C. (compare Judges 19 and 20). Saul's fortress was destroyed about 1100 B.C. The present-day site is Tell el-Ful, about four miles north of Jerusalem.

GIBEON (gĭb'ē-ōn). A Canaanite town (Josh. 9:3; 10:2) and the scene of Joshua's great victory (Josh. 10:1-14). It had a notable pool (2 Sam. 2:13). Illegitimate sacrifices were offered at its altar (1 Kings 3:4). The site exists today as El-Jib, about 11 miles northwest of Jerusalem.

GIDEON (gĭd'ē-ōn) ("hewer, feller"). A reformer, Baal exterminator, deliverer, and judge of Israel (Judg. 6:11 — 8:35). Relying upon the Lord, he routed the invading Amalekites and won a great victory with only 300 soldiers (Josh. 7:1-25).

GIER-EAGLE (Hebrew *rāhām*). Apparently the Egyptian vulture (*Neophron percnopterus*). It was common in Palestine, where it breeds during its northern migration. It was ceremonially unclean (Lev. 11:18; Deut. 14:17).

GIFTS OF THE SPIRIT. Sovereign bestowments of the Holy Spirit upon individual believers in the church. They are given in order to produce various spiritual ministries. Nine of these gifts operated in the early church before the New Testament was written. These are specified in 1 Corinthians 12:7-11. Three of these—direct inspirational prophecies, supernatural languages, and direct inspirational knowledge (1 Cor. 13:8)—were required only temporarily. Their need disappeared after the New Testament was completed. Thus the Apostle Paul explained that these temporary gifts would be superseded by "the completed (final) thing" (the completed New Testament) and would then pass out of use (1 Cor. 13:10-13). First Corinthians 14 regulated the use of these gifts in the early church.

GIHON (gī'hŏn). (1) A river associated with the Garden of Eden. It was presumably an ancient waterway that connected the Tigris and the Euphrates Rivers (Gen. 2:13). (2) A spring east of Jerusalem. See under "Springs, Wells, and Pools."

GILBOA (gĭl-bō'à). A range of hills southwest of Bethshan which overlooked the eastern end of the Plain of Jezreel (Esdraelon). It was the scene of Saul's death in his first clash with the Philistines (1 Sam. 28:4—31:6).

GILEAD (gĭl'ė-ăd). The mountainous country east of the Jordan Valley. It extends from the northern end of the Dead Sea to the River Yarmuk south of the Sea of Galilee. North of this territory, held by the tribes Reuben, Gad, and half-Manasseh, was the territory of Bashan (Deut. 3:12, 13; Josh. 13:24-31). The last interview between Jacob and Laban took place in this region (Gen. 31:20-25). It was famous for its cattle (1 Chron. 5:9) and balm (Jer. 8:22; cf. Gen. 37:25).

GILGAL (gĭl'găl). The place where the Israelites were circumcised and the reproach of Egypt was "rolled away" from them (Josh. 5:9). It lay between Jericho and the Jordan River (Josh. 4:19). It is mentioned in the time of the Judges (Judg. 2:1; 3:19) and in Samuel's era (1 Sam. 7:16; 1 Sam. 11:14, 15; 15:12-33). David's subjects met him at Gilgal with a homecoming welcome after Absalom's revolt (2 Sam. 19:15, 40).

GIRDLE. A sash or belt worn around the waist. It was an important accessory for ancients who wore long, flowing robes. Men frequently wore utilitarian belts (as the soldier's belt in 2 Samuel 20:8), while women wore more decorative girdles (Prov. 31:24; Isa. 3:24). Men's belts frequently held knives or weapons. The linen "sash" of a priest was a distinctive item of priestly attire (Exod. 28:4; 29:9; 39:29; Lev. 8:7; 16:4).

The leather belt or girdle (Greek *zōnē*) was originally the lower section of a double girdle worn by women. In the New Testament it also appears as an article of clothing worn by men (Matt. 3:4; Mark 1:6). "Girding the loins" involved tightening flowing garments securely about the body so that the wearer would not stumble as he walked. The expression also denotes a figure of speech for preparing for spiritual activity (1 Pet. 1:13).

GLASSMAKER. Before the Roman period glass items were a rare luxury. But by the eighteenth dynasty in Egypt (1546-1316 B.C.) a glass factory at El-Amarna in Egypt was producing imitations of stone and pottery wares. Samples of these have been found at Gezer, Lachish, Megiddo, and Hazor. Local products also appeared around this time. Glazes are mentioned in contemporary Assyrian and Hittite texts. Cobalt and manganese were employed as coloring agents. However, ancient glass products lacked transparency. Techniques to eliminate the impurities in glass were not perfected until the Roman period (cf. Rev. 4:6; 15:2; 21:18, 21).

GNAT. In biblical times, as now, gnats abounded in swamps and marshes. The Egyptians slept under nets to protect themselves from gnat bites (Herodotus 11:95). The Pharisees strained drinking water through a cloth to avoid swallowing an insect regarded as unclean (Matt. 23:24).

GOAT, DOMESTIC. Denoted by a number of different Hebrew and Greek words, the goat was one of the most common domestic animals in Bible times. The domestic goat (*Capra hircus*) belonged to the large family of hollow-horned ruminants. Every flock of goats had its own stately leader (cf. Jer. 50:8). The goat was admirably suited for a hilly and somewhat dry country. The flesh and milk of goats furnished food (Deut. 14:4; Prov. 27:27) and their hair was woven into cloth (Exod. 25:4; 35:26). They formed a very important part of a cattleman's wealth (Gen. 30:25-36). The goat served as an animal of sacrifice (Gen. 15:9; Exod. 12:5; Lev. 1:10).

GOAT, WILD. A species of ibex (*Capra beden*), which the Arabs call *badan* or *beden*. It is lighter in color than the European ibex, with slender, recurved horns. It was found in Egypt, Arabia, Persia, Moab, the Judean Wilderness, and the wilderness about Engedi.

GOD. God is a Spirit, infinite in being, glory, blessedness, and perfection. He is eternal, unchangeable, incomprehensible, and all-sufficient. He is omnipresent, omnipotent, and omniscient. He is gracious, absolutely loving, and slow to anger, but he "will not at all acquit the wicked" (Nah. 1:3). He is revealed in nature, the written Word, and the incarnate Word—Christ himself (John 1:1, 14). Through him God becomes visible to men (John 1:18). God can be "just and the justifier of him who believes in Jesus" (Rom. 3:26) because his holy Law—the Mosaic Decalogue—has been vindicated by Christ's death. See also "Adonai," "Adonai Jehovah," "Elohim," and "Jehovah."

GODS. The worship of pagan gods or their idol representations was strictly forbidden by the first commandment of the Law (Exod. 20:1-6). One reason for this stringent prohibition is that people who bow down to idol images are actually worshiping demons. These fallen spirit beings masquerade as "gods" and frequently indwell various idol images (Lev. 17:7; Deut. 32:17; Rev. 9:20). The Apostle Paul strongly cautions New Testament believers against falling into this severe sin (1 Cor. 10:19-21).

GOG (gŏg). The "chief prince" of Meshech and Tubal (Ezek. 38:2). He will lead the great Northern Confederacy in an invasion of Palestine in the end time (Ezek. 38, 39), before Christ's second advent and Israel's restoration (Ezek. 40−48).

Possible Golgotha, the "place of the skull," where Jesus Christ was crucified (*Russ Busby photo*)

GOLGOTHA (gŏl'gō-thá). Probably "Gordon's Calvary" near the Garden Tomb (Matt. 27:33; Mark 15:22; John 19:17). The word is the Aramaic equivalent of Latin *calvaria* (Calvary).

GOLIATH (gō-lī'áth) ("an exile"). The Philistine giant of Gath who taunted God and his people but was slain by David (1 Sam. 17).

GOMER (gō'mĕr). (1) The daughter of Diblaim and the wife of Hosea the prophet (Hos. 1:3). Her unfaithfulness in marriage was used by the prophet as a dramatic parable of Israel's unfaithfulness to God. Apparently the Lord commanded Hosea to marry a practicing harlot, though it is possible that she became a harlot only after his marriage. At any rate the prophet felt the sting and insult of his wife's infidelity, even as the Lord felt the pain of Israel's apostasy (Hos. 1:2-9).

The names of Gomer's children (Hos. 1:6-9) depict Israel's deserved sufferings. "*Lo-ruhamah*" means "unpitied" and "*Lo-ammi*" means "not my people." The name of Gomer's previous child, *Jezreel* (Hos. 1:3-5), means "the Lord sows." It pointed back to the blood shed by Jehu in Jezreel (2 Kings 10:1-11) and forward to the approaching punishment of the Jehu dynasty. It also intimated the future restoration of the nation (Hos. 2:21-23; cf. Rom. 9:25, 26). (2) The Japhetic progenitor of the Cimmerians (the *Gimirrai* of the Assyrian records), who inhabited "the uttermost parts of the north" (Ezek. 38:6; cf. 10:2, 3).

GOMORRAH (gṓ-mŏr′rȧ). A town now under the shallow waters of the southern end of the Dead Sea in the valley of Siddim, near Sodom (Gen. 14:2-11). It was destroyed by God because of its overwhelming wickedness (Gen. 18:20 – 19:25).

GOOSE. Geese were common in Egypt at an early period and were mentioned by Homer (ninth century B.C.).

GOPHER WOOD. The timber out of which Noah's ark was constructed (Gen. 6:14). Its precise identification is obscure, but the writer evidently refers to a conifer. The cypress tree, commonly used in shipbuilding, may have been intended.

GORGIAS (gôr′jĭ-ăs). A Syrian general whom Antiochus Epiphanes commanded to destroy the forces of the Maccabees (1 Macc. 3 – 5).

GOSHEN (gō′shĕn). A district in Egypt (in the Wadi Tumilat in the northeast part of the Nile Delta) where the cities of Raamses, Baal-zephon, Pibeseth, Pithom, and Succoth were located (Gen. 45:10; 46:28, 29; 47:1-6; Exod. 8:22).

GOSPEL. The word "gospel" means "good news." The good news is addressed to lost humanity and centers in God's grace, which rescues man from sin and restores him to God's image and fellowship. The gospel was first announced when God promised Adam and Eve that the "seed of the woman" would crush the serpent's head (Gen. 3:15). It was prefigured in the shed blood of the animal which God killed in order to clothe the naked sinners (Gen. 3:21). It was symbolized year after year in the blood of the animals that were offered in the Mosaic sacrificial system (Heb. 9:11-14, 19, 21).

When Christ, the true Sacrifice, was offered, the gospel in symbol became the gospel in reality (Heb. 9:11-15; 10:10-14). Sins which had previously been passed over were now instantly remitted for all those who had believed, whether before or after the Cross (Rom. 3:25, 26). The one human requirement for salvation is *faith in God's grace revealed in Christ's death and resurrection* (Rom. 10:8, 9; Eph. 2:8, 9). Absolutely no other requirement for salvation must be added or substituted. Any addition, change, or substitution corrupts the simple gospel of pure grace into "another gospel" – a heretical one which God's people are instructed to denounce (Gal. 1:6-9). This spurious gospel may parade under various seductive forms. The test, however, is simple. Does the alleged gospel question the total sufficiency of God's grace to save, keep, and perfect? If it does, perhaps by recommending some kind of human striving, it is to be branded "another gospel" and is to be rejected outright.

GOSPELS, THE FOUR. Precisely speaking, these are neither biographies of our Lord nor histories of his earthly life among men. They are rather feature portraits of the most unique personage ever to walk the paths of earth. Matthew presents Christ as the King of the Jews. Mark features him as the Perfect Servant. Luke portrays him as the Perfect Man. John shows that he is above all the Son of God. While each Gospel emphasizes a particular role of Christ, all four roles (and other characteristics as well) can be seen in every Gospel.

The four Gospels describe the Person who is the heart of the gospel (1 Cor. 15:1-4; 2 Pet. 1:16). They are not a doctrinal exposition of the gospel, although occasional expository notes are found.

GOURD. A plant which the Lord prepared for Jonah (Jonah 4:6). The castor-oil plant is suggested by some scholars. Others suggest the bottle gourd, a rapid-climbing vine, as in Isaiah 1:8. The "wild gourds" of 2 Kings 4:39 are commonly identified with the colocynth. It resembles the cucumber in appearance but is poisonous. It is useful as a cathartic when carefully administered.

GOVERNMENT. Human government was established by God after the Flood. Man was expected to govern his fellow man for God. The institution of capital punishment showed that man was to govern under divine moral law and to preserve order and safety (Gen. 9:5, 6). A contributing cause of the lawlessness and violence that necessitated the Flood may have been the complete absence of governmental authority. But after the Flood human governmental authority was to be exercised even to the point of capital punishment. This God-given authority was never rescinded in succeeding dispensations and is thus applicable even today. The ultimate breakdown of human authority will be seen in the rampant violence and unbridled lawlessness of the Tribulation Period.

GOVERNOR (Greek *hēgemōn*). A ruler set up by a king to administer a specific territory or province. In the New Testament the word is used for Roman legates, procurators, and proconsuls (who ruled for the Roman Emperor—1 Pet. 2:14). The Roman governor of the province of Syria was a legate. The governor of Judea, on the other hand, was only a procurator (Matt. 27:2). The Roman governor of Egypt was a prefect. Quirinius was a proconsul (Luke 2:2). Felix (Acts 23:24) and Festus (Acts 24:27) were procurators.

GOZAN (gō'zăn). (1) A town and district southeast of Haran in northern Mesopotamia. It was a site to which certain Israelites were deported (2 Kings 17:6; 19:12; 1 Chron. 5:26). The modern site, Tell Halaf, has been extensively excavated and is famous for its pottery. (2) The Habor River, a tributary of the Euphrates now known as the Habur. The town of Gozan mentioned above was situated on the upper Habur River. See "Habor."

GRACE. Grace is the manifestation of God's love and mercy toward sinful men (2 Cor. 8:9; Tit. 2:11). God's essential nature includes both love (1 John 4:16), manifested in mercy and grace, and holiness (1 John 1:5), manifested in righteous judgment of sin. God cannot display his love until sin has been judged. In the miracle of Calvary, Christ simultaneously paid the full penalty for sin and exhibited the ultimate manifestation of grace. Now God is able to freely save lost men (Rom. 3:24). Grace functions totally apart from human merit or works; it rests completely in Christ (Eph. 2:8, 9).

Divine grace provides not only salvation but security. This is accomplished by the continuation of the divine work of grace despite the believer's imperfections. Ephesian 2:8 reads literally "By grace you are saved and continue to be." Grace also leads the believer into the divine will and the good works which the Author of grace has previously planned

that he should accomplish (Eph. 2:10).

Grace versus Law. In Scripture grace as a principle is contrasted with law as a principle (John 1:17; Rom. 6:14, 15). Under law God demands righteousness; under grace he bestows it (Rom. 3:21-24; 8:3, 4; Gal. 2:16; Phil. 3:9). Law connects with Moses and works; grace ties in with Christ and faith (John 1:17; Rom. 10:4-10). Under law obedience brings blessing (Deut. 28:1-14). Under grace blessing is bestowed as a free gift. When obedience does not respond to love, grace teaches and disciplines (Tit. 2:11, 12; 1 Cor. 11:31, 32).

An Arab woman works in a vineyard near Taiyibeh, ancient Ephraim, northeast of Jerusalem. (© *MPS*)

GRAPE. The common grapevine (*Vitis vinifera*), indigenous to western Asia south of the Caspian Sea (cf. Gen. 9:20, 21). It was cultivated in Egypt (Gen. 40: 9-11; Psa. 78:47), as is abundantly attested by Old Empire sculptures and reliefs. The grape flourished in Palestine (Gen. 14:18), especially in the central highlands near Hebron, Shiloh, and Shechem (Num. 13:23; Judg. 9:27; 21:20; Jer. 31: 5), but also in Transjordan (Isa. 16:8-10; Jer. 48:32) and Lebanon (Hos. 14:7). See also "Vine."

GRASS. A term used in the Bible to include all herbage on which cattle could graze. Grass, herbs, and trees are basic divisions of the vegetable kingdom (Gen.

1:11). Man's brief life on earth is compared to grass (Psa. 37:2; 103:15, 16; Matt. 6:30).

GRASSHOPPER. A leaping orthopterous insect with a four-jointed tarsus and long tapering antennae. Some think that the Hebrew *hāgāb* (Lev. 11:22; Num. 13:33; Eccl. 12:5; Isa. 40:22) is a true grasshopper while others regard it as a locust.

GREEKS. A Japhetic or Indo-Germanic people who in the course of history occupied the Greek mainland and archipelago. They are listed as the descendants of Javan in Genesis 10:4. They consisted of various migrating tribes, notably the Ionians of Homer, who lived in the coasts of Lydia and Caria and whose cities became commercial centers several centuries before those on the mainland. "Javan" was the name under which the Hebrews first became acquainted with the Greeks. In Assyrian records the Greeks were first mentioned by Sargon II (721-705 B.C.), who encountered them in a naval battle.

In the New Testament the term "Greek" may refer either to a native of Greece (Acts 16:1; 17:4) or to any well-cultured Gentile (Rom. 1:14-16; 10:12).

The Greeks were eminent in art, science, philosophy, and human culture (cf. 1 Cor. 1:22).

GROVE. A sacred pole in the form of a branchless tree trunk is often found in remains of Canaanite shrines. The cult object is in some way connected with the Canaanite goddess Asherah and represents an intrusion of polluted Canaanite religion into Israelite worship (1 Kings 14:15; 2 Kings 23:6). The Book of Deuteronomy and the Hebrew prophets inveigh against the asherahs.

GUILT. Guilt is liability for sin committed or wrong enacted. Divine grace has triumphed over sin by removing the guilt of all who trust in Jesus Christ's atoning death (Rom. 8:1). Adam's sin and guilt passed upon the whole race (Rom. 5:12-21), but this guilt has been borne by Christ on the cross and is forgiven all who believe (Col. 2:13, 14). The guilt and condemnation of sins committed— past, present, and future—is removed entirely as soon as an individual receives Christ's free gift of salvation (Rom. 3:24). Sin in the life of the believer is judged on a Father-child basis by divine chastening (Heb. 12:5-13).

HABAKKUK (há-băk′ŭk) (perhaps "embrace"). One of the "Minor Prophets" who lived during the rise of the Chaldean Empire (625-615 B.C.). He stressed the truth that "the righteous shall live by his faith" (Hab. 2:4, RSV).

HABOR (hā′bôr). A river of Mesopotamia sometimes known as the River of Gozan. It flows southward through Gozan and

after a course of 190 miles meets the Euphrates. The River Balikh empties into the Euphrates, some 90 miles west of the Habor. The city of Haran, associated with Terah and Abraham (Gen. 11:31), is situated on the Habor River. The territory between these rivers was known as Padan-Aram ("field" or "plain" of Aram—Gen. 25:20; 31:18) and is identical with Aram Naharaim, "Aram of the Rivers."

HACHILAH (hà-kī'là). A hill between Engedi and Ziph in the Wilderness of Judah west of the Dead Sea. There David was hidden when the Ziphites plotted to betray him to Saul (1 Sam. 23:19; 26: 1, 3).

HADADEZER (hà-dăd-ē'zêr) ("Hadad is a help"). The king of the Aramaean state of Zobah in northern Syria. He was defeated by David (2 Sam. 8:3).

HADASSAH (hà-dăs'sà) (Hebrew "myrtle"). The Hebrew name of Esther, the wife of King Ahasuerus (Xerxes I, 486-465 B.C.). She saved her people from destruction. Her story is related in the Book of Esther.

HADES (hā'dēs). The unseen realm of the spirit world. In Old Testament times the soul and spirit of every person went there after death. The righteous, however, were separated from the wicked by a "great gulf" (Luke 16:25, 26). Since the time of Christ's resurrection, paradise or "Abraham's bosom" has apparently been transferred to "the third heaven" (2 Cor. 12:1-4). This is the immediate presence of God (1 Thess. 4:13-18; 2 Cor. 5:1-8).

All the unsaved, however, (both before and after Christ's resurrection) still go to Hades and are in conscious torment (Luke 16:22-24). At the Great White Throne Judgment, which preludes the eternal state (Rev. 20:11-15), the wicked will be raised. Then Hades becomes part of Gehenna or eternal hell. This eternal destiny of Satan, fallen angels, and unsaved humanity (Matt. 25:41) is called "the second death." It will consummate the first death and will involve eternal separation from God and his sin-cleansed universe (Rev. 20:14).

HAGAR (hā'gär) ("flight"). Sarah's Egyptian slave woman, evidently obtained during Abraham's visit to Egypt (Gen. 16:1; cf. 12:10). Despairing of a son of her own (at 76 years of age), Sarah gave Hagar to Abraham as a wife. Ishmael was born as a result. When Sarah finally gave birth to Isaac tension arose between the boys and their mothers. Eventually Sarah cast out both Hagar and Ishmael (Gen. 16:1-16; 21:1-21; Gal. 4:21-31). Muslim Arabs claim descent from Hagar.

HAGGAI (hăg'gà-ī) ("festal"). A post-captivity prophet who predicted the future millennial Temple (Hag. 2:1-19) and the final destruction of Gentile world power (Hag. 2:20-23).

HAGGITH (hăg'gĭth) ("festal"). One of David's eight wives and the mother of Adonijah (2 Sam. 3:4; 1 Kings 1:5). Adonijah's selfish attempts to exalt himself seem to be a reflection of his mother's character (cf. 1 Kings 1:5, 11; 2:13-25).

HALAH (hā'là). A place in Assyria to which Israelites were deported from Samaria in 722 B.C. (2 Kings 17:6; 18: 11). It is possibly the same as Halakku (near Kirkuk) or Halhu (near Gozan).

HALAK (hā'lăk). A mountain in southern Palestine on the way to Mount Seir (Josh. 11:17; 12:7). It is probably modern Jebel Halaq, west of the ascent of Akrabbim and southwest of the Dead Sea.

HAM (hăm) ("hot"). One of Noah's sons (Gen. 5:32; 6:10; 9:18). His display of uncleanness on the occasion of his father's drunkenness (Gen. 9:20-27) furnished prophetic insight into the moral character of his descendants, notably the Canaanites. Their moral debauchery reached its height at the time of the conquest by Israel.

HAMAN (hā'măn). One of King Ahasuerus' favorite court officers (Esth. 3:1). Because Mordecai the Jew refused to bow to him Haman plotted the destruction of all Jews in the kingdom (Esth. 3:2-15). However, Queen Esther (herself a Jew) frustrated his plan and Haman was hanged on the court gallows (4:1 – 7:10).

HAMATHITES (hăm'à-thīts). Citizens of the city-state of Hamath on the Orontes River (cf. Gen. 10:18). Hamath, the capital city, was located on one of the main trade routes to the south. King Toi was its ruler in David's day (2 Sam. 8:9, 10). Solomon controlled it as a vassal state (2 Chron. 8:4). Jeroboam II conquered it in about 778 B.C. (2 Kings 14:28), as did Sargon II in about 721 B.C. (2 Kings 18: 33, 34). Some of its inhabitants were settled in Samaria by the Assyrians (2 Kings 17:24). In classical times the city was known as Epiphaneia. Today it is known as Hamah. Extensive archeological diggings have been made at the site. "The entering in of Hamath" (modern Leb-weh, 14 miles northeast of Baalbeck) was the ideal northern boundary of Israel (Num. 34:8; Josh. 13:5; Amos 6:14).

HAMMOLEKETH (hă-mŏl'ē-kĕth ("the queen"). The mother of Abiezer, from whose line sprang the great hero and judge, Gideon (1 Chron. 7:18).

HAMMURABI (hàm-ōō-rä'bĕ). The sixth Amorite king of the first dynasty of Baby-lon (1790-1750 B.C.). He carved out the first Babylonian Empire, which included nearly all of Mesopotamia. He is famous for his Code of Laws, discovered at Susa in 1902.

HAMUTAL (hă-mū'tàl) (probably "fa-ther-in-law is dew"). The wife of King Josiah (641-609 B.C.) and the mother of Kings Jehoahaz and Jeremiah of Libnah.

HANNAH (hăn'à) ("grace, compassion"). The favorite of Elkanah's two wives. She devoted her son Samuel to the Lord be-fore he was born (1 Sam. 1:1-28). He be-came the last of the Judges and the first of the prophets—one of the truly great and godly men of Israel. Hannah's devo-tion to the Lord found fruition in her eminent son. Her trust has been an in-spiration to godly mothers through the centuries. Her triumphal ode (1 Sam. 2:1-10) glimpses the coming Messiah and the day of the Lord which precedes the establishment of his kingdom (1 Sam. 2:9, 10). Hannah's song was apparently in the mind of Mary when she voiced her gratitude upon learning that she was to give birth to Israel's promised Messiah (Luke 1:46-55).

HANUN (hā'nŭn) ("favored"). An Am-monite king who responded to David's overtures of kindness with gross insult, thus precipitating a disastrous war (2 Sam. 10:1-19).

HARAN, HARRAN (hā'răn) (from Ak-kadian *harranu*, "main road"). A town located about 20 miles southeast of Urfa (Edessa) on the river Balikh in northern Mesopotamia. It was on the main east-west trade routes (Ezek. 27:23). Terah settled there after leaving Ur (Gen. 11:31, 32). It was from Haran that Abraham journeyed to Canaan (Gen. 12:1-5). Like Ur, it was the center of worship for the moon-god, Sin. After the fall of Nineveh in 612 B.C. Haran became the capital of

Assyria until it fell to the Chaldeans in 609 B.C. The Greek form of the name is "Charran" (Acts 7:4).

HARP. See under "Music and Musical Instruments."

The hawk at rest (© *MPS*)

HAWK (Hebrew *nes*). Any of several small-to-medium-sized diurnal birds of prey of the suborder *Falcones*. Twenty species of the sparrow hawk alone exist. They were ceremonially unclean (Lev. 11:16).

HAZAEL (hăz'à-ĕl) ("God has seen"). An Aramaean courtier who murdered his master (Benhadad I or II) and seized the throne (1 Kings 19:15, 17). He became a terrible scourge to sinning Israel and re-sisted Assyrian advance westward.

HAZOR (hā'zŏr). An important Canaanite city (Josh. 11:1, 10-13; Judg. 4:2). It was fortified by Solomon (1 Kings 9:15) but was later taken by the Assyrians (2 Kings 15:29) and still later by the Babylonians (Jer. 49:28-30). The present-day site is Tell el-Qedah, about five miles south-west of Lake Huleh in Galilee.

HEALING. God heals today through both natural and supernatural means in re-sponse to the "prayer of faith" (James 5: 14-16). In order to be a "prayer of faith" a petition must be offered in harmony with God's Word and God's will. Sometimes it is not God's will to heal (cf. 2 Kings 13:14; 2 Cor. 12:7-9). Thus it is not al-ways possible to offer a "prayer of faith" with regard to healing. God has not made a healing covenant with the church, as he did with the nation Israel (Exod. 15:26).

Although "gifts of healings" (1 Cor. 12:9) are to be operative in the church today, God heals only on the basis of his highest glory and the greatest *ultimate* benefit for the believer. He often uses illness to chastise sinning saints (1 Cor. 11:30-32) and to test and refine victorious saints (2 Cor. 12:7-9; 2 Tim. 4:20). Multitudes of believers can testify to miraculous healing by God's power. But we must not ignore doctors and medical help. God does not perform miracles wastefully when he has provided effective natural methods of healing.

HEAVEN. The usual term for the eternal abode of the saved (Matt. 5:12; Col. 1:5; 1 Pet. 1:4). Heaven will apparently be only part of the future sin-cleansed universe. There will also be Gehenna (the Lake of Fire—Rev. 20:14, 15), "a new heaven and a new earth" (2 Pet. 3:13; Rev. 21:1), and a new Jerusalem (Rev. 21:2). See also "New Jerusalem."

HEBREWS. The term "Hebrew" is used in Scripture as a name for Abraham and his posterity (Gen. 14:13). The designation is derived from the name "Eber" (Gen. 10:21-31; 11:14-16). Some scholars think the term means "one from the other side, a crosser or nomad," referring to the Hebrews as men from the "other side" of the Euphrates (cf. Gen. 12:5; Josh. 24:2, 3). Others connect the term with the "Habiru" of antiquity. These were aliens, soldiers of fortune, mercenaries.

The Habiru are prominent in the Tell el Amarna Letters as a people who invaded Palestine. These Letters relate how Abdi-Heba of Jerusalem made frantic appeals to the Egyptian Pharaoh Akhnaton (1375 B.C.) in a situation which seems to correspond to the invasion under Joshua. The Israelites doubtless fitted the category of nomads or soldiers of fortune, but not all Habiru were Israelites. Israelites are clearly called Hebrews in Scripture (Gen. 40:15; 1 Sam. 4:6; 13:3; 2 Cor. 11:22). In the New Testament a Hebrew was a Jew who spoke the Hebrew or Aramaic language (in distinction to Jews who spoke Greek and were called Grecians—Acts 6:1). A "Hebrew of the Hebrews" (Phil. 3:5) was a thorough-going Hebrew in language, parentage, and religious custom.

Hebron shelters tombs of the patriarchs in Machpelah's Cave, covered by a mosque. (© *MPS*)

HEBRON (hĕb'rŭn). The highest town in Palestine, 3,040 feet above sea level. It lies 19 miles south-southwest of Jerusalem. Its older name was Kiriath-arba ("tetrapolis"). It was founded about 1720 B.C. in the era of Tanis (cf. Num. 13:22). The patriarchs had important associations with Hebron (Gen. 23). The *Haram el-Halil* (the "Enclosure of the Friend," i.e. Abraham) is the traditional site of the graves of Abraham, Sarah, Isaac, Rebekah, Jacob, and Leah (Gen. 49:29-32; 50:13). Hebron was visited by the Israelite spies (Num. 13:22) and was captured by Joshua (Josh. 10:36, 37). It was a city of refuge (Josh. 20:7) and David's first capital (2 Sam. 2:1-4, 11).

HEIFER, RED. The ordinance of the red heifer was instituted during the wilderness wanderings of the nation of Israel because of their wholesale contact with human death (cf. 1 Cor. 10:5-10). The use of the ashes of an animal for purification beautifully illustrates Christ's atonement as the basis for the believer's cleansing from defilement in his pilgrim walk (1 John 1:7–2:2; cf. John 13:3-10). The ashes were a memorial of an already accepted sacrifice. Death suggests the polluting effects of sin, which defile the believer's conscience and render him unworthy to "serve the living God" (Heb. 9:14).

HELAH (hē'là) ("ornament, necklace"). One of the two wives of Ashur, the ancestor of the inhabitants of Tekoa in Judah (1 Chron. 4:5, 7).

HELIOPOLIS (hē-lĭ-ŏp'ō-lĭs). (1) The famous Syrian cult city of Baalbeck. It lies on the lower slope of Antilebanus about 40 miles from Damascus. It is best known for its ruins of cultic temples. (2) The Greek name (meaning "City of the

Sun") for the temple city of "On" in Lower Egypt. The Hebrew name is Beth-shemesh (Jer. 43:13). See "On."

HELL. See "Gehenna" and "Hades."

HELMET. In early Israel helmets were apparently worn only by kings or prominent military leaders. King Saul gave David his own helmet of bronze (1 Sam. 17:38). Hittite helmets were similar to skull caps, as depicted on wall reliefs at Karnak, Egypt. In Uzziah's prosperous reign Hebrew soldiers were supplied with helmets which were probably made of leather (2 Chron. 26:14). When bronze became common, the ordinary soldier wore a bronze helmet (1 Macc. 6:35).

Roman armor in New Testament times consisted of helmet, cuirass, and greaves. The earliest Roman helmet was a leather cap (*galea*). Later the metal helmet (*cassis*) became prominent. It consisted of several parts: the cap itself, the elaborately decorated crest, two cheek pieces, and a hinged visor. Both metal and leather helmets were common in New Testament times. The helmet as a figure for salvation is part of the Christian warrior's equipment in Christ (Eph. 6:17).

HEMLOCK. Any of a group of poisonous weeds of the carrot family. It has small white flowers and finely divided leaves. True hemlock is apparently not mentioned in Scripture. See instead "Gall" and "Wormwood."

HENNA. A shrub that grows wild in Palestine. It has spiny branches with clusters of white, fragrant flowers. It originated in North India. Its leaves were pulverized into a paste and used as a cosmetic from earliest times. It was also used as a hair and fingernail dye. It is translated "camphire" in Song of Solomon 1:14 and 4:13.

HEPHZIBAH (hĕf'zĭ-bȧ) ("my delight is in her"). The wife of King Hezekiah (716-687 B.C.) and the mother of Manasseh (2 Kings 21:1). She knew the love and fellowship of a godly husband as well as the extreme waywardness and apostasy of an ungodly son (whose evil reign extended from about 686 to 642 B.C. and brought Judah to the brink of disaster).

HERDSMAN. In Bible times human wealth and the sacrificial worship of God revolved in large degree around cattle.

This was true under both nomadic and settled agricultural conditions. Tending sheep and goats was therefore a very common occupation. See also "Shepherd."

HERMES (hûr'mēz). The divine messenger of the gods in Greek mythology (Acts 14:12). He corresponded to Mercury in Roman mythology.

HERMON (hûr'mŭn). A 9100-foot-high mountain in the Antilebanon range. It is the highest mountain in the neighborhood of Palestine and is perpetually snowclad. Its melting ice provides a major source of water for the Jordan River. The summit has three peaks, with the southeast one being the highest. Mount Hermon was also called Mount Sion (Deut. 4:48), Sirion, and Senir or Shenir (Deut. 3:9). Its proximity to Caesarea Philippi has led some to suggest that Hermon was the "high mountain" of Christ's transfiguration (Mark 9:2).

HEROD THE GREAT (hĕr'ŭd). The king of Judea from 40 to 4 B.C. He was the son of Antipater, a Jew of Idumean descent. Through friendship with Antony and Octavian he was appointed "King of the Jews" by the Roman Senate in 40 B.C. By exercising shrewdness and duplicity as well as some native ability he secured his position as a loyal client king under Rome. He was detested by the Jews for his Idumean origin, his loyalty to Rome, and his devotion to pagan Greek culture. He was a lavish builder, the Temple in Jerusalem being but one of his many enterprises. It was during Herod's administration that Christ was born (Matt. 2:1).

HERODIAS (hĕ-rō'dĭ-ȧs). The daughter of Herod the Great's son Aristobulus. Her first marriage was to her uncle Herod Philip (a son of Herod the Great), by whom she had a daughter, Salome. She then married Herod the tetrarch while her first husband was still living. Herod in turn divorced his wife, a daughter of the Nabataean king Aretas, in order to indulge his guilty passion for Herodias. After John the Baptist reproved the guilty pair (Mark 6:18) Herodias began to plot the death of John and had him imprisoned. Then, after her daughter Salome had delighted Herod at a state banquet, Herodias extorted from Herod the head of John the Baptist. The king feared and respected John, but because of his foolish oath he sent a soldier to behead the Baptist and bring his head on a platter (Matt. 14:3-12; Mark 6:17-29). When the tetrarch was subsequently banished, Herodias went with him into exile.

HERODIUM (hĕ-rō'dĭ-ŭm). The fortress and burial site of Herod the Great. It is present-day Jebel Fureidis, located about three miles southeast of Bethlehem.

HERON. Any of a family (*Ardeidae*) of wading birds with a long thin neck and long legs. Its food is fish and other aquatic animals found in the lake regions of Palestine, on the Kishon River, and on the Palestinian seacoast.

HESHBON (hĕsh'bŏn). Originally a city of Moab but later taken by the Amorites and made a royal city of Sihon (Num. 21:26). Israel captured it and allotted it to Reuben (Num. 21:21-25; 32:1-37). Later it passed over to Gad (Josh. 31:39). Eventually Moab retook the city (Isa. 15:4; Jer. 48:2). The present site is Hisban, about fourteen miles east-northeast of the mouth of the Jordan River as it enters the Dead Sea.

HETH (hāth). The second son of Canaan and an ancestor of the Hittites (Gen. 10:15), an ancient imperial people whose civilization has been resurrected by modern archeological research.

HEZEKIAH (hĕz-ė-kī'ä) ("the Lord has strengthened"). A godly king of Judah from about 716 to 687 B.C. Because of his hatred of idolatry and faith in the Lord he was able to keep Jerusalem and Judah from collapsing under Assyrian advance in 701 B.C., as the Northern Kingdom had done in 722 B.C. (2 Kings 18−20; Isa. 36−39).

HIDDEKEL (hĭd'ė-kĕl). The ancient name of the Tigris River (Gen. 2:14; Dan. 10:4). The name derives from the Akkadian word *Idiglat*.

HIEL (hī'ĕl) (probably "God lives"). A native of Bethel who rebuilt Jericho and suffered the curse predicted by Joshua (Josh. 6:26; 1 Kings 16:34).

HIERAPOLIS (hĕ-ėr-ăp'ȯ-lĭs). A city of the Lycus Valley in the Roman province of Asia Minor. Hierapolis, Colosse, and Laodicea were the subjects of Epaphras' ministry (Col. 4:12, 13).

HIGH PLACES. Elevated sanctuaries of idolatrous cult worship. They were erected either on natural hills or on elevated structures. Mosaic law forbade these sanctuaries as an offense to the God of Israel (Deut. 12:2-4).

HIGH PRIEST. Aaron prefigures Christ as the Great High Priest who now represents us before God (Exod. 29:1-9; Heb. 3:1; 7:23-28; 9:11-24). Like Aaron, Christ bears our names on his shoulders and on his breast (Exod. 28:1-29).

In New Testament times the high priest was the president of the Sanhedrin. He presided at Jesus' trial (Matt. 26:57-65; Mark 14:53-63; John 18:19-24). The plural is used in the New Testament and by Josephus to denote 1) members of the Sanhedrin who belonged to high priestly families, 2) ruling or deposed high priests, and 3) adult male members of the most prominent priestly families (cf. Matt. 16:21; 26:47; 27:12, 41; Mark 14:1; Luke 23:13; John 7:32; 19:15; Acts 9:14; 22:30; 26:10).

HILKIAH (hĭl-kī'ä) ("the Lord is the portion"). A high priest during King Josiah's reign. He discovered the Book of the Law in the Temple and conveyed it to King Josiah through Shaphan the scribe. After hearing the words of the book Josiah instituted the greatest religious revival of any king of Judah (2 Kings 22:8−23:25).

HILLEL (hĭl'lĕl). A famous Jewish spiritual leader who lived from about 30 B.C. TO A.D. 10. He was a leader of the Pharisees, a member of the Sanhedrin, and a leader of a specific school of thought.

HIPPOPOTAMUS. See "Behemoth."

HIRAM (hī'răm) (probably abbreviated from *Ahiram*, "the brother is exalted"). (1) A king of Tyre and an ally and friend of David and Solomon. He helped supply materials and workmen for the construction of the Temple (1 Kings 5). (2) An architect and skilled craftsman sent by King Hiram to Solomon (1 Kings 7:13-46). He was also called "Huram."

HISTORY. See under "Archeology."

HITTITES (hĭt'īts). An Indo-European people who settled in Asia Minor about the beginning of the second millennium B.C. Their name derived from "Hatti," the earlier inhabitants of the area, whom they absorbed. The Hittites founded an empire (about 1800 B.C.) whose capital was at Boghaz-keui (ancient Hattushash) at the great bend of the Halys River. There are two chief periods of Hittite power: the earlier Old Kingdom (1800-1600 B.C.) and the New Kingdom (about 1400-1200 B.C.). The Hittites were practically unknown before the advent of modern archeology, which rediscovered this long-lost imperial people.

In the Old Testament the Hittites appear as a great nation which gave its name to the whole region of Syria (Josh. 1:4) and as an ethnic group which inhabited Canaan from patriarchal times until after the Israelite settlement (Gen. 15:20; Deut. 7:1; Judg. 3:5). They were known as "the children of Heth" because of their progenitor, Heth (Gen. 10:15).

After the collapse of the new Hittite kingdom, 24 city-states of the Tabali (the "Tubal" of Genesis 10:2) became heirs to the Hittite home territory in Asia Minor. In Syria, seven city-states which had once belonged to the Hittite Empire preserved the name "Hittite" for several centuries. Their rulers were called "kings of the Hittites" (cf. 1 Kings 10:28, 29; 2 Kings 7:6). Hamath on the Orontes and Carchemish on the Euphrates were among the most important of the Syrian Hittite states until they were conquered by Assyria in the late eighth century B.C.

HIVITES (hī'vīts). An ancient people listed as one of the sons of Canaan (Gen. 10:17) and as a separate group inhabiting Syria-Palestine. They are distinguished from the Canaanites, Jebusites, Perizzites, Gergashites, and Amorites (Exod. 3:8; Num. 13:29; Deut. 7:1). They were located principally in the Lebanon region and the Hermon range as far as the valley leading to Hamath (Judg. 3:3; Josh. 11:3; cf. 2 Sam. 24:7). They were conscripted for Solomon's building operations (1 Kings 9:20, 21). Hivites also settled in Shechem (Gen. 34:2) and near Gibeon (Josh. 9:7; 11:19).

HOGLAH (hŏg'là) (perhaps from Arabic *hajal*, "partridge"). One of the five daughters of Zelophehad (Num. 26:33). Because Zelophehad had no sons a law was enacted which gave the right of inheritance to a man's daughters in such cases (Num. 27:1-11). The daughters, however, were required to marry within their native tribe (Num. 36:1-12; cf. Josh. 17:1-6).

HOLINESS. The holiness of believers exists in three aspects. (1) *Positional.* God sees all believers as "in Christ" and thus regards them as possessing the holiness of Christ himself (Eph. 1:3-14; Rom. 4:22-25; Phil. 3:8, 9). (2) *Experiential.* Believers can translate their positional holiness into practical, everyday holy living as they rely on the power of Christ (Rom. 6:11-18). Faith translates positional holiness into experiential holiness. (3) *Ultimate.* Believers will experience complete perfection only after the rapture and first resurrection (1 Cor. 15:42-49; 1 John 3:2).

HOLY SPIRIT. The third Person of the triune God. He indwells and seals every believer (John 14:16, 17; Rom. 8:9-16; 1 Cor. 3:16; Eph. 1:13, 14) and glorifies Christ (16:13, 14).

HOMER. See under "Weights and Measures."

HOPE. Hope is faith that looks forward to the future fulfillment of God's promises contained in his Word. Israel's hope is centered in Messiah's advent and kingdom (Luke 1:67-75; 2:38; Acts 26:6, 7; 28:20; Eph. 2:12). The Christian's hope is centered in Christ's return for his own (Tit. 2:12, 13; 1 John 3:2, 3).

HOPHNI (hŏf'nī) (perhaps "hollow of hand"). The brother of Phinehas. Both brothers were slain when the ark was taken by the Philistines (1 Sam. 2:22 – 4:11). The tragedy was a judgment from God for their greed and immorality.

HOR (hōr). A mountain in the Wilderness of Kadesh northeast of Kadesh-barnea. It was here that Aaron died (Num. 20:22-29). Some scholars identify the site as present-day Jebel Madeira, northeast of Kadesh on the northwest border of Edom (since the detour around Edom began at Mount Hor – Num. 21:4).

HOREB (hōr'ĕb). Probably Mount Sinai, "the mount of God" (Jebel Musa). It is in the Sinai Peninsula, west of the Gulf of Aqaba and about 55 miles from the tip of the Peninsula (where the Gulf of Suez and the Gulf of Aqaba meet the Red Sea). There Moses received the Decalogue from God (Exod. 19:1–31:18). Elijah fled there from the wrath of Jezebel (1 Kings 19:1-8).

HORMAH (hôr'má). An important town southeast of Beersheba (Josh. 15:30; 1 Sam. 30:30). Its king was defeated by Joshua (Josh. 12:14; cf. Num. 21:1-3). It is identified with present-day Tell el-Mishash.

HORN. A symbol of power and authority. Compare "the horn of David" (Psa. 132: 17; 92:10) and "the horn of the house of Israel" (Ezek. 29:21). "The little horn" — the man of sin, the Antichrist—will appear at a future time (Dan. 7:8).

HORNET. Any of several types of large, stinging wasps. Hornets were well known in Bible lands. God helped Israel by driving out the Canaanites with hornets (Exod. 23:28; Deut. 7:20; Josh. 24: 12).

HORSE. The most important beast of burden, though not the first one to be domesticated. (The earlier domesticated ass came from the wild species in desert regions.) The horse was native to the grasslands of Europe and Asia. The first mention of a horse is found on a Babylonian tablet from the time of Hammurabi (about 1750 B.C.). Horses were employed in Egypt at the time of the Exodus (about 1440 B.C.), and the nations inhabiting Canaan used horses in battle (Josh. 11:1-4). David fought against these peoples (2 Sam. 10:18) but apparently observed the prohibition against multiplying horses (Deut. 17:16). Solomon disregarded the divine command and kept large numbers of horses at Hazor, Megiddo, and Gezer. They were specially imported from Egypt (1 Kings 10:28, 29). Horses drew war chariots (Josh. 11:4-9) and are mentioned prominently in the Book of Revelation (Rev. 6:2-8; 9:16, 17; 19:14-21).

HORSELEECH. A blood-sucking creature that clings to the body (Prov. 30:15). The leech is well known in Palestine and is used for medical treatment. The horseleech is a large variety (*Haemopsis sanguisuga*). The writer of Proverbs apparently refers to its insatiable thirst for blood (Prov. 30:15).

HOSEA (hó-zē'à) ("salvation"). A prophet of Israel in the latter part of the materially prosperous but morally declining era

of Jeroboam II (782-753 B.C.). His ministry was on the Lord's love for his sinning people.

HULDAH (possibly "weasel"). A prophetess during the reign of Josiah (640-609 B.C.). She was the wife of Shallum and the "keeper of the wardrobe" (2 Kings 22:14; 2 Chron. 34:22). The "wardrobe" doubtless included the priestly vestments and royal robes. She resided in the second or western quarter of Jerusalem. She was consulted on behalf of the king by Hilkiah, the chief priest, and others concerning the discovery of the Book of the Law in the Temple (2 Kings 22:14; 2 Chron. 34:22).

Huldah accepted the newly found Scriptures (doubtless lost during the idolatrous orgy of Manasseh's reign) as the Word of the Lord. With its authority she predicted approaching judgment upon Judah.

HULEH, LAKE (hoo'lē). The body of water which forms the headwaters of the Jordan River. It lies about 12 miles south of the ancient cult center of Dan.

HUMAN SACRIFICE. To propitiate the gods, especially in times of danger, the pagans of antiquity often sacrificed their children, especially the firstborn. This cruel custom was denounced and prohibited in the Mosaic Law (Lev. 18:21; 20:2). The obscene deities Molech and Baal were thought to be honored by this horrible practice (Jer. 19:5).

HUNTER. Hunting was not a common occupation or recreation in Palestine. It was usually practiced only to provide food or to defend against attacking wild animals (Exod. 23:29; Judg. 14:5, 6; 1 Sam. 17:34, 35). However, men like Ishmael (Gen. 21:20) and Esau (Gen. 25:27) were noted for their hunting prowess. By contrast, the Mesopotamians from the days of Nimrod (the mighty hunter of antiquity—Gen. 10:8) had a long record of hunting activity. Lions and other ferocious beasts were hunted avidly, as depicted on monuments and bas-reliefs.

Egyptians liked to hunt game and predatory birds, using dogs and cats to aid them. The mention of such delicacies as the partridge (1 Sam. 26:20), the gazelle, the hart (Deut. 12:15), and the roebuck (1 Kings 4:23) indicates hunting activity among these people. The hunter used bow and arrow (Gen. 27:3), nets (Isa. 51:20) and snares (Psa. 91:3). For dangerous animals such as bears he used pits (Ezek. 19:1-8). Hunting techniques were sufficiently familiar to biblical writers to be used in figurative speech (Job 18:10; Jer. 5:26; Rom. 11:9; Matt. 22:15).

HUR (hûr) ("splendor"). The man who held up Moses' arms during the battle with the Amalekites (Exod. 17:10-12). He assisted Aaron while Moses was absent on Mount Sinai (Exod. 24:14).

HURRIANS, HORITES (hŏŏr'ē-ɔns; hō'rīts). A Caucasian people who spread southward and westward from Lake Van into Mesopotamia at about the beginning of the second millennium B.C. They gradually infiltrated into Palestine Syria and occupied Edom in Abraham's time (Gen. 14:6) but were in turn driven out of Edom by the descendants of Esau (Deut. 2:12, 22). They also occupied places in central Palestine, including Shechem, according to the Septuagint.

Before archeology resurrected the Hurrians, the Horites were thought to be cave dwellers (derived from Hebrew *hor,* a hole or cave). But the Horites are now known to have been the same people as the Hurrians. They are well known from numerous tablets uncovered from A.D. 1925 to 1941 at Nazu, southeast of Nineveh and near modern Kirkuk. As part of the kingdom of Mitanni, they rose to dominant leadership in Syria at Alalah, Ras Shamra, Asia Minor (Boghaz-keui), and East Assyria (Nazu) from about 1550 to 1150 B.C., at which time they were subdued by Assyria.

HYKSOS (hĭk'sŏs). An ethnically composite group of people which dominated Upper Egypt and most of Syria Palestine from about 1792 to 1550 B.C., the interval between the strong twelfth and eighteenth dynasties. The Hyksos were "rulers of foreign countries" who took control of Egypt. Their capital was the Delta city of Avaris, though there is no evidence that the foreign invaders controlled Upper Egypt at Thebes and beyond.

The foreigners introduced the horse and chariot into Egypt and extended the use of bronze for weapons. Their domination of the Delta is concurrent with Israel's sojourn in Egypt. Their expulsion by Ahmose (1570-1545 B.C.), the first ruler of the eighteenth dynasty, is doubtless connected in some way with Israel's enslavement under and subsequent deliverance from Amenhotep II, one of the other pharaohs of the dynasty.

HYSSOP. A common plant of Egypt. The Israelites used it before the Passover to apply blood from a slain lamb to the lintels and doorposts of their houses (Exod. 12:1-13, 21-28). The ritual symbolized faith in the shed blood of Christ, the true Lamb of God (John 1:29, 36; 1 Pet. 1:18, 19; Rev. 5).

I

IBZAN (ĭb'zăn) ("swift"). One of the minor judges who succeeded Jephthah (Judg. 12:8-10).

ICHABOD (ĭk'ȧ-bŏd) ("the glory is not"). The posthumous son of Phinehas and the grandson of Eli. His name perpetuates the spiritual significance underlying the capture of the ark by the Philistines and the death of Eli and his sons (1 Sam. 4:19-22).

ICONIUM (ī-cō'nĭ-ŭm). A town on the borders of Phrygia and Lycaonia. It became part of the Roman province of Galatia in 25 B.C. It was visited by Paul and Barnabas on their first missionary tour (Acts 14:1-7; 16:2). Paul refers to it in 2 Timothy 3:11.

IDUMEANS (ĭd'ū-mē'ăns). The post-exilic name of those Edomites who were forced out of their ancient homeland southeast of the Dead Sea by the growing pressure of the Nabataeans (an Arab tribe who conquered Edom proper). The new region south of Judea became known as "Idumea" and its Edomite refugees as "Idumeans." Idumean power grew and eventually extended as far north as Beth-zur, only 15 miles south of Jerusalem. Throughout the Seleucid, Hasmonean, and Herodian periods Idumea changed hands frequently. In 164 B.C. Judas Maccabeus fortified Beth-zur to oppose an independent Idumea (1 Macc. 4:61) and ravaged its territory (1 Macc. 5:3, 65). Idumea was annexed to the Hasmonean state by John Hyrcanus in 125 B.C. Pompey separated it from Judea in 63 B.C.

In the Herodian line Idumea supplied the native ruling dynasty in Palestine for nearly a century and a half. Herod the Great, an Idumean, reannexed Idumea to Judea, but after his death it again exchanged hands. Not until after the First Revolt did the territory come under the rule of the procurator of Judea as a permanent part of the province of Syria. See also "Edomites."

ILLYRICUM (ĭ-lĭr'ĭ-kŭm). A Roman province (Rom. 15:19) also called Dalmatia. The latter designation eventually became the official one.

IMAGE. As representations of pagan gods, images were strictly prohibited to Israelites under the Mosaic Law (Exod. 20:1-6). Because of their connection with demonized pagan religion, these objects were an affront to the Lord. God's people were to love him supremely and remain completely separated from idolatry.

IMMANUEL (ĭ-măn'ū-ĕl). The prophetic name of the virgin-born Messiah (Isa. 7:14). The name portrayed both his humanity and his deity: "Immanu" means "with us" and "El" means "God."

IMMORTALITY. The perpetual life of the believer's resurrection body. Believers will receive an immortal body at the rapture (the coming of Christ to the air—1 Thess. 4:13-18; 1 Cor. 15:51-54). Christ's resurrected and glorified body in heaven is immortal. Believers will receive a body like his. He alone now has "immortality dwelling in the light" (1 Tim. 6:16). He brought "life and immortality to light through the gospel" (2 Tim. 1:10).

IMPUTATION. The word means "to reckon over to one's account." Scripture sets forth three major aspects of imputation. First, *Adam's sin is imputed to all mankind* (Rom. 5:12-21). In a sense all men sinned with Adam, the federal head of the race. In so doing mankind incurred the penalty of death (Rom. 5:12-21). This is a case of literal imputation, that is, reckoning to each person something that was his prior to his birth.

Second, *mankind's sin is imputed to Christ.* Christ "bore our sins" (1 Pet. 2:24), was "made . . . to be sin" (2 Cor. 5:21), and had "laid on him" our iniquity (Isa. 53:5, 6). This is *judicial* imputation: although Christ never sinned in any way, our guilt was transferred to him.

Third, *God's righteousness is imputed to the believer.* This is the righteousness of God reckoned to the believer by virtue of faith in Christ (Rom. 4:5-8). This aspect of imputation constitutes the believer's acceptance and standing before God. It is constituted legal before God since Christ offered himself without spot to God (Heb. 9:14). It is applied directly on the basis of the fact that the believer is "in Christ" (1 Cor. 1:30; 2 Cor. 5:21; Heb. 10:14).

INCARNATION. The process whereby Christ the Word, who was with God and was God (John 1:1), became man (John 1:14). The second Person of the triune Godhead became a theanthropic Person, lived a sinless life in a real human body on earth, and died a vicarious death to provide salvation for fallen men. As a result, every person who trusts Christ is guaranteed a sinless, deathless, glorified body like Christ's present glorified body.

INCENSE. Fragrant substances, such as

gums, spices, and resins, which release a fragrant smoke when burned. The burning of incense was a common practice in worship. Sweet incense was prominent in Israelite ritual (Exod. 25:6; 35:8; 37:29). It was offered on an "altar of incense" (Exod. 30:1-10; Luke 1:8-10). The divinely approved incense was compacted of opobalsamum, onycha, galbanum, and pure frankincense (Exod. 30:34-38). See also "Galbanum" and "Frankincense."

INNOCENCE. Man was created innocent of sin. He was placed in a perfect environment with only a single test, and was warned of the consequences of disobedience (Gen. 2:16, 17). Tempted by Satan, man chose to disobey God, thereby falling from his position of innocence. The woman was deceived, while the man transgressed deliberately (1 Tim. 2:14). The economy of innocence ended when God judged man by expelling him from Eden (Gen. 3:22-24). Being a sinner, man now needed redemption (Rom. 5:12-21).

INSECTS. Insects belong to a large group of invertebrate animals characterized in the adult state by division of the body into head, thorax, and abdomen and possessing three pairs of legs and membranous wings. Bees, beetles, flies, wasps, etc. are insects. The term is sometimes also popularly applied to other small animals (usually wingless), including spiders, snails, scorpions, etc. The mild and dry climate of Palestine encourages the growth of multitudes of insects and other small creatures. These normally help to maintain a proper balance in natural wildlife. In Old Testament times God sometimes used insects to upset this balance and thereby discipline his wayward people.

INSPIRATION. Holy Scripture is "God-breathed" in its very words as well as in its thoughts (Matt. 5:17-19; 2 Tim. 3:16, 17). The term "inspired" means "in-breathed," that is, by God. This applies to "all Scriptures" — that of the Old Testament as well as the New. The sound position has always been that of verbal and plenary inspiration, which teaches that in the original manuscripts every word of every portion of Scripture is fully inspired and bears full divine authority. Abandonment of this doctrine leads to a host of errors and false doctrines. This truth is the mother and guardian of all other theological truths. It is true that God used men to write his Word, but these human writers were borne along by the Holy Spirit and were infallibly guided to record everything God intended (2 Pet. 1:21).

INTERCESSION. A form of prayer in which the petitioner stands between God and some great need (Rom. 8:26, 27). Prayer in all its forms is to be offered to the Father (Matt. 6:9) in the name of the Son (John 16:23, 24), and in dependence on the Holy Spirit (Eph. 6:18; Jude 1:20).

ISAAC (ī′zăk) ("he laughs"). The child of faith and promise born to Abraham and Sarah in their advanced years (Gen. 21:1-3). He was in the line of the promised Redeemer and is a beautiful picture of Christ as the Son "obedient to death" (Gen. 22:1-10) and as the Bridegroom of a called-out bride (Gen. 24:1-67).

ISAIAH (ī-sā′á) ("the Lord saves"). A great Old Testament prophet, writer, statesman, teacher, reformer, and theologian. His ministry extended from about 740 to 687 B.C. His prophecies, which are literary masterpieces, abound in detailed messianic predictions; of all the prophetic books of the Old Testament, Isaiah is the most messianic.

ISHBOSHETH (îsh-bō′shĕth) ("man of shame"; originally Ishbaal, "man of Baal"). Saul's son, who contested the throne of Israel with David. He was ultimately deserted by Abner and murdered by two of his captains (2 Sam. 2:8 – 4:12).

ISHMAEL (îsh′mā-ĕl) ("God hears"). Abraham's son by Hagar (Gen. 16) and the progenitor of the Ishmaelites, who roamed the deserts like the "wild ass" (Gen. 16:12). Like Ishmael, their ancestor, the Ishmaelites were celebrated for their skill with the bow. Moslem Arabs claim descent from Ishmael.

ISHTAR (îsh′tăr). The Babylonian goddess corresponding to Ashtoreth of the Canaanites (Judg. 2:13; 10:6; 1 Sam. 7:3-4; 12:10; 1 Kings 11:5). See "Ashtoreth."

ISLAND. The islands of the biblical world are located in the Mediterranean Sea, also called "the great sea" (Josh. 1:4), "the uttermost sea" (Deut. 11:24), and "the sea of the Philistines" (Exod. 23:31).

These islands are called "the isles of the Gentiles" (Gen. 10:5) or "the isles of the sea." They consist principally of the land masses of the eastern half of the Mediterranean, notably Caphtor (Crete) and Chittim (Cyprus), but also include insular Tyre and Arvad. In the New Testament a number of islands receive special interest as the result of Paul's missionary travels. The island of Patmos in the Aegean is specified in the Book of the Revelation as the place where John received his apocalyptic visions.

ISRAEL (ĭz'rā-ĕl) ("God strives"). The new name given to Jacob, the supplanter, after his night of wrestling at Penuel (Gen. 32:28). The name also stands for the whole body of Jacob's descendants in their calling and destiny before God (Psa. 73:1; Rom. 11:26). See also "Israelites" below.

ISRAELITES. Those Hebrews who descended from Abraham through Isaac and Jacob (Israel). They became the divinely chosen line through which the Messiah-Redeemer would eventually come. Through their deliverance out of Egyptian bondage they became a symbol of redemption for the whole fallen race. The twelve tribes became a nation at Sinai. The Mosaic Law with its priesthood and sacrificial system was given to them so they could show to all nations both the necessity of redemption and the need to obey the eternal moral law of God.

The Israelite nation conquered Palestine and settled in it under covenant to serve and honor the Lord. Repeated violation of the covenant resulted in divine chastisement during the era of the judges and under the kingdoms of Saul, David, and Solomon. The most serious blow was the division of the kingdom under Rehoboam (931 B.C.) After this date the Northern Kingdom of ten tribes went its separate way until its fall to Assyria in 722 B.C. Judah continued until the fall of Jerusalem in 586 B.C. and the ensuing exile in Babylon.

Elements of the twelve tribes had become integrated with the Judeans or "Jews." The mixed Judeans or "Jews" in turn adopted the broader term of "Israelites." Their prophets foresaw a regathering of representatives from every tribe and the establishment of the converted and blessed nation under Messiah-Savior in the end time. This was viewed as a fulfillment of God's faithful covenants and promises made to the nation (Isa. 11, 12, 55; Ezek. 37). See also "Chosen People" and "Jews."

ISSACHAR (ĭs'à-kär) ("man of wages, a hired worker"). A son of Jacob by Leah and the progenitor of the tribe that bears his name (Gen. 30:17, 18; 35:23).

ITHAMAR (ĭth'à-mär) (possibly "land of palms"). The youngest son of Aaron (Exod. 6:23) and an ordained priest (Exod. 28:1). He was placed over the Gershonites and Merarites (Num. 4:28, 33).

ITALY (ĭt'à-lĭ) The name of the peninsula bordered on the east by the Adriatic Sea and on the south by the Ionian Sea (Acts 27:1, 6; Heb. 13:24).

ITTAI (ĭt'à-ī) ("with me"). A loyal follower of David; he was faithful through thick and thin (2 Sam. 15:18-22; 18:2-5).

ITUREA (ĭt'ū-rē'à). The territory of the Itureans (the "Jetur" of Gen. 25:15; 1 Chron. 1:31). It was located in the valley between Lebanon and Antilebanon. After the death of Herod the Great it became part of the tetrarchy of Philip (Luke 3:1).

J

JABBOK (jăb'ŏk). An eastern tributary of the Jordan River. It separated the Transjordan tribes of Gad and Manasseh. There Jacob wrestled with the celestial visitant (Gen. 32:22-24).

JABAL (jā'băl). A pre-flood patriarch and a progenitor of migrating cattle owners (Gen. 4:20).

JABESH-GILEAD (jā'bĕsh-gĭl'ė-ād). An Israelite town east of the Jordan River. Saul routed the Ammonites who were besieging it (1 Sam. 11:1-11). It is probably to be identified with present-day Tell Abu-Kharaz, nine miles from Bethshan and two miles from the Jordan.

JABEZ (jā'bĕz) ("he makes sorrow"). A man of Judah whose mother named him Jabez because she bore him in sorrow and pain. But after praying for and receiving a special blessing he became more honorable than his brothers (1 Chron. 4:9, 10).

JABIN (jā'bĭn) ("he perceives"). (1) A Canaanite king of Hazor who was defeated by Joshua (Josh. 11:1-14). (2) Another Canaanite king at Hazor who was defeated by Deborah and Barak (Judg. 4:1-24; cf. Psa. 83:9).

JACKAL. A carrion-eating mammal that inhabits wilderness areas (Isa. 34:13, 14; 35:7; 43:20; Jer. 49:33; 51:37). The jackal has been dubbed "the lion's provider" because its cry apprises the lion that food is at hand. See also "Fox."

JACOB (jā'kŭb) (popular etymology, "one who takes by the heel or supplants"). The son of Isaac and Rebekah and the twin brother of Esau (Gen. 25:21-26). He illustrates the conflict of the two natures in a believer. As Jacob he was crafty, deceitful, and selfish. As Israel he displayed faith and obedience as a chosen instrument of God. As such he was also affectionate (Gen. 29:18), industrious (Gen. 31:40, 41), prayerful (Gen. 32:9-12), and divinely disciplined (Gen. 37:31-35; 42:36-38). He became the founder of the Hebrew nation (Gen. 49:1-28) and a link in the messianic line.

JACOB'S WELL. See under "Springs, Wells, and Pools."

JAEL (jā'ĕl) ("wild goat"). The wife of the Kenite Heber. She slew Sisera by driving a tent pin through his head while he slept (Judg. 4:18-21). When the victorious Barak passed by, Jael called him to see her part in the battle (Judg. 4:22). Deborah praised Jael's deed (Judg. 5:1-6, 24-27), thereby revealing the cruelty of the human heart in times of war.

JAIR (jā'ēr) ("he enlightens"). A judge of Israel for 22 years, succeeding Tola (Judg. 10:1-3).

JAIRUS (jā'ĭ-rŭs) ("he enlightens"). A ruler of the synagogue. It was his daughter whom Jesus raised from death (Mark 5:22-42; Luke 8:41-56).

JAMBRES (jăm'brēz). One of the demon-energized magicians of Egypt (Exod. 7, 8). He opposed Moses, the true miracle-worker of God (Exod. 7:1-6). The names Jannes and Jambres do not occur in the Old Testament but are found in extra-biblical literature in other forms, as in the Zadokite Work. See also "Jannes."

JAMES (a form of the name "Jacob"). (1) James the son of Zebedee and the brother of John (Matt. 4:21; 17:1). He was one of the inner circle of Christ's disciples. (2) James the son of Alphaeus. He was also an apostle (Matt. 10:3; Mark 15:40; 16:1). (3) James the half brother of Jesus (Matt. 13:55; Mark 6:3; Gal. 1:19). He was a leader in the early church at Jerusalem (Acts 12:17; 15:13; 21:18; Gal. 2:9, 12) and the writer of the Epistle of James (1: 1).

JANNES (jăn'ēz). One of the two Egyptian magicians who attempted to counterwork Moses. See also "Jambres." Compare 2 Timothy 3:8 with Exodus 7 and 8.

JAPHETH (jā'fĕth) ("let him enlarge"). Noah's second son and the progenitor of the peoples that spread to the northern and western regions of the earth after the Flood—Medians, Greeks, Romans, Gauls, Germans, Russians, etc. (Gen. 9: 18, 19; 10:1-5).

JASON (jā'sŭn) ("healing"). (1) A Hebrew Christian (Rom. 16:21). (2) A believer at Thessalonica who befriended Paul and Silas (Acts 17:5-9).

JAVAN (jā'văn). The fourth son of Japheth (Gen. 10:2) and the progenitor of the Ionian Greeks (Ezek. 27:13; Joel 3:6).

JAVELIN. A type of light spear having a shaft of wood pointed with metal. It could be hurled at a target (1 Sam. 18:10, 11; 19:9, 10). An even lighter and shorter spear was also employed as a javelin (Josh. 8:18; Jer. 6:23; Job 39:23).

JAZER (jā'zêr). A town which was occupied by the tribe of Gad (Num. 32:1-5; Josh. 13:24, 25). It was a Levitical city (Josh. 21:39). It is identified with present-day Khirbet Jazzir, 10 miles east of the Jordan and about 12 miles south of the River Jabbok.

JEARIM (jē'à-rĭm). A mountain near Beth-shemesh whose northern shoulder formed a boundary of the tribe of Judah (Josh. 15:10). It is situated northwest of Jerusalem in the central highland ridge.

JEDIDAH (jē-dī'dà) ("beloved"). The wife of king Amon (642-640 B.C.) and the mother of Josiah. Her evil husband was struck down by palace servants for his wickedness. He was succeeded by his eight-year-old son, who became one of the godly kings of Judah (640-609 B.C.).

Since his father was wicked, it was apparently his mother who influenced the youthful king in the ways of the Lord.

JEHO-ADDAN (jē'hō-ăd'ăn) (perhaps "the Lord is delight"). The wife of King Joash of Judah (835-796 B.C.) and the mother of King Amaziah (796-767 B.C.). Joash did well in his youth under the guidance of the priest Jehoiada. Later on he apostatized from the Lord and was murdered, even as he had murdered Zechariah the son of Jehoiada for pronouncing judgment upon evildoers (2 Chron. 24:15-22; 2 Kings 12:20; 2 Chron. 24:25). Amaziah also began well but ended his reign in idolatry. Like his father, he was murdered (2 Kings 14: 17-20).

JEHOAHAZ (jē-hō'à-hăz) ("the Lord has laid hold of"). (1) A son and successor of Jehu. He reigned over the Northern Kingdom from about 813 to 798 B.C. Syrian aggression reduced his kingdom to its lowest ebb (2 Kings 13:1-9). (2) The son and successor of King Jehoram of Judah (2 Chron. 21:17). He was also called Ahaziah. (2) A son of King Josiah who was deposed by Pharaoh-necho (2 Kings 23:30-34). He was also called Shallum (1 Chron. 3:15).

JEHOASH, JOASH (jē-hō'ăsh, jō'ăsh) ("the Lord has bestowed"). (1) A king of Judah, a son of Ahaziah, and the father of Amaziah (2 Kings 11:21; 12:1-18). He escaped family massacre by being concealed until he was seven years old. His preservation provided continuance of the royal line. (2) The king of Israel from about 798 to 782 B.C. and a son and successor of King Jehoahaz (2 Kings 13:10, 25; 14:8-16). He raised the fortunes of Israel from their lowest ebb under Jehoahaz to greatness for his son, Jeroboam II.

JEHOIACHIN (jē-hoi'à-kĭn) ("the Lord establishes"). The king of Judah during 598 and 597 B.C. and a son of Jehoiakim. He was carried off to Babylon (2 Kings 24:8-16; 2 Chron. 36:9, 10). This event is also described in the Babylonian Chronicle. He was succeeded by his uncle Mattaniah, renamed Zedekiah (2 Kings 24: 17; Jer. 37:1).

JEHOIADA (jē-hoi'à-dà) ("the Lord knows"). The high priest who made Joash king and saved the infant Jehoash from massacre (2 Kings 11:4-17).

JEHOIAKIM (jĕ-hoi'ȧ-kĭm) ("the Lord has established"). A son of Josiah. Pharaoh-necho made him king instead of Jehoahaz. His reign (609-598 B.C.) was evil and he displayed himself as a frivolous and profane egotist (2 Kings 23:34-36; 24:1-4).

JEHORAM (jĕ-hō'răm; abbrev. **JORAM**) ("the Lord is exalted"). (1) The king of Israel during 852 and 851 B.C. He succeeded the brief reign of his brother Ahaziah (2 Kings 1:17). Elisha was active during his reign (2 Kings 1:17 — 9:28). (2) A son of Jehoshaphat and brother-in-law of Jehoram of Israel through marriage with Athaliah, Ahab's daughter (848-841 B.C.). His reign over Judah (2 Kings 8:16-24) stood in sad contrast to that of his godly father. His apostasy was rebuked by Elijah (2 Chron. 21:12-15).

JEHOSHAPHAT (jĕ-hŏsh'ȧ-făt) ("the Lord judges"). A king of Judah (870-848 B.C.) and son of Asa (1 Kings 22:41-50; 2 Chron. 17:1 — 21:1). He was a godly king, one of the best of Judah (1 Kings 22:43). However, he manifested weakness in allying himself with wicked kings (1 Kings 22:1-36).

JEHOSHEBA (jē-hŏsh'ē-bȧ) ("the Lord is an oath"). The daughter of King Jehoram of Judah and the wife of Jehoiada the high priest. When Ahaziah and the royal seed were slain by Athaliah, Jehosheba hid Ahaziah's infant son, Joash, in the Temple until he could safely be declared the rightful king in the Davidic line (2 Kings 11:2; 2 Chron. 22:11).

JEHOVAH (jĕ-hō'vȧ), **YAHWEH.** The personal name of Israel's God. The Hebrews connected the word with *hayah*, "to be." In Exodus 3:14 the name is explained as "I am that I am," indicating either the eternal, self-existent One or "I will be what I will be," that is, "I will be all that is necessary for every occasion." See also "Adonai Jehovah."

JEHU (jē'hū) ("the Lord is he"). The king of Israel from 841 to 814 B.C. With a massive bloodbath he exterminated the house of Ahab and stamped out the worship of Baal (2 Kings 9:1 — 10:28). But his true inner character appears in his toleration of the corrupt worship of the Lord linked with the bull images at Dan and Bethel (2

Kings 10:29-31). Israel did not prosper under Jehu, and Hazael of Syria overran all her territory in Transjordan (2 Kings 10:32, 33). Jehu's submission to Assyria is depicted on the Black Obelisk of Shalmaneser III, but the picture was doubtless rendered for the purpose of pitting Assyria against Hazael.

JEPHTHAH (jĕf'thȧ) ("God opens"). One of the later Hebrew judges (Judg. 11:1 — 12:7), who delivered Israel from Ammonite oppression. He made a rash vow and kept it (Judg. 11:29-40).

JEREMIAH (jĕr'ē-mī'ȧ) ("the Lord lifts up"). The great prophet of the last forty years of the Kingdom of Judah (626-586 B.C.) He is called "the weeping prophet." The sin and apostasy of Judah caused him to grieve inconsolably. His sufferings and persecutions were intense (Jer. 20:1-18; 38:6). His predictions of the fall of Jerusalem to the Chaldeans were fully realized, to the consternation of his foes.

Mound of ancient Jericho in foreground connects by road with modern Jericho to the south. (© *MPS*)

JERICHO (jĕr'ĭ-kō). An important city located in the Valley of the Jordan (Deut. 34:1, 3) on the west side of the river. It is situated about 10 miles from the north end of the Dead Sea and about 17 miles from Jerusalem. It guarded the gateway to Palestine from Transjordan. Jericho fell to Joshua and the Israelites but was placed under a curse (Josh. 6). It is mentioned in both the Old and New Testaments (Luke 10:30; 18:35; 19:1, 2; Matt. 20:29). Old Testament Jericho is identified with present-day Tell es-Sultan, about one mile northwest of er-Riha village. Herodian and New Testament Jericho are identified with the mounds of Tulul Abu el-ᶜAlayiq, one mile west of modern er-Riha. It was Herod's winter capital.

JERICHO, PLAINS OF. The city of Jericho was situated about five miles west of the Jordan River and about 10 miles from the northern tip of the Dead Sea. The low-lying terrain between the city, the river, and the Sea constituted "the plains of Jericho" (Josh. 4:13). These plains were part of the deep valley of the Jordan River (Deut. 34:3). The valley was called the Arabah and designated the Rift Valley, which extends from the Sea of Galilee to the Gulf of Aqabah. Today the Valley of the Jordan downstream to the Dead Sea is called the Ghor, meaning the "depression." The plural of the word "Arabah" describes certain wastelands around Jericho (Josh. 5:10; 2 Kings 25:5).

JEROBOAM I (jĕr-ō-bō'am) ("the people become numerous"). The first king of the Northern Kingdom (931-910 B.C.). He was the man who gave occasion for Israel

782 to 735 B.C. He was the son of Joash. During his reign Israel attained material prosperity and power but declined spiritually (2 Kings 14:23-28). Amos prophesied during this reign (Amos 1:1), calling the wayward people to come back to God and warning of impending judgment. Hosea also ministered during Jeroboam's lifetime (Hosea 1:1).

JERUBBAAL (jĕr'ŭb-bā'ăl) ("let Baal contend"). The name given to Gideon by his father (Judg. 6:32). Jerubbesheth ("Let *shame* contend") is the same name with the word "shame" (*bosheth*) substituted for the pagan deity (2 Sam. 11:21).

JERUSALEM. The sacred city and well-known capital of Judah, of Judea, and of world Jewry. It was called Urusalim in the Amarna Letters and was probably the "Salem" of Genesis 14:18. It was originally a Canaanite (Jebusite) city (Josh. 10:1-5). It was captured from the Jebu-

Airview of Jerusalem, looking southwest over Temple site near Muslim Dome of the Rock and toward distant Mediterranean (© *MPS*)

to sin by setting up the polluted worship of the Lord at Bethel and Dan (1 Kings 12:25 – 13:5; 13:33, 34). Jeroboam attempted to retain his kingdom through idolatry even though Solomon had lost his kingdom by committing this sin.

JEROBOAM II. The king of Israel from

sites by David (2 Sam. 5:6-9) and later became the capital of the United Kingdom (2 Sam. 20:3; 1 Kings 2:36). It was threatened by the Assyrians (2 Kings 18: 35) and plundered by the Babylonians (2 Kings 24:10-16; 25:1-21). It was restored after the exile (Ezra 1:1-4) and harassed by Antiochus Epiphanes (1 Macc. 4:36-60) and later became the Hasmonean capital. It was Herod the Great's capital (Matt. 2:1-3) and the religious center of Judea in Roman times (Luke 2:42-45; John 2:13, 23; Acts 2:5; 8:1; Gal. 1:18; 2:1).

JERUSALEM, NEW. The city is the glorious symbol of the eternal abode and destiny of the redeemed of all ages (Rev. 21:10 — 22:5). Such a city has always been foreseen by God's saints (Heb. 11:10; 13:14; cf. John 14:1-3). The inhabitants of the eternal city will include God the Father, glorified Old Testament saints (Heb. 11:10), New Testament church saints, myriads of unfallen angels, and our blessed Lord himself (Heb. 12:22, 23). Both Israel and the church appear prominently in the city (Rev. 21:12, 14). The great wall of the city symbolizes the security of its inhabitants, who are bathed in God's radiant, unveiled majesty (Rev. 21:23-25; 22:5). The city is distinct from the new heaven and earth of the eternal state, for it comes down from God out of heaven (Rev. 21:10). See also "Zion."

JERUSHAH (je-rū′shȧ) ("possessed"). The wife of Azariah king of Judah and the mother of his successor, Jotham (2 Kings 15:33; 2 Chron. 27:1), who reigned from about 739 to 731 B.C. It is recorded that this mother's son "became mighty, because he prepared his ways before the Lord" (2 Chron. 27:6).

JESSE (jĕs′ė) (perhaps "man"). The father of David and a descendant of Ruth the Moabitess (Ruth 4:18-22).

JESUS CHRIST. In addition to being the central character of the Bible, our Lord Jesus Christ is the greatest of all men everywhere. He fulfills this role because he is the eternal Word, God become man (John 1:1-18; Phil. 2:5-11). He is the Creator of all things; nothing was made apart from him (John 1:3; Col. 1:16, 17; Heb. 1:2). He was "before all things," and "in him all things consist (hold together)" (Col. 1:17). He is the appointed "heir of all things," the "brightness of (God's) glory," and the "express image of his person" (Heb. 1:2, 3).

As the eternal Word, Christ the preincarnate Son became a man by the power of the Holy Spirit in the womb of the virgin Mary (Isa. 7:14; Matt. 1:18-25; Luke 1:35). He thus possessed a human body, soul, and spirit that were united to deity to form a unique, divine-human personality. As the God-man, Christ lived a sinless life, died a vicarious and sin-atoning death, and was raised with a glorified body that forever unites redeemed mankind with God. For when Christ had "by himself purged our sins," he "sat down at the right hand of the majesty on high" (Heb. 1:3).

Thus this greatest of all men is now in heaven as the glorified Son of Man, Jesus Christ "come in the flesh" (1 John 4:2). The Greek perfect participle denotes that he possessed not merely a temporary humanity by virtue of his incarnation, but instead, a genuine, permanent, glorified human body for all eternity. This provides an eternal link between God and redeemed mankind.

Christ is greater than Adam because he is Adam's Creator. He is greater than Abraham because he existed in past eternity and was the object of Abraham's faith (John 8:56-58). He is greater than Solomon because he is "the wisdom of God" (Matt. 12:42; 1 Cor. 1:30) as well as the Creator and Owner of the universe and the "heir of all things" (Col. 1:15-17; Heb. 1:3). He is greater than Jacob in the liberality of his gift. Jacob gave his people a well (John 4:12), but Christ gave his people rivers of living waters (John 4:13, 14; 7:37-39).

Christ's Genealogies. Matthew and Luke present genealogies of Christ. Matthew, addressing Jews, presents Christ as the son of David, tracing his lineage back 2000 years to Abraham (Matt. 1:1-17). Matthew thus introduces the rightful Heir to the Kingdom and proclaims Christ as the King of Israel. Luke, addressing non-Jews, traces Christ's lineage to the first man, Adam, the father of the human race (Luke 3:23-38). Luke thus presents Christ as the Son of Man. Both genealogies link Christ to the Old Testament with its promises and prophecies of redemption.

Our Lord Jesus Christ bears many exalted names and titles. A few of these are herewith described.

Lord is the name that expresses Christ's sovereignty and majesty, both as Sovereign of life and Ruler of the earth (1 Cor. 12:3; Rev. 19:16). By the dual right of creation and redemption he is the absolute King and Ruler of the earth and its people. At his second advent he will fully assume this rightful dignity (Rev. 19:16).

Jesus is the human name of Christ, the Son of God. The name comes from the Greek form of the Hebrew word for "Joshua," meaning "Jehovah is salvation" (cf. Acts 7:45; Heb. 4:8). He was to be called Jesus because he was to "save his people from their sins" (Matt. 1:21). However, his full title is "Lord Jesus Christ." "Lord" relates him to his eternal deity, "Christ" to his threefold office (Prophet, Priest, and King), and "Jesus" to his incarnation and saviorhood as the God-man.

Christ (Greek *Christos*, Hebrew *Mashiah*) means "the anointed one" and is our Savior's official name. The title presents our Lord in the light of the Old Testament foreview of him as Prophet (Deut. 18:15-19), Priest (Psa. 110:4), and King (2 Sam. 7:12, 13; Psa. 2:1-12; Isa. 9:6, 7). Prophets, priests, and kings were anointed with oil (1 Kings 19:16; 1 Sam. 16:13), but Jesus was anointed with the Holy Spirit (Isa. 61:1-3; Matt. 3:16, 17; Mark 1:10, 11; Luke 3:21, 22; John 1:32, 33).

Shiloh, meaning "peace" (Gen. 49:10), presents Christ as our Peacemaker. He *preached* peace (Eph. 2:17), he *makes* peace (Eph. 2:15), and he *is* our peace (Eph. 2:14).

Immanuel (Isa. 7:14) is a name which describes Christ in his incarnation. The name is composed of two parts and means "with *us*" (*Immanu*) is "God" (*El*). Along with this highly significant name, Isaiah presented a sign which involved the miracle of the virgin birth. The sign was divinely given—"the Lord himself" gave it (Isa. 7:14). It was presented to David's house and not simply to Ahaz ("you" is plural in Isaiah 7:14). The sign included the element of the miraculous (Isa. 7:11). It foresaw the perpetuation of the house of David until the ultimate sign of the ages should be realized. It involved a virgin (Matt. 1:22, 23). Although divine, the child would also be human (Isa. 7:15).

Wonderful Counselor (Isa. 9:6) describes Christ in his infinite wisdom (cf. Prov. 8).

The Mighty God (Isa. 9:6) emphasizes Christ's deity. The title connotes "God-Champion," Christ as a champion in battle.

Everlasting Father (Isa. 9:6) is literally "father of eternity" or "the eternal one." The title connotes both Christ's eternal personal existence and his authorship of all eternal life.

Prince of Peace (Isa. 9:6) describes the sovereign Lord who will effect a warless world in the coming kingdom.

The Branch describes the coming Messiah in his Temple-building role (Zech. 6:12-15; Ezek. 40—42; Mic. 4:1, 2). He will be highly glorified (Psa. 8:1; Isa. 52:13; Rev. 19:16). Messiah will be the "second man" who regains that dominion over the earth which had been lost by the "first man," Adam (Psa. 8; Heb. 1:6-10; 1 Cor. 15:45-49). In the coming kingdom, Messiah will combine in one Person the two offices of King-Priest.

The Word of God is the rich title which John applies to Christ in Revelation 19:13. The name means "the full expression of God" and aptly epitomizes the infinite glory of the Person of Christ.

JETHRO (jĕth'rō) ("preeminence, excellence"). A priest of Midian and the father-in-law of Moses (Exod. 3:1; 4:18; 18:1-12). He was also called Reuel, which means "friend of God" (Exod. 2:18).

JEWELRY. See specific item of jewelry.

JEWS. As used in the Bible, the term "Jew" in the pre-exilic era referred to citizens of the southern state of Judah (Neh. 1:2; Jer. 32:12; 40:11). In post-exilic times the name denoted the people of Israel in contrast to the Gentiles (Esth. 9:15-19; Dan. 3:8; Zech. 8:23; John 4:9; Acts 14:1). In the New Testament the term applied to anyone who was Jewish by both nationality and religion. In a few cases Jewish Christians were also called Jews (John 8:31; Acts 21:39; Gal. 2:13). See also "Chosen People" and "Israelites."

JEZEBEL (jĕz'ĕ-bĕl). A pagan queen of

Israel and the wife of Ahab (873-853 B.C.). She was the daughter of Ethbaal, priest-king of Tyre and Sidon. She was an ardent devotee of Baal Melqart, and provision was made for her to continue her pagan cult in her new home in Samaria. Her staff numbered 450 Baal prophets and 400 prophets of the goddess Asherah (1 Kings 16:31-33; 18:19). Her zeal for Canaanite religion brought her into conflict with Elijah, who thoroughly discredited the cult worshipers on Mount Carmel (1 Kings 18:1-40).

Jezebel's idea of an absolute monarchy also collided with the Hebrew covenant relationship between the Lord, the king, and the people. Her ruthless treatment of Naboth was a highhanded violation of Hebrew law and morality and sealed her doom and that of the house of Ahab (1 Kings 21). Her name became proverbial for wickedness and symbolic of idolatrous lawlessness (Rev. 2:20-23).

JEZREEL (jĕz'rĕ-ĕl). A town at the head of the Valley of Jezreel. It was part of Solomon's fifth district (1 Kings 4:12). Ahab had a palace there (1 Kings 21:1-16).

JOAB (jō'ăb) ("the Lord is father"). A nephew of King David and a general in his army (1 Sam. 26:6; 2 Sam. 2:1 – 1 Kings 2:34). He was an overambitious man, whose apparent devotion to David was actually a cover-up for his own preeminence as commander of the army. Although a skilled general (attested by the many victories he won – 2 Sam. 2:12-32; 11:1; 12:26-29; 20:4-22; 1 Chron. 11:6-9), Joab was vindictive and ruthlessly cruel (2 Sam. 3:22-27; 18:14; 20:9, 10; 1 Kings 11:16).

JOANNA (jō-ăn'à) ("the Lord has been gracious"). A woman of position who supported Christ in his public ministry by giving of her material means (Luke 8:3). She was the wife of Chuza, an important official of Herod Antipas (Luke 8:3). She was one of the women who attempted to show final respects to Christ's body and shared in announcing the resurrection to the Twelve (Luke 24:1-11).

JOB (jōb) (meaning uncertain, but possibly "one who came back to God"). The great biblical example of the suffering saint. His experiences probe the question of why the righteous suffer. A prime answer to the question is that the godly suffer in order to be refined and purified to the ultimate glory of God (Job 42:1-6).

JOCHEBED (jŏk'ĕ-bĕd) ("the Lord is glory"). A daughter of Levi and the mother of Moses, Aaron, and Miriam (Exod. 6:20; Num. 26:59). Her name is not recorded in the actual narrative of Moses' birth and miraculous preservation (Exod. 2:1-10).

JOEL (jō'ĕl) ("the Lord is God"). A prophet in the days of King Uzziah (767-739 B.C.). He foresaw the future day of the Lord under the figure of a locust plague and the promised pre-kingdom outpouring of the Spirit (Joel 1, 2). This latter event bears resemblance to the pentecostal effusion upon believing Jews when the church was born (Acts 2:14-21). Joel also envisioned the judgment of the nations which precedes Israel's establishment in full kingdom blessing (Joel 3).

JOHN ("the Lord is gracious"). The "beloved Apostle," a son of Zebedee and brother of James (who was martyred under Herod Agrippa I). John belonged to a family of Galilean fishermen until he and his brother were called to follow Jesus (Matt. 4:21, 22; Mark 1:19, 20). Later they were appointed apostles (Matt. 10:2). Their vehemence won them the nickname "sons of thunder" (Mark 3:17). With his brother James, John belonged to the inner circle at the raising of Jairus' daughter (Mark 5:37; Luke 8:51), at the transfiguration (Matt. 17:1; Mark 9:2), and at the agony in Gethsemane (Matt. 26:37; Mark 14:33). John occupied the place next to Jesus at the Last Supper (John 13:23). He was a prominent witness of the resurrection and the ascension (John 20:1-10; Acts 1:1-13). John wrote the fourth Gospel, the three Johannine Epistles, and the Revelation (cf. Rev. 1:9).

JOHN THE BAPTIST. The rugged, fearless preacher who was the forerunner of the Messiah (Matt. 3:1). He preached the baptism of repentance (Matt. 3:11; Mark 1:8) which was preparatory to Messiah's baptism with the Holy Spirit (John 1:32, 33; Acts 1:5; 2:1-21).

JOKTAN (jŏk'tăn). The progenitor (through Eber of the family of Shem) of 13 Arab tribes (Gen. 10:26; 1 Chron. 1:19-23).

JONADAB, JEHONADAB (jŏn'a-dăb, jḗ-hŏn'a-dăb) ("the Lord is bounteous"). A son of Rechab (Jer. 35:6). He followed a strict ascetic life (Jer. 35:6, 7) and aided Jehu in exterminating Baal worship from Israel (2 Kings 10:15, 23).

JONAH (jō'nà) ("a dove"). The first Hebrew prophet to be sent as a missionary to a pagan nation (Jonah 1:1, 2; 2 Kings 14:25). He attempted to flee from the instructions and presence of God but was chastised in the stomach of a large marine animal (Jonah 1). Thereupon he repented, obeyed the call of God, and preached in Nineveh with astonishing response (Jonah 2, 3). He reluctantly learned about the mercy of God (Jonah 4). Jonah symbolizes Christ in death, resurrection, and witness (Matt. 12:38-41). His experiences also parallel the history of the Jewish nation.

JONATHAN (jŏn'a-thăn) ("the Lord has given"). The eldest son of Saul and a close friend of David. He was humble, loving, loyal, and unselfish. He was unswervingly devoted to David even though he knew that David would occupy the throne of Israel which would normally have been Jonathan's as the firstborn son (1 Sam. 18:1 — 20:42).

JOPPA (jŏp'pà). A town on the Mediterranean coast about 35 miles northwest of Jerusalem. It was the seaport for Jerusalem in Old Testament times (2 Chron. 2:16; Ezra 3:7). It was at Joppa that Jonah attempted to sail from the presence of God (Jonah 1:3). Peter had an extensive ministry in Joppa (Acts 9:36-43; 10:5-23). Joppa is now called Jaffa and still maintains a harbor.

JORAM, JEHORAM (jō'răm, jĕ-hō'răm). (1) The king of Judah from 848 to 841 B.C. He was the son of Jehoshaphat (2 Kings 8:16-19). (2) The king of Israel from 852 to 841 B.C. He was the son of Ahab (2 Kings 3:1-3).

JORDAN RIVER. The largest and most important river of the Holy Land. The name "Jordan" (Hebrew *yardēn*) has the appropriate meaning of "the Descender." Its spring-fed headwaters first collect in Lake Huleh, 230 feet above sea level. At Lake Tiberias, 10 miles south, the river descends to 700 feet below sea level. At the north end of the Dead Sea it plunges

Serpentine Jordan River twists between barren hills toward lowest spot on earth, the Dead Sea. (© *MPS*)

to 1,290 feet below sea level. The Jordan River is a snakelike stream, requiring more than 150 miles of riverbed to cover the 75 straight-line miles from Lake Huleh to the Dead Sea. No river is referred to more frequently in the Bible.

JOSEPH (jō'sĕf) ("may he add"). (1) The eleventh of Jacob's 12 sons (Gen. 30:22-24). He is a remarkable prefiguration of Christ. Both were special objects of a father's love (Gen. 37:3; Matt. 3:17; John 3:35). Both were hated by their brothers (Gen. 37:4; John 15:25). The superior claims of both were rejected by their brothers (Gen. 37:8; Matt. 21:37-39; John 15:24, 25). The brothers of both conspired to kill them (Gen. 37:18; Matt. 26:3, 4). Each became a blessing among the Gentiles and gained a Gentile bride (Gen. 41:1-45; Acts 15:14). Joseph reconciled his brothers to himself and afterward exalted them (Gen. 45:1-15). Christ will do the same with his Jewish brethren at the second advent (Deut. 30:1-10; Hos. 2:14-18; Rom. 11:1, 15, 25, 26).

(2) The husband of Mary and foster-father of our Lord Jesus Christ (Matt. 1:16-25). A humble carpenter (Matt. 13:55), Joseph was present at the manger where Jesus was born. Although the unborn infant which Mary carried was not Joseph's, he believed the angelic message about his wife's chastity (Matt. 1:18-24). He was blessed with the knowledge that the promised Messiah was to be a member of his own modest family and that

Mary was to bear the sinless Son of Man and Son of God.

JOSEPH OF ARIMATHEA (ăr'ĭ-mà-thē'à). The man who gave his tomb to Jesus (Matt. 27:57-60; Mark 15:43-46; Luke 23:50-53; John 19:38-42). By this gift the virgin-born Savior was buried in a virgin tomb.

JOSEPHUS, FLAVIUS (jō-sē'fəs, flā'vē-əs). A famous Jewish historian who lived from about A.D. 30 to 100. He was appointed commander of the army in Galilee at the outbreak of the Jewish revolt. He accompanied Vespasian's son Titus to Rome and received Roman citizenship and honors. His historical works include *The Jewish War* and *The Antiquities of the Jews.*

JOSHUA (jŏsh'ū-à) ("the Lord is salvation"). As a slave in Egypt Joshua knew the lash of the oppressor's whip. As a scout in the wilderness he believed God and prepared to possess the land of Canaan (Num. 13:1 – 14:10). As a servant he was unswervingly loyal to God and Moses. As a savior he led the people into the land and vanquished their foes. As a statesman he allotted the land, set up the Tabernacle, and established the cities of refuge. As a saint he was filled with the Spirit (Deut. 34:9), enjoyed the presence of God (Josh. 1:5; 6:27), and obeyed the will of God (Num. 32:11, 12; Josh. 5:13-15). He is a symbol of Christ as the captain of our salvation, the leader who gives us rest (Heb. 3:7 – 4:11).

JOSIAH (jō-zī'à) ("the Lord heals"). The king of Judah from 641 to 608 B.C. He was a good king, initiating revival and obeying the Word of God (2 Kings 22:1 – 23:30). He repaired the Temple, stamped out heathen worship, observed the Passover, and called the nation back to God. He met death at the hands of Pharaoh-Necho at the age of 39.

JUBILEE (jōo'bĭ-lē). Under the Mosaic Law every seventh year was a sabbatical year for the land. Sowing and pruning were forbidden. After seven sabbatical years or 49 years, the fiftieth year was a "jubilee year," when all slaves were released and all alienated property was returned to its ancestral owners (Lev. 25). This humane law showed that God owned the land, and that it was not to be alienated from the Lord's people permanently. Earth will one day celebrate its eternal jubilee in the new heaven and new earth (Rev. 21:1 – 22:5; cf. Rom. 8: 19-23).

JUDAH (jōo'dà) ("let him be praised"). The fourth son of Jacob and the founder of the kingly tribe of Israel (Gen. 29:35; Num. 26:19-22), from whom Messiah-King came. On account of their sins Reuben, Simeon, and Levi were passed over by Jacob and the blessing of the birthright was bestowed on Judah instead (Gen. 49:1-12).

JUDAISM (jōo'dà-ĭz'm). God's special relation with the Jews. The Apostle Paul refers to it as the religion of the Jews (Acts 26:5; Gal. 1:13; cf. James 1:26, 27). Although some similarities exist, Judaism is to be clearly distinguished from Christianity or what the New Testament writers designate as "the faith" (Jude 1:3) and "this way" (Acts 9:2; 22:4; cf. 18:26). Old Testament Judaism was conditioned by God's covenants with and promises to Israel, and looked forward to Christ. When Israel rejected Christ, God turned to the Gentiles to take out of them a heavenly people for his name (Acts 15:14). These are in contrast to God's earthly people, Israel. The latter will turn to Christ at his glorious second advent.

JUDAS (jōo'dàs, jōo'dà) (1) A half-brother of Jesus, a brother of James, and the writer of the Epistle of Jude (Matt. 13: 55; Mark 6:3; Luke 6:16; Acts 1:13; Jude 1:1). (Jude is the English form of Judas.) See "Jude." (2) A Galilean who fomented an anti-Roman rebellion shortly after the birth of Christ (Acts 5:37). (3) A man with whom Paul lodged at Damascus (Acts 9:11). (4) A prophet (surnamed Barsabas) who was dispatched with Silas to Antioch (Acts 15:22).

JUDAS ISCARIOT. The false disciple who betrayed Christ and then committed suicide. Iscariot means " a man of Kerioth" (a city in Moab). Judas Iscariot was the treasurer of the apostolic band (John 13:29) and pilfered the money entrusted to him (John 12:6). He was so controlled by Satan as to be called "a devil" (John 6: 70, 71). His acts, however, were included in God's foreknown plan, despite Judas' inclusion as one of the twelve apostles.

He was chosen "that the Scriptures might be fulfilled" (Matt. 26:47-56; Zech. 11:12, 13; Psa. 109:5-8; Acts 1:16). He is called " a son of perdition," the designation of the Antichrist, the Man of Sin (2 Thess. 2:3). Some scholars therefore believe that Judas was the Devil incarnate and feel that the Antichrist will be Judas brought back from "his own place" (Acts 1:25).

JUDAS MACCABEUS. The warrior son of Mattathias. He was the valiant leader of the revolt against enforced Greek paganism (166-160 B.C.). He was slain in the battle of Elasa (1 Macc. 9:1-18). "Judas" is the Greek form of "Judah."

JUDGE. The first judges in Jewish history were appointed at Jethro's advice to assist Moses in settling cases of dispute (Exod. 18:13-27). They were God's earthly representatives for justice (Exod. 21:6; 22:8; Psa. 82). The Mosaic Law made provision for the appointment of judges and officers to assist in dispensing justice (Deut. 16:18). Strict justice and absolute fairness were required (Deut. 1:16-18; 16:19, 20; 24:17, 18). In more important cases judges were assisted by priests who functioned as assessors (Deut. 17:8-13). During the period of the Conquest, the judges participated in the national assemblies (Josh. 8:33; 24:1).

During the period of the judges, the judge was more than simply a judicial arbiter representing God. He was first and foremost a "savior" and "deliverer" (Judg. 3:9), divinely raised up and charismatically empowered by God's Spirit to deliver Israel from her enemies (Judg. 6:34). The same word in kindred Semitic dialects was used for the chief magistrates of Carthage and as a synonym for "king" at Ugarit.

Under the monarchy, judges performed both judiciary and executive functions (1 Chr. 26:29). Jehoshaphat displayed zeal for righteousness and appointed judges and officers city by city (2 Chron. 19:4-7). Ezra set judges over the people after the exile (Ezra 7:25). See also "Officer."

In the New Testament, Christ is declared to be the Judge of all mankind (John 5:22, 23, 27, 30). This fact is emphasized in apostolic preaching (Acts 10:42; 17:31; Rom. 2:16). Christ will specif-

ically be the judge of believers' works (Rom. 14:10; 2 Cor. 5:10). The basis of judgment for the unsaved in Gehenna will also be their works (Rev. 20:12, 13). Thus *all men* will be judged for their works—their response to the eternal moral law of God.

JUDGMENT. The once-popular concept of a single general judgment cannot be sustained from a careful inductive study of God's Word. Eight well-defined and separate judgments appear in Scripture. These are briefly described below.

God's Judgment of Sin. When Christ died he bore all the sin and guilt of every believer (1 Cor. 15:3; Heb. 9:26-28; 1 Pet. 2:24; 3:18). When he was lifted up on the Cross, the world was judged and Satan was defeated (John 12:31). The result was the justification and security of every believer (John 5:24; Rom. 5:9; 8:1; 2 Cor. 5:21; Gal. 3:13).

The Believer's Judgment of Self. Believers must confess and forsake the sins they commit if they are to avoid chastisement by their heavenly Father (Heb. 12:7; 1 Cor. 11:31, 32). If confession is neglected, the Father's chastening follows, though never condemnation with the unsaved (1 Cor. 11:32; 5:5).

Christ's Judgment of the Believer's Works. This event is often termed "the judgment seat of Christ" (Rom. 14:10; 2 Cor. 5:10). At issue in this judgment is not the salvation of the believer but the rewards for his Christian service (1 Cor. 3:11-15). The event occurs immediately after the rapture (Christ's coming for his own). See 1 Corinthians 4:1-5 and 2 Timothy 4:8. This judgment is in no sense a condemnatory trial for sins, since even the least devoted believer will be saved "so as by fire" (1 Cor. 3:15).

The Judgment of All Unsaved. This event is often called the "Great White Throne judgment" (Rev. 20:11). It involves every unsaved person that has ever lived, and possibly angels and millennial saints as well. The unsaved are judged on the basis of their works (Rev. 20:12, 13). Everyone whose name is not written in the book of life is cast into the lake of fire (Rev. 20:15).

The Judgment of the Nations. This judgment takes place when Christ returns in glory to establish his kingdom over Israel (Matt. 25:31-33). The basis of judgment is the treatment of Christ's "brothers" (the Jewish remnant of the end time). The result will be admittance to or exclusion from the kingdom as individuals in the nations (Matt. 25:34-46).

The Judgment of Israel. The subjects of this judgment are Israelites regathered from worldwide dispersion at the end of the Tribulation period (Ezek. 20:33-38). At issue is the opportunity to enter the millennial kingdom (Mal. 3:2-5; 4:1-3).

The Judgment of Fallen Angels. Revelation 20:10 indicates that Satan (and presumably his angels) will be condemned with finality immediately following the millennial age. This judgment may include angels who cohabited with humanity prior to the Flood (Gen. 6:1-4; 2 Pet. 2:4; Jude 1:6). Evil angels will be cast into Gehenna, the Lake of Fire (Rev. 20:10).

JUDGMENT IN THE GATE. In Old Testament times, civil law cases were often heard at the gateway to a city. Either the elders of the city or the king himself would dispense justice at this location (Deut. 22:15; Ruth 4:1, 2; 2 Sam. 15:2; Prov. 31:23).

JUDITH (Hebrew feminine form of *Yehu-di,* "a Judean, a Jew"). (1) A wife of Esau and a daughter of Beeri the Hittite (Gen. 26:34). She is probably identical with the "Aholibamah" of Genesis 36:5. Esau's carnality and marriage to a pagan woman reveal his character and help explain why he was willing to forfeit his birthright (Gen. 25:29-34; 26:34, 35). (2) The heroine of the apocryphal book of Judith. By her valor this beautiful and devout Jewish widow of Bethulia (a pseudonym for Shechem) saved her city from Nebuchadnezzar's invading army under Holophernes.

JUNIPER. See "Broom."

JUSTICE. A virtue which God possesses in absolute perfection because of his infinite holiness. The gospel of grace, involving the death of Christ, is the solution to the problem of how God can remain just and nevertheless pardon guilty sinners (Rom. 3:25, 26).

JUSTIFICATION. A judicial act by which God declares a sinner righteous in his sight on the basis of Christ's substitutionary death on the Cross (Rom. 3:25, 26; 4:24, 25). Justification originates in the grace of God (Rom. 3:24; Tit. 3:4-7). It is received by faith alone, exclusive of works (Rom. 4:1-5; Gal. 2:16).

KADESH (kā'dĕsh). (1) A Canaanite city (Josh. 12:22) identified with present-day Tell Qades. It was a city of refuge and a Levitical city (Josh. 20:7). Barak lived there (Judg. 4:6). It was captured by Tiglath-Pileser III (2 Kings 15:29). (2) A city on the Orontes River (2 Sam. 24:6, RSV). It is identified with present-day Tell Nebi Mend.

KADESH-BARNEA. ꜥAin Qedeis or possibly Khirbet el-Qudeirat, a town in the desert of Paran south of Judah. From it the Israelite spies were sent out to explore Canaan (Num. 13:26).

KANAH (kā'nȧ). A river which runs west from the watershed at the heel of the Michmethath Valley, four miles south of Shechem. It constitutes the natural boundary between Ephraim and Manasseh (Josh. 16:8). The river is now known as Wadi Qana.

KASSITES (kăs'īts). An Indo-European people from the region of the Zagros mountains. They invaded and dominated Babylon from about 1500 to 1100 B.C., establishing a dynasty that ruled for half a millennium. The Kassite period is obscure historically, but it is known that the horse, which was a divine symbol of the Kassites, became common in Babylonia only after their entry.

KEILAH (kē-ī'lȧ). Khirbet Qila in the Shephelah of Judah (Josh. 15:44). It is associated with David (1 Sam. 23:1-13). The town was located about eight miles northwest of Hebron.

KENITES (kē'nīts). A Midianite tribe (Judg. 1:16; 4:11) who inhabited the copper-yielding region southeast of the Gulf of Aqabah. Since their name means "smith," they are thought to have been itinerant artisans in metal. Balaam's parable implies that the Kenites were at home in Edom and the Wadi Arabah (Num. 24:20-22). They in all likelihood exploited the rich mineral deposits of this region. Hobab the Midianite (of the family of the Kenites) accompanied the Israelites as a scout on their march from Mount Sinai to Canaan (Num. 10:29-32).

After the conquest of Canaan the Kenites cast their lot with Judah and settled southeast of Hebron (Judg. 1:16). In Abraham's time a branch of the Kenites had settled in Canaan or its vicinity (Gen. 15:18, 19; Num. 24:20-22). It was perhaps this group which maintained friendly relations with Israel in the Saul-David era (1 Sam. 15:6; 27:10; 30:29), perhaps as itinerant smiths (cf. 1 Chron. 2:55). See also "Midianites."

KETURAH (kē-tū'rȧ) ("incense"). Abraham's wife after Sarah's death (Gen. 25: 1). From her came the tribes of Zimram, Jokshan, Medan, Midian, and other Arabian peoples (1 Chron. 1:32). Her progeny were not placed on the same level with Isaac and were not in the line of the coming Redeemer. Abraham therefore endowed them with gifts and sent them eastward while he still lived (Gen. 25:6).

KEYS OF THE KINGDOM OF HEAVEN. A key is a symbol of power and authority (Isa. 22:22; Rev. 3:7). The keys given to Peter (Matt. 16:19) represent the divine authority granted him to open the gospel of grace to Jews at Pentecost (Acts 2:37-40), to racially mongrel Samaritans (Acts 8:14-17), and to pure Gentiles in the house of Cornelius (Acts 10:34-48). There was no other assumption of authority by Peter (Acts 15:7-11).

KHIRBET KERAZEH. See "Chorazin."

KIDRON, KEDRON (kĭd'rŏn, kē'drŏn). A seasonal stream which starts north of Jerusalem, flows past the Temple Mount and the Mount of Olives, and empties into the Dead Sea by way of the Wilderness of Judea. David passed over Kidron when he fled from Absalom (2 Sam. 15: 23). There Hezekiah and Josiah destroyed pagan idols (1 Kings 15:13). Our Lord passed over Kidron to Gethsemane (John 18:1). The brook is present-day Wadi en-Nar.

KING (Hebrew *melek*). A monarch who rules by birth or acclaim. In Old Testament times the king normally administered a large territory surrounding a central walled city. He was also head of the army, supreme arbiter, and absolute master of the lives of his subjects. He had power to impose taxes and exact personal labor. Pagans either equated the king with their chief god or made him his representative.

In Egypt the pharaoh was usually looked upon as identical with the god. In Assyria he was regarded as representing the god. But in Israel the king, as well as prophets, priests, and judges, was regarded simply as God's representative (1 Sam. 10:1). He was divinely chosen and was expected to follow God's laws and to administer justice in God's place (Isa. 11:1-5; Jer. 33:15). He also had responsibilities as a judge (1 Kings 3:28) and as a proclaimer of the Law (2 Kings 23:2; cf. Judg. 17:6).

The term "king" is also frequently applied to the ultimate Ruler of all creation, God himself (1 Sam. 12:12; Psa. 47:7; Isa. 6:5; 1 Tim. 1:17). Special emphasis is given by Scripture to Christ's kingly role (Psa. 2:6; Zech. 9:9; Matt. 2:2; 21:5; Rev. 17:14; 19:16). Every Old Testament prophecy of the coming millennial kingdom bears witness to this glorious role which Christ will assume. He will occupy the Davidic throne as David's Lord and Heir (2 Sam. 7:16; Psa. 89:20-37; Isa. 11:11-16; Jer. 33:19-21). Christ came as a king (Luke 1:32, 33), was rejected as the king of Israel (Mark 15:12, 13; Luke 19:14), and died as a king (Matt. 27:37). At his second advent he will come as King par excellence (Rev. 19:16). His earthly reign as King will be mediatorial until he has vanquished all his enemies (1 Cor. 15:25-28). Then his mediatorial kingdom will merge into the eternal kingdom (2 Sam. 7:16; Psa. 89:36, 37; Isa. 9:6, 7; Luke 1:33; 1 Cor. 15:28).

KINGDOM. A sphere of rule and authority. Before man's fall the dominion of the earth belonged to Adam and Eve (Gen. 1:26-28). When they sinned they lost this dominion and Satan became "prince of this world" (Matt. 4:8-10; John 14:30). After the Flood human government was instituted under the Noahic Covenant, which is still God's intended charter for all human government (Gen. 9:1-17).

KINGDOM OF GOD. The rule of God over all intelligences in heaven and on earth who willingly submit to the Creator. Among human beings, only those who are born again fall into this category.

KINGDOM OF HEAVEN. The rule of God over the earth at any given time. The kingdom of heaven has been manifested in various aspects throughout the centuries. In its theocratic aspect it was established by Moses (Exod. 19:3-6) and later continued under the judges (Josh. 1:1-5; Judg. 2:16-18) and the kings (1 Sam. 10:1; 16:1-13; 1 Kings 9:1-5). It ended at the captivities (Ezek. 21:25-27; cf. Jer. 27:6-8; Dan. 2:36-38).

The theocratic kingdom will one day be restored (2 Sam. 7:8-16; Psa. 89:3, 4, 20, 21, 28-37). The prophets expound features of the kingdom as follows. (1) It will be Davidic, established under David's virgin-born Heir (Isa. 7:13, 14; 9:6, 7; 11:1), who will also be Immanuel, the God-Man (Jer. 23:5, 6; Ezek. 34:23; 37:24; Hos. 3:4, 5). (2) It will be heavenly in origin and authority but will be estab-

lished on the earth (Isa. 2:2-4; 4:3-5; Joel 3:1-17). (3) It will be established first over regathered and converted Israel. Then it will become universal (Psa. 2:6-8; 22:22-31; 24:1-10). (4) The second advent of Christ will usher in the earthly kingdom (Deut. 30:3-5; Psa. 2:1-9; Matt. 24, 25). (5) The Davidic Covenant has not been set aside (Psa. 89:33-37); it is yet to be fulfilled (Acts 15:14-17).

The kingdom of heaven as announced by John, the Apostles, and Christ himself (Matt. 3:2; 4:17) was rejected (Matt. 12:1-50). This demonstrated that fallen man must have salvation provided for him before he could be ready for kingdom participation (Matt. 16:21). The kingdom was thus postponed until the risen, ascended, and glorified Redeemer would return (Rev. 19:11-16). Not until the millennial reign of Christ will the kingdom of heaven become a realization. Meanwhile the *mystery* form of the kingdom is already in existence (Matt. 13:11); Christ is already ruling in the hearts of his believers.

KING'S HIGHWAY. An important trade route from Ezion-geber (on the Red Sea) to Damascus. It passed through Edom and Transjordan. In later Roman times the route was called Trajan's Road. Under Turkish rule it was known as the Sultan's Road. It is the present-day Tariq es-Sultani. Note the ancient Israelites' attempted use of the route in Numbers 20:14-21; 21:21-23.

KINSMAN-REDEEMER. The *go'el* or kinsman redeemer beautifully typifies Christ. The redeemer had to be a relative (Lev. 25:48, 49; Ruth 3:12, 13; Gal. 4:4, 5; Heb. 2:14, 15). He had to be capable of redeeming (Ruth 4:1-12; Gal. 3:13; 4:4, 5; Rev. 5:9, 10). He effected redemption by paying the just demand in full (Lev. 25:25-27; Gal. 3:13; 1 Pet. 1:18, 19).

KISH (kish). (1) A Benjamite and the father of King Saul (1 Sam. 9:1, 2). (2) An important ancient Sumerian city of lower Babylonia. It was the center of kingship in the Early Dynastic period of Sumerian history.

KISHON (kī'shŏn). A river known today as Nahr el-Muqatta. It originates in the hills of Galilee, drains the plain of Esdraelon, and empties into the Bay of

Acre, east of Mount Carmel. Barak won his famous victory over Sisera at the Kishon River (Judg. 4:1-17; 5:21). It was at Kishon that Elijah slaughtered the prophets of Baal (1 Kings 18:40). The river was also known as "the waters of Megiddo" (Judg. 5:19).

KITTIM. See "Cypriots."

KOHATH (kō'hăth). The second son of Levi (Gen. 46:11). His descendants held special offices in sanctuary service (Num. 3:27-32).

KORAH (kō'rà) ("held"). A Levitical leader who with Dathan and Abiram rebelled against the authority of Moses and Aaron. They died under God's judgment in an earthquake (Num. 16:1-35).

KUE. See "Cilicia."

LABAN (lā'băn) ("white"). The grandson of Nahor (Abraham's brother). Laban lived at Haran in Padan-aram in the region of the Balikh and Habur Rivers of Mesopotamia (Gen. 28:5; 29:4, 5). His sister Rebekah married Abraham's son Isaac (Gen. 24). When Jacob fled Esau's wrath he went to his Uncle Laban, serving him twenty years for Laban's daughters Rachel and Leah and for a herd of cattle (Gen. 28:1–31:55). Laban mixed the true worship of Jehovah with the worship of household gods (Gen. 31:19, 30-35).

LACHISH (lā'kĭsh). A fortified city in the lowland of Judah (Josh. 15:33, 39). It is located at Tell ed-Duweir, five miles south-southwest of Beit Jibrin. It was captured by Sennacherib of Assyria in 701 B.C. and made the base of his operations against Jerusalem (2 Kings 18:14, 17; 19:8 cf. Isa. 36:2; 37:8). It was one of the last places to fall to the Babylonians before Jerusalem's destruction (Jer. 34:7). It was reoccupied after the Exile (Neh. 11:30). The mound of the city has been excavated, yielding the famous Lachish Letters of about 589 B.C.

LAMECH THE CAINITE (lā'měk). Born of a godless line of ancestors, Lamech practiced polygamy, boasted of self-defensive murder, and exulted in the use of the sword for that purpose (Gen. 4:18-24).

LAMECH THE SETHITE. The son of Methuselah and the father of Noah. A God-fearing man, Lamech rested his faith in the divine promise of the removal of the curse of sin (Gen. 5:25-31). He was in the line of the coming Messiah-Redeemer (Luke 3:36).

Bronze lamps used by Romans and Christians (© MPS)

LAMP. Ancient lamps were usually simple bowls made of wood, clay, or metal and containing oil and a wick. As time progressed lamps became more sophisticated. By the New Testament era a lamp would often have a long spout for the wick and a hole in which to pour the oil. Mass production of lamps was facilitated by the use of molds, one for the bowl and another for the lid.

LANCE (Hebrew *romaḥ*). A type of heavy spear (Num. 25:7; Judg. 5:8; 1 Kings 18:28; 2 Chron. 11:12). Troops with heavy armor carried this weapon, which was a feature of Egyptian soldiery (Jer. 46:4). It was a spear with a long shaft, and was employed for thrusting rather than hurling (Num. 25:7, 8). It is frequently mentioned in connection with the shield, since both were used in battle array. As the Assyrian monuments illustrate, the opposing front lines would face each other shield-to-shield with lances protruding.

LAODICEA (lȧ-ŏd′ĭ′sē-à) (in Anatolia). A city of Phrygia which was probably introduced to Christianity at the same time as Colosse (cf. Col. 4:13-17). It was the site of one of the seven churches of Asia mentioned in Revelation 2 and 3. See especially Revelation 3:14-22. The present-day site is Eski-Hissar, near Denizli.

LAUREL. The *Laurus nobilis,* an evergreen tree with elliptical leaves and cream-white flower clusters. Its fruit is a black berry somewhat smaller than an olive. Laurel oil is extracted from the plant for medicinal purposes. The leaves are used as a condiment in flavoring pickles. The laurel is native to Palestine and the Mediterranean regions. It is mentioned only once in the Bible (Isa. 44:14).

LAW. Israelites as well as other ancient peoples of Bible times had codes of laws. The Mosaic Code is roughly paralleled by the Accadian Laws of Eshnunna (about 1850 B.C.), the Sumerian Code of Lipit-Ishtar (about 1900 B.C.), the Code of Hammurabi (about 1700 B.C.), the Hittite Laws (about 1500 B.C.), and the Middle Assyrian Laws (twelfth century B.C.). The Law given by God through Moses was distinct from other laws of the ancient world in its divine origin and authority and its high moral and spiritual tone.

LAW, BIBLE DOCTRINE OF. The word "law" is used in several different ways in the Bible. Five of the more important uses are described below.

(1) *The Eternal Moral Law of God.* This is the eternal, unchangeable law of God which applies at all times to all of his created intelligences. It was first introduced in written form in the Ten Commandments of the Mosaic Law (Exod. 20:1-17). Nine of the commandments underly all governmental laws. The fourth commandment, the requirement to observe the Sabbath, was given to Israel alone.

(2) *Governmental Law.* This is human law, determined by society but based on God's eternal moral law. All human beings are subject to some kind of governmental law (Rom. 13:1-7).

(3) *The Law of Moses.* The Law of Moses consists of the entire set of ordinances given to the Israelites by God through Moses. The Law is commonly divided into three parts: the moral law, the civil law, and the ceremonial law.

The moral law comprises the Ten Commandments (Exod. 20:1-17) and embraces the moral government of Israel (and, in principle, all other societies as well). The Ten Commandments may be succinctly summarized in the law of love to God and man (Matt. 22:34-40; Rom. 13:10; Gal. 5:14; James 2:8). It is this underlying principle of love which makes the essence of the Decalogue applicable to all mankind.

The second part of the Mosaic Law, the civil law, outlines the requirements for correct social relationships for the nation Israel (Exod. 21:1 – 23:33).

The third part of the Mosaic Law, the ceremonial law (sometimes called "the ordinances"), provided detailed regulations for Israel's worship (Exod. 25:1 – 31:18).

When Christ died on the Cross, the entire Mosaic system of law was abrogated as a test of human obedience (John 1:17; Rom. 10:4; 2 Cor. 3:6-11). However, the eternal moral principles which underly the Law of Moses have never been abolished. It is these very principles which are amply re-expressed throughout the New Testament, especially in the Epistles. Thus the *righteousness* of the Law (its underlying ethic) is fulfilled in every believer (Rom. 8:4).

(4) *The Law of Christ.* The law of Christ

includes all the principles of the eternal moral law of God as adapted to the teachings of grace (1 Cor. 9:20, 21; Gal. 6:2). Far from being an outlaw, the believer has been "inlawed to Christ" (1 Cor. 9: 20, 21, literal translation). The Spirit-filled believer exhibits the righteousness of Christ himself (Rom. 6:13; 1 Cor. 1: 30; Phil. 3:9).

(5) *The Law as the Will of God.* This includes all of God's revealed will for all people at all times. Paul's discussion in Romans 7:1 – 8:4 goes beyond the Law of Moses to include this facet of law.

LAWYER (Greek *nomikos*, from *nomos*, "law"). In biblical usage, an Israelite who was trained in the Law of Moses. In the New Testament the title is used synonymously with "scribe" and "teacher of the law" (cf. Matt. 22:35; Mark 12:28). By Christ's time many Jewish lawyers had departed from the Word of God. They concerned themselves mostly with traditions of men that actually set aside the commandments of God. Hence they merited severe censure from Christ (Luke 11:45-52).

LAZARUS OF BETHANY (lăz'ȧ-rŭs). The brother of Mary and Martha. It was he whom Jesus resurrected from death (John 11:1-44). This stupendous miracle of Christ so antagonized the Sanhedrin that they plotted to kill both Jesus and Lazarus (John 11:45-54; 12:10, 11).

LAZARUS THE BEGGAR. The destitute man who went to "Abraham's bosom" upon his death (Luke 16:19-31). The lesson of the story is that the accumulation of riches without regard to eternal destiny represents the ultimate folly in life.

LEAH (lē'ȧ) ("wild cow" or "gazelle"). The elder daughter of Laban. She became Jacob's first wife and bore him six sons and a daughter. Laban tricked Jacob into marrying his less attractive elder daughter in addition to the younger and more beautiful Rachel (Gen. 29:15-30). To the less favored Leah were born Reuben, Simeon, Levi, and Judah (Gen. 29: 31-35), and later Issachar, Zebulun, and Dinah (Gen. 30:14-24). Her handmaid, Zilpah, bore Gad and Asher (Gen. 30:9-13). Leah and her children accompanied Jacob to Palestine (Gen. 31). She was buried with Abraham, Sarah, Isaac, and Rebekah in the Cave of Machpelah at Hebron (Gen. 49:31).

The majestic cedars of Lebanon (© *MPS*)

LEBANON (lĕb'ȧ-nŏn). A mountain range in Syria. The name is sometimes also applied to the surrounding regions (Josh. 13:5). The name is derived from a Hebrew root meaning "to be white," an appropriate description of the white limestone of the high ridge of Lebanon and of the glittering snow that caps its peak for six months of the year. The southernmost peaks (which are a continuation of the hills of North Galilee) rise to a height of nearly 6200 feet behind Sidon. The east-west gorge of the Litany River marks the beginning of the 100-mile-long Lebanon range, whose highest peak reaches a height of almost 10,000 feet at a point east-southeast of Tripoli.

LEBANON, TREES OF. See under "Forest."

LEBBAEUS (lĕ-bē'ŭs). One of the twelve apostles. He was also called Thaddeus (Matt. 10:3; Mark 3:18). He was apparently also the "Judas" of Luke 6:16 and Acts 1:13.

LEEK. A tall herb resembling garlic. Its leaves and bulb are widely eaten as both a vegetable and a flavoring. The leek, *Allium porrum*, has always been a favorite dish in both Palestine and Egypt. It was one of the delicacies which the discontented Israelites longed for in the desert (Num. 11:5). The leek is still commonly sold in the markets of the Near East.

LENTIL. An annual plant with pinnate leaves and white flowers with violet stripes. Lentil seeds have been a favorite food in Near Eastern countries since biblical times (Gen. 25:34; 2 Sam. 17:27-29). The parched seeds could be carried easily on a long journey and were suitable for emergency needs (Ezek. 4:9). The "red pottage" of Esau was made of lentils (Gen. 25:29-34), and lentils were among the staples offered to David at Mahanaim (2 Sam. 17:28). A field of lentils is referred to in 2 Samuel 23:11, 12.

LEOPARD (Hebrew *nārmēr*). Any of several kinds of spotted cats, including the true leopard of Africa and Southern Asia (*Felis pardus*), the cheetah or hunting leopard, and several other wild cats of Palestine. The leopard was very swift (Hab. 1:8) and fed on smaller animals (Isa. 11:6). It sometimes attacked humans (Hos. 13:7, 8), lurking for its victims near villages (Jer. 5:6). Its ordinary habitat was the mountains (Song 4:8).

LEVI (lē'vī) ("joined, attached"). (1) Jacob's third son and an ancestor of Moses and Aaron. It was from Levi's lineage that the Old Testament priestly service was staffed (Exod. 28:1; Num. 1:47-54). (2) An alternative name for the Apostle Matthew (cf. Matt. 9:9-13 with Luke 5:27-32). See "Matthew."

LEVIATHAN. A large aquatic animal described at length in Job 41 and mentioned in several other poetic passages of Scripture. It is usually assumed to be the crocodile.

LEVIRATE MARRIAGE (lĕv'ī-rāt). The Mosaic Code provided that if a man died childless, his brother or male next of kin should marry his widow. The firstborn of this second marriage would then continue the name of the deceased (Deut. 25:5-10). This "kinsman-redeemer" practice is beautifully illustrated in the Book of Ruth. The removal of the shoe (Deut. 25:7-10; Ruth 4:7) arose from the custom of walking on the soil as a declaration of one's right of acquired possession. If a man refused this obligation, the widow took off his shoe and spat in his face.

LEVITES (lē'vīts). Sometimes this name denotes the entire tribe of Levi, including the priests, the descendants of Aaron (Exod. 6:25; Lev. 25:32; Num. 35:2; Josh. 21:3). Frequently, however, the designation applies only to those descendants of Levi who were not priests. The priests offered the sacrifices and performed the ritual worship of the Tabernacle while the Levites handled the more routine duties.

LIBNAH (lĭb'nä) (in Judah). A Canaanite city captured by Joshua (Josh. 10:29, 30). It was located in the lowlands (Josh. 15:42) and was a Levitical town (Josh. 21:13). Its inhabitants revolted from Jehoram, king of Judah (2 Kings 8:22). Sennacherib attacked it (2 Kings 19:8). It is identified as present-day Tell es-Safi, about eight miles south of Ekron.

LIBYANS. The inhabitants of Libya, west of Lower Egypt. These hostile people first appear as "Lubim" in Egyptian texts of the twelfth and thirteenth centuries B.C. and in the Hebrew Bible (Nah. 3:9; cf. "Libyans" in Dan. 11:43). From the twelfth to the eighth century B.C. they entered Egypt as settlers, raiders, or soldiers in the armies of the Pharaohs. Lubim are prominent among the troops of Shishak (2 Chron. 12:3) and Zerah (2 Chron. 14:9; 16:8) and among the forces of the Ethiopian pharaohs that failed to protect No-Amon (Thebes) from Assyrian devastation (Nah. 3:9). Some scholars equate Phut or Put with Cyrenaica, the region around Cyrene (Gen. 10:6).

LICE (Hebrew *kinnām, kinnīm*). A small insect of somewhat uncertain identification. It has been variously identified as lice, gnats, sandflies, fleas, and mosquitoes.

LILY. A bulbous plant which produces a beautiful flower. A number of varieties flourish in Palestine, including the "lily of the valleys" (Song 2:1), the hyacinth, the anemone, and the madonna lily, as well as varieties of iris and gladioli (cf. Song 2:16; 4:5; 6:3; Matt. 6:28). The "lilies of the field" (Matt. 6:28; Luke 12:27) apparently refer to families of flowers which include the narcissus, the cyclamen, and the Palestinian chamomile (a common, daisy-like bloom).

LINEN EPHOD. A simple, white linen priestly robe (as distinguished from the more elegant high priestly garment). Samuel wore one (1 Sam. 2:18), as did the priests (1 Sam. 22:18; Hos. 3:4). David also wore such a garment when the ark of the Tabernacle was transferred to Jerusalem (2 Sam. 6:14).

LION. Lions are mentioned dozens of times in the Bible. They were once common in Europe and Asia and were also found in Palestine. The lion was proverbial for strength (2 Sam. 1:23; Prov. 30:30) and courage (2 Sam. 17:10). It had the habit of crouching before springing on its victim (Gen. 49:9). It preyed on small animals (1 Sam. 17:34, Isa. 11:6, 7) as well as man (1 Kings 13:24). The lion lurked in thickets and forests (Jer. 4:7; 5:6; 25:38). It was especially common in the Jordan jungle (Jer. 49:19). Satan is compared to a lion (1 Pet. 5:8). Our Lord is called "the Lion of the tribe of Judah" (Rev. 5:5; cf. Gen. 49:9).

LIZARD. In the warm, dry climate of Palestine lizards of many varieties exist. Some forty species are found. They were regarded as unclean and were thus not used as food by the Hebrews (Lev. 11:30, 31). The green lizard, the wall lizard, the sand lizard, the monitor lizard, and the gecko are especially numerous.

LO-AMMI (lō-ăm'ī) ("not my people"). A name given by Hosea to his son (Hos. 1:8-10; 2:23). It symbolized Israel's temporary rejection by the Lord because of her sin and apostasy.

Locust—food and foe of the Middle East (© *MPS*)

LOCUST (Hebrew *'arbeh;* Greek *'akris*). The locust is distinguished from the grasshopper by the shortness of its antennae. Locusts were clean insects (Lev. 11:21, 22) and are still used as food by the poor (cf. Matt. 3:4). They are prepared by roasting or drying in the sun and removing the head, wings, legs, and intestines. The locust was, and still is, the scourge of the Middle East. Locusts blown by the wind into the Nile Valley constituted the eighth plague in the days of the Exodus (Exod. 10:3-20). The female deposits her eggs in the earth in April or May. They hatch in June, producing wingless larvae.

These then enter the pupa state, where they develop rudimentary wings. At this stage (Joel 1:4) the insects are more voracious than in any other stage of their development. In a month or so they cast their pupas or nymph skins and become full-grown insects, ready to participate in another wave of destruction.

LOGOS. A Greek word which means "a thought" or "the expression or utterance of a thought." It is an appropriate designation of Christ, since all the treasures of the divine wisdom are embodied in him (Col. 2:2, 3). From past eternity and especially in the incarnation, Christ has perfectly expressed the inmost nature of God (John 1:1-18; 14:9-11; Col. 1:12-20; Heb. 1:1-4).

LOIS (lō'ĭs). The mother of Eunice and the grandmother of Timothy (2 Tim. 1:5). Both women were devout Christians. Their godly example in teaching Timothy has been a source of inspiration for countless mothers to "train up a child in the way he should go" and to believe that "when he is old he will not depart from it" (Prov. 22:6).

LORD. The English word "Lord" is a translation of the Hebrew words *Yahweh, Adonai,* and *Adon* as well as the Aramaic word *mar* and the Greek word *kurios. Kurios* is used in a number of ways in the New Testament. It can refer to God (Acts 2:34; cf. Psa. 110:1), to Christ (Luke 10:1), or to human masters (Matt. 18:23-35). It can mean simply "Rabbi" or "sir" (Matt. 8:6). Those who addressed Christ as "Lord" in the Gospels sometimes acknowledged his full deity by the title (as in John 20:28) while at other times they meant nothing more than the usual polite form of address (as in John 9:35, 36).

Because they were well versed in the vocabulary of the Old Testament, the early Christians associated the word "Lord" with God himself. They thus expressed the deity of Christ when they referred to him as "Lord." The Apostle Paul frequently alluded to Christ by his full and official title—the Lord Jesus Christ (1 Thess. 1:1; 2 Cor. 13:14; etc.).

LORD'S DAY. The weekly remembrance of our Lord's resurrection. It is identified with "the first day of the week" (Sunday).

Scripture says very little about this day (cf. Rev. 1:10). We do know, however, that the day represents the initiation of a new order rather than a change of the Sabbath. It celebrates the New Creation with the resurrected Christ as its Head. The Sabbath, by contrast, was connected with the Old Creation (Exod. 20:8-11; 31:12-17; Heb. 4:4). The Lord's day is in no sense a "Christian Sabbath." It has no connection with Mosaic legalism. It is a day to be honored solely by New Testament believers.

LORD'S SUPPER. One of two ordinances of the Christian church. It is intended to be a commemoration of Christ's atoning death and victorious resurrection (Matt. 26:26-28; Mark 14:22-24; Luke 22: 19, 20; 1 Cor. 11:23-28). The bread and the cup are beautiful, easily understood symbols of Christ's body and blood broken and shed for our sins (1 Cor. 11:24, 25).

LO-RUHAMAH (lō-rōo-há′má) ("not pitied"). The name given by the prophet Hosea to his second child. It symbolized God's anger against sinning Israel and warned that God would not pity his covenant people when he chastened them for their idolatry (Hos. 1:2, 6). The cruel lash of Assyria would be pitiless upon the back of God's wayward people.

LOT (probably "covering"). Abraham's nephew, who accompanied the patriarch from Mesopotamia to Canaan (Gen. 11: 27 – 12:5). He began his life experiences in faith as a justified believer (2 Pet. 2:8), but through unbelief and worldly greed he made a costly error of choice (Gen. 13: 5-13). As a result he lost everything except his own life and the lives of his two daughters (Gen. 19:1-30). Because of their pagan environment in childhood, even Lot's daughters ended up disgracing him (Gen. 19:31-38).

LOVE OF GOD. One of God's essential attributes is love (1 John 4:8, 16). His divine love embraces the whole world (John 3:16; Heb. 2:9; 1 John 2:2) but is directed especially toward the redeemed (Rom. 5:5). God's love is sacrificial (2 Cor. 8:9; 1 John 3:16, 17) and can be communicated toward his children (Rom. 5:5; 1 John 4:7, 11). If we love God we will reject the present evil world system (1 John 2:15-17). God also shows special love toward his eternally elect nation, Israel (Jer. 31:3). Though now temporarily set aside, Israel will be restored at Christ's second advent (Rom. 11).

LUCIFER (lū′sĭ-fēr) ("the light-bearer"). A name applied to the king of Babylon as a description of his glory and pomp (Isa. 14:12-14). The passage is a veiled reference to Satan, the real power behind the government of Babylon (Dan. 10:13; cf. Eph. 6:12).

LUD (lŭd) A region in Western Anatolia sometimes known as Ludu or Lydia. Its capital was Sardis. Gyges founded the Lydian kingdom in the seventh century B.C. Its last king, Croesus, was defeated by Cyrus the Persian. Lydian mercenaries were employed in Egyptian armies.

LUKE (meaning uncertain). A Christian physician and companion of Paul (Col. 4: 14; 2 Tim. 4:11). He was the inspired penman of the Gospel of Luke and the Book of the Acts. He was thus the first church historian. The Gospel of Luke presents Christ as the perfect man. It stresses themes of pardon and redemption and emphasizes joy and praise (Luke 1:14; 2:10, 13: 15:7). See especially the Magnificat of Mary (Luke 1:46-55), the Benedictus of Zechariah (Luke 1:67-79), the Gloria in Excelsis of the angels (Luke 2:14), and the Nunc Dimittis of Simeon (Luke 2:29-32).

LUMBERMAN. The modern lumberjack finds a parallel in the lumberman of antiquity, who hewed timber in the cedar forests of the Lebanon region. Together with firs and cypress trees, this area furnished the finest building materials in the ancient east. Hiram I of Tyre had timber cut in the Lebanon region for Solomon's Temple (1 Kings 5:6-9). The finest of Lebanon and Antilebanon (Sirion) were also felled to provide ships for Tyrian traders (Ezek. 27:5) and sacred barges for Egypt. Fine furniture was made from Lebanese cedar (Song 3:9). Wood for the second Temple at Jerusalem was also hewn in Lebanon (Ezra 3:7).

LUZ (lŭz). The ancient name for Bethel. The name was changed in Jacob's day (Gen. 28:19; 35:6; Josh. 18:13). It is now identified with Beitin, about a dozen miles north of Jerusalem. See "Bethel."

LYCAONIA (lĭk′á-ō′nĭ-à) The district of Asia Minor in which Lystra was located. Its natives were non-Greeks (Acts 14:6, 11).

LYDIA (lĭd′ĭ-à) (perhaps "a Lydian, woman of Lydia"). A businesswoman from Thyatira whom Paul met at Philippi. She became the first Christian convert in Europe (Acts 16:11-40). She and her household were baptized, and she acted as host to the apostle and his party. Lydia sold purple-dyed goods which she had brought to Philippi from Thyatira. She was a woman of means. Her generosity was characteristic of the Philippian church, from whom Paul accepted gifts because of his special love for them and their love for him (Phil. 1:3, 8; 4:1, 15-19).

LYSIAS (lĭs′ĭ-ăs). The chief captain of the Roman garrison at Jerusalem. He rescued Paul from the mob of hostile Jews (Acts 23:12 – 24:9).

LYSTRA (lĭs′trà). A city in Asia Minor in which Paul was stoned (Acts 14:8-20). It was also the home of Timothy (Acts 16:1, 2). It is present-day Zoldera, about 24 miles southwest of Iconium.

MAACHAH (mā′á-kà). (1) The wife of Machir son of Manasseh (1 Chron. 7:15, 16). (2) A concubine of Caleb son of Hezron (1 Chron. 2:48). (3) The wife of Jehiel and an ancestress of King Saul (1 Chron. 8:29; 9:35). (4) A daughter of Talmai king of Geshur. She became one of David's wives and bore him Absalom (2 Sam. 3:3). (5) The wife of King Rehoboam (930-913 B.C.). She was either the daughter or granddaughter of Absalom (1 Kings 15:2; 2 Chron. 11:20-22) and the mother of King Abijam (913-910 B.C.). After Abijam's death she remained queen mother. However, Asa, her grandson, removed her from this position because she made an idolatrous image of an Asherah, a Canaanite fertility goddess (2 Chron. 15:16).

MACEDONIANS (măs′ė-dō′nĭ-ȧns). The inhabitants of the country north of Greece. Macedonia came into prominence under Philip of Macedon (359-336 B.C.) and his world-conquering son, Alexander the Great (336-323 B.C.). Under Alexander's successors the country declined until it was conquered by the Romans in 168 B.C. It was made a province in 142 B.C. The Macedonian Empire is referred to in Daniel 8:5-8. Macedonia is prominent in the missionary call of Paul (Acts 16:6-10) and the introduction of the Christian gospel into Europe (Acts 16:11-40).

MACHPELAH (măk-pē′là). A cave and field near Hebron which Abraham purchased as a burial place (Gen. 23:9). Later Abraham, Isaac, Rebekah, and Jacob were buried here. The modern site of the burial cave is incorporated in the southern end of the sacred Haram al-Halil at Hebron.

MAGI (mā′jī). Originally an Iranian priestly order of wise men, astrologers, and soothsayers (similar to the Hindu Brahmin). Later the name was applied to any sage, especially eastern, such as the Magi who came to Jerusalem at Christ's birth (Matt. 2:1-10).

MAGIC. The operation of Satanic and demonic power in opposition to God's Word and will. Magic is the Satanic counterfeit of miracle. It attempts to use supernatural power independent of and in opposition to God (Exod. 7:10 – 8:7; 2 Thess. 2:7-10; Rev. 13). It is a phenomenon of demon-energized occultism.

MAGISTRATE. In the Old Testament the word occurs in Ezra 7:25 as the translation of the Hebrew word *shōphet* or "judge." In Judges 18:7 the word "magistrate" means a civil authority who exercised restraint against evil. Luke used the term to refer to civil authorities in general (Luke 12:11, 58). Paul was beaten by magistrates at Philippi (Acts 16:19-24, 35-38).

MAGOG (mā'gŏg). A son of Japheth and his descendants (Gen. 10:2). They are the Scythians. When Ezekiel employed the terms Gog and Magog (Ezek. 38:2; 39:6) he used them primarily in a historical sense but also applied them to the future rise of the Prince of the Northern Confederacy (Gog) and his scope of rule (Magog).

MAHALATH (mā'hă-lăth) ("sickness"). (1) One of Esau's wives. She was the daughter of Ishmael, Abraham's son (Gen. 28:9) and may have been the same person as Basemath. (2) A granddaughter of David and one of the eighteen wives of Solomon's son, King Rehoboam (2 Chron. 11:18).

MAHANAIM (mā'hà-nā'ĭm). A locality in Transjordan associated with Jacob (Gen. 32:2). David once took refuge there (2 Sam. 17:23-29). It was the center of Solomon's seventh district. It is perhaps located east of Penuel near the River Jabbok.

MAKKEDAH (mă-kē'dà). A cave where the defeated Amorite kings fled for refuge and were slain by Joshua. The town of Makkedah was located in the lowlands a few miles southwest of Bethshemesh and a few miles north of Azekah near the Vale of Elah (Josh. 10:10, 16).

MALACHI (māl'à-kī) ("my messenger"). The last of the Old Testament prophets and the author of the Book of Malachi (written about 400 B.C.). Malachi was the prophet who stressed God's electing love. He declares that Jacob's election was a demonstration of divine grace, and that Israel as a son had dishonored his Father by his sin (Mal. 1, 2). Judgment of the sinners and blessing for the penitent are shown to be certain. The coming day of the Lord is given as an example of judgment and the second advent of Christ is presented as the hope of blessing for the righteous (Mal. 3, 4).

MAMRE (măm'rè). A place in Hebron where Abraham and Isaac sojourned (Gen. 13:18; 18:1). The field of Machpelah was nearby (Gen. 25:9; 49:30).

MAN. God's special, direct creation, placed on earth in order to demonstrate God's plan of redemption (Gen. 1:1 – 3: 15). Through the redemption of man God will show to all creation how he will deal with sin and ultimately achieve a sinless universe (Rev. 21:1 – 22:5).

MAN OF SIN. The last-day Antichrist, the embodiment of Satan's power (Luke 4:5, 6). His rule on earth will be terminated by the glorious coming of Christ (2 Thess. 2:8-12; Rev. 20:10). He is the "little horn" of Daniel 7:8, the "willful king" of Daniel 11:36, the "abomination of desolation" of Matthew 24:15, and the first "beast" of Revelation 13:1-10.

MANASSEH (mà-năs'ĕ) ("causing to forget"). (1) Joseph's older son, born of Asenath. Like his brother, Ephraim, Manasseh was half Egyptian (Gen. 41: 50-52). In his dying prophecy Jacob conferred the primary blessing upon Ephraim instead of Manasseh (Gen. 48:8-20). (2) A wicked king of Judah from 687 to 643 B.C. He was the son of good King Hezekiah. He filled Jerusalem with idolatry and violence (2 Kings 21:1-16). He became subject to Assyria and paid tribute to Esarhaddon (680-669 B.C.). and Shalmaneser III (669-633 B.C.). Later he repented of his wickedness (2 Chron. 33:12-19).

MANDRAKE. The *Mandragora officinarum*, a stemless perennial herb with thick, branched roots which often resemble the lower parts of the human body. It was called the "love apple" and was sometimes used as an aphrodisiac (Gen. 30:14-16). In Palestine it is common in fields of the Mediterranean zone.

MANNA. A divinely provided food which constituted the main diet of the Israelites during their sojourn in the desert (Exod. 16). Attempts to explain the phenomenon on a natural basis have failed. Some authorities attempt to identify the manna with certain lichens, or with a substance exuded from tamarisk trees, or with the excrement of certain scale insects living on tamarisk trees. Although the identifications are based on substantial findings, the substances involved are quantitatively far insufficient to have supported the large number of people involved. The manna must therefore have been supernaturally provided, as stated in Scripture.

MANTLE OF DISTINCTION (*'addereth*). Such a garment was worn by kings and prophets (Jonah 3:6). Achan stole this kind of apparel (Josh. 7:20, 21). Elijah had such a mantle (1 Kings 19:13, 19; 2 Kings 2:8, 13, 14). It was a sign of the prophet's office (Zech. 13:4). John the Baptist wore a mantle of camel's hair (Matt. 3:4; Mark 1:6). The robe of mockery placed on Christ was the Roman soldier's mantle, simulating that of royalty (Matt. 27:28, 31; Mark 15:17; John 19:2, 5).

In the New Testament the robe or stole was worn as a mark of honor, as by the scribes (Mark 12:38; Luke 20:46), the restored prodigal (Luke 15:22), the martyrs (Rev. 6:11), and the redeemed (Rev. 7:9, 13). See also "Robe."

MARA (mä'rá) ("bitter, sad in spirit"). The name chosen by Naomi when she returned to Bethlehem. It expressed the sorrow that came to her while she sojourned in Moab (Ruth 1:20).

MARAH (mä'rá). See under "Springs, Wells, and Pools."

MARDUK (mär'dook). The Mesopotamian hero-god. He was thought to be the head of the Babylonian pantheon, the creator of mankind, and the ruler of human destiny.

MARESHAH (mà-rē'shà). A town in the lowlands of Judah (Josh. 15:44). It had been fortified by Rehoboam (2 Chron. 11:8) and was the scene of King Asa's victory over the Ethiopian invaders (2 Chron. 14:9-15). It was located at Tell Sandahanna, a few miles northeast of Lachish.

In the Hellenistic period the town was called Marisa.

MARI (mä'rē). A city-state on the Middle Euphrates. It was conquered by Hammurabi about 1765 B.C. Previously it was the capital of the kingdom of Mari. The administration and personal records of Mari, dating from the eighteenth century B.C., have been recovered. The modern site is Tell el-Hariri, near Abou Kemal.

MARK (Latin *marcus*, "a large hammer"). John Mark was a Jew and a son of Mary, a Christian matron at Jerusalem (Acts 12:12). Mark accompanied Paul and Barnabas on their first missionary tour (Acts 13:5) but later dropped out in failure (Acts 13:13; 15:38). However, Mark recovered himself and won back his place in apostolic esteem, becoming a valued colleague of Paul (Col. 4:10, 11; Philem. 1:24; 2 Tim. 4:11; 1 Pet. 5:13). Mark wrote the Gospel of Mark, presenting the Son of God as the Perfect Servant, an especially appealing theme for Roman readers.

MARRIAGE. An institution established by God from the beginning of human existence (Gen. 2:21-25) and designed for the welfare and happiness of mankind. Monogamy is God's ideal for man's highest happiness (Gen. 2:24). However, plural marriages are recorded in the Old Testament, sometimes even of the most prominent saints. With the advance in relationship between God and his saints in the New Testament, the more exalted ideal of one wife and one husband is clearly enjoined (Eph. 5:22, 33).

MARRIAGE, JEWISH. The betrothal was consummated by the wedding festivities. These were mostly social in character and ordinarily lasted from one to two weeks (Judg. 14:12, 17). Guests were invited and summoned by special messenger (Luke 14:17). When the wedding day arrived, the bridegroom went in procession to the bride's house to bring her to his own house or that of his father. Special groomsmen, called "friends of the bridegroom," attended him in New Testament times and later. The "children of the bridechamber" (Matt. 9:15) refer to another class, the guests invited to the wedding. At the actual wedding no services of a priest were thought necessary.

Deeply veiled, the bride was led away from her home amid the well wishes of parents and friends (Ruth 4:11, 12). Sometimes, if circumstances required, the wedding festivities were celebrated at the bride's house (Gen. 29:22). A wealthy bridegroom sometimes distributed garments suitable for the occasion among his guests (Matt. 22:11). The bridal procession sometimes took place at night amid the blaze of torches and accompanied by singing, dancing, and merrymaking (Matt. 25:1-10). Under the Law of Moses the bridegroom was exempt from all public duties for one year following his marriage (Deut. 24:5).

In view of the sanctity of marriage God provided special laws to protect the marital union from violation. The sin of adultery was originally punished by stoning both participants to death (Lev. 20:10; Deut. 22:22). Nor did the Mosaic Law condemn only the outward act. Like our Lord (Matt. 5:27, 28), it also condemned the inner sin of lust (Exod. 20:17).

Under Mosaic Law a husband who suspected his wife of infidelity could subject her to a grueling ordeal which no guilty person could well pass through without betraying her guilt (Num. 5:11-31). Conversely, the Law protected the wife from unfounded suspicions of premarital infidelity (Deut. 22:13-21). See also "Engagement."

MARRIAGE OF THE LAMB. The marriage of Christ and his bride, the church (Rev. 19:7-9). The figure of marriage symbolizes the glory which redeemed church saints will share with Christ through all eternity (Rev. 21:9 — 22:5).

On Mars Hill in Athens the Greeks' wisest men concluded that Jesus' resurrection was only a fairy tale (Acts 17). (*Russ Busby photo*)

MARS HILL ("Hill of Ares," the god of war). The place at Athens where the Apostle Paul addressed the Court of the Areopagus (Acts 17:19). It was one of the lower hills west of the Acropolis. The seats of the judges and others connected with the court can still be seen in the rocks.

MARTHA (mär'thà). (Aramaic, "lady, mistress"). The woman to whom Christ first proclaimed, "I am the resurrection and the life" (John 11:24, 25). With her brother Lazarus and her sister Mary she resided at Bethany, a small town on the Mount of Olives (about two miles from Jerusalem). The trio loved Jesus sincerely, but of the two sisters Mary had the greater appreciation of spiritual things while Martha concerned herself more about the routine duties of hospitality. For this she was gently rebuked by Christ (Luke 10:38-42). Both sisters were true believers (John 11:21-32) and were honored by one of Christ's most celebrated miracles, the raising of their brother Lazarus from death (John 11:1-44). The supper where Mary anointed Christ's head (John 12:1-3) was at the house of Simon the leper (Matt. 26:6, 7; Mark 14:3). It is possible that Martha may have been the wife or widow of Simon.

MARY (mâr'ĭ) (from Hebrew *Miryam;* same as "Miriam"). (1) Mary the mother of Jesus. With respect to the birth of Jesus Christ, Mary was a virgin. She was "found with child of the Holy Spirit" (Matt. 1:18) before she had sexual union with Joseph (Matt. 1:24, 25). This was the fulfillment of the "virgin birth" prophecy made 700 years earlier by the Prophet Isaiah (Isa. 7:14; Matt. 1:22, 23). Christ's miraculous conception and virgin birth are also proclaimed by Luke (Luke 1:34-38) and are required by John's account, for God could become man (John 1:1-5, 14) only by such supernatural conception.

After Jesus' birth Mary had other children who were Christ's half brothers and sisters and the natural offspring of her husband, Joseph (Matt. 12:46-50; Mark 3:31-35; Luke 8:19-21). Mary appeared at the marriage in Cana of Galilee (John 2:1-11) and with other women at the Cross (John 19:25-27). After the ascension she was with the apostles in the upper room in Jerusalem (Acts 1:12-14). This is the last notice of her in Scripture. (2) Mary of Bethany. She with her sister Martha and brother Lazarus were close friends of Jesus and frequently entertained him in their home at Bethany (Luke 10:38-42). Mary also anointed the Lord with ointment (John 11:2; 12:1-8) in anticipation of his approaching death. (3) Mary Magdalene. Magdala was a town near Tiberias at the southern end of the fertile Plain of Gennesaret on the shore of the Sea of Galilee. It was a prosperous town, predominantly Gentile, and had a reputation for licentiousness. When Mary met Christ she was saved from both her sins and her severe demonic oppression (Luke 8:2; Mark 16:9). She became a devoted disciple of Christ (Luke 8:1-3; Mark 15:40, 41). Mary Magdalene appeared at the crucifixion (Mark 15:40; John 19:25), came to the tomb to anoint Jesus' body (Mark 16:1; Luke 23:55 – 24:1), reported the fact of the empty tomb to the Eleven (Luke 24:1-11), and saw the risen Christ (John 20:11-18). (4) Mary the wife of Clopas. She was one of the women standing near the Cross (John 19:25). Clopas or Cleophas is apparently to be identified with Alphaeus (Matt. 10:3; Mark 3:18; Luke 6:15), the two names being variant forms of the same Aramaic original. Thus Mary and her husband Clopas were the parents of the Apostle James (Mark 3:18), Joses (Mark 15:40), and Levi (Mark 2:14). (5) Mary the mother of Mark. It was her son who authored the second Gospel and accompanied Paul and Barnabas in their missionary work (Acts 12:25; 15:36-41; cf. 2 Tim. 4:11). The sole reference to this Mary occurs in Acts 12:12. Her house in Jerusalem was a meeting place for Christians, and Peter went there after his escape from prison (Acts 12:6-19). (6) Mary of Rome. A resident of Rome, she greatly assisted the missionary cause (Rom. 16:6).

MASADA (mȧ-sā'dȧ). An ancient Hasmonean stronghold on the west side of the Dead Sea. It lies about 11 miles south of En-gedi and opposite El Lisan. It was formidably fortified by Herod the Great. Like the Herodium and Machaerus, it held out tenaciously but unsuccessfully against the Romans. It is present-day es-Sebbeh, which has been carefully excavated.

MASON. Stonemasons worked on fine public buildings and sumptuous private dwellings (Amos 5:11). Palestinian limestone being soft and destructible, blocks of harder stones for the Temple and other public buildings were cut and worked in the Lebanon region (1 Kings 6:7). The stones were cut with saws (1 Kings 7:9) and trimmed with picks or axes.

The stonemason also quarried out hillside tombs at various locations, as well as rock cisterns for water storage at Jericho, Lachish, Megiddo, and Gibeon. Under Herod the Great's regime, massive blocks of stone were used for building purposes and were so carefully dressed that they could be aligned without mortar. Masons also cut inscriptions in rocks, as in the case of the Siloam Tunnel at Jerusalem.

MATTATHIAS OF MODIN (măt-ȧ-thī′ as, mō′dĭn). An aged Jewish priest who refused to compromise with the paganization program of Antiochus Epiphanes. He killed Antiochus' officer and the Jew who was willing to offer a profane sacrifice. Escaping with his five sons, he initiated the Maccabean revolt. The uprising was led by his sons – Judas (166-160 B.C.), Jonathan (160-142 B.C.), and Simon (142-134 B.C.). The latter inaugurated a period of Jewish independence (143-63 B.C.).

MATTHEW ("gift of the Lord"). A Jewish tax-collector who was also named Levi (cf. Matt. 9:9 with Luke 5:27). When Christ called him he immediately left all to follow the Lord (Luke 5:28). To celebrate the occasion, Matthew entertained Christ and others at a feast in his own house (Luke 5:29). Matthew wrote the Gospel which bears his name. He presents Christ as the Son of David and the King of the Jews.

MATTHIAS (mȧ-thī′ȧs) (probably shortened from Mattathias, "gift of the Lord"). A disciple chosen by lot to succeed Judas Iscariot (Acts 1:23, 26). Tradition identifies him with the Seventy (Luke 10:1).

MEDES (mēdz). An Indo-European people who conquered and settled the country of Media east of the Zagros Mountains, south of the Caspian Sea, and north of Elam. They are the "Madai" of the "table of the nations" (Gen. 10:2). The Medes became prominent in Assyrian records beginning with Shalmaneser III in the ninth century. Under Cyaxares (650-612 B.C.) Media allied itself with Babylonia, and with Scythian aid they were able to overthrow Assyria between 616 and 612 B.C. Meanwhile Persia, which lay south and east of Media, rebelled against Median power and Cyrus the Great became king of Media and Persia. The conquerors and the conquered were both of the fine Aryan race. The result was a dual nation, Media-Persia, which became a world empire until destroyed by Alexander the Great (cf. Dan. 2:39; 7:5). The two-horned ram of Daniel (Dan. 8:3-7, 20) symbolizes Media and Persia. One horn (Persia) was higher than the other (Media) and came up last. Though the Median power arose first, the Persian power later attained the ascendancy. See also "Persians."

MEDIATION. A ministry of reconciling persons at odds with each other. Christ is the great Mediator between God and man (1 Tim. 2:5). As a Prophet he represents God to man. As a Priest he represents man to God (Heb. 9:15). As a King he will reign as God over the earth (Psa. 2).

MEGIDDO (mḗ-gĭd'ō). A strategic fortified town which once guarded the mountain pass leading to the Plain of Esdraelon. It was taken by Thutmose III in the fifteenth century B.C. Its people opposed Joshua but remained in Canaanite control (Josh. 12:21; 17:11; Judg. 1:27). The city fell into Solomon's fifth district (1 Kings 4:12) and was fortified by him (1 Kings 9:15; cf. 2 Kings 9:27; 23:29). The modern site, Tell el-Mutesselim, has been extensively excavated and reveals occupational levels from the early fourth millennium until about 350 B.C.

MELCHIZEDEK (mĕl-kĭz'ē-dĕk) ("king of righteousness"). The priest and king of Salem or "peace" (Heb. 7:2). Melchizedek met Abraham and blessed him (Gen. 14:18-20; Heb. 7:1-3). He thus prefigures Christ's priesthood (Heb. 7). Christ alone can bring us peace, since he is our righteousness (1 Cor. 1:30). Melchizedek's genealogy is purposely omit-

ted to make him typify more strikingly the mystery of Christ's birth and the eternity of his priesthood. Christ had no human father and no divine mother. As the only-begotten of the Father, Christ was without priestly pedigree. Melchizedek's greatness is seen in the tithes which Abraham paid him. Christ himself is infinitely greater than Melchizedek and thus deserves our all.

MELITA (mĕl'ĭ-tà). Modern Malta, a central Mediterranean island about 60 miles south of Sicily. It is about 95 square miles in area. Paul's ship was driven there from Crete and wrecked (Acts 27:9—28:1). The Apostle spent three months on the island before resuming his journey to Rome via Syracuse, Rhegium, and Puteoli (Acts 28:11-13). In the tenth century B.C. Melita was occupied by the Phoenicians. The island's name in that language means "refuge," a reminder that the island has often proved a haven to storm-battered sailors. The site of Paul's shipwreck is probably "Saint Paul's Bay," eight miles northwest of the modern town of Valetta.

MELON. The plant commonly named watermelon (*Citrullus vulgaris*), which the Hebrews ate in Egypt (Num. 11:5). Melons of all sorts were grown in Egypt, and these are included in the reference to the watermelon.

MEMPHIS. An ancient Egyptian city on the west side of the Nile River and about 19 miles above the apex of the delta. It was the capital of the earlier dynasties until power was transferred to Thebes. To the Hebrews it was known as Noph (Isa. 19:13) and Moph (Hebrew text of Hosea 9:6). Some Jews settled there after the fall of Jerusalem and Gedaliah's murder (Jer. 44:1). Most of the ruins of Memphis have been carried to Cairo for construction purposes, so that the ancient city is now almost non-existent. However, 20 pyramids and the celebrated sphinx still remain.

MENAHEM (mĕn'à-hĕm) ("comforter"). A murderer and usurper of the throne of Israel. He reigned for about 10 years, from 752 to 742 B.C. (2 Kings 15:14-22). He rose to power in the period of civil war that marked the end of the Jehu dynasty.

MEPHIBOSHETH (mḗ-fĭb'ō-shĕth). A

son of Jonathan and grandson of King Saul. He is also called "Meribbaal," "striver against Baal." (The "Baal" element was changed to *bosheth*, Hebrew for "shame.") Mephibosheth became crippled as a child when his nurse dropped him while fleeing from the news of the death of Saul and Jonathan (2 Sam. 4:4). He at first lived in exile under David, the new king, but was later reinstated because of a previous covenant between David and Jonathan (1 Sam. 20:11-17; 2 Sam. 9). The story of Mephibosheth illustrates God's grace to the redeemed sinner.

MEROM (mē'rŏm), **WATERS OF.** Copious springs situated between Lake Huleh (Semechonitis) and the Lake of Galilee. The springs lie about 10 miles west of the Jordan River in Upper Galilee at the village of Merom. The Waters of Merom flow southeastward into the Lake of Galilee. Joshua routed the Hazor confederacy there (Josh. 11:5-8).

MESHECH (mē'shĕk). A son of Japheth and progenitor of the "Mushki" of the Assyrian records of the ninth century B.C. They inhabited the regions northeast of Cilicia (Gen. 10:2; cf. Ezek. 27:13; 32: 26; 38:2; 39:1) and will participate in the great Northern Confederacy that will attack Palestine in the future.

MESHULLEMETH (mē-shŭl'ē-mĕth) ("recompensed, repaid"). The wife of King Manasseh of Judah (686-642 B.C.). She became the mother of King Amon (642-640 B.C.). The Bible states that her son "did that which was evil in the sight of the Lord, as Manasseh his father had done" (2 Kings 21:19-22). The implication is that Meshullemeth, too, was an ungodly person.

MESSIAH (mē-sī'à). The ancient custom of consecrating priests, prophets, and kings by anointing them with oil led to the description of such persons as "anointed ones" (messiahs). The promised "Seed of the woman," the virgin-born Christ (Gen. 3:15; Isa. 7:14), held the three offices of Prophet, Priest, and King and was thus the Messiah par excellence.

As the suffering Messiah our Lord experienced rejection and death at his first advent (Isa. 53; Psa. 22:1-21). At his second advent he will appear as the ruling Messiah-King and Lord supreme (Rev. 19:11-16).

METHUSELAH (mē-thū'zĕ-là) (probably "man of a javelin"). The oldest of the pre-flood patriarchs (Gen. 5:21-27).

MICAH THE EPHRAIMITE (mī'kà, ē'frà-ĭm-īt). An Israelite idolater during the time of the judges. He hired a Levite to act as priest for an image, thus linking idolatry to the ancient Levitical order in open violation of the Word of God (Judges 17, 18).

MICAH THE PROPHET. A native of Moresheth near Gath, about 20 miles southwest of Jerusalem in North Philistia (Mic. 1:1). He ministered from about 750 to 700 B.C. He espoused the cause of the poor and called for social righteousness (Mic. 6:8). He foresaw Christ's birth in Bethlehem as the coming Prince of Peace (Mic. 5:2; 4:3).

MICAIAH (mī-kā'yà) ("who is like the Lord?"). A prophet who foretold the death of Ahab at Ramoth-gilead (1 Kings 22). He ranks with all true and faithful spokesman for God.

MICHAL (mī'kāl) ("who is like God?"). The younger daughter of Saul (1 Sam. 14:49). Saul had offered Michal to David on the condition that he kill 100 Philistines. David performed the feat and received Michal as his wife (1 Sam. 18:22-27). When Michal helped David escape from Saul's plot to kill him, the unscrupulous king gave her to another man despite her marriage to David (1 Sam. 25: 44). Eventually David retrieved his wife (2 Sam. 3:12-16). Later Michal despised David as he danced before the Lord when the ark was brought up to Jerusalem. As a result she died childless (2 Sam. 6:12-23).

MICHMASH (mĭk'măsh). The location of a Philistine encampment about seven miles northeast of Jerusalem (1 Sam. 13: 1-5). Exiles from Michmash returned from the Captivity (Ezra 2:27; Neh. 7:31; Neh. 11:31). Jonathan Maccabaeus exercised judgeship there (1 Macc. 9:73). The pass still retains the name "Mukhmas."

MIDIANITES (mĭd'ĭ-àn-īts). A nomadic desert people who had descended from Abraham through Keturah (Gen. 25:1-6). It was Midianite traders (with a caravan of Ishmaelites) who bought Joseph and carried him to Egypt (Gen. 37:25-28, 36).

The Midianites joined with the Moabites in hiring Balaam to curse Israel (Num. 22—24). See also "Kenites."

MIDWIFE. Midwives are first mentioned in the Bible in the story of Jacob. They assisted Rachel (Gen. 35:16, 17) and Tamar (Gen. 38:28). The Hebrew word denotes "one who helps to bear" by cutting the umbilical cord, washing the infant, and salting and wrapping it (Ezek. 16:4). Women in childbirth customarily crouched down on a pair of stones or on a birthstool of similar design (Exod. 1:16). The process is well illustrated from ancient Egyptian sources.

MILCAH (mĭl′kȧ) ("counsel"). (1) A daughter of Haran and a sister of Lot. She became the wife of Nahor (Gen. 11:29) and the grandmother of Rebekah (Gen. 22:20-23). (2) One of the five daughters of Zelophehad (Num. 26:33; 27:1; Josh. 17:3).

MILE. See under "Weights and Measures."

MILETUS (mī-lē′tŭs). A principal seaport city of Ionia. It was founded by Ionian Greeks in the tenth century B.C. In New Testament times it was a city of the Roman province of Asia (Acts 20:15, 17; 2 Tim. 4:20). Miletus was about 36 miles south of Ephesus on the south shore of the bay of Latmus.

MILLENNIUM. The thousand-year period of Christ's royal reign on earth. It is the time during which God will fulfill all the covenants and promises which he has made to Israel. The millennium occurs after the church age and the Tribulation and prior to eternity itself.

MILLER. After threshing and winnowing, grain was either crushed in a mortar with a pestle or ground in a stone mill. This process of reducing grain to flour was usually done in the home. In large households or in a royal court like Solomon's the services of a miller were required. The miller was usually a member of the baking staff.

MILLO (mĭl′ō) (Hebrew "a fill"). Apparently a citadel or fortress at Shechem (Judg. 9:6, 20) and at Jerusalem. It existed at the time of David (2 Sam. 5:9) and was rebuilt by Solomon (1 Kings 9:15, 24; 11:27). Hezekiah strengthened it against attack by the Assyrians (2 Chron. 32:5).

Sluice gate regulates flow of mineral-laden Dead Sea for mining of potash. (© *MPS*)

MINING. Copper and iron were mined within the confines of Solomon's empire (Deut. 8:9). His extensive mining operations at Ezion-geber required large numbers of laborers for both the mining and the refining of these ores. Silver was usually mined in the form of the sulphide ore of lead (galena) but was also occasionally mined in its native state (Jer. 6:29, 30). Sources of silver and lead were Asia Minor, Southern Greece, Armenia, Persia, and the islands of the Aegean Sea. Tin alloyed with copper produced bronze. Gold was mined and used for jewelry and currency from early times. Turquoise was mined before 3000 B.C. at Magharah and Serabit el-Khadim in West Sinai. See Job 28:1-11 for a vivid description of ancient mining practices.

MINOANS (mĭ-nō′ɔns). A people on the island of Crete who attained a high degree of culture in the second millennium B.C. Their capital was at Knossos. See also "Cretans."

MINT. An herb of the genus *Mentha*, of which there are several species (Matt. 23:23). Horsemint grows wild and is the commonest species in Syria.

MIRACLE. A supernatural act in which God temporarily transcends the laws of nature in order to accomplish some special purpose.

MIRIAM ("rebellion, stubbornness"). The sister of Aaron and Moses (Exod. 15:20; Num. 26:59). Though she was gifted as a prophetess, her career was tarnished by insubordination to Moses as God's spokesman. When Moses married a Cushite woman, Miriam and Aaron used the occasion to criticize their brother's superior influence and position as God's mouthpiece. They claimed that God had spoken by them as well (Num. 12). For this serious breach of God's order Miriam was struck with leprosy. Later she was healed through Moses' intercession.

Although not actually mentioned by name, it was certainly Miriam who watched over the ark that held the infant Moses (Exod. 2:1-11). It was also Miriam who led the women of Israel in triumphal song after crossing the Red Sea (Exod. 15:20, 21). She did not enter Canaan, but died at Kadesh and was buried there (Num. 20:1).

MITHRAISM (mĭth'rṛ-ĭz'ĕm). A religion which blended worship of the Iranian sun-god, Mithras, with the Fertility Cult. It produced a mystery faith that observed a Lord's Day on Sunday and a sacrament of bread and wine. It resembled Christianity in so many ways that it was regarded by the early church as a demonic counterfeit invented to delude mankind. Mithraism was formally suppressed in the fourth century A.D. It left many monuments which were destroyed in lands which Mohammedans overran, but which remain in parts of Germany.

MIZPAH, MIZPEH (mĭz'pà). (1) Tell en-Nasbeh, eight miles north of Jerusalem (Josh. 18:26). It was an early sanctuary site (Judg. 20:1). It was later associated with Samuel (1 Sam. 7:5, 15, 16; 10:17) and was fortified by King Asa (1 Kings 15:22). It was the seat of Gedaliah's government after the fall of Jerusalem in 586 B.C. (2 Kings 25:23; Jer. 40:6-12). It was reoccupied in the post-exilic period (Neh. 3:19). Excavations reveal Asa's fortifications. (2) The place in Gilead where the pillar called Mizpeh was set up by Laban (Gen. 31:48, 49). The place also figures in the career of Jephthah (Judg. 10:17; 11:29). (3) Mizpeh in Moab (1 Sam. 22:3). It has not been located in modern times.

MIZRAIM (mĭz'rà-ĭm). The second son of Ham and the progenitor of the Egyptians and other Hamitic peoples (Gen. 10:6, 13).

MOABITES. The descendants of Lot through an incestuous union with his older daughter (Gen. 19:30-37). They occupied the territory east of the Dead Sea from the Brook Zered to the Arnon. At the time of Israel's entrance into Palestine Moab refused Israel permission to travel along the "King's Highway" which crossed the plateau (Judg. 11:17). Balak king of Moab hired Balaam to curse Israel (Num. 22–24; Josh. 24:9). In the period of the judges Eglon, king of Moab, overran part of Israel (Judg. 3:12-30). Elimelech of Bethlehem migrated to Moab and his sons married Moabite women, Orpah and Ruth. Ruth married Boaz and became the ancestress of David (Ruth 4:13-22) and of Christ (Matt. 1:5-16). Saul fought the Moabites (1 Sam. 14:47), David subdued them, and Solomon ruled them. After Solomon's death Moab broke free and remained so until subdued by Omri, as the Moabite Stone recounts.

During the reign of Jehoshaphat, Judah was invaded by a confederacy of Moabites, Ammonites, and Edomites (2 Chron. 20:1-30). Moab was tributary to Assyria and was later subdued by the Chaldeans, Persians, and various Arab groups.

MOLE. The reference in Isaiah 2:20 is not to the common mole (which does not exist in Palestine) but to the mole rat (*Spalax typhlus*), a common animal in the Holy Land. It is mole-like in appearance but is not of the same order, being a rodent. Unlike the mole, it feeds on vegetables rather than insects. It is also larger than the mole.

MOLECH, MOLOCH (mō'lĕk, mō'lŏk). A degraded deity worshiped by the Ammonites and associated with the sacrifice of children in fire. The Mosaic Law prescribed death for any Israelite who offered his child to Molech (Lev. 18:21; 20:2-5).

MONEY. See "Coins and Money."

MONEY-CHANGERS. The trade arose because money for the Temple, including the required half-shekel (Exod. 30:13), had to be in Tyrian standard coin and not in the current Roman standard (the Roman coins had pagan embellishments). An exchange surcharge was made, leading to various bad practices. The "exchangers" (Matt. 25:27) were regular bankers (*trapezitai*). A specialized class of currency exchangers had a concession in the Temple precincts, most likely in the Court of the Gentiles (Matt. 21:12; Mark 11:15; John 2:14, 15). Our Lord overthrew the counters of these dealers at the lucrative Passover season, thus cleansing the holy precincts of commercialism tainted with covetousness and materialism.

MONOTHEISM. Belief in a single Supreme Being. This was the original faith of the human race and has been held by a faithful minority throughout world history. Monotheism formed the basis of the Mosaic Covenant (Exod. 20:1-7). It repudiated all idolatry and all physical representations of Deity.

MONTH. See under "Calendar, Hebrew."

MORDECAI (from Akkadian "Marduk," the chief Babylonian deity). A Jew of the Exile who reared his uncle's daughter, Hadassah (Esther). She in turn became queen of Persia under Xerxes (486-464 B.C.). Through the queen, Mordecai saved Xerxes' life by informing him of a plot (Esth. 2:21-23). Later, when Mordecai's enemy, Haman (a court favorite), determined to murder Mordecai and exterminate all Jews in the kingdom, God used Esther and Mordecai to save them and to have Haman executed (Esth. 2 – 10).

MOREH (mō′rĕ). A hill south of Mount Tabor (Judg. 7:1) at the entrance of the northern side of the Valley of Jezreel. It is about one mile south of Nain and about eight miles northwest of Gilboa. It is present-day Jebel Dahi. In the Gideon story the Midianites encamped in the valley by the Hill of Moreh to the north of Gideon's camp (Judg. 7:1).

MORESHETH-GATH (mō′rĕsh-ĕth-gāth). The home town of Micah (1:1, 14; Jer. 26:18). ("Morasthite" means "of Moresheth."). Moresheth is identified with present-day Tell el Gudeideh, not far from Gath in Philistia.

MORIAH (mō-rī′à). One of the hills of Jerusalem on which Solomon built the Temple. It was traditionally believed to be the spot where Abraham offered his son Isaac (Gen. 22:2; cf. 2 Chron. 3:1).

MOSES. One of the greatest of all Bible heroes. He was educated in Egypt and could have attained great power and prestige there. But he chose to identify himself with God's persecuted people rather than to enjoy the pleasures of sin for a season (Exod. 2 – 5; Heb. 11:23-28). As Israel's leader he rose to his great destiny as deliverer, administrator, commander-in-chief, lawgiver, judge, author, and intermediary between God and his people. As a member of the tribe of Levi he consecrated his brother Aaron to the high priesthood and, under God's direction, constituted him the forefather of the priestly line.

Moses is a prefigurement of Christ. Both were preserved from perils in infancy (Exod. 2:2-10; Matt. 2:12-15). Both were great deliverers (Heb. 11:24-30; Matt. 1:21). Both fasted forty days (Exod. 34:28; Matt. 4:2). Both had power to control the sea (Exod. 14:21; Matt. 8:26). Both fed a multitude (Exod. 16:4-8; Matt. 14:14-21). Both were powerful intercessors (Exod. 32:11-14; John 17). Both spoke as the oracles of God (Deut. 18:15-22; John 7:46). Both left memorials (Exod. 12:14; Luke 22:19, 20). Both reappeared after death (Matt. 17:1-4; John 20: 11 – 21:25; Acts 1:3).

MOTH (Hebrew ʿash, Greek sēs). The common clothes moth, as shown by the context of the Scripture references (Job 4:19; 13:28; 27:18; Psa. 39:11; Isa. 50:9; 51:8; Hos. 5:12; Matt. 6:19, 20; Luke 12: 33; James 5:2). The larva feeds on wool (Isa. 51:8). The moth flourishes in the mild climate of Palestine.

MOTHER. The Bible emphasizes the importance of the home and of godly family life. The influence of a mother in the rearing of children is repeatedly emphasized in Scripture. Ezekiel declares the proverb "Like mother, like daughter" (Ezek. 16:44, RSV). The Decalogue obligates children to honor the mother as well as the father (Exod. 20:12). Honoring parents demonstrates obedience to the will of God and results in divine blessing, since parents stand in the place of God until their children grow to maturity (Col. 3:20; Eph. 6:1-3; Exod. 20: 12b).

Both godly and ungodly mothers figure prominently in many of the Scripture accounts. While they are often mentioned by name, mothers also frequently remain unnamed. Some of the more significant unnamed mothers of Scripture are briefly described below.

David's Mother. She was a woman who shared the dangers as well as the triumphs of her illustrious son. While David was being hunted like a wild animal by King Saul, the safety of David's parents was also seriously threatened. He and his men therefore visited the king of Moab and requested asylum for his parents. This was granted and David's parents were protected as the king's guests while they were in danger of reprisals from King Saul (1 Sam. 22:3, 4).

Ichabod's Mother. She was the wife of the undisciplined and immoral priest, Phinehas (son of Eli). She represents a mother without hope. She received word of her husband's death in battle shortly before her son was to be born. She thereupon named him "Ichabod," meaning "inglorious, no glory," in commemoration of the tragic departure of Israel's glory (the ark of the Tabernacle had been captured by the Philistines). She then died in childbirth. The incident is related in 1 Samuel 4:19-22.

Micah's Mother. She represents a religiously confused and spiritually disoriented mother, unable to guide her son in the ways of the Lord (Judg. 17:1-6). Both she and her son lived in the lawless era of the Judges, when everyone "did what was right in his own eyes" (Judg. 17:6). Her son had stolen 1100 pieces of silver from her, but had returned them out of fear for the curse which she had pronounced on the thief. She thereupon pronounced the Lord's blessing on her son and commissioned a metal-worker to convert 200 pieces of the silver into two images!

Micah then prepared a shrine for the images, complete with priest, ephod, and teraphim (household deities). Though Micah's mother is not mentioned again after this incident, her idolatry corrupted a whole tribe of Danites, who stole the images and carried them to Laish-Dan (Judg. 18:7-31).

Peter's Wife's Mother. After Jesus had cleansed a leper (Matt. 8:1-4) and healed the servant of a centurion (Matt. 8:5-13), he healed Peter's wife's mother of a fever. The Savior simply touched her hand and "the fever left her" (Matt. 8:14, 15). Luke the physician calls it a "great" or "high" fever, probably indicating acute malaria, then common in the region of Capernaum and Bethsaida.

After being healed, Simon Peter's mother-in-law "ministered unto them." The writers of all three synoptic Gospels report this remarkable detail. It is not surprising that she who owed her life and strength to Christ should be eager to serve him. She represents a great host of mothers who have become outstanding servants of the Savior after being healed by his touch.

The Mother from Shunem. Called the Shunnamite because of her residence in Shunem (near Jezreel), she is called "great" in the King James Version (2 Kings 4:8). This indicates that she was wealthy and influential. But her story shows that she was also great in faith, wisdom, and generosity. She offered hospitality to the prophet Elisha and prepared a "prophet's chamber" for him. Her generosity was rewarded by the Lord when the prophet informed her that she was to have a son.

Later, when the boy was about 12 years old, he died of apparent sunstroke after helping his father in the fields. With the poise of faith his mother hurried 16 miles to Carmel to get Elisha. He returned with her and restored the child to life.

During a very severe famine Elisha urged the woman to go to Philistia. She did so, remaining away seven years. Upon returning home she found that her house had been appropriated by others. Through Elisha's mediation it was restored to her by the king. The mother from Shunem represents the generous and faithful mother who allows God's blessings to flood her life. Her story is told in 2 Kings 4:1-37 and 8:1-6.

The Mother from Tekoa. A wise and clever woman who was engaged by David's general, Joab, to effect the recall of Absalom from his banishment. Because Absalom had murdered his half-brother, Amnon, for defiling his sister Tamar, the king had banished him to the Aramean principality of Geshur (his mother's native land). The mother from Tekoa presented herself before the king as a suppliant for mercy for one of her two sons. When the woman obtained a decision in favor of her own son, she quickly showed the king the parallel to his son Absalom. By this means she secured Absalom's recall (2 Sam. 14).

The Harlot Mothers. During Solomon's reign (971-931 B.C.) two prostitutes appeared before the king in a dispute over the possession of a child. A baby had been born to each of these women, both of whom lived in the same house. One child was smothered to death at night when the mother accidentally overlaid it. Boldly this woman took her own dead child and laid it beside the other woman, taking the living child as her own.

When the two appeared before Solomon, the king devised a clever test to reveal the true mother. He called for a sword and ordered that the living child be cut in two, with half to be given to each mother. The real mother showed her love by relinquishing her child to the other woman. The false mother, on the other hand, agreed to have the baby cut in two. In addition to illustrating the wisdom of Solomon, the story shows the triumph of motherly love over even the most severe test (1 Kings 3:16-28).

The Model Mother. Her price is "far above rubies" and her excellencies are eloquently portrayed in Proverbs 31:10-31. The preceding chapters in Proverbs sound a solemn warning against the woman who is not virtuous. But this portrait paints the ideal woman in her most glorious role of housewife and mother. She is fully trustworthy (v. 11). She does only good to her husband (v. 12). She is industrious and provident (vv. 13-19). She is considerate, kind, and generous (v. 20). She is thrifty, prosperous, strong, and happy of disposition (vv. 21-25). She is wise and kind of speech (v. 26). She is busy in doing good and is never idle (v. 27). She wins the love and respect of her husband and children (v. 28) and excels in virtue (v. 29). Her crowning grace is her fear of the Lord, which is reflected in her words and deeds (vv. 30, 31).

MOUNTAIN. A large part of the charm of Palestine and Transjordan lies in its mountains and rolling hills. The central highlands of Palestine consist of a moun-

tain range beginning at the Lebanons where peaks of over 6000 feet above sea level are found. The highest peak in Palestine is Jebel Jermaq in Upper Galilee (3962 ft.). Lower Galilee consists of a number of ridges not exceeding 2000 feet in height. The "hill country of Ephraim" is a broad limestone ridge interspersed with fertile valleys and plains. Mount Ebal (3083 ft.) and Mount Gerizim (2889 ft.), with the city of Shechem nestled between them, was the place where the coastal road and the north-south trunkline met.

The mountains of Ephraim present no marked difference from the hill country of Judah except that they are not quite as high. As they approach Jerusalem the hills decrease to an altitude of about 2600 feet; they rise again as they go south until the highest point, 3346 feet, is reached just north of Hebron. East of this central ridge between Jerusalem and Hebron is the desolate Wilderness of Judah, a wild, arid wasteland. On the west the terrain declines gently to the lowlands or "shephelah." This area was important for both agriculture and defense. Such fort towns as Lachish, Debir, Libnah, Azekah, and Beth-shemesh guarded the interior territories. To the south the hills descend gently to the semi-arid *negeb* or southland between Beer-sheba and Kadesh Barnea.

The eastern hills of Transjordan form a plateau or tableland cut by four rivers: the Yarmuk, the Jabbok, the Arnon, and the Zered. Because of its elevation this region receives considerable rainfall and is thus fertile and agriculturally productive. But the rainfall decreases eastward as the terrain changes rapidly from steppe to desert. Mountains reach to 3900 feet in Gilead and rise nearly as high in Ammon and Moab.

Other important mountains in Bible lands are those of the Sinai Peninsula. Mount Sinai is located here, as well as other peaks up to 8600 feet in elevation. Other lofty mountain ranges include the Taurus range of Asia Minor (with peaks of over 12,000 feet), the Mountains of Armenia (where Noah's Ark rested), and the Zagros Mountains east of Mesopotamia. The Pindus Mountains of central

Looking from the ruins of Jericho to traditional Mount of Temptation *(Russ Busby photo)*

Greece and the Apennines of Central Italy are also significant.

MOURNING RITES. Acts of lamentation included weeping, wailing, tearing of garments, gashing the body, wearing sackcloth, heaping dust or ashes on the head, sitting in an ash heap, and playing dirges on musical instruments (cf. Jer. 16:6-8; 2 Sam. 1:11, 12; 13:31; 14:2; Ezek. 7:18; Amos 8:10). See also under "Funerals, Jewish."

MULE (Hebrew *pered*). The mule is a crossbreed between the horse and the ass (1 Kings 18:5). It is frequently mentioned with horses (Psa. 32:9). It became popular for riding and transportation (2 Sam. 13:29; 2 Kings 5:17). It was well known from David's time onward. Mules were obtained from Armenia by the Tyrians (Ezek. 27:14).

MUSIC AND MUSICAL INSTRUMENTS. Though music did not attain the level of development in Israel which it attained elsewhere, especially among the Greeks, its importance was nevertheless great in both the social and religious life of the Israelites. To Jubal is ascribed the invention of music (Gen. 4:21), while his brother Jabal is said to be the ancestor of shepherds. Shepherds have always been fond of music. David was famous as a skilled lyrist. In Greek mythology Pan, the patron of shepherds, was credited with inventing the flute.

Music was popular and indispensable at public feasts and family festivities. Singing and dancing brightened every festive occasion (Gen. 31:27; Judg. 11:34). Singing men and women and skilled instrumentalists graced every royal court and every home of the great (2 Sam. 19:35; Amos 8:3), as shown by tomb paintings and archeological remains. Singing to the accompaniment of lyre and tambourine was an intrinsic part of feasting (Job 21:12). Such festivities sometimes led to drunkenness and immorality (Isa. 5:12; Amos 6:5, 6).

Music also played a prominent role in times of mourning. It may have originally been intended to drive away evil spirits. David's lyre-playing relieved Saul of demonic pressure (1 Sam. 16:23).

Music played a dominant role in the worship of the Lord. Israelites knew how to sing to God and praise him in song and dance. As newly freed slaves from Egypt they worshiped God with a full array of musical instruments (Exod. 15:20). The subsequent history is repeatedly highlighted by joyful music in the worship of the Lord (2 Sam. 6:5; Psa. 150:1-6).

The musical instruments of the Bible are somewhat better known today than when the King James Version was translated, though precise knowledge of the various instruments is still somewhat scant despite the contributions of modern archeological research.

The instruments mentioned in the Bible can be divided into three main groups: strings, wind, and percussion.
Strings: *harp, psaltery, sackbut.*
Wind: *clarinet, flute, horn, trumpet.*
Percussion: *bells, cymbals, gong, sistrum, timbrel.*

These instruments are listed and described in alphabetical order below.
Bells. Two types are mentioned. One type is literally "strikers," from the Hebrew root "to strike." It was fastened to the hem of the high priest's robe (Exod. 28: 33; 39:25, 26). These bells apparently had no clappers, but produced a pleasant sound simply by striking against each

other at every movement of the high priest. The other type, literally "jingle bells" (from a Hebrew root meaning "to rattle, to jingle"), were used as ornaments or amulets on horses (Zech. 14:20). These produced both melody and rhythm.

Clarinet (from Hebrew *ḥālal*, "to pierce"). This was an actual reed woodwind (not merely a pipe or flute). It was the most popular of the woodwinds in the ancient Near East (1 Sam. 10:5; Isa. 5:12; 30:29; Jer. 48:36). Its Greek counterpart is mentioned in Matthew 9:23 and 11:17, Luke 7:32, 1 Corinthians 14:7, and Revelation 18:22. It was practically identical with the Greek *aulos* (1 Cor. 14:7). Long before Israel's existence the double clarinet is mentioned in Akkadian tablets; many ancient representations of this instrument have been found.

Cymbals. In certain ritual and priestly functions two round metal plates were clashed together (1 Chron. 13:8; 15:19; 16:5, 42; 2 Chron. 5:12, 13; 29:25; Ezra 3:10; Neh. 12:27). Another type of cymbal consisted of two cups, one held stationery in the hand and the other brought down upon it (2 Sam. 6:5; Psa. 150:5).

Flute. This is the King James translation of the Aramaic word *mashrōqitha* (Dan. 3:5). It is derived from the root *shāraq*, meaning "to hiss" or "to whistle." The word describes the hissing sound characteristic of pipe or flute music. The instrument mentioned in Daniel 3:5 is probably of this general type.

Gong. A bronze gong was commonly used at weddings and other joyous occasions. It was the "sounding brass" of 1 Corinthians 13:1. In its smaller form it appeared as a kind of handbell.

Harp. The *kinnor* (usually translated "harp" in the King James Version) is the first musical instrument mentioned in the Bible (Gen. 4:21). It is used in this passage as a general description for all stringed instruments. When used in other passages it is uncertain whether the word denotes the simple lyre (which has a sounding box under the upper part of the strings) or an actual harp. (A harp is triangular, is held upright, and usually has at least nine strings. The lyre usually had only five to eight strings).

Ancient Egyptian tomb paintings represent foreigners playing lyres with plectrum in their hands. Elaborate ten-stringed harps were also depicted on tomb paintings.

Horn (Hebrew *shōphār*, from Akkadian *shapparu*, "wild ibex"). The ram's horn (Josh. 6:4, 8, 13) was the Jewish signaling instrument par excellence. It sounded all signals in both war and peace. It announced the new moon, the beginning of the sabbath, the death of a notable, and many other events. In its strictly ritual usage it carried the cry of the people to God. At special occasions God or his angels also sound the *shōphār* (Isa. 27:13; Zech. 9:14; Rev. 8:2, 6, 12; 9:1, 13). It was not so much a true musical instrument as a signaling device.

The *yobēl* (Exod. 19:13) was also a ram's horn used for signaling. Its special function was to announce the beginning of the Year of Jubilee (Lev. 25:9-17).

Psaltery (Hebrew *nēbel*). A stringed instrument, either a portable harp, lute, or guitar with a bulging resonance body at the lower end (1 Sam. 10:5; Psa. 71:22; Isa. 14:11; Amos 5:23; 2 Chron. 5:12; Neh. 12:27). The cithara, harp, lyre, and psaltery were all very similar stringed instruments. It is no longer possible to differentiate between them clearly in every Scripture reference.

Sackbut (Aramaic *sabbekâ*). A stringed instrument of uncertain appearance. It may have been a large, many-stringed harp. (The word incorrectly translated "sackbut" in the King James Version was a trombone-like wind instrument.)

Sistrum. A small, hand-held noisemaker which was fitted with metal pieces that rattled when it was shaken. The oldest sistrums were found at Ur, Kish, and other early sites. It came to Palestine and Egypt from Mesopotamia. The only biblical mention of this is in 2 Samuel 6:5, where it is incorrectly translated "cornet" in the King James Version.

Timbrel (Hebrew *toph*). A percussion instrument known from remote antiquity. It was a type of tambourine and was generally played by women as an accompaniment to songs and dances at festivals. It is mentioned frequently in the Old Testament, both alone and with other instruments (Gen. 31:27; Exod. 15:

20; Judg. 11:34; 1 Sam. 10:5; 18:6; Job 21:12; Isa. 5:12; Jer. 31:4). It was sometimes used in religious services (Psa. 68:25; 81:2; 149:3; 150:4).

Trumpet (Hebrew *ḥaṣoṣerâ,* from a root meaning "to shatter"). A priestly instrument par excellence. Its function was almost the same as that of the horn (*shophar*). Trumpets were employed in pairs (Num. 10:1-10) and were made of silver and other metals. The question of whether the pitch of the trumpet could be standardized so that groups of trumpeters could play simultaneously (as in 2 Chronicles 5:12) has been settled by the Dead Sea Scrolls. The Scroll of the War of the Sons of Light and the Sons of Darkness assigns numerous complicated signals in unison. Trumpets were used to terrorize an enemy (Judg. 7:19, 20) and to introduce rituals and sacrifices.

MUSTARD. The plant whose seed was used by Christ as an illustration of something which develops rapidly from small beginnings, such as the kingdom of heaven (Matt. 13:31, 32; Mark 4:31, 32; Luke 13:19) or the faith of a person (Matt. 17:20; Luke 17:6). Some equate the plant with the black mustard (*Sinapis nigra*), since in New Testament times its seeds were cultivated for their oil and for culinary purposes. Others identify it with white mustard (*Sinapis alba*). Though both varieties have reportedly attained a height of 15 feet, they normally do not exceed four feet at maturity.

MUTILATION. Religious frenzy in demon-oriented pagan religions often caused the priests and devotees to gash themselves with knives (1 Kings 18:28) and to otherwise mutilate themselves.

MYCENAE. A prominent city of Bronze Age Greece. It is known for its tombs of Achaean kings. The site gives its name to "Mycenaean" civilization, which spread over the Aegean region after the fall of the empire of the Minoans and reached as far as Rhodes and Asia Minor.

MYRA (mī′rȧ). A seaport of Lycia (Acts 27:5), Myra was a province of southwestern Asia Minor bordered on the north by Caria and Pisidia and on the east by Pamphylia. On his voyage to Rome, Paul landed at Myra and subsequently took an Alexandrian freighter bound for Italy.

MYRRH (Hebrew *mōr,* Akkadian *murru*). The resin exuded from the stems and branches of a low, shrubby tree, either the *Commiphora myrrha* or the closely related *Commiphora kataf*. The gum hardens to form an oily, yellowish-brown resin as it exudes from the shrub. Myrrh was an ingredient of the sacred anointing oil (Exod. 30:23-33). It was used in cosmetics and perfumery, being highly valued for its aromatic qualities (Psa. 45:8; Prov. 7:17; Song 3:6; 4:14; 5:5, 13). It was presented by the Magi as a present to the infant Jesus (Matt. 2:11) and was mixed with the wine which was offered to Christ on the Cross (Mark 15:23). It was also one of the spices employed at his burial (John 19:39). The myrrh carried by the Ishmaelites to Egypt was apparently the resin of the *Cistus villosus,* commercial ladanum (Gen. 37:25; 43:11).

MYRTLE TREE (Hebrew *hadas*). A beautiful Palestinian evergreen with fragrant leaves and scented white flowers. It attains a height of about 30 feet. The tree flourished in mountain glens (Zech. 1:8-11). Booths were made of its branches at the Feast of Tabernacles (Neh. 8:15). It symbolizes the Israelite nation preserved through humiliation and suffering for future kingdom glory (Zech. 1:8-11; cf. Isa. 41:19; 55:13). The tree still adorns the hills of Palestine.

MYSTERIES. (1) Secrets of the ancient cults of Babylon and Rome. (2) Any work or purpose of God which was revealed for the first time in the New Testament Canon. Instead of consisting of secrets to be withheld, New Testament mysteries are wonderful truths to be revealed to believers (1 Cor. 4:1). Before the New Testament was established in permanent written form, the temporary spiritual gifts of direct inspirational prophecies, knowledge, and languages (1 Cor. 13:8-13) operated in the apostolic church in order to enable believers to receive these truths in public services (1 Cor. 13:2). As the written New Testament began to be circulated among the churches these mysteries became available through biblical study and exposition. The temporary gifts were then superseded by the completed New Testament canon, the "completed thing" of 1 Corinthians 13:10.

N

NAAMAH (nā′ȧ-mȧ) ("sweet, pleasant"). (1) A daughter of Lamech and a sister of Tubal-cain (Gen. 4:22). She is the first daughter cited by name in the Bible. Her brother was the originator of the ancient craft of metalworking. (2) One of Solomon's 700 wives. She was an Ammonite woman and became the mother of Rehoboam, Solomon's successor on the throne of Israel (1 Kings 14:21, 31; 2 Chron. 12:13). As an Ammonite princess born of Israel's inveterate enemies, Naamah was a corrupting force. Solomon built for her a high place for the worship of her national god, Molech. Her son Rehoboam's life and death was a monument to his father's sin and folly and a reflection of his mother's hatred for the true God of Israel.

NAAMAN (nā′ȧ-măn) ("pleasant"). A captain in the army of Benhadad, king of Damascus. He was cured of leprosy by Elisha the prophet (2 Kings 5).

NABAL (nā′bȧl) ("foolish"). A wealthy but churlish sheepmaster. He was as foolish as his name implied (1 Sam. 25:1-43). He was temporarily saved from death (for refusing to help David in a time of distress) by his beautiful wife. But God subsequently struck Nabal dead, and his widow became a wife of David (25:39-42).

NABATEANS (năb′ȧ-tē′ȧnz). An Arab people apparently descended from Ishmael and Edom (Gen. 25:13; 29:9). Their capital was at Petra. From the time of their first known king, Aretus I (170 B.C.), they became influential through the control of trade routes from India and China across Arabia. They brought silks, spices, and other luxuries to the Greco-Roman world. The Nabateans developed not only commerce but agriculture and the arts as well. They were a remarkably gifted people and had good relations with the Jews in the period of the Hasmoneans and Herodians. Several of their kings with the dynastic name of Haretath (Aretas) came in contact with biblical history. Aretas IV was the father-in-law of Herod Antipas. He attempted to seize Paul at Damascus (2 Cor. 11:32).

NABONIDUS (năb′ō-nī′dŭs) (Akkadian *Nabunaᶜid*, "the god Nabu is exalted"). The last king of the Neo-Babylonian Empire (556-539 B.C.), whose son Belshazzar (Dan. 5) was co-regent from the third year of his reign to the fall of the city in 539 B.C.

NABOPOLASSAR (năb′ō-pō-lăs′ȧr) (Akkadian, "Nabu protect the son"). The king of Babylon from 625 to 605 B.C. He created the Neo-Babylonian Empire upon the ruins of the Assyrian Empire. He was the father of Nebuchadnezzar.

NABOTH (nā′bŏth) (from the Arabic *nabata*, "grow, sprout"). The man whom Jezebel arranged to have murdered in order to obtain his vineyard (1 Kings 21:1-14).

NADAB (nā′dăb) ("liberal"). A son of Aaron who, with his brother Abihu, was slain by the Lord for offering priestly sacrifices in an unauthorized manner (Lev. 10:1, 2).

NAHUM (nā'hŭm) ("consolation, comfort"). A Hebrew prophet (c. 620 B.C.) who predicted the fall of Nineveh and the Assyrian Empire.

NAIN (nā'ĭn). A town where Jesus raised a widow's son to life (Luke 7:11-15). It is still called Nein and is located in the northwest corner of the eminence called Little Hermon. Nein is about two miles west-southwest of Endor and five miles south-southeast of Nazareth.

NAMES. Bible names frequently have a significant meaning and often carry a character designation, as in the case of Jacob (Gen. 27:36). The various names of deity describe God's character. To believe on Christ's name means to trust him as Redeemer-Savior. Works done "in his name" are accomplished directly by his power (Acts 16:18; cf. Luke 24:47). Prayer "in Christ's name" identifies the petitioner with him, so that the petition is as effective as though Christ himself had made the request (John 14:14; 16:23; cf. Rom. 10:13).

NAOMI (nā'ô-mī; nà-ō'mī) ("my pleasantness"). An Israelite woman who emigrated to Moab with her husband, Elimelech, because of famine. There their two sons, Mahlon and Chilion, took wives. But Elimelech and the two sons died in Moab, leaving three widows. Ruth, one of the daughters-in-law, elected to go back to Bethlehem with Naomi, but Orpah, the other daughter-in-law, chose to remain in Moab.

Back in Bethlehem, Naomi introduced Ruth to Boaz, her kinsman, and a levirate marriage between the two was consummated. Ruth beautifully portrays the believing remnant of the nation Israel, which will ultimately come in touch with the mighty Kinsman-Redeemer. Through him they will inherit the kingdom blessings. Naomi pictures the nation Israel in her sorrows outside the land and her ultimate restoration to the land through the believing remnant of the last days (cf. Isa. 10:21, 22; Mic. 4:7). Little wonder that Ruth became, through Boaz's child Obed, the ancestress of both David and David's Lord, the divine Kinsman-Redeemer (Ruth 4:17-22).

NAPHTALI (năf'tà-lī) ("my wrestling"). A son of Jacob and the progenitor of an Israelite tribe (Gen. 30:8; Gen. 46:24).

NATHAN (nā'thăn) ("he has given"). A prophet in the time of David and Solomon. He confronted David with his scandalous sin (2 Sam. 12:1-14). Nathan wrote a history of the period (1 Chron. 29:29).

NAZARETH (năz'à-rĕth). A Galilean town situated in a high valley among the most southerly limestone hills of the Lebanon range. To the south is a magnificent view and a sharp descent to the Plain of Esdraelon. The village of Nazareth was Christ's home for about 30 years (Luke 2:39; 4:16).

NAZARITE, NAZIRITE (năz'à-rīt; năz'ĭ-rīt) ("dedicated, separated"). A designation given to an Israelite who vowed special consecration to the Lord. Abstinence from wine (a symbol of natural joy—Psa. 104:15) symbolized the Nazarite's joy in the Lord alone (cf. Psa. 97:12; Hab. 3:18; Phil. 3:1; 4:4, 10). Long hair, naturally a reproach to man (1 Cor. 11:14), symbolized the Nazarite's willingness to bear reproach for the Lord.

The Nazarite symbolism was perfectly fulfilled in Christ, who was "holy, harmless, undefiled, and separate from sinners" (Heb. 7:26). He was completely separated to the Father (John 1:18; 6:38). He allowed no mere natural claim to direct him from God's will (Matt. 12:46-50; John 2:2-4).

NEAPOLIS (nē-ăp'ō-lĭs) (in Italy). Naples, near Pompeii on the bay of Naples (on the west-central coast of Italy).

NEAPOLIS (in Macedonia). The port of Philippi, which lay on Paul's route during his second missionary tour (Acts 16:11).

NEAPOLIS (in Palestine). The site of ancient Nablus (near Shechem). In the Roman period the city was called Colonia Julia Neapolis.

NEBO (nē'bō). (1) The mountain in the range of Abarim from which Moses viewed the promised land (Num. 27:12; Deut. 32:49; 34:1). Christian tradition identifies it with Jebel en-Neba (2,630 ft.) 17 miles east of the northern end of the Dead Sea. However, some scholars prefer Jebel Osha, a considerably higher mountain (3,303 ft.) which is farther to the north, overlooking Jericho. This site would better fit the description in Deuteronomy 34:1, 2. The mountain was named from the Babylonian god Nabu. (2) The Babylonian deity Nabu, son of Bel (Marduk). He symbolized the national power of Babylon (Isa. 46:1). He was considered the god of learning—writing, astronomy, and all science. A temple, Ezida ("the House of Knowledge"), was dedicated to him in each of the larger cities of Babylonia and Assyria.

NEBUCHADNEZZAR (nĕb'ů-kàd-nĕz'ĕr) (Akkadian *Nebuchadrezzar*, "Nabu defend the boundary"). The king of Babylon from 605 to 562 B.C. He was used by God as an instrument to chastise his disobedient people. He inaugurated "the times of the Gentiles" (Luke 21:24; cf. Dan. 4:34-37; Rev. 11:15-17). Nebuchadnezzar was one of the greatest builders and rulers of ancient times (cf. Dan. 4:29, 30).

NECHO II (nē'kō). The second ruler of Egypt's twenty-sixth dynasty. He reigned from 609 to 593 B.C. He slew Josiah of Judah at Megiddo in 608 B.C. He set Jehoiakim on the throne of Judah (2 Kings 23:29-34). He was completely routed from Asia by Nebuchadnezzar.

NECKLACE. Neck-pendants (Song 4:9; cf. Judg. 8:26; Prov. 1:9) were common in the ancient Near-Eastern world of antiquity. The tombs of Egypt and the excavated sites of Babylonia and Assyria have yielded necklaces of fine workmanship and beauty.

NEHEMIAH (nē'hĕ-mī'à) ("the Lord has comforted"). The cup-bearer of the king of Persia at Shushan (Susa). He obtained royal permission and help to rebuild the walls of Jerusalem. He was both a soldier and a statesman. As the governor of Jerusalem he overcame all types of difficulties in the completion of his patriotic task (see the Book of Nehemiah).

NEHUSHTA (nĕ-hŭsh'tà) ("of bronze"). The wife of King Jehoiakim (609-598 B.C.) and the mother of King Jehoiachin (598-597 B.C.—2 Kings 24:8). She was taken prisoner with her son when the Babylonians took possession of Jerusalem in 597 B.C. and was carried away with other leading citizens to Babylon (2 Kings 24:12-15). Nehushta suffered severely in these terrible times. She saw her

wicked husband revolt against the Babylonians and perish in disgrace (Dec. 6, 598 B.C.). Her son Jehoiachin ruled only three months and ten days. His evil reign is described in 2 Kings 24:8, 9 and 2 Chronicles 36:9, 10. Jeremiah predicted the end of his rule and dynasty (Jer. 22: 24-30).

Evidently Nehushta and her son were treated as royal hostages in Babylon, for he is named in Babylonian tablets as receiving rations with his five sons. Nebuchadnezzar's successor in 561 B.C. transferred Jehoiachin from prison to the royal palace (2 Kings 25:27-30; Jer. 52:31-34). Whether Nehushta was still living and shared this good fortune is not known.

NERO (nē'rō). The Roman Emperor from A.D. 54 to 68. He was a monster of iniquity. He accused Christians of setting the great fire in Rome in A.D. 54 and had them tortured and killed. Doubtless Paul and perhaps Peter met death under him. When the Jewish Revolt broke out in Judea, Nero dispatched Vespasian to quell it. While the war raged, he was forced from the throne and committed suicide.

NETHINIM (nĕth'ĭ-nĭm). The name means "those who are given." David and the princes had given these people for the service of the Levites (Ezra 8:20). They are called "temple slaves" in 1 Esdras 5: 29 and Josephus (*Antiquities* XI:5, 1).

NETTLE. A number of related weeds with stinging hairs (Job 30:7). This weed overspreads the sluggard's unworked garden (Prov. 24:31) and an untilled countryside (Zeph. 2:9). The plant is not further identified. The Roman pill nettle (*Urtica pilulifera*) is common in Palestine. It is referred to in Isaiah 34:13 and Hosea 9:6. See also Proverbs 24:31, where a modification of the word in the plural is rendered "thorns."

NEW COVENANT. Secured in Christ's blood, this covenant guarantees the personal revelation of the Lord to every believer (Heb. 8:11) and the complete removal of sins (Heb. 8:12; 10:17). It rests on an accomplished redemption (Matt. 26:27, 28; 1 Cor. 11:25). It assures the perpetuity, future conversion, and kingdom blessing of a repentant Israel, with whom the new covenant will also someday be ratified (Jer. 31:31-34; Heb. 10:9).

NEW JERUSALEM. The eternal residence and destiny of the redeemed of all ages (Rev. 21:9 – 22:5). The city will be part of the new heaven and new earth (Rev. 21:1, 2) in the sin-cleansed universe.

NICODEMUS (nĭk'ṓ-dē'mŭs) ("victor over the people"). A Pharisee and Jewish teacher who came to Jesus by night and was instructed in the necessity of experiencing the new birth (John 3:1-21). Nicodemus must have experienced this new birth, for he later spoke for Christ (John 7:45-52) and honored him (John 19:39, 40).

NICOLAITANS (nĭk'ṓ-lā'ĭ-tănz). A religious sect that lived licentiously while professing to be Christians (Rev. 2:6, 15). They apparently advocated pagan sexual laxity. References in Irenaeus, Clement, and Tertullian trace this heretical group as far back as A.D. 200.

NICOPOLIS (nĭ-kŏp'ṓ-lĭs). A city on the southwestern tip of Epirus (northwest of Achaia). It was founded by Augustus in 31 B.C. to commemorate his victory at nearby Actium. Paul hoped to winter there when he penned the Epistle to Titus (Tit. 3:12).

NIGHT HAWK (Hebrew *tahmās*). An unidentified bird listed as unclean (Lev. 11.16; Deut. 14:15). Though most English versions render it "night hawk," the bird is better known as the night jar or goatsucker (*Caprimulgus europaeus*). The Septuagint and Vulgate identify the Hebrew word with the owl.

The Nile River in Old Cairo, an area familiar to Joseph (© *MPS*)

NILE (nīl). The longest and most navigable river in Bible lands, a 4000-mile waterway to the heart of Africa. It was called "the Nile" by the Greek and Romans. This life-giving stream with its annual inundation was the life of Egypt and made possible a mighty nation in the heart of a scorching desert. In it Moses was hid in a papyrus boat (Exod. 2:3). The Hebrews referred to the river as *Yeor*, which in the plural refers to the Nile River system (Isa. 7:18).

NIMROD (nĭm'rŏd) (from the Hebrew root *marad*, "to rebel"). An ancient Hamitic ruler and the founder of imperial power in Babylonia (Gen. 10:8, 9). This power is intimated to be evil in the sense of rebellion against God.

NINEVEH (nĭn'ĕ-vĕ). The ancient capital of the Assyrian Empire (Gen. 10:11; 2 Kings 19:36; Jonah 1:2; Nah. 1:1). It was situated on the Upper Tigris River above the Great Zab tributary. It is represented by the tells (mounds) of Quyunjik and Nabi Yunus. In its heyday it embraced a great metropolitan area including Calah (Nimrud) and Dur-Sharrukin (Khorsabad). The "three days' journey" of Jonah 3:3 probably refers to the whole administrative district, which was about 30 to 60 miles across (Hatra-Khorsabad-Nimrud). The city was destroyed by the Babylonians and Medes in 612 B.C. (cf. Nah. 2:8; 3:7; Zeph. 2:13) and was lost in oblivion until resurrected by modern archeology.

NIPPUR. A religious and cultural center of Sumer from about 4000 B.C. It has yielded much information to the excavator. It is present-day Nuffar, southeast of Babylon, between Kish and Isin.

NO. The capital of Upper and Lower Egypt in the Middle Kingdom and under the Eighteenth Dynasty. It is 330 miles upstream from Cairo. Its site on the two banks of the Nile is marked on the eastern side by two vast temple-precincts of the god Amun, now known by the Arabic names Karnak and Luxor. The western side is marked by a row of royal funerary temples from modern Qurneh to Medinet Habu. Behind this extends a vest necropolis of rock-cut tombs. Ashurbanipal of Assyria sacked Thebes in 663 B.C. (Nah. 3:8). But the city still remained important (Jer. 46:25; Ezek. 30:14-16). It was finally destroyed completely by the Roman prefect Gallus, in 30 and 29 B.C.

NOAH (nō′à) ("rest"). (1) The man who, with his wife and his sons and his sons' wives, was saved out of the deluge to begin life anew on a cleansed earth (Gen. 6—9). The biblical account of the Flood finds remarkable parallels in Sumerian and Babylonian cuneiform accounts of the same event. (2) One of the five daughters of Zelophehad who asked for and received an inheritance even though their father was deceased and they had no brothers (Num. 26:33; 27:1-11; 36:10-12; Josh. 17:3-6).

NOB (nōb). A priestly city in Benjamin (1 Sam. 21:1; 22:9; Isa. 10:32). It is identified with et-Tor, a few miles east-northeast of Jerusalem.

NOPH (nŏf). See "Memphis."

NOSE RING. A woman's ornament commonly worn on the nose (Gen. 24:22, 30, 47, RSV). Proverbs 11:22 speaks of a "ring in a swine's snout" (cf. Hos. 2:13, RSV; Ezek. 16:12).

NUMBERS. The numbers of Scripture undoubtedly possess spiritual significance.

One denotes unity—one Lord, one faith, etc. (Deut. 6:4; Eph. 4:3-6). It is the unity between Christ and the Father (John 10:30), the union between believers and the Godhead (John 17:20, 21), the oneness existing among Christians (Gal. 3:28), and the union of man and woman in marriage (Matt. 19:6).

Two prefigures both unity and diversity. Man and woman comprise the basic family unit (Gen. 1:27; 2:20-24). Animals entered the ark two-by-two (Gen. 7:9). Two people can work together in companionship (e.g. Joshua's two spies and the two witnesses of Revelation 11:3-12). The Twelve and the Seventy were sent out two-by-two (Mark 6:7; Luke 10:1). The Law was given on two tablets. Sometimes the number two designates opposing forces (1 Kings 18:21; Matt. 7: 13, 14).

Three relates to the perfection of God in the Trinity (Matt. 28:19), the three heavens (2 Cor. 12:2), and God's mighty acts (Exod. 19:11; Hos. 6:2; Jonah 1:17; Matt. 12:40; 1 Cor. 15:4).

Four speaks of the earth and creative works. The name "Jehovah," which has only four letters in its original form (YHWH), connects God redemptively with man and the earth. There are four quarters or "corners" of the earth (Rev. 7:1; 20:8), as well as four winds (Jer. 49:36; Ezek. 37:9; Dan. 7:2). The number four is prominent in prophetic symbolism about the earth and its judgments (Zech. 1:18-21; 6:1-8; Rev. 9:13). Four major kingdoms constitute world history from Nebuchadnezzar (605 B.C.) till the second advent of Christ (cf. Dan. 2 and 7).

Five as a divisor of ten denotes a portion of a complete unit. The ten virgins represent the nation Israel before Christ's advent in glory (Matt. 25:1). The five wise virgins symbolize the believing remnant while the five foolish ones represent the unbelieving segment.

Six is the number of man. He was created on the sixth and final day of creation (Gen. 1:27); six days constitute his work week (Exod. 20:9; 23:12; 31:15); 666 denotes man's complete rebellion against God (Rev. 13:18).

Seven denotes fullness or completion (not perfection per se). The seventh or sabbath day marked God's rest upon completion of creation (Gen. 2:2, 3; Exod. 20:10). Compare the seventh year (Lev. 25:2-6) and the Jubilee year, which follows seven times seven years (Lev. 25: 8). The Feast of Unleavened Bread and the Feast of Tabernacles each lasted seven days (Exod. 12:15, 19; Num. 29:12). The latter foreshadowed Israel's kingdom rest and the completion of the divine economies in time, before the advent of eternity. The Day of Atonement, prefiguring completed redemption, fell in the seventh month (Lev. 16:29). Seven is prominent in Old Testament ritual (Lev. 4:6; 14:7; Num. 28:11; cf. 2 Kings 5:10). The Tabernacle candlestick had seven flames (a stem and six branches), symbolizing Christ as the full light of God (Exod. 25:32).

Eight appears to denote resurrection (Matt. 28:1) and the spiritual power released in the putting off of the flesh by circumcision (Gen. 17:1, 12; Phil. 3:5; Col. 2:10-13). It looks forward to the eternal state, as typified by the eighth day which ends the Feast of Tabernacles

(Lev. 23:39).

Nine (three times three) suggests perfection and completeness that looks forward to God as all in all in the eternal state. The basis of this is the death of Christ that occurred at the ninth hour (Mark 15:34).

Ten, the sum of seven and three, indicates completeness. Ten pre-flood patriarchs represent the complete messianic line. The 10 Egyptian plagues embrace the full divine judgment against the gods of Egypt. The Ten Commandments reflect the complete moral law of God required of Israel. The 10 virgins represent the entire nation Israel at Christ's coming (Matt. 25:1-10). Ten powers which cannot separate the believer from God's love (Rom. 8:38, 39) stand for *all* powers.

Eleven (twelve minus one) signifies a missing of God's elective purpose (Acts 1:26).

Twelve, like three, seven, and ten, is a number of completeness and is connected with the elective purposes of God—for example, the 12 tribes of Israel and the 12 Apostles (Gen. 49:28; Matt. 10:1). The Hebrew year was divided into 12 months and the day into 12 hours (John 11:9).

NUTS. Pistachio nuts (Hebrew *botnim*) are referred to in Genesis 43:11. They were not grown in Egypt and thus constituted an acceptable gift to Joseph (they were considered a delicacy in the land of the Nile). The pistachio is native to western Asia but was introduced into southern Europe and Palestine. It is no longer common in Bible lands. The nut referred to in Song of Solomon 6:11 is apparently the walnut (*Juglans regia*), referred to in the United States as the English walnut. It is cultivated in Galilee and along the slopes of Mount Lebanon and Mount Hermon.

OAK (Hebrew *'alla, 'allōn, 'ēla*). These three common Hebrew words designate only a few of the many species of the genus *Quercus* found in Palestine. The oak is a sturdy hardwood tree which lives to a great age. Its fruit is the acorn. Some Palestinian species are evergreen while others are deciduous. Bashan, the fertile region north of Gilead in Transjordan, was famous for its oaks (Isa. 2:13; Ezek. 27:6; Zech. 11:2). Absalom was caught in an oak (2 Sam. 18:9, 10). Dead people were frequently buried under an oak (Gen. 35:8).

OATH. A solemn adjuration employed to ratify an assertion and usually sealed by appeal to divine authority (cf. Heb. 6:16). Swearing in biblical times took the following common forms: (1) placing the hand under the thigh of the person to whom the promise was made (Gen. 24:2; 47:29); (2) dividing a slain animal and distributing the pieces (Gen. 15:10, 17; Jer. 34:18); (3) lifting up the hand or placing the hand on the head of the accused (Gen. 14:22; Lev. 24:14; Deut. 17:7); and (4) standing before the altar or (if distant from Jerusalem) positioning oneself toward the Temple (1 Kings 8:31; 2 Chron. 6:22). The sanctity of the oath was protected by the Law. The crime of perjury was very severe (Exod. 20:7; Lev. 19:12).

OBADIAH (ō′bà-dī′à) ("servant of the Lord"). One of the Hebrew prophets who foretold Edom's destruction.

OFFICER. (1) *Old Testament usage.* The Hebrew word *shoter* signifies "one who writes or records." Officers apparently acted as overseers over the people (Prov. 6:7). At the same time they functioned as assistants or recorders, helping those under whom they served. It was such foremen who supervised the enslaved Israelites in Egypt and monitored the number of bricks they made. This type of supervisory function is abundantly illustrated in Egyptian records from the Mosaic era and earlier. It is therefore not surprising that officers were appointed alongside judges in the Mosaic Law (Deut. 16:18) and held prominent positions in subsequent Israelite history (Josh. 1:10; 8:33; 1 Chron. 26:29, 30; 2 Chron. 19:11; 26:11; 34:13). (2) *New Testament usage.* Luke refers to a police "officer" or bailiff (Greek *praktor* — Luke 12:58) whose duty it was, after sentence was passed, to collect debts under orders from the judge. The term in classical Greek denoted tax collectors and other officials of finance.

Other minor officers or servants (Greek *huperetēs*) are frequently referred to in the New Testament. John Mark was such an assistant or helper of Paul and Barnabas (Acts 13:5). Such assistants (RSV, "guards") performed duties for a board or court, such as the Sanhedrin (Matt. 5:25; 26:58; Mark 14:54; John 7:32; 19:6; Acts 5:22). Synagogue attendants belonged to this category (Luke 4:20). The apostles were such servants of Christ (Acts 26:16; 1 Cor. 4:1).

OG (ŏg). A king of the Amorites of Bashan (Deut. 3:1, 8). His rule extended from the River Jabbok to Mount Hermon (Deut. 3:8; Num. 21:23, 24). He was conquered by the invading Israelites (Num. 21:32-35; Deut. 3:14) and his territory was allotted to the half-tribes of Manasseh (Deut. 3:13).

OIL TREE. Some identify this tree with the oleaster (*Elaeagnus angustifolia*), a shrub common in Palestine. It yields an inferior oil and a small fruit. But it is difficult to see how a mere shrub like the oleaster could furnish wood of large enough dimensions to construct the cherubim (1 Kings 6:23, 26), the doors of the oracle, and the door posts for the Temple entrance (1 Kings 6:31-33). The oil tree may well be the Aleppo pine (*Pinus halepensis*). It is called "oil tree" because of the tar and turpentine obtained from it.

OLEANDER (*Apocynaceae*). A beautiful evergreen tree with pink or white blossoms. It was enjoyed by Palestinians in both biblical and modern times. It is a stream-loving tree that keeps a ribbon of refreshing green alive along sun-baked stream beds in the summer. The oleander is thought by some to be the "rose of Sharon" of Song of Solomon 2:1.

OLIVE DRESSER. The olive was one of the most valuable trees in Palestine. With the vine, its cultivation constituted an important and lucrative industry (1 Sam. 8:14; 2 Kings 5:26) which employed many workers. But the task of cultivating the trees and harvesting the fruit was only part of the work connected with the olive crop. The harvest had to be transported to the presses in baskets on the backs of donkeys. The berries were then crushed in a shallow rock cistern by an upper millstone or simply by the feet of the harvesters (Deut. 33:24; Mic. 6:15). The oil was then cleansed of impurities by a settlement process and stored in jars or rock cisterns.

OLIVE TREE. The olive tree of Palestine is the common *Olea europaea*. It has leathery, dusty, green leaves and small, whitish flowers. It is a distinct feature of the Palestinian landscape. It is a long-lived, gnarled tree, often surviving for centuries. The fruit furnished food to eat and oil to illuminate ancient homes. In order to remain fruitful an olive tree has to be cultivated. If its care is neglected it degenerates into a wild olive tree. The process of grafting a cutting from a wild olive tree into a cultivated tree is alluded to in Romans 11:17, 24. In horticulture the reverse procedure was normally followed. A cutting from the cultivated tree was grafted into the wild (uncultivated) olive tree in order to alter its nature. The olive tree is a symbol of peace, prosperity, beauty, and divine blessing (Psa. 52:8; Jer. 11:16; Hos. 14:6).

The Mount of Olives and Garden of Gethsemane, across the Kidron Valley from the Temple site (© MPS)

OLIVET. A small range of four summits which overlooks Jerusalem and the Temple area from the east across the Kidron Valley (Zech. 14:4; Matt. 21:1). In Christ's day the Mount of Olives (as Olivet was frequently known) was thickly wooded with olive trees. But it was stripped bare when Jerusalem was destroyed by Titus.

OMRI (ŏm'rī). The king of Israel from 880 to 873 B.C. and the founder of a dynasty which was continued in his son Ahab (873-853 B.C.) and Ahab's sons, Ahaziah (853-852 B.C.) and Joram (852-841 B.C.). Omri transferred his capital from Tirzah to Samaria. He followed the idolatries of Jeroboam (1 Kings 16:26). As the founder of the Omride dynasty he was well known by the Moabites (as the Moabite Stone attests), but his reputation among the Assyrians is proved by their reference to Jehu (a king of a different dynasty) as *mār Ḥumri* or "successor of Omri."

ON (ŏn). Present-day Tell Husn, northeast of Memphis in Lower Egypt. It was a center for sun-worship. The Greek form of the name, Heliopolis, means "City of the Sun" (cf. Isa. 19:18, RSV; 43:13, RSV). The city was the home of Joseph's Egyptian wife (Gen. 41:45, 50).

ONESIMUS (ô-nĕs'ĭ-mŭs) ("useful, profitable"). A slave of Philemon whom Paul led to Christ at Rome and whom the Apostle returned to his Christian master as a brother beloved (Philem. 1:10-19). A native of Colosse, Onesimus accompanied Tychicus from Rome to that city with the letters of Colossians and Philemon (Col. 4:7-9).

ONESIPHORUS (ŏn'ĕ-sĭf'o-rŭs) ("profit-bringer"). A believer at Ephesus who befriended Paul (2 Tim. 1:16; 4:19).

ONIAS III (ô-nī'ās). A Jewish high priest who suffered exile and death because of his loyalty to Judaism and opposition to Hellenism on the eve of the Maccabean Revolt (second century B.C.). He became a legendary figure (2 Macc. 3, 4).

ONION. A bulbous-root plant popular in Egypt as an article of food (Num. 11:5). It is the *Allium cepa*, cultivated from earliest times in Egypt and other parts of the East.

ONO (ō'nō). A town in the Plain of Ono (Neh. 6:2) near Lydda. The town is first mentioned in the lists of Thutmose III (1490-1436 B.C.). The Benjamites rebuilt it after the conquest of Canaan (1 Chron. 8:12) and reoccupied it after the Exile (Neh. 11:31-35).

OPHEL (ō'fĕl). The southeast hill of Jerusalem and the original Jebusite settlement and citadel at that city. It was captured by David. Its fortifications were improved by Jotham (2 Chron. 27:3). In a city of Moab, according to the Moabite Stone, Mesha built the wall of "the ophel," that is, "the bulge or hill" of the citadel.

OPHIR (ō'fēr). A source of gold in the Arabian Peninsula or possibly on the East African Coast (Gen. 10:29; 1 Kings 9:28; 10:11; 22:48; cf. Job 22:24; Isa. 13:12).

ORACLE. According to pagan belief, either the utterances which the gods delivered or the temple chambers in which these messages were given. The oracular shrine of Apollo at Delphi was the most famous of these pagan temples. In contrast to the pagan usage, the Bible employs the word "oracle" in a much more exalted sense. In Old Testament usage the oracle was the inner shrine or Holiest Place. In New Testament usage oracles *(logia)* refer to the inspired Old Testament Scriptures in whole or in part (Acts 7:38; Rom. 3:2; Heb. 5:12; cf. 1 Pet. 4:11).

ORPAH (ôr'pä) ("neck"). The wife of Chilion and the sister-in-law of Ruth. She chose to remain in her native Moab while Ruth determined to follow her mother-in-law to Palestine (Ruth 1:14-22). In the beautiful typology that underlies this romance of redemption, Orpah symbolizes the unbelieving majority of the Jewish people that will choose to remain scattered among the nations in the day of Israel's return to her homeland. Ruth portrays the believing remnant of Israel that will trust in God's redemptive provision and will come in contact with the great Kinsman-Redeemer, Christ.

ORDINATION. In an ecclesiastical sense this term refers to setting men apart to a particular spiritual service (Mark 3:14; John 15:16; Acts 6:1-6; 13:2; Gal. 1:1; 1 Tim. 4:14; Tit. 1:5). Those who carry on the Christian ministry are apparently vested with the authority to ordain men to carry on the work of the gospel.

OSPRAY, OSPREY. An unclean bird (Lev. 11:13; Deut. 14:12). It is probably to be identified with a dark brown eagle, *Pandion haliaetus,* found along the Maritime Coast and the marshy lagoons of the Kishon.

OSSIFRAGE (Latin for "bone-breaker"; Hebrew *peres,* "breaker"). An unclean bird (Lev. 11:13; Deut. 14:12) commonly identified with the bearded eagle, whose chief haunts are the ravines of the Arnon. The ossifrage stands over three feet high and has about a nine-foot wingspread. It crushes its victim, often by dropping it on a rock from a great height.

OTHNIEL (ŏth'nĭ-ĕl). The first of the judges of Israel (Josh. 15:17; Judg. 1:13; 3:9).

OWL (Hebrew *kōs*). A ceremonially unclean bird (Lev. 11:17; Deut. 14:16) which frequents desolate places (Psa. 102:6). The reference is likely to the little owl (*Athene glaux*), which is very common in Palestine in ruins, tombs, rocks, thickets, and olive orchards. Another

species (Hebrew *yanshūph*), also ceremonially unclean (Lev. 11:17; Deut. 14:16) and frequenting waste places, was the great owl (Isa. 34:11). This bird is apparently to be identified with the Egyptian eagle owl (*Bubo ascalapus*), common in caves and ruins in the Petra area and around Beer-sheba. Some scholars think the night owl is referred to in Isaiah 34: 14.

Strong oxen pull together under a yoke, as they have for centuries. (*Russ Busby photo*)

OX. The male of the species *Bos taurus*. It was domesticated early in human history. So common was the ox that the plural (oxen) was frequently used to denote cattle in general. The ox was in common use in Palestine in the time of Abraham, about 2000 B.C. (Gen. 12:16; 21:27; 20: 14), and in Egypt at the time of the Exodus (1440 B.C.). This patient beast was used for plowing (1 Kings 19:19), for transport (Num. 7:3; 2 Sam. 6:6), and for trampling out grain at the threshing floor (Deut. 25:4). The ox was sometimes used for food (1 Kings 1:25; cf. Matt. 22:4) and was one of the sacrificial animals (Num. 7:87, 88; 2 Sam. 24:22).

P

PADAN-ARAM (pā'dăn-ā'răm) ("field or plain of Aram"). The Balikh-Habur region of northern Mesopotamia (Gen. 25: 20; 28:5-7; 31:18; 33:18). It is the same as Aram-Naharaim, "Aram of the two rivers."

PAINTER. Skilled artists were employed in antiquity to paint scenes on walls. A notable example is the Investiture fresco from Mari on the Middle Euphrates. Doubtless the Hebrew followed the same custom, although no examples have survived. However, excavations have uncovered pigments. Red ocher was used for painting on walls and wood (Jer. 22: 14; Ezek. 23:14).

PALM TREE (Hebrew *tāmār*, Greek *phoinix*). The date palm (*Phoenix dactylifera*) has a single upright stem and towers to a height of 60 to 80 feet, terminating at the top in a circle of feathery, perennially green leaves. The fruit of the palm was an important article of food (Joel 1:12). It was a tree of beauty and furnished the motif for carvings in various parts of Solomon's Temple and other sanctuaries (1 Kings 6:29, 32, 35; Herodotus II:169). Its expansive leaves were used as tokens of victory and peace (John 12:13; Rev. 7:9). In biblical times the palm tree flourished in Egypt and Palestine. Phoenicia took its Greek name from the date palm. The psalmist compared the righteous to the palm tree (Psa. 92: 12).

PALMERWORM. The migratory locust at a certain stage of its growth. See "Locust."

PALMYRA (păl-mī'rᴏ). An oasis in the desert between Syria and Iraq. It was Old Testament Tadmor (2 Chron. 8:4), apparently also called "Tadmor in the wilderness" (1 Kings 9:18). It is located about 140 miles east-northeast of Damascus and about 120 miles from the Euphrates. Its surviving ruins are impressive.

PAMPHYLIA (păm-fĭl'ĭ-à). A Roman province west of Lycia and east of the Kingdom of Antiochus and Cilicia Trachea on the southern coast of Asia Minor. Paul landed at its seaport, Attalia, after his voyage from Paphos in Cyprus during his first missionary tour (Acts 13: 13). He departed from Attalia to return to Syrian Antioch (Acts 14:24). The city of Perga was located just northeast of Attalia. Paul preached there (Acts 14:25).

PANEAS. Modern Baniyas, located at one of the sources of the Jordan. It was renamed by Herod Philip, who took it as his capital. See "Dan" and "Caesarea Philippi."

PAPHOS (pā'fŏs). A Hellenistic Roman town (modern Kuklia) in the southwest extremity of Cyprus. It was called Old Paphos to distinguish it from the newer seaport town about 10 miles to the northwest. New Paphos was the capital of the Roman province of Cyprus and the residence of the proconsul. It was the center of Aphrodite worship and contained a celebrated temple dedicated to the goddess. Paul visited the town on his first tour (Acts 13:6-13). New Paphos is modern Baffo.

141

PAPYRUS (pà-pī'rŭs) (Hebrew *gōmē*). A giant sedge with a triangular stock which rises eight to ten feet and is terminated by a tuft of flowers. It grows in the Sharon plain (near the Sea of Galilee) and in the Huleh swamps. In antiquity it flourished on the Nile. The Egyptians used it to make baskets, boats, shoes, and paper as early as the third millennium B.C. Papyrus grows in mire (Job 8:11). The tiny ark of the baby Moses was made of papyrus, as were many larger boats (Isa. 18:2). See also "Flags."

PARACLETE (păr'à-klēt). The Greek word which designates one of the roles of the Holy Spirit (John 14:16, 17, 26; 15:26; 16:7). It means "someone called alongside to help" and is frequently translated "comforter." The word sometimes also describes the personal intercessory work of Christ in heaven (1 John 2:1).

PARADISE. A Greek word derived from ancient Iranian and meaning "a garden with a wall." The Jews identified paradise with that part of hades to which the soul and spirit of the righteous went between death and the resurrection. Christ mentioned paradise in the account of the rich man and Lazarus (Luke 16:19-31). Since the resurrection of Christ, however, paradise has apparently been transferred to the third heaven, where Christ sits enthroned (Eph. 4:8-10; 2 Cor. 12:4; Rev. 2:7). Paul was evidently caught up to paradise when he was stoned at Lystra (2 Cor. 12:1-6).

Now the spirits of departed believers are "with the Lord" in heaven (2 Cor. 5:8; Phil. 1:23). Their bodies await resurrection or translation (Rom. 8:23; 1 Cor. 15:35-57; Phil. 3:20, 21).

PARAN (pā'răn). A mountain mentioned in the Song of Moses (Deut. 33:2). It was apparently a prominent peak in the mountain range on the west shore of the Gulf of Aqabah in the Wilderness of Paran.

PARTHIANS (pàr'thī-ănz). An Iranian people who originally inhabited the territory southeast of the Caspian Sea. They were a subject people under the Persians, but revolted under the Seleucids and became an independent state in the third century B.C. under Arsaces I. Mithridates

I (174-138 B.C.) founded the Parthian Empire, which extended westward to the Euphrates and adjoined the eastern provinces of the Roman Empire. From 64 B.C. to A.D. 226 the Parthians set limits to the Roman rule in the east. From 40 to 37 B.C. Parthian forces overran Asia Minor and Syria. They plundered Jerusalem and placed Antigonus, the last ruler of the Hasomeans, on the throne. Jews from Parthia were present at Jerusalem at Pentecost (Acts 2:9). Parthian power was not broken till the Persian family of Sassan instituted the second Persian or Sassanian Empire in A.D. 226.

PARTRIDGE (Hebrew *qōrē*, "crier" or "caller"). The rock partridge (*Alectoris graeca*). It is commonly hunted in the mountains of Palestine (1 Sam. 26:20). The partridge, of which several species exist in Palestine, was a large, fine bird. Jeremiah compares those who amass ill-gotten gain to a partridge (Jer. 17:11).

PATARA (păt'à-rà). A seaport city of southwest Lycia. Paul took ship there for Phoenicia on his last trip to Palestine (Acts 21:1). It possessed a famous shrine to Apollo.

PATHROS (păth'rŏs). The region of Upper Egypt (Isa. 11:11; Jer. 44:1, 15; Ezek. 29:14; 30:14). Pathros is Egyptian for "Southland."

PATMOS (păt'mŏs) One of the Sporades islands in the Greek Archipelago. It lies off the southwest coast of Asia Minor and is about 30 miles south of Samos. It is about ten miles long and six miles wide and is barren and rocky. There John was banished and received the visions recorded in the Book of the Revelation (Rev. 1:9).

PAUL ("little"). The great Apostle to the Gentiles, whose original name was Saul. He was one of the great men of the Bible and of all history. He was a convert from Pharisaic Judaism to Christ (Phil. 3:5) and was a tentmaker by trade (Acts 18:3). He was highly educated under Gamaliel (Acts 22:3). He became transformed from a rabid persecutor of Christianity to the world's greatest expositor of Christ. He was both a missionary of the Cross and the writer of 13 of the New Testament Epistles. The spread of Christianity to Europe and the western world is due in large part to the indefatigable zeal and labors of this mighty herald of the Cross.

PEACOCK (Hebrew *tukkiyīm*). The peacock is a native of India. Solomon's ships of Tarshish brought them from Ophir (India or Arabia). However, some scholars identify Ophir with the northeastern African Coast or Somaliland (Egyptian Punt) and identify the *tukkiyīm* as a type of monkey or baboon.

PEKAH (pē'kä) ("he has opened"). A conspirator against King Pekahiah. After seizing the throne he reigned from 739 to 731 B.C. He allied himself with Rezin of Damascus against Judah under Ahaz (Isa. 7:1-9). Pekah was subsequently murdered by Hoshea, who then seized the throne (731 B.C.).

PEKAHIAH (pĕk'à-hī'à) ("the Lord has opened"). The son and successor of Menahem (741-739 B.C.). He was assassinated by Pekah, who usurped the throne (2 Kings 15:23-26).

PELEG (pē'lĕg) ("division"). A son of Eber. In his time the earth "was divided" (Gen. 10:25). Possibly the division referred to the scattering of the descendants of Noah. Some associate the division with the incident at the tower of Babel, when the Lord scattered the builders over the face of the earth (Gen. 11:7-9).

PELICAN. A ceremonially unclean bird (Lev. 11:18; Deut. 14:17). It lived "in the wilderness" (Psa. 102:6), a description for swampland as well as arid desert. The drained swamps of the northern Jordan valley are still visited by migratory flocks of white pelicans.

PELLA (pĕl'à). Canaanite Pehel. It is mentioned in early Egyptian records and in the Amarna Letters. It was rebuilt by the Greeks under the name Pella. It was a city of the Decapolis, located in Transjordan about seven miles southeast of Scythopolis. After the fall of Jerusalem it became the center of a Christian community as a result of refugees from Judea.

PELOPONNESUS (pĕl'ạ-pạ-nē'sŭs). The peninsula south of the Isthmus of Corinth. It was part of the Roman province of Achaia.

PELUSIUM (pė-lū'shĭ-ŭm). A fortress town east of the Nile Delta. It guarded the approach to Egypt. It is called "Sin" in the King James Version (Ezek. 30:15).

PENNINAH (pē-nĭn'à) ("coral"). One of Elkanah's two wives, the other being Hannah (1 Sam. 1:1, 2). Penninah taunted Hannah because the latter was childless. She displayed an ungracious spirit and had an unpleasant disposition. But Hannah was a woman of faith, and her trust in God resulted in the birth of Samuel, one of the greatest leaders and men of God that graced Israel's history (1 Sam. 1:1-20).

PENNY. See "Denarius" under "Coins and Money."

PENUEL, PENIEL (pė-nū'ĕl). The place where Jacob wrestled with the angel (Gen. 32:30). It was plundered by Gideon (Judg. 8:8-17) and fortified by Jeroboam I (1 Kings 12:25). It is identified with Tulul edh-Dhanab, north of the River Jabbok and about four miles east of Succoth in Transjordan.

PEOR (pē'ôr). A mountain east of the Jordan River that overlooked the desert. It was the place from which Balaam blessed Israel (Num. 23:28). The site is somewhere to the north of the Dead Sea and opposite Jericho, but its exact location is uncertain.

PERATH. See "Euphrates."

PERFECTION. In the sense of sinlessness in experience, perfection is not attainable in this life, for the sin nature is not removed until the glorification of the body at the Lord's coming and the resurrection (Phil. 3:20, 21). However, perfection in position (God's assessment of the believer) is assured by the Christian's position "in Christ" (Heb. 10:14). In this respect every believer is regarded as absolutely and infinitely perfect — as perfect as Christ himself.

Although sinless perfection is not possible in an unglorified body, progressive maturity and spiritual adulthood are to be experienced by every Spirit-filled believer (1 Cor. 2:6; 13:11; 14:20; Phil. 3:15; 2 Tim. 3:17). Ultimate perfection will be realized by the believer when his body is glorified and conformed to the image of Christ (Col. 1:28; Eph. 4:12, 13; 1 Thess. 3:13; 1 John 3:1-3; 1 Pet. 5:10; Jude 1:24, 25).

PERFUMER. Cosmetics and perfumery constituted an important industry in antiquity. Painting of the face and the body was common, particularly of the eyes and lashes (cf. 2 Kings 9:30; Jer. 4:30; Ezek. 23:40). Such eye paint consisted of lead sulphide rather than antimony, as is commonly supposed. Red ocher (oxide of iron) may have served as rouge and lipstick. Nails were dyed from a product made from the henna plant. Even face powder was used by the Sumerians. Perfumes figure prominently in the Song of Solomon (cf. 1:3, 12; 3:6; 4:6; 5:1; 8:14). See also "Apothecary."

PERGA (pûr′gả). A city of Pamphylia visited by Paul on his first tour (Acts 13: 13, 14; 14:25). It is northeast of the seaport Attalia. The present-day site is Murtana.

PERGAMUM (pûr′gả-mŭm). The splendid ancient capital of the Attalid kingdom. In Roman times it was in the province of Asia and was the center of the emperor-worship cult (Rev. 2:12, 13). Its church was one of the seven churches of Asia (Rev. 1:11; 2:12-17). Pergamum is modern Bergama.

PERSEPOLIS (pûr-sĕp′ō-lĭs). The Persian capital from the reign of Darius I the Great (521-486 B.C.). It displaced Pasargadae. It was destroyed by Alexander the Great and resurrected by modern archeological excavations. Persepolis is located about 175 miles east of the northern extremity of the Persian Gulf in the heart of Persia (modern Iran).

Mound of Susa—biblical Shushan—in Iran, the site of the winter residence of Darius the Great; spire among buildings at left marks traditional tomb site of Daniel. (*OI-UC photo*)

PERSIANS. An Indo-European people who established a great empire that dominated the ancient world from 550 B.C. to 330 B.C. The empire eventually stretched from the coast of Europe to the borders of India and from the Black Sea and the Caspian Sea to Ethiopia. Cyrus the Great was its founder. The Persians were noble-minded and generous and revered one supreme God. They had few temples and no altars or images. When Cyrus conquered Babylon he found an oppressed race who abhorred idols (like the Persians) and embraced a religion somewhat like his own. Cyrus thus determined to restore this people to their own country. This is recorded in the remarkable edict appearing in the first chapter of Ezra (1:2-4).

Darius I (the Great, 521-486 B.C.) granted the Jews the privilege of completing their Temple and even aided the work by grants from his own revenues (Ezra 6:1-5). Darius was succeeded by Xerxes (486-465 B.C.), who was apparently the Ahasuerus of Esther. Artaxerxes I (465-423 B.C.) is the monarch who showed favor toward Ezra (Ezra 7:11-28) and Nehemiah (Neh. 2:1-9). Other Persian kings reigned until the Empire collapsed under the attack of Alexander the Great in 330 B.C.

PERSIS (pûr′sĭs) (Greek for "Persian"). A Christian woman whom Paul commended for her labor for the Lord (Rom. 16:12). The name is frequently found in the papyrii and inscriptions, especially in connection with female slaves.

PETER (a "rock, a stone," the Greek form of the Aramaic surname "Cephas"). The great fisherman-apostle (Matt. 4:18; John 1:40). He was introduced to Christ by his brother, Andrew. Contact with the Lord transformed him from a reed to a rock. He became the leader and spokesman of the Twelve and, along with James and John, one of the inner circle of Jesus' friends. These three were privileged to witness the raising of Jairus' daughter (Mark 5:37), the transfiguration (Matt. 17:1-13), and the agony in Gethsemane (Matt. 26:37-46). He confessed Christ's deity (Matt. 16:16-19) and was given "the keys of the kingdom of heaven" to loose the gospel to Jews at Pentecost (Acts 2: 16), Samaritans in Samaria (Acts 8:14), and Gentiles at Caesarea (Acts 10:34-48). The outpoured gift of the Spirit transformed him into a fearless witness. He wrote First and Second Peter.

PETRA (pē'trȧ) (Greek equivalent of the Hebrew word *selaᶜ*, "rock"). A site in Edom (Isa. 16:1; cf. Obad. 1:3) situated in a rock basin on the eastern side of the Wadi Arabah. It is about 50 miles south of the southern end of the Dead Sea. About 300 B.C. the Nabataeans took over the site and converted the great valley to the north (some 4500 feet long and 740 to 1500 feet across) into the amazing rock-cut city of Petra. The massive rock plateau, Umm el-Biyara, which towers 1000 feet above the city, was the site of the great high place. Other altars stood on neighboring heights. The dynasty of Nabataean kings that ruled in Petra contained several kings with the name "Aretas." One of these is mentioned in 2 Corinthians 11:32.

PHARAOH (fâr'ō) A biblical title employed as a name of the king of Egypt. The word means "the great house" and derives from the Old Kingdom designation of the royal palace as "The Great House." This became a common exponent of authority in such titles as "Superintendent of the Domain of the Great House." By 1800 B.C. this name for the palace had attracted to itself some of the divine titles attributed to the name of the king. By 1500 B.C. the term came to be applied to the occupant of the palace, the king of Egypt himself.

PHARISEES (fâr'ĭ-sēz). A lay fellowship originating in the second century B.C. and dedicated to the strict observance of the Mosaic Law. The name comes from the Hebrew word *Perushim*, meaning "those separated" from sinners and lawbreakers. In Christ's day the Pharisees had degenerated into self-righteous, hypocritical religionists (cf. Matt. 23:13-36). But in their earlier days they had exerted great influence for good because of their purity, piety, and championship of national independence during the Maccabean period. They laid the foundations of orthodox Judaism.

PHAROS (fâr'ōs). An island which had a usable port prior to the founding of Alexandria. It later became the site of a lighthouse called "pharos" that marked the harbor of Alexandria.

PHARPAR (fär'pär). One of the two streams of Damascus mentioned by Naaman (2 Kings 5:12). It is present-day Awaj. Some 40 miles in length, it flows eastward from Hermon south of Damascus.

PHEBE, PHOEBE (fē'bė) ("radiant"). A Christian deaconness in the church at Cenchrea, the eastern seaport of Corinth (Rom. 16:1, 2). She evidently relocated to Rome and was a helper or patron to many.

PHILADELPHIA (fĭl'ȧ-dĕl'fĭ-ȧ). (1) A city in Asia Minor founded by Attalus Philadelphus. It lies about 28 miles southeast of Sardis. It was one of the seven churches of the Revelation (Rev. 1:11; 3:7-13). It is present-day Alashehir. (2) A city of the Decapolis, former Rabbah, or Rabbath Ammon. It was captured by Ptolemy II and renamed Philadelphia. See "Rabbah."

PHILEMON (fĭ-lē'mŏn) ("loving"). A believer at Colosse to whom Paul returned a runaway but converted slave. Paul addressed one of the New Testament Epistles to Philemon.

PHILETUS (fĭ-lē'tŭs) ("worthy of love"). A first-century heretic who taught that the resurrection had already occurred (2 Tim. 2:17, 18).

PHILIP (fĭl'ĭp). (1) One of the twelve apostles (Matt. 10:3; John 1:43-48; 6:5, 6; 12:20-23; 14:8-12; Acts 1:13). (2) A son of Herod the Great and the husband of Herodias. He was disinherited by his father and lived a private life (Matt. 14:3; Mark 6:17; Luke 3:19).

PHILIP OF MACEDON. The father of Alexander the Great. By conquest he raised Macedonia to a dominant position (359-336 B.C.) in Greek affairs.

PHILIP THE DEACON. One of the seven Greek-speaking believers chosen to manage the material needs of the church at Jerusalem (Acts 6:5). He became an evangelist (Acts 8:4-8; 21:8). He won and baptized the eunuch of Ethiopia (Acts 8:26-39). He resided in Caesarea and had four unmarried daughters (Acts 8:40; 21:8, 9).

PHILIP THE TETRARCH. The ruler of Iturea and Trachonitis (Luke 3:1). He enlarged Paneas and named it Caesarea. It became known as Caesarea Philippi

(Matt. 16:13) to distinguish it from Caesarea on the Mediterranean.

PHILIPPI (fĭ-lĭp'ī). A city of Macedonia rebuilt by Philip II of Macedon and named after himself (it had originally been called Krenides). It was evangelized by Paul on his second tour (Acts 16:11-40; 20:6; 1 Thess. 2:2; Phil. 4:15). The site is called Filibedjik today.

PHILISTIA (fĭ-lĭs'tĭ-á). The southern maritime plain of Palestine. It received its name from the Philistines (Exod. 15:14; Psa. 60:8; Joel 3:4).

PHILISTINES (fĭ-lĭs'tēnz). A people descended from Casluhim, the son of Mizraim (Egypt), the son of Ham (Gen. 10:14). These people had settled in southeastern Palestine as early as the patriarchal age. But the great wave of them came from Caphtor (Crete) in the early twelfth century B.C. They settled in five main cities — Gaza, Ashkelon, Ekron, Ashdod, and Gath. They became a formidable power in the era of Saul and David, but were decisively defeated by David. They reasserted their aggressiveness in the time of Ahaz (Isa. 9:8-12). Their last scriptural mention is in Zechariah's prophecy, during the post-exilic period (Zech. 9:5-7). The Philistines were eventually assimilated by the Jews, for they are not mentioned in the New Testament.

PHILO (fī'lō). A famous Jewish and Hellenistic philosopher of Alexandria, Egypt (20 B.C. – A.D. 50). His ministry was to present biblical truth in categories that would appeal to the educated Greek. He employed allegory and personified divine wisdom as the "Logos." Philo's writings proved useful to the church and have been preserved through the centuries.

PHINEHAS (fĭn'ē-ăs) ("Egyptian, Nubian"). (1) A faithful priest and the grandson of Aaron (Exod. 6:25; Num. 25:1-18). (2) The younger of Eli's two degenerate sons, who was killed in battle when the ark was taken by the Philistines (1 Sam. 1:3; 2:34; 4:11-22).

PHOENICIANS (fê-nĭsh'ĭ-ánz). A seafearing people who occupied the coastal strip of the Mediterranean from the Ladder of Tyre (about 14 miles south of Tyre) to Ugarit on the north. Important Phoenician towns were Tyre, Sidon, Gebal (Byblus), Arvad, and Ugarit (Ras Shamra). The Phoenicians were apparently the product of the mingling of Canaanites and Achaeans. The Semitic element predominated. As artisans, traders, and skilled seamen, the Phoenicians were the merchant marine of antiquity. They established colonies in North Africa and Spain, even venturing as far as Britain.

The heyday of Phoenician history spanned from about 1150 to 880 B.C. Sidon was the most powerful city-state in the period of the Judges. But by the time of David and Solomon Tyre had gained the ascendancy. Hiram (979-945 B.C.) was the ally of Solomon. He furnished craftsmen and materials for constructing the Temple at Jerusalem (1 Kings 5:1-18). Western civilization owes its alphabet to the Phoenicians.

PHYLACTERIES. Small leather pouches which contained passages from the Pentateuch inscribed with Exodus 13:2-16 and Deuteronomy 6:4-9, 13-23. They were worn on the forehead and upper left arm during morning prayer, except on sabbaths and holy days. They were a literal representation of Deuteronomy 6:8: "The sign upon thy hand and frontlets between thine eyes." The term "phylactery" derives from a Greek word connoting an amulet. The practice of wearing them tended to substitute ritual for reality and even degenerated into a pagan superstition in some cases.

PHYSICIAN. The word for physician is rarely used in the Bible (Hebrew *rapha*ʾ, "healer"; e.g. Exod. 15:26; Jer. 8:22; Greek *iatros*; Mark 5:26; Luke 8:43). The biblical terms imply substantially the same meaning as "doctor" in present-day parlance. Israel's faith differed sharply from pagan religions in its clear-cut separation between the offices of priest and physician.

Remedies varied with the times. Poultices and local applications were frequently used (Isa. 1:6; 38:21; cf. Luke 10:34; Mark 5:26). Sometimes the remedy was linked with superstition (Gen. 30:14-16). Wine is mentioned as a stimulant (Prov. 31:6) and a remedy (1 Tim. 5:23).

PIGEON. A number of doves are found in Palestine. The Hebrew word *yōnāh* is usually translated "dove." However, in the passages in Leviticus and Numbers it is rendered "pigeon." The dove was domesticated in antiquity and was widely used for both food and message-carrying. See also "Dove."

PILLARS. Stones, whether naturally occurring or artificially erected, attracted Semitic peoples as places of worship. Jacob set up a stone and poured oil over it (Gen. 28:18). Some of these stones were commemorative, marking covenants, boundaries, or battles (Gen. 31:45). Others were funeral monuments (Isa. 19:19; Gen. 35:20). The twelve stones taken by Moses to build an altar (Exod. 24:4) and the twelve stones set up by Joshua after crossing the Jordan (Josh. 4:1-9) probably became relics, eventually to be linked with pagan deities. The prophets inveighed against these dangers (Jer. 2:26-28). King Hezekiah was praised because he destroyed the pillars from the high places (2 Kings 18:4).

PILATE (pī'lat). The Roman procurator of Judea and Samaria from A.D. 26 to 36, a period that included the public ministry of Christ (Luke 3:1). He was intolerant of the religious scruples of his subjects and ruthless in asserting Rome's authority. His treatment of Jesus resulted from a shriveled conscience and a withdrawal from official responsibility. His insistence on crucifying Jesus as "King of the Jews" evidenced his scorn of the Jewish Sanhedrin (Matt. 27:36, 37; Mark 15:1-14; Luke 23:1-4, 38; John 18:28 – 19:22).

PINE TREE. The translation of the Hebrew word *tidhar* (Isa. 41:19; 60:13). The fir tree and the pine are botanically in the genus *Pinus*, and the reference is doubtless to one of the species of evergreen coniferous trees native to the hills of Palestine and Lebanon.

PISGAH (pĭz'gà). A ridge crowning a hill or mountain. Such ridges or "pisgahs" are common in Transjordan (Num. 21:20; cf. Num. 23:13, 14). The "pisgah" to which Moses was bidden to ascend in order to view the Promised Land from every point of the compass (Deut. 3:27) is carefully described in Deuteronomy 34:1 as "the mountain of Nebo to the top of (the) Pisgah, that is over against Jericho." If Nebo is Jebel Osha, Moses was able to see the entire Promised Land from this vantage point.

PISHON, PISON (pī'shŏn). The Pishon and the Gihon were associated with the Garden of Eden (Gen. 2:10-14). They were presumably canals which connected the ancient Tigris and Euphrates riverbeds.

PITHOM (pī'thŏm). A stone city built by the oppressed Israelites in Egypt (Exod. 1:11). It was located in Goshen, the extreme northeast portion of the Delta. It was about 30 miles east of Pibeseth (Bubastis). Probably Tell er-Retabeh.

PLAIN. The principal region of flat or gently rolling plains in Palestine is the coastal plain, along the Mediterranean Sea. From Sidon southward to the Ladder of Tyre is the Plain of Phoenicia, varying from four to ten miles in width. The plain of Acco extends from the Ladder of Tyre southward to Mount Carmel. It is bordered by the hills of Upper and Lower Galilee and is scarcely wider than the Phoenician Plain. Cradled in the Central Highland ridge to the southwest of the Plain of Acco is the Plain of Megiddo or Esdraelon, called also the Great Plain. South of Mount Carmel to the Wadi Zerqah is the narrow Plain of Dor. From the Wadi Zerqah to Joppa is the beautiful, fertile Plain of Sharon and south of it to the Brook Besor the large Plain of Philistia.

PLANE TREE. A deciduous tree (*Platanus orientalis*) which stands 30 to 50 feet high and has a broad, ovate crown and large, deep-lobed, hairy leaves (Gen. 30:37; Ezek. 31:8). It thrives on riverbanks in the northern part of Palestine.

POLITARCHS (pŏl'ĭ-tärks). The senior board of magistrates, five in number and later six, at Thessalonica. They were technically called politarchs. This title is attested for a number of Macedonian states. The King James Version calls them "rulers of the city" (Acts 17:6, 8). Since Thessalonica was a free city and the capital of the province of Macedonia, the politarchs of Thessalonica carried heavy responsibilities. As the Acts passage shows, the politarchs controlled the city under Roman supervision. This consisted of a proconsul of praetorian rank supported by a legate and a quaestor.

POLYGAMY. The custom of having more than one wife at the same time. The practice was a violation of the original monogamous standard set by the Creator at the beginning (Gen. 2:24). Fallen man very early disregarded this divine arrangement and entered into polygamous unions (Gen. 4:19). Polygamy soon became common, especially among men of rank and wealth. Even certain men in the godly messianic line practiced polygamy (cf. Gen. 16:3, 4; 25:1, 6; 28:9; 29:23, 28). However, the practice of the patriarchs was devoid of the shameful degradation associated with polygamy in pagan lands.

The Mosaic Law discouraged polygamy. Everywhere it recognized the original, divinely instituted principle of monogamy in distinguishing between the first or legitimate wife and those taken in addition to her. It prohibited second marriages in certain cases. If a man took more than one wife, his matrimonial obligations were clearly prescribed (Exod. 21:10, 11).

Polygamy persisted down to New Testament times, but with diminishing prevalence. It disappeared rapidly in the face of the clearer light and higher claims of Christianity.

POMEGRANATE (Hebrew *rimmon*). A small tree (*Punica granatum*) which grows wild in many eastern countries. It was much prized and cultivated in Bible lands from earliest times. It has bright green leaves, blossoms with scarlet petals, and a large, leathery calyx. The orange-like fruit has a hard red rind fitted with innumerable seeds in a bright red pulp. Several places in the Bible bear its name: Rimmon (Josh. 15:32), Gath-rimmon (Josh. 19:45), and En-rimmon (Neh. 11:29). A refreshing drink is made from pomegranate juice; a syrup called grenadine is squeezed from its seeds; and an astringent medicine is extracted from its blossoms. The pomegranate is as prominent in Palestinian art as the lotus is in Egyptian motifs. Ornamental pomegranates adorned the high priests' vestments (Exod. 28:33), the capitals of Solomon's Temple pillars (1 Kings 7:20), and the silver shekel of Jerusalem struck in Maccabean times (143-135 B.C.).

POMPEII. A Roman city southeast of Naples in Italy. It was destroyed by the eruption of Vesuvius in A.D. 79. It was covered with volcanic ash and resurrected by modern archaelogy.

PONTUS (pŏn'tŭs). The southern coastal region of the Black Sea (Pontus Euxinus) east of Bithynia. Part of it was incorporated into the province of Galatia and part united with Bithynia to form another province (Acts 2:9; 18:2; 1 Pet. 1:1).

POOL. See "Springs, Wells, and Pools."

POPLAR TREE (Hebrew *libneh*, "white"). Rods of this tree were peeled by Jacob in deceiving Laban (Gen. 30:37). It appears to be the white poplar (*Populus albus*), so named because the undersides of its leaves are white. It has thick foliage and provides dense shade.

PORTER. As used in the King James Version this word denotes a gatekeeper, from the Latin *portarius*, the attendant at the *porta* or gate (cf. Mark 13:34; John 10:3).

Levitical porters were a class of servants (together with the Nethinim) who assisted the priests and Levites in duties at the Temple (Ezra 7:7), including guarding the gates (2 Chron. 8:14; 35:15).

POTIPHAR (pŏt'ĭ-fêr) (Egyptian, "he whom Re has given"). The captain of Pharoah's guard (Gen. 39:1). His wife tried to seduce Joseph (Gen. 39:7-20).

Sensitive and strong fingers mold fine pottery. (© MPS)

POTTER. The potter was an important artisan in Bible lands after the invention of the potter's wheel in the late fourth millennium B.C. The professional potter's workshop is illustrated by discoveries at such cities as Lachish and Qumran. The potter sat on the edge of a small pit in which the wheels were located. These were customarily two stones, one pivoted over the other, which were turned with the potter's feet. Pottery assumed various styles during successive periods, thereby helping the archeologist to date the various strata of excavated sites.

PRAETOR (prē'tôr). Almost a synonym for the Greek word *strategoi*. It is used five times in Acts 16 to designate the highest officials of the Roman Colony of Philippi. In general it denotes the *duumviri* or chief magistrates of Roman Colonies.

PRAETORIUM (prē-tō'rĭ-ŭm). The palace occupied by Pontius Pilate at Jerusalem. In it the judgment seat was erected (Mark 15:16; Matt. 27:27; John 18:28; 19:9). Some take it to be the castle of Antonia. Herod's palace at Caesarea also had a praetorium (the "judgment hall" of Acts 23:35). The Praetorium Guard at Rome guarded the imperial palace and its occupant, the Emperor.

PREDESTINATION. God's total plan with respect to humanity is called predestination or foreordination. His purpose to act in such a manner that certain men will believe and be saved is called election. His purpose to act in such a manner that certain will disbelieve and therefore be lost is called reprobation.

PREFECT. The Praetorium prefect was a Roman military officer who commanded the Praetorian guards. The office came to have a civil aspect and the prefect, like a proconsul, ruled a province. Egypt was administered by a prefect.

PRESBYTER. See "Elder."

PRIEST. Although not technically a worker or artisan, both the high priest and the ordinary priests played a very significant role in the religious and social life of Israel under the Mosaic Covenant. Only when apostasy from God's Law developed did the people treat the priesthood and its sacrificial system with negligence or disrespect. In Israel the worship of God was intimately bound up with every phase of life, ennobling and purifying it. By contrast, in pagan Semitic cultures the veneration of heathen deities debased virtually every phase of life.

Engraving of Hebrew priest and Ark of the Covenant (*HPS photo*)

PRIESTHOOD. The priest is man's representative before God. In Old Testament times the patriarch functioned as the priest over his household (Gen. 8:20; Job 1:5). Melchizedek the priest symbolized Christ's priesthood in both person and order (Gen. 14:17-20; Psa. 110:1-4; Heb. 6:20−7:28). The Aaronic high priest likewise symbolizes Christ, while the regular priest symbolizes the believer. The New Testament believer is constituted a priest on the basis of the once-for-all, efficacious sacrifice of Christ. He offers worship, sacrifice, and intercession (Heb. 13:15, 16).

PRIESTHOOD OF CHRIST. Christ was set apart as Priest (as well as Prophet and King) at his baptism (Matt. 3:15-17; Heb. 5:1, 2; 7:23-25; 9:24). Christ's earthly service, bodily sacrifice, and heavenly intercession are all comprehended by his priesthood.

PRISON-KEEPER. In Egypt the "keeper of the prison" elevated Joseph to be in charge of all the prisoners there (Gen. 39: 20-23). In Jeremiah's time the palace guardrooms served as a temporary prison (Jer. 32:2, 8, 12; 33:1). Ahab had Micaiah imprisoned on rations of bread and water (1 Kings 22:27). Defeated kings were often imprisoned by their conquerors (cf. Jer. 24:1, 5; 52:11).

John the Baptist was incarcerated in Herod's fortress at Machaerus (east of the Dead Sea). The Apostles were imprisoned in "a public place of watching"

(Acts 5:18). Peter was imprisoned and guarded by four soldiers (Acts 12:3-6). At Philippi Paul was placed in custody in the town jail under the charge of a jail-keeper (Acts 16:24). At Caesarea Paul was imprisoned in Herod's castle (Acts 23:35). At Rome he was allowed to remain in his own house, but with a soldier chained to him (Acts 28:16, 30).

PRISCA (pris'ká) ("old woman"). Same person as Priscilla.

PRISCILLA (pri-sil'á) ("little old woman"). The wife of Aquila, a tentmaker by trade. Paul met these Jewish Christians at Corinth (Acts 18:1-3). They were his fellow-passengers from Corinth to Ephesus, as Paul traveled to Syria (Acts 18:18, 19). They were instructed accurately in the gospel and were able to show the disciples of Apollos the difference between the baptism of John and the baptism of the Spirit (Acts 18:24 – 19:7). Paul regarded Priscilla very highly. In three out of five verses she is named before her husband (Acts 18:1-3, 18, 26; Rom. 16:3; 2 Tim. 4:19).

PROCONSUL (prō'kŏn-sŭl). In the Roman Empire as organized by Augustus, "proconsul" became the title of governors of provinces which required no standing army and were ruled by the Senate. Sergius Paulus was proconsul of Cyprus when Paul and Barnabas visited that island in about A.D. 47 (Acts 13:7). Gallio was proconsul of Achaia (A.D. 51-52) while Paul ministered in Corinth (Acts 18:12-17).

PROCURATOR (prŏ-cū-rā'tèr). The designation of the financial officer of a province in Roman imperial administration. The title was also used of a Roman province of the third class, such as Judea. But in the New Testament the procurator of Judea is described as "governor" (Greek *hēgemōn*). The procurators were commonly of the equestrian order. They had auxiliary troops to assist them. They were free to exercise necessary authority but were subject to the superior authority of the imperial legate of Syria. Caesarea was their capital, though they took up residence in Jerusalem on important occasions.

During A.D. 6-41 and 44-66 Judea was administered by imperial procurators.

Three are listed in the New Testament. Of these, Pontius Pilate (A.D. 26-36) is the best known. Antonius Felix (A.D. 52-59) is mentioned in Acts 23:24-35 and Porcius Festus (A.D. 59-62) is referred to in Acts 24:27 and 25:12.

PROPHET. Like the priest, the prophet represented God to the people and constituted a characteristic feature of early Hebrew society. Because of the ever-present threat of the false prophet and the pagan counterpart, the diviner (cf. Deut. 18:20-22), constant vigilance had to be exercised against the incursion of false religion and demon-energized paganism with its threat of occult supernaturalism (Deut. 18:9-14). The coming Great Prophet (the Messiah) was constantly held out as the expectation of every godly Israelite (Deut. 18:15-19; cf. John 1:21, 45; 6:14; Acts 3:22, 23; 7:37).

PROPITIATION. Propitiation is in no sense the placating of a vengeful God. It is instead the satisfying of the righteousness of a holy God, so that it is possible for him to show mercy without compromising his infinite holiness. This satisfaction was procured by Christ's death on the Cross. In prospect of the Cross God righteously forgave sins in the Old Testament period (Rom. 3:25).

Propitiation (Greek *hilastērion*) means "that which expiates or makes propitious." The place of propitiation in the Old Testament was the mercy seat sprinkled with atoning blood on the Day of Atonement (Lev. 16:14; Heb. 9:11-15). Christ is our "propitiation" (1 John 2:2; 4:10), indicated by the Greek word *hilasmos*. Christ's New Testament fulfillment of the Old Testament sacrifices demonstrates that he completely satisfied the demands of a holy God for judgment on sin.

PROSTITUTION, SACRED. A concomitant of debased Canaanite paganism. Both male and female prostitutes were attached to the heathen temples as devotees of the polluted gods and goddesses. Canaanite religion features violence, war, and sexual immorality. Sacred prostitution in times of apostasy desecrated the holy Temple at Jerusalem (1 Kings 15:12; 2 Kings 23:7).

PSALTERY. See under "Music and Musical Instruments."

PTOLEMAIS (tŏl'ĕ-mā'ĭs). The Hellenistic city and port, formerly known as Acre or Acco. It was built during Ptolemaic rule over Palestine (1 Macc. 5:22; 11:22; 12:45; Acts 21:7).

PUAH (pū'á) (probably Ugaritic *pgt*, "girl"). One of the two Hebrew midwives ordered by the Pharaoh to kill all male children (Exod. 1:15). They were probably heads of a larger group of midwives. Puah had the courage to defy the tyrant's commands.

PUBLICAN. A tax collector for the Roman government. Jews who held this position were hated by their countrymen.

PUL (pŭl; pōōl). Another name for Tiglathpileser III (745-727 B.C.). He was the "Pulu" of the Babylonian dynastic tablets.

PUNT. The east coast of Africa in Egyptian records. It was the source of myrrh and other exotic products. It corresponds today to Somaliland and perhaps also the coast of Arabia.

PURIFICATION. Any legal or ritual uncleanness among the Jewish people had to be removed by various washings or sacrifices (Lev. 11:24; 15:1, 2; 17:15). This pointed to the defilement of sin and the necessity of its eventual remission by the sacrifice of Christ on the Cross. The Day of Atonement, which most graphi-cally sets forth these truths, was therefore the supreme feast of purification for the Temple and the whole nation (Lev. 16).

PURIM (pū'rĭm), **FEAST OF.** This post-exilic festival was observed on the four-teenth and fifteenth day of the month Adar. It celebrates the deliverance of the Jews from the plot of their enemy, Ha-man, a minister of Xerxes I (485-465 B.C.). The execution was fixed by lot or "Pur" for the thirteenth of Adar. After the Jews had permission to massacre their enemies, they rested and made the fourteenth of Adar a day of joyful feast-ing (Esther 9:20-32). The Second Book of Maccabees mentions the feast.

PURPLE. A color prominent in the tabernacle and its ritual. It typifies Christ in his kingship (Exod. 25:4; 26:1; 39:3; Num. 4:13). See also "Blue," "Scarlet," and "Gold."

PUTEOLI (pū-tē'ô-lī). The port where Paul landed in Italy (Acts 28:13). The present-day site is Pozzuoli, near modern Naples.

PYGARG (pī'gärg) (Hebrew *dīshōn*). A clean animal (Deut. 14:5) identified with the white-rumped antelope or addax. It has twisted and ringed horns. It is native to northeast Africa, but its range extend-ed to the southeastern frontier of Pales-tine.

QANTIR. A town in Lower Egypt in the northeast part of the Nile Delta. It is con-sidered by some to be the site of Raamses.

QARQAR. A town south of Hamath on the Orontes River. It is the place where the famous battle was fought in 853 B.C. be-tween Shalmaneser III and a coalition of 12 kings of Syria-Palestine, including Ahab of Israel. The present-day site is Khirbet Qarqur.

QUAIL. The smallest species of the par-tridge subfamily. (The quail is about

151

eight inches long.) It is migratory, arriving in Palestine and Sinai in immense numbers in March. Quail fly with the wind, and if the wind changes course and the birds become exhausted in flight, a whole flock of them may fall to the ground and lie stunned (Num. 11:31-34; Psa. 78:26-31; cf. Josephus, *Antiquities*

III; 1, 5).

QUIRINIUS (kwĭ-rĭn'ĭ-ŭs). The Roman legate of Syria who instituted the census of the Jews decreed by Caesar Augustus (Luke 2:1-3). (This census apparently took place in 6 B.C., when Quirinius was first associated with the government of Syria.)

R

RA (rä). The national god of Egypt during the greater part of its history. His veneration was a form of sun-worship, and was carried out under the insignia of the solar disc encircled by the poisonous uraeus serpent.

RAAMSES (rä'ăm-sēz). A town in Egypt built by the Israelites (Exod. 1:11; Num. 33:3, 5). It was also called Zoan, Avaris, and Tanis at various times. It was located in the northeast section of the Nile Delta and is commonly identified with present-day San el-Hagar.

RAB (răb) (Hebrew *rab*, "great one, a chief, captain"). A title employed of certain Assyrian and Babylonian officers (2 Kings 25:8-20; Jer. 39:9–52:30). See also "Captain."

RABBAH (răb'à). The capital of Ammon (Deut. 3:11; Josh. 13:25). It was captured by David's army (2 Sam. 11:1; 12:26-31). It was sometimes called Rabbath-ammon.

RABBI. A Jewish title of honor used during the New Testament period. It comes from the Hebrew word *rab*, meaning "great," "master," or "teacher." *Rabbi* means "my teacher." The word eventually became a stereotyped form of reverential address for recognized Jewish

teachers. *Rabboni* is a heightened form of *rabbi* and was used in addressing Christ (Mark 10:51; John 20:16). *Rabbi* was applied once to John the Baptist (John 3: 26) and some 12 times to our Lord (e.g. John 1:38, 50; 3:2, 26; 6:25).

RACHEL (rā'chĕl) ("ewe, a female sheep"). The younger daughter of Laban and Jacob's favorite wife. She became the mother of Joseph and Benjamin. Jacob worked seven years for Rachel (Gen. 29: 27-30) after being duped into marrying Jacob's older daughter, Leah (Gen. 29: 15-26). Rachel was barren for years and eventually gave Jacob her handmaid, Bilhah, to bear him children (Gen. 30:1-8). Bilhah gave birth to Dan and Naphtali. Then Rachel bore Joseph (Gen. 30:22-24). Later, in Canaan, she also bore Benjamin but died in childbirth and was buried near Ramah (Gen. 35:16-20).

RAHAB (rā'hăb) ("wide, broad"). The harlot who sheltered the men dispatched by Joshua to spy out Jericho (Josh. 2:1-21). She hid the two men on the roof of her house in stalks of flax. While she gave a false lead to the king's police, she let down the men from her house (which was built on the city wall) and enabled them to escape. She confessed to them that she knew the Lord to be the God of heaven and asked the spies to swear that when Israel took Jericho they would spare her house. The identification would be a scarlet cord tied to her window. In the subsequent conquest of the city only Rahab and her family were spared (Josh. 6:17, 22-25). Rahab is included among the heroes of faith in Hebrews 11 (v. 31). She is also cited as an example of saving faith in action (James 2:25). She is included in our Lord's genealogy (Matt. 1:5).

RAMAH (rā'mȧ). A town in Benjamin (Josh. 18:25) fortified by Baasha, king of Israel, but demolished by King Asa of Judah (1 Kings 15:17-22). It is associated with Rachel, the mother of Joseph and Benjamin (Jer. 31:15; Matt. 2:18). It is present-day er-Ram, about five miles north of Jerusalem.

RAMOTH-GILEAD (rā'mōth-gĭl'ė-ăd). A city of refuge in the tribe of Gad (Deut. 4:43; Josh. 20:8; 21:38). It was in northern Transjordan, in Solomon's sixth district (1 Kings 4:13). It was in Ramoth-Gilead that the Syrians defeated Israel under Ahab (1 Kings 22:3-40) and Joram (2 Kings 8:28; 9:14-26). The site is present-day Tell Ramith, about 30 miles due east of Bethshan.

RAS-SHAMRA (räs-shäm'rȧ). The present-day site of the Canaanite-Phoenician city of Ugarit. Excavations here have uncovered a temple, library, and royal archives. The Ugaritic literature, rendered in alphabetic cuneiform, is of immense importance in evaluating the religion and morality of the Canaanites.

RAVEN. The bird referred to in Scripture is black in color (Song 5:11), feeds on carrion (Prov. 30:17), and is ceremonially unclean (Lev. 11:15). It is the common raven (*Corvus corax*). It is found all over Palestine. The name is also applied to the hooded crow, which is very similar in appearance. Noah sent a raven from the ark (Gen. 8:7). Elijah was fed by ravens (1 Kings 17:2-7).

REBEKAH, REBECCA (rĕ-bĕk'ȧ) (probably from the root "to tie fast"). The daughter of Bethuel, Abraham's nephew in Padan-Aram (Gen. 22:23). Abraham sent his steward to Mesopotamia to find a bride for Isaac (Gen. 24). He found Rebekah as the result of divine leading. She proved barren, but in answer to prayer she finally bore twins, Esau and Jacob (25:20-26).

RECHABITES (rē'kăb-ītz). The descendants of Rechab (2 Kings 10:15-28). They formed an association to return to simple nomadic life, rejecting the comforts of sedentary life and advocating an austere and godly manner of living (Jer. 35). The Rechabites differed from the prophets. They protested the dangers which religious faith faces in an advanced civilization and sought to flee from them. The prophets, however, demonstrated that the essence of faith resides in the heart and cannot be quenched by external circumstances.

RECONCILIATION. The change which Christ's death produced in the relationship between God and fallen men. As a result of Calvary, God can justly show mercy where previously only judgment could be rendered. This reconciliation was totally God's undertaking. Man had no part in it (2 Cor. 5:19). This aspect of reconciliation constituted the lost race salvable.

There is another aspect of reconciliation, however, that actually saves men. This is accomplished by God in the believing sinner himself. As a result he becomes changed in his rebellion toward God and appropriates the reconciliation provided by Christ on the Cross (Rom. 5:11). Christians can participate in the ministry of reconciliation by imploring sinners to be "reconciled to God" (2 Cor. 5:19, 20).

RECORDER (Hebrew *mazkir*, "one who causes to remember"). An aide to the king whose responsibilities included the chronicling of state events (cf. 2 Kings 21:25). Some scholars construe the office as that of an executive administrator or prime minister. Others take it to mean simply a herald or court announcer.

RED HEIFER. The sacrifice of the red heifer symbolized the death of Christ as the basis for the believer's cleansing from the daily defilement of sin (Num. 19). Death was required (Num. 19:2, 3), as well as sevenfold sprinkling of the blood before the tabernacle (Num. 19:4). (The sprinkled blood signifies the believer's public confession of faith in the finished work of Christ—Heb. 9:12-14; 10:10-12.) Then the slain heifer was burned. Its ashes were preserved and mixed with water as needed to sprinkle those defiled by sin (Num. 19:5-22). This pictures the Holy Spirit using the Word of God to convict the believer of the defilement of sin (water being a type of both the Spirit and the Word—John 7:37-39; Eph. 5:26). The convicted believer then acknowledges that the guilt of his sin has been met by Christ's death (1 John 1:7). He accordingly confesses the evil as unworthy of a saint, and is forgiven and cleansed (John 13:3-10; 1 John 1:7-10).

The Red Sea, near traditional area of Moses' crossing with Israelites (© *MPS*)

RED SEA. In modern geography, the large body of water that separates northeast Africa from Arabia. Its northern two arms, the Gulf of Suez and the Gulf of Aqabah, continue the sea northward on the western and eastern sides of the Sinai Peninsula. However, the term which is used in the Hebrew Old Testament is not the *Red* Sea but the *Reed* Sea—the *yam suph* or "sea of (papyrus) reeds." The term designates (a) the region of the Bitter Lakes in the Egyptian Delta north of Suez along the line of the Suez Canal

(Exod. 13:18; 14:1, 2); (b) the Gulf of Suez (Num. 33:10, 11 and possibly Exod. 23:31); and (c) the Gulf of Aqabah (Num. 14:25; Deut. 1:40; 2:1; Num. 21:4; Judg. 11:16; cf. 1 Kings 9:26).

REDEEMER. The first promise of the Redeemer given to the fallen race envisioned both the incarnation and the virgin birth of the eternal Word of God in his appearance as "the Seed of the Woman" (Gen. 3:15). The messianic line begins at this point and continues through Abel, Seth, Noah (Gen. 6:8-10), Shem (Gen. 9:26, 27), Abraham (Gen. 12:1-4), Isaac (Gen. 17:19-21), Jacob (Gen. 28:10-14), Judah (Gen. 49:10), and David (2 Sam. 7:5-17) and then culminates in Christ himself (Isa. 7:10-14; Matt. 1:20-23).

REDEMPTION, NEW TESTAMENT. The central idea of redemption is "deliverance by payment of a price." Christ's work in fulfilling Old Testament types and promises of redemption is summarized by three Greek words. (1) *Agorazo* means "to buy in the market" and pictures man as a slave "sold under sin" (Rom. 7:14) and condemned to death (Gen. 2:17; John 3:18, 19; Rom. 6:23). However, fallen man is subject to redemption by the purchase price of the blood of the Redeemer (1 Cor. 6:20; 7:23; 2 Pet. 2:1; Rev. 5:9). (2) *Exagorazo* means "to buy out of the market" by purchasing and removing from sale. This is what Christ did for us (Gal. 3:13; 4:5). His deliverance is final and complete. (3) *Lutroō* means "to set loose or free" and is used commonly to indicate the release of a slave (Luke 21:28; Rom. 3:24; 8:23; 1 Cor. 1:30; Eph. 1:7; 4:30; Col. 1:14; Heb. 9:15). After the redemption by Christ's blood the Holy Spirit empowers the believer to experience the deliverance in his daily life (Rom. 8:2).

REDEMPTION, OLD TESTAMENT. Israel's national redemption out of Egypt illustrates all human redemption. All redemption is based entirely on God's grace (Exod. 3:7, 8) and is implemented solely by the blood of Christ (Exod. 12: 13, 23, 27; 1 Pet. 1:18, 19) and by divine power (Exod. 6:6; 13:14; Rom. 1:16; 1 Cor. 1:18, 24).

A lost estate could be redeemed by a

kinsman (Lev. 25:25). This custom furnishes a beautiful picture of Christ's redemption, as in the Book of Ruth. A redeemer must be a near relative (fulfilled in the incarnation). He must be capable of redeeming (fulfilled in the all-efficacious blood of Christ—Acts 20:28; 1 Pet. 1:18, 19). He must be willing to redeem (witnessed in Christ's delight in the Father's will and his voluntary obedience in death—Phil. 2:5-8; Heb. 10:4-10). He must be free from the calamity which made redemption necessary (fulfilled in Christ's sinlessness and Saviorhood). See also "Kinsman-Redeemer."

REGENERATION. A vital aspect of salvation in which the divine nature is imparted to the believer (John 3:1-6; Tit. 3:5; 1 Pet. 1:23; 2:2) and he becomes a son in the Father's family (Gal. 3:26). In regeneration the believer is reborn by the Spirit through the Word (John 3:5) and receives a new, eternal life. He thereupon becomes an heir of God and a joint heir with Christ (Rom. 8:17). The sole condition of the new birth is unreserved faith in the crucified Christ (John 3:14-18).

REHOBOAM (rē'hō-bō'ăm) ("the people is enlarged"). The son and successor of Solomon. His folly split the kingdom. He followed the false philosophy that the subjects existed for the sovereign instead of the sovereign for the subjects. He heeded unsound advice and failed to give God first place (1 Kings 12:1—14:31; 2 Chron. 10:1—12:16).

REMNANT. A minority of humanity that has remained faithful to the Lord in every age since the fall of Adam. In Elijah's day it was seven thousand people who had not been corrupted by Baal worship (1 Kings 19:18; Rom. 11:1-5). In Isaiah's day it was "very small" (Isa. 1:9). Today it is composed of members of the true Church (cf. Rom. 11:4, 5). In the tribulation it will be the 144,000 Israelites (Rev. 7:3-8) and a great number of Gentiles (Rev. 7:9). A remnant will enter the kingdom age (Zech. 12:6—13:9).

REPENTANCE. Repentance is that change of attitude toward sin that enables a person to trust Christ as Savior. Repentance is inseparable from saving faith. Nor can saving faith ever be exercised apart from repentance. This vital newness of mind is a part of believing and is therefore sometimes used as a synonym for believing (cf. Acts 17:30; 20:21; 26:20; Rom. 2:4; 2 Tim. 2:25; 2 Pet. 3:9). Repentance cannot be *added* to faith as a condition of salvation (John 3:16; Acts 16:31; Eph. 2:8, 9), for repentance and faith are two sides of the same coin. The one cannot occur without the other (Acts 20:21).

Believers who have sinned may repent as a separate act. But this is totally different from being saved over again (cf. 2 Cor. 7:8-11). Israel, God's covenant nation, was also called on to repent (Matt. 3:2). As in the case of the New Testament believer, this was not a gospel call but rather a challenge to return to a prior spiritual relationship (cf. Matt. 4:12-17).

RESURRECTION, THE FIRST. The raising of the new and heavenly body to reunion with the redeemed soul and spirit. This resurrection occurs in stages and will ultimately embrace all of God's elect saints from Adam to the end of the kingdom age (1 Cor. 15:22, 23; 1 Thess. 4:13-17; Rev. 20:4-6, 12, 13).

The final phase of the first resurrection occurs at the same time as the second resurrection—at the end of the kingdom age. It includes saints who have died during the millennium. Their names will appear in the "book of life" (Rev. 20:12, 13). Christ himself constituted the "firstfruits" of the first resurrection (1 Cor. 15:23).

RESURRECTION, THE SECOND. This is the "resurrection of condemnation" (John 5:28, 29). It constitutes the "great white throne" judgment (Rev. 20:11-15) and includes every unsaved person, from the fall of Adam to the creation of the new heavens and earth. These unsaved will be judged according to their works (deeds), that is, according to their response to the moral law of God, and will suffer degrees of punishment. This sentence involves eternal separation from God rather than simple annihilation (cf. Rev. 19:20 with 20:10).

RETURN OF CHRIST. Scripture declares the certainty of this event (John 14:1-3; Acts 1:10, 11). Christ's return will be an actual occurrence and not simply a process. It is to be personal and corporeal or bodily (Matt. 23:39; 24:30; Phil. 3:20, 21; 1 Thess. 4:13-17). It occurs in two distinct stages: first, Christ's coming *for* his saints, when he raises the dead and transforms the living (1 Thess. 4:13-17; 1 Cor. 15:51-53; Phil. 3:20, 21; 1 John 3: 1-3); second, Christ's coming *with* his saints, when he conquers his enemies, destroys the Satanic world system, and establishes his earthly kingdom over Israel and the nations (Rev. 19:11 – 20:4; cf. Zech. 14:1-9; Luke 1:31-33; 1 Cor. 15: 24-28).

REUBEN (rōō'bĕn) ("behold a son"). Jacob's firstborn son. He forfeited his family status through gross misconduct (Gen. 29:31, 32; 35:22). This cost him his birthright (Gen. 49:3, 4). He fathered the Jewish tribe that bore his name (Num. 26:5-7).

REUEL (rōō'ĕl) ("God is a friend"). An alternate name for Jethro, Moses' father-in-law (Exod. 2:18).

REUMAH (rōō'mȧ) ("exalted"). A concubine of Nahor, Abraham's brother (Gen. 22:24). Her four sons were ancestors of Aramean tribes located in the regions north of Damascus.

RHEGIUM (rē'jĭ-ŭm). A city on the coast of Italy opposite Messina in Sicily. Paul's vessel touched at this port after leaving Syracuse (Acts 28:13). Rhegium is present-day Reggio.

RHODA (rō'dȧ) (Greek for "rose"). A maid in the house of John Mark's mother in Jerusalem. She announced Peter's arrival after the angel had released him from prison (Acts 12:13). Rhoda served both her mistress and the larger fellowship of the church.

RHODES (rōdz). The southernmost large island of the Aegean Sea. It lies off the southwestern extremity of Asia Minor and points toward Crete, about 95 miles to the southwest. The city of Rhodes, situated at the northeast tip of the island (about 65 miles from the mainland), was passed by Paul on his last journey to Palestine (Acts 21:1). The city was famed as a commercial mecca and for the huge statue of Apollo known as the "Colossus of Rhodes."

RIBLAH (rĭb'lȧ). A city south of Hamath in Syria (Ezek. 6:14, RSV). Here the Babylonians punished captive kings of Judah (2 Kings 23:33; 25:6, 20; Jer. 39:5; 52:9).

RIGHTEOUSNESS. God's righteousness is absolute, being the expression of his infinitely holy character. His divine righteousness is seen in his person (James 1:17; 1 John 1:5) as well as his purposes and plans (Rom. 3:25, 26). Imputed righteousness is the intrinsic righteousness of God imputed to the believer through Christ at conversion (1 Cor. 1:30; 2 Cor. 5:21; cf. Rom. 3:21, 22). God's righteousness was also imputed to Old Testament saints by virtue of their prospective faith in Christ (Gen. 15:6; Rom. 4:3; Gal. 3:6; James 2:23; cf. John 8:56; Heb. 11:13).

RIVERS AND STREAMS. The usual word for river in Hebrew is *nāhār*, signifying a constantly flowing stream, such as the rivers of Eden (Gen. 2:10, 13, 14), the Euphrates (Deut. 1:7), the rivers of Ethiopia (Isa. 18:1), and the rivers of Damascus (2 Kings 5:12). Sometimes the word is applied to canals, like the Chebar (Ezek. 1:1, 3; 3:15; 10:15). The great rivers of the Bible are the Nile, the Tigris, the Euphrates, and the Jordan. In the New Testament the missionary journeys of Paul are associated with important cities located on rivers. (However, the rivers themselves, such as the Cydnus at Tarsus, the Orontes at Syrian Antioch, and the Tiber at Rome, are not named in Scripture.)

Another frequent Hebrew word, *nahal*, denotes a seasonal watercourse known as a *wadi*. In summer it is a dry riverbed or ravine. In the rainy season, however, it may become a raging torrent. The Jabbok was such a wadi (Deut. 2:37), as well as the brook Cherith (1 Kings 17:3).

Among the rivers of Palestine not named in the Bible are the Yarmuk, an eastern tributary of the Jordan River south of the Sea of Galilee, and the Auja (present-day Yarkon), which flows into the Mediterranean Sea at modern Tel-Aviv. The Nile is also unnamed in Scripture. "The river of Egypt" (Gen. 15:18) is probably not the Nile but rather the *Wadi el ᶜArish*, south of Gaza.

RIZPAH (rĭz'pȧ) ("hot stone or coal"). A concubine of Saul. After Saul's death, Abner, the head of the army, took Rizpah as his wife (2 Sam. 3:7). This act was tantamount to a claim to the throne (cf. 1 Kings 2:22). Consequently Ishbosheth, Saul's son and nominal ruler, challenged Abner's loyalty. Abner in retaliation began negotiations to support David as king (2 Sam. 3:7-21).

Later, when famine came as a divine punishment for Saul's treacherous murder of the Gibeonites, David made recompense to the aggrieved Gibeonites by handing over seven of the sons of Saul (the two sons of Rizpah and five of Merab) to be hanged (2 Sam. 21:1-9). Then Rizpah showed intense love and fortitude by protecting the bodies from birds and beasts of prey until burial could be made (2 Sam. 21:10-14). This devotion led David to undertake proper burial of the bones of Jonathan and Saul along with those of the men who had been hanged.

ROBE (*simlah*). The ordinary outergarment of biblical times. It is still worn by modern *fellahin*. The robe was essentially a square piece of cloth thrown over one or both shoulders. There were openings for the arms at the sides. A cloak, which even the poorest person possessed, could not be given in loan, since it was used at night as a covering (Exod. 22:25-27; Deut. 24:13). It was removed during manual labor (Matt. 24:18; Mark 10:50). It was often used to hold a variety of objects (Exod. 12:34; Judg. 8:25; 2 Kings 4:39). A variety of the robe, a *sadin*, was a shawl-like wrap (Judg. 14:12, 13; Prov. 31:24).

ROBE (*me^cil*). This, too, was an outer, coat-like garment. Samuel's mother made one each year for her son (1 Sam. 2:19), and he wore one on significant occasions (1 Sam. 15:27; 28:14). Saul (1 Sam. 24:4, 11) and Jonathan (1 Sam. 18:4) wore one, as did David on the occasion of the transfer of the ark to Jerusalem (1 Chron. 15:27). This was the garment which was customarily ripped in times of grief or distress (Ezra 9:3, 5; Job 1:20; 2:12). The ephod of the priest was worn over the *me^cil* (Lev. 8:7; cf. Exod. 29:5). This garment may be similar to the *qumbaz* of modern Palestine — the long, loosely-fitting robe worn over all other clothing.

ROCK. Rocks abound in the hilly and mountainous sections of Palestine. Often the rocks are of such size and formation as to constitute well-known landmarks. They also afford shelter, shade, and defense. Little wonder that God is often described as a Rock!

Relief sculpture on Arch of Titus in Rome portrays Roman soldiers plundering treasures of Jerusalem Temple in A.D. 70. (*HPS photo*)

ROMANS. A Latin people strongly influenced by Etruscan culture. Rome, the center of their power and expansion, was founded about 753 B.C. Gradually this people extended their control over Italy and the entire Mediterranean world. The term "Roman" gradually acquired a broader meaning then simply an inhabitant of Rome (1 Macc. 8:1; Acts 2:10) or a representative of the Roman government (Acts 25:16; 28:17). It came to include anyone who had rights of citizenship in the Empire (Acts 16:21, 37, 38; 22:25-29). According to Valerian and Porcian laws no magistrate could arrest, scourge, or kill a Roman citizen. The life of one so privileged could not be taken except by the vote of a general assembly.

Rome became dominant in Jewish affairs from the time of Pompey in 63 B.C. Herod the Great was the vassal king of Rome, having been enthroned through Antony and Octavian. After the dethronement of Herod's son, Archelaus, Rome ruled Judea through procurators, except for the brief reign of Herod Agrippa I (A.D. 41-44).

Christianity was outlawed by the Romans, and early believers frequently suffered great persecution. The Emperor cult was diametrically opposed to the Christian faith. Although Rome resisted the gospel, Christianity nevertheless made great strides throughout the Empire, finally attaining imperial favor in the fourth century A.D. under Emperor Constantine.

ROME. The famous city on the Tiber River in Italy. It was the residence of the Emperor and the seat of the Roman government (Acts 28:14-16; Rom. 1:7, 15).

ROSE, ROSE OF SHARON (Hebrew *ḥabaṣṣeleth*). This is apparently not a true rose but instead the white narcissus, the crocus, the meadow saffron, or the anemone. (However, true roses apparently existed in Palestine in the biblical period. At least four wild species are still found in Palestine.) But the "rose" of the Old Testament was some common, bulbous plant that carpeted the Plain of Sharon.

RUE (Greek *peganon*). A plant which the Pharisees scrupulously tithed. It is native to Bible lands and was cultivated as a medicine and a condiment. It is identified as the *Ruta gaveolens,* a shrub with pinnate, bluish-green leaves and yellow flowers (Luke 11:42).

RULER OF THE SYNAGOGUE. During the Hellenistic period, Jewish synagogues were normally governed by a council of elders under the leadership of a "ruler of the synagogue." Several such rulers are mentioned: (1) Jairus, whose daughter Jesus raised from death (Mark 5:22-43); (2) an unnamed man who was angered because Jesus healed on the sabbath (Luke 13:10-17); (3) those who allowed Paul to speak in the synagogue at Antioch of Pisidia (Acts 13:14, 15); (4) Crispus, a convert at Corinth (Acts 18:8); and (5) Sosthenes, a ruler of the Corinthian synagogue at the time of Paul's first visit (Acts 18:17).

RUTH (rŏŏth) (apparently a contraction from *reᶜuth,* "a female companion"). The Moabite woman who by faith clung to Naomi and her God and accompanied Naomi back to Bethlehem (Ruth 1:1-22). In her act of faith Ruth illustrates how the believing remnant of the Israelite nation will someday return to the land in a saving relationship with Christ, the great Kinsman-Redeemer (portrayed by Ruth's marriage to Boaz). Naomi represents the sorrowing Israelite nation outside the land in dispersion, as well as her eventual return to Messiah through a believing remnant. The Book of Ruth illustrates God's redemptive ways with Israel and the nations through the Kinsman-Redeemer.

SACRIFICE. Fallen man's divinely appointed avenue of approach to God was always through animal-sacrifice until Christ himself died as the ultimate offering. Animal sacrifice was instituted immediately after the fall of Adam and was reiterated on several occasions thereafter (Gen. 3:21; 4:3-7; 8:20-22; 12:7; 33: 18-20; Exod. 12:3-14). The slain animals in all cases prefigured Christ as the substitute sufferer for our sins. This is why they had to die through the shedding of blood (Heb. 9:22).

The death of Christ fulfilled all sacrificial types. The Father made the sacrifice (John 3:16; Rom. 8:32). It was substitutional (Lev. 1:4; Isa. 53:5, 6; 2 Cor. 5:21; 1 Tim. 2:6; 1 Pet. 2:24), voluntary (John

10:18), redemptive (1 Cor. 6:20; Gal. 3: 13; Eph. 1:7), propitiatory (Rom. 3:25; 1 John 2:2), reconciling (Rom. 5:10; 2 Cor. 5:18, 19; Col. 1:21, 22), efficacious (John 12:32, 33), and revelatory (1 John 4:9, 10).

The spiritual sacrifices which believers offer involve the priestly functions of self-dedication (Rom. 12:1, 2), praise (Eph. 5:20; Heb. 13:15), and giving of substance (Phil. 4:18).

The animal sacrifices in the future millennial kingdom (Ezek. 43:19-27) will be purely retrospective or commemorative — they will look back to the finished work of Christ.

SAFFRON (Hebrew *karkōm*). A fragrant plant with light violet flowers veined with red. The dried and pulverized stigmas yield a yellow dye. Olive oil was perfumed with saffron and food was spiced with it. It also served as a medicine (Song 4:14).

SAILOR. The Hebrews displayed little enthusiasm for the sea. Throughout their history they had few ports, the best harbors being held by alien maritime peoples (particularly the Phoenicians). However, Solomon did build a navy at Ezion-geber which required many sailors (1 Kings 9:26-28). Jehoshaphat did the same, but his venture was frustrated (1 Kings 22:48). These ships were apparently manned mainly by Phoenician sailors in cooperation with the Phoenician fleet.

SAINT (Greek *hagios*, "a holy one"). A frequent New Testament designation of a believer in Christ. Every believer is a saint because of his holy standing in Christ. According to Scripture, sainthood depends not on personal merit but on the finished work of Christ. Sainthood is thus not a vague future possibility but a present privilege in Christ (1 Cor. 1:2).

SALAMIS (săl'á-mĭs). A Greek city on the east coast of Cyprus (the island which Paul and Barnabas began evangelizing on their first missionary tour — Acts 13:4-6). It is located north of present-day Famagusta.

SALEM (sā'lĕm). The name "Salem" as used in Genesis 14:18 apparently refers to the city of Jerusalem. This identification is supported by Psalm 76:2 and by ancient Jewish tradition.

SALOME (sà-lō'mē) (feminine form of Solomon, "peaceable"). (1) Zebedee's wife and the mother of James and John (Mark 15:40; 16:1). She was one of the women who witnessed the crucifixion (Matt. 27:56). She also took sweet spices to the sepulchre on the morning of the resurrection (Mark 16:1). (2) The daughter of Herodias by her first husband, Herod Philip. She is not actually named in the Gospel accounts but is certainly the girl who danced before Herod Antipas (Matt. 14:6; Mark 6:22). Josephus identifies her as Salome. Her evil mother used the occasion and the foolish oath of Herod to have John the Baptist beheaded. Salome later married her great-uncle, Philip the Tetrarch.

SALT SEA. See "Dead Sea."

SAMARIA (sà-mâr'ĭ-à) (1) The capital of the Hebrew Northern Kingdom. It was founded by Omri in the ninth century B.C. (1 Kings 16:24). The Assyrians took it in 722 B.C. (2 Kings 17:5, 6). The native population was displaced by foreigners (2 Kings 17:24), who practiced a mixed worship of the Lord (2 Kings 17: 29). It later became the capital of an Assyrian and then of a Persian province (Ezra 4:17). Herod the Great rebuilt it and renamed it Sebaste. (2) The central highland ridge extending from Galilee in northern Palestine to Judea in southern Palestine (Jer. 31:5). "The hill of Samaria," on which Omri built the capital of the Northern Kingdom, was purchased for two talents of silver (about four thousand dollars) from a man named Shemer (1 Kings 16:23, 24).

SAMARITANS (sà-măr'ĭ-tăns). The descendants of the colonists whom Shalmaneser V, king of Assyria, brought from Cutha, Babylon, Hamath, and other foreign places after he had conquered Samaria in 722 B.C. (2 Kings 17). Two later Assyrian kings, Esarhaddon and Ashurbanipal, added other pagan deportees. The first settlers were overrun by lions and appealed for a priest of the Lord to teach them the faith of Israel. The result was a mixed worship of Jehovah. The Jews despised the Samaritans for this (John 4:9). The Samaritans in turn obstructed the efforts of Ezra and Nehe-

Samaritan chief priest and ancient scroll in Nablus, ancient Shechem (© *MPS*)

miah to rebuild Jerusalem and reestablish the sanctuary (cf. Ezra 4:2-24). Jews contemptuously called Samaritans "Cuthites" because they came from Cutha and other pagan cities.

SAMOS (sā′mŏs). One of the larger islands in the Aegean Sea. It is situated off the coast of Asia Minor southwest of Ephesus. A narrow strait runs between Samos and the mainland at Trogillium. Paul sailed through this body of water on his way home from his third missionary journey (Acts 20:15). Emperor Augustus made Samos a free state in 17 B.C.

SAMOTHRACE (săm′ō-thrās). A small, mountainous island of the northeastern Aegean Sea off the coast of Thrace. A town by the same name was situated on the northern side. Paul sailed northwest from Troas to Neapolis, reaching Samothrace in one day and Neapolis the next (Acts 16:11).

SAMSON (săm′sŭn) ("little sun"). A judge of Israel who rescued God's people from the Philistines (Judg. 13:1 – 16:31). As long as Samson kept his Nazarite vow he was invincible. But his ultimate violation of his vow culminated in a tragic ending (Judg. 16:30). Samson was a man of contrasts. He was occasionally Spirit-possessed (Judg. 13:25; 15:14), but he

frequently yielded to carnal appetites (Judg. 16:1-4). He was mighty in physical strength (Judg. 16:3-14) but weak in resisting temptation (Judg. 16:15-17). He was courageous in battle with the Philistines (Judg. 15:1-4) but cowardly in resisting the world, the flesh, and the Devil.

SAMUEL (săm′ū-ĕl) ("asked of God"). The last of the judges and the first of the prophets (Acts 3:24; 13:20). As a judge he exercised spiritual discernment and enforced the law and authority of the Lord (1 Sam. 7:15-17). As a prophet (1 Sam. 2:27-36; 3:19-21) his faithfulness rebuked the unfaithfulness of Eli. As a priest he interceded (1 Sam. 7:9), offered sacrifices (1 Sam. 7:9, 10), and anointed kings (1 Sam. 10:1; 16:13).

SANDALS. For the protection of the feet the Hebrews, like other eastern peoples, wore sandals. In their simplest form sandals consisted simply of pieces of leather bound to the soles of the feet by thongs (Gen. 14:23; Isa. 5:27; Mark 1:7; John 1:27). Tomb paintings and other archeological remains reveal that sandals varied greatly in style, even resembling shoes or boots at times.

SAPPHIRA (să-fī′rà) (Aramaic "fair one"). A Christian in the first church in Jerusalem. She was the wife of Ananias (Acts 5:1). Like Samson and Saul, Ananias and Sapphira committed the "sin unto (physical) death" (Acts 5:1-11; cf. 1 John 5:16). They yielded themselves to Satan by lying to the Holy Spirit regarding their financial commitment.

SAR (Assyrian *sharru*, "king"). A leader or chieftain of Israel (Num. 21:18), of Midian (Judg. 7:25; 8:3), or of the Philistines (1 Sam. 29:3). The word is also used of a noble or official under a king (Gen. 12:15; Isa. 30:4) or of a military captain or general (1 Sam. 12:9; 1 Kings 1:25). It was sometimes employed as a term of rank and dignity (Isa. 23:8).

SARAH (sā′rà) ("a princess"). The wife of Abraham and the mother of Isaac, the child of promise in the line of Messiah (Gen. 11:29-31; 21:1-5). Sarai (the earlier form of her name) was childless for years. When she was about 76 years old, she doubted that God's promise of posterity would ever be fulfilled. She therefore prevailed upon her husband to take Hagar, her handmaid, as a secondary wife. Abraham yielded to her unbelief and became the father of Ishmael (Gen. 16). Several years later Sarai gave birth to Isaac through divine promise and power. Sarai's name was then changed to Sarah, meaning "princess" (Gen. 17:15).

Sarah died at Hebron at the age of 127 years. She is listed as a hero of faith despite her doubts (Heb. 11:11).

SARDIS (sär'dĭs). The brilliant capital city of Lydia. Its position of wealth and power under Croesus ended abruptly when the city fell to Cyrus the Persian (549 B.C.). Now only a small village (Sart) remains near the site of the ancient city. One of the seven letters of the Revelation is addressed to the church in Sardis (Rev. 3:1-6). Excavations have uncovered the ancient splendor of the city.

SARGON (sär'gŏn) (Assyrian *Sharruukin*, "he has established the kingship"). The Assyrian emperor from 722 to 705 B.C. He is described in some detail in the inscriptions at his palace at Khorsabad. He is named only once in Scripture, in Isaiah 20:1.

SATAN. See "Devil."

SATRAP. A designation of various grades of governor under the Persian Empire. The word is derived from the Old Persian and means "protector of the realm." The satraps had their own courts and were endowed with considerable authority (cf. Esth. 8:9; 9:3).

SAUL (sôl) ("asked for, demanded"). The first king of Israel (1030-1010 B.C.). He was a man who began well but finished in tragedy and untimely death. Although God-anointed (1 Sam. 10:1), humble (1 Sam. 9:21), and self-controlled (1 Sam. 10:27) in his early years, Saul later became disobedient and self-willed (1 Sam. 13:8-14). He rejected God's sovereignty over his kingship, and God in turn rejected him as king. He committed "the sin unto (physical) death" (1 John 5:16) and sealed his doom by resorting to occultism (1 Sam. 28:7-14).

SAUL OF TARSUS. The name of the Apostle Paul before his conversion and dedication to Christ (Acts 7:58).

SCAPEGOAT. The goat which symbolically carried away the sins of the Jewish people on the Day of Atonement (Lev. 16:10). The scapegoat typifies that aspect of Christ's work which puts away our sins from God's presence (Heb. 9:26). The goat slain (the Lord's lot—Lev. 16: 8, 9) portrays that facet of Christ's atonement which vindicates the divine holiness as expressed in the Law (Rom. 3:24-26).

SCARLET. A color which symbolizes safety through sacrifice (as in the scarlet line of Rahab—Josh. 2:21; Heb. 9:19-22). Scarlet was a prominent color in the Tabernacle ritual and symbolism (Exod. 25:4; 28:5, 6; 35:6, 23, 25; 38:18; Lev. 14:4; Num. 4:8). See also "Blue" and "Purple."

SCORPION. An anthropod commonly found in hot, dry countries. About a dozen kinds are found in Palestine. The scorpion's tail is armed with a poisonous sting which inflicts great pain (Rev. 9:5, 10). Rehoboam threatened to punish his subjects with scorpions (1 Kings 12:11), which were probably whips armed with sharp points to cause pain like a scorpion sting.

SCRIBE (Hebrew *sopher;* Greek *grammateus, nomikos*). Jewish experts in the Law of Moses. They originated after the Exile. The scribes instituted the synagogue service. Some were members of the Sanhedrin (Matt. 16:21; 26:3). They transmitted unwritten legal decisions (oral law) in their effort to apply the Mosaic Law to daily life. However, they eventually claimed that their oral law was more important than the written Law, thereby substituting human tradition for the Word of God (Mark 7:6-13).

SCULPTURE. The Canaanites possessed considerable artistic ability, and examples of their skill in sculpture have been recovered in Canaanite ruins in various Palestinian sites, such as Hazor and Tell Beit Mirsim. However, the works of their neighbors (such as the sculptured sarcophagus of Ahiram of Byblos) are much better known. Volute capitals found at Megiddo and Samaria were the forerunners of the Ionic type. Ossuary workers at Jerusalem have left us several chests engraved with six-pointed stars, rosettes, and flowers.

SCYTHIA (sĭth'ĭ-à). The region north of the Black Sea. It was the home of the uncivilized people known as Scythians. They were proverbially "barbarians" to Greeks and Romans (cf. Col. 3:11).

SCYTHOPOLIS (sĭth-ŏp'ɔ-lĭs). The Greek name of ancient Beth-shan (present-day Tell el-Husn). It is mentioned in the apocryphal books of Judith and Maccabees. In the time of Christ it was a city of the Decapolis. Scythopolis was thoroughly Hellenic and had a hippodrome, theater, and pagan temples.

SEA. The most prominent sea in the Bible is the Mediterranean. It lies west of Palestine, forming its entire western border. The Hebrew word for sea (yām) also means "west" or "westward," that is, "seaward." This large and beautiful body of water provided a most important means of travel and trade, linking the Holy Land with the civilized world of the time through such seaports as Joppa in Old Testament times and Caesarea in New Testament times. The Mediterranean Sea made accessible the long southern seaboard of Europe and the opposite coast of North Africa. Venturesome mariners passed through the straits of Gibraltar and out into the Atlantic, thereafter sailing to Africa or the British Isles. The Red Sea and the Persian Gulf opened up exploration of the east coast of Africa and the coastal regions of Arabia. Points in Asia were accessible across the Indian Ocean.

The Hebrews displayed little enthusiasm for the sea. Solomon depended heavily on Phoenician craftsmen both to build and operate his commercial fleet at Ezion-geber on the Red Sea (1 Kings 9: 26-28). Once every three years this fleet of vessels transported refined copper to Africa and South Arabia in exchange for gold, silver, ivory, apes, peacocks, and other exotic products (1 Kings 10:22). The Phoenicians, Israel's neighbors on the northwest, were thus the true sailors of antiquity. Egyptians, Greeks, Romans, and Carthaginians also plied the sea. Numerous accounts of voyages of these various peoples have come down to us. Paul's famous voyage to Rome in New Testament times shows how important sea traffic was.

SEAL. A symbol of the indwelling Holy Spirit as the security of the believer (Eph. 1:13, 14; 4:30; 2 Cor. 1:22). A seal signifies a finished transaction (Jer. 32:9, 10; John 17:4; 19:30), ownership (Jer. 32:11, 12; 2 Tim. 2:19), and security (Esth. 8:8; Dan. 6:17).

SEASONS. See under "Calendar, Hebrew."

SECOND DEATH. The "lake of fire," the eternal isolation ward for all sin and sinners (Rev. 21:8). It is called the *second* death because it follows physical death. The second death involves everlasting separation from God in sins (Matt. 25:41-46; 2 Thess. 1:7-9).

SEIR (sē'ĭr). (1) A mountain south of the Dead Sea in the land of Edom (Gen. 14: 6; Ezek. 35:15). (2) The mountainous land of Edom itself (Gen. 32:3; 36:21). This was Esau's home (Gen. 32:3). (3) Esau's descendants, who overcame the original inhabitants, the Horites (Gen. 14:6; 36:20; Deut. 2:12).

SELA (sē'là). The capital of Edom (2 Kings 14:7; Isa. 16:1). It was later called Petra by the Greeks. See "Petra."

SENNACHERIB (sĕ-năk'ĕr-ĭb). The king of Assyria from 705 to 681 B.C. He was the son and successor of Sargon II. Sennacherib overran Judah under Hezekiah in 701 B.C. He besieged Jerusalem but failed to take the city, as his own records confirm (2 Kings 18:13 – 19:34). God miraculously delivered Jerusalem and Judah (2 Kings 19:35, 36). The tyrant was murdered by two of his sons. Esarhaddon, a third son, succeeded him (2 Kings 19:37).

SEPARATION. God's people are to separate themselves from every sinful or defiling activity. Separation represents the human side of sanctification. Old Testament illustrations include Abraham's separation from Ur with its idolatry and Israel's separation from Egypt by the Exodus.

The New Testament teaches that the believer has been separated from his old position of slavery to sin in Adam by the redemptive work of Christ (Rom. 5:12 – 6:23). Believers are expected to shun unholy alliances of any kind (2 Tim. 2: 20, 21; 2 John 1:9-11). Separation from all sin must be followed by joining oneself actively to God in dedicated service (Rom. 12:1, 2).

SERAPHIM. See "Cherubim and Seraphim."

SERPENT. A reptile which creeps on its belly (Gen. 3:14). Palestine has some eighteen species of snakes. The "fiery serpents" of Numbers 21:6 were a poisonous species found in Arabia and the Sinai Peninsula. Their bite caused burning fever and thirst. The serpent symbolized sin and its outcome — death. The bronze replica of the serpent portrayed Christ's judgment and conquest of sin (Num. 21:9; John 3:14-16). See also "Adder," "Asp," and "Viper."

SETH (sĕth) ("appointed, substituted"). The third son of Adam and Eve. He was born after Cain had murdered Abel. Seth served as Abel's substitute in the perpetuation of the messianic line (Gen. 4:25, 26).

SHALMANESER (shăl-măn-ē′zẽr) (Assyrian, "the god Shulman is chief"). The name of several Assyrian emperors. Shalmaneser III (859-824 B.C.) clashed with a coalition of kings at Qarqar in 853 B.C. "Ahab the Israelite" was a member of this federation. Shalmaneser III received tribute from "Jehu, son of Omri," an event not mentioned in the Old Testament but portrayed on the Black Obelisk. Shalmaneser V (727-722 B.C.) vanquished Hoshea of Israel (2 Kings 17:3) and besieged Samaria for three years, until it fell in 722 B.C. (2 Kings 17:5, 6). This event is also recorded in the Babylonian Chronicle.

SHARON (shăr′ŭn). A large, fertile plain which spans 50 miles between Carmel and Joppa and extends ten miles back to the hills of Samaria. It is fertile (Isa. 35:2) and rich in vegetation (1 Chron. 27:29). Lydda was at its southern limits (Acts 9:35). The Plain of Sharon is the garden spot of Palestine.

SHEAR-JASHUB (shē′ăr-jä′shŭb) ("a remnant shall come back"). The infant son of Isaiah, whom he had with him (probably in his arms) when he announced the virgin-birth prophecy (Isa. 7:13-16). The child served to make the prophecy relevant to King Ahaz.

SHEBA (shē′bà). A region in South Arabia. Her queen visited Solomon (1 Kings 10:1-13). Sheba was a proverbial source of gold (Psa. 72:15) and incense (Jer. 6:

20; Isa. 60:6; Ezek. 27:22). At the capital city, Marib, archeology has unearthed examples of Sabaean art and architecture, notably the temple of the moon-god.

SHECHEM (shĕ′kĕm). (1) A city in central Palestine in the hill country of Ephraim (Josh. 20:7). It is in the vicinity of Mount Gerizim (Judg. 9:7) and lies about 31 miles north of Jerusalem and 6 miles southeast of Samaria. Shechem had patriarchal associations (Gen. 12:6; 33:18; 37:12). It was a city of refuge and a Levitical town (Josh. 20:7; 21:21). Joseph was buried there (Josh. 24:32). Shechem was the focal point for the assembly of Israel (Josh. 24:1; 1 Kings 12:1). It was fortified by Jeroboam I (1 Kings 12:25) and was the first capital of the Northern Kingdom. (2) A Hivite prince who disgraced his princely dignity and suffered the consequences at the hands of Jacob's sons, Simeon and Levi (Gen. 34).

SHEEP. Sheep and goats were the most common of the small domestic animals in Bible times. Sheep were raised from earliest human history (Gen. 4:2). The sheep was a ceremonially clean animal under Mosaic Law and could therefore be used for food (Lev. 11:1-3). Its milk supplied many dairy products (Deut. 32:14; Isa. 7:21, 22). Cloth was woven from its wool (Job 31:20; Prov. 27:26; Ezek. 34:3). As a clean animal the sheep was used in sacrifice (Exod. 20:24; Num. 22:40). The sheep and the sheepcote furnish much of the redemptive imagery of the Bible (cf. Isa. 53:7; John 1:29; 1 Pet. 1:18, 19).

SHEKEL. See under "Weights and Measures" and "Coins and Money."

SHEKINAH (shĕ-kī′nà). The radiant and glorious light which denoted the presence of the invisible God among his people (Exod. 40:34-38; Ezek. 43:2-4). The Shekinah resided beneath the overspread wings of the cherubim, above the mercy seat in the most holy place. God's glory also appears in the New Testament (Luke 2:9; 2 Cor. 3:18; Rev. 15:8; Rev. 21:23).

SHELOMITH (shĕl′ŏ-mīth) (feminine form of *Shelomi*, "peaceful, complete"). A Danite woman whose son was stoned to death in the wilderness for blaspheming the name of the Lord (Lev. 24:10-23).

The incident shows the gravity of cursing God's name.

SHEM (shĕm) ("name, renown"). A son of Noah and a perpetuator of the messianic line. The Jewish people are "Shemites" or "Semites."

SHEMA (shē'mȧ). The initial Hebrew word of Deuteronomy 6:4. *Shema^c* means "Hear!" The full verse forms a concise Jewish confession of faith. In Hebrew liturgy the *Shema^c* refers to Deuteronomy 6:4-9 and 11:13-21 and Numbers 15:37-41. Deuteronomy 6:4 has become a slogan of Judaism, emphasizing its monotheistic faith.

SHEPHERD. Shepherding is probably the most sentimentally appealing occupation of Bible countries, since it pictures the guarding of human souls. Shepherds have existed since the time of Abel (Gen. 4:2). A shepherd's responsibility is clearcut and challenging. He must find pasturage and water in an arid, stony land (Psa. 23:2). He must protect his charges from the storm and the wild beast (Amos 3:12) and must retrieve any lost animal (Ezek. 34:8; Matt. 18:12). Christ is pictured as the Shepherd of Israel (Gen. 49:24; Psa. 23:1; Isa. 40:11), the Good Shepherd (John 10:1-18), and the Chief Shepherd (Heb. 13:20; 1 Pet. 2:25; 5:4). Christ's pastors are his under-shepherds (1 Pet. 5:2).

SHEOL (shē'ōl). An Old Testament Hebrew word meaning "grave" (Gen. 42:38; Job 14:13; Psa. 88:3). It is a place of sorrow (2 Sam. 22:6; Psa. 18:5; 116:3) to which the wicked are consigned while fully conscious (Psa. 9:17; Ezek. 32:21). *Sheol* is equivalent to the New Testament word *hades* (Luke 16:19-31). See also "Gehenna."

SHIELD (Hebrew *ṣinnâ*). A large shield designed to cover the whole body. It was either oval or rectangular in shape and was as large as a door. Hence the Greek name was *thureos*, derived from *thyra*, "a door." (This large shield is inaccurately rendered "buckler" or "target" in the King James Version.)

All nations of antiquity employed shields in heavy-armed infantry (2 Chron. 14:8). Goliath, the Philistine champion, had a special shield-bearer (1 Sam. 17:7). Shields were usually made of wood or wickerwork overlaid with leather. Sometimes shields of gold or bronze were used (1 Kings 10:16, 17; cf. 14:26, 27).

SHILOH (shī'lō). (1) A city located about nine miles north of Bethel. It was an early assembly place of Israel (Josh. 18:1). The tabernacle was erected in Shiloh (Josh. 18:1; 1 Sam. 1:3). The site is present-day Seilun. (2) A symbolic name for Messiah. Rule in Judah will not depart until he comes; then his sovereignty will include the whole world (Gen. 49:10).

SHILOAH. See under "Springs, Wells, and Pools."

SHIMEI (shĭm'ė-ī) (shortened from *Shima^cyahu*, "the Lord has heard"). The man who cursed David maliciously (2 Sam. 16:5-14). David bore the insult patiently, but Solomon later executed Shimei (1 Kings 2:36-46).

SHINAR (shī'när). The lower alluvial plain of the Tigris-Euphrates Rivers. In this region were located such ancient cities as Babylon, Erech, (Uruk), Akkad (Agade), and Calneh (Gen. 10:10). It was here that the Tower of Babel was attempted (Gen. 11:2-4).

SHIPHRAH (shĭf'rȧ) ("fair one"). One of the Hebrew midwives in Egypt who refused to obey the royal command to kill all Jewish male babies (Exod. 1:15-17). The name appears in a list of Egyptian slaves. The Aramaic form, Sapphira, occurs in the New Testament (Acts 5:1). God blessed Shiphrah and her companions for their integrity (Exod. 1:20, 21).

Egypt's pharaoh Shishak recorded here his battle victory over Judah's Rehoboam. (© *MPS*)

SHISHAK (shī'shăk). Pharaoh Sheshonq

I (945-924 B.C.), the founder of the twenty-second Egyptian dynasty. He invaded Palestine in the fifth year of Rehoboam (925 B.C.) and subdued Judah (1 Kings 14:25, 26; 2 Chron. 12:2-12). He also overran Israel, as is evident from his stele found at Megiddo and from his exploits recorded at the temple of Amun in Thebes.

SHIRT-TUNIC (Hebrew *kuttoneth*, Greek *chitōn*). A linen or woolen frock made short or long and with or without sleeves. It was worn next to the skin and frequently reached to the knees or ankles. It became prominent about 1400 B.C. and was the normal dress after 1200 B.C. The garment was similar for both sexes, though the woman's garment was fuller and of richer material than the man's.

The Bible also refers to a long, half-sleeved, shirtlike tunic which reached to the ankles (Gen. 37:3, 23, 31-35). The famous Benihasan painting illustrates such garments in white and various colors. It was worn by princes (2 Sam. 13:18, 19), by Christ (John 19:23), and by the high priest at Christ's trial (Mark 14:63).

SHITTIM (shĭt'ŭm). See "Acacia."

SHOMER (shō'mēr) ("keeper, guard"). The mother of Jehozabad, one of the servants who murdered King Joash (Jehoash) of Judah (2 Kings 12:21; 2 Chron. 24:26). The name is also spelled Shamer (1 Chron. 7:34) and Shimrith (2 Chron. 24:26). Shomer was a Moabite woman.

SHUNEM (shoo'nĕm). A town in the territory of Issachar near Jezreel (Josh. 19:18). It was the site of the Philistine camp before the battle of Gilboa (1 Sam. 28:4). It was here that Elisha miraculously raised the son of the Shunamite woman (2 Kings 4:8-37). Abishag was brought to David from this city (1 Kings 1:3, 15). The site is identified with present-day Solem.

SHUSHAN, SUSA (shoo'shăn, soo'sà). One of the three royal cities of the Persian Empire (Dan. 8:2; Neh. 1:1). The palace which Darius I built in Shushan constitutes one of the outstanding architectural features of the fifth century B.C. (cf. Esth. 1:2, 5; 2:3; 3:15).

SICILY. A large island at the toe of the foot of Italy. Paul sailed the narrow straits between this island and the Italian mainland on his trip to Puteoli and Rome. The famous city of Sicily was Syracuse, located at the southeastern extremity of the island.

SIDDIM (sĭd'ĭm), **VALLEY OF.** Originally a fertile, well-watered region south of the Lisan peninsula of the Dead Sea. It was later submerged by earthquake action (Gen. 14:3, 10).

SIDON (sī'dŏn). The chief Phoenician city before the rise of Tyre in the tenth century B.C. (Gen. 10:19; 1 Chron. 1:13). The city lay 25 miles northeast of Tyre. The present-day site is Saida in Lebanon. The city is prominent in both the Old Testament (Judg. 1:31; 1 Kings 17:9; Isa. 23:2; Joel 3:4-8) and the New Testament (Matt. 11:21; Acts 27:3).

SILAS (sī'làs). Apparently the same person as Silvanus (2 Cor. 1:19; 1 Thess. 1:1; 2 Thess. 1:1; 1 Pet. 5:12), the Latinized form of the name Silas. He was a member and prophet of the church at Jerusalem (Acts 15:32) and a delegate of the apostolic council (Acts 15:22). Silas was apparently a Roman citizen (Acts 16:37) and spiritually qualified to take Barnabas' place as Paul's companion (Acts 15:40; cf. 16:19-29). He was also associated with Peter (1 Pet. 5:12).

SILOAM, POOL OF. See under "Springs, Wells, and Pools."

SILVER. In the Tabernacle symbolism, silver pictures redemption. When the Tabernacle was first constructed Moses was commanded to collect from every Israelite a half-shekel of silver (Exod. 30:11-16), called "atonement money." Its purpose was "to make atonement for your souls" (Exod. 30:16). The silver collected in this manner was used for the sockets of the sanctuary and for the rods and hooks. As a result the Tabernacle rested on silver sockets. The curtains of the door (the way of access) were hung from silver rods and hooks (Exod. 27:17). But the atonement money was only a *token* payment. The actual redemption was not by silver or gold but by Christ's own blood (1 Pet. 1:18, 19).

SIMEON (sĭm'ē-ŭn) ("hearing"). One of Jacob's sons (Gen. 29:33). He took part in the massacre at Shechem (Gen. 34) and was rebuked for his bloody act by the dying Jacob (Gen. 49:5-7).

SIMEON OF JERUSALEM. A devout believer at Jerusalem who awaited the coming of the Messiah and saw his faith rewarded (Luke 2:25-34).

SIMON (sī'mŏn) **THE JUST.** A famous high priest of the third century B.C. He was lauded by Jesus Ben Sira in the apocryphal book of Ecclesiasticus.

SIMON THE MACCABEE. One of the five sons of the priest Mattathias, who fought for the Jewish faith against Hellenistic paganism. Simon became the successor of his brother Jonathan and established the Hasmonean dynasty (143-135 B.C.), which lasted till the rise of Herod the Great (37 B.C.).

SIMON MAGUS. A magician and sorcerer of Samaria who attempted to purchase the gifts of the Spirit with money (Acts 8: 9-24).

SIN. God is infinitely holy and is not the author of sin (Hab. 1:13; Tit. 1:2; James 1:13; 1 John 1:5). The "evil" God is said to create (Isa. 45:7) connotes "adversity" or "calamity." He has ordered that sorrow and misery shall be the inescapable results of sin. God did not create sinners, either angelic or human. The original universe was sinless (Job 38:4-7). Sin began among the angels in Lucifer's revolt (Isa. 14:12-14; Ezek. 28:11-19). Man was created in innocence and freedom of choice. But he fell and introduced sin into the human family (Gen. 3:1-19; Rom. 5:12-21; 1 Cor. 15:22). Because God is infinitely holy and separate from sin, fallen angels and Christ-rejecting men must face eternal separation from God. Unbelievers who regard hell as inconsonant with a God of love fail to comprehend God's full-orbed character (Nah. 1:3).

SIN. A city at the extreme northeast of the Nile Delta. The Greeks called it Pelusium. It is present-day Tell Farama and is located about 32 miles east of Raamses across Lake Menzaleh.

SINAI (sī'nī). The mountain in the Sinai Peninsula where the Law was given to Moses (Exod. 19:1-6; Gal. 4:24). It is the same as Mount Horeb. The precise identification of Mount Sinai is uncertain. Jebel Musa (7,370 feet) or Jebel Serbal (6,825 feet) are the most likely possibilities.

SINGER. Both men and women singers had a prominent part in the tabernacle and temple worship as developed by David and subsequent kings (cf. 1 Chron 9:33; 15:19; 2 Chron. 5:13). Singers and instrumentalists graced all the royal courts of antiquity.

SION, SIRION (sī'ŭn, sīr'ĭ-ŏn). A synonym for Mount Hermon or one of its three peaks (Deut. 4:48). Sirion was the Canaanite name for Mount Hermon, as used in the Old Testament by the Sidonians (Deut. 3:9; cf. Psa. 29:6).

SISERA (sĭs'ĕr-à). A Canaanite general who commanded the army of Jabin, king of Hazor (Judg. 4:2), in battle against Deborah and Barak. He was slain by Jael after his army suffered defeat (Judg. 4:1-31).

SLAVERY. The practice of slavery was regulated but not instituted by the Mosaic Law. The Law mitigated the hardship of slavery and guaranteed certain rights to everyone. A Hebrew could be reduced to servitude by selling himself in order to pay his debts and support his family (Lev. 25:25, 39). He could also fall into slavery as the result of theft (Exod. 22:1, 3). Sometimes a person became a servant through the exercise of paternal authority. This was limited to the sale of a daughter as a servant, frequently with the hope that she would become the concubine of the purchaser (Exod. 21:7-11).

The Mosaic Law humanely provided for the termination of all servitude at the end of six years of service (Exod. 21:2; Deut. 15:12). The Year of Jubilee (every fiftieth year) also ended all servitude (Lev. 25:39-41). Of course, the satisfaction or remission of all valid claims against the servant also resulted in his freedom. A servant who preferred to remain perpetually in the service of his master could signify his intention by having his ear pierced with an awl in the presence of judicial authorities (Exod. 21:6).

The Law prohibited cruel and inhumane treatment of servants (Lev. 25:39-43) and enjoined kindness and liberality (Deut. 15:12-15). However, some aspects of slavery in Israel might seem stringent when compared with modern, Christianized practices. For example, a father

could sell his young daughter to a Hebrew with the hope that the purchaser or
his son would marry her (Exod. 21:7-9).
In this case the purchase money was considered a dowry given to the parents of
the bride. Doubtless the consent of the
maid had to be obtained, as the later Rab-
bis contend. In any case she was protected by law against exploitation (Exod. 21:
7-11).

Enslavement of Hebrews by fellow
Hebrews fell into gradual disuse, especially after the exile. Great numbers of
Jews, however, were reduced to slavery as
war prisoners by Phoenicians, Philistines, Romans, etc.

Non-Hebrew slaves were commonly
war captives of the Canaanites and other
foreign nations (cf. Num. 31:26-30).
Some were purchased from foreign slave-
dealers (Lev. 25:44, 45). The children of
slaves remained slaves, being "born in
the house" (Gen. 14:14; 17:12; Eccl.
2:7). The average price of a slave was 30
shekels (Exod. 21:32). He was the property of his master and could be sold freely
as an article of personal possession (Lev.
25:45, 46).

Provision was made for the physical
protection of the slave (Exod. 21:20; Lev.
24:17, 22). Loss of bodily members was
to be recompensed by granting the servant liberty (Exod. 21:26, 27). Religious
provision was also made for him in circumcision (Gen. 17:12) and participation
in the Passover and other religious festivals (Exod. 12:44; Deut. 12:12, 18; 16:11,
14). The Mosaic legislation thus made
slavery similar to hired service. As a result slavery almost disappeared among
the Jews long before the Christian era.
Christianity itself announced the full
freedom in Christ which eventually abolished slavery completely as an institution
in Christianized lands.

SLING. A simple weapon used chiefly by
shepherds to ward off prowling beasts
from their flock. David was armed with a
sling and developed great skill in using it
(1 Sam. 17:40, 49, 50). It was also used as
a weapon of war among the Assyrians,
Babylonians, and Egyptians. Stones for
ammunition were abundant in Palestine,
and Israelites employed companies of
slingers as an important sector of their

armed forces (Zech. 9:15). The Benjamites were famous as skilled slingers (1
Chron. 12:2).

The sling was made of a strip of leather
which was broadened in the center to
form a cavity for the stone. Both ends of
the leather strip were held firmly in one
hand while the loaded sling was whirled
rapidly around the head. Then one end
was released suddenly. With proper control the stone could strike its target with
deadly force.

SMITH. Fine work in gold, silver, and
copper was executed by Palestinians long
before the advent of the iron age (about
1200 B.C.). When iron smelting methods
were learned by Israelites in the Davidic-
Solomonic era, a variety of metal instruments began to be produced by smiths.
Plow blades, axes, forks, tips for ox-
goads, knives, swords, daggers, lances,
spears, and other weapons of war became
common under David and Solomon.

Smiths' workshops began to dot the
land. Metal was melted in a furnace heated by coals (Isa. 54:16). The molten
metal was beaten on an anvil while still
hot (Isa. 41:7). Joints were soldered or
riveted together (Isa. 41:7). See also "Artisan."

SMYRNA (smûr′nà). A city of the Roman
province of Asia. Smyrna was the site of
one of the seven churches of the Revelation (Rev. 1:11; 2:8-11). It is present-day
Izmir, located on a bay opening to the
Aegean Sea.

SOCIAL LIFE, JEWISH. The ancient
Hebrews, like most Orientals, were a
highly social people. Their spiritual calling and organization contributed to this
result. The entire family was expected to
appear before the Lord at the sanctuary
during pilgrimage festivals (Deut. 16:14).
Other occasions for social gatherings
were sheep-shearings, grain and fruit
harvests, the weaning of children, the
wedding seasons, and the normal enter-
taining of guests. The private home, the
city gate, the marketplace, and the public
well all served as places of social inter-
change.

Hospitality was normal for a people
bound to each other and the Lord in a
covenant relationship. Hospitality was
exemplified by the earliest patriarchs

(Gen. 18:1-8) and was repeatedly enjoined by the Mosaic Law (e.g. Deut. 10:19). The greeting of guests was ordinarily warm and profuse (Gen. 23:7, 12). "Peace be to you" was a common greeting, equivalent to our "Hello" (1 Sam. 25:6; 1 Chron. 12:18).

SOCOH (sō'kō). (1) A town in Solomon's third district (1 Kings 4:10). It is probably present-day Tell er-Ras, near the Plain of Sharon. (2) A town in the lowlands of Judah (Josh. 15:35; 1 Sam. 17:1). (3) A town in the hill country of Judah (Josh. 15:48). It is probably present-day Khirbet Shuweikeh, between Hebron and Beersheba.

SODOM. A city formerly located south of the Dead Sea (Gen. 10:19; 14:2-12). It was apparently submerged by the waters of the Dead Sea when it was destroyed by God (Gen. 19:24, 25).

SOLDIER. In early Israel there was no regular army. Recruits were enlisted on a voluntary basis when a crisis arose. Military leaders were raised up by God in the theocracy and were enabled to muster men quickly for battle, sometimes as the result of performing a heroic deed (Judg. 6:24-34). When the theocracy gave way to the monarchy, a standing army was formed. King Saul selected a contingent of private warriors. Under David the same policy prevailed, but the force was greatly increased (2 Sam. 15:18). The general levy of nonprofessional military men was divided into thousands, hundreds, fifties, and tens. Each category had its own commander. (This order apparently dated from Moses' time but had fallen into temporary disarray during the chaotic Period of the Judges.)

The archer was prominent in battle. Cavalry became important in the Solomonic era despite the prohibition of Deuteronomy 17:16. Solomon employed horses and chariots on a huge scale (1 Kings 10:26), as his stables at Megiddo attest (1 Kings 4:26). Soldiers were maintained by booty, by the produce of the land where they camped, and (under David and Solomon) by regular pay (1 Kings 4:27).

SOLOMON ("peaceable"). A son of David and his successor to the throne of Israel (971-931 B.C.). He was the wisest, wealth-iest, and most famous king of Israel, but in the end his sensuality and apostasy became his undoing. Though he was the wisest of men, sin turned him into a fool. He became a disillusioned man of the world, as seen in the book of Ecclesiastes. His earlier brilliant reign under God's blessing witnessed great commercial expansion and building operations, notably the magnificent Temple (1 Kings 3:1 – 11:43).

SONSHIP. The relation into which a person enters when he is saved and admitted to God's family (John 1:12, 13; 3:5; Rom. 8:16, 17). This is effected by regeneration (the new or second birth, accomplished by the Holy Spirit through God's Word).

With regard to the elect nation Israel, sonship expresses the covenant relationship of this people with the Lord (Exod. 4:22, 23; Hos. 11:1). With regard to God's relation to the human race as a whole, sonship expresses the *creatorial* relationship of man to God (Luke 3:38; Acts 17:28). This does not mean that all men are *spiritually* related to God, for Scripture teaches that they are not (Eph. 4:17, 18).

SONSHIP OF CHRIST. Christ bears five distinct relationships of sonship: Son of God, Son of Adam, Son of Abraham, Son of David, and Son of Mary. As the Son of God Christ is the unique Son from all eternity, coeternal and coequal with the Father (Matt. 16:16). As the Son of Adam or Son of man Christ is revealed in his human aspect (Matt. 8:20). As the Son of Abraham Christ appears in the messianic line and is therefore related to the Abrahamic Covenant (Matt. 1:1). As the Son of David Christ is associated with the Davidic Covenant (Matt. 21:9). As the Son of Mary Christ is related to the incarnation (Matt. 1:25).

SOPATER (sō'pà-tēr) ("of sound parentage"). A believer from Berea who accompanied Paul on his return from his third missionary tour (Acts 20:4; Rom. 16:21).

SORCERY. A general term for the practice of the occult arts (fortune-telling, divination, magic, spiritism, witchcraft, etc.). Sorcery was practiced at the Egyptian court (Exod. 7:11; 8:7, 18). The "magicians" resisted Moses by appealing to demonic powers masquerading as Egyptian deities. By this means they were able to counterfeit some of God's miracles displayed through Moses. Daniel also encountered occult workers in Babylonia in the sixth century B.C. (Dan. 2:2). They also tried to imitate the power of God through demonic means. Such demon-energized practitioners of false religions constantly threatened the pure faith of God's people (Isa. 2:6; Jer. 27:9; Mic. 5:12).

The clairvoyant medium with whom Paul clashed at Philippi (Acts 16:16-18), as well as Simon of Samaria (Acts 8:9-11) and Bar-Jesus of Paphos in Cyprus (Acts 13:6-11), practiced the occult arts in demonized religionism. All employment of sorcery was sternly forbidden by the Mosaic Law (Lev. 19:31; 20:6; Deut. 18:9-12).

SOUL AND SPIRIT. The immaterial part of man. The soul is related to life, action, and emotion. The spirit knows (1 Cor. 2:11) and is capable of communication with God when enlivened by the Holy Spirit (Job 32:8; Prov. 20:27; Psa. 18:28). The terms "soul" and "spirit" are sometimes used interchangeably, but they are nevertheless distinct (Heb. 4:12; 1 Cor. 15:44).

SOWER. Since sowing was done by hand in Bible days, the sower was a common figure in Palestine. Christ used this phase of the farmer's work to illustrate the Word of God planted in men's hearts (Matt. 13:1-9, 18-23).

SPARROW (Hebrew *ṣippōr*). Several species of sparrows are common in Palestine, such as the house sparrow, the Italian sparrow, the tree sparrow, and the rock sparrow. The Greek *strouthion* (Matt. 10:29; Luke 12:6, 7) implies not only the sparrow but a group of other small birds such as were, and still are, killed and offered for sale in Palestinian markets.

SPEAR. A weapon used from very ancient times. Metal-tipped spears became popular after the advent of metallurgy. Spears were often carried by kings and princes, military leaders, and individual warriors (1 Sam. 17:45; 19:9; 2 Sam. 2:23; cf. 2 Sam. 21:16).

The *logchē*, the spear which pierced

Christ's side (John 19:34), was almost certainly the Roman *pilum*, a javelin with a three-foot iron shaft inserted into a wooden shaft of the same length. In New Testament times all legionnaires were equipped with such a weapon.

SPICES (Hebrew *bōsem*). A vegetable substance which has aromatic and pungent qualities (Song 4:16; cf. Exod. 25:6; 1 Kings 10:10; Song 4:10). The chief spices were myrrh, calamus, cassia, and cinnamon (Exod. 30:23, 24). Arabia was the principal producer of spices (1 Kings 10:2; Ezek. 27:22).

SPIDER (Hebrew *ʿakkābīsh*). There are innumerable species of Spiders in Palestine. The "spider" in Proverbs 30:28, however, is probably actually the gecko. See "Lizard."

SPIKENARD (Hebrew *nērd;* Greek *nardos*). A fragrant oil obtained from the *Nardostachys jatamansi*, native to North India. In Bible times spikenard was very precious because of the long distance it had to be imported. It was sealed in alabaster containers, which were opened only on very special occasions (John 12:3).

SPIRITISM. Alleged communication with the dead through a spirit medium. The practice is a form of the occult arts and actually consists of the impersonation of dead persons by demonic spirits. This occult activity is severely condemned by God's Word (Lev. 19:31; 20:6, 27; Deut. 18:9-12; 1 Sam. 28:1-25).

SPIRITUAL GIFTS. Endowments given by the Holy Spirit to individual believers for the purpose of benefiting the church (1 Cor. 12:8-11; Rom. 12:3-8; Eph. 4:7-11). Certain gifts were meant to be temporary (1 Cor. 13:8) and were to be superseded by "the completed (final) thing" (1 Cor. 13:10), the completed New Testament Scriptures (1 Cor. 13:9-13).

SPRINGS, WELLS, AND POOLS. Water is a precious commodity in Palestine, since rainfall is not abundant. However, the geological structure of Palestine has provided it with many springs (Deut. 8:7). Since the presence of a permanent spring frequently made a particular site habitable for human beings, the Hebrew or Arabic words for "spring" often occur as a common element in place names.

For example, ᶜAin es Sultan is the fountain that determined the site of ancient Jericho.

Unlike a spring or fountain, which is provided by nature, a well is a manmade phenomenon. Successful wells are obtained by sinking a shaft or boring a hole into a natural underground spring (Gen. 24:11-14; John 4:11). Rainwater or well water was often stored in a cistern—a natural or manmade rock storage tank. The Pool of Siloam was supplied by both rainwater and springs. Sometimes water was conducted through channels from a cistern to nearby towns and gardens (Eccl. 2:6). In certain dry regions water was nearly as precious as gold. For this reason wells were sometimes the objects of fierce disputes (Gen. 21:25).

Some of the more significant springs, wells, and pools of Scripture are described below.

Beer-lahai-roi (bē′ĕr-là-hī′roi) ("well of the Living One who sees me"). A well on the road through the wilderness between Kadesh and Bered (Gen. 16:7, 14; 24:62). Bedouins identify it with present-day Ain Muweileh, about 12 miles northwest of Kadesh and 50 miles south of Beersheba.

Beer-sheba (bē′ĕr-shē′bà) ("well of the seven"). A place in south Judah where Abraham dug a well and where he and the king of Gerar made a treaty (Gen. 21: 22-32). The present city is 48 miles southwest of Jerusalem and two miles west of Tell es-Sebaᶜ, the original site of the ancient town.

Bethesda (bĕ-thĕz′dà). A pool at Jerusalem where Jesus healed an infirm man (John 5:2). It had five porticoes. Excavators have discovered in the northeast sector of the city a five-porched pool which appears to be this site.

Elim (ē′lĭm) ("large trees"). The second stopping place of the Israelites after crossing the Red (Reed) Sea. It was an oasis with twelve springs (Exod. 15:27; 16:1; Num. 33:9, 10). Biblical references suggest that it is situated on the west side of the Sinai Peninsula, on the Gulf of Suez. It is probably presentday Wadi Gharandel, about 40 miles southeast of Suez.

En-dor (ĕn′dôr) ("spring of habitation"). Modern ᶜIndur, on the north shoulder of

Little Hermon and six miles southeast of Nazareth in the tribe of Manasseh (Josh. 17:11). Fugitives from Sisera's defeated army perished there (Psa. 83:9, 10). The spirit medium consulted by Saul lived there (1 Sam. 28:7).

En-gedi (ĕn-gē′dĭ) ("spring of the goat"). A small oasis with a fresh-water spring located on the west mid-shore of the Dead Sea. The site was allotted to Judah (Josh. 15:62). En-gedi was a fertile spot in the midst of a desolate wilderness. It was a favorite hiding place for fugitives because food and caves were found nearby (Song 1:14; 1 Sam. 23:29; 24:1-7).

Gihon (gī′hŏn). A spring to the east of Jerusalem at which Solomon was anointed king (1 Kings 1:33, 38, 45). Hezekiah cut a tunnel through solid rock to conduct the water of Gihon to the pool of Siloam (2 Chron. 32:30). About 2000 B.C. the Jebusites cut a passage through the rock so that buckets could be let down a shaft to collect the water from the underground conduit.

Jacob's Well. This was located near Sychar. The site is identified with the village of Askar on the southeastern slope of Mount Ebal, about a half-mile to the north of Jacob's well. However, some scholars identify Sychar with ancient Shechem. Jesus met the woman of Samaria at Jacob's well and led her to a knowledge of salvation (John 4:5-29).

King's Pool. Probably the Lower or Old Pool of Jerusalem. See "Old Pools."

Marah (mä′rà). A spring of brackish water in the desert of Shur on the way to Sinai. Here Moses was divinely directed to cast a certain tree into the waters in order to make them potable (Exod. 15:23-25). Marah is probably to be located at Ain Hawarah, about 47 miles from Suez and a few miles inland from the Red Sea.

Old Pool. The Lower Pool or King's Pool, located near the Fountain Gate. The Old Pool is situated about 35 feet southeast of the Upper Pool and opens into the Kidron Valley. Modern buildings prevent archeologists from verifying that the Upper Pool was really Hezekiah's or that its waters overflowed directly to the Lower Pool. John 9:7-11 probably refers to the Old Pool.

Pool of Hebron (hē′brŭn). Hebron was

originally named Kiriath-arba, "tetrap-olis." It is 19 miles south-southwest of Jerusalem and is the highest town in Palestine, rising 3,040 feet above sea level. There are 25 springs of water and 10 large wells in the area. The pool was doubtless a rock-hewn reservoir.

Pool of Samaria (sȧ-mā'rĭ-ȧ). A reservoir on the north side of the city. It was cut out of rock and cemented. It was beside this pool that Ahab's servants washed the bloodstained chariot in which Ahab's body was brought home from Ramoth-Gilead (1 Kings 22:38).

Siloam (sĭ-lō'ăm) ("conducted"). The Upper Pool of Jerusalem. It is located near a bend in the old wall beneath Ophel. It is a rectangular reservoir measuring 58 feet long by 18 feet wide by 19 feet deep. It was the termination of Hezekiah's tunnel, which had been cut through the rock from the spring of Gihon. In 1880 bathers in the Upper Pool found the entrance to Hezekiah's tunnel and the famous inscription commemorating the cutting of the 1,777-foot aqueduct.

Solomon's Pools. These were located in the valley of Etam (Urtas) near Bethlehem and supplied water to Jerusalem. Three in number, the pools are about 200 feet wide, as much as 600 feet long, and 50 feet deep. They supplied water for Jerusalem from at least as early as Roman times.

Waters of Shiloah (shĭ-lō'ȧ). The gently flowing stream from the Gihon spring. It originally flowed outside the city wall to the Old Pool, but was later diverted by Hezekiah's tunnel to the Upper Pool of Siloam, within the city limits. Shiloah or Siloah is apparently identical with the Old or Lower Pool, the Pool of Shelah, and the King's Pool. See also "Old Pool."

STACTE (stăk'tē) (Hebrew *nāṭāph;* Greek *stactē*). One of the ingredients of the sacred anointing oil (Exod. 30:34). It is probably the gum of the storax tree.

STAFF (Hebrew *shēbeṭ*). A support carried by travelers (Gen. 32:10; Mark 6:8), shepherds (Psa. 23:4), old men (Zech. 8:4), and men of rank (Gen. 38:18). This accessory was a walking stick and was frequently carved and ornamented. It was as welcome a companion and support to the ancient Hebrews on the hilly roads of Palestine as the Alpine stick is to climbers of the Alps. It was also a kind of protective weapon (1 Sam. 17:43; 2 Sam. 23:21). The disciples of our Lord, despite the meagerness of their outfit, were allowed to carry a staff (Mark 6:8).

STEPHANAS (stĕf'ȧ-nȧs) ("crowned"). A convert of Paul's at Corinth (1 Cor. 1:16). He also visited the apostle later and brought him aid (1 Cor. 16:15, 17).

STEPHEN (stē'vĕn) ("wreath or crown"). The first Christian martyr. He was one of the seven deacons appointed to supervise benevolent work (Acts 6:5-8). He was also a powerful preacher (Acts 7:1-53). Stephen was stoned to death by Jewish leaders (Acts 7:54 – 8:3). He was full of faith (Acts 6:5), grace (Acts 6:8, RV), power, the Scriptures (Acts 7:1-53), wisdom (Acts 6:3, 10), courage (Acts 7:51-56), and love (Acts 7:60).

STEWARD. An official who manages the affairs of a large household, overseeing the service of the master's table, directing the household servants, and controlling the household expenses on behalf of the master. Jesus employed the figure in parables (Luke 16:1-9). The master of a vineyard is also called a steward (Matt. 20:8; Luke 8:3).

STOICISM. A school of philosophy founded by Zeno (300 B.C.). Stoicism taught that men should cultivate moral virtue and be masters of themselves under every circumstance. The important thing was growth in character – not pleasure or the pursuit of happiness. Stoicism was possibly the most noble of the pagan philosophies, even paralleling Christian teachings in some points. However, Stoicism could not offer Christ's deliverance from sin or the Holy Spirit's dynamic for righteousness. Paul encountered disciples of Stoic and Epicurean thought at Athens (Acts 17:18).

STONE. A prominent scriptural symbol portraying Christ. Christ became a stumblingstone to Israel because he came to earth as a servant instead of a conquering king (Isa. 8:14, 15; Matt. 21:44; Rom. 9:32, 33; 1 Cor. 1:23; 1 Pet. 2:8). Christ is related to the church as her foundation (1 Cor. 3:11) and chief cornerstone (Eph. 2:

20-22; 1 Pet. 2:4, 5). He is related to the nations in judgment as "the stone cut without hands" (Dan. 2:34), who will destroy the Satanic world system at the second advent. Whoever falls on this stone in faith and contrition will be broken and will find salvation. But those on whom the stone falls in judgment will be ground to dust (Matt. 21:44). See also "Rock."

STONECUTTER. The art of carving and setting precious stones was an important occupation in Bible times. The jewels on the breastplate of the high priest (Exod. 28:15-21) were cut with the names of the twelve tribes of Israel. Jewels for the noble and wealthy (Exod. 11:2; Isa. 3:18-21) also called for the skilled gem cutter. Precious and semiprecious stones were not cut in facets, as in contemporary art, but were rounded and polished and sometimes engraved and sculptured.

Another kind of stonecutter worked not as a jeweler but as a mason, dressing large blocks of building stone. Hiram of Tyre and Solomon obtained large groups of workmen to cut cedar and other trees in Lebanon and to dress fine building stones, which had to be measured and cut to very exact dimensions (1 Kings 6:7; 7:9).

STORAX TREE (*Styrax officinalis*). A resinous shrub or tree which abounds in Galilee. It grows to a height of 15 or 20 feet and produces fragrant flowers. The extracted juice of the bark is called storax and is used in medicine and perfumery.

STORK (Hebrew *ḥāsīdāh*, "affectionate"). The *Ciconia alba*, a white, heron-like bird which migrates through Palestine in the Spring. There is also the black stork, *Ciconia nigra*, which is common in the Dead Sea area. It is a ceremonially unclean bird (Lev. 11:19; Deut. 14:18).

SUCCOTH (sŭk'ŏth). A town in Goshen on the northeast frontier of Egypt. It lay along the route of the Exodus (Exod. 12: 37; 13:20; Num. 33:5, 6). Succoth is identified with present-day Tell el Mashkuta, east of Pithom and not far from Lake Timsah. There was also a Succoth in the Arabah. It is mentioned in Genesis 33:17, Joshua 13:27, Judges 8:5, 1 Kings 7:46, and Psalm 60:6.

SUFFERING. The doctrine of suffering wrestles with the question of why the righteous suffer. Elihu's idea, that suffering is educational and disciplinary (Job 32 — 37), was apparently all that Job himself ever recognized (Job 42:5, 6).

The New Testament teaches that Christ's sufferings were infinite. What he suffered from the Father was humanly incomprehensible and cannot be shared by anyone else (Psa. 22:1; Matt. 27:46; 2 Cor. 5:21). What Christ suffered from men may be shared by others (John 15: 18-20).

The believer may suffer with Christ (Acts 9:15, 16; Rom. 8:16-18; 1 Pet. 4:12-16). He may also suffer because of chastening from the Father. This may be corrective (John 15:2; 1 Cor. 11:29-32; Heb. 12:3-13) or preventive (2 Cor. 12:1-10). In either case it refines and matures the saint, educates him in obedience, and enlarges his spiritual life and ministry.

SUMERIANS (sū-mĕr'ē-ənz). A remarkable non-Semitic people who came from the far east (Gen. 11:2) and settled in the rich alluvial plain of southern Babylonia before 3000 B.C. They called their new home Shumer or Sumer (biblical Shinar — Gen. 11:2). Prehistoric dynasties of Sumerian rulers were associated with such ancient cities as Erech, Ur, Nippur, Kish, and Lagash. Each city-state had its own local god, who was regarded as the actual ruler. Sumerian history flourished from 3000 to 2000 B.C., until it was interrupted by Akkadian (Semitic) domination under Sargan of Agade (2380-2160 B.C.).

After 2000 B.C. Sumer, like Akkad, fell to the Amorites. The conquerors eventually adopted Sumerian laws and culture. The Sumerians were intellectual and inventive and influenced all subsequent civilization on the Tigris-Euphrates Valley and the Fertile Crescent.

SURVEYOR. The builder or architect needed the services of a surveyor to lay out the site of a new edifice. This was done with a measuring line consisting of a rope or cord (2 Sam. 8:2; Zech. 2:1), single-filament string (1 Kings 7:15), or twisted linen thread (Ezek. 40:3). The space was marked in cubits (1 Kings 7: 15, 23). In New Testament times a reed rod was similarly employed (Rev. 11:1; 21:15).

SUSANNA (sū-zăn'à). A woman who gave Christ some of her material possessions (Luke 8:3). She is listed with Joanna, the wife of Herod's steward, and others who had been blessed both spiritually and physically by Christ's ministry.

SWEET CANE. See "Calamus."

SWINE. A ceremonially unclean animal (Lev. 11:7; Deut. 14:8). It was prohibited as food to Jews by the Mosaic Law. The pig was the emblem of filth and coarseness (Prov. 11:22; Matt. 7:6; 2 Pet. 2:22). To feed swine was the lowest state to which a Jew could sink (Luke 15:15). Partaking of pork at idolatrous feasts was the height of degeneration and apostasy among Jews (Isa. 65:4; 66:17).

SWORD (Hebrew *hereb*). The most frequently mentioned weapon in the Bible. The straight blade was made of iron (1 Sam. 13:19) and was at times two-edged (Psa. 149:6). It was usually kept in a sheath fastened to the left side of the waist-belt.

SYCAMINE TREE (Greek *sykaminos*). The black mulberry (*Morus nigra*), a small, stocky tree with edible fruit (Luke 17:6).

SYCAMORE. See "Sycamore tree."

SYCHAR (sī'kàr). Modern Askar, the place where Jacob's Well was located (John 4:5). It is on the eastern slope of Mount Ebal, about a half-mile north of Jacob's Well. Some scholars suggest a location at ancient Shechem.

SYCOMORE TREE (Hebrew *shiqma*; Greek *sykomōraia*). The sycomore-fig, a tree with a short trunk but a total height of 30 to 40 feet. It has evergreen leaves. The sycomore flourishes in Egypt and the lowlands of Palestine (1 Kings 10:27; 2 Chron. 1:15; 9:27). It produces edible fruit (1 Chron. 27:28; Psa. 78:47). Amos was a tender or dresser of the fruit (Amos 7:14). The dressing operation consisted in cutting off the top of each fig to aid its ripening. Zaccheus climbed a sycomore to see Jesus (Luke 19:4). The Bible sycomore is not to be confused with the North American plane tree (Platanus), also known as sycamore.

SYNAGOGUE (*sunagōgē*, "a bringing together, an assembly"). The traditional place at which Jews met to read the Scripture and pray. Archeologically, the oldest synagogue attested by an inscription is the one near Alexandria, Egypt, and dates from the reign of Ptolemy II (247-221 B.C.). For such an institution to have been formed abroad, it must already have existed in Israel itself. By New Testament times the synagogue was an established institution both in Palestine and throughout the Roman world—wherever Jews resided (Mark 1:21, 39; Luke 4:20, 28; 6:6; Acts 13:5; 14:1; 17:1; 18:4). The synagogue appears prominently in the ministry of both Christ and the apostles.

SYNTYCHE (sĭn'tĭ-chē) ("coincidence, success"). A woman believer at the church in Philippi who was exhorted by Paul to settle her differences with another woman believer, Euodia (Phil. 4:2).

SYRIA (sĭr'ĭ-à) See "Damascus."

SYRIANS. See "Arameans."

T

TABERNACLE AND TEMPLE. The Old Testament Tabernacle contains a vast array of biblical typology and appears prominently in New Testament interpretation (e.g., Heb. 9:1–10:39). The Tabernacle lasted almost 500 years, until it was replaced by Solomon's Temple. No typology of the Temple is expounded in the New Testament, but the figure of a temple is employed to symbolize the believer's body (1 Cor. 3:16, 17; 6:19). Both the local church (2 Cor. 6:16) and the entire mystical Church (Eph. 2:21) are also pictured as a temple.

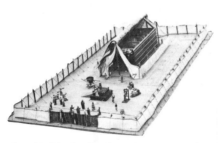

A model of the Israelite tabernacle, prepared by Shick (© *MPS*)

Solomon's magnificent edifice endured for about 376 years, until it was destroyed by Nebuchadnezzar II in 486 B.C. Zerubbabel completed a temple in 515 B.C. It was replaced by Herod's magnificent edifice, which was destroyed by the Romans in A.D. 70, only a few years after its completion. In the end times the Jews will build a temple which will ultimately become occupied by the man of sin (2 Thess. 2:4). The millennial Temple (Ezek. 40–44) will be established by Christ himself and will be used for the duration of the kingdom age (Isa. 2:1-5). The unveiled presence of God will constitute the "temple of God" in the New Jerusalem of the eternal state (Rev. 21:3, 22).

TABERNACLE, FEAST OF. See "Booths, Feast of."

TABITHA (tăb′ĭ-thá). The Aramaic name for Dorcas. See "Dorcas."

TABOR (tā′bėr). A rounded mountain rising from the Plain of Jezreel to 1,843 feet above sea level. Deborah summoned Barak and his army to assemble at Mount Tabor (Judg. 4:6). The view from its summit is breathtaking. A fourth-century tradition connects this mountain with the site of Christ's transfiguration. However, this identification is unlikely, since a town crowned the summit in New Testament times.

TAHPANHES (tä′păn-hēz). An important Egyptian settlement in the east Delta (Jer. 2:16; 44:1; 46:14; Ezek. 30:18). It is identified with present-day Tell Defneh, southeast of Tanis. Later the Greek trading settlement of Daphnae was established there. Jeremiah went to Tahpenhes with Jewish refugees (Jer. 43:7-13).

TAHPENES (tä′pė-nēz) (probably "the wife of the king"). An Egyptian queen, probably one of the rulers of the Twenty-first Dynasty at Tanis in the Delta (during the Davidic-Solomonic era, 980-931 B.C.). During David's reign young Hadad of Edom had fled to Egypt. The reigning Pharaoh received him cordially and wedded him to the sister of the queen. After David's death Hadad returned to Edom and opposed Solomon (1 Kings 11:19, 20).

TALENT. See under "Weights and Measures."

TALMAI (tăl'mī) ("plowman" or possibly "big"). (1) A son of Anak who was ousted from Hebron by Caleb (Num. 13:22; Josh. 15:14; Judg. 1:10). (2) A king of the Aramean principality of Geshur. His daughter was one of David's wives and the mother of Absalom (2 Sam. 3:3; 13:37).

TAMAR (tā'mēr) ("date palm"). (1) Judah's daughter-in-law, the Canaanite wife of his eldest son, Er. After Er's death she remained a widow for a long time because Judah's second son, Onan, refused to marry her and his third son was withheld beyond the promised time (Gen. 38:1-23). In anger and impatience Tamar, disguised as a harlot, offered herself to Judah. As a result she bore him twins, Perez and Zerah (Gen. 38:24-30). She is recalled as the ancestress of the tribe of Judah in Ruth 4:12, 1 Chronicles 2:4, and Matthew 1:3. Tamar was a quick-witted widow who protected herself and her family rights under the Mosaic Law of Levirate marriage. She was not a promiscuous woman and was more righteous and honorable than Judah himself (Gen. 38:26). As the mother of Perez she became an ancestor of King David. (2) A daughter of King David by Maacah. She was Absalom's full sister. Tamar was raped and grossly insulted by Amnon, her half-brother (son of Ahinoam). Absalom took Tamar to his house, where she remained. When King David failed to punish his son for the despicable crime. Absalom took the matter into his own hands and had Amnon murdered (2 Sam. 13:1-39). This story is an awesome sequel to David's own sin (2 Sam. 11:1 — 12:23) and represents part of the divine chastisement upon the king himself. (3) A daughter of Absalom and a beautiful woman (2 Sam. 14:27). She was doubtless named after Absalom's sister,

who had been so shamefully treated by Amnon. Tamar apparently became the wife of Uriel and the mother of Maacah (King Rehoboam's wife — 2 Chron. 13:2).

TAMARISK. A small tree with minute, scale-like, evergreen leaves and striking pink flowers. It is considered a holy tree by Arabs. Three common species are found in desert areas of southern Palestine and Beersheba. Saul resided beneath a tamarisk in Ramah (1 Sam. 22:6, RSV) and the bones of Saul and his sons were interred beneath one in Jabesh-Gilead (1 Sam. 31:13).

TANIS. An Egyptian city on the Tanitic branch of the Nile (in the eastern part of the Delta). It was built seven years after Hebron and was thus in existence during Abraham's time (Num. 13:22). Later certain kings of the Twelfth Egyptian Dynasty made Tanis their capital in order to repel invasions from the east. The Hyksos also used it as their capital, fortifying it and renaming it Avaris. Rameses II (1290-1224 B.C.) later named the city Raamses in his own honor. The modern site is San el-Hagar.

TANNING. Treating the skins of animals in order to obtain leather. Tanning was an important craft in Bible times. The common method was to remove the hairs by soaking in lime, then to treat the sun-dried skins with sumach pods, pine bark, oak bark, or leaves. The finest leathers were treated with mineral salts (usually alum) procured from the Dead Sea or imported from Egypt.

Leather was used for many articles, including sandals and girdles (2 Kings 1:8; Matt. 3:4), containers for water or other liquids (Gen. 21:14; Matt. 9:17; Judg. 4:19), and numerous military items (2 Sam. 1:21; Isa. 21:5).

TAPHATH (tā'fāth) ("a drop"). A daughter of King Solomon. She became the wife of the son of Abinadab, one of the king's officials in charge of the region of Dor (1 Kings 4:11).

TARES (Greek *zizanion*). The bearded darnel (*Lolium temulentum*). It is a poisonous grass which is practically indistinguishable from wheat while both are in the blade. However, it is easily distinguished (though hard to separate) when they both come into ear (Matt. 13:25-30).

TARSUS. The capital of Cilicia and the home of the Apostle Paul (Acts 21:39; 22:3). The city lies on the Cydnus or Tarsus River and was prominent from Mycenean Times.

TAX COLLECTOR. The "publican" (Greek *telōnēs*) collected taxes or customs for the Roman Empire. As early as 212 B.C. such an order of publicans had existed and become active in a number of provinces. The system was vulnerable to abuse. Although the worst cases were apprehended and brought to justice, extortion and malpractice were characteristic of the *publicani* system from its inception.

The word *architelōnēs* in Luke 19:2 seems to suggest that Zacchaeus had contracted for the taxes of Jericho and supervised various collectors. If these were Jews, they were particularly despised (Matt. 5:46) and were classed with "sinners" because of their free association with Gentiles (Matt. 11:19; Luke 5: 30; 15:1).

TEIL TREE. See "Terebinth."

TEKOA (tĕ-kō′á). A town six miles south of Bethlehem. Tekoa was near the Wilderness of Tekoa (2 Chron. 20:20) and was the home of the prophet Amos (Amos 1:1). The town was fortified by Rehoboam (2 Chron. 11:5, 6). Tekoa is present-day Tekua.

TEMA (tē′má). A city in Arabia about 225 miles southeast of Petra (Job 6:19; Isa. 21:14).

TEMAN (tē′măn). A district inhabited by a tribe descended from Esau (Gen. 36:11). The territory was in Edom (Jer. 49:20), apparently in the northern part (Ezek. 25: 13), where the inhabitants were noted for their wisdom (Jer. 49:7). Teman was on the King's Highway about five miles southeast of Petra (modern Tawilan).

TEMPLE. See "Tabernacle and Temple."

TEMPTATION OF CHRIST. Temptation is not sin, for Christ was tempted as we are but remained sinless (Heb. 4:15; Matt. 4:1-11). Because Christ was impeccable (incapable of sinning), his temptations can be likened to an attack on an impregnable fortress. Christ's victory over all temptations demonstrated his sinlessness (John 8:46; 14:30).

TEMPTATION OF GOD. Men tempt or test God when they challenge him to prove the truth of his words or the justice of his ways (Exod. 17:2-7; Num. 14:22; Psa. 78:18, 41, 56; 95:9; 106:14; Acts 15: 10). The place name "Massah" was a memorial to such an instance of tempting God (Exod. 17:7; Deut. 6:16). The sin is sternly forbidden (Deut. 6:16; Matt. 4:7; 1 Cor. 10:9).

TEMPTATION OF MEN. Satan tests God's people within certain limits established by God himself (Job 1:12; 2:6; 1 Cor. 10:13). Satan is "the tempter" (Matt. 4:3; 1 Thess. 3:5) and a perpetual enemy of God's saints (1 Pet. 5:8). However, God overrules Satan's temptations for his own beneficent purposes (Matt. 4:1; 6:13). God also tests his people in order to reveal the condition of their hearts (Gen. 22:1; Exod. 16:4; 20:20; Deut. 8:2). Through trials he purifies them (Psa. 66: 10; Isa. 48:10; Zech. 13:9; 1 Pet. 1:6, 7), matures them (James 1:2-12), and leads them into an enlarged assurance of his love (Gen. 22:15-18; Rom. 5:3-5). Men also test their fellow men in order to explore their capacities (1 Kings 10:1). Christ's opponents tempted him in order to test the validity of his Messiahship (Mark 8:11), examine his doctrines (Luke 10:25), and dissect his assertions (Mark 12:15).

Soldier touches stones considered part of the Temple in Jesus' day. (*Russ Busby photo*)

TEN LOST TRIBES. The idea of ten lost tribes which are "known only to God and later to be found by him" is a misconception of 2 Kings 17:7-23 (compare 2 Chronicles 6:6-11). The notion has given rise to serious errors which identify these alleged "lost tribes" with the Anglo-Saxon peoples, various gypsy groups, or certain people of Central Asia or Africa. Those "cast out" in the Northern Kingdom were excluded from the promise of restoration to the land (2 Kings 17:23). But this does not mean that only the tribes of Judah and Benjamin remained. From the division of the kingdom in 931 B.C. until the fall to Assyria in 722 B.C. multitudes of the ten tribes returned to the Davidic dynasty and the true worship of the Lord (1 Kings 12:16-20; 2 Chron. 11:16, 17; 2 Chron. 19:4; 20:1, 10, 11; 34: 5-7; etc.).

In God's view *all* the tribes were represented in the kingdom of Judah when it was taken to and repatriated from Babylon. Our Lord came to the entire nation (Matt. 10:5, 6) and was rejected by the entire nation. Tribes other than Judah are mentioned in the New Testament (Matt. 10:5, 6; Luke 2:36; Acts 4:36; 26: 7; Phil. 3:5; James 1:1).

Israel is still in age-long rejection, but she is being supernaturally preserved by God even though she does not acknowledge his divine care (Isa. 11:11-13; Hos. 3:4, 5; Rom. 11:1-12). Some of Israel has already returned to the land. A thorough spiritual restoration will eventually follow, and the ancient political rift will be healed (Ezek. 37:15-28). Then the kingdom will be established by the returning Messiah (Amos 9:13-15; Zech. 12:9-14; Rom. 11:25-27).

TERAH (tē'rà) (Akkadian *turahu*, "ibex"). The father of Abraham. He evidently worshiped Sin, the moon god (Josh. 24:2), who had temples at both Ur and Haran. Terah failed to renounce his idolatry and died in Haran (Gen. 11:25-32).

TERAPHIM (tĕr'à-phēm). Images of deities kept in homes for family protection (Gen. 31:19; 1 Sam. 19:13). The law against graven images (Exod. 20:1-6) forbade this pagan-influenced custom.

TEREBINTH (Hebrew *'ela*, A.V. "teil tree" Isa. 6:13 and "elm" Hos. 4:13). The tree referred to is now generally recognized as the Palestinian terebinth (*Pistacia terebinthus*) or turpentine tree.

TETRARCH. The Romans gave this title to the ruler of part of a province. It originally denoted the ruler of one-fourth (Greek *tetrarchos*) of a region, especially the four regions of Thessaly. When Herod the Great's will was contested by his sons after the death of the client king in 4 B.C., Caesar Augustus gave the title of tetrarch to two of them. Antipas was appointed tetrarch of Galilee and Perea, and Philip was appointed tetrarch of Gaulonitis, Batanea, and other areas northeast of the Sea of Galilee.

In the New Testament the term *tetrarch* is actually used only in reference to Herod Antipas (Matt. 14:1; Luke 3:19; 9:7; Acts 13:1). However, the cognate verb is applied to Antipas, Philip, and Lysanias (Luke 3:1).

THADDAEUS (thă-dē'ŭs). One of Christ's Twelve Apostles (Matt. 10:3; Mark 3:18). He was also called Lebbaeus and is sometimes identified with the Jude who wrote the Epistle of Jude.

THEBES (thēbz). See "No."

THEOCRATIC KINGDOM. When the times of the Gentiles have run their course, the mediatorial kingdom of God on earth will be restored to Israel (Acts 1: 6). This will take place when Messiah returns in power and glory to reign over the nations (Rev. 19:11–20:6; Mic. 4:1-8; Psa. 2:1-12). Christ's millennial rule will be a phase of the universal kingdom of God (1 Cor. 15:24). The theocratic kingdom was established at Sinai, with the Shekinah glory (the visible symbol of God's presence) as the divine Ruler (Exod. 40:34-38). The glory also entered and filled Solomon's Temple (2 Chron. 7:1, 2). The Shekinah departed from Jerusalem when the kingdom collapsed at the Babylonian captivity (Ezek. 11:23).

THEOPHANY. Any preincarnate appearance of God the Son. The form was angelic or human (Gen. 12:7; 18:1, 2), manifested glory (Isa. 6:1-4; Ezek. 1:4-28), or unspecified (Gen. 17:1).

THEOPHILUS (thĕ-ŏf'ĭ-lŭs) ("loved by God"). The Christian of position and prominence to whom Luke addressed both his Gospel (Luke 1:3) and the Acts (1:1).

THESSALONICA (thēs'à-lô-nī'kà). The capital of one of the Macedonian districts during the Roman period. The city was originally called Thermae ("Hot

Springs") but was renamed Salonica or Thessalonica in honor of the wife of Cassander of Macedon. Thessalonica was a free city from 42 B.C. onward. Paul had an effective ministry there (Acts 17:1-13; Phil. 4:16; 1 Thess. 1:1; 2 Thess. 1:1).

THEUDAS (thū'dàs). (1) A Jewish insurrectionist before A.D. 6 (cf. Acts 5:36). His precise identity is a historical puzzle. (2) A magician who led many followers to the Jordan River with the promise that the river would be divided at his command. The Roman procurator Fadus (A.D. 44-46) dispersed the crowd and beheaded Theudas.

THISTLE. Numerous thistles with flowerets of various colors are found in Bible lands. The milk thistle, the star thistle, the cocklebur, and the teasel are only a few. Thorny weeds and bushes of various kinds also abound. The thorny burnet, the thorny caper, the prickly pear, and the acanthus are common. The box thorn and the bramble are used for hedges. Various hawthorns flourish. In most passages where thistles and thorns are alluded to, the terms are generic rather than specific.

THOMAS ("twin"). One of the Twelve Apostles of Christ. He was also called Didymus (Greek "twin"). He earned the title of "Doubting Thomas" because of his hesitance in accepting the witness of Christ's resurrection (John 20:19-29). Yet he had previously been willing to go with Jesus to Lazarus' tomb at the risk of death at the hands of the Jews (John 11: 16). Thomas' great confession of faith (John 20:28) is a highwater mark in the Gospel of John.

THORN. See "Thistle."

THRACE (thrās). The non-Greek "barbarian" country north of the Aegean Sea. It was overrun by the Persians and became part of the Persian Empire. It did not become a Roman Province until the time of Vespasian (A.D. 69-70).

THRONE. Various thrones are named in Scripture. The throne of God represents the seat of God's universal government (Isa. 2:2; Matt. 5:34; Acts 7:49; Heb. 8:1; Rev. 4:2; 3:21). The throne of David is the earthly seat of power which Christ will occupy as a "throne of glory" (Matt. 19:28; 25:31; Psa. 2:6; 2 Sam. 7:16; Psa.

89:36; Luke 1:32). The great white throne (Rev. 20:11, 12) is the site at which God will judge the wicked before the eternal state. The throne of Satan (Matt. 12:26; Col. 1:16; Rev. 2:13) represents the earthly power which Satan exercises. The throne of the Twelve Apostles represents their sphere of kingdom authority (Luke 22:30). The throne of grace is the immediate presence of God's power available to the petitioning saint in this age (Heb. 4:16). The throne of the church is represented by the session of the 24 elders in heaven (Rev. 4:4).

THUTMOSE III. The most powerful of the Egyptian pharaohs (1500-1450 B.C.). He was probably the oppressor of the enslaved Israelites. In fifteen campaigns he conquered Syria-Palestine and most of Western Asia. With his spoils he built great temples at Karnak.

THYATIRA (thī-à-tī'rà). A Greek city of proconsular Asia (Acts 16:14). It was one of the seven churches addressed in the Revelation (Rev. 2:18-29).

THYINE WOOD (Greek *thyinos*). This is thought to be wood from the sanderac-tree (*Tetraclinis articulata*), a small, coniferous tree native to North Africa. The wood is handsome, dark, and fragrant. It was used extensively in the Greco-Roman world for cabinetmaking. Some scholars have identified thyine with the wood of the almug-tree.

The city of Tiberias clings to the western shore of the Sea of Galilee. (© *MPS*)

TIBERIAS (tī-bēr'ī-ūs). A town constructed by Herod Antipas, tetrarch of Galilee. It was named in honor of then-reigning

Emperor Tiberius (John 6:1, 23; 21:1). The present site is Tabariyeh, about 12 miles from the point at which the Jordan River enters the Lake of Galilee.

TIBERIUS CAESAR. The Roman Emperor from A.D. 14 to 37. This period spanned the ministry and crucifixion of Christ. One of the last actions of this elderly stepson of Augustus was to recall Pontius Pilate from Judea. In his later career Tiberius was under the influence of the villanous schemer Sejanus until the latter's execution.

TIGLATHPILESER (tĭg'lȧth-pĭ-lē'zẽr) ("my trust is in the son of Esharra," i.e. the god Ninib). The king of Assyria from 745 to 727 B.C. He was also called Pul or Pulu (2 Kings 15:19-29; 16:7, 10; 1 Chron. 5:6, 26; 2 Chron. 28:20). He was a great warrior and conqueror and acted as God's scourge to punish the sinning Northern Kingdom.

TIGRIS (tī'grĭs). One of the four streams associated with the Garden of Eden. It is also called the Hiddekel (Gen. 2:14). With the Euphrates, it formed the two great rivers of Mesopotamia in antiquity. From its source in the Mountains of Armenia the Tigris runs 1,146 miles to become a tributary of the Euphrates 40 miles from the Persian Gulf. However, in antiquity the Tigris emptied separately into the Persian Gulf, which extended much farther inland. Centuries of silting have extended the coastline of lower Babylonia out to sea. Nineveh, Assur, and Calah were among the ancient cities located on the Tigris River.

TIME. See under "Calendar, Hebrew."

TIMES OF THE GENTILES. The period during which non-Jews dominate God's chosen people. The period extends from the time of Nebuchadnezzar (605 B.C.) to the advent of Christ and his establishment of the kingdom (Luke 21:24; Dan. 2:34, 35, 44).

TIMNA (tĭm'nȧ). A woman listed as the concubine of Eliphaz the son of Esau in order to show the close relationship between Edomites and Horites (Hurrians). Timna was the sister of Lotan, one of the native Horite inhabitants of Edom (Gen. 36:22; 1 Chron. 1:39).

TIMNAH (tĭm'nȧ). A town near Philistia on the border of Judah (Josh. 15:10; 19:

43; Judg. 14:1, 5; 2 Chron. 28:18). It is identified with present-day Tell el-Batashi, about five miles south of Gezer. (2) A town in the hill country of Judah (Josh. 15:57; Gen. 38:12-14. It is present-day Tibnah, about fourteen miles southeast of Jerusalem.

TIMNATH-SERAH (tĭm'nȧth-sē'rȧ). Joshua's place of burial in the hill country of Ephraim (Josh. 24:29, 30). It is identified with present-day Khirbet Tibneh, about thirteen miles southwest of Shiloh.

TIMOTHY (tĭm'ō-thē) ("honored by God"). A young believer of Lystra who became Paul's companion and son in the faith (Acts 16:1). Paul addressed 1 and 2 Timothy to this young pastor. His name is joined with the Apostle's in a number of Paul's Epistles. Timothy was sent to various churches as a special pastor.

TIRZAH (tûr'zȧ) ("pleasantness"). (1) The youngest of Zelophehad's five daughters (Num. 26:33; 27:1; Josh. 17:3). (2) A Canaanite city whose king was defeated by Joshua (Josh. 12:24). It was the capital of the Northern Kingdom until Omri moved the seat of government to Samaria (1 Kings 15:21, 33; 16:6, 8, 15, 23; 2 Kings 15:14-16). It is identified with present-day Tell Farᶜah, about seven miles northeast of Nablus.

TISHBE (tĭsh'bė). The home of Elijah "the Tishbite" (1 Kings 17:1). Tishbe was located just north of the Brook Cherith and about eight miles east of the Jordan River. It is identified with present-day Lisdib.

TITHING. The ancient custom (Gen. 14: 17-20) of giving a tenth of one's income to God. Under the Mosaic Law tithing was the primary means of supporting the Levitical priesthood (Lev. 27:30-33; Num. 18:21-26; Deut. 14:22-29). Under grace, giving is to be performed spontaneously — not out of necessity or legal pressure (2 Cor. 9:7). Giving is to be proportionate to God's blessing (1 Cor. 16:2). Grace giving ought to exceed the tithe rather than to justify dodging it or coming short of it.

TITUS (tī'tŭs). (1) The Roman Emperor from A.D. 79 to 81. He succeeded his father, Vespasian. When Vespasian was proclaimed Emperor he left Titus in Palestine to complete the task of crushing the Jewish revolt. Titus captured Jerusalem and destroyed the Temple, although it is said that he tried to restrain his troops from the Temple destruction. (2) A companion of Paul and a faithful pastor in Crete (Gal. 2:3; Tit. 1:4). The Epistle of Titus was written to him, probably after Paul's release from his first imprisonment.

TOB (tŏb). A city and district in South Hauran (Judg. 11:3-5). The town is apparently preserved in present-day et-Taiyibeh, between Bozrah and Edrei (near the sources of the Yarmuk River). Tob was an Aramean city (2 Sam. 10:6-13).

TOBIAH (tô-bī′à) ("the Lord is good"). An Ammonite who opposed the rebuilding of the walls of Jerusalem by Nehemiah (Neh. 2:10; 4:3, 7).

TONGUES. A supernatural sign to Jews in the Book of Acts. At Pentecost (Acts 2:1-8) it was a sign to the Jews (together with the wind and the fire) of a change from the Mosaic economy to the age of the church and grace. At Caesarea (Acts 10:46) supernatural languages were a sign to Peter and the Jews with him that the Gentiles had received identically the same gift of the Spirit as the Jews at Pentecost (Acts 11:17). At Ephesus (Acts 19:6) the sign of tongues demonstrated to the Jews that, no matter what their religious activity or fidelity to Old Testament religious ceremonies or beliefs might be, salvation was now possible only on the ground of faith in Christ's atoning sacrifice ministered to them by the outpoured Spirit.

In the early church (1 Cor. 12:7-11) tongues were a gift or sovereign bestowment of the Spirit. Along with the gift came extrabiblical prophecies and knowledge directly from God himself. These temporary provisions met the need for teaching in the primitive assembly (1 Cor. 13:8). After the New Testament Scriptures were written, they provided the *permanent* instruction in righteousness for the churches. Chapter 14 of 2 Corinthians regulates the gifts of tongues and direct inspirational prophecy and knowledge in the primitive assembly.

TOPHET (tō′fĕt). The name for the high place in the Valley of Hinnom (south of Jerusalem) where human sacrifices and other idolatrous abominations were practiced (2 Chron. 33:6; Jer. 7:31). King Josiah defiled the place (2 Kings 23:10). As a result of its idolatrous connections and its defilement (perhaps as the site of the city dump), the names for the valley (Hebrew *Ge-Hinnon*, Greek *Gehenna*) came to symbolize sin and its eternal punishment (Matt. 5:22; 10:28; Mark 9:43, 45, 47; Luke 12:5; James 3:6). Theologically, Gehenna is identical with the lake of fire (Rev. 19:20; 20:10-15) and the second death (John 8:24; Rev. 21:8).

TOWN CLERK. The *grammateus* (Acts 19:35) was customarily the secretary of a board of magistrates. His duty was to make an accurate record of official decisions. In the large and influential city of Ephesus he was evidently the president of the assembly. As such he was the principal municipal officer, the executive responsible for such situations as the riot over Paul (Acts 19:21-41). His important position is attested by coins and inscriptions from Ephesus and by the fact that his administration dated the year.

TRACHONITIS (trăk-ō-nī′tĭs). The Greek designation of the rugged country north of the Hauran. Herod the Great subdued its turbulent tribes and added the country to the Tetrarchy of Philip (Luke 3:1).

TRANSFIGURATION. A portrayal in miniature of Christ's second advent in glory (Matt. 17:1-9). All the elements of this great coming event were present: (1) Christ was seen as the glorified Son of man. (2) Moses appeared in glorified form, representing the redeemed who have entered the kingdom through death. (3) Elijah, likewise glorified, represented the redeemed who have entered the kingdom by translation (1 Thess. 4:14-17). (4) Peter, James, and John were seen unglorified, representing the Jewish remnant who will then enter the kingdom in unglorified bodies. (5) The multitude at the foot of the mountain (Matt. 17:14-21) represented the nations who will be ushered into the blessings of the kingdom after its restoration to Israel (Acts 1:6; Isa. 11:10-12).

TRIBULATION. The Greek word for tribulation, *thlipsis*, may denote (1) a trial of any kind or (2) the Great Tribulation. The latter usage refers to the seventieth week of Daniel (Dan. 9:24-27), the period of worldwide trouble and anguish following the rapture of the church (2 Thess. 2: 1-7). Then the mystery of iniquity will unfold and the Antichrist, the Man of Sin, will be manifested (2 Thess. 2:8-12; cf. John 5:43). This period represents the time of God's judgments on a Christ-rejecting world (Psa. 2:5). The period will witness the casting of Satan into the earth and his restriction to this sphere (Rev. 12:9-12). He will be joined by myriads of wicked demons now confined in the abyss (Rev. 9:1-20).

The awful suffering and bloodshed of the Tribulation will be climaxed by the battle of Armageddon (Rev. 16:13-16). Christ will return in glory to slay his enemies, destroy the Satanic world system (Rev. 19:11–20:3), and inaugurate his kingdom reign (Rev. 20:4-10). The Tribulation period is foretold in detail by both the major and minor prophets of the Old Testament (e.g., Jer. 30:5-7; Zech. 12:1–14:3).

TROAS (trō'ăz). A seaport of Mysia in northwest Asia Minor. Troas lies on the Aegean Sea about ten miles south of ancient Troy. It was an important city in New Testament times. It was here that the Apostle Paul experienced the missionary vision which called him to Europe (Acts 16:8-10; 2 Cor. 2:12). Paul stayed at Troas briefly on his third tour (Acts 20:6; cf. 2 Tim. 4:13).

TROPHIMUS (trŏf'ĭ-mŭs) ("nourishing"). A Gentile believer at Ephesus who accompanied Paul to Jerusalem. The Apostle was falsely accused of having brought Trophimus into the Temple in violation of the Mosaic Law (Acts 20:4; 21:29). Trophimus later became ill at Miletum (2 Tim. 4:20).

TRUMPETS, FEAST OF. A feast known as the "day of blowing the trumpets" (Num. 29:1) or the "memorial of blowing of trumpets" (Lev. 23:24). Held on the first day of the civil year, this feast prefigures the future regathering of Israel.

TRYPHENA (trī-fē'nà) ("dainty"). A Christian worker in the early church at Rome. Paul sent greetings to her and commended her for faithful service to

God (Rom. 16:12).

TRYPHOSA (trī-fō'sà) ("delicate"). A woman linked with Tryphena as a worker in the Lord (Rom. 16:12). Possibly they were sisters or even twins, since their names are derived from the same Greek root. Both names also occur in extrabiblical literature.

TYRANNUS (tī-răn'ŭs) ("an absolute sovereign, a tyrant"). An Ephesian teacher of philosophy or rhetoric. Paul discussed Christianity in Tyrannus' school when he no longer had access to the synagogue (Acts 19:9).

TWO WITNESSES. Evidently two Jewish witnesses of the latter-day remnant who are endued with power to perform miracles like Moses and Elijah (Rev. 11: 3-13). They command drought (cf. 1 Kings 17:1), turn water to blood (cf. Exod. 7:19), and perform other signs (cf. Exod. 7–10). Their message stresses Christ's lordship over the earth and his imminent kingly reign.

After the two witnesses have completed their testimony, they are killed by the Beast (the head of the revived Roman Empire–Rev. 13:1-10; 17:8), who ascends out of the abyss. Their bodies, however, are resurrected and translated to heaven and their enemies are punished (Rev. 11:11-13).

TYCHICUS (tĭk'ĭ-kŭs) ("fortuitous"). A missionary companion of Paul (Acts 20: 4). He carried several Pauline Epistles to their recipients (Eph. 6:21; Col. 4:7). Paul proposed to send him as a messenger to Titus in Crete (Tit. 3:12). Later he was sent to Ephesus (2 Tim. 4:12).

TYPE. An illustration of truth woven into the fabric of Scripture. Most types occur in the Old Testament and prefigure various aspects of the life, death, and resurrection of Christ. Types form an important unifying bond between the Old and New Testaments and constitute an important evidence for the divine inspiration of Scripture. Some biblical personages who typify Christ include Adam (by contrast as well as parallelism), Melchizedek, Isaac, Moses, Aaron, Joshua, David, Solomon, and Jonah. All Old Testament sacrifices offered in obedience to God typify some aspect of the person or work of Christ. The tabernacle with all its rich symbolism also pointed dramatically to the promised Savior. Christ has totally fulfilled the Old Testament types in his life, death, resurrection, and ascension. Now the spiritual realities prevail.

TYRE (tīr). An ancient Phoenician city and fortress situated on an island. Tyre was close to the Palestinian coast and about 25 miles south of Sidon (Josh. 19: 29). Alexander the Great captured the insular city in 333 B.C. by constructing a causeway from the mainland to the island. Hiram of Solomon's time built a breakwater that made the harbor one of the best on the entire coast. Tyre was still important in New Testament times (Matt. 15:21; Mark 7:31; Acts 12:20; 21: 3). The "Ladder of Tyre" was a pass through the mountains to the Plain of Phoenicia.

ULAI (ū'lī). A river east of Susa in southwest Persia (Dan. 8:2). It is Assyrian Ulai and classical Eulaeus. The river has changed its course in modern times. The present Upper Kherkhah and Lower Karun rivers were apparently once a single stream which flowed into the delta at the north of the Persian Gulf.

UNICORN. "See "Aurochs.""

UR (ûr). The city in South Iraq (ancient Sumer) which Terah and Abraham left in order to go to Haran (Gen. 11:28, 31; 15: 7). Ur is identified with modern Tell el-Muqayyar, near Eridu. The site has yielded a rich store of objects from Sumerian royal tombs and a famous ziggurat or temple tower.

URARTU (ŏŏ-rär'tŏŏ). See "Ararat."

URIAH (ů-rī'á) ("the Lord is light"). The Hittite husband of Bathsheba and one of David's generals. He was sent to his death by David in order to conceal David's sin of adultery (2 Sam. 11:1-25).

URUK (ŏŏ'rŏŏk). See "Erech."

UZAL (ū'zăl). An Arabian trading center located on the incense route through Sheba (in southeast Arabia). Uzal was connected with other similar trading centers, such as Muza, Eden, Timna, Marib, Shabwa, and Canneh in Sheba and Hazarmaveth in the southern extremity of the Arabian Peninsula.

UZZAH (ŭz'á) ("the Lord is strength"). A man of an unknown tribe who was struck dead for touching the Ark in violation of the Law (2 Sam. 6:2-7).

UZZIAH (ŭ-zī'á) ("the Lord is strength"). The king of Judah from 767 to 739 B.C. Uzziah (also called Azariah) brought Judah to the height of power and prosperity (2 Chron. 26:1-15). However, he intruded into the priests' office and was stricken with leprosy (2 Chron. 26:16-23).

V

VALLEYS OF SCRIPTURE. The primary valley of Palestine is the Rift Valley or the *Arabah.* The Jordan River descends rapidly through this valley. The narrow flood plain (the Zor) is covered with dense thickets of tamarisk and thorn scrub. The Zor is separated by the higher Rift Valley floor, called the Ghor, by badlands of grey saline marl. The northern (Syrian) part of the Rift Valley contains the Orontes and Leontes Rivers in the plain between the Lebanon and Anti-Lebanon Mountains. The southern part of the Rift Valley consists of the Dead Sea, 1,285 feet below sea level, and that portion of the Arabah that extends to the Gulf of Aqaba. Other significant valleys of Scripture are described briefly below.

Achor. A valley in northeast Judah where Achan was put to death (Josh. 7:24-26). It is the first place name on the copper scroll from Qumran. It is about four miles in length and is centered on the Wadi Qumran, northeast of the Dead Sea and ten miles south of Jericho.

Baca. A narrow valley mentioned in Psalm 84:6. Its name means "valley of the balsam tree." Baca poetically symbolizes a waterless place of testing and trial.

Decision, Valley of. A symbolic name given to a valley outside Jerusalem. It is apparently the same as the Valley of Jehoshaphat (Joel 3:2, 12, 14), where the judgment of the nations takes place.

Eshcol. The valley or wadi a few miles north of Hebron. There the scouts who had been sent out by Moses gathered a huge cluster (Hebrew *eshkol*) of grapes (Num. 13:23, 24).

Gibeon, Valley of. A narrow stretch of level terrain between the hills near the city of Gibeon. The valley is about six miles north of Jerusalem and is the site at which Joshua's army mustered for a great victory over the Amorite kings (Josh. 10:1-15).

Hebron, Valley of. The region from which Jacob sent the lad Joseph to visit his brothers in Shechem (Gen. 37:14). The city of Hebron is situated partly in a valley and partly on a slope about 3000 feet above sea level. Hebron lies about 19 miles south-southwest of Jerusalem in a well-watered area of vineyards and olive groves.

Hinnom. A narrow valley to the south of Jerusalem. It is also called "the valley of the sons of Hinnom." Hinnom is identified with the Wadi er-Rababeh, which encircles the city on the west and meets the Kidron Valley on the southeast (Josh. 15:8; 18:16). It was defiled by gross idolatry (2 Chron. 33:6) and later became a burning ground for garbage and dead bodies (2 Kings 23:10). The name *Gehinnom* became shortened to *Gehenna,* which eventually came to symbolize the eternal fires of hell (Matt. 5:22; 18:9).

Jehoshaphat, Valley of. The designation which the prophet Joel gives to the place where Christ will judge the nations before his glorious return (Joel 3:2, 12). The name means "the Lord judges" and is apparently used symbolically rather than topographically. However, the great end-time earthquake will change the topography of the land to make the Kidron "a very great valley" (Zech. 14:4) and a suitable theater for judgment. See also "Decision, Valley of."

Jezreel, Valley of. The southeastern part of the plain of Esdraelon (the Greek form of Jezreel). The Vale of Jezreel proper is the valley that slopes down from the city of Jezreel to Bethshan, the fortress town commanding the Jordan Rift Valley. The Hill of Moreh lies to the north and Mount Gilead to the south. Esdraelon is the triangular, alluvial plain guarded on the east by Bethshan. At the northwest, on the slopes of the Carmel spur, the towns of Megiddo, Joknean, Taanach, and Ibleam controlled the main mountain passes and the north-south routes through West Palestine. These towns, together with Jezreel and Bethshan, also controlled the vital road running east and west from the Jordan Valley (the only route not blocked by ranges of hills).

Jordan. The "Vale of Siddim," the circular area of land at the southern end of the Dead Sea. Before the destruction of Sodom and Gomorrah the Jordan Valley was luxuriant in vegetation (Gen. 13:10). Since this cataclysm the region has been covered by the Dead Sea.

Kidron. A small valley through which the Brook Kidron flowed. Christ and his disciples crossed Kidron to get to the Garden of Gethsemane (John 18:1). On the west side of the Kidron is the Gihon or "Virgin's Fountain," a spring whose waters were diverted into a reservoir to supply the needs of Jerusalem.

Lebanon, Valley of. The plain between the two parallel ranges of mountains that extend northward parallel with the coast of Phoenicia. The coastal range is Lebanon and the inland range is Anti-Lebanon. The valley was called the *Biqaᶜ*, the Hebrew word for a wide valley between mountain ranges.

Rephaim. A valley which extends southwest from Jerusalem in the general direction of Bethlehem (Josh. 15:8; 18:16; 2 Sam. 23:13, 14). Rephaim was quite fertile and was presumably once inhabited by the Rephaim, a people of large stature.

Shittim, Valley of. The camping place of the Israelites before the invasion of Canaan (Num. 25:1; Josh. 2:1; 3:1). It is probably to be identified with Tell Kefren, an eight-by-fifteen-mile area east of the Jordan River on the plains of Moab opposite Jericho. Joel mentions "the valley of Shittim" ("the vale of acacia trees"). Some scholars identify the area with the Kidron ravine or the Wadi es-Sant (Joel 3:18).

VASHTI (văsh′tī) (possibly Persian *vashti*, "one who is desired"). The wife of King Ahasuerus (Xerxes I, 486-465 B.C.), according to the Book of Esther (1:9-22). On the seventh day of a great banquet King Ahasuerus sent for Queen Vashti to parade her beauty before his guests. When Vashti refused to appear, the king banished her and proclaimed throughout his realm that every man should be lord in his own house (Esth. 1:22). Vashti's deposal occasioned a search for other beautiful maidens and the eventual selection of Esther as the new queen.

VEIL (*saᶜiph*). Some kind of covering (probably a shawl or scarf) which Rebekah put on when she approached Isaac prior to their marriage (Gen. 24:65). It seems that the veil identified a marriageable maiden and that it was removed at the marriage ceremony. Such a veil was used by Tamar to trick Judah (Gen. 38:14-19).

The mantle (*redid*) worn by the women of Jerusalem (Isa. 3:23) and the young women in Canticles (Song 5:7) was apparently a summer dress (Septuagint *theristron*), like the stoles worn by women in modern times. The mask with which Moses covered his face (Exod. 34:33-35) is termed a "veil" or "hood" (*kalumma*) in 2 Corinthians 3:13-16.

The veils worn by Muslim women in the East today have little parallel in the Bible. They are largely the offshoot of Mohammed's teachings concerning the status of women.

VEIL OF THE TABERNACLE. The curtain of blue, purple, and scarlet that separated the Holy Place from the Most Holy Place (Exod. 26:31) in the Old Testament Tabernacle. The veil symbolized Christ's human body (Heb. 10:20), showing that only through Christ's vicarious death could fallen man be justified (Rom.

3:24; 5:1, 2, 9-11). When Christ died on the Cross the veil was torn down the middle supernaturally (Matt. 27:51), thereby providing unhampered access to the Holy of Holies in the Temple. Now faith in Christ gives instant approach to God, showing that "by the deeds of the law shall no flesh be justified in God's sight" (Rom. 3:20).

VESPASIAN (vĕ-spā'zhē-ən). The Roman emperor from A.D. 70 to 79. He was called by Nero to put down the Jewish Revolt in Palestine. In the midst of his task, which he carried out with grim relentlessness, he was called to Rome to become Emperor. His son, Titus, finished the war in Judea.

VINE. The word usually designates the common grapevine *(Vitis vinifera)*. In Bible times Palestine was a land of vineyards and olive orchards. Prophets like Isaiah (5:1-7), poets like Asaph (Psa. 80: 8-19), and Christ himself (John 15:1-8) often used the figure of the vine to teach spiritual truths. See also "Grapes."

Muscle power turned these stones into a productive winepress. *(Russ Busby photo)*

VINEDRESSER. Keeping vineyards and oliveyards was a major phase of agriculture in Palestine. Sitting under one's vine and fig tree was a figure of contentment and of security against enemy invasion (1 Kings 4:25). In preparing a vineyard a good site had to be chosen (Isa. 5: 1) and the soil had to be prepared. The stones taken out of the soil were used as a wall to keep out larger animals. (Isa. 5:2, 5). A hedge of prickly thorn was also planted to keep out smaller animals (Isa. 5:5). A tower or house for the householder was erected, where a watch was maintained throughout the vintage period (Isa. 1:8; 5:2). The vines were chosen for fine quality and were arranged in rows about eight feet apart for easy cultivation. Pruning was done in the spring (Lev. 25: 3; John 15:2). After the grapes were picked, they were carried to nearby winepresses, where the juice was trampled out by foot (Amos 9:13). The juice was stored in new, expandable goatskin bags (Matt. 9:17) or in large pottery or stone containers. Appropriate time was then provided for the juice to ferment adequately. Large quantities of grapes were also dried and molded into raisin cakes (1 Sam. 25:18).

VIPER (Hebrew *'eph^eh*). A poisonous snake which was common in the Negeb (Isa. 30:6; 59:5). Job refers to its deadly nature (Job 20:16). This or a closely related poisonous reptile (Greek *echidna*) attacked the Apostle Paul's hand while he was on the Island of Melita (Acts 28:3). The *echidna* was well known to the Jews (Matt. 3:7). It was probably the common viper *(Vipera communis* or *Pelias berus)*, common on the Mediterranean coast.

VIRGIN BIRTH. The virgin birth of Christ is a necessary link in the whole golden chain of marvels that cluster around the person and work of our Lord Jesus Christ. To deny the fundamental fact of Christ's sinless conception is to invalidate all the other glorious realities of his unique career. His virgin birth is implicit in the first redemption prophecy, which specifies the Seed of the *woman* (Gen. 3:15). Isaiah clearly foretold Christ's virgin birth in the great messianic sign of Isaiah 7:14. This involved the miracle of the virgin birth because it was *divinely* given — "the Lord himself" gave it. It was given to the Davidic house — "to *you*" (plural) — not merely to Ahaz. It involved a stupendous miracle — "deep as Sheol" and "high as heaven."

The child's name, Immanuel, means *"with us"* (humanity) *"is God"* (deity), thereby declaring Christ's incarnation. *All* references to Christ in the New Testament presuppose him to be God incarnate, possessing a sinless human body generated in the womb of the virgin Mary by the Holy Spirit (Luke 1:35).

VOW. A specific dedication of oneself or one's possessions to the Lord. Vows were common in the Old Testament era (1 Sam. 1:11, 21; 2 Sam. 15:7, 8; Job 22:27; Psa. 65:1; etc.). Usually the vow was in the nature of a pious bargain, with the person making the vow expecting some specific deliverance or favor from God (Gen. 28:20-22; Judg. 11:30, 31). Vows were common under the Mosaic Law (Lev. 7:16; 22:18, 21, 23; 27:2-29; Num. 15:3). They were not to be made lightly (Prov. 20:25; Eccl. 5:4, 5). Vows were totally voluntary (Deut. 12:6), but once made they were to be conscientiously fulfilled (Deut. 23:21-23).

The Apostle Paul made at least one vow (Acts 18:18). He also assumed liability for a vow which four of his associates had taken (Acts 21:23-26). Paul's enemies also made a conspiracy under oath (similar to a vow) with the intent of killing the Apostle (Acts 23:12-14).

WADI. See "Rivers and Streams."

WAISTCLOTH. A garment which reached from the waist to the knee. It was a common item of dress in the Near Eastern world before the Israelite period. It disappeared as civilian attire during the latter part of the Bronze Age and survived only as a military garment (Isa. 5:27). Other primitve garments included animal skins and hairy cloaks or mantles. These were sometimes worn by poor people (Ecclesiasticus 40:4), as a badge of other-worldliness (2 Kings 1:8; Matt. 3:4), or as a symbol of grief (Gen. 37:24; Jonah 3:6).

Breeches or pants covering the hips and thighs were required for Hebrew priests (Exod. 28:42; 39:28), but were otherwise unknown in antiquity except among the Persians. The *paṭish* ("hosen") of Daniel 3:21 may have been breeches or pants, but the meaning of the word is uncertain.

WALK. A very common metaphor in both the Old Testament (Psa. 1:1) and the New Testament (Rom. 6:4; Eph. 4:1). Since walking is performed a step at a time, it furnishes a very apt illustration of living moment by moment (Col. 1:10; 1 Thess. 4:12).

WASHINGS. Old Testament washings typify both regeneration and daily cleansing of the redeemed (from day-to-day defilements). The washing of Aaron and his sons (Exod. 29:4) symbolizes regeneration (Tit. 3:5). The washing at the laver, on the other hand, signifies daily cleansing (Exod. 30:18, 21; cf. 1 John 1:9). Both appear in John 13:10.

WATCHMAN. Watchmen in Bible lands were of two types—those who guarded vineyards against thieves or marauding animals and those who manned watchtowers on city walls to warn of human enemies. Such watchtowers have been unearthed at Tell Beit Mirsim and Tell en-Nasbeh. Herod the Great erected three massive defense towers in Jerusalem, called Hippicus, Phasael, and Mariamne. Watchmen were sometimes also stationed on city walls (2 Sam. 18:24-27).

Watchtowers were erected in pastures or vineyards from earliest times (Gen. 35: 21). Sometimes the structures were used as living quarters during the harvest season.

WATER. See "Springs, Wells, and Pools."

WEAPON. Both offensive and defensive armor and weapons of war are summarized in the Hebrew term *kēlim* (Gen. 27: 3; 1 Sam. 17:54) and the Greek term *hopla* (2 Cor. 10:4). The Hebrew term *nesheq*, "weapons," is also sometimes employed (2 Kings 10:2).

WEASEL (Hebrew *ḥōlēd*). An unclean quadruped (Lev. 11:29) found in Palestine. The weasel is a flesh-eating mammal with short legs and a long, bushy tail.

WEAVER. Weaving provided work for both men and women (Exod. 35: 35; 2 Kings 23:7). The hangings of the Tabernacle in linen and goats' hair were produced by a weaver (Exod. 26:1, 7), as were the priestly robes (Exod. 39:1) and our Lord's seamless garment (John 19: 23). Guilds of weavers were formed (1 Chron 4:21). Egyptian and Babylonian weavers possessed great skill (Josh. 7:21; Isa. 19:9).

Spinning was known before weaving and consists of the production of yarn from short fibers by the use of a spindle. Weaving, on the other hand, involves two series of threads. The longitudinal thread is called the warp and the transverse one is labeled the woof. The weaving of the two sets of threads is accomplished on a loom. Weaving was such a common feature of everyday life that numerous figures of speech were derived from it (1 Sam. 17:7; 2 Sam. 21:19; Job 7:6). Yarn was produced in linen and wool (Lev. 13: 47), in byssus or fine Egyptian linen (Prov. 31:22), and in goats' hair or camel's hair (Exod. 35:26; Matt. 3:4).

WEEKS, FEAST OF. The Jewish Feast of the Harvest, celebrated seven weeks after the sickle was put to the grain (Deut. 16:9, 10). The one-day event, also called Pentecost, is observed on the fiftieth day after the offering of the sheaf of grain during the Passover celebration.

WEIGHTS AND MEASURES.

Early Standards of Weight. Everyday transactions between people demanded some system of weighing things. In early times almost any object could be employed as a standard. Stones and pieces of metal became popular weights. These were frequently carved into shapes of various animals and other configurations. Many of these weights have been recovered from excavated sites. Weights were commonly carried in a bag (Deut. 25:13; Prov. 16:11; Mic. 6:11). This enabled a buyer to compare his own weights with those at the place of purchase. Tomb paintings show that balances equipped with plummets were used in Egypt and elsewhere before Israelite times.

Common Old Testament Weights. The Hebrew weights closely followed the Babylonian, consisting principally of the shekel, the mina, and the talent. In earlier times the proportion was 60 shekels to a mina and 60 minas to a talent. Later the proportion of 50 shekels to a mina was adopted. The shekel was also divided into the half-shekel, the quarter-shekel, and the twentieth-shekel.

However, under the Babylonian system there were two standards, the Royal and the Popular, with the former being somewhat heavier. Each of these was in turn divided into a heavy and a light form, the latter being half the weight of the former. The following tables of Babylonian and Israelite weights are derived from recovered artifacts and provide approximate conversions to modern measures.

For convenience the Israelite shekel may be considered about the same weight as an American half-dollar, the mina about one and one-fourth pounds in weight, and the talent about 75 pounds. The discovery of the pim (equal to two-thirds of a shekel) has clarified a once-obscure biblical passage (1 Sam. 13:19-21).

The beka (Gen. 24:22) is defined in Scripture as a half-shekel (Exod. 38:26). This is substantially confirmed by archeological findings. The gerah is one-twentieth of a shekel (Exod. 30:13; Lev. 27:25). A "third of a shekel" is referred to in 1 Samuel 13:21.

New Testament Weights. Only two weights are alluded to in the New Testament. The litra (John 12:3; 19:39) was a

TABLE OF BABYLONIAN WEIGHTS, ROYAL STANDARD		
Unit	Metric Weight	U. S. Weight
Light Talent	30.6 kilograms	69.6 pounds
Light Mina	525 grams	1.2 pound
Light Shekel	8.4 grams	0.3 ounce
Heavy Talent	61.2 kilograms	138 pounds
Heavy Mina	1.05 kilograms	2.3 pounds
Heavy Shekel	16.7 grams	0.6 ounce

TABLE OF BABYLONIAN WEIGHTS, COMMON STANDARD		
Unit	Metric Weight	U. S. Weight
Light Talent	30 kilograms	66 pounds
Light Mina	500 grams	1.1 pound
Light Shekel	8.3 grams	0.3 ounce
Heavy Talent	60 kilograms	132 pounds
Heavy Mina	1.0 kilogram	2.2 pounds
Heavy Shekel	16.7 grams	0.6 ounce

TABLE OF OLD TESTAMENT WEIGHTS		
Unit	Metric Weight	U. S. Weight
Talent (3000 shekels)	34.3 kilograms	75.6 pounds
Mina (50 shekels)	571 grams	1.26 pound
Shekel	11.4 grams	0.4 ounce
Pim (2/3 shekel?)	7.6 grams	0.3 ounce
Beka (1/2 shekel)	5.7 grams	0.2 ounce
Third of a shekel	3.8 grams	0.1 ounce
Gerah (1/20 shekel)	0.6 gram	8.8 grains

Roman measure of weight equal to 327.45 grams (just under 12 ounces avoirdupois). (The King James Version renders litra as "libra," from which we have acquired the abbreviation "lb." for pound.)

The hailstones of Revelation 16:21 are said to weigh a talent. If this refers to the Old Testament talent of 3000 shekels, the hailstones would weigh about 75 pounds. Some scholars maintain that this talent equalled 125 librae, about 90 pounds. Others construe a light talent of 45 pounds.

A stone weight of one talent (© MPS)

Old Testament Dry Measures. The Old Testament terms were the same as those used throughout the ancient Near East. They were derived from various types of containers.

roughly seven liters or 1½ gallons (dry measure).

Omer. One-tenth of an ephah (Exod. 16:36), equivalent to about two liters or two quarts (dry measure).

Issaron. Apparently the equivalent of an omer or one-tenth of an ephah (Exod. 29:40; Lev. 14:10).

Cab (Hebrew *kab*). According to Rabbinical sources, one-eighteenth of an ephah, roughly the same as a liter or a quart (dry measure).

New Testament Dry Measures.

Koros. The Greek name for the Hebrew kor, equivalent to about 50 U.S. gallons (dry measure).

TABLE OF OLD TESTAMENT DRY MEASURES		
Unit	*Metric Volume*	*U.S. Volume (Dry Standard)*
Homer or Cor	220 liters	50 gallons
Half-Homer	110 liters	25 gallons
Ephah	22 liters	5.0 gallons
Seah	7.3 liters	6.6 quarts
Omer or Issaron	2.2 liters	2.0 quarts
Cab	1.2 liter	1.1 quart

Homer (Hebrew *homer*, Akkadian *imēr*). "A donkey's load," a standard dry measure (Ezek. 45:11). The homer was equal to the cor and contained ten baths or ephahs (Ezek. 45:11-14). This was equivalent to about 220 liters or 50 U.S. gallons (dry measure).

Cor (Hebrew *kor*, Akkadian *gur*). A large dry measure equal to the homer (cf. 1 Kings 4:22; 2 Chron. 2:10; 27:5).

Half-Homer (Hebrew *lethek*, Ugaritic *lth*). About 110 liters or 25 gallons (dry measure). The term occurs only in Hosea 3:2.

Ephah (Hebrew *'ephah*). A measure equal to the liquid *bath* or one-tenth of a homer (Ezek. 45:11). This is equivalent to about 22 liters or five gallons (dry measure).

Seah (Hebrew *seah*, Akkadian *sutu*). Probably one-thirtieth of a cor or one-third of an ephah (Isa. 40:12). This is

Modius. The "bushel" of Matthew 5:15, Mark 4:21, and Luke 11:33. It contained about 2.3 U.S. gallons (dry measure).

Choinix. A measure mentioned in Revelation 6:6 and equivalent to a little less than a quart (dry measure).

Saton. The Greek name (Matt. 13:33; Luke 13:21) for the Hebrew seah, equivalent to about 1.5 pecks.

Old Testament Liquid Measures. In addition to dry measures of capacity there were liquid measures. These varied as much as the dry measures. Even today the English gallon differs from the American gallon and the Connecticut bushel of 2,748 cubic inches differs from the Colorado bushel of 2500 cubic inches. In fact no worldwide, uniform standard of measures existed until the metric system was formulated. However, the numerical values of ancient measures have been

189

TABLE OF OLD TESTAMENT LIQUID MEASURES		
Unit	*Metric Volume*	*U.S. Volume*
Cor	220 liters	58 gallons
Bath	22 liters	5.8 gallons
Hin	3.7 liters	3.9 quarts
Log	1.8 liter	1.9 quart

determined closely enough to be of value to the Bible student.

Cor (Hebrew *kor*). A measure equal to the homer. It was used to measure oil, and, like the homer, it was said to contain ten baths (Ezek. 45:14). This is equivalent to about 220 liters or 58 liquid gallons.

Bath (Hebrew *bath*; Greek *batos*, Luke 16:6 only). The liquid equivalent of the ephah (Ezek. 45:11, 14). It was an exact and standard measure (Ezek. 45:10). Its modern equivalent is best calculated as 22 liters (about 6 gallons). The recovered examples from Lachish and Tell Beit Mirsim are fragmentary, however, and cannot be reconstructed with certainty. The estimated equivalents thus range between 20.9 and 46.6 liters.

Hin. The Hebrew hin ("a pot") was originally the designation of the vessels employed as a measure of oil (Exod. 29: 40), of wine (Lev. 23:13), and of water (Ezek. 4:11). The hin was one-sixth of a bath, according to Josephus.

Log (Hebrew *log*). One-twelfth of a bath, according to Jewish tradition. It occurs only in Leviticus 14:10 as a measure of oil.

New Testament Liquid Measures.

Xestes. One-sixteenth of the Latin modius, or slightly less than a pint (Mark 7: 4, 8).

Batos. The Greek counterpart of the Hebrew bath. It is referred to as a measure of oil in Luke 16:6. Josephus says the bath contained 72 sextarii or 4.5 modii. This would be equivalent to about 40 liters or 10 U.S. gallons.

Metretes. A Greek liquid measure referred to in John 2:6. It was approximately equal to the Hebrew bath (about 6 U.S. gallons).

Old Testament Units of Length. In ancient times units of length were derived from members of the human body (such as the finger, hand, palm, forearm, or foot) or from such loosely determined distances as a bowshot, a stone's throw, or the distance one could legally travel on a Sabbath day (Acts 1:12).

The following conversions were commonly used in Old Testament times:

4 fingerbreadths	= 1 handbreadth
3 handbreadths	= 1 span
2 spans	= 1 cubit
6 cubits	= 1 reed

When measurements became more precise, a standardized unit of length had to be agreed upon. The cubit was selected for this purpose.

Cubit (Hebrew *ʾamma*; Akkadian *ammatu*; Latin *cubitus*). The distance from the elbow to the fingertip. Four of these "natural" cubits constitute the height of a typical man.

However, a more precisely defined cubit was used as the standard of Hebrew measurements. The best calculations yield a value of 17.5 inches. This commonly accepted value agrees well with the ancient figure for the length of the Siloam tunnel, 1200 cubits. Based on the configuration of a half-sphere, Solomon's bronze laver of 1000 baths yields a cubit of 17.51 inches (see 1 Kings 7:23-26). The Egyptians used a cubit of 17.6 inches, a value only slightly larger than that of the standard Hebrew cubit.

The "long" or royal cubit was a handbreadth ("palm") longer than the standard cubit of six palms (Ezek. 40:5). It measured 20.4 inches. The Babylonian

TABLE OF OLD TESTAMENT LINEAR MEASURES		
Unit	*Metric Length*	*U.S. Length*
Reed	2.64 meters	8 feet, 8 inches
Reed (Ezekiel)	3.1 meters	10 feet, 2 inches
Cubit	44.5 centimeters	17.5 inches
Cubit (Ezekiel)	52 centimeters	20.5 inches
Span	22 centimeters	8.7 inches
Palm	7.4 centimeters	2.9 inches
Finger	18 millimeters	0.7 inch

cubit was 19.8 inches, attested by thirty fingers marked on a statue of Gudea. This was "three fingers" shorter than the Egyptian royal cubit, which, according to Herodotus, was 20.65 inches.

Reed (Hebrew *ganeh*). A unit equal to six cubits. It was exact enough to be mentioned in Scripture as a unit of length (Ezek. 40:5).

Span (Hebrew *zereth*). The distance from the thumb to the little finger in the outstretched hand. It was considered half a cubit (1 Sam. 17:4; Exod. 28:16; Ezek. 43:13).

Palm (Hebrew *tephah*). A "handbreadth," the width of the hand at the base of the four fingers (about 2.9 inches). See Exod. 25:25; 37:12; Ezek. 40:5; Psa. 39:5.

Finger (Hebrew *esba*). One-fourth of a handbreadth (Jer. 52:21). It was the smallest unit in everyday use in the ancient biblical world. It is commonly computed to be 0.73 inches.

Distance. Unlike the measurement of objects, which could be accomplished with a fair degree of precision, the ancient computation of distances was a much more approximate undertaking. Examples of distance standards include a bowshot (Gen. 21:16), a day's journey (Num. 11:31; 1 Kings 19:4), and the length of a plowed furrow (1 Sam. 14:14).

New Testament Units of Length.

Cubit. The custom of relating measurements to parts of the human body was continued in New Testament times. The basic unit remained the "forearm" (Greek *pēchys*), that is, the cubit. However, the length of the Jewish cubit under the Roman Empire evidently measured 21.6 inches.

Fathom (Greek *orgyia*). The length of the outstretched arms (about 6 feet). The term was derived from the verb *orego*, "I stretch."

Furlong (Greek *stadion*). One hundred orgiai (about 607 feet), supposedly the exact length of the Olympian race course. Compare the English word stadium.

Mile (Greek *milion*). The Greek transliteration of the Roman *mille pasuum*, "a thousand paces." It consisted of 8 stadia (1,618 English yards). It was calculated on the basis of 5 Roman feet (each of 11.65 inches) to the pace (4 feet, 10.25 inches).

Sabbath Day's Journey. This was fixed at 2000 cubits in the Talmud. It is referred to in Acts 1:12.

Measures of Area. In Egypt the cubit of square measure was employed for area measurements. This was defined as an area one linear cubit wide and 100 linear cubits long. One hundred cubits of area constituted approximately two-thirds of an acre. Babylonian and Assyrian criteria for measuring area were frequently computed by units of agricultural capacity. An area was measured by the quantity of seed, such as barley, necessary to sow it properly.

In Israel areas were customarily measured by the *ṣemed*, translated "acre" in the King James Version (1 Sam. 14:14;

Isa. 5:10). It was defined as the amount of land which a pair of yoked animals could plow in one day. In Babylonia this amount was stipulated as 6,480 square cubits (about two-fifths of an acre). In later times this constituted essentially the Latin *jugerum* of 28,800 square Roman feet (about five-eighths of an acre).

WELL. See "Springs, Wells, and Pools."

WHALE. As used in the King James Version of the Old Testament, this term signifies any large marine animal (Gen. 1:21). The same is true of the Greek word *kētos* (Matt. 12:40). The rhinodon, the shark, the whale, the dolphin, the sea dog, and the seal are included in this general term. True whales are found in both the Mediterranean Sea and the Red Sea. The Hebrew term for "great fish," *dāg gādhōl* (Jonah 1:17), is rendered by the Septuagint as "great whale," *kētos mega*. Hence the word *kētos* passed into Matthew 12:40, giving rise to the idea that Jonah was necessarily swallowed by an actual whale.

Wheat mixed with tares gave Jesus a poignant spiritual illustration, told in Matthew 13. (© MPS)

WHEAT. Wheat was cultivated throughout the biblical world. Egypt was the granary of the Mediterranean region. Vast quantities of wheat were shipped annually to Rome from Alexandria (Acts 27:6, 38). Wheat cultivated in Palestine was of the common variety, *Triticum vulgare*. It was sown in November or December, after the rains began. Harvest came from April till June, depending on weather and locality.

WIDOW. In Old Testament times widows were the special object of the Lord's care.

They were not to be wronged or neglected (Exod. 22:22; Isa. 1:17; Prov. 15:25; Mal. 3:5). The New Testament denounces those who "devour widows' houses" (Matt. 23:14; Mark 12:40; Luke 20:47). The neglect of widows became a temporary problem in the early church (Acts 6:1). Paul had much to say to Timothy, the young pastor, concerning the care of widows (1 Tim. 5:3-6). James declares that "pure religion and undefiled before God and the Father is to visit . . . widows in their affliction" (James 1:27). Some especially significant widows are briefly described below.

The Widow of Zarephath. This good woman of great faith gave the prophet Elijah a home, providing for him during the famine that raged in Israel at the time. As a reward of her trust in the Lord her oil and meal did not diminish and her boy was restored to life (1 Kings 17:8-24).

The Widow Whose Oil Multiplied. She was a recipient of the considerate ministry of Elisha (2 Kings 4:1-7). Her godly husband had died, and her two sons were in danger of being sold into slavery to satisfy creditors. All the woman had in her house was a pot of oil. The prophet directed her to borrow as many containers as she could, shut herself and her sons in their house, and empty the pot of oil into these vessels. In obedient faith she did so. The oil did not stop until all the containers were full. Her blessing was proportionate to her faith in gathering pots.

Elisha then directed her to sell the oil, pay her debts, and live on the remaining money. Her faith saved her family and brought the blessing of God into her life.

The Widow with Two Mites. She is enshrined among the spiritual heroes of the Bible because of the sacrifice and love for God that prompted her total giving. This widow's "mite" was a very small coin, worth scarcely one-eighth of a cent. But even though this impoverished widow seemed unnoticed in the swarming crowds that cast gifts into the Temple treasury during Passover Week, Jesus did not leave her devotion unnoticed, but preserved it for all future generations in the safekeeping of his praise. "This poor widow has cast more in than all they who have cast into the treasury. For all they did cast in of their abundance, but she of her want did cast in all she had, even all her living" (Mark 12:43-44; cf. Luke 21: 1-4).

The Importunate Widow. She appears as a figurative character in one of Jesus' parables (Luke 18:1-8). Her grievance was brought before a godless and callous judge who had no compassion for her or regard for the justice of her cause. Only by dint of dogged persistence did she finally get the judge to act in her behalf. Christ used the illustration to show that God, the righteous and compassionate Judge, will surely hear the cry of his persecuted people during the Great Tribulation preceding Christ's second advent (Luke 18:7, 8). He will answer them speedily, despite his seeming delay and the apparent triumph of evil.

The Hellenistic Jewish Widows. These women were widows of Hellenists, that is, Jews who spoke Greek and adopted many Greek customs. Even in the early church a tension existed between the Hellenists and the more conservative Hebrews. The Hellenists complained that their widows were being neglected in the philanthropic activities of the church (Acts 6:1).

The problem was resolved by appointing seven deacons (Acts 6:2-7). These officers were entrusted with the temporal responsibilities of the church. The apostles were thereby freed to devote themselves to prayer and Bible teaching.

WIFE. Wives play a very important role in the Bible; the word "wife" or "wives" is found almost 400 times. The monogamous standard was God's order from the beginning. "Therefore shall a man leave his father and his mother, and shall cleave unto his wife; and they shall be one flesh" (Gen. 2:24). But after Adam's fall polygamy with its attendant evils became common. Beginning with Lamech of the godless line of Cain (Gen. 4: 19), polygamy spread even to some of God's choicest saints. It invariably introduced trial and grief into the family circle. Monogamy has always been God's pattern for the greatest family happiness.

The Law of Moses forbade coveting a neighbor's wife (Exod. 20:17) and discouraged divorce (Deut. 24:1-4). The

New Testament stipulated monogamy for believers (1 Cor. 7:2). Divorce is permitted only under certain circumstances (Matt. 5:32; Mark 10:2-12; 1 Cor. 7:10-17). Nowhere, however, does God's Word penalize an innocent marital partner for the sin of the mate.

Many wives mentioned in Scripture played important roles of various types, some good and some evil. In a number of cases the names of these wives are not given. Some of the more significant unnamed wives are briefly described below.

Cain's Wife. "And Cain knew his wife; and she conceived and bore Enoch" (Gen. 4:17). Bible skeptics often want to know who Cain's wife might have been. The question is based on the assumption that there were no women available to Cain, since his parents were the first human beings to appear on earth. This presupposition overlooks several important facts. It fails to take into account the phenomenal fertility of Adam and Eve after the fall. God greatly multiplied the conception and childbearing activity of the woman after she had sinned (Gen. 3: 16). Eve bore many children in addition to Cain, Abel, and Seth. In fact, Adam did not father Seth until he was 130 years old (Gen. 5:3). (Seth took the murdered Abel's place as the son in the messianic line—Gen. 4:25). In all probability Adam fathered many sons and daughters during this period of well over a century. In addition to numerous sons and daughters, he probably had many generations of descendants. By the time Adam was 130 years old there may well have been thousands of women from which Cain could have selected a wife!

Lot's Wife. Christ referred to Lot's wife in warning believers against the perils of worldliness and materialism. His stark words were, "Remember Lot's wife" (Luke 17:32). The Old Testament summarizes her tragic career with the words, "But (Lot's) wife looked back from behind him, and she became a pillar of salt" (Gen. 19:26). Lot's wife had lived in Sodom, enjoying all the luxuries and pleasures that her wealthy and compromising husband could provide. When destruction overtook the city, her heart remained with her possessions and pleasures. As a result she became engulfed in God's judgment on those wicked cities.

Moses' Ethiopian Wife. Apparently a second wife whom Moses married in the wilderness. She is distinct from Zipporah, his first wife (a daughter of the Midian priest, Jethro), whom Moses had married before he became the deliverer and leader of Israel. His sister, Miriam, and brother, Aaron, rebelled against Moses' leadership because of his marriage to this woman of a different race. But the Lord severely rebuked them and reaffirmed Moses' leadership and authority (Num. 12:1-16).

Peter's Wife. She remains strictly in the background, though she doubtlessly witnessed her mother's healing by Christ (Mark 1:30; Luke 4:38, 39). She must have entertained Christ often, since their home in Capernaum appears to have been Jesus' headquarters while there. Commonly referred to as Simon's (Cephas') wife, she frequently traveled with her husband, as did the wives of the other apostles (1 Cor. 9:5).

Pilate's Wife. After a dream on the night of Christ's arrest, the wife of the Roman procurator of Judea dispatched a message to her husband, imploring him not to condemn Jesus of Nazareth. She held strong convictions of right and wrong. Moreover, she had the courage to testify of Christ's innocence when the forces of evil were clamoring for his death. The few quoted words of Pilate's wife have immortalized her: "Have thou nothing to do with that just man" (Matt. 27:19).

Potiphar's Wife. A woman remembered solely for her wickedness (Gen. 39:1-20). She was an Egyptian of high social position, the wife of the chief of Pharaoh's bodyguard. Hence she moved in a circle of elegance and splendor (about 1870 B.C.). A spoiled, selfish woman, Potiphar's wife knew nothing of Joseph's God and the high standards of morality of those who worshiped him. Serving only the gods of sensual pleasures, she tried to seduce Joseph. When Joseph resisted her advances, she seized his outer garment and falsely accused him to her husband. Her husband, believing her, cast Joseph into prison.

Potiphar's wife represents the evil of humanity apart from the redemptive grace of God. Both she and Jezebel represent pagan women who manifest utter disregard of right and wrong — the basis of the eternal moral law of God. Both women dramatize the close relationship of idolatry and immorality.

Samson's Wife. This Philistine woman, whom Samson insisted on marrying because she "pleased him well" (Judg. 14:3), ended up giving him nothing but trouble (Judg. 14:15-20). However, the Lord overruled the hero's folly and ultimately used Samson to deliver Israel from the encroachments of the Philistines (Judg. 15:1-8).

Solomon's Many Wives. Solomon's enormous harem of 700 wives and 300 concubines testified to both his wealth and his growing apostasy from the Lord (1 Kings 11:1-8). Solomon's many marriages, first with the Pharaoh's daughter (1 Kings 3:1) and then with various foreign princesses, cemented his political ties with various countries. All of Solomon's wives lived in luxury and splendor. He built a special palace for Pharaoh's daughter (1 Kings 7:8-12).

However, the Bible does not indicate that a single one of Solomon's wives learned to trust the God of Israel. Instead, these pagan women turned the king's heart away from God. This "wisest of men" played the part of a fool by forsaking the Lord (1 Kings 11:1-13). The king violated God's law (Deut. 17:17) and paid a terrible price for his folly.

The Unbelieving Wife. The Apostle Paul declares that such a wife is sanctified by her believing husband (1 Cor. 7:14). Though he is a Christian and she is not, his faith stamps the marriage as holy and in a sense sanctifies the offspring of the union. The children are not, of course, saved by their parents' faith. However, in a certain sense they enjoy the blessings of the converted parent's Christian faith. (The Apostle presupposes that the believing parent will lead the child to accept the gospel of redemption and will rear him in Christian truth.)

The same principle applies to unsaved husbands. "The unbelieving husband is sanctified by the wife" (1 Cor. 7:14). This truth is meant to encourage a Christian husband or wife to claim his or her entire family for the Lord and to trust God to save all its unconverted members.

WILDERNESS. Since large areas of Palestine and the Near East are arid and mountainous, desert or wilderness conditions are common. The commonest Hebrew word for such a region, *midbar*, denotes barren areas of sand dunes or rock as well as steppes and pasture lands (Deut. 32:10; Job 38:26; Psa. 65:12; Joel 2:22). The same description applies to *erēmos*, the Greek word for wilderness regions (Matt. 14:15; Luke 9:10).

The term "Jeshimon" (Hebrew *yeshimon*, "a waste" or "desert") is identified principally with the Wilderness of Judah, a barren, rugged region extending from Masada to Khirhet Qumran (1 Sam. 23:24; 26:1). The designation is also sometimes applied to the rugged region north of the Dead Sea and east of the Jordan River (Num. 21:20; 23:28).

The term "Arabah," in addition to its use as a proper name for the long, barren Rift Valley from the Dead Sea to the Gulf of Aqabah, is also sometimes used in a general way of steppe and scrubland or of barren desert (Jer. 17:6; Job 39:6). Exceptionally arid regions are specifically designated as such by the words *ṣiyya* (Job 30:3; Psa. 78:17) or *tōhu* (Job 6:18; 12:24).

The more significant wildernesses of Bible lands are described briefly below.

Damascus. The semi-desert region beyond the fertile city of Damascus. It was the site at which Elijah anointed Hazael to be the king of Aram.

Edom. Edom proper is a rugged, mountainous region which extends about 100 miles southward from Moab on both sides of the Arabah (the great depression from the Dead Sea to the Gulf of Aqabah). The Wilderness of Edom was the Arabah at the southern extremity of the Dead Sea.

En-gedi. The rugged, mountainous country around En-gedi proper. Because it abounded in caves and deep ravines, the Wilderness of En-gedi was a frequent hiding place for hunted people.

Judah. A portion of the region between the Central Highland Ridge and the Dead Sea. It included the Valley of Berachah, the Ascent of Ziz, the Wadi Murab-

baʿat, and part of the Brook Kidron. It was in the Wilderness of Judah that the Dead Sea Scrolls were found.

Kadesh-Barnea. The desert region in the vicinity of the city of Kadesh-Barnea. The locale is the same as Meribah (Exod. 17:7; Num. 20:13) and Meribath-Kadesh (Deut. 32:51). It was in Kadesh-Barnea that the people of Israel chose to disbelieve God and wander in the desert for a whole generation.

Paran. The desert plateau region in which Israel wandered for 38 years. It included practically the entire eastern half of the Sinai Peninsula. The region was bounded roughly by Mount Sinai, the Wilderness of Shur, the Wilderness of Zin, and the Gulf of Aqabah.

Shur. The barren country through which Israel marched for three days immediately after crossing the Red Sea. It was also called the Wilderness of Etham (Num. 33:8). The region extended from the frontier fortresses of Egypt to the River of Egypt.

Sin. The wilderness through which the Israelites passed on their journey from Elim (by the Red Sea) to Rephidim and Mount Sinai (Num. 33:11, 12). It was the general region northwest of Mount Sinai.

Life is precarious in wilderness regions, such as this in the Sinai Peninsula. (© *MPS*)

Sinai. The territory in the general vicinity of Mount Sinai. The Wilderness of Sinai included the south-central portion of the tip of the Sinai Peninsula, about midway between the Gulf of Suez and the Gulf of Aqabah. Some scholars locate Mount Sinai at Jebel Helal, south and east of the Brook of Egypt.

Tekoa. The region surrounding the city of Tekoa (about six miles south of Bethlehem). The Prophet Amos came from this area (Amos 1:1).

Zin. The rugged country ranging from Kadesh-Barnea in northeast Sinai to the Ascent of Akrabbim, between Edom and Judah (Josh. 15:1-4; cf. Num. 34:1-5).

Ziph. The rugged country near the town of Ziph in the hill country of Judah (Josh. 15:55). David fled from King Saul to the Wilderness of Ziph on at least two occasions (1 Sam. 23:12-18; 26:1-25).

WILFUL KING. Evidently the "little horn" of Daniel 7:24-26, the head of the revived Roman power preceding Christ's glorious advent. Some expositors, however, identify the wilful king as an apostate Palestinian Jew in league with the Roman beast. The wilful king will flout the God of Israel, ridicule the messianic hope, and honor the Roman beast (Rev. 13:11-18). The wilful king will be destroyed at Christ's second coming (Dan. 11:45).

WILL. The ability of conscious, rational creatures to choose and accomplish a course of action. The relationship of God's sovereignty and man's will has always challenged the ingenuity of theologians. Attempts to harmonize this relationship have resulted in two major schools of thought on the issue: Calvinism and Arminianism.

It is quite clear, however, that the will of man is a faculty designed and created by God to execute his purposes. Human will (as well as angelic will) thus *accomplishes* divine purposes rather than thwarting them. Satan's introduction of sin into the universe took the form of rebellion against God in five "I wills" thundered against the divine will (Isa. 14:13, 14).

Scripture teaches that Satan dominates the wills of unsaved men (Eph. 2:2). The saved are urged to yield their redeemed bodies to the Lord in order to be able to know and do God's perfect will (Rom. 12:1, 2). There is nothing higher for a believer than to find the will of God and to walk in it. This is God's gracious goal in saving him (Eph. 2:8-10).

God's will is either directive or permissive. His directive will includes the doctrines of decrees, election, predestination, and foreordination. God's permissive will allows man his own choice. This often results in second best or even outright sin.

God's will is the correct standard of comparison for every motive, thought, and action. Man's highest purpose in life is achieved when he finds and fulfills God's perfect will. Christ himself came to perform fully the will of the Father (John 6:38). Every yielded believer should say, as Christ did, "Not my will, but thine, be done" (Luke 22:42).

WILLOWS. The willow tree is commonly found alongside streams in Palestine (Job 40:22; Isa. 15:7; 44:4; Ezek. 17:5). The "willows of the brook" (Lev. 23:40) and the "willows" of Babylon (Psa. 137:2) are now usually regarded as species of the poplar. A few scholars, however, identify them with the aspen.

WINNOWER. In biblical days grain was harvested with a sickle, tied into sheaves, and carried to the threshing floor. Threshing floors were usually located on soil coated with marly clay or on rocky hilltops. The sheaves were laid about a foot deep and were trampled by animals until the grain was separated and the stocks chopped into bits. Sometimes a wooden sled with stones or nails was used to loosen the grain. The winnower then tossed the mass into the wind with a wooden pitchfork. The chaff was blown away and the remaining grain was put into bags.

WOLF. The Palestinian wolf is a variety of the European species (*Canis lupus*). It belongs to the same genus as the dog, but cannot bark (it howls instead). The wolf is fierce and carnivorous (Heb. 1:8). It seeks its prey, often sheep (John 10:12), in the evening (Zeph. 3:3). Violent rulers and false teachers are compared to wolves (Ezek. 22:27; Matt. 7:15; Acts 20:29).

WOMAN. In a certain biblical sense woman plays a secondary role to man. Because of both creation and the fall, man bears a certain responsibility of headship over woman. Man was created before woman. Moreover, woman was made from man and for man (Gen. 2:7, 18-24; 1 Cor. 11:8, 9). Woman was also the first to sin (Gen. 3:6; 1 Tim. 2:14), thereby becoming subject to the rule of her husband (Gen. 3:16; 1 Cor. 11:3). However, the headship of man over woman does not imply that woman is inferior to man. It simply means that God has given man a broader and more defined sphere of leadership in human affairs than woman. For this reason male characters are more numerous and more prominent in biblical history (and world history) than female characters.

However, the prominence of male characters over female characters does not detract from the importance of women in Scripture. In their own sphere women, like men, often become God's instrument to accomplish certain divine purposes. If unbelieving and disobedient, women can become agents of Satan to oppose God's will. God's Word describes its women as candidly as it does the men.

In general, Hebrew women were held in the highest respect by Israelite men. Two women were prophetesses (Exod. 15:20; 2 Kings 22:14), and one was both a prophetess and a judge (Judg. 4:4). Hebrew women enjoyed full legal rights in the execution of justice (Num. 27:1-11; 1 Kings 3:16-28). They are portrayed in every virtue and excellence of character as mothers and wives in the home. The highly beneficent influence of mothers on their offspring, especially their sons, is emphasized in Scripture (2 Tim. 1:5).

Women of the Old Testament era were active in both indoor and outdoor responsibilities. They spun yarn (Exod. 35:26; Prov. 31:19), made clothing (1 Sam. 2:19), served as water-carriers (Gen. 24:15; 1 Sam. 9:11) or shepherdesses (Gen. 29:6; Exod. 2:16), gleaned in the harvest fields (Ruth 2:17), and prepared bread (Matt. 24:41).

The sacrifice, zeal, and fidelity of Hebrew women are exemplified in the devoted group that supported Jesus' ministry and ministered to him of their material possessions (Luke 8:2, 3). The noblest features of Hebrew womanhood are seen in such biblical personalities as Mary, Elisabeth, Anna, Eunice, Lois, and many more.

The great New Testament revelation that all believers of both sexes enjoy identical spiritual privileges in Christ gave womanhood a dignity and glory that it had never enjoyed even in ancient Israel (Gal. 3:28). Every region of the world that has accepted the rudiments of Christianity has elevated womanhood under the principle of the headship of man. Modern "woman's liberation" movements usually ignore the teachings of Christ and reject the order of the sexes which God established in the beginning of human history.

As with certain men of Scripture, numerous women are referred to but not named in the pages of the Bible. These include mothers, wives, daughters, and various others. Some of these unnamed personalities actually fulfill more important roles than certain other women who are mentioned by name.

Some of the more significant unnamed women of Scripture are briefly described below.

An Adulterous Woman. Probably a young woman, likely a first offender. However, she was apprehended in the act of adultery (John 8:3-11) and could therefore have been stoned to death, according to the Law of Moses (Lev. 20:10). In dealing with the woman and her accusers Christ raised new standards for marriage. Both men and women were expected to honor their marriage vows. Christ in no sense condoned the guilty woman's sin, but he did provide opportunity for repentance and a renewed life.

The Elect Lady. John's Second Epistle is addressed to "the elect lady and her children" (1:1). She was evidently a Christian matron who resided somewhere in the circuit of churches over which the aged Apostle John exercised spiritual oversight. Some consider the designation a name—"Lady Elect." Other scholars feel the title refers to a church and its members.

The Great Harlot of Revelation 17. A

figure of the final form of religious rebellion against God's Word (Rev. 17:1-18). The woman's harlotry symbolizes corrupt religionism, which compromises the truth of God's Word for worldly power. The woman rides into power on the beast, the final form of Gentile world government. She represents in fullest scope all apostate religious movements and mergers from their inception in ancient Babylon (Gen. 11:1-9) to their end-time consummation in apostate Christendom (Rev. 17:5).

The woman's crimes are enumerated (Rev. 17:6) and her destruction at the hands of the beast (governmental authority) which she rode into power is described (17:7-18).

The Lamb's Wife. The bride of Christ, a symbol of the New Testament church (Rev. 21:9). The figure of a wife symbolizes the church in glorious union with Christ in the kingdom. The figure of marriage represents the outward, public consummation of the inner spiritual union between Christ and his church (Eph. 5:22-32).

The bride's preparation for marriage presupposes her sanctification through Christ's imputed righteousness and follows the evaluation of her works at the judgment seat of Christ (Rom. 14:10; 2 Cor. 5:10). The bride's robes portray the righteousness of Christ graciously imputed to her by God on the basis of Christ's death (Rev. 19:8).

The Queen of Heaven. An ancient Semitic fertility goddess (Jer. 7:18; 44:17-19). She was worshiped by the apostates of Judah in the last terrible forty years before the Babylonian captivity.

The Shulamite. The young woman in the Song of Solomon (Song 6:13). The name is best interpreted as the feminine form of Solomon and a descriptive title, "the Solomoness." Solomon wooed and apparently won her.

The Sun-Clothed Woman. A supernatural symbol which apparently portrays the nation Israel clothed in regal and governmental splendor (Rev. 12:1, 2). The twelve stars signify her twelve tribes, as Joseph's dream suggests (Gen. 37:9). Her travail reflects the nation's suffering during the Great Tribulation (Jer. 30:5-7;

Isa. 26:15-18; 66:7), when she will give birth to the godly remnant.

The Ten Virgins. The five wise virgins symbolize the believing remnant of the nation Israel during the nation's judgment just prior to the establishment of the kingdom (Matt. 25:1-13). The five foolish virgins prefigure the unbelieving part of the nation. They are not ready for the coming of the Messiah; their profession proves to be a false one. Their lack of the Holy Spirit (symbolized by the oil) will exclude them from participation in the coming kingdom.

The Woman of Endor. A spiritistic medium whom Saul brazenly consulted after he himself had outlawed spiritism from his realm (1 Sam. 28:3, 9), in accord with the warnings of the Mosaic Law (Lev. 19:31; 20:6, 27; Deut. 18:9-11). God unexpectedly intervened in the visit, bringing up the actual spirit of Samuel to pronounce doom upon Saul for this last step toward ruin (1 Sam. 28:12-20).

The Woman with Leaven. A symbol of false teaching. The leaven which she hides in the meal represents erroneous doctrine propagated by false Christianity during this present age (Matt. 16:11, 12; Mark 8:15; 1 Cor. 5:6-8; Gal. 5:9).

The Woman of Samaria. The woman who met Christ at the well at Sychar in the plain of Shechem. Jesus displayed toward her a compassionate concern which transcended all social and religious prejudices. He recalled her sinful life but did not censure her. She opened her heart to his message of life and carried it back to others in Samaria. The result was an ingathering of souls (John 4:7-42).

The Woman with Seven Husbands. The hypothetical woman who married each of seven brothers, every one of whom died without leaving a child (Matt. 22:23-30). Her marriages were in accord with the early Levirate law, which obligated a man to marry his deceased brother's widow (Deut. 25:5-10). The hypocritical Pharisees and Sadducees tried to embarrass Christ by contriving the situation of a woman with seven successive husbands. Whose wife would she be in the resurrection? Christ responded by revealing their ignorance of the spiritual realm, where God grants glorified bodies to all his saints (Matt. 22:29, 30).

WOOD CARVER. Bezaleel and Aholiab performed intricate wood carving for the Old Testament Tabernacle (Exod. 35:30-35). The walls and doors of Solomon's Temple were executed in bas-relief of lotus flowers, lilies, and cherubim (1 Kings 6:18, 29, 32-35). Ezekiel's Temple also reveals elaborate carving (Ezek. 41:16-26). In its heyday Egypt boasted exquisite and highly developed wood carving.

WORD OF GOD. The beauties and excellencies of the written Word of God are extolled in Psalm 119 in a manner found nowhere else in the Bible. Scripture bears its own witness that it is God-breathed and fully authoritative (2 Tim. 3:16, 17). This full inspiration and authority extends not merely to parts of Scripture, but to every word in the entire Book.

The process by which God communicated his thoughts to inspired writers is outlined in 1 Corinthians 2:9-14. Unsaved men cannot discover the unseen things of God (1 Cor. 2:9, 14). God has, however, revealed these truths to his saints (1 Cor. 2:10-12). They are communicated in Spirit-taught words (1 Cor. 2:13). The Holy Spirit sovereignly chose words from the writer's own vocabulary (1 Cor. 2:13). These words are properly understood by the believer only through the illumination of the Holy Spirit (1 Cor. 2:15, 16).

WORLD (Greek *kosmos*). The present world system, organized and controlled by Satan. It is erected upon Satan's principles of greed, force, selfishness, ambition, lust, and war (Matt. 4:8, 9; Eph. 2:2;

6:12). The believer is warned against loving this evil system (1 John 2:15-17). To love it is to be at enmity with God (James 4:1-4). Accommodation to this evil system is a constant threat to the spiritual life of the believer.

The Greek word *aiōn*, often translated "world" in the King James Version, actually refers to an age or a period of time (Mark 10:30; Matt. 12:32; 24:3; 28:20). The Greek word *oikoumenē* means the inhabited earth, as referred to in prophetic and kingdom teaching (Luke 2:1; Matt. 24:14).

WORLD EMPIRES. In his visions Daniel saw four great world Empires which spanned the centuries from Nebuchadnezzar to the second advent of Christ (Dan. 2:31-45; 7:1-28). The fourth Empire will be revived in the end time (Rev. 13:3), only to be shattered by Christ (the Stone supernaturally cut out of the mountain) at his second coming (Dan. 2:34). The stone will in turn become "a great mountain" (the millennial kingdom) and will fill the whole earth (Dan. 2:35).

WORMWOOD. Any of several species of strong-smelling plants that yield a bitter, dark-green oil used in making absinthe (an alcoholic liquor). The biblical references to wormwood are either to *Artemisia herba-alba* or to *Artemesia judaica*. Every species of wormwood has a strong, bitter taste (Prov. 5:4; Lam. 3:15, 19).

WORSHIP. Old Testament worship centered around the altar of incense, a symbol of Christ as our Intercessor (John 17:1-26; Heb. 7:25). It is through him that our prayers and praises ascend to God. The altar of incense also symbolizes the believer-priest's sacrifice of praise and worship to God (Heb. 13:15; Rev. 8:3, 4).

Z

ZACCHAEUS (ză-kē′ŭs) (Greek form of Hebrew *Zaccai*). A prosperous tax collector for the Roman government who lived in Jericho. He overcame obstacles to come to Christ and later became his devoted disciple (Luke 19:1-10).

ZACHARIAH (zăk′à-rī′à). The king of Israel during part of 753 and 752 B.C. He was the son of Jeroboam II. Zachariah was assassinated after only a six-month reign (2 Kings 14:29; 15:8-12).

ZACHARIAS (zăk′à-rī′às) ("the Lord has remembered"). (1) A righteous man who was murdered at the insistence of King Joash (835-796 B.C.) in the court of the Temple (2 Chron. 24:20-22). Christ referred to the event in Luke 11:51. (2) The father of John the Baptist (Luke 1:5-79).

ZALMON (zăl′mŏn). A mountain in the vicinity of the town of Shechem (Judg. 9: 48). It is probably to be identified with the southern part of Mount Gerizim or with Jabal al-Kabir. A different mountain is rendered "Salmon" in Psalm 68:14, KJV. This mountain is possibly one of the high peaks of Bashan.

ZAREPHATH (zăr′ě-făth). A town belonging to Sidon (1 Kings 17:9; Luke 4: 26). Here lived the widow who fed Elijah and for whom the Lord performed miracles (1 Kings 17:8-24). The name of the town still lingers in the form of "Sarafend," a present-day village near the ruins of ancient Zarephath.

ZEBEDEE (zĕb′ě-dē) ("the Lord has given"). The father of James and John. Like his sons, Zebedee was a Galilean fisherman (Matt. 4:21, 22) and a man of enough wealth to retain hired servants (Mark 1:20).

ZEBOIM (zě-bō′ĭm). One of the five cities of the Plain of Genesis 10:19. Its king was defeated by Chedorlaomer (Gen. 14: 2, 8, 10). Zeboim was destroyed with Sodom and Gomorrah and now lies buried beneath the shallow southern waters of the Dead Sea.

ZEBULUN (zĕb′ū-lŭn) ("habitation, dwelling"). Jacob's tenth son and the progenitor of one of the twelve tribes of Israel (Gen. 30:19, 20; Num. 26:26, 27).

ZECHARIAH (zĕk-à-rī′à) ("the Lord remembers"). A prophet of the restoration who (with Haggai) encouraged God's people to complete the Temple during 520 to 515 B.C. Zechariah foresaw the first and second comings of Messiah. He particularly envisioned Israel's final regathering and establishment in millennial blessing under Messiah-King-Priest (Zech. 3:1 – 6:15; 9:1 – 14:21).

ZEDEKIAH (zĕd′ě-kī′à) ("the Lord is righteous"). (1) A false prophet who encouraged King Ahab to go up to Ramoth-Gilead. He clashed with the true prophet of God, Micaiah (1 Kings 22:11-28). (2) The last king of Judah (597-586 B.C.) before the fall of Jerusalem to the Babylonians. He was an evil king and his career ended in tragedy. First his sons were slain before his eyes, and then his eyes were put out and he was carried to Babylon in chains (2 Kings 24:18 – 25:7).

ZEPHANIAH (zĕf′à-nī′à) ("the Lord has hidden"). One of the minor prophets. He was a contemporary of Jeremiah (640-608

B.C.). Zephaniah had access to the royal court and was therefore doubtless instrumental in Josiah's religious reformation (2 Kings 22:1 – 23:30). Zephaniah warned of approaching judgment upon both Israel (Zeph. 1) and the nations (Zeph. 2:1 – 3:8). He also foresaw Israel's kingdom blessing (Zeph. 3:9-20).

ZEPHATH (zē'făth). A Canaanite city which was destroyed and later renamed Hormah ("destruction"). Zephath was situated southeast of Beersheba, toward the borders of Edom. It is identified with present-day Tell el-Mishash. It was in Zephath that the presumptuous Israelites suffered defeat (Num. 14:39-45; Deut. 1:44; cf. Num. 21:1-3). Zephath was originally allotted to the tribe of Judah but was later transferred to Simeon (Josh. 15:30; 19:4). See also "Hormah."

ZERED (zē'rĕd). A brook which flows eastward into the south end of the Dead Sea. The Israelites crossed this wadi on their journey around the frontiers of Edom and Moab (Num. 21:12; Deut. 2:13-14).

ZERUAH (zē-rōō'à) ("having a skin disease"). The mother of Jeroboam I, first king of the Northern Kingdom (931-910 B.C.). Zeruah was a widow at the time of Jeroboam's birth. Her husband, Nebat, had apparently been an official under King Solomon, and her son became an overseer of heavy work. As king of Israel Jeroboam introduced the idolatrous worship of the golden bulls at the cult centers of Dan and Bethel (1 Kings 12:25-33). No doubt Zeruah, being a widow at the time of Jeroboam's birth, was responsible for molding Jeroboam's life in a pattern of expediency and opportunism.

ZERUBBABEL (zē-rŭb'à-bĕl) (Akkadian, "seed of Babylon"). The governor of the Jewish remnant who returned from Babylon in 539 B.C. It was under his administration that Haggai and Zechariah prophesied and preached and that the Temple was rebuilt (515 B.C.). Zerubbabel was a son of Shealtiel and a relative of King David. He was also an ancestor of Christ (Matt. 1:12, 13; Luke 3:27).

ZERUIAH (zēr'ōō-ī'à) (probably "one perfumed with mastix"). The mother of Joab, Abishai, and Asahel, three loyal supporters of David and commanders of his army (2 Sam. 2:18). The fact that her name appears some 25 times in connection with her sons seems to indicate that she exercised a beneficent influence on her sons' lives (1 Sam. 26:6; 2 Sam. 2:13, 18; 3:39; 8:16; etc.). Zeruiah was David's half-sister; like her sister Abigail, Zeruiah was a daughter not of Jesse but of Jesse's wife by an earlier marriage with Nahash (1 Chron. 2:16; cf. 2 Sam. 17:25).

ZIBIAH (zĭb'ĭ-à) ("gazelle"). The mother of Joash, king of Judah (835-796 B.C.), and the wife of King Ahaziah (841 B.C.). Zibiah's infant son was rescued from Athaliah's plot to kill all the royal seed. His aunt hid Joash in the Temple until he was seven years old. He was proclaimed king by the high priest, Jehoiada, after Athaliah was slain. His reign was good because of the influence of his mother and the high priest, Jehoiada (2 Kings 12:1-21).

ZIKLAG (zĭk'lăg). A town in south Judah (Josh. 15:31) which belonged to Simeon (Josh. 19:5). David took refuge there (1 Sam. 27:6; 30:1-6; 2 Sam. 1:1). It was settled after the exile (Neh. 11:28).

ZILPAH (zĭl'pà). The mother of Gad and Asher. Laban gave her to Leah as her maidservant (Gen. 29:24; 46:18). Leah, on the other hand, gave Zilpah to Jacob as his wife (Gen. 30:9; 37:2). She bore the patriarch two of his twelve sons (Gen. 30:10-13; 35:26).

ZION (zī'ŭn). The fortified hill southeast of Jerusalem which David captured from the Jebusites and made the capital of the United Kingdom (2 Sam. 5:7; 1 Kings 8:1). In the Old Testament the name is used poetically for Jerusalem, and probably means "citadel" or "stronghold" (cf. 2 Kings 19:21; Psa. 48:1-14; 69:35; 133:3; Isa. 1:8; 52:1).

The New Testament use of Zion refers not only to Jerusalem as a whole but to the entire nation of Israel (Rom. 11:26, 27). It also embraces the New Jerusalem, the symbolized abode and destiny of all the redeemed in eternity (Heb. 12:22, 23; Rev. 21:9 – 22:5).

Zion also has reference to the capital city of the millennial kingdom in the coming age (Isa. 1:27; 2:3; 4:1-6; Joel 3:16; Zech. 1:16, 17; 8:3-8; Rom. 11:26).

ZIPPORAH (zĭ-pō'rà) ("swallow"). The

first wife of Moses and the mother of Gershom and Eliezer (Exod. 2:16-22). Moses met Zipporah in Midian. She was one of the seven daughters of Reuel (another name for Jethro). She and Moses apparently had little compatibility, she being a Midianite and he a Hebrew. She apparently opposed circumcising their son. This was a serious matter because circumcision was the symbol of the covenant between God and his people. Now called to deliver God's people out of Egypt, Moses recognized the seriousness of this reluctance. At an inn Moses evidently became violently ill. Zipporah in fright circumcised the child herself, and Moses' life was spared (Exod. 4:24-26). After this she became a nonentity until she, her sons, and her father, Jethro, joined Moses at Mount Sinai (Exod. 18: 5). Zipporah seems to have been prejudiced and rebellious and of little help to her husband.

ZOAN (zō'ăn). A city of northeast Egypt known as Avaris in the Hyksos period, as Raamses under Rameses II, and as Tanis still later. See Num. 13:22; Psa. 78:12, 43; Isa. 19:11, 13; 30:4; Ezek. 30:14.

ZOAR (zō'ẽr). One of the cities of the Plain, probably the smallest of the five (Gen. 19:20, 22). Its original name was Bela (Gen. 14:2). Lot first interceded for Zoar, then fled from its impending destruction (Gen. 19:20−22:30). The site was in existence in the days of Isaiah and Jeremiah, apparently on the east (Moabite) side of the Dead Sea (Isa. 15:5; Jer. 48:34). Zoar is located a few miles from the present south-southeast shoreline of the Dead Sea.

ZOBAH (zō'bà). A powerful Aramean kingdom in the days of Saul and David. It lay west of the Euphrates (1 Sam. 14:47; 2 Sam. 8:3). It was also called Aram-Zobah (2 Sam. 10:6). David subdued the region and Solomon controlled it (cf. 1 Kings 11:23).

ZOPHAR (zō'fẽr) (perhaps "chirper," from Arabic *safara*, "to whistle"). One of Job's friends who boasted of his knowledge of God. Zophar was of little comfort or help to Job, for his dogmatism rested not upon God's Word but on what he thought he knew (Job 2:11; 11:1; 20:1; 42:9).

ZORAH (zō'rà). A town in the lowlands of Judah (Josh. 15:33). It was inhabited by the tribe of Dan (Josh. 19:41). Samson's father was a native of the place (Judg. 16: 31). Some of the Danites who captured Laish were from Zorah (Judg. 18:2, 8, 11). Rehoboam fortified the town (2 Chron. 11:10). It was inhabited in the post-captivity period (Neh. 11:29). Zorah is located at Sarᶜa, on the north side of the Valley of Sorek and about 14 miles west of Jerusalem.

Pronunciation Guide

Dedication:

In loving memory of my parents—
Lillian Scarboro Severance
Willard Murray Severance, Sr.

Acknowledgments

Authors do not work in a vacuum. Support comes from many quarters in the form of research, resources, professional services, management, and personal advice and support. My special thanks go to the following persons for their help and assistance in the creation of this book:

- Clifton J. Allen, the instigator, who gave me the concept, helped me see the need, and then encouraged me in the initial work on this idea.

- John Durham, Malcolm Tolbert, and Johnnie Godwin for their assistance with the Hebrew and Greek languages.

- Ernie Couch, from Consultx, for his enthusiastic response to the book and his suggestions for format, typography, and design.

- John Nehlig of Holman Bible Publishers, who guided me professionally and zealously through the tedious process of book publishing.

- Ann Severance, my wife, for her loving support and patience during the months of manuscript preparation.

I also breathe a prayer of thanks to the good Lord for granting me health to persist, patience to endure, and insight to fulfill.

W. Murray Severance

Introduction

No two scholars in any field agree one hundred percent. In fact, no two persons agree totally about any subject. That's a clear indication of individuality. People don't think alike, speak alike, look alike, or do anything else exactly alike. The author of this guide recognizes that distinctiveness. He realizes that some of those seeking to pronounce Bible names "properly" will not agree with the conclusions set forth in this book. And that's okay. It is a guide, not the final authority. Usage is! Britons spell the same word differently from Americans. Southerners pronounce words unlike Westerners. Heritage, environment, era, and other principles influence pronunciation.

Pronunciation continues to be influenced by the three languages in which the Bible was written. Two dominate—Hebrew and Greek. One is minor by volume—Aramaic. Hebrew and Aramaic are sister languages. The Koiné Greek, the language of the common man, contains a different number of letters from the two Semitic languages and has distinctive rules for accenting and pronunciation. When these three languages are translated to English, other drastic changes appear. Colloquial spellings and pronunciations come as no real surprise, and they do occur. For instance, even the name Palestine is pronounced in various ways. The last syllable of the Middle Eastern country rhymes with "tine," like a prong of a fork. Yet, the last syllable of Palestine as spoken by many Texans rhymes with "teen," a young person!

To a great extent we learn our rules of language and speech from our parents, teachers, and peers. Change comes about slowly, but change does occur continually. Proof of this statement is easily witnessed when a student picks up a copy of Chaucer or Shakespeare and then turns to one of the modern writers. Even the poorest reader can easily discern the difference.

As a producer of religious audiovisuals for more than thirty years, I have produced literally hundreds of products directly based on the Bible. Most filmstrip scripts, motion picture and videotape dialogues, and audiocassette narrations include proper Bible names. Audiovisuals represent a marriage of video (picture) and audio (sound) components that approach real life more closely than any other medium. Only the third dimension is missing, but the illusion of depth is there nevertheless. When dialogue is added to tape or film, it is immediately preserved, not only the words themselves, but also the manner in which the words were recorded. That fact motivated a serious student of the Bible to come by my office several years ago to ask my opinion about pronunciation of a rather obscure Bible name. He, like preachers, teachers, and other lecturers, realized that a successful presentation depends on how he presents the material perhaps as much as what he says!

This person was highly respected as a teacher, editor, writer, and Christian gentleman. For him to come to me was flattering. After I gave my opinion, he left to record some Sunday School lessons for radio. Suddenly it dawned on me that if an educator of his stature needed help, what about others with less training?

For years I have been a follower of Frank C. Laubach and his relentless campaign to spread his philosophy of "each one teach one." He spent his life searching out remote areas of the world and developing methods to help natives read in their own language. In order to accomplish this task, Dr. Laubach had to develop an alphabet, where there was none, that harmonized with each language he discovered. Charts were constructed and natives were trained to teach themselves. Then Dr. Laubach and his colleagues moved on to other fields. From his experience came some basic rules for pronunciation in the various languages.

Using a method for pronouncing Bible names which paralleled Laubach's experience and other existing systems, I produced an audio product entitled *Pronunciation of Bible Names*. The accompanying manual contained all 3,492 proper names from the King James Version. Three definite ways to pronounce practically guaranteed that the method developed could be faithfully reproduced. One column in the manual consisted of Bible names with diacritical marks and the other presented phonetic or a respelling system. For the third method, a narrator pronounced each proper name in sequence for the audiocassettes. Since its publication, this product has been distributed widely.

As author, I hope this guide will help many people in the crucial responsibility of "handling accurately the word of truth" (2 Tim. 3:15, NASB).

The Author

Explanation of Phonetic Spelling

This book goes a step further than the initial product on Bible names with the addition of all proper names from four widely distributed versions of the Bible: New American Standard Bible, New International Version, Revised Standard Version, and Today's English Version, or the Good News Bible. In the pursuit of bringing all the names together from the various versions, an interesting pattern emerged. As in the earlier product, the basic version used was the King James. A comparison of each of the other versions with the King James reveals 752 differences in the NASB, 1039 differences in the NIV, 933 differences in the RSV, and 1188 differences in the TEV! Out of fewer than 4,000 names, how could up to a third of the names vary?

All versions began with the texts available at the time of publication. Scholars today know more about the original languages than in 1611 when the KJV first appeared. Like current events versus history, the farther an analyst gets away from the event, the better and more accurate the conclusions can be drawn. To date, no known original manuscripts of the Bible have been found, even though great archaeological discoveries like the Dead Sea Scrolls have proved again that later manuscripts are very faithful to any earlier ones.

Changes do occur, however, in biblical names from one translation to another in the following ways:

1. Doubling or undoubling of letters: Bezaleel vs. Bezalel
2. Substitution of letters in transliteration: Chebar vs. Kebar
3. Combining names: Abel Maim vs. Abelmaim
4. Colloquial spellings: e.g. American or British: Judea vs. Judaea
5. Interpreting rather than naming names: Father vs. Abba
6. Deletions from one version to another: (about one-third)

These changes are facts. No scholastic degree is needed to compare versions. These changes do not destroy or change the basic texts. Differences in purpose, audience, time of publication, and other selective factors produce those changes. Acceptance by readers is expressed graphically in sales of specific versions. The KJV continues to be the traditional favorite. As in pronunciation, selection of translations is a highly individualistic choice. What appeals to one person leaves another dissatisfied. Therefore, students of the Bible choose different translations for their own purposes.

Most of the principles listed above that cause name changes are very obvious. But the principle of deletions needs a little more explanation. Deletions actually include all of the other factors. If a British version translates the term as Judaea, that choice automatically eliminates Judea. Both are correct, and neither affects the original text. Substitution of various letters from one language to another, as well as other factors, all speak to deletions. Thus, deletions are all-encompassing, comprehensive, or include "all of the above."

Alphabet Chart

Another way of recognizing the problems in translation from any language to another is to study the alphabet chart on the facing page. It includes the Hebrew and Greek alphabets with English equivalents. All three start with "a" and "b." Greek points out most graphically where the term "alphabet" (alpha beta) comes from. From that point on, no two alphabets agree completely, either in number of letters or in the sounds produced. A simple study reveals the difficulty in transferring any name from one language to another.

To illustrate, in recent years the thrilling story of Masada beside the Dead Sea has been reported in archaeological journals, novelized, and produced for television. Present-day Israelis mention Masada in a slogan concerning national pride. The "s" in Masada has no direct equivalent in English from the Hebrew. A better transliteration of the name to English would be *Metzada* or *Metsada*. Since there were no written vowels in Hebrew until the Massoretes added them in the ninth century A.D., vowels affecting pronunciation changed through the centuries, adding even another dimension or problem. This fact is graphically demonstrated in the origin of the word "Palestine" being a corruption from "Philistine!" Harden the "P" by removing the "h," change the vowels, and Palestine appears almost magically. Concerning Masada, the middle consonant of the triconsonantal root is a *tsade* (צ), that when anglicized, appears as a simple "s."

Comparison of English, Hebrew, and Greek Alphabets

ENGLISH (Equivalent)	HEBREW Character	Name	Pronunciation	GREEK Character	Name	Pronunciation
a (')	א	aleph	AH leff (glottal stop)	α	alpha	AL fuh
b	ב*	beth	BAYTH	β	beta	BAY tuh
g	ג*	gimel	GHEE mehl	γ	gamma	GAM muh
d	ד*	daleth	DAH lehth	δ	delta	DEHL tuh
e				ε	epsilon	EP sih lahn
h	ה	he	HAY			
v	ו	waw	WAUGH			
z	ז	zayin	ZA yihn	ζ	zeta	ZAY tuh
h	ח	heth	HAYTH	η	eta	AY tuh
t	ט	teth	TAYTH	θ	theta	THAY tuh
y	י	yodh	YOHDTH	ι	iota	ih OH tuh
k	ך, כ*	kaf	KAFF	κ	kappa	KAP puh
l	ל	lamedh	LAH medh	λ	lambda	LAMB duh
m	ם, מ	mem	MAYM	μ	mu	MEW
n	ן, נ	nun	NOON	ν	nu	NEW
s	ס	samekh	SAH mek			
				ξ	xi	ZEE
	ע	ayin	A yihn (rough breath)			
o				ο	omicron	AH mih krahn
p	פ*, ף	pe	PAY	π	pi	PIGH
	ץ, צ	tsade	TSAH deh			
q	ק	qof	QOHF			
r	ר	resh	RAYSH	ρ	rho	ROH
s, sh	ש, שׂ	sin, shin	SEEN, SHEEN	σ, ς	sigma	SIHG muh
t	ת*	taw	TAW	τ	tau	TAW
u				υ	upsilon	OOP sih lahn
				φ	phi	FIGH
				χ	chi	KIGH
				ψ	psi	puh SIGH
				ω	omega	oh MAY guh

26 letters · 22 letters · 24 letters

*ב, ג, ד, כ, פ, ת—so-called "beghadkephat" letters. Hard sound with dot in bosom of letter.

Key to Pronunciation

When it comes to language study, Americans in general are far behind some other nations. Europeans who live in the midst of compacted countries sometimes speak four or five languages fluently. Not so many years ago the "universal" or international language was French. A shift to English has developed in recent years.

English continues to be one of the very few languages that can be set without accents, diacritics, or special alphabetic characters. English also uses extensive capitalization. Nevertheless, some method has to be finally adopted which offers a solution to the problem of pronunciation in spite of the differences and comparisons.

Criteria for determining the pronunciation of each biblical name from the five different versions in this book are based on several important factors, as follows:

1. Accurately translated
2. Graphically visible
3. Obviously pronounceable
4. Simply expressed
5. Consistently stable
6. Currently acceptable

This guide developed because of a distinct need to present a definite way to pronounce Bible names easily. Various opinions are acknowledged and alternate pronunciations often appear.

Study the key on pages 216-217. Two paralleling methods appear: diacritical marks and phonetic spelling or respelling. The respelling system is the major contribution of this book. Nevertheless, the user of this guide will be exposed to the diacritical marks and may even learn them by simple exposure. One system supports the other. Phonetic or respelling is simply that. Rules are ignored for clarity and visibility. Problems such as double vowels, or diphthongs, must be eliminated. In English, when a vowel appears, it and the consonants around it form a syllable. The key to phonetic spelling is to spell a word as it sounds. Spell so as not to be mispronounceable!

Language experts agree generally that there are at least forty different sounds in English. Some find sixty. Many agree on forty-two. The tiny sound-making muscles with smacks, clicks, clacks, etc. are capable of making thousands of sounds, but no language requires that many. Since there are only twenty-six letters in the English alphabet, some must do double duty. Vowels take care of most of the extra sounds. While that offers a solution, it is also a paradox and a problem. The International Phonetic Alphabet was developed so that one symbol stands for one sound, but the system requires extensive learning of new signs. Nevertheless, the IPA is being taught in a number of American colleges.

Russian and Spanish words are not difficult to spell for those who know the languages. Each letter has a sound to match, and each letter always stands for the same sound. Spelling in English is highly inconsistent with its pronunciation. That's why other symbols like diacritical marks developed. But, they can be cumbersome, especially for the casual student. English has this one great difficulty—its chaotic spelling. It is perhaps the most irregularly spelled phonetic language. A famous American writer once said that he felt sorry for the person who didn't have enough imagination to spell a word more than one way! Coming from so many roots of so many lands, the English language has the richest vocabulary in the world. The English alphabet reflects this same flexibility, and confusion. Perhaps you have heard how one witty person spelled "fish." He claimed that *ghoti* is perfectly logical for "fish!" Observe:

gh from enou<u>gh</u> = f
o from w<u>o</u>men = i
ti from na<u>ti</u>on <u>= sh</u>
        fish

The genius of the respelling system used in this book is that a standard typewriter contains all the symbols. Accented syllables appear in all caps; spaces indicate syllable division; unaccented syllables consist of lower case letters.

Returning to the factor of "obviously pronounceable," logic prevails. Vowels require the most attention because of their flexibility in pronunciation. The letter "a" provides the best example because it varies in sound more than any other vowel. Note:

ā	long a with the mācrŏn, (MAY krahn), retains the letter sound as in hāy, sāy	= ay	= SAY
ă	short a with the brēve (BREEV), as in hăt, căt	= a	= KAT
ä	with the dieresis (DIGH ehr eh sihs) as in fär	= ah	= FAHR
â	with the circumflex (SUHR kuhm flehx) as in fâre	= eh	= FEHR
å	with the short macron, as in åbout	= uh	= uh BOWT
a	unmarked, as in call	= aw	= CAWL
à	with the single dot, as in Annà	= uh	= AN nuh
āē	diphthong, with double macron, as in Cāēsar	= ee	= SEE zuhr
ah	unmarked, as in Elijah	= uh	= ih LIGH juh
âî	diphthong, with double circumflex, as in âîsle	= igh	= IGHL
ai	underlined, as in h<u>ai</u>l, m<u>ai</u>l	= ay	= MAYL
am	unmarked, as in Adam	= uhm	= A duhm
an	unmarked, as in Canaan	= uhn	= KAY nuhn
āū	diphthong, with the double macron, as in Esāū	= aw	= EE saw

All other vowels follow the same pattern. The only diacritical mark not appearing on an "a" is the tilde (TEEL dih) which comes from a Spanish background (ñ). Each equivalent for long vowels is made up of letters, not only pronounceable, but combinations of letters or sounds found in everyday words: Long a = ay from sāy; long e = ee from frēē; long i = igh from hīgh; long o = oh from nōte; long u = yoo from tūne, (TYOON). As mentioned, these symbols are already known to every reader in words observed every day. This guide only shifts the attention a little.

A familiar example of the genius of the respelling system is represented in the Hebrew name of Israel's first king, Saul. Transliterated from the Hebrew, it appears as "Shaul" with a soft "s" or "sh." The letters "au" make up a diphthong which Webster claims is a "gliding monosyllabic speech sound," treated as a single vowel even though when spoken it "moves from one vowel sound toward the position of another." In Hebrew, however, the name appears as שָׁאוּל and is pronounced shah UHL, recognizing the two vowels, which in this case means two syllables. In English, Saul has two vowel letters, but is treated as one syllable. This guide recognizes the possible problem, but works around it by ignoring the rules for clarification and granting only one way to pronounce. First, the diphthong had to be changed to get rid of the two-syllable possibility. Letter substitutions were considered which would result in the acceptable pronunciation. SAWL, with the "w," a consonant, substituting for the second vowel fulfils all the requirements. Some New Yorkers may call it SAWRL, but that "R" just isn't there. It's part of their colloquial speech pattern. "Saw," otherwise, can be pronounced but one way in English. SAWL appears in all caps as being the accented syllable, but in this case, the only syllable. The same philosophy was applied to all the proper names, using the key as a guide. This same theory can be used to transfer any foreign language into English words that can be pronounced. A prominent singer who knows very little if any Russian transposes that language and pronounces or sings it precisely while not necessarily knowing what he is singing!

Some consonants possess more than one sound possibility. They, too, appear in the key with a more consistent substitute. The letter "c" in cat has a "k" sound, whereas in cell it has an "s" sound.

Exceptions seem to occur in every situation. Special rules must originate to care for particular problems. The name of the second Old Testament patriarch, Isaac, gives perfect example. No diacritical markings existing can produce the "proper" sound, but the phonetic spelling or respelling does the job beautifully. The long ī part is easy (IGH); but "saac" defies all rules, so it must be respelled as it sounds—zik or zihk, with a short i.

Can you imagine what confusion abounds for one who was not raised in an English-speaking country and migrates? We Americans often use the phrase, "It's all Greek to me." Actually the Chinese language is more complicated, but some consider that if you know English, you've mastered the most difficult language in the world!

Key to Pronunciation

MARK	EXAMPLE	SIGN
ā	dāy, lāy	ay
ă	hăt, căt	a
ä	äre, fär	ah
â	câre, fâre	e, eh
å	åbout, åbet	u, uh
a	(unmarked) call	aw
à	àfraid	u, uh
āē	daēmon, dēmon	ee
ah	(unmarked) Elijah	uh
aî	aîsle	igh
ai	mail, hail	ay
am	(unmarked) adam's apple	uhm
an	(unmarked) roman	uhn
c, ch	cord, chorus	k
ç	çity	s, ss
ē	mēte, Crēte	ee
ĕ	mĕt, lĕt	e, eh (uh)
ē	tērm	u, uh
ė	ėlastic	i, ih
ḡ	ḡet	g
ġ	ġerm	gh, j
ī	pīne, fīne	igh
ĭ	hĭm, pĭn	ih
î	machîne	ee
ī	fīrm	u, uh (uhr)
ō	nōte, rōde	o, oh
ŏ	nŏt, rŏt	ah
o	(unmarked) amok	uh
ô	ôr, fôr	aw
ph	(unmarked) alpha	f
ṣ	hiṣ, muṣe	z
s	(unmarked) kiss	ss
ū	tūne, mūte	yoo, ew
ŭ	ŭp, tŭb	uh
û	hûrl, fûrl	u, uh
ü	trüth	oo, ew
th	(unmarked) thin	th
th̄	th̄yme	t
ti, ci, si	attraction	sh
y	city	i, ih

Seldom Used Marks

a̲a̲	Balaam	uh
a̲e̲	Colossae koh LAHS sih	ih
ao	(unmarked) pharaoh (ant)	oh
au	(unmarked) author	aw
e̅a	sea	ee
e̲a̲	zealous	eh
e̅e	gee	ee
e̅u, e̅w	brew	oo, ew
ia	(unmarked)	ya
ī̲o	legion	uh
i̲o̲	savior	yaw
oî	boil	oy
on	(unmarked) onion	uhn
ou	(unmarked) out	ow

- Signifies the joining of two words to form a compound name.
· Indicates a break between syllables.
' Indicates an accented syllable.
BAH (Syllables in capital letters) indicates the strongest, accented syllable.

This book began as a pronunciation guide to proper names in the King James Version of the Bible. The scope of the book, however, broadened to include pronunciation guidance for five major translations. Each of the translations has its own unique style or system of capitalization, spelling, and pronunciation. Since this is the case *Pronouncing Bible Names* will be especially helpful. All you have to do is look in alphabetical order for the name you want to pronounce. Then, regardless of variations in style from version to version, you can determine the essential and primary phonetic spelling and pronunciation.

Pronouncing Bible Names will give you both confidence and authority as you speak, teach, or preach by enabling you to pronounce correctly the often-difficult proper names from five of the most-often-used versions of the Bible.

Aâr′on ER′n, AIR′n *KJV, NAS, NIV,*
RSV, TEV

Aâr′on·ic ER uhn ihk, AIR uhn ihk
NIV

Aâr′on·ite ER′n ight *KJV, NAS, TEV*

A·băd′don uh BAD uhn *KJV, NAS, NIV,*
RSV, TEV

A·băg′thà uh BAG thuh *KJV, NAS, NIV,*
RSV, TEV

Ăb′à·nà AB uh nuh *KJV, NIV, RSV, TEV*

Ăb′à·nah AB uh nuh *NAS*

Ăb′à·rĭm AB uh rim *KJV, NAS, NIV,*
RSV, TEV

Ăb′bà AB buh *KJV, NAS, NIV, RSV, TEV*

Ăb′dà AB duh *KJV, NAS, NIV, RSV, TEV*

Ăb′dĕ·ĕl AB dih el *KJV, NAS, NIV, RSV,*
TEV

Ăb′dĭ AB digh *KJV, NAS, NIV, RSV, TEV*

Ăb′dĭ·ĕl AB dih el *KJV, NAS, NIV, RSV,*
TEV

Ăb′dŏn AB dahn *KJV, NAS, NIV, RSV,*
TEV

A·bĕd′nê·gō uh BED nih go *KJV, NAS,*
NIV, RSV, TEV

Ā′bĕl AY bel *KJV, NAS, NIV, RSV, TEV*

Ā′bĕl-bĕth-mā′à·cah AY bel-beth-MAY
uh kuh *NAS, NIV, RSV*

Ā′bĕl-bĕth-mā′à·chah AY bel-beth-
MAY uh kuh *KJV, TEV*

Ā′bĕl-cher′à·mĭm AY bel-KER uh
mim *KJV*

Ā′bĕl-kĕr′à·mĭm AY bel-KER uh mim
NAS, NIV, RSV, TEV

Ā′bĕl-mā′ĭm AY bel-MAY im *KJV,*
NAS, NIV, RSV, TEV

Ā′bĕl-mĕ·hō′lah AY bel-meh HO luh
KJV, NAS, NIV, RSV, TEV

Ā′bĕl-mĭz′rà·ĭm AY bel-MIZ ray im
KJV, NAS, NIV, RSV, TEV

Ā′bĕl-shĭt′tĭm AY bel-SHIT tim *KJV,*
NAS, NIV, RSV

Ā′bĕz AY bez, AY buhz *KJV*

Ā′bĭ AY bigh *KJV, NAS, RSV, TEV*

A·bī′à (A·bī′ah) uh BIGH uh *KJV, TEV*

Ā′bī-ăl′bŏn AY bigh-AL bahn *KJV,*
NAS, NIV, RSV, TEV

A·bī′à·săph uh BIGH uh saf *KJV, NAS,*
NIV, RSV, TEV

A·bī′à·thär uh BIGH uh thahr *KJV,*
NAS, NIV, RSV, TEV

Ā′bĭb AY bib *KJV, NAS, NIV, RSV, TEV*

A·bī′dà uh BIGH duh *KJV, NAS, NIV,*
RSV, TEV

Ăb′ĭ·dăn AB ih dan, uh BIGH dan
KJV, NAS, NIV, RSV, TEV

A·bī′ĕl uh BIGH el, AY bih el *KJV,*
NAS, NIV, RSV, TEV

Ā′bĭ-ē′zēr AY bigh-EE zur *KJV, NAS,*
NIV, RSV, TEV

Ā′bĭ-ĕz′rīte AY bigh-EZZ right *KJV,*
NAS, NIV, RSV

Ăb′ĭ·ḡail AB ih gayl *KJV, NAS, NIV,*
RSV, TEV

Ăb′ĭ·găl AB ih gal *KJV, RSV*

Ăb′ĭ·hail AB ih hayl *KJV, NAS, NIV,*
RSV, TEV

A·bī′hū uh BIGH hyoo *KJV, NAS, NIV,*
RSV, TEV

A·bī′hŭd uh BIGH huhd *KJV, NAS,*
NIV, RSV, TEV

A·bī′jah uh BIGH juh *KJV, NAS, NIV,*
RSV, TEV

A·bī′jăm uh BIGH jam *KJV, NAS, RSV*

Ăb′ĭ·lē′nē ab ih LEE nee *KJV, NAS,*
NIV, RSV, TEV

A·bĭm′à·ĕl ah BIM ay el *KJV, NAS, NIV,*
RSV, TEV

A·bĭm′ĕ·lĕch uh BIM eh lek *KJV, NAS,*
NIV, RSV, TEV

A·bĭn′à·dăb uh BIN uh dab *KJV, NAS,*
NIV, RSV, TEV

A·bĭn′o·am uh BIN uh uhm *KJV, NAS,*
NIV, RSV, TEV

A·bī′răm uh BIGH ram *KJV, NAS, NIV,*
RSV, TEV

Ăb′ĭ·shăg AB ih shag *KJV, NAS, NIV,*
RSV, TEV

A·bish′à·ī uh BISH ay igh, AB ih shigh
KJV, NAS, NIV, RSV, TEV

A·bĭsh′à·lŏm uh BISH uh luhm, uh
BIGH shah lohm *KJV, NAS, NIV,*
RSV, TEV

A·bĭsh′ū·à uh BISH yoo uh, AB ih shoo
uh *KJV, NAS, NIV, RSV, TEV*

A·bĭ′shûr uh BIGH shur *KJV, NAS,*
NIV, RSV, TEV

Ā·bī′tăl   uh BIGH tal, AB ih tal   *KJV,*
NAS, NIV, RSV, TEV
Ā·bī′tŭb   uh BIGH tuhb, AB ih tuhb
KJV, NAS, NIV, RSV, TEV
Ā·bī′ŭd   uh BIGH uhd   *KJV, NAS, NIV,*
RSV, TEV
Ăb′nēr   AB nur   *KJV, NAS, NIV, RSV,*
TEV
Ā′brȧ·hăm   AY bruh ham   *KJV, NAS,*
NIV, RSV, TEV
Ā′bram   AY bruhm   *KJV, NAS, NIV, RSV,*
TEV
Ā·brō′nah   a BROH nuh   *KJV, NAS, NIV,*
RSV, TEV
Ăb′sȧ·lom   AB suh luhm   *KJV, NAS, NIV,*
RSV, TEV
Ạb′shā·ī   AB shay igh, AB shigh   *NAS*
Ạ·cā′çiȧ   uh KAY shuh   *TEV*
Ạ·cā′çiȧ-Cī′tў   uh KAY shuh-SIH tih
TEV
Ăc′bôr   AK bawr   *NIV*
Ăc′căd   AK ad   *KJV, NAS, RSV, TEV*
Ăc′chō   AHK oh, AK oh   *KJV*
Ăc′cō   AHK oh, AK oh   *NAS, NIV, RSV,*
TEV
Ā·çĕl′dȧ·mà   uh SELL duh muh   *KJV*
Ā·chā′iȧ   uh KAY yuh, uh KIGH uh
KJV, NAS, NIV, RSV, TEV
Ā·chā′ĭ·cŭs   uh KAY ih kuhs   *KJV, NAS,*
NIV, RSV, TEV
Ā′chàn   AY kuhn   *KJV, NAS, NIV, RSV,*
TEV
Ā′chär   AY kahr   *KJV, NAS, NIV, RSV,*
TEV
Ā′chăz   AY kaz   *KJV*
Ăch′bôr   AK bawr   *KJV, NAS, RSV, TEV*
Ā′chīm   AY kim   *KJV, NAS, RSV, TEV*
Ā′chĭsh   AY kish   *KJV, NAS, NIV, RSV,*
TEV
Ăch′mē·thà   AK mee thuh   *KJV*
Ā′chôr   AY kawr   *KJV, NAS, NIV, RSV,*
TEV
Ăch′sà   AK suh   *KJV*
Ăch′sah   AK suh   *KJV, NAS, RSV, TEV*
Ăch′shăph   AHK shaf   *NIV*
Ăch′zĭb   AK zib   *KJV, NAS, RSV, TEV*
Ăc′sah   AK suh   *NIV*
Ăc′shăph   AK shaf   *NIV*
Ăc′zĭb   AK zihb   *NIV*
Ăd′ȧ·dah   AD uh duh, uh DAY duh
KJV, NAS, NIV, RSV, TEV
Ā′dah   AY duh   *KJV, NAS, NIV, RSV, TEV*

Ā·daĭ′ah   uh DIGH uh, uh DAY yuh
KJV, NAS, NIV, RSV, TEV
Ăd·ȧ·lī′ȧ   ad uh LIGH uh, uh DAY lih
uh   *KJV, NAS, NIV, RSV, TEV*
Ăd′am   AD duhm   *KJV, NAS, NIV, RSV,*
TEV
Ăd′ȧ·mah   AD uh muh   *KJV, NAS, NIV,*
RSV, TEV
Ăd′ȧ·mī   AD uh migh   *KJV*
Ăd′ȧ·mī-nē′keb   AD uh migh-NEE keb
KJV, NAS, NIV, RSV, TEV
Ā′där   AY dahr, UH dahr   *KJV, NAS,*
NIV, RSV, TEV
Ăd′bē·ēl   AD bih el   *KJV, NAS, NIV, RSV,*
TEV
Ăd′dan   AD uhn   *KJV, NAS, RSV, TEV*
Ăd′där   AD ahr   *KJV, NAS, NIV, RSV,*
TEV
Ăd′dī   AD igh   *KJV, NAS, NIV, RSV, TEV*
Ăd′dŏn   AD ahn   *KJV, NAS, NIV, RSV,*
TEV
Ā′dĕr   AY dur   *KJV*
Ăd′ĭ·ĕl   AD ih el, AY dih el   *KJV, NAS,*
NIV, RSV, TEV
Ā′dĭn   AY din   *KJV, NAS, NIV, RSV, TEV*
Ăd′ĭ·nà   AD ih nuh, uh DIGH nuh   *KJV,*
NAS, NIV, RSV, TEV
Ā·dī′nō   uh DIGH no, AD ih no   *KJV,*
NAS
Ăd·ĭ·thā′ĭm   ad ih THAY im   *KJV, NAS,*
NIV, RSV, TEV
Ăd′lā·ī   AD lay igh, ad LAY igh   *KJV,*
NAS, NIV, RSV, TEV
Ăd′mäh   AD mah   *KJV, NAS, NIV, RSV,*
TEV
Ăd·mā′thà   ad MAY thuh, AD muh
thuh   *KJV, NAS, NIV, RSV, TEV*
Ăd′mĭn   AD mihn   *NAS, RSV, TEV*
Ăd′nà   AD nuh   *KJV, NAS, NIV, RSV, TEV*
Ăd′näh   AD nah   *KJV, NAS, NIV, RSV,*
TEV
Ăd′ō·nī-zē′dĕk   AD oh nigh-ZEE dek
KJV, NAS, NIV, RSV, TEV
Ăd·ō·nī′jah   ad oh NIGH juh   *KJV, NAS,*
NIV, RSV, TEV
Ăd·ō·nī′kam   ad oh NIGH kuhm   *KJV,*
NAS, NIV, RSV, TEV
Ăd·ō·nī′ram   ad oh NIGH ruhm   *KJV,*
NAS, NIV, RSV, TEV
Ăd′ō·nī-zē·dĕk   AD oh nigh-ZEE dek
KJV, NAS, NIV, RSV, TEV
Ăd·ō·rā′ĭm   ad oh RAY im   *KJV, NAS,*
NIV, RSV, TEV
Ā·dō′răm   uh DOH ram   *KJV, NAS, RSV*

Á·drăm′mê·lĕch   uh DRAM uh lek *KJV, NAS, NIV, RSV, TEV*

Ăd·râ·mўt′tĭ·an   ad ruh MIT ih uhn *NAS*

Ăd·râ·mўt′tĭ·ŭm   ad ruh MIT ih uhm *KJV, NIV, RSV, TEV*

Ā′drĭ·à   AY drih uh *KJV, RSV*

Ā·drĭ·ă′tĭc   ay drih A tihk *NAS, NIV*

Ā′drĭ·ĕl   AY drih el *KJV, NAS, NIV, RSV, TEV*

Á·dŭl′lam   uh DUHL uhm *KJV, NAS, NIV, RSV, TEV*

Á·dŭl′lam·īte   uh DUHL uhm ight *KJV, NAS, NIV, RSV, TEV*

Á·dŭm′mĭm   uh DUHM im *KJV, NAS, NIV, RSV, TEV*

Āe·nē′às   ee NEE uhs *KJV, NAS, NIV, RSV, TEV*

Āe′non   EE nuhn *KJV, NAS, NIV, RSV, TEV*

Ăḡ′â·bŭs   AG uh buhs *KJV, NAS, NIV, RSV, TEV*

Ā′ḡăg   AY gag *KJV, NAS, NIV, RSV, TEV*

Ā′ḡăg·īte   AY gag ight, AG uh gight *KJV, NAS, NIV, RSV*

Ā′ḡär   AY gahr *KJV*

Ā′ḡēē   AY gee *KJV, NAS, NIV, RSV, TEV*

Á·ḡrĭp′pà   uh GRIP uh *KJV, NAS, NIV, RSV, TEV*

Ā′ḡûr   AY guhr *KJV, NAS, NIV, RSV, TEV*

Ā′hăb   AY hab *KJV, NAS, NIV, RSV, TEV*

Á·hâr′ah   uh HEHR uh *KJV, NAS, NIV, RSV, TEV*

Á·här′hĕl   uh HAHR hel *KJV, NAS, NIV, RSV, TEV*

Á·hā′saì   uh HAY sigh, uh HAY say igh *KJV*

Á·hăṣ′baì   uh HAZ bigh *KJV, NAS, NIV, RSV, TEV*

Á·hăṣ·ū·ē′rŭs   uh haz yoo EE russ *KJV, NAS, RSV*

Á·hā′và   uh HAY vuh *KJV, NAS, NIV, RSV, TEV*

Ā′hăz   AY haz *KJV, NAS, NIV, RSV, TEV*

Ā·hâ·zī′ah   ay huh ZIGH uh *KJV, NAS, NIV, RSV, TEV*

Äh′băn   AH ban *KJV, NAS, NIV, RSV, TEV*

Ā′hĕr   AY hur *KJV, NAS, NIV, RSV*

Ą′hī   AY high *KJV, NAS, NIV, RSV, TEV*

Á·hī′ah   uh HIGH uh *KJV, NAS, NIV, RSV*

Á·hī′ăm   uh HIGH am *KJV, NAS, NIV, RSV, TEV*

Á·hī′ăn   uh HIGH an *KJV, NAS, NIV, RSV, TEV*

Ā·hī·ē′zĕr   ay high EE zur *KJV, NAS, NIV, RSV, TEV*

Á·hī′hŭd   uh HIGH huhd *KJV, NAS, NIV, RSV, TEV*

Á·hī′jah   uh HIGH juh *KJV, NAS, NIV, RSV, TEV*

Á·hī′kăm   uh HIGH kam *KJV, NAS, NIV, RSV, TEV*

Á·hī′lŭd   uh HIGH luhd *KJV, NAS, NIV, RSV, TEV*

Á·hĭm′â·ăz   uh HIM uh az *KJV, NAS, NIV, RSV, TEV*

Á·hī′man   uh HIGH muhn *KJV, NAS, NIV, RSV, TEV*

Á·hĭm′ē·lĕch   uh HIM eh lek *KJV, NAS, NIV, RSV, TEV*

Á·hī′mŏth   uh HIGH mahth *KJV, NAS, NIV, RSV, TEV*

Á·hĭn′â·dăb   uh HIN uh dab *KJV, NAS, NIV, RSV, TEV*

Á·hĭn′ō·ăm   uh HIN oh am *KJV, NAS, NIV, RSV, TEV*

Á·hī′ō   uh HIGH oh *KJV, NAS, NIV, RSV, TEV*

Á·hī′rà   uh HIGH ruh *KJV, NAS, NIV, RSV, TEV*

Á·hī′ram   uh HIGH ruhm *KJV, NAS, NIV, RSV, TEV*

Á·hī′râm·īte   uh HIGH ruhm ight *KJV, NAS, NIV, RSV*

Á·hĭṣ′â·măch   uh HIZ uh mak *KJV, NAS, NIV, RSV, TEV*

Á·hī′shā·här   uh HIGH shay hahr, uh HISH uh hahr *KJV, NAS, NIV, RSV, TEV*

Á·hī′shär   uh HIGH shahr *KJV, NAS, NIV, RSV, TEV*

Á·hĭth′ō·phĕl   uh HITH oh fel *KJV, NAS, NIV, RSV, TEV*

Á·hī′tŭb   uh HIGH tuhb *KJV, NAS, NIV, RSV, TEV*

Äh′lăb   AH lab *KJV, NAS, NIV, RSV, TEV*

Äh′lā·ī   AH lay igh *KJV, NAS, NIV, RSV, TEV*

Á·hō′ah   uh HOH uh *KJV, NAS, NIV, RSV, TEV*

Á·hō′hīte   uh HOH hight *KJV, NAS, NIV, RSV, TEV*

Á·hō′lah   uh HOH luh *KJV*

Á·hō′lĭ·ăb   uh HOH lih ab *KJV*

Á·hō′lĭ·bah   uh HOH lih buh *KJV*

Á·hō·lĭ·bā′mah   uh hoh lih BAY muh

KJV, NAS

A·hū′maî   uh HYOO migh, uh HYOO may igh   *KJV, NAS, NIV, RSV, TEV*

A·hū′zăm   uh HYOO zam   *KJV, NAS*

A·hūz′zăm   uh HYOO zam   *NIV, RSV, TEV*

A·hŭz′zàth   uh HUHZ uhth   *KJV, NAS, NIV, RSV, TEV*

Äh′zaî   AH zigh   *KJV, NAS, NIV, RSV, TEV*

Ā′ī   AY igh   *KJV, NAS, NIV, RSV, TEV*

Ā·ī′ah (Ā′jah)   ay IGH uh, AY yuh   *KJV, NAS, NIV, RSV, TEV*

Ā·ī′àth   ay IGH uhth, AY yath   *KJV, NAS, NIV, RSV, TEV*

Ā·ī′jà   ay IGH juh, IGH juh   *KJV, NAS, NIV, RSV, TEV*

Äi′jà·lŏn   A juh lahn   *KJV, NAS, NIV, RSV, TEV*

Äi′jĕ·lĕth shā′här   AY jeh leth SHAY hahr   *KJV, NAS*

Ā′ĭn   AY in   *KJV, NAS, NIV, RSV, TEV*

Ā′jah   AY juh   *KJV*

Äj′à·lŏn   AJ uh lahn   *KJV, TEV*

Ā′kan   AY kuhn   *KJV, NAS, NIV, RSV, TEV*

A·kĕl′dà·mà   uh KEHL duh muh   *NIV, RSV, TEV*

Ā′kīm   AY kim   *NIV*

Äk′kad   AK ad   *NIV*

Äk′kŭb   AK uhb   *KJV, NAS, NIV, RSV, TEV*

Äk·ràb′bīm   ak RAB im, ah KRAB im   *KJV, NAS, RSV, TEV*

Äl′à·mĕth   AL uh meth   *KJV*

A·lăm′mĕ·lĕch   uh LAM eh lek   *KJV*

Äl′à·môth   AL uh mawth   *KJV, NAS, NIV, RSV*

Äl′ĕ·mĕth   AL ih meth   *KJV, NAS, NIV, RSV, TEV*

Äl·ĕx·än′dĕr   al eg ZAN dur   *KJV, NAS, NIV, RSV, TEV*

Äl·ĕx·än′drĭ·à   al eg ZAN drih uh   *KJV, NIV, RSV, TEV*

Äl·ĕx·än′drĭ·an   al eg ZAN drih uhn   *NAS*

Ă·lī′ah   a LIGH uh, AL ih uh   *KJV, NAS, RSV*

A·lī′an   uh LIGH uhn, AL ih uhn   *KJV, NAS, RSV*

Äl·lăm′mĕ·lĕch   uh LAM eh lek   *NAS, NIV, RSV, TEV*

Äl′lĕ·mĕth   AL eh meth   *KJV*

Äl′lŏn   AL ahn   *KJV, NAS, NIV, RSV, TEV*

Äl′lŏn-băch′ŭth   AL lahn-BAK uhth AL lahn-BAY kuhth   *KJV*

Äl′lŏn-băc′ŭth   AL lahn-BAK uhth   *NAS, NIV, RSV, TEV*

Äl·mō′dăd   al MOH dad   *KJV, NAS, NIV, RSV, TEV*

Äl′mŏn   AL mahn   *KJV, NAS, NIV, RSV, TEV*

Äl′mŏn-dīb·là·thā′ĭm   AL mahn-dib luh THAY im   *KJV, NAS, NIV, RSV, TEV*

Ā′lŏth   AY lahth   *KJV, NIV*

Äl′phà   AL fuh   *KJV, NAS, NIV, RSV*

Äl·phāe′ŭs   al FEE uhs   *NAS, NIV, RSV, TEV*

Äl·phē′ŭs   al FEE uhs   *KJV*

Äl-tăsh′hĕth   al-TASH heth   *KJV*

Äl-tăs′chĭth   al-TASS keeth   *KJV*

Ā′lŭsh   AY luhsh   *KJV, NAS, NIV, RSV, TEV*

Äl′vah   AL vuh   *KJV, NAS, NIV, RSV, TEV*

Äl′van   AL vuhn   *KJV, NAS, NIV, RSV, TEV*

Ā′măd   AY mad   *KJV, NAS, NIV, RSV, TEV*

Ā′măl   AY mal   *KJV, NAS, NIV, RSV, TEV*

Äm′à·lĕk   AM uh lek   *KJV, NAS, NIV, RSV, TEV*

Äm′à·lĕk·īte   AM uh lek ight, uh MAL uh kight   *KJV, NAS, NIV, RSV, TEV*

Ā′măm   AY mam   *KJV, NAS, NIV, RSV, TEV*

A·mā′nà   uh MAY nuh, uh MAH nuh   *KJV, NAS, NIV, RSV, TEV*

Äm·à·rī′ah   am uh RIGH uh   *KJV, NAS, NIV, RSV, TEV*

A·mā′sà   uh MAY suh, AM uh suh   *KJV, NAS, NIV, RSV, TEV*

A·mā′saî   uh MAY sigh   *KJV, NAS, NIV, RSV, TEV*

A·măsh′aî   uh MASH igh, uh MASH ay igh   *KJV, NIV, RSV*

A·măsh′saî   uh MASH sigh   *NAS, TEV*

Äm·à·sī′ah   am uh SIGH uh   *KJV, NAS, NIV, RSV, TEV*

Äm′aw   AM aw   *RSV, TEV*

Äm·à·zī′ah   am uh ZIGH uh   *KJV, NAS, NIV, RSV, TEV*

Ā′mī   AY migh   *KJV, NAS, NIV, RSV, TEV*

Äm′ĭ·ĕl   AM ih el   *KJV*

A·mīn′à·dăb   uh MIN uh dab   *KJV*

A·mĭt′taî   uh MIT igh   *KJV, NAS, NIV, RSV, TEV*

222

Å·mĭz′a·băd   uh MIHZ uh bad, uh
   MIGH zuh bad *TEV*
Ăm′mah   AM uh *KJV, NAS, NIV, RSV,*
   TEV
Ăm′mī   AM igh *KJV, NAS*
Ăm′mi·ĕl   AM ih el *NAS, RSV, NIV, TEV*
Ăm·mī′hŭd   uh MIGH huhd, AM ih
   huhd *KJV, NAS, NIV, RSV, TEV*
Ăm·mī′hûr   uh MIGH hur *KJV*
Ăm·mĭn′å·dăb   uh MIN uh dab *KJV,*
   NAS, NIV, RSV, TEV
Ăm′mi·nå′dĭb   AM ih-NUH dib, uh
   MIN uh dib *KJV*
Ăm′mi·shăd′daì   AM ih-SHAD igh
   KJV, NAS, NIV, RSV, TEV
Ăm′mĭz′å·băd   uh MIZ uh bad, uh
   MIGH zuh bad *KJV, NAS, NIV, RSV,*
   TEV
Ăm′mon   AM uhn *KJV, NAS, NIV, RSV,*
   TEV
Ăm′mon·ite   AM uhn ight *KJV, NAS,*
   NIV, RSV, TEV
Ăm′mon-i′tĕss   AM uhn IGHT ess *RSV,*
   NAS
Ăm′nŏn   AM nahn *KJV, NAS, NIV, RSV,*
   TEV
Ā′mŏk   AY mahk *KJV, NAS, NIV, RSV,*
   TEV
Ā′mon   AY muhn *KJV, NAS, NIV, RSV,*
   TEV
Ăm′o·rīte   AM uh right *KJV, NAS, NIV,*
   RSV, TEV
Ā′mos   AY muhs *KJV, NAS, NIV, RSV,*
   TEV
Ā′mŏz   AY mahz *KJV, NAS, NIV, RSV,*
   TEV
Ăm·phĭp′o·lis   am FIP uh lihs *KJV, NAS,*
   NIV, RSV, TEV
Ăm·plĭ·às   AM plih uhs *KJV*
Ăm·plĭ·ā′tŭs   am plih AY tuhs *KJV,*
   NAS, NIV, RSV, TEV
Ăm′răm   AM ram *KJV, NAS, NIV, RSV,*
   TEV
Ăm′răm·ite   AY ram ight *KJV, NAS,*
   NIV, RSV
Ăm′rå·phĕl   AM ruh fel *KJV, NAS, NIV,*
   RSV, TEV
Ăm′zī   AM zigh *KJV, NAS, NIV, RSV,*
   TEV
Ā′năb   AY nab *KJV, NAS, NIV, RSV, TEV*
Ā′nah   AY nuh *KJV, NAS, NIV, RSV, TEV*
Å·nā′hå·răth   uh NAY huh rath *KJV,*
   NAS, NIV, RSV, TEV

Å·naì′ah   uh NIGH uh *KJV, NAS, NIV,*
   RSV, TEV
Ā′năk   AY nak *KJV, NAS, NIV, RSV, TEV*
Ăn′å·kĭm   AN uh kim *KJV, NAS, RSV,*
   TEV
Ăn′å·kites   AN uh kights *NIV*
Ā′năm   AY nam *NAS, TEV*
Ăn′å·mim   AN uh mim *KJV, NAS, RSV,*
   TEV
Ăn′å·mites   AN uh mights *NIV*
Å·năm′mĕ·lĕ<u>ch</u>   uh NAM uh lek *KJV,*
   NAS, NIV, RSV, TEV
Ā′năn   AY nan *KJV, NAS, NIV, RSV, TEV*
Å·nā′nī   uh NAY nigh *KJV, NAS, NIV,*
   RSV, TEV
Ăn·å·nī′ah   an uh NIGH uh *KJV, NAS,*
   NIV, RSV, TEV
Ăn·å·nī′às   an uh NIGH uhs *KJV, NAS,*
   NIV, RSV, TEV
Ā′năth   AY nath *KJV, NAS, NIV, RSV,*
   TEV
Ăn′å·thôth   AN uh thawth *KJV, NAS,*
   NIV, RSV, TEV
Ăn′å·thôth·ite   AN uh thawth ight *KJV,*
   NAS, NIV, TEV
Ăn′drew   AN droo *KJV, NAS, NIV, RSV,*
   TEV
Ăn·dro·nī′cŭs   an druh NIGH kuhs *KJV,*
   NAS, NIV, RSV, TEV
Ā′nĕm   AY nem *KJV, NAS, NIV, RSV,*
   TEV
Ā′nĕr   AY nur *KJV, NAS, NIV, RSV, TEV*
Ăn′ĕ·thôth·ite   AN ih thawth ight *KJV*
Å·nī′am   uh NIGH uhm, AY nih uhm
   KJV, NAS, NIV, RSV, TEV
Ā′nim   AY nim *KJV, NAS, NIV, RSV, TEV*
Ăn′nà   AN uh *KJV, NAS, NIV, RSV, TEV*
Ăn′nàs   AN uhs *KJV, NAS, NIV, RSV,*
   TEV
Ăn·thô·thī′jah   an thoh THIGH juh
   KJV, NAS, NIV, RSV, TEV
Ăn′ti·ô<u>ch</u>   AN tih ahk *KJV, NAS, NIV,*
   RSV, TEV
Ăn′ti·pàs   AN tih puhs *KJV, NAS, NIV,*
   RSV, TEV
Ăn·ti·pät′ris   an tih PAHT riss, an TIP
   uh triss *KJV, NAS, NIV, RSV, TEV*
Ăn·tô·thī′jah   an toh THIGH juh *KJV,*
   NAS
Ăn′tô·thite   AN toh thight *KJV*
Ā′nŭb   AY nuhb *KJV, NAS, RSV, NIV,*
   TEV
Å·pĕl′lĕs   uh PEL ehz *KJV, NAS, NIV,*

RSV, TEV
A·phär′săch·ītes   uh FAR sak ights   *KJV*
A·phär·săth′chītes   uh far SATH kights *KJV*
A·phär′sītes   uh FAR sights   *KJV*
A′phĕk   AY fek   *KJV, NAS, NIV, RSV, TEV*
A·phē′kah   uh FEE kuh   *KJV, NAS, NIV, RSV, TEV*
Ā·phī′ah   uh FIGH uh   *KJV, NAS, NIV, RSV, TEV*
Ā′phĭk   AY fik   *KJV, NAS, RSV*
Ā′pĭs   AY pihs   *RSV, TEV*
Āph′rah   AF ruh   *KJV*
Āph′sēs   AF seez   *KJV*
Ap·ol·lō′nĭ·à   ap uh LOH nih uh   *KJV, NAS, NIV, RSV, TEV*
A·pŏl′los   uh PAHL uhs   *KJV, NAS, NIV, RSV, TEV*
A·pŏll′yon   uh PAHL yuhn, uh PAHL ih uhn   *KJV, NAS, NIV, RSV, TEV*
Ăp′pā·ĭm   AP ay im   *KJV, NAS, NIV, RSV, TEV*
Ăp′phĭ·à   AF ih uh, AP fih uh   *KJV, NAS, NIV, RSV, TEV*
Ăp′pĭ·ī Fō′rŭm   AP ih igh FOH ruhm *KJV*
Ăp′pĭ·ŭs   AP pih uhs   *NAS, NIV, RSV, TEV*
Ā′qå·bä   A kuh bah   *TEV*
A·quĭl·à   uh KWIL uh, AK wuh luh   *KJV, NAS, NIV, RSV, TEV*
Är   AHR   *KJV, NAS, NIV, RSV, TEV*
Ā′rà   AY ruh   *KJV, NAS, NIV, RSV, TEV*
Ā′răb   AY rab, AR uhb   *KJV, NAS, NIV, RSV, TEV*
Är′å·bah   AR uh buh   *KJV, NAS, NIV, RSV, TEV*
A·rä′bĭ·à   uh RAY bih uh   *KJV, NAS, NIV, RSV, TEV*
A·rä′bĭ·an   uh RAY bih uhn   *KJV, NAS, NIV, RSV, TEV*
Är′å·bĭm   AHR uh bihm   *NAS*
Ā′răd   AY rad   *KJV, NAS, NIV, RSV, TEV*
Ā′rah   AY ruh   *KJV, NAS, NIV, RSV, TEV*
Ā′răm   AY ram   *KJV, NAS, NIV, RSV, TEV*
Ăr·å·mā′ĭc   ar uh MAY ihk   *NAS, NIV, RSV, TEV*
Ăr·å·mē′an   ar uh ME uhn   *NAS, NIV, RSV, TEV*
Är′å·mĭt·ĕss   AHR uh might ess   *KJV*
Ā′răm-Mā′å·cah   AY ram-MAY uh kuh   *KJV, NAS, NIV, RSV, TEV*

Ā′răm-Nā·hå·rā′ĭm   AY ram-nay huh RAY im   *KJV, NIV, TEV*
Ā′răm-Zō′bah   AY ram-ZOH buh   *KJV*
Ā′ran   AY ruhn   *KJV, NAS, NIV, RSV, TEV*
Âr′å·răt   ER uh rat   *KJV, NAS, NIV, RSV, TEV*
Âr′å·rīte   ER uh right   *KJV, NAS, TEV*
A·raū′nah   uh ROO nuh, uh RAW nuh   *KJV, NAS, NIV, RSV, TEV*
Är′bà   AHR buh   *KJV, NIV, RSV, TEV*
Är′bah   AHR buh   *TEV*
Är′bāth·īte   AHR bath ight   *KJV, NAS, NIV, RSV, TEV*
Är′bīte   AHR bight   *KJV, NAS, NIV, RSV, TEV*
Är·chè·lā′ŭs   ahr kih LAY uhs   *KJV, NAS, NIV, RSV, TEV*
Är′chè·vītes   AHR kih vights   *KJV*
Är′chī   AHR kigh   *KJV*
Är·chĭp′pŭs   ahr KIP uhs   *KJV, NAS, NIV, RSV, TEV*
Är′chīte   AHR kight   *KJV, NAS, RSV, TEV*
Ärc·tū′rŭs   ark TOO ruhs   *KJV*
Ärd   AHRD   *KJV, NAS, NIV, RSV, TEV*
Är′dīte   AHR dight   *KJV, NAS, NIV, RSV*
Är′dŏn   AHR dahn   *KJV, NAS, NIV, RSV, TEV*
A·rē′lī   uh REE ligh   *KJV, NAS, NIV, RSV, TEV*
A·rē′līte   uh REE light   *KJV, NAS, NIV, RSV*
Âr·ê·ŏp′å·gīte   er ih AHP uh gight   *KJV, NAS, RSV*
Âr·ê·ŏp′å·gŭs   er ih AHP uh guhs   *KJV, NAS, NIV, RSV, TEV*
Âr′ê·tăs   ER uh tass   *KJV, NAS, NIV, RSV, TEV*
Är′gŏb   AHR gahb   *KJV, NAS, NIV, RSV, TEV*
A·rīd′å·ī   uh RID ay igh, AHR ih digh   *KJV, NAS, NIV, RSV, TEV*
Är·ĭ·dā′thà   ar ih DAY thuh, uh RID uh thuh   *KJV, NAS, NIV, RSV, TEV*
A·rī′ĕh   uh RIGH uh, ER ih eh   *KJV, NAS, NIV*
Â′rĭ·ĕl   ER ih el   *KJV, NAS, NIV, RSV, TEV*
Är·ĭ·må·thē′à   ar ih muh THEE uh   *KJV, NAS, NIV, RSV, TEV*
Âr′ĭ·ŏch   ER ih ahk   *KJV, NAS, NIV, RSV, TEV*
A·rĭṣ′å·ī   uh RIZ ay igh, AHR ih sigh

Âr·ĭs·tär′chŭs   er iss TAHR kuhs   *KJV, NAS, NIV, RSV, TEV*

Â·rĭs·tō·bū′lŭs   uh riss toh BYOO luhs   *KJV, NAS, NIV, RSV, TEV*

Är′kīte   AHR kight   *KJV, NAS, NIV, RSV, TEV*

Är·mȧ·gĕd′dŏn   ahr muh GED uhn   *KJV, NIV, RSV, TEV*

Är·mē′nĭ·à   ahr MEE nih uh   *KJV*

Är·mō′nī   ar MOH nigh   *KJV, NAS, NIV, RSV, TEV*

Är′năn   AHR nan   *KJV, NAS, NIV, RSV, TEV*

Är′nī   AHR nigh   *KJV, RSV, TEV*

Är′nŏn   AHR nahn   *KJV, NAS, NIV, RSV, TEV*

Ā′rŏd   AY rahd, ER ahd   *KJV, NAS, RSV, TEV*

Â·rō′dī   uh ROH digh, ER oh digh   *KJV, NAS, NIV, RSV*

Ā′rŏd·īte   AY rahd ight, ER ahd ight   *KJV, NAS, NIV, RSV*

Â·rō′ẽr   uh ROH ur   *KJV, NAS, NIV, RSV, TEV*

Â·rō′ẽr·īte   uh ROH ur ight   *KJV, NAS, NIV, RSV, TEV*

Är·pặch′shặd   ahr PAK shad   *KJV, NAS, RSV, TEV*

Är′pặd   AHR pad   *KJV, NAS, NIV, RSV, TEV*

Är′phặd   AHR fad   *KJV*

Är·phặx′ặd   ahr FAX ad   *KJV, NAS, NIV, RSV*

Är·tȧ·xẽr′xẽṣ   ahr tuh ZURK seez   *KJV, NAS, NIV, RSV, TEV*

Är′tĕ·màs   AHR tih muhs   *KJV, NAS, NIV, RSV, TEV*

Ặr′tĕ·mĭs   AHR tih mihs   *NAS, NIV, TEV*

Â·rūb′bōth   uh ROO bohth   *KJV, NAS, NIV, RSV, TEV*

Â·rū′mah   uh ROO muh   *KJV, NAS, NIV, RSV, TEV*

Är′vặd   AHR vad   *KJV, NAS, NIV, RSV, TEV*

Är′vặd·ites   AHR vuhd ights   *KJV, NAS, NIV, RSV, TEV*

Är′zà   AHR zuh   *KJV, NAS, NIV, RSV, TEV*

Ā′sà   AY suh   *KJV, NAS, NIV, RSV, TEV*

Ăs′ȧ·hĕl   ASS uh hel, AY suh hel   *KJV, NAS, NIV, RSV, TEV*

Ặs·ȧ·hī′ah   ass uh HIGH uh   *KJV, RSV*

Â·ṣai′ah   uh ZAY uh   *NAS, NIV, RSV, TEV*

Ā′săph   AY saf, AY suhf   *KJV, NAS, NIV, RSV, TEV*

Â·sā′rẽl   uh SAY rehl   *NAS, NIV, RSV, TEV*

Â·sā′rė·ĕl   uh SAY rih el, ASS uh reel   *KJV*

Ặs·ȧ·rē′lah   ass uh REE luh   *KJV, NIV*

Ặs′ė·năth   ASS eh nath   *KJV, NAS, NIV, RSV, TEV*

Ā′sẽr   AY sur   *KJV*

Ā′shan   AY shuhn   *KJV, NAS, NIV, RSV, TEV*

Ăsh·ȧ′rē′lah   ash uh REE luh   *NAS, RSV, TEV*

Ặsh·bē′à   ash BEE uh   *KJV, TEV*

Ặsh′bĕl   ASH bel   *KJV, NAS, NIV, RSV, TEV*

Ặsh′bĕl·īte   ASH bel ight   *KJV, NAS, NIV, RSV*

Ặsh′chė·năz   ASH kih naz   *KJV*

Ặsh′dŏd   ASH dahd   *KJV, NAS, NIV, RSV, TEV*

Ặsh′dŏd·īte   ASH dahd ight   *KJV, NAS, RSV*

Ặsh′dŏth-Pĭṣ′gah   ASH dahth-PIZ guh   *KJV*

Ặsh′ẽr   ASH ur   *KJV, NAS, NIV, RSV, TEV*

Â·shē′rah   uh SHEE ruh, ASH uh ruh   *KJV, NAS, NIV, RSV, TEV*

Ặsh′ė·rĭm   ASH uh reem   *KJV, NAS, RSV*

Ặsh′ẽr·īte   ASH ur ight   *KJV, NAS, RSV*

Ặsh′ẽr·ŏth   ASH ur rahth   *KJV, NAS, RSV*

Ặsh′hŭr   ASH uhr   *NAS, NIV, RSV, TEV*

Â·shī′mà   uh SHIGH muh, ASH ih muh   *KJV, NAS, NIV, RSV, TEV*

Â·shī′mah   uh SHIGH muh, ASH ih muh   *RSV*

Ặsh′kė·lŏn   ASH kih lahn   *KJV, NAS, NIV, RSV, TEV*

Ặsh′kė·lŏn·īte   ASH kih lahn ight   *KJV, NAS*

Ặsh′kė·năz   ASH kih naz, ash KEE naz   *KJV, NAS, NIV, RSV, TEV*

Ặsh′nah   ASH nuh   *KJV, NAS, NIV, RSV, TEV*

Ặsh′pė·năz   ASH peh naz   *KJV, NAS, NIV, RSV, TEV*

Ặsh′rĭ·ĕl   ASH rih el   *KJV*

Ặsh′tȧ·rŏth   ASH tuh rahth   *KJV, NAS, NIV, RSV, TEV*

Ặsh·tē′rȧ·thite   ash TEE ruh thight,

ASH tuh rath ight *KJV. NAS. NIV. RSV*
Ăsh'tĕ·rŏth Kär'nā·ĭm ASH tuh rahth kahr NAY im *KJV. NAS. NIV. RSV. TEV*
Ăsh'to·rĕth ASH tuh reth *KJV. NAS. NIV. RSV. TEV*
Ăsh'ŭr ASH ur *KJV. TEV*
Ā'shŭr·băn'ĭ·pal a shuhr BAN ih pal *NIV. RSV. TEV*
Ăsh'ŭr·ĭ ASH ur ih *NIV*
Ăsh'ŭr·īte ASH ur ight *KJV. NAS. RSV. TEV*
Ăsh'văth ASH vath *KJV. NAS. NIV. RSV. TEV*
Ā'sià AY shuh *KJV. NAS. NIV. RSV. TEV*
Ā'sị·archs AY zih arks *NAS. RSV*
Ăs'ĭ·ĕl ASS ih el, AY sih el *KJV. NAS. NIV. RSV. TEV*
Ăs'kĕ·lŏn ASS kuh lahn *KJV*
Ăs'nah ASS nuh *KJV. NAS. NIV. RSV. TEV*
Ăs·năp'pēr ass NAP ur *KJV*
Ăs·pā'thà ass PAY thuh *KJV. NAS. NIV. RSV. TEV*
Ăs'rĭ·ĕl ASS rih el *KJV. NAS. NIV. RSV. TEV*
Ăs'rĭ·ĕl·īte ASS rih uhl ight *KJV. NAS. NIV. RSV. TEV*
Ăs'shŭr ASH uhr *KJV. NAS. NIV. RSV. TEV*
Ăs·shū'rĭm uh SHOO rim *KJV. NAS. RSV. TEV*
Ăs·shū'rītes uh SHOO rights *NIV*
Ăs'sĭr AZ ur *KJV. NAS. NIV. RSV. TEV*
Ăs'sŏs ASS ahs *KJV. NAS. NIV. RSV. TEV*
Ăs'sŭr ASS ur *KJV*
Ăs·sўr'ĭ·à uh SIHR ih uh *KJV. NAS. NIV. RSV. TEV*
Ăs·sўr'ĭ·an uh SIHR ih uhn *KJV. NAS. NIV. RSV. TEV*
Ăs'tå·rŏth ASS tuh rahth *KJV*
Ăs·tär'tĕs as TAHR teez *TEV*
Ā·sūp'pīm a SUHP im *KJV*
Ā'swän A swahn, AZ swahn *NIV. TEV*
Ā·sўn'crĭ·tŭs uh SIN krih tuhs *KJV. NAS. NIV. RSV. TEV*
Ā'tăd AY tad *KJV. NAS. NIV. RSV. TEV*
Ăt'å·rāh AT uh rah *KJV. NAS. NIV. RSV. TEV*
Ăt'å·rŏth AT uh rawth *KJV. NAS. RSV. TEV*

Ăt'å·rŏth-Ăd'där AT uh rawth-AD ahr *KJV, NAS, NIV, RSV, TEV*
Ā'tēr AY tur *KJV. NAS. NIV. RSV. TEV*
Ā'thăch AY thak *KJV. NAS. NIV. RSV. TEV*
Ā·thaï'ah uh THIGH uh, uh THAY yuh *KJV. NAS. NIV. RSV*
Ăth·å·lī'ah ath uh LIGH uh *KJV. NAS. NIV. RSV. TEV*
Ăth'å·rĭm ATH uh rim *KJV. NAS. NIV. RSV*
Ā·thē'nĭ·an uh THEE nih uhn *KJV. NAS. NIV. RSV. TEV*
Ăth'ĕnṣ ATH inz *KJV. NAS. NIV. RSV. TEV*
Ăth'laï ATH ligh, ATH lay igh *KJV. NAS. NIV. RSV. TEV*
Ăt'rŏth AT rahth *KJV*
Ăt'rŏth-bĕth-Jō'ăb AT rahth-beth-JOH ab *KJV. NAS. NIV. RSV. TEV*
Ăt'rŏth-shō'phăn At rahth-SHOH fan *KJV. NAS. NIV. RSV. TEV*
Ăt'tā·ī AT ay igh, AT igh *KJV. NAS. NIV. RSV. TEV*
Ăt·tå·lī'à at uh LIGH uh *KJV. NAS. NIV. RSV. TEV*
Āu·gŭs'tan aw GUHS tuhn *NAS. RSV*
Āu·gŭs'tŭs aw GUHS tuhs *KJV. NAS. NIV. RSV. TEV*
Ā'và AY vuh *KJV*
Ā'vĕn AY vuhn *KJV. NAS. NIV. RSV. TEV*
Ā'vĭm AY vim *KJV*
Ā'vīte AY vight *KJV*
Ā'vīth AY vith *KJV. NAS. NIV. RSV. TEV*
Āv'và AY vuh *NAS. NIV. RSV*
Āv'vĭm AY vihm *NAS. NIV. RSV. TEV*
Āv'vīte AY vight *NAS. NIV. RSV. TEV*
Ăy'yah A yuh *NAS. NIV. RSV. TEV*
Ā'zăl AY zal *KJV*
Ăz·å·lī'ah az uh LIGH uh *KJV. NAS. NIV. RSV. TEV*
Ăz·å·nī'ah az uh NIGH uh *KJV. NAS. NIV. RSV. TEV*
Ăz·å·rā'ĕl az uh RAY el, uh ZAY ray el *KJV. TEV*
Ăz'å·rĕĕl AZ uh reel *KJV*
Ăz'å·rĕl AZ uh rehl *NAS. NIV. RSV. TEV*
Ăz·å·rī'ah az uh RIGH uh *KJV. NAS. NIV. RSV. TEV*
Ăz·å·rī'å·hü az uh RIGH uh hoo *NIV. TEV*

Ă·zăr·yä′hü   a zuhr YAH hoo   *NAS*
Ā′zăz   AY zaz   *KJV, NAS, NIV, RSV, TEV*
Å·zā·zĕl   uh ZAY zel, AZ uh zel   *KJV, RSV, TEV*
Ăz·å·zī′ah   az uh ZIGH uh   *KJV, NAS, NIV, RSV, TEV*
Ăz′bŭk   AZ buhk   *KJV, NAS, NIV, RSV, TEV*
Å·zē′kah   uh ZEE kuh   *KJV, NAS, NIV, RSV, TEV*
Ā′zĕl   AY zel   *KJV, NAS, NIV, RSV, TEV*
Ā′zĕm   AY zuhm   *KJV*
Ăz′găd   AZ gad   *KJV, NAS, NIV, RSV, TEV*
Ā·zī′ĕl   AY zih el   *KJV, NAS, NIV, RSV*
Å·zī′zà   uh ZIGH zuh   *KJV, NAS, NIV, RSV, TEV*
Ăz·mā′vĕth   az MAY veth   *KJV, NAS, NIV, RSV, TEV*
Ăz′mŏn   AZ mahn   *KJV, NAS, NIV, RSV, TEV*
Ăz′nŏth-Tā′bôr   AZ nahth-TAY bawr   *KJV, NAS, NIV, RSV, TEV*
Ā′zôr   AY zawr   *KJV, NAS, NIV, RSV, TEV*
Å·zō′tŭs   uh ZOH tuhs   *KJV, NAS, NIV, RSV*
Ăz′rĭ·ĕl   AZ rih el   *KJV, NAS, NIV, RSV, TEV*
Ăz·rī′kăm   az RIGH kam, AZ rih kam   *KJV, NAS, NIV, RSV, TEV*
Å·zū′bah   uh ZYOO buh   *KJV, NAS, NIV, RSV, TEV*
Ā′zûr   AY zur   *KJV*
Ăz′zah   AZ uh   *KJV*
Ăz′zan   AZ uhn   *KJV, NAS, NIV, RSV, TEV*
Ăz′zŭr   AZ ur   *KJV, NAS, NIV, RSV, TEV*

Bā′àl   BAY uhl   *KJV, NAS, NIV, RSV, TEV*
Bā′å·lah   BAY uh luh   *NAS, RSV*
Bā′å·lăth   BAY uh lath   *NAS, RSV*
Bā′å·lăth·bē′ēr   BAY uh luhth BEE uhr   *NAS, RSV*
Bā′àl-bē′rĭth   BAY uhl-BEE rith   *KJV, NAS, NIV, RSV*
Bā′å·lē   BAY uh lee   *KJV*
Bā′å·lē·jū′dah   BAY uh lee JOO duh   *NAS, RSV*
Bā′àl-găd   BAY uhl-GAD   *KJV, NAS, NIV, RSV, TEV*
Bā′àl-hā′mŏn   BAY uhl-HAY muhn   *KJV, NAS, NIV, RSV, TEV*
Bā′àl-hā′năn   BAY uhl-HAY nan   *KJV, NAS, NIV, RSV, TEV*
Bā′àl-hā′zôr   BAY uhl-HAY zawr   *KJV, NAS, NIV, RSV, TEV*
Bā′àl-hĕr′mon   BAY uhl-HUR muhn   *KJV, NAS, NIV, RSV, TEV*
Bā′å·lĭm   BAY uh lim   *KJV, NAS*
Bā′å·lĭs   BAY uh liss   *NAS, NIV, RSV*
Bā′àl-mē′on   BAY uhl-ME uhn   *KJV, NAS, NIV, RSV, TEV*
Bā′àl-pē′ôr   BAY uhl-PEE awr   *KJV, NAS, NIV, RSV*
Bā′àl-pĕr′å·zĭm   BAY uhl-PER uh zim, puh RAY zim   *KJV, NAS, NIV, RSV, TEV*
Bā′àl-shăl′ĭ′shah   BAY uhl-SHAL ih shuh   *KJV, NAS, NIV, RSV, TEV*
Bā′àl-tā′mär   BAY uhl-TAY mahr   *KJV, NAS, NIV, RSV, TEV*
Bā′àl-zē′bŭb   BAY uhl-ZEE buhb   *KJV, NAS, NIV, RSV, TEV*
Bā′àl-zē′phon   BAY uhl-ZEE fuhn   *KJV, NAS, NIV, RSV, TEV*
Bā′å·nà   BAY uh nuh   *KJV, NAS, NIV, RSV, TEV*
Bā′å·nàh   BAY uh nuh   *KJV, NAS, NIV, RSV, TEV*
Bā′å·rà   BAY uh ruh   *KJV, NAS, NIV, RSV, TEV*
Bā·å·seî′ah   bay uh SIGH uh   *KJV, NAS, NIV, RSV, TEV*
Bā′å·shà   BAY uh shuh   *KJV, NAS, NIV, RSV, TEV*
Bā′bĕl   BAY buhl   *KJV, NAS, NIV, RSV*
Băb′y·lŏn   BAB ih lahn   *KJV, NAS, NIV, RSV, TEV*
Băb·y·lō′nĭ·à   bab ih LOH nih uh   *NIV, RSV, TEV*
Băb·y·lō′nĭ·an   bab uh LOH nih uhn   *KJV, NAS, NIV, RSV, TEV*
Băb·y·lō′nĭsh   bab uh LOH nish   *KJV, NAS*
Bā′cà   BAY kuh   *KJV, NAS, NIV, RSV, TEV*

Băch′rīte   BAK right   *KJV*
Bȧ·hā′rŭm   buh HAY ruhm   *RSV, TEV*
Bȧ·hā′rŭm·īte   buh HAY ruhm ight
 KJV, NAS, NIV
Bȧ·hū′rĭm   buh HYOO rim   *KJV, NAS,
 NIV, RSV, TEV*
Bā′jĭth   BAY jith   *KJV*
Băk·băk′kär   bak BAK ahr   *KJV, NAS,
 NIV, RSV, TEV*
Băk′bŭk   BAK buhk   *KJV, NAS, NIV,
 RSV, TEV*
Băk·bū·kī′ah   bak byoo KIGH uh   *KJV,
 NAS, NIV, RSV, TEV*
Bā′lȧam   BAY luhm   *KJV, NAS, NIV, RSV,
 TEV*
Bā′lăc   BAY lak   *KJV*
Băl′ȧ·dăn   BAL uh dan   *KJV, NAS, NIV,
 RSV, TEV*
Bā′lah   BAY luh   *KJV, NAS, NIV, RSV,
 TEV*
Bā′lăk   BAY lak   *KJV, NAS, NIV, RSV,
 TEV*
Bā′mah   BAY muh   *KJV, NAS, NIV, RSV,
 TEV*
Bā′mŏth   BAY mahth   *KJV, NAS, NIV,
 RSV, TEV*
Bā′mŏth-bā′al   BAY mahth-BAY uhl
 KJV, NAS, NIV, RSV, TEV
Bā′nī   BAY nigh   *KJV, NAS, NIV, RSV,
 TEV*
Băp′tĭst   BAP tist   *KJV, NAS, NIV, RSV,
 TEV*
Bȧ·räb′bȧs   buh RAB uhs   *KJV, NAS,
 NIV, RSV, TEV*
Bär′a·chĕl   BAHR uh kel, buh RAY k′l
 KJV, NAS, RSV
Bär′ȧ·chī′ah   bahr uh KIGH uh   *KJV,
 RSV*
Bär·a·chī′as   bahr uh KIGH uhs   *KJV*
Bā′răk   BAY rak   *KJV, NAS, NIV, RSV,
 TEV*
Bär′ȧ·kĕl   BAHR uh kehl   *NIV, TEV*
Bär·hū′mīte   bahr HYOO might   *KJV,
 NAS, NIV, TEV*
Bȧ·rī′ah   buh RIGH uh   *KJV, NAS, NIV,
 RSV, TEV*
Bär-jē′ṣŭs   bahr-JEE zuhs   *KJV, NAS,
 NIV, RSV, TEV*
Bär-jō′nȧ   bahr-JOH nuh   *KJV, NAS, RSV*
Bär′kŏs   BAHR kahs   *KJV, NAS, NIV,
 RSV, TEV*
Bär′nȧ·bȧs   BAHR nuh buhs   *KJV, NAS,
 NIV, RSV, TEV*
Bär′sȧ·bȧs   BAHR suh buhs   *KJV, RSV*

Bär·sȧb′bȧs   bar SAB uhs, BAHR suh
 buhs   *NAS, NIV, TEV*
Bär·thŏl′ō·mew̄   bar THAHL uh myoo
 KJV, NAS, NIV, RSV, TEV
Bär·tĭ·mae′ŭs   bahr tih MEE uhs   *NAS,
 NIV, RSV, TEV*
Bär·tĭ·mē′ŭs   bahr tih MEE uhs   *KJV*
Bā′rŭch   BAY rewk, BAR uhk   *KJV,
 NAS, NIV, RSV, TEV*
Bär·zĭl′lā·ī   bahr ZIL ay igh   *KJV, NAS,
 NIV, RSV, TEV*
Băs′ĕ·măth   BASS eh math   *KJV, NAS,
 NIV, RSV*
Băs′ĕ·măth   BASS uh math   *TEV*
Bā′shăn   BAY shan   *KJV, NAS, NIV, RSV,
 TEV*
Bā′shăn-hā′vŏth-jā′ir   BAY shan-HAY
 vahth-JAY ir   *KJV*
Băsh′ĕ·măth   BASH uh math   *KJV*
Băs′măth   BASS math   *KJV*
Băth-răb′bĭm   bath-RAB im   *KJV, NAS,
 NIV, RSV*
Băth·shē′bȧ   bath SHEE buh, BATH shi
 buh   *KJV, NAS, NIV, RSV, TEV*
Băth′shū·ȧ   BATH shoo uh, bath SHOO
 uh   *KJV, NAS, NIV, RSV, TEV*
Bā′vā·ī   BAY vay igh, BAV ay igh   *KJV*
Băv′vaı   BAV igh, BAV ay igh   *NAS*
Băv′vā·ı   BAY vay igh   *RSV, TEV*
Băz′lĭth   BAZ lith   *KJV, NAS, RSV, TEV*
Băz′lŭth   BAZ luhth   *KJV, NAS, NIV,
 RSV, TEV*
Bē·ȧ·lī′ah   bee uh LIGH uh   *KJV, NAS,
 NIV, RSV, TEV*
Bē′ȧ·lŏth   BEE uh lahth   *KJV, NAS, NIV,
 RSV, TEV*
Bē′bā·ī   BEE bay igh, BEB ay igh, bee
 BAY igh   *KJV, NAS, NIV, RSV, TEV*
Bē′cher   BEE kur   *KJV, NAS, RSV, TEV*
Bē′cher·īte   BEE kur ight   *KJV, NAS,
 RSV, TEV*
Bē·chō′răth   bee KOH rath   *KJV, RSV*
Bē·cō′răth   bee KOH rath   *NAS, NIV,
 TEV*
Bē′dăd   BEE dad   *KJV, NAS, NIV, RSV,
 TEV*
Bē′dăn   BEE dan   *KJV, NAS, NIV, RSV,
 TEV*
Bē·dē′iah   bee DEE yuh   *KJV, NAS, NIV,
 RSV, TEV*
Bēè·lī′ȧ·dȧ   bee LIGH uh duh   *KJV, NAS,
 NIV, RSV, TEV*
Bē·ĕl′zē·bŭb   bee EL zee buhb   *KJV, NIV*

Bḗ·ĕl′zē·bŭl   bee EHL zee buhl   *NAS,*
   RSV, TEV
Bḗ′ĕr   BEE ehr   *KJV, NAS, NIV, RSV, TEV*
Bḗ·ē′rà   bee EE ruh, BEER uh   *KJV,*
   NAS, NIV, RSV, TEV
Bḗ·ē′rah   bee EE ruh   *KJV, NAS, NIV,*
   RSV, TEV
Bḗ′ĕr-ē′lĭm   BEE ur-EE lim   *KJV, NAS,*
   NIV, RSV, TEV
Bḗ·ē′rī   bee EE righ, BEER igh   *KJV,*
   NAS, NIV, RSV, TEV
Bḗ′ĕr-là·haĭ′roì   BEE ehr-luh HIGH
   roy   *KJV, NAS, NIV, RSV*
Bḗ·ē′rŏth   bee EE rahth   *KJV, NAS, NIV,*
   RSV, TEV
Bḗ·ē′rŏth·īte   bee EE rahth ight, BEER
   oth ight   *KJV, NAS, NIV, RSV*
Bḗ·ē′rŏth-bē′nē-jā′à·kan   bee EE rahth-
   BEE nee-JAY uh kuhn   *KJV*
Bḗ′ĕr·shē′bà   BEE ehr SHE buh   *KJV,*
   NAS, NIV, RSV, TEV
Bḗ·ĕsh′tĕ·rah   bee ESH tih ruh   *KJV,*
   NAS, RSV, TEV
Bḗ′hē·mŏth   BEE hih mahth, bee HEE
   mahth   *KJV, NAS, NIV, RSV, TEV*
Bḗ′kĕr   BEHK uhr   *NIV*
Bḗ′kĕr·īte   BEHK uhr ight   *NIV*
Bĕl   BELL   *KJV, NAS, NIV, RSV, TEV*
Bḗ′là (Bḗ′lah)   BEE luh   *KJV, NAS, NIV,*
   RSV, TEV
Bḗ′là·īte   BEE luh ight   *KJV, NAS, NIV,*
   RSV
Bḗ′lĭ·àl   BEE lih uhl, BEL yuhl   *KJV,*
   NAS, NIV, RSV
Bĕl·shăz′zàr   bel SHAZ ur   *KJV, NAS,*
   NIV, RSV, TEV
Bĕl·tē·shăz′zàr   bel teh SHAZ ur   *KJV,*
   NAS, NIV, RSV, TEV
Bĕn   BEN, BEHN,   *KJV, NAS*
Bĕn·à·bĭn′à·dăb   ben uh BIN uh dab
   KJV, NAS, NIV, RSV, TEV
Bḗ·naì′ah   bee NIGH uh, bee NAY
   yuh   *KJV, NAS, NIV, RSV, TEV*
Bĕn·ăm′mi   ben-AM igh   *KJV, NAS, NIV,*
   RSV, TEV
Bĕn·dē′kĕr   ben-DEE kur   *KJV, NAS,*
   NIV, RSV, TEV
Bĕn′ē-bē′răk   BEN ih-BEE rak   *KJV,*
   NAS, NIV, RSV, TEV
Bĕn′ē-jā′à·kan   BEN ih-JAY uh kuhn
   KJV, NAS, NIV, RSV, TEV
Bĕn·ġē′bĕr   ben-GHEE bur   *KJV, NAS,*
   NIV, RSV, TEV
Bĕn·hā′dăd   ben-HAY dad   *KJV, NAS,*

NIV, RSV, TEV
Bĕn·hā′ĭl   ben-HAY ihl, ben-HAYL
   KJV, NAS, NIV, RSV, TEV
Bĕn·hā′năn   ben-HAY nan   *KJV, NAS,*
   NIV, RSV, TEV
Bĕn·hē′sĕd   ben-HEE sed   *KJV, NAS,*
   NIV, RSV, TEV
Bĕn-Hĭn′nom   ben-HIHN nuhm   *NIV*
Bĕn-hûr′   ben-HUR   *KJV, NAS, NIV,*
   RSV, TEV
Bĕ·nī′nū   bee NIGH nyoo, BEN ih
   nyoo   *KJV, NAS, NIV, RSV, TEV*
Bĕn′jà·mĭn   BEN juh min   *KJV, NAS,*
   NIV, RSV, TEV
Bĕn·jà·mĭn′īte   bihn juh MIHN ight   *RSV*
Bĕn′jà·mīte   BEN juh might   *KJV, NAS,*
   NIV, TEV
Bḗ′nō   BEE no   *KJV, NAS, NIV, RSV, TEV*
Bĕn-ō′nī   ben-OH nigh   *KJV, NAS, RSV,*
   TEV
Bĕn·zō′hĕth   ben ZOH heth   *KJV, NAS,*
   NIV, RSV, TEV
Bḗ′ŏn   BEE ahn   *KJV, NAS, NIV, RSV,*
   TEV
Bḗ′ôr   BEE awr   *KJV, NAS, NIV, RSV,*
   TEV
Bḗ′rà   BEE ruh   *KJV, NAS, NIV, RSV,*
   TEV
Bĕr′à·cah   BER uh kah   *NAS, NIV, RSV,*
   TEV
Bĕr′à·chäh   BER uh kah   *KJV*
Bĕr·à·chī′ah   ber uh KIGH uh   *KJV, TEV*
Bḗ·raì′ah   buh RIGH uh, ber ay IGH
   uh   *KJV, NAS, NIV, RSV, TEV*
Bĕr·à·kī′ah   behr uh KIGH uh   *NIV, TEV*
Bḗ·rē′à   buh REE uh   *KJV, NAS, NIV,*
   TEV
Bĕr·ē·chī′ah   behr uh KIGH uh, behr ih
   KIGH uh   *KJV, NAS, RSV*
Bḗ′rĕd   BEE red   *KJV, NAS, NIV, RSV,*
   TEV
Bḗ′rī   BEE righ   *KJV, NAS, NIV, RSV,*
   TEV
Bḗ·rī′ah   buh RIGH uh   *KJV, NAS, NIV,*
   RSV, TEV
Bḗ·rī′īte   buh RIGH ight   *KJV, NAS, NIV,*
   RSV
Bḗ′rīte   BEE right   *KJV, NAS, NIV*
Bḗ′rĭth   BEE rith   *KJV, NAS*
Bĕr·nī′cè   bur NEE sih, bur NEES
   KJV, NAS, NIV, RSV, TEV
Bḗ·rō′dăch Băl′à·dăn   bih ROH dak
   BAL uh dan   *KJV, NAS*
Bḗ·rōe′à   bih REE uh   *KJV, RSV*

229

Bḗ·rō′thah   bih ROH thuh   *KJV, NAS, NIV, RSV, TEV*

Bḗ·rō′thaî   buh ROH thigh   *KJV, NAS, NIV, RSV, TEV*

Bē′rŏth·īte   BEE rahth ight   *KJV, NAS, NIV*

Bē′saî   BEE sigh   *KJV, NAS, NIV, RSV, TEV*

Bĕs·ô·deî′ah   bess oh DIGH uh, bess oh DEE yuh   *KJV, NAS, NIV, RSV, TEV*

Bē′sôr   BEE sawr   *KJV, NAS, NIV, RSV, TEV*

Bē′tah   BEE tuh   *KJV, NAS, RSV, TEV*

Bē′tēn   BEE tuhn   *KJV, NAS, NIV, RSV, TEV*

Bĕth-ăb′å·rà   beth-AB uh ruh   *KJV*

Bĕth-ā′năth   beth-AY nath   *KJV, NAS, NIV, RSV, TEV*

Bĕth-ā′nŏth   beth-AY nahth   *KJV, NAS, NIV, RSV, TEV*

Bĕth′å·nў   BETH uh nih   *KJV, NAS, NIV, RSV, TEV*

Bĕth-är′å·bah   beth-AR uh buh   *KJV, NAS, NIV, RSV, TEV*

Bĕth-ā′răm   beth-AY ram   *KJV*

Bĕth-är′bĕl   beth-AHR bel   *KJV, NAS, NIV, RSV, TEV*

Bĕth-ăsh′bĕ·à   beth-ASH bih uh   *NAS, NIV, RSV, TEV*

Bĕth-ā′vēn   beth-AY vuhn   *KJV, NAS, NIV, RSV, TEV*

Bĕth-ăz·mā′vĕth   beth-az MAY veth   *KJV, NAS, NIV, RSV, TEV*

Bĕth-bā′àl-mē′ŏn   beth-BAY uhl-MEE ahn   *KJV, NAS, NIV, RSV, TEV*

Bĕth-bâr·ah   beth-BEHR uh   *KJV, NAS, NIV, RSV, TEV*

Bĕth-bĭr′ê·ī   beth-BIR ih igh   *KJV*

Bĕth-bĭr′ī   beth-BIHR igh   *NAS, NIV, RSV, TEV*

Bĕth′cär   BETH kahr   *KJV, NAS, NIV, RSV, TEV*

Bĕth-dā′gŏn   beth-DAY gahn   *KJV, NAS, NIV, RSV, TEV*

Bĕth-dĭb·là·thā′ĭm   beth-dib luh THAY im   *KJV, NAS, NIV, RSV, TEV*

Bĕth-ē′dĕn   beth-EE dehn   *NAS, NIV, RSV, TEV*

Bĕth-ē′kĕd   beth-EE kid   *NAS, NIV, RSV*

Bĕth′ĕl   BETH uhl   *KJV, NAS, NIV, RSV, TEV*

Bĕth′ĕl·īte   BETH uhl ight   *KJV, NAS*

Bĕth-ē′mĕk   beth-EE mek   *KJV, NAS, NIV, RSV, TEV*

Bē′thēr   BEE thur   *KJV, NAS, TEV*

Bḕ·thĕṣ′dà   buh THEZ duh   *KJV, NAS, NIV, TEV*

Bĕth·ē′zĕl   beth EE z′l   *KJV, NAS, NIV, RSV, TEV*

Bĕth-ḡā′dĕr   beth-GAY dur   *KJV, NAS, NIV, RSV, TEV*

Bĕth-ḡā′mŭl   beth-GAY m′l   *KJV, NAS, NIV, RSV, TEV*

Bĕth-Gĭl′găl   beth-GIHL gal   *NAS, NIV, RSV, TEV*

Bĕth-hăc′cē·rĕm   beth-HAK kuh rem   *KJV, NAS*

Bĕth-hăc·chê′rĕm   beth-hak KIH rem   *NAS, RSV, TEV*

Bĕth·hăg′gan   beth HAG guhn   *NIV, RSV, TEV*

Bĕth-Hā′năn   beth-HAY nan   *TEV*

Bĕth-hā′răm   beth-HAY ram   *NAS, NIV, RSV, TEV*

Bĕth-hā′ran   beth-HAY ruhn   *KJV, NAS, NIV, RSV, TEV*

Bĕth-hŏg′lah   beth-HAHG luh   *KJV, NAS, NIV, RSV, TEV*

Bĕth-hō′rŏn   beth-HOH rahn   *KJV, NAS, NIV, RSV, TEV*

Bĕth-Jĕsh′ĭ·mŏth   beth-JESH ih mahth   *NAS, NIV, TEV*

Bĕth-jĕs′ĭ·mŏth   beth-JESS ih mahth   *KJV, RSV, TEV*

Bĕth-lĕ-Áph′rah   beth-lih-AF ruh   *KJV, RSV, TEV*

Bĕth-lĕb′ā·ŏth   beth-LEB ay ahth, beth-lih BAY ahth   *KJV, NAS, NIV, RSV, TEV*

Bĕth′lĕ·hĕm   BETH lih hem   *KJV, NAS, NIV, RSV, TEV*

Bĕth′lĕ·hĕm Ĕph′rå·tah   BETH lih hem EF ruh tuh   *KJV*

Bĕth′lĕ·hĕm-Ĕph′rå·thăh   BETH lih hehm-EF ruh thuh   *TEV*

Bĕth′lĕ·hĕm·īte   BETH lih hem ight   *KJV, NAS, NIV, RSV*

Bĕth-mā′å·cah   beth-MAY uh kuh   *NAS, RSV*

Bĕth-mā′å·chah   beth-MAY uh kuh   *KJV*

Bĕth-mär′cà·bŏth   beth-MAHR kuh bahth   *KJV, NAS, NIV, RSV, TEV*

Bĕth-mē′ŏn   beth-MEE ahn   *KJV, NAS, NIV, RSV, TEV*

Bĕth-Mîl′lō   beth-MEEL oh, beth-MIHL oh   *NAS, RSV, TEV*

Bĕth-nĭm′rah   beth-NIM ruh   *KJV, NAS, NIV, RSV, TEV*

Bĕth-Ŏph′ràh beth-OHF ruh *NIV*
Bĕth-pā′lĕt beth-PAY luht *KJV*
Bĕth-păz′zĕz beth-PAZ ez *KJV, NAS,
NIV, RSV, TEV*
Bĕth-pē′lĕt beth-PEE luht *KJV, NAS,
NIV, RSV, TEV*
Bĕth-pē′ôr beth-PEE awr *KJV, NAS,
NIV, RSV, TEV*
Bĕth′phà·ġē BETH fuh jee, BETH
fayg *KJV, NAS, NIV, RSV, TEV*
Bĕth-phē′lĕt beth-FEE luht *KJV*
Bĕth-rā′phà beth-RAY fuh *KJV, NAS,
NIV, RSV, TEV*
Bĕth-rē′hŏb beth-REE hahb *KJV, NAS,
NIV, RSV, TEV*
Bĕth·sā′ĭ·dà beth SAY ih duh *KJV,
NAS, NIV, RSV, TEV*
Bĕth′shän BETH shahn *KJV, NAS, NIV,
RSV*
Bĕth-shē′an beth-SHEE uhn *KJV, NAS,
RSV, TEV*
Bĕth-shē′mĕsh beth-SHEE mesh *KJV,
NAS, NIV, RSV, TEV*
Bĕth·shē′mīte beth-SHEE might *KJV,
NAS*
Bĕth-shĭt′tah beth-SHIT uh *KJV, NAS,
NIV, RSV, TEV*
Bĕth-tăp′pū·ah beth-TAP yoo uh *KJV,
NAS, NIV, RSV, TEV*
Bĕth-tō·gär′mah beth-toh GAHR muh
NAS, NIV, RSV
Bĕ·thū′ĕl beh THYOO ′l *KJV, NAS,
NIV, RSV, TEV*
Bē′thŭl BEE thuhl, BETH uhl *KJV,
NAS, NIV, RSV, TEV*
Bĕth·zā′thà beth ZAY thuh *RSV, TEV*
Bĕth-zûr beth-ZUR *KJV, NAS, NIV,
RSV, TEV*
Bĕt′ō·nĭm BET oh nim *KJV, NAS, NIV,
RSV, TEV*
Beù′lah BYOO luh *KJV, NIV*
Bē′zā·ī BEE zay igh, bee ZAY igh
KJV, NAS, NIV, RSV, TEV
Bĕz′á·leèl BEZ uh leel, beh ZAL eh el
KJV
Bĕz′á·lĕl BEHZ uh lehl *NAS, NIV, RSV,
TEV*
Bē′zĕk BEE zek *KJV, NAS, NIV, RSV,
TEV*
Bē′zêr BEE zur *KJV, NAS, NIV, RSV,
TEV*
Bĭch′rī BIK righ *KJV, NAS, RSV*
Bĭch′rīte BIHK right *RSV*
Bĭc′rī BIK righ *NIV*

Bĭd′kär BID kahr *KJV, NAS, NIV, RSV,
TEV*
Bĭḡ′thà BIG thuh *KJV, NAS, NIV, RSV,
TEV*
Bĭḡ′thăn BIG than *KJV, NAS, RSV*
Bĭḡ·thā′nà big THAY nuh, BIG thuh
nuh *KJV, NAS, NIV, RSV, TEV*
Bĭg′vā·ī BIG vay igh, BIG vigh *KJV,
NAS, NIV, RSV, TEV*
Bĭk′rī BIHK rih *TEV*
Bĭl′dăd BIL dad *KJV, NAS, NIV, RSV,
TEV*
Bĭl′ē·am BIL, ee uhm, BIGH lih uhm
KJV, NAS, NIV, RSV, TEV
Bĭl′ḡah BIL guh *KJV, NAS, NIV, RSV,
TEV*
Bĭl′ḡā·ī BIL gay igh, bil GAY igh *KJV,
NAS, NIV, RSV, TEV*
Bĭl′häh BIL hah *KJV, NAS, NIV, RSV,
TEV*
Bĭl′hăn BIL han *KJV, NAS, NIV, RSV,
TEV*
Bĭl′shăn BIL shan *KJV, NAS, NIV, RSV,
TEV*
Bĭm′hăl BIM hal *KJV, NAS, NIV, RSV,
TEV*
Bĭn′è·à BIN ih uh *KJV, NAS, NIV, RSV,
TEV*
Bĭn′nū·ī BIN yoo igh *KJV, NAS, NIV,
RSV, TEV*
Bĭr′shà BIHR shuh *KJV, NAS, NIV,
RSV, TEV*
Bĭr·zā′ĭth bihr ZAY ihth *NAS, NIV,
RSV, TEV*
Bĭr·zā′vĭth bihr ZAY vith *KJV*
Bĭsh′lăm BISH lam *KJV, NAS, NIV,
RSV, TEV*
Bĭ′thĭ′à BIH thih uh *NAS*
Bĭth′ĭ·ah BITH ih uh *KJV, NIV, RSV,
TEV*
Bĭth′rŏn BITH rahn *KJV, NIV, TEV*
Bĭ·thўn′ĭ·à bih THIN ih uh *KJV, NAS,
NIV, RSV, TEV*
Bĭz′ĭ·ō·thĭ′ah BIZ ih oh THIGH uh
NAS, NIV, RSV, TEV
Bĭz·jŏth′jah biz JAHTH juh *KJV, TEV*
Bĭz′thà BIZ thuh *KJV, NAS, NIV, RSV,
TEV*
Blăs′tŭs BLASS tuhs *KJV, NAS, NIV,
RSV, TEV*
Bō·á·nêr′ġĕṣ boh uh NUR jeez *KJV,
NAS, NIV, RSV, TEV*
Bō′ăz BOH az *KJV, NAS, NIV, RSV, TEV*
Bŏ<u>ch</u>′ė·rū BAHK ih roo, BOH kuh

roo *KJV, NAS, RSV, TEV*
Bō′chĭm   BOH kim   *KJV, NAS, RSV, TEV*
Bō′hăn   BOH han   *KJV, NAS, NIV, RSV, TEV*
Bō′kĕ·rü   BOH keh roo   *NIV*
Bō′kĭm   BOH kihm   *NIV*
Bō′ŏz   BOH ahz   *KJV*
Bôr·ā′shăn   bohr AY shan   *NAS, NIV, RSV*
Bŏs′căth   BAHS kath   *KJV*
Bō′sôr   BOH sawr   *KJV*
Bō′zĕz   BOH zez   *KJV, NAS, NIV, RSV, TEV*
Bŏz′kăth   BAHZ kath   *KJV, NAS, NIV, RSV, TEV*
Bŏz′rah   BAHZ ruh   *KJV, NAS, NIV, RSV, TEV*
Bū′băs·tĭs   BYOO bas tihs   *NIV, TEV*
Bŭk′kī   BUHK igh   *KJV, NAS, NIV, RSV, TEV*
Bŭk·kī′ah   buh KIGH uh   *KJV, NAS, NIV, RSV, TEV*
Bŭl   BUL, BOOL   *KJV, NAS, NIV, RSV, TEV*
Bū′nah   BYOO nuh   *KJV, NAS, NIV, RSV, TEV*
Bŭn′nī   BUHN igh   *KJV, NAS, NIV, RSV, TEV*
Bŭz   BUHZ   *KJV, NAS, NIV, RSV, TEV*
Bū′zī   BYOO zigh   *KJV, NAS, NIV, RSV, TEV*
Būz′īte   BYOO zight   *KJV, NAS, NIV, RSV*
Bў′blōs   BIH blohs   *TEV*

Căb′bon   KAB uhn   *KJV, NAS, NIV, RSV, TEV*
Cā′būl   KAY bul   *KJV, NAS, NIV, RSV, TEV*
Çāe′sàr   SEE zur   *KJV, NAS, NIV, RSV, TEV*
Çaĕs·å·rē′à   sess uh REE uh   *KJV, NAS, NIV, RSV, TEV*

Çaĕs·å·rē′à Phĭl′ĭp·pī   sess uh REE uh FIL ih pigh, fih LIP igh   *KJV, NAS, NIV, TEV*
Caì′å·phàs   KIGH uh fuhs, KAY yuh fuhs   *KJV, NAS, NIV, RSV, TEV*
Cain   KAYN   *KJV, NAS, NIV, RSV, TEV*
Cā·ī′nan   kay IGH nuhn   *KJV, NAS, NIV, RSV, TEV*
Cā′lah   KAY luh   *KJV, NAS, NIV, RSV, TEV*
Căl′cöl   KAL kahl   *KJV, NAS, NIV, RSV, TEV*
Cā′lĕb   KAY luhb   *KJV, NAS, NIV, RSV, TEV*
Cā′lĕb Ĕph′rå·tah   KAY luhb EF ruh tuh   *KJV*
Cā′lĕb-ĕph′rå-thah   KAY luhb-EF ruh thuh   *NAS, NIV*
Cā′lĕb·īte   KAY luhb ight   *NAS, NIV, RSV*
Căl′nĕh   KAL neh   *KJV, NAS, NIV, RSV*
Căl′nō   KAL no   *KJV, NAS, NIV, RSV, TEV*
Căl′vå·rў   KAL vuh rih   *KJV, NAS*
Cā′mŏn   KAY mahn   *KJV*
Cā′nà   KAY nuh   *KJV, NAS, NIV, RSV, TEV*
Cā′năan   KAY nuhn   *KJV, NAS, NIV, RSV, TEV*
Cā′năan·īte   KAY nuhn ight   *KJV, NAS, NIV, RSV, TEV*
Cā′năan·ī·tĕss   KAY nuhn ight tehs   *NAS, RSV*
Cā′năan·nī·tĭsh   KAY nuhn nigh tish   *RSV*
Cā·nå·nāē′an   kay nuh NEE uhn   *KJV, RSV*
Căn′då·cē   KAN duh see   *KJV, NAS, NIV, RSV, TEV*
Căn′nĕh   KAN eh   *KJV, NAS, NIV, RSV, TEV*
Cå·pêr′nā·um   kuh PURR nay uhm   *KJV, NAS, NIV, RSV, TEV*
Cāpe-Săl·mō′nė   KAYP-sal MOH nih   *TEV*
Căph′tôr   KAF tawr   *KJV, NAS, NIV, RSV*
Căph′tō·rĭm   KAF toh rim   *KJV, NAS, RSV*
Căph′tō·rītes   KAF toh rights   *NIV*
Căp·på·dō′cĭ·à   kap uh DOH shih uh   *KJV, NAS, NIV, RSV, TEV*
Cär′càs   KAHR kuss   *KJV, NIV, TEV*
Cär′chĕm·ĭsh   KAHR kem ish   *KJV, NAS, NIV, RSV, TEV*

Că·rē′ah   kuh REE uh *KJV*

Cär′ĭ·tēṣ   KAR ih teez *KJV, NAS, NIV, RSV, TEV*

Cär′kàs   KAHR kuss *NAS, NIV, RSV, TEV*

Car′mel   KAHR m'l *KJV, NAS, NIV, RSV, TEV*

Cär′mĕl·īte   KAHR muhl ight *KJV, NAS, NIV*

Cär′mĕl·ĭ·tĕss   KAHR muhl ight ess *NAS, RSV*

Cär′mī   KAHR migh *KJV, NAS, NIV, RSV, TEV*

Cär′mīte   KAHR might *KJV, NAS, NIV, RSV*

Cär′pŭs   KAHR puhs *KJV, NAS, NIV, RSV, TEV*

Cär·shē′na   kahr SHE nuh, KAHR she nuh *KJV, NAS, RSV, TEV*

Că·sĭph′ĭ·à   kuh SIF ih uh *KJV, NAS, NIV, RSV, TEV*

Căs′lŭh   KASS luh *NAS, TEV*

Căs′lū·hĭm   KASS lyoo him, kass LYOO him *KJV, NAS, RSV*

Căs′lū·hites   KASS lyoo hights, kass LYOO hights *NIV*

Căs′tôr   KASS tawr *KJV, NIV*

Caū′dà   KAW duh *KJV, NIV, RSV, TEV*

Çĕ′drŏn   SEE druhn *KJV*

Çĕn′chrĕ·à   SEN krih uh, sen KREE uh *NAS, NIV*

Cĕn·chrē′ae   kihn KREE uh, sihn KREE igh *KJV, RSV, TEV*

Çĕ′phàs   SEE fuhs *KJV, NAS, NIV, RSV, TEV*

Chăl′cŏl   KAL kahl *KJV*

Chăl·dē′à   kal DEE uh *KJV, NAS, NIV, RSV*

Chăl·dē′àn   kal DEE uhn *KJV, NAS, NIV, RSV, TEV*

Chăl′dēēṣ   KAL deez *KJV, NAS*

Chär′à·shīm   KAHR uh shim *KJV*

Chär′chĕm·ĭsh   KAHR kem ish *KJV*

Chär′ran   KAR uhn *KJV*

Chē′bär   KEE bahr *KJV, NAS, RSV, TEV*

Chĕd·ôr·lā′ō·mēr   ked awr-LAY oh muhr *KJV, NAS, RSV, TEV*

Chē′lăl   KEE lal *KJV, NAS, RSV, TEV*

Chĕl′lŭh   KEL yoo *KJV*

Chē′lŭb   KEE luhb *KJV, NAS, RSV, TEV*

Chĕ·lū′baì   kih LOO bigh *KJV, NAS, RSV, TEV*

Chĕl′ŭh·ï   KEHL yoo ih *NAS, RSV, TEV*

Chĕm′à·rĭm   KEM uh rim *KJV, TEV*

Chē′mŏsh   KEE mahsh *KJV, NAS, RSV, TEV*

Chĕ·nà′à·nah   kih NAY uh nuh *KJV, NAS, RSV, TEV*

Chĕ·na′nĭ   kih NAY nigh, KEN uh nigh *KJV, NAS, RSV, TEV*

Chĕn·à·nī′ah   ken uh NIGH uh *KJV, NAS, RSV, TEV*

Chē′phär·ăm′mō·nī   KEE fahr AM oh nigh *RSV, TEV*

Chē′phär-ăm′mo·nī   KEE fur-AM uh nigh *NAS*

Chē′phär Hă-ăm′mō·naì   KEE fahr ha-AM oh nigh *KJV*

Chĕ·phī′rah   kih FIGH ruh *KJV, NAS, RSV, TEV*

Chĕph′ï·rīm   KEFF ih rim *NAS*

Chē′ran   KEE ruhn *KJV, NAS, RSV, TEV*

Chĕr′ĕ·thītes   KER ih thights *KJV, NAS, RSV*

Chē′rith   KEE rith *KJV, NAS, RSV, TEV*

Chĕr′ŭb   (angel) CHEH rub *KJV, NAS, NIV, RSV, TEV*

Chĕr′ŭb   (town or person) KER uhb *NAS*

Chĕs′à·lŏn   KESS uh lahn *KJV, NAS, RSV, TEV*

Chē′sĕd   KEE sed, KEES uhd *KJV, NAS, RSV, TEV*

Chē′sĭl   KEE suhl *KJV, NAS, RSV, TEV*

Chĕ·sŭl′lŏth   kih SUHL ahth *KJV, NAS, RSV, TEV*

Chē′zĭb   KEE zib *KJV, NAS, RSV, TEV*

Chī′don   KIGH d'n *KJV, NAS, RSV, TEV*

Chīl′ĕ·ab   KIL ih ab, KIGH lih ab *KJV, NAS, RSV, TEV*

Chīl′ĭ·ŏn   KIL ih ahn *KJV, NAS, RSV, TEV*

Chīl′măd   KIL mad *KJV, NAS, RSV, TEV*

Chĭm′hăm   KIM ham *KJV, NAS, RSV, TEV*

Chĭn′nĕ·rĕth   KIN ih reth *KJV, NAS, RSV, TEV*

Chĭn′nĕ·rŏth   KIN ih rahth *KJV, NAS, RSV, TEV*

Chī′ös   KIGH ahs, KEE ahs *KJV, NAS, RSV, TEV*

Chīs′lĕu   KISS lew *KJV*

Chĭṣ′lĕv   KIZZ lehv, KISS lehv *NAS, RSV*

Chĭṣ′lŏn   KIZ lahn, KISS lahn *KJV, NAS, RSV, TEV*

Chĭs′lŏth-tā′bôr   KISS lahth-TAY

bawr *KJV, NAS, RSV, TEV*
Chit′lish KIT lish *NAS, RSV, TEV*
Chit′tim KIT im *KJV*
Chi′un KIGH uhn *KJV*
Chlō′ē KLOH ee *KJV, NAS, NIV, RSV, TEV*
Chôr·ash′an kawr ASH uhn *KJV*
Chō·ra′zin koh RAY zin *KJV, NAS, RSV, TEV*
Chō·zē′bà koh ZEE buh *KJV, NAS*
Christ KRIGHST *KJV, NAS, NIV, RSV, TEV*
Chris′tian KRISS chuhn *KJV, NAS, NIV, RSV, TEV*
Chrŏ′ni·clĕs KRAN nih kuhls *KJV, NAS, NIV, RSV, TEV*
Chub KUHB, CHUHB *KJV*
Chun KUHN *KJV*
Chu′shăn-rish·â·thā′im KYOO shan-rish uh THAY im *KJV, NAS*
Chu′zà KYOO zuh *KJV, NAS, RSV, TEV*
Çi·lic′ï·à sih LISH ih uh *KJV, NAS, NIV, RSV, TEV*
Çin′nē·rŏth SIN uh rahth *KJV*
Çis SIS *KJV*
Claū′dà KLAW duh *KJV, NAS*
Claū′di·à KLAW dih uh *KJV, NAS, NIV, RSV, TEV*
Claū′di·ŭs KLAW dih uhs *KJV, NAS, NIV, RSV, TEV*
Clĕm′ēnt KLEM uhnt *KJV, NAS, NIV, RSV, TEV*
Clē′ō·pàs KLEE oh puhs *KJV, NAS, NIV, RSV, TEV*
Clē′ō·phàs KLEE oh fuhs *KJV*
Clō′pàs KLOH puhs *NAS, NIV, RSV, TEV*
Cnī′dŭs NIGH duhs *KJV, NAS, NIV, RSV, TEV*
Cŏl·hō′zĕh kahl HOH zeh *KJV, NAS, NIV, RSV, TEV*
Cŏ·lŏs′saê koh LAHS sih *NAS, RSV, TEV*
Cŏ·lŏs′sē koh LAHS ee *KJV, NIV*
Co·lŏs′sians kuh LAHS uhns, *NAS*
Cŏn·â·ni′ah kahn uh NIGH uh, koh nuh NIGH uh *KJV, NAS, NIV, RSV, TEV*
Cŏ·ni′ah coh NIGH uh *NAS, RSV*
Cŏ′ŏs KOH ahs *KJV*
Côr·ash′an kawr ASH uhn *KJV*
Côr′băn KAWR ban *NAS, NIV, RSV*
Cŏ′rĕ KOH rih *KJV*
Côr′inth KAWR inth *KJV, NAS, NIV,*

RSV, TEV
Cŏ·rin′thi·an koh RIN thih uhn *KJV, NAS, NIV, RSV*
Côr·nē′li·ŭs kawr NEE lih uhs *KJV, NAS, NIV, RSV, TEV*
Cŏş KAHS *NAS, NIV, RSV*
Cō′săm KOH sam *KJV, NAS, NIV, RSV, TEV*
Coun′çil KOWN sihl *NAS, NIV, TEV*
Cov′ĕ·nănt-Bŏx KUHV ih nuhnt-BAHX *TEV*
Cov′ĕ·nănt-Tĕnt KUHV ih nuhnt-TIHNT *TEV*
Cŏz KAHZ *KJV, TEV*
Cŏz′bī KAHZ bigh *KJV, NAS, NIV, RSV, TEV*
Cō·zē′bà koh ZEE buh *NAS, NIV, RSV, TEV*
Crĕs′cĕnş KRES uhnz *KJV, NAS, NIV, RSV, TEV*
Crē′tanş KREE tuhnz *KJV, NAS, NIV, RSV, TEV*
Crēte KREET *KJV, NAS, NIV, RSV, TEV*
Crētes KREETS *KJV*
Crē′tians KREE shuhnz *KJV, NAS*
Cris′pŭs KRIS puhs *KJV, NAS, NIV, RSV, TEV*
Cūn KYOON *NAS, NIV, RSV*
Cūsh KUHSH *KJV, NAS, NIV, RSV, TEV*
Cū′shăn KYOO shan *KJV, NAS, NIV, RSV, TEV*
Cū′shăn·rish·â·thā′im KYOO shan rish uh THAY ihm *NAS, NIV, RSV, TEV*
Cū′shī KYOO shigh *KJV, NAS, NIV, RSV, TEV*
Cū′shite KYOO shight *KJV, NAS, NIV, RSV*
Cŭth KUHTH *KJV, NAS, RSV, TEV*
Cū′thàh KYOO thuh *KJV, NAS, NIV, RSV, TEV*
Cü′zà KOO zuh *NIV*
Cȳ′pri·an SIH prih uhn *NAS*
Cȳ′prŭs SIGH pruhs *KJV, NAS, NIV, RSV, TEV*
Cȳ·rē′nē sigh REE nee *KJV, NAS, NIV, RSV, TEV*
Cȳ·rē′ni·an sigh REE nih uhn *KJV, NAS, RSV*
Cȳ·rē′ni·ŭs sigh REE nih uhs *KJV*
Cȳ′rŭs SIGH ruhs *KJV, NAS, NIV, RSV, TEV*

Dăb'å·reh   DAB uh reh   *KJV*

Dăb'bå·shĕth   DAB uh sheth   *KJV, RSV, TEV*

Dăb'bĕ·shĕth   DAB eh sheth   *NAS, NIV*

Dăb'ĕ·răth   DAB eh rath   *KJV, NAS, NIV, RSV, TEV*

Dā'g̣ŏn   DAY gahn   *KJV, NAS, NIV, RSV, TEV*

Då·laí·ah   duh LIGH uh, dal ay IGH uh   *KJV*

Dăl·må·nū'thà   dal muh NYOO thuh   *KJV, NAS, NIV, RSV, TEV*

Dăl·mā'tǐ·à   dal MAY shih uh   *KJV, NAS, NIV, RSV, TEV*

Dăl'phon   DAL fahn   *KJV, NAS, NIV, RSV, TEV*

Dăm'å·rǐs   DAM uh riss   *KJV, NAS, NIV, RSV, TEV*

Dăm'å·scēne   DAM uh seen, dam uh SEEN   *KJV, NAS, NIV*

Då·măs'cŭs   duh MASS kuss   *KJV, NAS, NIV, RSV, TEV*

Dăn   DAN   *KJV, NAS, NIV, RSV, TEV*

Dăn'iĕl   DAN yuhl   *KJV, NAS, NIV, RSV, TEV*

Dăn'ite   DAN ight   *KJV, NAS, NIV, RSV, TEV*

Dăn·jā'an   dan JAY uhn   *KJV, NAS, NIV*

Dăn'nah   DAN uh   *KJV, NAS, NIV, RSV, TEV*

Dâr'à   DER uh   *KJV, NAS, RSV*

Där'dà   DAHR duh   *KJV, NAS, NIV, RSV, TEV*

Då·rī'ŭs   duh RIGH uhs   *KJV, NAS, NIV, RSV, TEV*

Där'kŏn   DAHR kahn   *KJV, NAS, NIV, RSV, TEV*

Dā'than   DAY thuhn   *KJV, NAS, NIV, RSV, TEV*

Dā'vĭd   DAY vid   *KJV, NAS, NIV, RSV, TEV*

Dē'bīr   DEE bur   *KJV, NAS, NIV, RSV, TEV*

Dĕb'o·rah   DEB uh ruh   *KJV, NAS, NIV, RSV, TEV*

Dĕ·căp'ō·lĭs   dih KAP oh liss   *KJV, NAS, NIV, RSV*

Dē'dan   DEE duhn   *KJV, NAS, NIV, RSV, TEV*

Dĕd'å·nǐm   DED uh nim, DEE dah nim   *KJV*

Dĕd'ån·ite   DED uhn ight   *KJV, NAS, NIV, RSV*

Dĕ·hā'vĭte   dih HAY vight   *KJV*

Dē'kär   DEE kahr   *KJV*

Dĕ·laí'ah   dih LIGH uh, dih LAY yuh   *KJV, NAS, NIV, RSV, TEV*

Dĕ·lī'lah   dih LIGH luh   *KJV, NAS, NIV, RSV, TEV*

Dē'màs   DEE muhs   *KJV, NAS, NIV, RSV, TEV*

Dĕ·mē'trǐ·ŭs   dih MEE trih uhs   *KJV, NAS, NIV, RSV, TEV*

Dêr'bê   DUR bih   *KJV, NAS, NIV, RSV, TEV*

Dĕu'ĕl   DYOO el   *KJV, NAS, NIV, RSV, TEV*

Dī·ăn'à   digh AN uh   *KJV*

Dĭb'lah   DIB luh   *KJV, NAS, NIV*

Dĭb·lā'ĭm   dib LAY im, DIB lay im   *KJV, NAS, NIV, RSV, TEV*

Dĭb'lath   DIB lath   *KJV*

Dī'bŏn   DIGH bahn   *KJV, NAS, NIV, RSV, TEV*

Dī'bŏn-găd   DIGH bahn-gad   *KJV, NAS, NIV, RSV*

Dĭb'rī   DIB righ   *KJV, NAS, NIV, RSV, TEV*

Dĭd'y̆·mŭs   DID ih muhs   *KJV, NAS, NIV*

Dĭk'läh   DIK lah   *KJV, NAS, NIV, RSV, TEV*

Dī'lē·an   DIGH lih uhn, DIL ih uhn   *KJV, NAS, NIV, RSV, TEV*

Dĭm'nah   DIM nuh   *KJV, NAS, NIV, RSV, TEV*

Dī'mŏn   DIGH mahn   *KJV, NAS, NIV*

Dī·mō'nah   digh MOH nuh   *KJV, NAS, NIV, RSV, TEV*

Dī'nah   DIGH nuh   *KJV, NAS, NIV, RSV, TEV*

Dī'nå·ite   DIGH nuh ight   *KJV*

Dĭn'hå·bah   DIN huh buh   *KJV, NAS, NIV, RSV, TEV*

Dī·ō·ny̆s'ǐ·us   digh oh NISH ih uhs, digh oh NIGH sih uhs   *KJV, NAS, NIV, RSV, TEV*

Dī·ŏt'rē·phēs   digh AHT rih feez   *KJV,*

NAS, NIV, RSV, TEV

Dī′phăth   DIGH fath   *KJV, NAS, RSV, TEV*

Dī′shăn   DIGH shan   *KJV, NAS, NIV, RSV, TEV*

Dī′shŏn   DIGH shahn   *KJV, NAS, NIV, RSV, TEV*

Dĭz′å·hăb   DIZ uh hab, DIGH zuh hab   *KJV, NAS, NIV, TEV*

Dō′daı   DOH digh, DOH day igh   *KJV, NIV, RSV, TEV*

Dō′dä·nĭm   DOH dah nim, DAHD uh nim   *KJV, NAS, RSV*

Dŏd′å·vah   DAHD uh vuh, DOH duh vuh   *KJV*

Dō·dăv′å·hū   doh DAV uh hyoo, DOH duh VAY hyoo   *NAS, NIV, RSV*

Dō·dăv′hū   doh DAV hyoo, DAHD uh hyoo   *TEV*

Dō′do   DOH duh   *KJV, NAS, NIV, RSV, TEV*

Dō′ĕğ   DOH ehg   *KJV, NAS, NIV, RSV, TEV*

Dŏph′kah   DAHF kuh   *KJV, NAS, NIV, RSV, TEV*

Dôr   DAWR   *KJV, NAS, NIV, RSV, TEV*

Dôr′càs   DAWR kuhs   *KJV, NAS, NIV, RSV, TEV*

Dō′than   DOH thuhn   *KJV, NAS, NIV, RSV, TEV*

Drŭ·sĭl′là   droo SIL uh   *KJV, NAS, NIV, RSV, TEV*

Dū′mah   DYOO muh   *KJV, NAS, NIV, RSV, TEV*

Dū′rà   DYOO ruh   *KJV, NAS, NIV, RSV, TEV*

Ē′bàl   EE buhl   *KJV, NAS, NIV, RSV, TEV*

Ē′bĕd   EE bed   *KJV, NAS, NIV, RSV, TEV*

Ē′bĕd-mē′lĕch   EE bed-MEE lek   *KJV, NAS, NIV, RSV, TEV*

Ĕb′ĕn-ē′zĕr   EB uhn-EE zur, eb uh NEE zur   *KJV, NAS, NIV, RSV, TEV*

Ē′bĕr   EE buhr   *KJV, NAS, NIV, RSV, TEV*

Ē′bĕz   EE behz   *NAS, NIV, RSV, TEV*

Ē·bī′å·săph   ih BIGH uh saf   *KJV, NAS, NIV, RSV, TEV*

Ē′brŏn   EE bruhn   *NAS, RSV, TEV*

Ē·brō′nah   ih BROH nuh, eb ROH nuh   *KJV, NAS*

Ĕc′băt·å·nà   EHK bat uh nuh, ehk BAT uh nuh   *NAS, NIV, RSV, TEV*

Ĕd   ED   *KJV, RSV, TEV*

Ē′där   EE dahr   *KJV*

Ē′dĕn   EE d′n   *KJV, NAS, NIV, RSV, TEV*

Ē′dĕr   EE dur   *KJV, NAS, NIV, RSV, TEV*

Ē′dom   EE duhm   *KJV, NAS, NIV, RSV, TEV*

Ē′dom·īte   EE duhm ight   *KJV, NAS, NIV, RSV, TEV*

Ĕd′rê·ī   ED rih igh   *KJV, NAS, NIV, RSV, TEV*

Ĕğ′lah   EG luh   *KJV, NAS, NIV, RSV, TEV*

Ĕğ′lā·ĭm   EG lay im   *KJV, NAS, NIV, RSV, TEV*

Ĕğ′làth-Shĕ·lĭsh′ĭ·yah   EGG luhth-sheh LISH ih yuh   *NAS, NIV, RSV, TEV*

Ĕğ′lŏn   EG lahn   *KJV, NAS, NIV, RSV, TEV*

Ē′ğўpt   EE jipt   *KJV, NAS, NIV, RSV, TEV*

Ē·ğўp′tian   ee JIP shuhn   *KJV, NAS, NIV, RSV, TEV*

Ē′hī   EE high   *KJV, NAS, NIV, RSV, TEV*

Ē′hŭd   EE huhd   *KJV, NAS, NIV, RSV, TEV*

Ē′kēr   EE kur   *KJV, NAS, NIV, RSV, TEV*

Ĕk′rŏn   EK rahn   *KJV, NAS, NIV, RSV, TEV*

Ĕk′rŏn·īte   EK rahn ight   *KJV, NAS*

Ĕl   EHL   *TEV*

Ē′là   EE luh   *KJV, NAS, NIV, RSV, TEV*

Ĕl′å·dah   EL uh duh   *KJV*

Ē′lah   EE luh   *KJV, NAS, NIV, RSV, TEV*

Ē′lam   EE luhm   *KJV, NAS, NIV, RSV, TEV*

Ē′làm·īte   EE luhm ight   *KJV, NAS, NIV, RSV, TEV*

Ĕl-ā′sah   el-AY suh, EL uh suh   *KJV, NAS, NIV, RSV, TEV*

Ē′läth   EE lath   *KJV, NAS, NIV, RSV, TEV*

Ĕl-bĕr′ĭth   el-BIHR ith   *NAS, NIV, RSV*

Ĕl-bĕth′ĕl   el-BETH uhl   *KJV, NAS, NIV, RSV*

Ĕl·dā′äh   el DAY ah   *KJV, NAS, NIV, RSV, TEV*

Ĕl′dăd   EL dad   *KJV, NAS, NIV, RSV, TEV*

Ĕl′ê·àd   EL ih uhd, EE lee ad   *KJV,*

NAS, NIV, RSV, TEV

Ěl'ė·ā'dah   EL ih AY duh   *NAS, NIV, RSV, TEV*

Ē'lė·ā'·lěh   EE lih AY leh, el eh AY leh   *KJV, NAS, NIV, RSV, TEV*

Ěl-ė·ā'sah   EL-ih AY suh, ih LEE uh suh   *KJV, NAS, NIV, RSV, TEV*

Ěl-ė·ā'zàr   EL-ih AY zur, el ih AY zur   *KJV, NAS, NIV, RSV, TEV*

Ěl-ė·lō'hě-Ĭs'rā·ël   EL-ih LOH heh-IZ ray el   *KJV, NAS, NIV, RSV*

Ē'lěph   EE lef   *KJV*

Ěl-hā'nan   el-HAY nuhn   *KJV, NAS, NIV, RSV, TEV*

Ē'lī   EE ligh   *KJV, NAS, NIV, RSV, TEV*

Ė·lī'ăb   ih LIGH ab   *KJV, NAS, NIV, RSV, TEV*

Ė·lī'å·dà   ih LIGH uh duh   *KJV, NAS, NIV, RSV, TEV*

Ė·lī'å·dah   ih LIGH uh duh   *KJV, TEV*

Ė·lī'ah   ih LIGH uh   *KJV*

Ė·lī'áh·bà   ih LIGH uh buh   *KJV, NAS, NIV, RSV, TEV*

Ė·lī'å·kĭm   ih LIGH uh kim   *KJV, NAS, NIV, RSV, TEV*

Ė·lī'am   ih LIGH uhm   *KJV, NAS, NIV, RSV, TEV*

Ė·lī'às   ih LIGH uhs   *KJV*

Ė·lī'å·săph   ih LIGH uh saf   *KJV, NAS, NIV, RSV, TEV*

Ė·lī'å·shĭb   ih LIGH uh shib   *KJV, NAS, NIV, RSV, TEV*

Ė·lī'å·thah   ih LIGH uh thuh   *KJV, NAS, NIV, RSV, TEV*

Ė·lī'dăd   ih LIGH dad   *KJV, NAS, NIV, RSV, TEV*

Ěl'ĭ·ē·hō·ē'naì   EL ih ee hoh EE nigh   *NAS, NIV, RSV*

Ė·lī'ěl   ih LIGH el, EE lih el   *KJV, NAS, NIV, RSV, TEV*

Ē'·lī-Ē'lī-lä'mä-sä·bäch·thä·nī'   EE ligh-EE ligh-LAH mah-sah bahk thah NEE (NIGH)   *KJV, NAS, RSV, TEV*

Ěl·ĭ·ē'naì   el ih EE nigh   *KJV, NAS, NIV, RSV, TEV*

Ěl·ĭ·ē'zēr   el ih EE zur   *KJV, NAS, NIV, RSV, TEV*

Ěl·ĭ·hō·ē'naì   el ih hoh EE nigh, el ih hoh EE nay igh   *KJV, TEV*

Ěl'ĭ-hō'rěph   EL ih-HOH ref   *KJV, NAS, NIV, RSV, TEV*

Ė·lī'hū   ih LIGH hyoo   *KJV, NAS, NIV, RSV, TEV*

Ė·lī'jah   ih LIGH juh   *KJV, NAS, NIV,*

RSV, TEV

Ė·lī'kà   ih LIGH kuh, EL ih kuh   *KJV, NAS, NIV, RSV, TEV*

Ē'lĭm   EE lim   *KJV, NAS, NIV, RSV, TEV*

Ė·lĭm'ē·lěch   ih LIM uh lek   *KJV, NAS, NIV, RSV, TEV*

Ěl·ĭ·ō·ē'naì   el ih oh EE nigh, ih ligh oh EE nigh   *KJV, NAS, NIV, RSV, TEV*

Ė·lī'phăl   ih LIGH fal, EL ih fal   *KJV, NAS, NIV, RSV, TEV*

Ė·lĭph'å·lět   ih LIF uh let   *KJV, TEV*

Ěl'ĭ·phăz   EL ih faz   *KJV, NAS, NIV, RSV, TEV*

Ė·lĭph'ē·lěh   ih LIF uh leh   *KJV, RSV, TEV*

Ė·lĭph'ē·lē'hū   ih LIHF eh LEE hyoo, eh LIF ih leh hyoo   *NAS, NIV, RSV, TEV*

Ė·lĭph'ē·lět   ih LIHF eh let   *NAS, NIV, RSV, TEV*

Ė·lĭs'å·běth   ih LIZ uh beth   *KJV*

Ěl·ĭ·sē'ŭs   el ih SEE uhs   *KJV*

Ė·lī'shà   ih LIGH shuh   *KJV, NAS, NIV, RSV, TEV*

Ė·lī'shah   ih LIGH shuh   *KJV, NAS, NIV, RSV, TEV*

Ė·lĭsh'å·mà   ih LISH uh muh, EE ligh shah mah   *KJV, NAS, NIV, RSV, TEV*

Ė·lĭsh'å·phăt   ih LISH uh fat, ee ligh SHAY fat   *KJV, NAS, NIV, RSV, TEV*

Ė·lĭsh'ė·bä   ih LISH ih bah, ee LIGH shih buh   *KJV, NAS, NIV, RSV, TEV*

Ěl'ĭ-shū'à   EL ih-SHOO uh, ih LISH oo uh   *KJV, NAS, NIV, RSV, TEV*

Ė·lī'ūd   ih LIGH uhd   *KJV, NAS, NIV, RSV, TEV*

Ė·līz'å·běth   ih LIHZ uh beth, ih LIHZ uh buhth   *NAS, NIV, RSV, TEV*

Ěl'ĭ-zā'phan   EL ih-ZAY fuhn, EE ligh-ZAY fan   *KJV, NAS, NIV, RSV, TEV*

Ė·lī'zûr   ih LIGH zur   *KJV, NAS, NIV, RSV, TEV*

Ěl·kā'nah   el KAY nuh, EL kuh nuh   *KJV, NAS, NIV, RSV, TEV*

Ěl'kěsh   EHL kesh   *TEV*

Ěl'kŏsh   EHL kahsh   *RSV*

Ěl·kŏsh'īte   el KAHSH ight, el KOH shight   *KJV, NAS, NIV*

Ěl·lā'sär   el LAY sahr, el LAH sahr   *KJV, NAS, NIV, RSV, TEV*

Ěl·mā'dam   ehl MAY duhm   *NAS, NIV, RSV, TEV*

Ěl·mō'dăm   el MOH dam   *KJV, TEV*

Ěl·nā'ăm   el NAY am   *KJV, NAS, NIV,*

Ĕl·nā'than el NAY thuhn *KJV, NAS,*
NIV, RSV, TEV
Ė·lō'ī ih LOH igh *KJV, NAS, NIV, RSV,*
TEV
Ē'lŏn EE lahn *KJV, NAS, NIV, RSV, TEV*
Ē'lŏn-bĕth-hā'năn EE lahn-beth-HAY
nan *KJV, NAS, NIV, RSV*
Ē'lŏn-īte EE lahn ight *KJV, NAS, NIV,*
RSV, TEV
Ē'lŏth EE lahth *KJV, NAS, RSV*
Ĕl-pā'ăl el-PAY al *KJV, NAS, NIV, RSV,*
TEV
Ĕl-pā'lĕt el-PAY let *KJV, NAS*
Ĕl-pā'ran el-PAY ruhn *KJV, NAS, RSV,*
TEV
Ĕl-pĕl'ĕt el-PEL uht *KJV, NAS, NIV,*
RSV, TEV
Ĕl'tĕ·kĕ EL teh keh *NAS, RSV*
Ĕl'tĕ·kēh EL tih kuh *KJV, NAS, NIV,*
RSV, TEV
Ĕl'tĕ·kŏn EL tih kahn *KJV, NAS, NIV,*
RSV, TEV
Ĕl·tō'lăd el TOH lad *KJV, NAS, NIV,*
RSV, TEV
Ė'lūl ih LOOL *KJV, NAS, NIV, RSV, TEV*
Ė·lū'zā·ī ih LYOO zay igh, ih LYOO
zigh *KJV, NAS, NIV, RSV, TEV*
Ĕl'ÿ·măs EL ih mass *KJV, NAS, NIV,*
RSV, TEV
Ĕl·zā'băd el ZAY bad, EL zay bad
KJV, NAS, NIV, RSV, TEV
Ĕl·zā'phan el ZAY fuhn, EL zuh fan
KJV, NAS, NIV, RSV, TEV
Ē'mĕk-kē'zīz EE mek-KEE ziz *KJV,*
NAS, NIV, RSV, TEV
Ē'mĭm EE mim *KJV, NAS, RSV, TEV*
Ē'mītes EE mights *NIV*
Ĕm·măn'ū·ĕl ih MAN yoo el *KJV, RSV*
Ĕm·mā'ŭs eh MAY uhs *KJV, NAS, NIV,*
RSV, TEV
Ĕm'môr EM awr *KJV*
Ė·nā'ĭm ih NAY im *KJV, NAS, NIV,*
RSV, TEV
Ē'năm EE nam *KJV, NAS, NIV, RSV,*
TEV
Ē'năn EE nan *KJV, NAS, NIV, RSV, TEV*
Ĕn'dôr EN dawr *KJV, NAS, NIV, RSV,*
TEV
Ė·nē'ăs ih NEE uhs *KJV*
Ĕn-ĕg'lā·ĭm en-EGG lay im *KJV, NAS,*
NIV, RSV
Ĕn-găn'nĭm en-GAN nim *KJV, NAS,*
NIV, RSV, TEV

Ĕn'gĕ·dī en GED ih, en GHEE digh
KJV, NAS, NIV, RSV, TEV
Ĕn-hăd'dah en-HAD uh *KJV, NAS, NIV,*
RSV, TEV
Ĕn-hăk'kō·rĕ en-HAK oh rih *KJV, NAS,*
NIV, RSV, TEV
Ĕn-hā'zôr en-HAY zawr *KJV, NAS,*
NIV, RSV, TEV
Ĕn-mĭsh'pat en-MISH pat *KJV, NAS,*
NIV, RSV, TEV
Ē'nŏch EE nuk *KJV, NAS, NIV, RSV,*
TEV
Ē'nŏn-Çī'tÿ EE nahn-SIH tih *TEV*
Ē'nŏs EE nahs, EE nuhs *KJV, NIV, RSV*
Ē'nŏsh EE nahsh *KJV, NAS, NIV, RSV,*
TEV
Ĕn-rĭm'mon en-RIM uhn *KJV, NAS,*
NIV, RSV, TEV
Ĕn-rō'gĕl en-ROH gehl *KJV, NAS, NIV,*
RSV, TEV
Ĕn-shē'mĕsh en-SHEE mesh *KJV, NAS,*
NIV, RSV, TEV
Ĕn-tăp'pū·ah en-TAP yoo uh *KJV,*
NAS, NIV, RSV, TEV
Ė·pāe'nĕ·tŭs ih PEE neh tuhs *NAS,*
RSV, TEV
Ĕp'ȧ·phrăs EP uh frass *KJV, NAS, NIV,*
RSV, TEV
Ė·păph'rō·dī'tŭs ih PAF roh DIGH
tuhs *KJV, NAS, NIV, RSV, TEV*
Ė·pē'nĕ·tŭs ih PEE nih tuhs *KJV, NIV*
Ē'phàh EE fuh *KJV, NAS, NIV, RSV,*
TEV
Ē'phaì EE figh, EE fay igh *KJV, NAS,*
NIV, RSV, TEV
Ē'phĕr EE fur *KJV, NAS, NIV, RSV, TEV*
Ē'phĕs-dăm'mĭn EE fess-DAM in *KJV,*
NAS, NIV, RSV, TEV
Ē'phē'ṣian ih FEE zhuhn *KJV, NAS,*
NIV, RSV, TEV
Ėph'ē·sùs EF uh suhs *KJV, NAS, NIV,*
RSV, TEV
Ėph'lăl EF lal *KJV, NAS, NIV, RSV, TEV*
Ē'phŏd EE fahd, EF ahd *KJV, NAS,*
NIV, RSV, TEV
Ėph'phȧ·thȧ EF uh thuh *KJV, NAS,*
NIV, RSV, TEV
Ė·phrä·ĭm EE frih ihm *KJV, NAS, NIV,*
RSV, TEV
Ē'phrä·im·īte EE frih ihm ight *KJV,*
NAS, NIV, RSV, TEV
Ē'phrä·ĭn EE fray in *KJV*
Ėph'rȧ·tah EF ruh tuh *KJV, NIV*

Ē′phrăth   EE frath   *KJV, NAS, NIV, RSV,*
TEV
Ĕph′ra·thah   EF ruh thuh   *NAS, NIV,*
RSV
Ĕph′ra̍·thīte   EF ruh thight   *KJV, NAS,*
NIV, RSV, TEV
Ē′phrŏn   EE frahn   *KJV, NAS, NIV, RSV,*
TEV
Ĕp·ĭ·cū·rē′an   ep ih kyoo REE uhn   *KJV,*
NAS, NIV, RSV, TEV
Ēr   UR   *KJV, NAS, NIV, RSV, TEV*
Ē′răn   EE ran   *KJV, NAS, NIV, RSV, TEV*
Ē·răn·ite   EE ran ight   *KJV, NAS, NIV,*
RSV
Ē·răs′tŭs   ih RASS tuhs   *KJV, NAS, NIV,*
RSV, TEV
Ē′rĕch   EE rek, ER ek   *KJV, NAS, NIV,*
RSV, TEV
Ē′rī   EE righ   *KJV, NAS, NIV, RSV, TEV*
Ē′rīte   EE right   *KJV, NAS, NIV, RSV,*
TEV
Ē·s̲a̲i̲′as   ih ZAY uhs, ih ZIGH uhs   *KJV*
Ē′sär·hăd′don   EE sahr-HAD ′n   *KJV,*
NAS, NIV, RSV, TEV
Ē′saū   EE saw   *KJV, NAS, NIV, RSV, TEV*
Ē′sĕk   EE sek   *KJV, NAS, NIV, RSV, TEV*
Ē′shăn   EE shan, EE shuhn   *NAS, NIV,*
RSV, TEV
Ĕsh-bā′ăl   esh-BAY uhl   *KJV, NAS, NIV,*
RSV, TEV
Ĕsh′băn   ESH ban   *KJV, NAS, NIV, RSV,*
TEV
Ĕsh′cŏl   ESH kahl, ESH kawl   *KJV,*
NAS, NIV, RSV, TEV
Ĕsh′ē·an   ESH ih uhn, EE shih uhn
KJV
Ē′shĕk   EE shek   *KJV, NAS, NIV, RSV,*
TEV
Ĕsh′ka̍·lŏn·īte   ESH kuh lahn ight   *KJV*
Ĕsh′tā·ŏl   ESH tay ahl   *KJV, NAS, NIV,*
RSV, TEV
Ĕsh′ta·o·lītes   ESH tuh uh lights   *NAS,*
NIV, RSV
Ĕsh′ta̍·rah   ESH tuh ruh   *NIV*
Ĕsh·ta̍·ū′līte   esh tuh YOO light   *KJV,*
TEV
Ĕsh·tĕ·mō′a̍   esh tih MOH uh   *KJV, NAS,*
NIV, RSV, TEV
Ĕsh′tĕ·mōh   ESH tih moh   *KJV, NAS,*
NIV, RSV, TEV
Ĕsh′tŏn   ESH tahn   *KJV, NAS, NIV, RSV,*
TEV
Ĕs′lī   ESS ligh   *KJV, NIV, RSV, TEV*

Ĕs′rŏm   ESS rahm   *KJV*
Ĕs′thĕr   ESS thur, ESS tur   *KJV, NAS,*
NIV, RSV, TEV
Ē′tăm   EE tam   *KJV, NAS, NIV, RSV, TEV*
Ē′thăm   EE tham   *KJV, NAS, NIV, RSV,*
TEV
Ē′than   EE thuhn   *KJV, NAS, NIV, RSV,*
TEV
Ĕth′a̍·nĭm   ETH uh nim   *KJV, NAS, NIV,*
RSV, TEV
Ĕth-bā′ăl   eth-BAY uhl   *KJV, NAS, NIV,*
RSV, TEV
Ē′thĕr   EE thur   *KJV, NAS, NIV, RSV,*
TEV
Ē·thĭ·ō′pĭ·a̍   ee thih OH pih uh   *KJV,*
NAS, RSV, TEV
Ē·thĭ·ō′pĭ·an   ee thih OH pih uhn   *KJV,*
NAS, NIV, RSV, TEV
Ĕth-Kā′zĭn   eth-KAY zihn   *NIV*
Ĕth·kā′zĭn   eth KAY zin   *KJV, NAS, RSV,*
TEV
Ĕth′năn   ETH nan   *KJV, NAS, NIV, RSV,*
TEV
Ĕth′nī   ETH nigh   *KJV, NAS, NIV, RSV,*
TEV
Ēu·bū′lŭs   yoo BYOO luhs   *KJV, NAS,*
NIV, RSV, TEV
Ēu′nĭce   YOO niss, yoo NIH seh
KJV, NAS, NIV, RSV, TEV
Ēu·ō′dĭ′a̍   yoo OH dih uh   *NAS, NIV,*
RSV, TEV
Eu·ō′dĭ·as   yoo OH dih uhs   *KJV*
Ēu·phrā′tēs̲   yoo FRAY teez   *KJV,*
NAS, NIV, RSV, TEV
Ēu·rŏc′ly̍·dŏn   yoo RAHK lih dahn
KJV
Ēu·răq′uĭ·lō   yoo RAK wih loh   *KJV,*
NAS
Ēu′ty̍·chŭs   YOO tih kuhs   *KJV, NAS,*
NIV, RSV, TEV
Ēve   EEV   *KJV, NAS, NIV, RSV, TEV*
Ē′vī   EE vigh   *KJV, NAS, NIV, RSV, TEV*
Ē′vĭl-mê·rō′dăch   EE vil-mih ROH dak,
MER oh dak   *KJV, NAS, NIV, RSV,*
TEV
Ē′zàr   EE zur   *KJV*
Ĕz′bā·ī   EZ bay igh, EZ bigh   *KJV, NAS,*
NIV, RSV, TEV
Ĕz′bŏn   EZ bahn   *KJV, NAS, NIV, RSV,*
TEV
Ĕz·ē·kī′a̍s   ez uh KIGH uhs   *KJV*
Ē·zē′kī·ĕl   ih ZEE kih ehl, ih ZEEK
yuhl   *KJV, NAS, NIV, RSV, TEV*

Ē′zĕl   EE zel *KJV, NAS, NIV, TEV*
Ē′zĕm   EE zem *KJV, NAS, NIV, RSV, TEV*
Ē′zēr   EE zur *KJV, NAS, NIV, RSV, TEV*
Ē′zĭ·ŏn-ĝā′bēr   EE zih ahn-GAY bur *KJV*
Ē′zĭ·ŏn-ĝē′bēr   EE zih ahn-GEE bur *KJV, NAS, NIV, RSV, TEV*
Ĕz′nīte   EZ night *KJV, NAS*
Ĕz′rà   EZ ruh *KJV, NAS, NIV, RSV, TEV*
Ĕz′rah   EHZ ruh *NAS, NIV, RSV, TEV*
Ĕz′rå·hīte   EZ ruh hight *KJV, NAS, NIV, RSV, TEV*
Ĕz′rī   EZ righ *KJV, NAS, NIV, RSV, TEV*

F̲air-Hā′vĕn̲ṣ   FAYR-HAY vehnz *NAS, NIV*
Fē′lĭx   FEE liks *KJV, NAS, NIV, RSV, TEV*
Fēs′tŭs   FESS tuhs *KJV, NAS, NIV, RSV, TEV*
Fôr·tū·nā′tŭs.   fawr tyoo NAY tuhs *KJV, NAS, NIV, RSV, TEV*

Ḡā′àl   GAY uhl *KJV, NAS, NIV, RSV, TEV*
Ḡā′ăsh   GAY ash *KJV, NAS, NIV, RSV, TEV*
Ḡā′bà   GAY buh *KJV*
Ḡăb′bā·ī   GAB bay igh, gah BAY igh *KJV, NAS, NIV, RSV, TEV*
Ḡăb′bå·thà   GAB uh thuh *KJV, NAS,*

NIV, RSV, TEV
Ḡā′brĭ·ēl   GAY brih uhl *KJV, NAS, NIV, RSV, TEV*
Ḡăd   GAD *KJV, NAS, NIV, RSV, TEV*
Ḡăd′å·rà   GAD uh ruh *TEV*
Ḡăd′å·rēne   GAD uh reen, GAD uh ree nee *KJV, NAS, NIV, RSV, TEV*
Ḡăd′dī   GAD igh *KJV, NAS, NIV, RSV, TEV*
Ḡăd′dĭ·ēl   GAD ih uhl *KJV, NAS, NIV, RSV, TEV*
Ḡā′dī   GAY digh *KJV, NAS, NIV, RSV, TEV*
Ḡăd′īte   GAD ight *KJV, NAS, NIV, RSV, TEV*
Ḡā′hăm   GAY ham *KJV, NAS, NIV, RSV, TEV*
Ḡā′här   GAY hahr *KJV, NAS, NIV, RSV, TEV*
Ḡā′iŭs   GAY yuhs *KJV, NAS, NIV, RSV, TEV*
Ḡā′lăl   GAY lal *KJV, NAS, NIV, RSV, TEV*
Ḡå·lā′tià   guh LAY shuh *KJV, NAS, NIV, RSV, TEV*
Ḡå·lā′tian   guh LAY shuhn *KJV, NAS, NIV, RSV*
Ḡăl′ĕ·ĕd   GAL ih ed *KJV, NAS, NIV, RSV, TEV*
Ḡăl·ĭ·lē′àn   gal ih LEE uhn *KJV, NAS, NIV, RSV, TEV*
Ḡăl′ĭ·lēe   GAL ih lee *KJV, NAS, NIV, RSV, TEV*
Ḡăl′lĭm   GAL im *KJV, NAS, NIV, RSV, TEV*
Ḡăl′lĭ·ō   GAL ih oh *KJV, NAS, NIV, RSV, TEV*
Ḡā′măd   GAY mad *RSV, TEV*
Ḡå·mā′lĭ·ĕl   guh MAY lih ehl, guh MAYL yuhl *KJV, NAS, NIV, RSV, TEV*
Ḡăm′mad   GAM mud *NIV*
Ḡăm′må·dĭm   GAM uh dim *KJV, NAS, TEV*
Ḡā′mŭl   GAY muhl *KJV, NAS, NIV, RSV, TEV*
Ḡā′rĕb   GAY reb *KJV, NAS, NIV, RSV, TEV*
Ḡär′mīte   GAHR might *KJV, NAS, NIV, RSV, TEV*
Ḡăsh′mū   GASH myoo *KJV, NAS, TEV*
Ḡā′tăm   GAY tam, GAY tuhm *KJV, NAS, NIV, RSV, TEV*
Ḡăth   GATH *KJV, NAS, NIV, RSV, TEV*
Ḡăth-hē′phēr   gath-HEE fur *KJV, NAS,*

NIV, RSV, TEV
Găth-rĭm'mon   gath-RIM uhn   KJV,
NAS, NIV, RSV, TEV
Gā'zà   GAY zuh, GAH zuh   KJV, NAS,
NIV, RSV, TEV
Gā'zăth·īte   GAY zuhth ight   KJV
Gā'zēr   GAY zur   KJV
Gā'zēz   GAY zez   KJV, NAS, NIV, RSV, TEV
Gā'zīte   GAY zite   KJV, NAS, RSV
Găz'zam   GAZZ uhm   KJV, NAS, NIV,
RSV, TEV
Gē'bà   GHEE buh   KJV, NAS, NIV, RSV,
TEV
Gē'bàl   GHEE buhl   KJV, NAS, NIV,
RSV, TEV
Gē'bàl·īte   GHEE buhl ight   KJV, NAS,
NIV, RSV, TEV
Gē'bēr   GHEE bur   KJV, NAS, NIV, RSV,
TEV
Gē'bĭm   GHEE bim   KJV, NAS, NIV,
RSV, TEV
Gĕd·à·lī'ah   ged uh LIGH uh   KJV, NAS,
NIV, RSV, TEV
Gĕd'ē·on   GED ih uhn   KJV
Gē'dēr   GHEE dur   KJV, NAS, NIV, RSV,
TEV
Gē·dē'rah   gih DEE ruh   KJV, NAS, NIV,
RSV, TEV
Gē·dē'rà·thīte   gih DEE ruh thight   KJV,
NAS, NIV
Gē·dēr'īte   gih DEER ight, GED ih
right   KJV, NAS, NIV, RSV
Gē·dē'rŏth   gih DEE rahth   KJV, NAS,
NIV, RSV, TEV
Gĕd'ē·rō·thā'im   GED ih roh THAY im
KJV, NAS, NIV, RSV, TEV
Gē'dôr   GHEE dawr   KJV, NAS, NIV,
RSV, TEV
Gē·hä·rā'shim   ghee-hah RAY shim
ghee-HAHR uh shim   KJV, NAS, RSV
Gē·hā'zī   gih HAY zigh   KJV, NAS, NIV,
RSV, TEV
Gēl'ĭ·lŏth   GEL ih lahth, gih LIGH
lahth   KJV, NAS, NIV, RSV, TEV
Gē·māl'lī   gih MAL ligh   KJV, NAS, NIV,
RSV, TEV
Gēm·à·rī'ah   gem uh RIGH uh   KJV,
NAS, NIV, RSV, TEV
Gĕn·nēs'à·rĕt   geh NESS uh ret   KJV,
NAS, NIV, RSV, TEV
Gĕn'tīle   JEN tighl   KJV, NAS, NIV, RSV,
TEV
Gē·nū'băth   gih NYOO bath   KJV, NAS,
NIV, RSV, TEV

Gē'rà   GHEE ruh   KJV, NAS, NIV, RSV,
TEV
Gē'rah   GHEE ruh   KJV, NAS, RSV
Gē'rär   GHEE rahr   KJV, NAS, NIV, RSV,
TEV
Gĕr'à·sà   GEHR uh suh   TEV
Gĕr'à·sēnes   GER uh seens   KJV, NAS,
NIV, RSV
Gĕr'gē·sēnes   GUR guh seens   KJV
Gĕr'ĭ·zĭm   GER ih zim, gih RIGH zim
KJV, NAS, NIV, RSV, TEV
Gĕr'shom   GUR shuhm   KJV, NAS, NIV,
RSV, TEV
Gĕr'sho·mītes   GUHR shuh mights   RSV
Gĕr'shŏn   GUR shahn   KJV, NAS, NIV,
RSV, TEV
Gĕr'shŏn·īte   GUR shahn ight   KJV,
NAS, NIV, RSV, TEV
Gē'rüth   GHEE rooth   NAS, RSV
Gē'rüth-chĭm'hăm   GHEE rooth-KIM
ham   KJV
Gē'rüth-Kĭm'ham   GHEE ruth-KIM
huhm   NIV
Gĕsh'äm   GESH uhm, GEE shuhm
KJV, TEV
Gĕsh'àn   GESH uhn   KJV, NAS, NIV,
RSV, TEV
Gĕsh'ĕm   GESH ehm, GHEE shuhm
KJV, NAS, NIV, RSV, TEV
Gē'shûr   GEE shur   KJV, NAS, NIV, RSV,
TEV
Gē·shū'rī   gih SHOO righ, GESH yoo
righ   KJV
Gĕsh'ū·rīte   GESH yoo right   KJV, NAS,
NIV, RSV, TEV
Gē'thēr   GEE thur   KJV, NAS, NIV, RSV,
TEV
Gĕth·sĕm'à·nē   geth SEM uh nih   KJV,
NAS, NIV, RSV, TEV
Gē·ū'ēl   gih YOO uhl   KJV, NAS, NIV,
RSV, TEV
Gē'zēr   GEE zur   KJV, NAS, NIV, RSV,
TEV
Gĕz'rīte   GEZ right   KJV
Gī'ah   GIGH uh   KJV, NAS, NIV, RSV,
TEV
Gĭb'bär   GIB ahr   KJV, NAS, NIV, RSV,
TEV
Gĭb'bē·thŏn   GIB uh thahn   KJV, NAS,
NIV, RSV, TEV
Gĭb'ē·à   GIB ih uh   KJV, NAS, NIV, RSV,
TEV

Ḡĭb'ė·ăh   GIB ih uh   *KJV, NAS, NIV, RSV, TEV*

Ḡĭb'ė·ăth   GIB ih ath   *KJV, NAS*

Ḡĭb'ė·ăth·ė·lō'hĭm   GIHB ih ath eh LOH him   *RSV*

Ḡĭb'ė·ăth-hä·är'å·lŏth   GIB ih ath-hah AHR uh lahth   *KJV, NAS, NIV, RSV*

Ḡĭb'ė·å·thīte   GIB ih uh thight   *KJV, NAS, NIV*

Ḡĭb'ė·on   GIB ih uhn   *KJV, NAS, NIV, RSV, TEV*

Ḡĭb'ė·on·īte   GIB ih uhn ight   *KJV, NAS, NIV, RSV*

Ḡĭb'līte   GIB light   *KJV*

Ḡĭd·dăl'tī   gih DAL tigh   *KJV, NAS, NIV, RSV, TEV*

Ḡĭd'dĕl   GID uhl   *KJV, NAS, NIV, RSV, TEV*

Ḡĭd·ė·on   GID ih uhn   *KJV, NAS, NIV, RSV, TEV*

Ḡĭd·ė·ō'nī   gid ih OH nigh   *KJV, NAS, NIV, RSV, TEV*

Ḡī'dŏm   GIGH dahm   *KJV, NAS, NIV, RSV, TEV*

Ḡī'hon   GIGH hahn, GEE hohn   *KJV, NAS, NIV, RSV, TEV*

Ḡĭl'å·laĭ   GILL uh ligh   *KJV, NAS, NIV, RSV, TEV*

Ḡĭl·bō'å   gill BOH uh   *KJV, NAS, NIV, RSV, TEV*

Ḡĭl'ė·ăd   GILL ih uhd   *KJV, NAS, NIV, RSV, TEV*

Ḡĭl'ė·ăd·ite   GILL ih uhd ight   *KJV, NAS, NIV, RSV, TEV*

Ḡĭl'găl   GILL gal   *KJV, NAS, NIV, RSV, TEV*

Ḡī'lō   GIGH loh   *RSV, TEV*

Ḡī'lōh   GIGH loh   *KJV, NAS, NIV, RSV, TEV*

Ḡī'lō·nīte   GIGH loh night   *KJV, NAS, NIV, RSV, TEV*

Ḡĭm'zō   GIM zoh   *KJV, NAS, NIV, RSV, TEV*

Ḡī'năth   GIGH nath   *KJV, NAS, NIV, RSV, TEV*

Ḡĭn'nė·thō   GIHN ih thoh   *KJV, RSV*

Ḡĭn'nė·thoĭ   GIHN ih thoy   *NAS, TEV*

Ḡĭn·nė·thŏn   GIHN nih thahn   *KJV, NAS, NIV, RSV, TEV*

Ḡĭr'gå·shīte   GUR guh shight   *KJV, NAS, NIV, RSV, TEV*

Ḡĭr'gå·sīte   GUR guh sight   *KJV, RSV*

Ḡĭr'zīte   GUR zight   *KJV, NAS, NIV, RSV, TEV*

Ḡĭsh'på   GISH puh   *KJV, NAS, NIV, RSV, TEV*

Ḡĭs'på   GISS puh   *KJV*

Ḡĭt'tăh-hē'phēr   GIT tah-HEE fur   *KJV*

Ḡĭt'tā·ĭm   GIT ay im, gih TAY im   *KJV, NAS, NIV, RSV, TEV*

Ḡĭt'tīte   GIT ight   *KJV, NAS, NIV, RSV*

Ḡĭt'tĭth   GIT ith   *KJV, NAS*

Ḡī'zō·nīte   GIGH zoh night   *KJV, NAS, NIV, RSV, TEV*

Ḡō'äh   GO ah   *KJV, NAS, NIV, RSV, TEV*

Ḡō'äth   GO ath   *KJV*

Ḡŏb   GAHB   *KJV, NAS, NIV, RSV, TEV*

Ḡŏd   GAHD   *KJV, NAS, NIV, RSV, TEV*

Ḡŏg   GAHG   *KJV, NAS, NIV, RSV, TEV*

Ḡoĭ·ĭm   GOY im   *KJV, NAS, NIV, RSV, TEV*

Ḡō'lăn   GO lan   *KJV, NAS, NIV, RSV, TEV*

Ḡŏl'gō·thå   GAHL guh thuh, gahl GAHTH uh   *KJV, NAS, NIV, RSV, TEV*

Ḡo·lī'ăth   guh LIGH uhth   *KJV, NAS, NIV, RSV, TEV*

Ḡō'mēr   GO muhr   *KJV, NAS, NIV, RSV, TEV*

Ḡo·môr'rah   guh MAWR uh   *KJV, NAS, NIV, RSV, TEV*

Ḡō'shĕn   GO shuhn   *KJV, NAS, NIV, RSV, TEV*

Ḡō'zăn   GO zan   *KJV, NAS, NIV, RSV, TEV*

Ḡrē'cī·å   GREE shih uh, GREE shuh   *KJV*

Ḡrē'cian   GREE shuhn   *KJV, NIV, TEV*

Ḡrēece   GREES   *NAS, NIV, RSV*

Ḡrēek   GREEK   *NAS, NIV, RSV, TEV*

Ḡŭd·gō'dah   guhd GO duh   *KJV, NIV, RSV, TEV*

Ḡŭ'nī   GYOO nigh   *KJV, NAS, NIV, RSV, TEV*

Ḡŭ'nīte   GYOO night   *KJV, NAS, NIV, RSV, TEV*

Ḡŭr   GUHR   *KJV, NAS, NIV, RSV, TEV*

Ḡŭr-bā'al   guhr-BAY uhl   *KJV, NAS, NIV, RSV, TEV*

Hā′å·hăsh′tå·rī HAY uh HASH tuh righ *KJV, NAS, NIV, RSV, TEV*

Hå·bā′iåh huh BAY yuh, huh BIGH uh *KJV, NAS, RSV, TEV*

Hå′băk′kŭk huh BAK uhk *KJV, NAS, NIV, RSV, TEV*

Hăb′å·zĭ·nī′ah HAB uh zih NIGH uh, huh baz ih NIGH uh *KJV*

Hăb′åz·zĭ·nī′ah hab uh zih NIGH uh *NAS, NIV, RSV, TEV*

Hā′bôr HAY bawr *KJV, NAS, NIV, RSV, TEV*

Hăc·å·lī′ah hak uh LIGH uh *NAS, NIV, RSV, TEV*

Hăch·å·lī′ah hak uh LIGH uh *KJV*

Hå·chī′lah huh KIGH luh, HAK ih luh *KJV, NAS, RSV, TEV*

Hăch′mon HAK muhn *TEV*

Hăch′mō·nī HAK moh nigh, hak MOH nigh *KJV, NAS, RSV, TEV*

Hăch′mō·nīte HAK moh night *KJV, NAS, RSV*

Hăc′mo·nī HAK muh nigh *NIV*

Hăc′mo·nīte HAK muh night *NIV*

Hā′dăd HAY dad *KJV, NAS, NIV, RSV, TEV*

Hăd′åd-ē′zĕr HAD ad-EE zur, HAD ah DEE zuhr *KJV, NAS, RSV, TEV*

Hā′dăd-rĭm′mon HAY dad-RIM uhn *KJV, NAS, NIV, RSV, TEV*

Hā′där HAY dahr *KJV, NAS, RSV*

Hăd′är-ē′zĕr HAD ahr-EE zur, HAD uh REE zur *KJV, TEV*

Hå·dăsh′ah huh DASH uh *KJV, NAS, NIV, RSV, TEV*

Hå·dăs′sah huh DASS uh *KJV, NAS, NIV, RSV, TEV*

Hå·dăt′tah huh DAT uh *KJV, TEV*

Hā′dĕṣ HAY deez *NAS, NIV, RSV, TEV*

Hā′dĭd HAY did *KJV, NAS, NIV, RSV, TEV*

Hăd′lā·ī HAD lay igh *KJV, NAS, NIV, RSV, TEV*

Hå·dō′răm huh DOH ram *KJV, NAS, NIV, RSV, TEV*

Hā′drăch HAY drak, HAD rak *KJV, NAS, NIV, RSV, TEV*

Hă·ē′lĕph ha EE lef, hay EE lihf *NAS, NIV, RSV, TEV*

Hā′găb HAY gab *KJV, NAS, NIV, RSV, TEV*

Hăḡ′å·bȧ HAG uh buh *KJV, NAS, NIV, RSV, TEV*

Hăḡ′å·bah HAG uh buh *KJV, NAS, NIV, RSV, TEV*

Hā′găr HAY gahr *KJV, NAS, NIV, RSV, TEV*

Hăḡ′å·rēne HAG uh reen *KJV*

Hăḡ′är·ite HAG ahr ight *KJV*

Hā′ḡĕr·ite HAY guhr ite, HAG uh right *KJV*

Hăḡ′găi HAG igh, HAG ay igh *KJV, NAS, NIV, RSV, TEV*

Hăḡ′ḡē·dō′lĭm HAG eh DOH lihm, hag gih DOH lihm *NAS, NIV, RSV*

Hăḡ·ḡē′rī huh GHEE righ *KJV*

Hăḡ′ḡī HAG igh *KJV, NAS, NIV, RSV, TEV*

Hăḡ·ḡī′ah huh GIGH uh *KJV, NAS, NIV, RSV, TEV*

Hăḡ′ḡīte HAG ight *KJV, NAS, NIV, RSV*

Hăḡ′ḡīth HAG ith *KJV, NAS, NIV, RSV, TEV*

Hăḡ′rī HAG righ *KJV, NAS, NIV, RSV, TEV*

Hăḡ′rīte HAG right *KJV, NAS, NIV, RSV, TEV*

Hå·hī′rŏth huh HIGH rahth *NAS, RSV*

Hā′ī HAY igh *KJV*

Hå·kĕl′då·mȧ huh KEHL duh muh *NAS*

Hå·kī′lah huh KIGH luh *NIV*

Hăk·kå′tăn HAK uh tan *KJV, NAS, NIV, RSV, TEV*

Hăk′kō·rĕ HAK oh rih *TEV*

Hăk′kŏz HAK ahz *KJV, NAS, NIV, RSV, TEV*

Hå·kū′phȧ huh KYOO fuh *KJV, NAS, NIV, RSV, TEV*

Hā′lah HAY luh *KJV, NAS, NIV, RSV, TEV*

Hā′lăk HAY lak *KJV, NAS, NIV, RSV, TEV*

Hăl′hŭl HAL huhl *KJV, NAS, NIV, RSV, TEV*

Hā′lī HAY ligh *KJV, NAS, NIV, RSV,*

TEV
Hăl·lō′hĕsh   huh LOH hesh   *KJV, NAS, NIV, RSV, TEV*
Hăm   HAM   *KJV, NAS, NIV, RSV, TEV*
Hā′man   HAY muhn   *KJV, NAS, NIV, RSV, TEV*
Hā′măth   HAY math   *KJV, NAS, NIV, RSV, TEV*
Hā′măth·īte   HAY muhth ight   *KJV, NAS, NIV, RSV, TEV*
Hā′măth-zō′bah   HAY math-ZOH buh   *KJV, NAS, NIV, RSV*
Hăm′ītes   HAM ights   *NIV*
Hăm′màth   HAM uhth   *KJV, NAS, NIV, RSV, TEV*
Hăm·mê·dā′thà   ham mih DAY thuh   *KJV, NAS, NIV, RSV, TEV*
Hăm′mĕ·lĕch   HAM uh lek   *KJV*
Hăm·mŏl′ĕ·chĕth   hah MAHL eh keth, hah MOH lih keth   *NAS, RSV, TEV*
Hăm·mō′lĕ·kĕth   hah MOH lih keth, hah MAHL ih keth   *KJV, TEV*
Hăm′mon   HAM uhn   *KJV, NAS, NIV, RSV, TEV*
Hăm′moth-dôr   HAM uhth-dawr   *KJV, NAS, NIV, RSV, TEV*
Hăm′mū·ĕl   HAM yoo el   *KJV, NAS, NIV, RSV, TEV*
Hå·mō′nah   huh MOH nuh   *KJV, NAS, NIV, RSV, TEV*
Hā′mŏn-gŏg̱   HAY mahn-gahg   *KJV, NAS, NIV, RSV, TEV*
Hā′môr   HAY mawr   *KJV, NAS, NIV, RSV, TEV*
Hăm′răn   HAM ran   *KJV, NAS, RSV, TEV*
Hăm′ū·ĕl   HAM yoo el, huh MYOO uhl   *KJV*
Hā′mŭl   HAY muhl   *KJV, NAS, NIV, RSV, TEV*
Hā′mŭl·īte   HAY muhl ight, HAM yoo light   *KJV, NAS, NIV, RSV*
Hå·mū′tăl   huh MYOO t′l   *KJV, NAS, NIV, RSV, TEV*
Hå·năm′ê·ĕl   huh NAM ih el, HAN uh meel   *KJV, TEV*
Hăn′å·mĕl   HAN uh mehl   *NAS, NIV, RSV, TEV*
Hā′năn   HAY nan   *KJV, NAS, NIV, RSV, TEV*
Hăn′å·nĕl   HAN uh nehl, huhn NAN ehl   *NAS, NIV, RSV, TEV*
Hå·năn′ê·ĕl   huh NAN ih el, HAN uh neel   *KJV*
Hå·nā′nī   huh NAY nigh   *KJV, NAS, NIV,*

RSV, TEV
Hăn·å·nī′ah   han uh NIGH uh   *KJV, NAS, NIV, RSV, TEV*
Hā′nĕş   HAY neez   *KJV, NAS, NIV, RSV, TEV*
Hăn′ī·ĕl   HAN ih el   *KJV*
Hăn′nah   HAN uh   *KJV, NAS, NIV, RSV, TEV*
Hăn·nå′thŏn   HAN uh thahn   *KJV, NAS, NIV, RSV, TEV*
Hăn′nī·ĕl   HAN ih el   *KJV, NAS, NIV, RSV, TEV*
Hā′nŏch   HAY nahk   *KJV, NAS, NIV, RSV, TEV*
Hā′nŏch·īte   HAY nahk ight   *KJV, NAS, NIV, RSV*
Hā′nŭn   HAY nuhn   *KJV, NAS, NIV, RSV, TEV*
Hăph·rā′īm   haf RAY im   *KJV*
Hăph·å·rā′īm   haf uh RAY im   *KJV, NAS, NIV, RSV, TEV*
Hăp·pīz′zĕz   HAP ih zez   *KJV, NAS, NIV, RSV, TEV*
Hā′rà   HAY ruh   *KJV, NAS, NIV, RSV, TEV*
Hå·rā′dah   huh RAY duh, HAR uh duh   *KJV, NAS, NIV, RSV, TEV*
Hā′răn   HAY ran   *KJV, NAS, NIV, RSV, TEV*
Hā′rår   HAY ruhr   *TEV*
Hā′rå·rīte   HAY ruh right   *KJV, NAS, NIV, RSV, TEV*
Här′bĕl   HAHR behl   *TEV*
Här·bō′nà   hahr BOH nuh   *KJV, NAS, NIV, RSV*
Här·bō′nah   hahr BOH nuh   *KJV, NAS, TEV*
Hā′rĕph   HAY ref   *KJV, NAS, NIV, RSV, TEV*
Hā′rĕth   HAY reth, HER uhth   *KJV*
Här·haī′ah   hahr HIGH uh, hahr HAY uh   *KJV, NAS, NIV, RSV, TEV*
Här′hăs   HAHR hass   *KJV, NAS, NIV, RSV, TEV*
Här·hē′rĕş   hahr HEE reez   *RSV*
Här′hŭr   HAHR hur   *KJV, NAS, NIV, RSV, TEV*
Hā′rīm   HAY rim   *KJV, NAS, NIV, RSV, TEV*
Här′īph   HAHR if, HER if   *KJV, NAS, NIV, RSV, TEV*
Här-Mȧ·gĕd′ŏn   hahr-muh GED ′n   *KJV, NAS*
Här′mon   HAHR muhn   *NAS, NIV, RSV*

Här′nē·phēr   HAHR nuh fur *KJV, NAS,*
NIV, RSV, TEV

Hā′rŏd   HAY rahd *KJV, NAS, NIV, RSV,*
TEV

Hā′rŏd·īte   HAY rahd ight *KJV, NAS,*
NIV

Hả·rō′ĕh   huh ROH eh *KJV, NAS, NIV,*
RSV, TEV

Hā′rō·rīte   HAY roh right *KJV, NAS,*
NIV

Hả·rō′shĕth   huh ROH sheth *KJV, NIV*

Hả·rō′shĕth-hả·goı̄′ı̆m   huh ROH sheth-
huh GOY ı̆hm *RSV*

Hả·rō′shĕth-hả·goy′ı̆m   huh ROH sheth-
huh GOY ı̆hm *RSV*

Här′shà   HAHR shuh *KJV, NAS, NIV,*
RSV, TEV

Här′sı̆th   HAHR sith *KJV*

Hā′rŭm   HAY ruhm *KJV, NAS, NIV,*
RSV, TEV

Hả·rū′măph   huh ROO maf *KJV, NAS,*
NIV, RSV, TEV

Hả·rū′phīte   huh ROO fight *KJV, NAS,*
NIV, RSV

Hā′rŭz   HAY ruhz, HER uhz *KJV,*
NAS, NIV, RSV, TEV

Hăs·ả·dī′ah   hass uh DIGH uh *KJV,*
NAS, NIV, RSV, TEV

Hăs·ė·nū′ah   hass ih NYOO uh *KJV*

Hăsh·ả·bī′ah   hash uh BIGH uh *KJV,*
NAS, NIV, RSV, TEV

Hả·shăb′nah   huh SHAB nuh *KJV, NAS,*
NIV, RSV, TEV

Hăsh′ăb·nē′ah   HASH uhb NEE uh
TEV

Hăsh′ăb·nēı̄′ah   HASH uhb NEE uh
NAS, NIV, TEV

Hăsh·ăb·nī′ah   hash ub NIGH uh *KJV*

Hăsh·bá·dā′na   hash buh DAY nuh,
hash BAD uh nuh *KJV*

Hăsh·băd·dả·nah   hash BAD uh nuh
NAS, NIV, RSV, TEV

Hā′shĕm   HAY shem *KJV, NAS, NIV,*
RSV, TEV

Hăsh·mō′nah   hash MOH nuh *KJV,*
NAS, NIV, RSV, TEV

Hăsh′ŭb   HASH uhb, HAY shuhb *KJV*

Hả·shū′bah   huh SHOO buh *KJV, NAS,*
NIV, RSV, TEV

Hā′shŭm   HAY shuhm *KJV, NAS, NIV,*
RSV, TEV

Hăṣ′rah   HAZ ruh *KJV, NAS, NIV, RSV*

Hăs·sė·nā′ah   hass ih NAY uh *KJV,*
NAS, NIV, RSV, TEV

Hăs·sė·nū′ah   hass ih NYOO uh *KJV,*
NAS, NIV, RSV, TEV

Hăs′shŭb   HASS shuhb *KJV, NAS, NIV,*
RSV, TEV

Hăs·sō′phė·rĕth   hass SOH fib reth, hah
SOHF uh reth *NAS, NIV, RSV,*
TEV

Hả·sū′phà   huh SOO fuh *KJV, NAS, NIV,*
RSV, TEV

Hā·tă<u>ch</u>   HAY tak *KJV*

Hā′thă<u>ch</u>   HAY thak *NAS, NIV, RSV,*
TEV

Hā′thăth   HAY thath *KJV, NAS, NIV,*
RSV, TEV

Hả·tī′phà   huh TIGH fuh *KJV, NAS,*
NIV, RSV, TEV

Hả·tī′tà   huh TIGH tuh *KJV, NAS, NIV,*
RSV, TEV

Hăt′tı̆l   HAT il *KJV, NAS, NIV, RSV, TEV*

Hăt′tŭsh   HAT uhsh *KJV, NAS, NIV,*
RSV, TEV

Haūr′ăn   HAWR an *KJV, NAS, NIV,*
RSV, TEV

Hăv′ı̆·lah   HAV ih luh *KJV, NAS, NIV,*
RSV, TEV

Hā′vŏth-jā′ı̆r   HAY vahth-JAY ir *KJV*

Hăv′vŏth-jā′ı̆r   HAY vahth-JAY ihr
NAS, NIV, RSV

Hăz′ă·ĕl   HAZ ay el, huh ZAY el *KJV,*
NAS, NIV, RSV, TEV

Hả·zaı̄′ah   huh ZIGH uh, huh ZAY yuh
KJV, NAS, NIV, RSV, TEV

Hā′zär-ăd′där   HAY zahr-AD ahr *KJV,*
NAS, NIV, RSV, TEV

Hā′zär-ē′nan   HAY zahr-EE nuhn *KJV,*
NAS, NIV, RSV, TEV

Hā′zär-ē′nŏn   HAY zahr-EE nohn *KJV,*
RSV

Hā′zär-găd′dah   HAY zahr-GAD duh
KJV, NAS, NIV, RSV, TEV

Hā′zär-hăt′tı̆·cŏn   HAY zahr-HAT ih
kahn *KJV, NAS*

Hā′zär-mā′vĕth   HAY zahr-MAY veth
KJV, NAS, NIV, RSV, TEV

Hā′zär-shū′ăl   HAY zahr-SHOO uhl
KJV, NAS, NIV, RSV, TEV

Hā′zär-sū′sah   HAY zahr-SOO suh
KJV, NAS, NIV, RSV, TEV

Hā′zär-sū′sı̆m   HAY zahr-SOO sim
KJV, NAS, NIV, RSV, TEV

Hăz′ả·zŏn   HAZ uh zahn *TEV*

Hăz′ả·zŏn-Tā′mår   HAZ uh zahn-TAY

245

muhr *NAS, RSV*

Hăz′ĕ·lĕl·pō′nī HAZ uh lel POH nigh *KJV*

Hā′zĕr-Hăt′tĭ·cŏn HAY zuhr-HAT ih kahn *NAS, NIV, RSV*

Hȧ·zē′rĭm huh ZEE rim *KJV*

Hȧ·zē′rŏth huh ZEE rahth *KJV, NAS, NIV, RSV, TEV*

Hăz′ȇ·zŏn-tā′mȧr HAZ ih zahn-TAY mur *KJV, TEV*

Hā′zĭ·ĕl HAY zih el *KJV, NAS, NIV, RSV, TEV*

Hā′zō HAY zoh *KJV, NAS, NIV, RSV, TEV*

Hā′zôr HAY zawr *KJV, NAS, NIV, RSV, TEV*

Hā′zôr-hȧ·dăt′tah HAY zawr-huh DAT uh *KJV, NAS, NIV, RSV, TEV*

Hăz·zē·bā′ĭm haz uh BAY ihm *TEV*

Hăz·zĕ·lĕl·pō′nī haz zih lehl POH nigh *NAS, RSV, TEV*

Hē′bȇr HEE buhr *KJV, NAS, NIV, RSV, TEV*

Hĕb′ȇr·īte HEB ur ight *KJV, NAS, NIV, RSV*

Hē′brēw HEE broo *KJV, NAS, NIV, RSV, TEV*

Hē′brŏn HEE bruhn *KJV, NAS, NIV, RSV, TEV*

Hē′brŏn·īte HEE bruhn ight *KJV, NAS, NIV, RSV*

Hē′gȧì HEE gigh, HEG ay igh *KJV, NAS, NIV, RSV, TEV*

Hē′gē HEE ghee *KJV*

Hĕg′lam HEHG luhm *RSV*

Hē′läh HEE lah *KJV, NAS, NIV, RSV, TEV*

Hē′lam HEE luhm *KJV, NAS, NIV, RSV, TEV*

Hĕl′bah HEHL buh *KJV, NAS, NIV, RSV, TEV*

Hĕl′bŏn HEHL bahn *KJV, NAS, NIV, RSV, TEV*

Hĕl′dā·ī HEHL day igh, HEL digh *KJV, NAS, NIV, RSV, TEV*

Hē′lĕb HEE leb *KJV, NAS, RSV, TEV*

Hē′lĕch HEE lek *NIV, RSV*

Hē′lĕd HEE led *KJV, NAS, NIV, RSV*

Hē′lĕk HEE lek *KJV, NAS, NIV, RSV, TEV*

Hē′lĕk·īte HEE lek ight *KJV, NAS, NIV, RSV*

Hē′lĕm HEE lem *KJV, NAS, NIV, RSV*

Hē′lĕph HEE lef *KJV, NAS, NIV, RSV, TEV*

Hē′lĕz HEE lez *KJV, NAS, NIV, RSV, TEV*

Hē′lī HEE ligh *KJV, NIV, RSV, TEV*

Hē·lĭ·ŏp′o·lĭs hee lih AHP uh lihs *NAS, NIV, RSV, TEV*

Hĕl′kā·ī HEL kay igh, hel KAY igh *KJV, NAS, NIV, RSV, TEV*

Hĕl′kăth HEL kath *KJV, NAS, NIV, RSV, TEV*

Hĕl′kăth-hăz·zū′rĭm HEL kath-haz YOO rim *KJV, NAS, NIV, RSV*

Hĕl·lĕ·nĭs′tĭc hehl lih NIHS tihk *NAS*

Hĕl′·lĕ·nĭsts HEHL lih nihsts *KJV, RSV*

Hē′lŏn HEE lahn *KJV, NAS, NIV, RSV, TEV*

Hē′măm HEE mam *KJV, NAS, TEV*

Hē′man HEE muhn *KJV, NAS, NIV, RSV, TEV*

Hē′măth HEE math *KJV*

Hĕm′dăn HEM dan *KJV, NAS, NIV, RSV, TEV*

Hĕn HEN *KJV, NAS, NIV*

Hē′nȧ HEE nuh *KJV, NAS, NIV, RSV, TEV*

Hĕn′ȧ·dăd HEN uh dad, hen AY dad *KJV, NAS, NIV, RSV, TEV*

Hē′nŏch HEE nahk *KJV*

Hē′phȇr HEE fur *KJV, NAS, NIV, RSV, TEV*

Hē′phȇr·īte HEE fur ight *KJV, NAS, NIV, RSV*

Hĕph′zĭ·bah HEF zi buh *KJV, NAS, NIV, RSV, TEV*

Hē′rĕs Hee ress, HEE reez *KJV, NAS, NIV, RSV, TEV*

Hē′rĕsh HEE resh *KJV, NAS, NIV, RSV, TEV*

Hē′rĕth HEE reth *KJV, NAS, NIV, RSV, TEV*

Hēr′mȧs HUR muhs *KJV, NAS, NIV, RSV, TEV*

Hēr′mēs HUR meez *KJV, NAS, NIV, RSV, TEV*

Hēr·mŏg′ȇ·nēṣ hur MAHJ ih neez *KJV, NAS, NIV, RSV, TEV*

Hēr′mon HUR muhn *KJV, NAS, NIV, RSV, TEV*

Hēr′mon·īte HUR muhn ight *KJV*

Hēr′od HAIR uhd *KJV, NAS, NIV, RSV, TEV*

Hȇ·rō′dĭ·an hih ROH dih uhn *KJV, NAS, NIV, RSV, TEV*

Hȇ·rō′dĭ·às hih ROH dih uhs *KJV, NAS.*

NIV, RSV, TEV
Hĕ·rō′dĭ·on   hih ROH dih uhn   *KJV,
  NAS, NIV, RSV, TEV*
Hē′sĕd   HEE sed   *KJV*
Hĕsh′bŏn   HESH bahn   *KJV, NAS, NIV,
  RSV, TEV*
Hĕsh′mŏn   HESH mahn   *KJV, NAS, NIV,
  RSV, TEV*
Hĕs′lī   HESS ligh   *NAS*
Hĕth   HETH   *KJV, NAS, RSV, TEV*
Hĕth′lŏn   HETH lahn   *KJV, NAS, NIV,
  RSV, TEV*
Hĕz′ê·kī   HEZ ih kigh   *KJV*
Hĕz·ê·kī′ah   hez ih KIGH uh   *KJV, NAS,
  NIV, RSV, TEV*
Hē′zī·ŏn   HEE zi ahn   *KJV, NAS, NIV,
  RSV, TEV*
Hē′zĭr   HEE zur   *KJV, NAS, NIV, RSV,
  TEV*
Hĕz′rā·ī   HEZ ray igh   *KJV*
Hĕz′rō   HEZ roh   *KJV, NAS, NIV, RSV,
  TEV*
Hĕz′rŏn   HEZ rahn   *KJV, NAS, NIV, RSV,
  TEV*
Hĕz′rŏn·īte   HEZ rahn ight   *KJV, NAS,
  NIV, RSV, TEV*
Hĭd′dā·ī   HID day igh, hih DAY igh
  KJV, NAS, NIV, RSV, TEV
Hĭd′dê·kĕl   HID ih kel   *KJV, RSV*
Hī′ĕl   HIGH el   *KJV, NAS, NIV, RSV, TEV*
Hī·êr·ăp′ō·lĭs   high ur AHP oh liss   *KJV,
  NAS, NIV, RSV, TEV*
Hĭg·gā′iŏn   hih GAY yahn, hih GIGH
  ahn   *KJV, NAS, NIV, RSV, TEV*
Hī′lĕn   HIGH len   *KJV, NAS, NIV, RSV,
  TEV*
Hĭl·kī′ah   hil KIGH uh   *KJV, NAS, NIV,
  RSV, TEV*
Hĭl′lĕl   HIL el   *KJV, NAS, NIV, RSV, TEV*
Hĭn′nŏm   HIN ahm   *KJV, NAS, NIV, RSV,
  TEV*
Hī′rah   HIGH ruh   *KJV, NAS, NIV, RSV,
  TEV*
Hī′ram   HIGH ruhm   *KJV, NAS, NIV,
  RSV, TEV*
Hĭt′tīte   HIT tight   *KJV, NAS, NIV, RSV,
  TEV*
Hī′vīte   HIGH vight   *KJV, NAS, NIV,
  RSV, TEV*
Hĭz′kī   HIZ kigh   *KJV, NAS, NIV, RSV,
  TEV*
Hĭz·kī′ah   hiz KIGH uh   *KJV, NAS, NIV,
  RSV, TEV*
Hĭz·kī′jah   hiz KIGH juh   *KJV, RSV*

Hō′băb   HOH bab   *KJV, NAS, NIV, RSV,
  TEV*
Hō′bah   HOH buh   *KJV, NAS, NIV, RSV,
  TEV*
Hō·bā′iah   hoh BAY yuh, hoh BIGH
  uh   *KJV, NIV, RSV, TEV*
Hŏd   HAHD   *KJV, NAS, NIV, RSV, TEV*
Hō·dā′iah   hoh DAY yuh, hoh DIGH
  uh   *KJV*
Hō·dă·vī′ah   hoh duh VIGH uh   *KJV,
  NAS, NIV, RSV, TEV*
Hō′dĕsh   HOH desh   *KJV, NAS, NIV,
  RSV, TEV*
Hō′dĕ·văh   HOH dih vah, hoh DEE
  vah   *KJV, NAS, RSV*
Hō·dī′ah   hoh DIGH uh   *KJV, NAS, NIV,
  RSV, TEV*
Hō·dī′jah   hoh DIGH juh   *KJV*
Hŏg′lah   HAHG luh   *KJV, NAS, NIV,
  RSV, TEV*
Hō′hăm   HOH ham   *KJV, NAS, NIV, RSV,
  TEV*
Hō′lŏn   HOH lahn   *KJV, NAS, NIV, RSV,
  TEV*
Hō′măm   HOH mam   *KJV, NAS, NIV,
  RSV, TEV*
Hŏph′nī   HAHF nigh   *KJV, NAS, NIV,
  RSV, TEV*
Hŏph′rà   HAHF ruh   *NIV, RSV, TEV*
Hôr   HAWR   *KJV, NAS, NIV, RSV, TEV*
Hō′răm   HOH ram   *KJV, NAS, NIV, RSV,
  TEV*
Hō′rĕb   HOH reb   *KJV, NAS, NIV, RSV*
Hō′rĕm   HOH rem   *KJV, NAS, NIV, RSV,
  TEV*
Hō′rĕsh   HOH resh   *NAS, NIV, RSV, TEV*
Hôr-hăg·gĭd′găd   hawr-huh GIHD gad
  NAS, NIV, RSV
Hôr-hă·gĭd′găd   hawr-huh GID gad
  KJV, TEV
Hō′rĭ   HOH righ   *KJV, NAS, NIV, RSV,
  TEV*
Hō′rĭm   HOH rim   *KJV*
Hō′rīte   HOH right   *KJV, NAS, NIV, RSV,
  TEV*
Hôr′mah   HAWR muh   *KJV, NAS, NIV,
  RSV, TEV*
Hŏr·ō·nā′ĭm   hahr oh NAY im   *KJV,
  NAS, NIV, RSV, TEV*
Hŏr′ō·nīte   HAHR oh night   *KJV, NAS,
  NIV, RSV*
Hō′sah   HOH suh   *KJV, NAS, NIV, RSV,
  TEV*
Hō·şăn′nà   hoh ZAN nuh   *NAS, RSV*

Hō·sē′à hoh ZEE uh, hoh ZAY uh
KJV, NAS, NIV, RSV, TEV

Hō·shaî′ah hoh SHIGH uh, hoh SHAY
yuh *KJV, NAS, NIV, RSV, TEV*

Hŏsh′å·mà HOSH uh muh *KJV, NAS,
NIV, RSV, TEV*

Hō·shē′à hoh SHE uh *KJV, NAS, NIV,
RSV, TEV*

Hō′thăm HOH tham *KJV, NAS, NIV,
RSV, TEV*

Hō′thăn HOH than *KJV*

Hō′thĭr HOH thur *KJV, NAS, NIV, RSV,
TEV*

Hō′zā·ī HOH zay igh *KJV, NAS*

Hŭb′bah HUB uh *NIV*

Hŭk′kŏk HUHK ahk *KJV, NAS, NIV,
RSV, TEV*

Hū′kŏk HYOO kahk *KJV, NAS, NIV,
RSV, TEV*

Hŭl HUHL *KJV, NAS, NIV, RSV, TEV*

Hŭl′dah HUHL duh *KJV, NAS, NIV,
RSV, TEV*

Hŭm′tah HUHM tuh *KJV, NAS, NIV,
RSV, TEV*

Hū′phăm HYOO fam *KJV, NAS, NIV,
RSV, TEV*

Hū′phăm·īte HYOO fam ight *KJV,
NAS, NIV, RSV*

Hŭp′pah HUHP uh *KJV, NAS, NIV,
RSV, TEV*

Hŭp′pĭm HUHP im *KJV, NAS, NIV,
RSV, TEV*

Hûr HER *KJV, NAS, NIV, RSV, TEV*

Hū′rā·ī HYOO ray igh, hyoo RAY igh
KJV, NAS, NIV, RSV, TEV

Hū′răm HYOO ram *KJV, NAS, NIV,
RSV, TEV*

Hū′răm·à′bĭ HYOO ram AH bih *NAS,
NIV, RSV*

Hū′rī HYOO righ *KJV, NAS, NIV, RSV,
TEV*

Hū′shah HYOO shuh *KJV, NAS, NIV,
RSV, TEV*

Hū′shaì HYOO shigh *KJV, NAS, NIV,
RSV, TEV*

Hū′shăm HYOO sham *KJV, NAS, NIV,
RSV, TEV*

Hū′shåth·īte HYOO shuhth ight *KJV,
NAS, NIV, RSV*

Hū′shĭm HYOO shim *KJV, NAS, NIV,
RSV, TEV*

Hū′shītes HYOO shights *NIV*

Hŭz HUHZ *KJV*

Hŭz′zăb HUHZ ab *KJV*

Hȳ′mĕ·nāē′ŭs HIGH muh NEE uhs
NAS, NIV, RSV, TEV

Hȳ·mĕ·nē′ŭs high meh NEE uhs *KJV*

Ĭb′här IB hahr *KJV, NAS, NIV, RSV, TEV*

Ĭb′lĕ·am IB lih uhm *KJV, NAS, NIV,
RSV, TEV*

Ĭb·neì′ah ib NIGH uh, ib NEE yuh
KJV, NAS, NIV, RSV, TEV

Ĭb·nī′jah ib NIGH juh *KJV, NAS, NIV,
RSV, TEV*

Ĭb′rī IB righ *KJV, NAS, NIV, RSV, TEV*

Ĭb′săm IHB sam *NAS, NIV, RSV, TEV*

Ĭb′zăn IB zan *KJV, NAS, NIV, RSV, TEV*

Ĭch′å·bŏd IK uh bahd *KJV, NAS, NIV,
RSV, TEV*

Ī·cō′nĭ·um igh KOH nih uhm *KJV, NAS,
NIV, RSV, TEV*

Ĭd′å·lah ID uh luh, IGH duh luh *KJV,
NAS, NIV, RSV, TEV*

Ĭd′băsh ID bash *KJV, NAS, NIV, RSV,
TEV*

Ĭd′dō ID oh *KJV, NAS, NIV, RSV, TEV*

Ĭd′ū·mē′à ID yoo ME uh, IGH dyu ME
uh *KJV, NAS, NIV, RSV*

Ī·ē′zĕr igh EE zur *KJV, NAS, NIV, RSV,
TEV*

Ī·ē′zĕr·ītes igh EE zur ights *KJV, NAS,
NIV, RSV*

Ī′găl IGH gal *KJV, NAS, NIV, RSV, TEV*

Ĭg·då·lī′ah ig duh LIGH uh *KJV, NAS,
NIV, RSV, TEV*

Ī′gĕ·al IGH gih uhl *KJV*

Ī′im IGH im *KJV, NAS, NIV, RSV, TEV*

Ī′jĕ·àb′å·rĭm IGH jih-AB uh rim *KJV*

Ī′jŏn IGH jahn *KJV, NAS, NIV, RSV,
TEV*

Ĭk′kĕsh IK esh *KJV, NAS, NIV, RSV, TEV*

Ī′lā·ī IGH lay igh *KJV, NAS, NIV, RSV,
TEV*

Ĭl·lȳr′ĭ·cŭm ih LIHR ih kuhm *KJV,
NAS, NIV, RSV, TEV*

Ĭm′là IM luh *KJV, NAS*
Ĭm′lah IM luh *KJV, NAS, NIV, RSV, TEV*
Ĭm·män′ū·ĕl ih MAN yoo ehl *KJV, NAS, NIV, RSV, TEV*
Ĭm′mēr IM ur *KJV, NAS, NIV, RSV, TEV*
Ĭm′nà IM nuh *KJV, NAS, NIV, RSV, TEV*
Ĭm′nàh IM nuh *KJV, NAS, NIV, RSV, TEV*
Ĭm′mīte IM ight *KJV*
Ĭm′nītes IHM nights *NAS, NIV*
Ĭm′rah IM ruh *KJV, NAS, NIV, RSV, TEV*
Ĭm′rī IM righ *KJV, NAS, NIV, RSV, TEV*
Ĭn′dĭ·à IN dih uh *KJV, NAS, NIV, RSV, TEV*
Ĭ·ōb IGH ohb *NAS, RSV*
Ĭph·dē′iah if DEE yuh *NIV, RSV, TEV*
Ĭph·ė·dėí′ah if ih DIGH uh, if ih DEE yuh *KJV*
Ĭph′tah IF tuh *NAS, NIV, RSV, TEV*
Ĭph′tah-ĕl IF tuh-el *KJV, NAS, NIV, RSV, TEV*
Îr UR, ER *KJV, NAS, NIV, RSV, TEV*
Ĭ′rà IGH ruh *KJV, NAS, NIV, RSV, TEV*
Ĭ′răd IGH rad, IGH ruhd *KJV, NAS, NIV, RSV, TEV*
Ĭ′răm IGH ram *KJV, NAS, NIV, RSV, TEV*
Ĭ′rī IGH righ *KJV, NAS, NIV, RSV, TEV*
Ĭ·rī′jah igh RIGH juh *KJV, NAS, NIV, RSV, TEV*
Ĭr-nā′hăsh ur-NAY hash *KJV, NAS, NIV, RSV*
Ĭ′rŏn IGH rahn *KJV*
Ĭr′pė·ĕl UHR pih uhl *KJV, NAS, NIV, RSV, TEV*
Ĭr-shē′mĕsh ur-SHEE mesh *KJV, NAS, NIV, RSV, TEV*
Ĭ′rū IGH roo *KJV, NAS, NIV, RSV, TEV*
Ĭ·şāac IGH zik *KJV, NAS, NIV, RSV, TEV*
Ĭ·şal′ah igh ZAY uh *KJV, NAS, NIV, RSV, TEV*
Ĭs′cah ISS kuh *KJV, NAS, NIV, RSV, TEV*
Ĭs·câr′ĭ·ot iss KER ih uht *KJV, NAS, NIV, RSV, TEV*
Ĭsh′bah ISH buh *KJV, NAS, NIV, RSV, TEV*
Ĭsh′băk ISH bak *KJV, NAS, NIV, RSV, TEV*
Ĭsh′bī-bē′nŏb ISH bigh-BEE nahb *KJV, NAS, NIV, RSV, TEV*
Ĭsh-bō′shĕth ish-BOH sheth, ISH boh sheth *KJV, NAS, NIV, RSV, TEV*
Ĭsh′hŏd ISH hahd *KJV, NAS, NIV, RSV*

Ĭsh′ī ISH igh *KJV, NAS, NIV, RSV, TEV*
Ĭsh·ĭ′ah ish IGH uh *KJV*
Ĭsh·ĭ′jah ish IGH juh, igh SHIGH juh *KJV, NIV*
Ĭsh′mà ISH muh *KJV, NAS, NIV, RSV, TEV*
Ĭsh′mā·el ISH may el *KJV, NAS, NIV, RSV, TEV*
Ĭsh′mā·ĕl·īte ISH may el ight *KJV, NAS, NIV, RSV, TEV*
Ĭsh·maî′ah ish MIGH uh, ish MAY yuh *KJV, NAS, NIV, RSV, TEV*
Ĭsh·mê·raî ISH mih righ *KJV, NAS, NIV, RSV, TEV*
Ĭ′shŏd IGH shadh *KJV*
Ĭsh′pah ISH puh *KJV, NAS, NIV, RSV, TEV*
Ĭsh′păn ISH pan *KJV, NAS, NIV, RSV, TEV*
Ĭsh′tŏb ISH tahb *KJV*
Ĭsh′ū·ah ISH yoo uh *KJV*
Ĭsh′ū·ī ISH yoo igh *KJV*
Ĭsh′vah ISH vuh *KJV, NAS, NIV, RSV, TEV*
Ĭsh′vī ISH vigh *KJV, NAS, NIV, RSV, TEV*
Ĭsh′vīte ISH vight *KJV, NAS, NIV, RSV*
Ĭs·mà·chī′ah iss muh KIGH uh *KJV, NAS, RSV, TEV*
Ĭs·mā′iah iss MAY yuh, iss MIGH uh *KJV*
Ĭs·mà·kī′ah iss muh KIGH uh *NIV*
Ĭs′pah ISS puh *KJV*
Ĭş′rā·ĕl IZ ray el *KJV, NAS, NIV, RSV, TEV*
Ĭş′rā·ĕl·īte IZ ray el ight *KJV, NAS, NIV, RSV, TEV*
Ĭs′sà·chär ISS uh kahr *KJV, NAS, NIV, RSV, TEV*
Ĭs·shī′ah iss SHIGH uh *KJV, NAS, NIV, RSV, TEV*
Ĭs·shī′jah iss SHIGH juh *KJV, NAS, RSV, TEV*
Ĭs′ū·ah ISS yoo uh *KJV*
Ĭs′ū·ī ISS yoo igh *KJV*
Ĭ·tăl′ĭ·an igh TAL ih uhn *KJV, NAS, NIV, TEV*
Ĭt′à·lў IT uh lih *KJV, NAS, NIV, RSV, TEV*
Ĭ′thā·ī IGH thay igh, ITH ay igh, ITH igh *KJV, NAS, NIV, RSV, TEV*
Ĭth′à·mär ITH uh mahr *KJV, NAS, NIV, RSV, TEV*

Ĭth′ĭ·ĕl   ITH ih el   *KJV, NAS, NIV, RSV, TEV*

Ĭth′lah   ITH luh   *KJV, NAS, NIV, RSV, TEV*

Ĭth′mah   ITH muh   *KJV, NAS, NIV, RSV, TEV*

Ĭth′năn   ITH nan   *KJV, NAS, NIV, RSV, TEV*

Ĭth′rà   ITH ruh   *KJV, NAS, RSV*

Ĭth′răn   ITH ran   *KJV, NAS, NIV, RSV, TEV*

Ĭth′rē·ăm   ITH rih am   *KJV, NAS, NIV, RSV, TEV*

Ĭth′rīte   ITH right   *KJV, NAS, NIV, RSV, TEV*

Ĭt′tåh-kā′zĭn   IT uh-KAY zin   *KJV*

Ĭt′tā·ī   IT ay igh, ih TAY igh   *KJV, NAS, NIV, RSV, TEV*

Ĭt′ū·rāē′à   IHT yoo REE uh, igh tyoo REE uh   *NAS, RSV*

Ĭt·ū·rē′à   it yoo REE uh, igh tyoo REE uh   *KJV, NIV, TEV*

Ī′vah   IGH vuh   *KJV*

Ĭv′vah   IGH vuh   *NAS, NIV, RSV, TEV*

Ī·yē·ăb′å·rĭm   igh ee AB uh rim   *KJV, NAS, NIV, RSV*

Ī′yĭm   IGH yim   *KJV, NAS, NIV, RSV*

Ī′zē·här   IGH zih hahr, IZ ih hahr   *KJV*

Ĭz′ē·här·īte   IZ ih hahr ight   *KJV, TEV*

Ĭz′här   IZ hahr   *KJV, NAS, NIV, RSV, TEV*

Ĭz′här·īte   IHZ hahr ight, IHZ huh right   *NAS, NIV, RSV*

Ĭz·lī′ah   iz LIGH uh   *KJV, NAS, NIV, RSV, TEV*

Ĭz·rä·hī′ah   iz rah HIGH uh   *KJV, NAS, NIV, RSV, TEV*

Ĭz′rå·hīte   IZ ruh hight   *KJV, NAS, NIV, RSV, TEV*

Ĭz′rī   IZ righ   *KJV, NAS, NIV, RSV, TEV*

Ĭz·zī′ah   iz IGH uh   *KJV, NAS, NIV, RSV, TEV*

Jā′å·kăn   JAY uh kan   *KJV, NAS, RSV, TEV*

Jā′å·kå·nītes   JAY uh kuh nights   *NIV*

Jā′å·kō′bah   JAY uh KOH buh   *KJV, NAS, NIV, RSV, TEV*

Jā′å·là   JAY uh luh, jay AY luh   *KJV, NAS, NIV, RSV, TEV*

Jā′å·lah   JAY uh luh, jay AY luh   *KJV, NAS, RSV, TEV*

Jā′å·lăm   JAY uh lam, juh AY luhm   *KJV*

Jā′å·naì   JAY uh nigh   *KJV*

Jā′är   JAY ahr   *NAS, NIV, RSV*

Jā′å·rē·ôr′ē·ğĭm   JAY uh rih-AWR ih gim   *KJV, NAS, NIV, RSV*

Jā′å·rē·shī′ah   JAY uh rih SHIGH uh   *KJV, NAS, NIV, RSV, TEV*

Jā′å·sáū   JAY uh saw   *KJV*

Jā·äs′ī·ĕl   jay ASS ih el, jay AY sih el   *KJV, NAS, NIV, RSV, TEV*

Jā′å·sū   JAY uh soo, jay UH soo   *NAS, NIV, RSV, TEV*

Jā·äz′å·nī′ah   jay az uh NIGH uh   *KJV, NAS, NIV, RSV, TEV*

Jā′å·zēr   JAY uh zur, jay AY zur   *KJV*

Jā·å·zī′ah   jay uh ZIGH uh   *KJV, NAS, NIV, RSV, TEV*

Jā·ā′zī·ĕl   jay AY zih el   *KJV, NAS, NIV, RSV, TEV*

Jā′băl   JAY bal   *KJV, NAS, NIV, RSV, TEV*

Jăb′bŏk   JAB ahk   *KJV, NAS, NIV, RSV, TEV*

Jā′bĕsh   JAY besh   *KJV, NAS, NIV, RSV, TEV*

Jā′bĕsh-gĭl′ē·àd   JAY besh-GIL ih uhd   *KJV, NAS, NIV, RSV*

Jā′bĕz   JAY bez   *KJV, NAS, NIV, RSV, TEV*

Jā′bĭn   JAY bin   *KJV, NAS, NIV, RSV, TEV*

Jăb′nē·ĕl   JAB nih el, JAB neel   *KJV, NAS, NIV, RSV*

Jăb′nĕh   JAB neh   *KJV, NAS, NIV, RSV*

Jā′căn   JAY kan   *NAS, NIV, RSV, TEV*

Jā′chăn   JAY kan   *KJV*

Jā′chĭn   JAY kin   *KJV, NAS, RSV, TEV*

Jā′chĭn·īte   JAY kihn ight   *KJV, NAS, RSV*

Jā′cob   JAY kuhb   *KJV, NAS, NIV, RSV, TEV*

Jā′dà   JAY duh   *KJV, NAS, NIV, RSV, TEV*

Jā′dah   JAY duh   *NIV*

Jăd′daì   JAD digh   *NAS, NIV, RSV*

Jăd′dū·à JAD yoo uh, ja DYOO uh
 KJV, NAS, NIV, RSV, TEV
Jā′dŏn JAY dahn *KJV, NAS, NIV, RSV, TEV*
Jā′ĕl JAY uhl *KJV, NAS, NIV, RSV, TEV*
Jā′gŭr JAY gur *KJV, NAS, NIV, RSV, TEV*
Jäh JAH, YAH *KJV*
Jā′häth JAY hath *KJV, NAS, NIV, RSV, TEV*
Jā′hăz JAY haz *KJV, NAS, NIV, RSV, TEV*
Já·hä′zà juh HAY zuh *KJV*
Jā′hå·zī′ah JAY huh ZIGH uh *KJV*
Já·hä′zī·ĕl juh HAY zih el *KJV, NAS, NIV, RSV, TEV*
Jäh′dā·ī JAH day igh *KJV, NAS, NIV, RSV, TEV*
Jäh′dĭ·ĕl JAH dih el *KJV, NAS, NIV, RSV, TEV*
Jäh′dō JAH doh *KJV, NAS, NIV, RSV, TEV*
Jäh′lĕ·ĕl JA lih el, JA leel *KJV, NAS, NIV, RSV, TEV*
Jäh′lĕ·ĕl·īte JA lih el ight *KJV, NAS, NIV, RSV*
Jäh′mā·ī JA may igh *KJV, NAS, NIV, RSV, TEV*
Jäh′zah JA zuh *KJV, NAS, NIV, RSV, TEV*
Jäh′zĕ·ĕl JA zih el *KJV, NAS, NIV, RSV, TEV*
Jäh′zĕ·ĕl·īte JA zih el ight *KJV, NAS, NIV, RSV*
Jäh·zē′iah ja ZEE yuh *KJV, NAS, NIV, RSV, TEV*
Jäh′zĕ·rah JA zeh ruh *KJV, NAS, NIV, RSV, TEV*
Jäh′zĭ·ĕl JA zih el *KJV, NAS, NIV, RSV, TEV*
Jā′ir JAY ur *KJV, NAS, NIV, RSV, TEV*
Jā·ir·īte JAY ur ight *KJV, NAS, NIV, RSV*
Jaī′rŭs JIGH ruhs, JAY uh ruhs *KJV, NAS, NIV, RSV, TEV*
Jā′kan JAY kuhn *KJV*
Jā′kĕh JAY keh *KJV, NAS, NIV, RSV, TEV*
Jā′kĭm JAY kim *KJV, NAS, NIV, RSV, TEV*
Jā′kĭn JAY kin *NIV*
Jā′kĭ·nītes JAY kih nights *NIV*
Jā′lam JAY luhm *KJV, NAS, NIV, RSV, TEV*
Jā′lŏn JAY lahn *KJV, NAS, NIV, RSV, TEV*

Jăm′brĕṣ JAM breez *KJV, NAS, NIV, RSV, TEV*
Jāmeṣ JAYMZ *KJV, NAS, NIV, RSV, TEV*
Jā′mĭn JAY min *KJV, NAS, NIV, RSV, TEV*
Jā′mĭn·īte JAY min ight *KJV, NAS, NIV, RSV, TEV*
Jăm′lĕch JAM lek *KJV, NAS, NIV, RSV, TEV*
Jā′nä·ī JAY nay igh *KJV, NAS, NIV, RSV, TEV*
Jā′nĭm JAY nim *KJV, NIV, RSV, TEV*
Jăn′nà JAN uh *KJV*
Jăn′naì JAN igh, jah NAY igh, JAN nuh igh *NAS, NIV, RSV, TEV*
Jăn′nĕṣ JAN eez *KJV, NAS, NIV, RSV, TEV*
Já·nō′ah juh NOH uh *KJV, NAS, NIV, RSV, TEV*
Já·nō′hah juh NOH huh *KJV*
Jā′nŭm JAY nuhm *KJV, NAS*
Jā′phĕth JAY feth *KJV, NAS, NIV, RSV, TEV*
Já·phī′à juh FIGH uh *KJV, NAS, NIV, RSV, TEV*
Jăph′lĕt JAF let *KJV, NAS, NIV, RSV, TEV*
Jăph·lē′tī jaf LEE tigh, JAF li tigh *KJV*
Jăph′lē·tīte JAF lee tight, JAF lih tight *NAS, NIV, RSV, TEV*
Jā′phō JAY fo *KJV, TEV*
Jā′rah JAY ruh *KJV, NAS, RSV, TEV*
Jā′rĕb JAY reb *KJV, NAS, RSV, TEV*
Jā′rĕd JAY red *KJV, NAS, RSV, NIV*
Jâr·e·sī′ah jehr uh SIGH uh *KJV*
Jär′hà JAHR huh *KJV, NAS, NIV, RSV, TEV*
Jā′rĭb JAY rib *KJV, NAS, NIV, RSV, TEV*
Jär′mŭth JAHR muhth *KJV, NAS, NIV, RSV, TEV*
Já·rō′ah juh ROH uh *KJV, NAS, NIV, RSV, TEV*
Jäsh′år JASH uhr *NAS, NIV, RSV, TEV*
Jā′shĕn JAY shen *KJV, NAS, NIV, RSV, TEV*
Jā′shĕr (Jā′shàr) JAY shur *KJV, NAS*
Já·shō′bĕ·ăm juh SHOH bih am *KJV, NAS, NIV, RSV, TEV*
Jā′shŭb JAY shuhb, JASH uhb *KJV, NAS, NIV, RSV, TEV*
Já·shū′bī·lē′hĕm juh SHOO bigh-LEE

251

hem *KJV, NIV*
Jā'shŭb·īte   JAY shuhb ight, JASH uhb
  ight *KJV, NAS, NIV, RSV*
Jăs'ĭ·ĕl   JAS ih el, JAY sih el *KJV*
Jā'son   JAY suhn *KJV, NAS, NIV, RSV,*
  TEV
Jăth'nĭ·ĕl   JATH nih el *KJV, NAS, NIV,*
  RSV, TEV
Jăt'tĭr   JAT ur *KJV, NAS, NIV, RSV, TEV*
Jā'văn   JAY van *KJV, NAS, NIV, RSV,*
  TEV
Jā'zẽr   JAY zur *KJV, NAS, NIV, RSV,*
  TEV
Jā'zĭz   JAY ziz *KJV, NAS, NIV, RSV, TEV*
Jĕ'å·rĭm   JEE uh rim *KJV, NAS, NIV,*
  RSV, TEV
Jĕ·ăt'ĕ·raì   jih AT uh righ *KJV, NIV*
Jĕ·ăth'ĕ·raì   jee ATH uh righ, jee ATH
  ih righ *NAS, RSV, TEV*
Jĕ·bẽr·ĕ·chī'ah   jih ber ih KIGH uh *KJV,*
  NAS, RSV, TEV
Jĕ·bẽr·ĕ·kī'ah   jeh buhr ih KIGH uh *NIV*
Jē'bŭs   JEE buhs *KJV, NAS, NIV, RSV,*
  TEV
Jĕb'ū·sī   JEB yoo sigh *KJV*
Jĕb'ū·sīte   JEB yoo sight *KJV, NAS, NIV,*
  RSV, TEV
Jĕc·å·mī'ah   jek uh MIGH uh *KJV, TEV*
Jĕch·ĭ·lī'ah   jek ih LIGH uh *NAS*
Jĕch·ō·lī'ah   jek oh LIGH uh *KJV*
Jĕch·o·nī'ah   jehk uh NIGH uh *RSV*
Jĕch·ō·nī'ăs   jek oh NIGH uhs *KJV*
Jĕc·ō·lī'ah   jek oh LIGH uh *KJV, NAS,*
  NIV, RSV, TEV
Jĕc·ō·nī'ah   jek oh NIGH uh *KJV, NAS,*
  NIV, RSV
Jĕ·daì'ah   jih DIGH uh, jih DAY yuh
  KJV, NAS, NIV, RSV, TEV
Jĕ·dī'ā·ĕl   jih DIGH ay el *KJV, NAS,*
  NIV, RSV, TEV
Jĕ·dī'dah   jih DIGH duh *KJV, NAS, NIV,*
  RSV, TEV
Jĕd·ĭ·dī'ah   jed ih DIGH uh *KJV, NAS,*
  NIV, RSV, TEV
Jĕ·dû'thŭn   jih DYOO thuhn *KJV, NAS,*
  NIV, RSV, TEV
Jĕ·ē'zẽr   jih EE zur *KJV*
Jĕ·ē'zẽr·īte   jih EE zur ight *KJV*
Jē'gär-sā·hå·dū'thà   JEE gahr-say huh
  DYOO thuh *KJV, NAS, NIV, RSV,*
  TEV
Jĕ·hå·lē'lĕ·ĕl   jih huh LEE lih el *KJV*
Jĕ·hăl'lĕ·lĕl   jeh HAL lih lehl *NAS, NIV,*

RSV, TEV
Jē'hăth   JEE hath *NIV*
Jĕ·hăz'ĭ·ĕl   jih HAZ ih ehl *TEV*
Jĕh·dē'iah   jeh DEE yuh *KJV, NAS, NIV,*
  RSV, TEV
Jĕ·hĕz'ĕ·kĕl   jih HEZ ih kel, jih HEZ ek
  el *KJV, RSV*
Jĕ·hĕz'kĕl   jih HEHZ kehl *NAS, NIV,*
  TEV
Jĕ·hī'ah   jih HIGH uh *KJV, NAS, NIV,*
  RSV, TEV
Jĕ·hī'ĕl   jih HIGH el *KJV, NAS, NIV,*
  RSV, TEV
Jĕ·hī'ĕ·lī   jih HIGH uh ligh *KJV, NAS,*
  NIV, RSV, TEV
Jĕ·hī'ĕ'līte   jeh HIGH uh light *NAS*
Jĕ·hĭz·kī'ah   jee hiz KIGH uh *KJV, NAS,*
  NIV, RSV, TEV
Jĕ·hō'å·dah   jih HOH uh duh *KJV*
Jĕ·hō'ăd·dah   jeh HOH ad duh *NAS,*
  NIV, RSV, TEV
Jĕ·hō·ăd'dan   jee hoh AD uhn *KJV,*
  NAS, RSV
Jĕ·hō·ăd'din   jee hoh AD in *KJV, NAS,*
  NIV, RSV, TEV
Jĕ·hō·å·hăz   jih HOH uh haz *KJV, NAS,*
  NIV, RSV, TEV
Jĕ·hō'ăsh   jih HOH ash *KJV, NAS, NIV,*
  RSV, TEV
Jē·hō'hā·năn   jee huh HAY nan *KJV,*
  NAS, NIV, RSV, TEV
Jĕ·hoì'å·chin   jih HOY uh kin *KJV, NAS,*
  NIV, RSV, TEV
Jĕ·hoì'å·dà   jih HOY uh duh *KJV, NAS,*
  NIV, RSV, TEV
Jĕ·hoì'å·kĭm   jih HOY uh kim *KJV, NAS,*
  NIV, RSV, TEV
Jĕ·hoì'å·rĭb   jih HOY uh rib *KJV, NAS,*
  NIV, RSV, TEV
Jĕ·hŏn'å·dăb   jih HAHN uh dab *KJV,*
  NAS, NIV, RSV
Jĕ·hŏn'å'than   jih HAHN uh thuhn
  KJV, NAS, NIV, RSV, TEV
Jĕ·hō'ram   jih HOH ruhm *KJV, NAS,*
  NIV, RSV, TEV
Jĕ·hō·shăb'ĕ·ăth   jee hoh SHAB ih ath
  KJV, NAS, RSV
Jĕ·hŏsh'å·phăt   jih HAHSH uh fat *KJV,*
  NAS, NIV, RSV, TEV
Jĕ·hŏsh'ĕ·bà   jih HAHSH ih buh *KJV,*
  NAS, NIV, RSV, TEV
Jĕ·hŏsh'ū·à   jih HAHSH yoo uh *KJV*
Jĕ·hō'vah   jeh HOH vuh *KJV*
Jĕ·hō'vah-jī'rĕh   jeh HOH vuh-JIGH

reh *KJV*
Jĕ·hō′vah-nĭs′sī   jeh HOH vuh-NISS
igh *KJV*
Jĕ·hō′vah-shä lom′   jeh HOH vuh-shah
LOHM *KJV*
Jĕ·hŏz′å·băd   jih HAHZ uh bad *KJV,
NAS, NIV, RSV, TEV*
Jĕ·hŏz′å·dăk   jih HAHZ uh dak *KJV,
NAS, NIV, RSV, TEV*
Jĕ′hū   JEE hyoo *KJV, NAS, NIV, RSV,
TEV*
Jĕ·hŭb′bah   jih HUHB uh *KJV, NAS,
RSV, TEV*
Jĕ·hū′căl   jih HYOO kal *KJV, NAS, NIV,
RSV, TEV*
Jĕ′hŭd   JEE huhd *KJV, NAS, NIV, RSV,
TEV*
Jĕ·hū′dī   jih HYOO digh *KJV, NAS, NIV,
RSV, TEV*
Jĕ·hū·dī′jah   JEE hyoo DIGH juh *KJV*
Jĕ·hū·ĕl   jih HYOO el *KJV, RSV, TEV*
Jĕ′hŭsh   JEE huhsh *KJV, RSV*
Jĕ·ī′ĕl   jee IGH ehl *KJV, NAS, NIV, RSV,
TEV*
Jĕ·kăb′zēĕl   jih KAB zeel, jih KAB zih
el *KJV, NIV, RSV, TEV*
Jĕ·kăm′ē·ăm   jeh KAM eh am, jek uh
MEE am *KJV, NAS, NIV, RSV, TEV*
Jĕk·å·mī′ah   jek uh MIGH uh *KJV, NAS,
NIV, RSV, TEV*
Jĕ·kū′thī·ĕl   jih KYOO thih el *KJV, NAS,
NIV, RSV, TEV*
Jĕ·mī′må   jeh MIGH muh *KJV*
Jĕ·mī′mah   jeh MIGH muh *NAS, NIV,
RSV*
Jĕ·mī′nah   jeh MIGH nuh *TEV*
Jĕ·mū′ĕl   jih MYOO el *KJV, NAS, NIV,
RSV, TEV*
Jĕph′thāē   JEF thee *KJV*
Jĕph′thah   JEF thuh *KJV, NAS, NIV,
RSV, TEV*
Jĕ·phŭn′nĕh   jih FUN ee *KJV, NAS, NIV,
RSV, TEV*
Jĕ′rah   JEE ruh *KJV, NAS, NIV, RSV,
TEV*
Jĕ′răh′mē·ĕl   jih RAH mih el *KJV, NAS,
NIV, RSV, TEV*
Jĕ·răh′mē·ĕl·ite   jih RAH mih uhl ight
KJV, NAS, NIV, RSV
Jĕ′rĕd   JEE red *KJV, NAS, NIV, RSV,
TEV*
Jĕr′ĕ·maї   JER ih migh, jer ih MAY igh
KJV, NAS, NIV, RSV, TEV
Jĕr·ĕ·mī′ah   jer ih MIGH uh *KJV, NAS,
NIV, RSV, TEV*

Jĕr·ĕ·mī′às   jer ih MIGH uhs *KJV*
Jĕr′ĕ·mŏth   JER ih mahth *KJV, NAS,
NIV, RSV, TEV*
Jĕr′ĕ·mў   JER uh mih *KJV*
Jĕ·rī′ah   jih RIGH uh *KJV, NIV, RSV,
TEV*
Jĕr·ĭ′bā·ī   JER ih bay igh, jer ih BAY
igh *KJV, NAS, NIV, RSV, TEV*
Jĕr′ĭ·chō   JER ih koh *KJV, NAS, NIV,
RSV, TEV*
Jĕr′ĭ·ĕl   JER ih el, JEE rih el *KJV, NAS,
NIV, RSV, TEV*
Jĕ·rī′jah   jih RIGH juh *KJV, NAS, RSV,
TEV*
Jĕr′ĭ·mŏth   JER ih mahth *KJV, NAS,
NIV, RSV, TEV*
Jĕr′ĭ·ŏth   JER ih ahth *KJV, NAS, NIV,
RSV, TEV*
Jĕr·o·bō′am   jer uh BOH uhm *KJV,
NAS, NIV, RSV, TEV*
Jĕ·rō′hăm   jih ROH ham *KJV, NAS, NIV,
RSV, TEV*
Jĕr·ŭb·bā′àl   jer uh BAY uhl *KJV, NAS,
NIV, RSV, TEV*
Jĕ·rŭb′bĕ·shĕth   jih RUHB bih sheth
KJV, NAS, NIV, RSV
Jĕ·rū′ĕl   jih ROO el, JER oo el *KJV,
NAS, NIV, RSV*
Jĕ·rū′så·lĕm   jih ROO suh lem *KJV,
NAS, NIV, RSV, TEV*
Jĕ·rū′shà   jih ROO shuh *KJV, NAS, NIV,
RSV, TEV*
Jĕ·rü′shàh   jeh ROO shuh *NAS, RSV*
Jĕ·saï′ah   jih SIGH uh *KJV*
Jĕs·å·rē′lah   jess uh REE luh *NIV*
Jĕ·shaï′ah   jih SHIGH uh, jih SHAY
yuh *KJV, NAS, NIV, RSV, TEV*
Jĕ·shā′nah   jih SHAY nuh, JESH uh
nuh *KJV, NAS, NIV, RSV, TEV*
Jĕsh·å·rē′lah   jesh uh REE luh *KJV,
NAS, RSV*
Jĕ·shĕb′ĕ·ăb   jih SHEB ih ab *KJV, NAS,
NIV, RSV, TEV*
Jĕ′shĕr   JEE shur *KJV, NAS, NIV, RSV,
TEV*
Jĕ·shī′mŏn   jih SHIGH mahn, JESH ih
mahn *KJV, NAS, NIV, RSV*
Jĕ·shĭsh′aï   jih SHISH igh *KJV, NAS,
NIV, RSV, TEV*
Jĕsh·ō·haï′ah   jesh oh HIGH uh, jesh oh
HAY uh *KJV, NAS, NIV, RSV*
Jĕsh′ū·à (Jĕsh′ū·ah)   JESH yoo uh *KJV,
NAS, NIV, RSV, TEV*
Jĕ·shū′rŭn   jih SHOO ruhn, JESH yoo
ruhn *KJV, NAS, NIV, RSV*

Jĕ·sī′ah   jih SIGH uh   *KJV*

Jĕ·sĭm′ĭ·ĕl   jih SIM ih el   *KJV, NAS, NIV, RSV, TEV*

Jĕs′sĕ   JESS ih   *KJV, NAS, NIV, RSV, TEV*

Jĕs′ū·ī   JESS yoo igh   *KJV*

Jĕs′ū·īte   JESS yoo ight   *KJV*

Jĕ·sū′rŭn   jih SOO ruhn, JES yoo ruhn   *KJV*

Jē′sŭs   JEE zuhs   *KJV, NAS, NIV, RSV, TEV*

Jē′thēr   JEE thur   *KJV, NAS, NIV, RSV, TEV*

Jē′thĕth   JEE theth   *KJV, NAS, NIV, RSV, TEV*

Jĕth′lah   JETH luh   *KJV*

Jĕth′rō   JETH roh, JEE throh   *KJV, NAS, NIV, RSV, TEV*

Jē′tŭr   JEE tur   *KJV, NAS, NIV, RSV, TEV*

Jēu′ĕl   JOO el, jeh YOO el   *KJV, NAS, NIV, RSV, TEV*

Jē′ŭsh   JEE uhsh   *KJV, NAS, NIV, RSV, TEV*

Jē′ŭz   JEE uhz   *KJV, NAS, NIV, RSV, TEV*

Jēw   JOO   *KJV, NAS, NIV, RSV, TEV*

Jēw′ĕss   JOO ehs   *KJV, NAS, NIV, RSV*

Jēw′ĭsh   JOO ihsh   *NAS, NIV, RSV, TEV*

Jĕz·â·nī′ah   jez uh NIGH uh   *KJV, NAS, NIV, RSV, TEV*

Jĕz′ĕ·bĕl   JEZ uh bel   *KJV, NAS, NIV, RSV, TEV*

Jē′zēr   JEE zur   *KJV, NAS, NIV, RSV, TEV*

Jē′zēr·īte   JEE zur ight   *KJV, NAS, NIV, RSV*

Jĕ·zī′ah   jeh ZIGH uh, JEZ yuh   *KJV*

Jē′zĭ·ĕl   JEE zih el   *KJV, NAS, NIV, RSV, TEV*

Jĕz·lī′ah   jez LIGH uh   *KJV*

Jĕ·zō′ar   jih ZOH ur   *KJV*

Jĕz·râ·hī′ah   jez ruh HIGH uh   *KJV, NAS, NIV, RSV, TEV*

Jĕz′rēel   JEZ reel   *KJV, NAS, NIV, RSV, TEV*

Jĕz′rēel·īte   JEZ reel ight   *KJV, NAS, NIV, RSV*

Jĭb′săm   JIB sam   *KJV*

Jĭd′lăph   JID laf   *KJV, NAS, NIV, RSV, TEV*

Jĭm′nà   JIM nuh   *KJV*

Jĭm′nah   JIM nuh   *KJV*

Jĭm′nīte   JIM night   *KJV*

Jĭph′tah   JIF tuh   *KJV*

Jĭph′thah-ĕl   JIF thuh-el   *KJV*

Jō′äb   JOH ab   *KJV, NAS, NIV, RSV, TEV*

Jō′ah   JOH uh   *KJV, NAS, NIV, RSV, TEV*

Jō′å·häz   JOH uh haz, joh AY haz   *KJV, NAS, NIV, RSV, TEV*

Jō·ā′nan   joh AY nuhn, joh AN uhn   *NAS, NIV, RSV, TEV*

Jō·än′nà   joh AN uh   *KJV, NAS, NIV, RSV, TEV*

Jō′äsh   JOH ash   *KJV, NAS, NIV, RSV, TEV*

Jō′å·thäm   JOH uh tham   *KJV*

Jōb   JOHB   *KJV, NAS, NIV, RSV, TEV*

Jō′băb   JOH bab   *KJV, NAS, NIV, RSV, TEV*

Jŏch′ĕ·bĕd   JAHK uh bed   *KJV, NAS, NIV, RSV, TEV*

Jō′dà   JOH duh   *KJV, NAS, NIV, RSV, TEV*

Jō′ĕd   JOH ed   *KJV, NAS, NIV, RSV, TEV*

Jō′ĕl   JOH el   *KJV, NAS, NIV, RSV, TEV*

Jō·ē′lah   joh EE luh   *KJV, NAS, NIV, RSV, TEV*

Jō·ē′zēr   joh EE zur   *KJV, NAS, NIV, RSV, TEV*

Jŏg′bĕ·häh   JAHG bih ha   *KJV, NAS, NIV, RSV, TEV*

Jŏg′lī   JAHG ligh   *KJV, NAS, NIV, RSV, TEV*

Jō′hà   JOH huh   *KJV, NAS, NIV, RSV, TEV*

Jō·hä′nan   joh HAY nuhn   *KJV, NAS, NIV, RSV, TEV*

Jō·hän′nan   joh HAY nuhn   *TEV*

Jŏhn   JAHN   *KJV, NAS, NIV, RSV, TEV*

Jŏhn-Märk   JAHN-MAHRK   *TEV*

Joı′å·dà   JOY uh duh   *KJV, NAS, NIV, RSV*

Joı′å·kĭm   JOY uh kim   *KJV, NAS, NIV, RSV*

Joı′å·rĭb   JOY uh rib   *KJV, NAS, NIV, RSV, TEV*

Jŏk′dĕ·äm   JAHK dih am   *KJV, NAS, NIV, RSV, TEV*

Jō′kĭm   JOH kim   *KJV, NAS, NIV, RSV, TEV*

Jŏk′mĕ·äm   JAHK mih am   *KJV, NAS, NIV, RSV, TEV*

Jŏk′nĕ·äm   JAHK nih am   *KJV, NAS, NIV, RSV, TEV*

Jŏk′shăn   JAHK shan   *KJV, NAS, NIV, RSV, TEV*

Jŏk′tăn   JAHK tan   *KJV, NAS, NIV, RSV, TEV*

Jŏk′thĕ·ĕl   JAHK thih el, JAHK theel   *KJV, NAS, NIV, RSV, TEV*

Jŏn′å·dăb   JAHN uh dab   *KJV, NAS, NIV, RSV, TEV*

Jō′nah   JOH nuh   *KJV, NAS, NIV, RSV, TEV*

Jō′nam   JOH nuhm   *NIV, RSV, TEV*

Jō′năn   JOH nan   *KJV, TEV*

Jō′nàs   JOH nuhs   *KJV*

Jō′năth-ē′lĕm-rĕ·chō′kĭm   JOH nath-EE lem-rih KOH kim   *KJV, NAS*

Jŏn′å·than   JAHN uh thuhn   *KJV, NAS, NIV, RSV, TEV*

Jŏp′pà   JAHP uh   *KJV, NAS, NIV, RSV, TEV*

Jō′rah   JOH ruh   *KJV, NAS, NIV, RSV, TEV*

Jō′rā·ī   JOH ray igh   *KJV, NAS, NIV, RSV, TEV*

Jō′ram   JOH ruhm   *KJV, NAS, NIV, RSV, TEV*

Jôr′dan   JAWR d'n   *KJV, NAS, NIV, RSV, TEV*

Jō′rĭm   JOH rim   *KJV, NAS, NIV, RSV, TEV*

Jôr′kĕ·ăm   JAWR kih am   *KJV, NIV, RSV, TEV*

Jôr′kō·ăm   JAWR koh am   *KJV*

Jŏs′å·băd   JAHS uh bad   *KJV*

Jŏs′å·phăt   JAHS uh fat   *KJV*

Jō′sĕ   JOH sih   *KJV*

Jō′sĕch   JOH sek   *KJV, NAS, NIV, RSV, TEV*

Jŏs′ĕ·dĕch   JAHS uh dek   *KJV*

Jō′sĕph   JOH zif   *KIV, NAS, NIV, RSV, TEV*

Jō′sēṣ   JOH seez   *KJV, NAS, NIV, RSV*

Jō′shah   JOH shuh   *KJV, NAS, NIV, RSV, TEV*

Jŏsh′å·phăt   JAHSH uh fat   *KJV, NAS, NIV, RSV, TEV*

Jŏsh·å·vī′ah   jahsh uh VIGH uh   *KJV, NAS, NIV, RSV, TEV*

Jŏsh·bĕ·kā′shah   jahsh bih KAY shuh   *KJV, NAS, NIV, RSV, TEV*

Jō′shĕb   JOH sheb   *TEV*

Jō′shĕb-Băs·shē′bĕth   JOH sheb-bass SHE beth   *NAS, NIV, RSV, TEV*

Jŏsh·ĭ·bī′ah   jahsh ih BIGH uh   *KJV, NAS, NIV, RSV, TEV*

Jŏsh′ū·à   JAHSH yoo uh   *KJV, NAS, NIV, RSV, TEV*

Jō·sī′ah   joh SIGH uh   *KJV, NAS, NIV, RSV, TEV*

Jō·sī′as   joh SIGH uhs   *KJV*

Jŏs·ĭ·bī′ah   jahs ih BIGH uh   *KJV*

Jŏs·ĭ·phī′ah   jahs ih FIGH uh   *KJV, NAS, NIV, RSV, TEV*

Jŏt′bah   JAHT buh   *KJV, NAS, NIV, RSV, TEV*

Jŏt′băth   JAHT bath   *KJV*

Jŏt′bå·thah   JAHT buh thuh   *KJV, NAS, NIV, RSV, TEV*

Jō′tham   JOH thuhm   *KJV, NAS, NIV, RSV, TEV*

Jŏz′å·băd   JAHZ uh bad   *KJV, NAS, NIV, RSV, TEV*

Jō′zå·cär   JOH zuh kahr   *NAS, RSV, TEV*

Jŏz′å·chär   JAHZ uh kahr, JOH zuh kahr   *KJV*

Jŏz′å·dăk   JAHZ uh dak   *KJV, NAS, NIV, RSV, TEV*

Jū′bàl   JOO buhl   *KJV, NAS, NIV, RSV, TEV*

Jū′căl   JOO kal   *KJV, NAS, RSV*

Jū′dà   JOO duh   *KJV*

Jū·dāē′à   joo DEE uh   *TEV*

Jū′dah   JOO duh   *KJV, NAS, NIV, RSV, TEV*

Jū′dā·ĭsm   JYOO day ihsm   *NAS, NIV, RSV, TEV*

Jū′dàs   JOO duhs   *KJV, NAS, NIV, RSV, TEV*

Jū′das-Ĭs·căr′ĭ·ŏt   JOO duhs-iss KAR ih aht   *TEV*

Jūde   JOOD   *KJV, NAS, NIV, RSV, TEV*

Jū·dē′à   joo DEE uh   *KJV, NAS, NIV, RSV, TEV*

Jū·dē′an   joo DEE uhn   *NAS, NIV, TEV*

Jū′dĭth   JOO dith   *KJV, NAS, NIV, RSV, TEV*

Jū′lĭ·à   JOO lih uh, JOOL yuh   *KJV, NAS, NIV, RSV, TEV*

Jū′lĭ·ŭs   JOO lih uhs, JOOL yuhs   *KJV, NAS, NIV, RSV, TEV*

Jū′nĭ·à   JOO nih uh   *KJV*

Jū′nĭ·às   JOO nih uhs   *KJV, NAS, NIV, RSV, TEV*

Jū′pĭ·tēr   JOO pih tuhr   *KJV*

Jū′shăb-hē′sĕd   JOO shab-HEE sed   *KJV, NAS, NIV, RSV, TEV*

Jūs′tŭs   JUHS tuhs   *KJV, NAS, NIV, RSV, TEV*

Jŭ′tah   JUHT uh   *KJV*

Jŭt′tah   JUHT uh   *KJV, NAS, NIV, RSV, TEV*

Kăb′zė·ĕl   KAB zih el, KAB zeel *KJV, NAS, NIV, RSV, TEV*

Kā′dĕsh   KAY desh *KJV, NAS, NIV, RSV, TEV*

Kā′dĕsh-bär·nē′à   KAY desh-bahr NEE uh *KJV, NAS, NIV, RSV, TEV*

Kā′dĕsh-Mĕr′ĭ·bäh   KAY desh-MEHR ih bah *TEV*

Kăd′mĭ·ĕl   KAD mih el *KJV, NAS, NIV, RSV, TEV*

Kăd′mon·īte   KAD muhn ight *KJV, NAS, NIV, RSV, TEV*

Kain   KAYN *KJV, NAS, NIV, RSV, TEV*

Kaĭ′wän   KIGH wahn *RSV, TEV*

Kăl′lā·ī   KAL ay igh, KAL igh *KJV, NAS, NIV, RSV, TEV*

Kā′mŏn   KAY mahn *KJV, NAS, NIV, RSV, TEV*

Kā′nah   KAY nuh *KJV, NAS, NIV, RSV, TEV*

Kȧ·rē′ah   kuh REE uh *KJV, NAS, NIV, RSV, TEV*

Kär′kà   KAHR kuh *NAS, NIV, RSV, TEV*

Kär·kā′à   KAHR kay uh *KJV*

Kär′kôr   KAHR kawr *KJV, NAS, NIV, RSV, TEV*

Kär·nā·ĭm   kahr NAY ihm *NAS, NIV, RSV, TEV*

Kär′tah   KAHR tuh *KJV, NAS, NIV, RSV, TEV*

Kär′tăn   KAHR tan *KJV, NAS, NIV, RSV, TEV*

Kăt′tah   KAT uh *NAS*

Kăt′tăth   KAT ath *KJV, NIV, RSV, TEV*

Kē′bär   KEE bahr *NIV*

Kē′dàr   KEE duhr *KJV, NAS, NIV, RSV, TEV*

Kĕd′ė·mah   KED ih muh *KJV, NAS, NIV, RSV, TEV*

Kĕd′ė·mŏth   KED ih mahth, kih DEE moth *KJV, NAS, NIV, RSV, TEV*

Kē′dĕsh   KEE desh *KJV, NAS, NIV, RSV, TEV*

Kē′dĕsh-năph′tȧ·lī   KEY desh-NAF tuh ligh *NAS*

Kĕd·ôr·lā′ō·mēr   ked awr LAY oh muhr *NIV*

Kē·hė·lā′thah   kee hih LAY thuh, keh HEL uh thuh *KJV, NAS, NIV, RSV, TEV*

Kė·ī′lah   kih IGH luh *KJV, NAS, NIV, RSV, TEV*

Kė·laĭ′ah   kih LIGH uh, kih LAY yuh *KJV, NAS, NIV, RSV, TEV*

Kē′lăl   KEE lal *NIV, TEV*

Kė·lī′tà   kih LIGH tuh, KEL ih tuh *KJV, NAS, NIV, RSV, TEV*

Kē′lŭb   KEE luhb *NIV, TEV*

Kĕl′ü·hī   KEHL yoo high *NIV*

Kė·mū′ĕl   kih MYOO el, KEM yoo el *KJV, NAS, NIV, RSV, TEV*

Kē·nā′ȧ·nah   keh NAY uh nuh *NIV*

Kē′nan   KEE nuhn *KJV, NAS, NIV, RSV, TEV*

Kė·nā′nī   kih NAY nigh *NIV*

Kĕn·ȧ·nī′ah   ken uh NIGH uh *NIV*

Kē′năth   KEE nath *KJV, NAS, NIV, RSV, TEV*

Kē′năz   KEE naz *KJV, NAS, NIV, RSV, TEV*

Kē′nĕz   KEE nez *KJV*

Kē′nĕz·īte   KEE nez ight *KJV*

Kĕn′īte   KEN ight, KEE night *KJV, NAS, NIV, RSV, TEV*

Kĕn′ĭz·zīte   KEN iz zight *KJV, NAS, NIV, RSV, TEV*

Kē′phär-Ăm′mō·nī   KEE fahr-AM oh nigh *NIV*

Kė·phī′rah   kih FIGH ruh *NIV*

Kē′ran   KEE ruhn *NIV*

Kĕr′ĕn-hăp′pŭch   KER uhn-HAP uhk *KJV, NAS, NIV, RSV, TEV*

Kĕr′ė·thītes   KER ih thights *NIV*

Kē′rĭ·ŏth   KEE rih ahth *KJV, NAS, NIV, RSV, TEV*

Kē′rĭ·ŏth-hĕz′rŏn   KEE rih ath-HEZ rahn, KER ih ohth *KJV, NAS, NIV, RSV*

Kē′rĭth   KEE rith *NIV*

Kē′rŏs   KEE rahs *KJV, NAS, NIV, RSV, TEV*

Kē′rŭb   KEE ruhb *NIV*

Kĕs′ȧ·lŏn   KEHS uh lahn *NIV*

Kē′sĕd   KEE sed, KESS ed *NIV*

Kē′sĭl   KEE sihl *NIV*

256

Kĕ·sŭl′lŏth   kih SUHL ahth *NIV*
Kĕ·tū′rah   keh TYOO ruh *KJV, NAS, NIV, RSV, TEV*
Kĕ·zī′a   kih ZIGH uh *KJV*
Kĕ·zī′ah   keh ZIGH uh *NAS, NIV, RSV, TEV*
Kē′zĭb   KEE zib *NIV*
Kē′zĭz   KEE ziz *KJV, TEV*
Kĭb′rŏth-hăt·tā′å·vah   KIB rahth-hat TAY uh vuh *KJV, NAS, NIV, RSV, TEV*
Kĭb′zā·ĭm   KIB zay im, kib ZAY im *KJV, NAS, NIV, RSV, TEV*
Kĭ′don   KIGH d′n, KIGH dahn *KJV*
Kĭd′ron   KID ruhn *KJV, NAS, NIV, RSV, TEV*
Kĭl′ĕ·ab   KIHL ih ab, KIGH lih ab *NIV*
Kĭl′ĭ·on   KIHL ih ahn *NIV*
Kĭl′măd   KIHL mad *NIV*
Kĭm′hăm   KIM ham *NIV*
Kĭ′nah   KIGH nuh *KJV, NAS, NIV, RSV, TEV*
Kĭn′nĕ·rĕth   KIN ih reth *NIV*
Kĭ′ŏs   KIGH ahs *NIV*
Kĭr   KUR *KJV, NAS, NIV, RSV, TEV*
Kĭr-hâr′ĕ·sĕth   kur-HAR uh seth *KJV, NAS, NIV, RSV*
Kĭr-hā′rĕsh   kur-HAY resh *KJV*
Kĭr-hē′rĕs   kur-HEE ress *KJV, NAS*
Kĭr′ĭ·ath   KIR ih ath *KJV, NAS, NIV*
Kĭr·ĭ·å·thā′ĭm   kir ih uh THAY im *KJV, NAS, NIV, RSV, TEV*
Kĭr′ĭ·ăth-Är′bà   KIHR ih ath-AHR buh, KUHR ih ath *NAS, NIV, RSV, TEV*
Kĭr′ĭ·ăth-Ā′rĭm   KIHR ih ath-AY rihm, KUHR ih ath *NAS, RSV*
Kĭr′ĭ·ăth-Bā′ål   KIHR ih ath-BAY uhl, KUHR ih ath *NAS, NIV, RSV, TEV*
Kĭr′ĭ·ăth-Hū′zŏth   KIHR ih ath-HYOO zahth, KUHR ih ath *NAS, NIV, RSV*
Kĭr′ĭ·ăth-Jē′å·rĭm   KIHR ih ath-JEE uh rim, KUHR ih ath *NAS, NIV, RSV, TEV*
Kĭr′ĭ·ăth-Săn′nah   KIHR ih ath-SAN nuh, KUHR ih ath *NAS, NIV, RSV*
Kĭr′ĭ·ăth-Sē′phêr   KIHR ih ath-SEE fur, KUHR ih ath *NAS, NIV, RSV, TEV*
Kĭr′ĭ·ŏth   KIR ih ahth *KJV*
Kĭr′jăth   KIR jath *KJV*
Kĭr·jå·thā′ĭm   kir juh THAY im, kir jath AY im *KJV*
Kĭr′jăth-är′bà   KIR jath-AHR buh *KJV*
Kĭr′jăth-ā′rĭm   KIR jath-AY rim *KJV*

Kĭr′jăth-bā′ål   KIR jath-BAY uhl *KJV*
Kĭr′jăth-hū′zŏth   KIR jath-HYOO zahth *KJV*
Kĭr′jăth-jē′å·rĭm   KIR jath-JEE uh rim *KJV*
Kĭr′jăth-săn′nah   KIR jath-SAN uh *KJV*
Kĭr′jăth-sē′phêr   KIR jath-SEE fur *KJV*
Kĭsh   KISH *KJV, NAS, NIV, RSV, TEV*
Kĭsh′ī   KISH igh *KJV, NAS, NIV, RSV, TEV*
Kĭsh′ĭ·ŏn   KISH ih ahn *KJV, NAS, NIV, RSV, TEV*
Kĭ′shŏn   KIGH shahn *KJV, NAS, NIV, RSV, TEV*
Kĭs′lĕv   KISS lehv *NIV, TEV*
Kĭş′lŏn   KIZ lahn, KISS lahn *NIV*
Kĭs′lŏth-Tā′bôr   KISS lahth-TAY bawr *NIV*
Kĭ′sŏn   KIGH sahn *KJV*
Kĭth′lĭsh   KITH lish *KJV*
Kĭt′lĭsh   KIT lish *NIV*
Kĭt′rŏn   KIT rahn *KJV, NAS, NIV, RSV, TEV*
Kĭt′tĭm   KIT im *KJV, NAS, NIV, RSV*
Kīy′yŭn   KIGH yuhn *NAS*
Kō′à   KOH uh *KJV, NAS, NIV, RSV, TEV*
Kō′hăth   KOH hath *KJV, NAS, NIV, RSV, TEV*
Kō′hăth·īte   KOH hath ight *KJV, NAS, NIV, RSV, TEV*
Kō·laì′ah   koh LIGH uh, koh LAY yuh *KJV, NAS, NIV, RSV, TEV*
Kō′rah   KOH ruh *KJV, NAS, NIV, RSV, TEV*
Kôr′å·hītes   KAWR uh hights, KOH ruh hights *NAS, NIV, RSV*
Kō′răth·īte   KOH rath ight *KJV*
Kō·rā′zĭn   koh RAY zihn *NIV*
Kō′rĕ   KOH rih *KJV, NAS, NIV, RSV, TEV*
Kôr′hīte   KAWR hight *KJV*
Koüm   KOOM *NIV*
Kŏz   KAHZ *KJV, NAS, NIV, RSV, TEV*
Kŭb   KUHB *TEV*
Kü′ĕ   KOO eh *NAS, NIV, RSV*
Kūn   KOON *TEV*
Kū·shaì′ah   kyoo SHIGH uh *KJV, NAS, NIV, RSV, TEV*

257

Lā'a·dah   LAY uh duh   *KJV, NAS, NIV, RSV, TEV*

Lā'a·dan   LAY uh dan   *KJV*

Lā'ban   LAY buhn   *KJV, NAS, NIV, RSV, TEV*

Lă·bā'ŏth   la BAY ahth   *TEV*

Lā'chish   LAY kish   *KJV, NAS, NIV, RSV, TEV*

Lā'dan   LAY duhn   *NAS, NIV, RSV, TEV*

Lā'ĕl   LAY uhl   *KJV, NAS, NIV, RSV, TEV*

Lā'hăd   LAY had   *KJV, NAS, NIV, RSV, TEV*

Lå·haı'roı   luh HIGH roy, luh HAY roy   *KJV*

Lăh'măm   LA mam   *KJV, RSV, TEV*

Läh'màs   LAH muhs   *NAS, NIV*

Lăh'mī   LAH migh   *KJV, NAS, NIV, RSV, TEV*

Lā'ĭsh   LAY ish   *KJV, NAS, NIV, RSV, TEV*

Lā'ish·ah   LAY ish uh   *KJV, NAS, NIV, RSV, TEV*

Lā'kŭm   LAY kum   *KJV*

Lăk'kŭm   LAY kuhm, LAK uhm   *NAS, NIV, RSV, TEV*

Lā'mĕch   LAY mek   *KJV, NAS, NIV, RSV, TEV*

Lă·mĕn·tā'tions   la mehn TAY shuhnz   *NAS*

Lā·ŏd·ĭ·cē'a   lay ahd ih SEE uh   *KJV, NAS, NIV, RSV, TEV*

Lā·ŏd·ĭ·cē'an   lay ahd ih SEE uhn   *KJV, NAS, NIV, RSV*

Lăp'ĭ·dŏth   LAP ih dahth   *KJV*

Lăp'pĭ·dŏth   LAP pih dahth   *NAS, NIV, RSV, TEV*

Lå·sē'a   luh SEE uh   *KJV, NAS, NIV, RSV, TEV*

Lā'shà   LAY shuh   *KJV, NAS, NIV, RSV, TEV*

Lå·shâr'on   luh SHER uhn   *KJV, NAS, NIV, RSV, TEV*

Lă'tĭn   LA tihn   *NAS, NIV, TEV*

Lăz'å·rŭs   LAZ uh ruhs   *KJV, NAS, NIV, RSV, TEV*

Lē'ah   LEE uh   *KJV, NAS, NIV, RSV, TEV*

Lĕ·ăn'nŏth   lih AN ahth   *KJV*

Lĕ·bā'nà   lih BAY nuh   *KJV, NAS, NIV, RSV, TEV*

Lĕ·bā'nah   lih BAY nuh   *KJV, NAS, NIV, RSV, TEV*

Lĕb'å·non   LEB uh nuhn   *KJV, NAS, NIV, RSV, TEV*

Lĕ·bā'ŏth   lih BAY ahth, LEB ay ahth   *KJV, NAS, NIV, RSV*

Lĕb·bē'ŭs   luh BEE uhs   *KJV*

Lĕb·kă'maı   leb KAY migh, leb KUH may igh   *NAS, NIV*

Lē'bō-hā'măth   LEE boh-HAY math   *NAS, NIV*

Lĕ·bō'nah   lih BOH nuh   *KJV, NAS, NIV, RSV, TEV*

Lē'cah   LEE kuh   *KJV, NAS, NIV, RSV, TEV*

Lē'gīon   LEE juhn   *KJV, NAS, NIV, RSV, TEV*

Lē'hăb   LEE hab   *NAS, TEV*

Lē'hā·bīm   LEE hay bim, lih HAY bim   *KJV, NAS, RSV*

Lē'hå·bītes   LEE huh bights   *NIV*

Lē'hĕm   LEE hem   *RSV*

Lē'hī   LEE high   *KJV, NAS, NIV, RSV, TEV*

Lĕm'ū·ĕl   LEM yoo uhl   *KJV, NAS, NIV, RSV, TEV*

Lē'shĕm   LEE shem   *KJV, NAS, NIV, RSV*

Lĕ·tū'shĭm   lih TYOO shim, LET oo shim   *KJV, NAS, RSV, TEV*

Lĕ·tū'shītes   leh TYOO shights   *NIV*

Lĕ·ŭm'mīm   lih UHM mim   *KJV, NAS, RSV, TEV*

Lĕ·ŭm'ō·nītes   lih UHM oh nights   *NIV*

Lē'vī   LEE vigh   *KJV, NAS, NIV, RSV, TEV*

Lĕ·vī'å·than   lih VIGH uh thuhn   *NAS, NIV, RSV, TEV*

Lē'vīte   LEE vight   *KJV, NAS, NIV, RSV, TEV*

Lē·vīt'ĭ·căl   leh VIT ih kuhl   *NIV, RSV*

Lĭb'ĕr·tīne   LIB ur teen   *KJV*

Lĭb'nah   LIB nuh   *KJV, NAS, NIV, RSV, TEV*

Lĭb'nī   LIB nigh   *KJV, NAS, NIV, RSV, TEV*

Lĭb'nīte   LIB night   *KJV, NAS, NIV, RSV*

Lĭb′y̆·à   LIB ih uh, LIB yuh *KJV, NAS, NIV, RSV, TEV*

Lĭb·y̆·an   LIB ih uhn *KJV, NAS, NIV, RSV, TEV*

Lĭk′hī   LIK high *KJV, NAS, NIV, RSV, TEV*

Lī′nŭs   LIGH nuhs *KJV, NAS, RSV, TEV*

Lō·ăm′mī   loh AM igh *KJV, NAS, NIV*

Lōd   LOHD *KJV, NAS, NIV, RSV, TEV*

Lō-dē′bär   lo-DEE bahr *KJV, NAS, NIV, RSV, TEV*

Lō′ĭs   LOH iss *KJV, NAS, NIV, RSV, TEV*

Lôrd   LAWRD *KJV, NIV, RSV, TEV*

Lō-rū·hă′mah   loh-roo HA muh *KJV, NAS*

Lŏt   LAHT *KJV, NAS, NIV, RSV, TEV*

Lō′tăn   LOH tan *KJV, NAS, NIV, RSV, TEV*

Lū′bĭm   LYOO bim *KJV, NAS*

Lū′căs   LYOO kuhs *KJV*

Lū′çĭ·fer   LYOO sih fur *KJV*

Lū′çĭŭs   LYOO shuhs *KJV, NAS, NIV, RSV, TEV*

Lŭd   LUHD *KJV, NAS, NIV, RSV, TEV*

Lū′dĭm   LOO dim *KJV, NAS, RSV*

Lū′dītes   LYOO dights *NIV*

Lū′hĭth   LYOO hith *KJV, NAS, NIV, RSV, TEV*

Lūke   LYOOK *KJV, NAS, NIV, RSV, TEV*

Lŭz   LUHZ *KJV, NAS, NIV, RSV, TEV*

Ly̆c·ā·ō′nĭ·à   lik ay OH nih uh, ligh kay OH nih uh *KJV, NAS, RSV, TEV*

Ly̆c·ā·ō′nĭ·an   LIK ay OH nih uhn, lik ih OH nih uhn, ligh COH nih uhn *NAS, NIV, RSV*

Ly̆c′ĭ·à   LISS ih uh, LISH uh *KJV, NAS, NIV, RSV, TEV*

Ly̆d′dà   LID uh *KJV, NAS, NIV, RSV, TEV*

Ly̆d′ĭ·à   LID ih uh *KJV, NAS, NIV, RSV, TEV*

Ly̆d′ĭ·an   LID ih uhn *KJV, NAS, NIV*

Ly̆·sā′nĭ·as   ligh SAY nih uhs *KJV, NAS, NIV, RSV, TEV*

Ly̆s′ĭ·às   LISS ih uhs *KJV, NAS, NIV, RSV*

Ly̆s′trà   LISS truh *KJV, NAS, NIV, RSV, TEV*

Mā′à·cah   MAY uh kuh *KJV, NAS, NIV, RSV, TEV*

Mā′à·căth   MAY uh kath *NAS, RSV*

Mā′ăc·à·thīte   MAY ak uh thight *KJV, NAS, RSV*

Mā′à·chah   MAY uh kuh *KJV*

Mā·ăch′à·thīte   may AK uh thight *KJV*

Mā·à·dā′ī   may uh DAY igh, MAY uh digh *KJV, NAS, NIV, RSV, TEV*

Mā·à·dī′ah   may uh DIGH uh *KJV, NAS, NIV, RSV, TEV*

Mā·ā′ī   may AY igh, MAY igh *KJV, NAS, NIV, RSV, TEV*

Mā′à·lĕh-ă·crăb′bīm   MAY uh leh-a KRAB im *KJV*

Mā′à·răth   MAY uh rath *KJV, NAS, NIV, RSV, TEV*

Mā′à·rēh-gē′bà   MAY uh reh-GHEE buh *KJV, NAS, TEV*

Mā′à·saì   MAY uh sigh *NAS, NIV, RSV, TEV*

Mā·à·seì′ah   may uh SIGH uh, may uh SEE yuh *KJV, NAS, NIV, RSV, TEV*

Mā·à·sī′aì   may uh SIGH igh *KJV*

Mā′ăth   MAY ath *KJV, NAS, NIV, RSV, TEV*

Mā′ăz   MAY az *KJV, NAS, NIV, RSV, TEV*

Mā·à·zī′ah   may uh ZIGH uh *KJV, NAS, NIV, RSV, TEV*

Măc′băn·naì   MAK buh nigh *KJV, NIV*

Măc·bē′nah   mak BEE nuh *KJV, NIV*

Măç·ē·dō′nĭ·à   mass uh DOH nih uh *KJV, NAS, NIV, RSV, TEV*

Măç·ē·dō·nĭ·an   mass uh DOH nih uhn *NAS, NIV, RSV, TEV*

Măch′bà·naì   MAK buh nigh *KJV, NAS, RSV*

Măch′băn·naì   MAK buh nigh *TEV*

Măch·bē′nà   mak BEE nuh *NAS*

Măch·bē′nah   mak BEE nuh *KJV, RSV, TEV*

Mā′chī   MAY kigh *KJV, NAS, RSV, TEV*

Mā′chĭr   MAY kir *KJV, NAS, RSV, TEV*
Mā′chĭr-īte   MAY kir ight *KJV, NAS, RSV*
Măch·năd′ê·baı̈   mak NAD ih bigh *KJV, NAS, NIV, RSV, TEV*
Măch·pē′lah   mak PEE luh *KJV, NAS, NIV, RSV, TEV*
Măc·năd′ê·baı̈   mak NAD ih bigh *NIV*
Mā′daı̈   MAY digh, MAD ay igh *KJV, NAS, NIV, RSV, TEV*
Mā′dı̆·an   MAY dih uhn, muh DIGH uhn *KJV*
Măd·măn′nah   mad MAN nuh *KJV, NAS, NIV, RSV, TEV*
Măd′mĕn   MAD men *KJV, NAS, NIV, RSV, TEV*
Măd·mē′nah   mad MEE nuh *KJV, NAS, NIV, RSV, TEV*
Mā′dŏn   MAY dahn *KJV, NAS, NIV, RSV, TEV*
Măg′a·dăn   MAG uh dan *KJV, NAS, NIV, RSV, TEV*
Măg′bı̆sh   MAG bish *KJV, NAS, NIV, RSV, TEV*
Măg′då·là   MAG duh luh *KJV, NIV*
Măg′då·lĕn   MAG duh len *KJV*
Măg·då·lē′nê   mag duh LEE nih, MAG duh leen *KJV, NAS, NIV, RSV, TEV*
Măg′dı̆·ĕl   MAG dih el *KJV, NAS, NIV, RSV, TEV*
Mā′gı̄   MA jigh *KJV, NIV*
Mā′gŏg   MAY gahg *KJV, NAS, NIV, RSV, TEV*
Mā′gŏr-mı̆s·sā′bı̆b   MAY gahr-mih SAY bib, MISS uh bib *KJV, NAS, NIV*
Măg·pı̄′ăsh   MAG pih ash *KJV, NAS, NIV, RSV, TEV*
Mā′gūs   MAY guhs *KJV*
Må·hā′lab   muh HAY luhb *RSV, TEV*
Må·hā′lah   muh HAY luh *KJV, RSV, TEV*
Må·hā′lå·lē·ĕl   muh HAY luh lee el *KJV, NAS, NIV, RSV, TEV*
Mä·hăl′å·lêl   ma HAL uh lihl *NAS, NIV, TEV*
Mā′hå·lăth   MAY huh lath, ma HAY lath *NIV, RSV*
Mā′hå·lăth-lĕ·än′nŏth   MAY huh lath-lih AN ahth *KJV, TEV*
Mā′hå·lı̄   MAY huh ligh *KJV*
Mā·hå·nā′ı̆m   may huh NAY im *KJV, NAS, NIV, RSV, TEV*
Mā′hå·nĕh-dăn   MAY huh neh-dan *KJV, NAS, NIV, RSV*

Må·hâr′ā·ı̄   muh HEHR ay igh *KJV, NAS, NIV, RSV, TEV*
Mā′hăth   MAY hath *KJV, NAS, NIV, RSV, TEV*
Mā′hå·vı̄te   MAY huh vight *KJV, NAS, NIV, RSV*
Må·hā′zı̆·ŏth   muh HAY zih ahth *KJV, NAS, NIV, RSV, TEV*
Mā′hĕr-shăl′ăl-hăsh′băz   MAY her-SHAL al-HASH baz *KJV, NAS, NIV, RSV*
Măh′lah   MA luh *KJV, NAS, NIV, RSV, TEV*
Măh′lı̄   MA ligh *KJV, NAS, NIV, RSV, TEV*
Măh′lı̄te   MA light *KJV, NAS, NIV, RSV*
Măh′lŏn   MA lahn *KJV, NAS, NIV, RSV, TEV*
Mā′hŏl   MAY hahl *KJV, NAS, NIV, RSV, TEV*
Măh′sēı̈·ah   MAH see uh *NAS, NIV, RSV, TEV*
Mā′kăz   MAY kaz *KJV, NAS, NIV, RSV, TEV*
Măk·hē′lŏth   mak HEE lahth *KJV, NAS, NIV, RSV, TEV*
Mā′kı̄   MAY kigh *NIV*
Mā′kı̆r   MAY kuhr *NIV*
Mā′kı̆·rı̄tes   MAY kih rights *NIV*
Măk·kē′dah   ma KEE duh *KJV, NAS, NIV, RSV, TEV*
Măk′tĕsh   MAK tesh *KJV*
Măl′å·chı̄   MAL uh kigh *KJV, NAS, NIV, RSV, TEV*
Măl′căm   MAL kam, MAL kuhm *NAS, NIV, RSV, TEV*
Măl′chăm   MAL kam *KJV*
Măl′chı̄′ah   mal KIGH uh *KJV, RSV, TEV*
Măl′chı̄·ĕl   MAL kih el *KJV, NAS, RSV, TEV*
Măl′chı̄·ĕl·īte   MAL kih el ight *KJV, NAS, RSV, TEV*
Măl′chı̄′jah   mal KIGH juh, mal KIGH uh *NAS, RSV, TEV*
Măl′chı̄′răm   mal KIGH ram *KJV, NAS, RSV, TEV*
Măl′chı̄·shū′å   mal kigh SHOO uh *KJV, NAS, RSV, TEV*
Măl′chŭs   MAL kuhs *KJV, NAS, RSV, TEV*
Må·lē′lê·ĕl   muh LEE lih el, MAL ih leel *KJV*

Măl′kĭ-Shü′ä MAL kigh-SHOO ah *NIV*

Măl′kĭ-ĕl MAL kih ehl *NIV*

Măl′kĭ-ĕ-lītes MAL kih ih lights *NIV*

Măl-kī′jah mal KIGH juh *NIV*

Măl-kī′răm mal KIH rahm *NIV*

Măl′lŏ-thī MAL oh thigh *KJV, NAS, NIV, RSV, TEV*

Măl′lŭch MAL uhk *KJV, NAS, NIV, RSV, TEV*

Măl′lū-chī MAL yoo kigh *KJV, NAS, RSV, TEV*

Mal′tä MAWL tuh *NAS, NIV, RSV, TEV*

Măm′rĕ MAM rih *KJV, NAS, NIV, RSV, TEV*

Măn′å-ĕn MAN uh en *KJV, NAS, NIV, RSV, TEV*

Măn′å-hăth MAN uh hath *KJV, NAS, NIV, RSV, TEV*

Măn′å-hăth-ītes MAN uh HATH ights, man uh HAY thights *NAS, NIV, RSV*

Må-nä′hĕth-īte muh NAY heth ight *KJV*

Må-năs′sĕh muh NASS uh *KJV, NAS, NIV, RSV, TEV*

Må-năs′sīte muh NASS ight *KJV, NAS, NIV, RSV*

Må-nō′ah muh NOH uh *KJV, NAS, NIV, RSV, TEV*

Mā′ŏch MAY ahk *KJV, NAS, NIV, RSV, TEV*

Mā′ŏn MAY ahn *KJV, NAS, NIV, RSV, TEV*

Mā′ŏn-īte MAY ahn ight *KJV, NAS, NIV, RSV, TEV*

Mā′rà MAY ruh, MER uh *KJV, NAS, NIV, RSV*

Mā′räh MAH rah, MAY ruh *KJV, NAS, NIV, RSV, TEV*

Măr′å-lah MAHR uh luh *KJV, NAS, NIV*

Măr-å-năth′ä mahr uh NATH uh *KJV, NAS, TEV*

Măr′dŭk MAHR dyook *NAS, NIV*

Măr′ĕ-ăl MAR ih uhl *RSV, TEV*

Må-rē′shah muh REE shuh *KJV, NAS, NIV, RSV, TEV*

Măr′cŭs MAHR kuhs *KJV*

Märk MAHRK *KJV, NAS, NIV, RSV, TEV*

Mā′rŏth MAY rahth *KJV, NAS, NIV, RSV, TEV*

Măr-sē′nà mahr SEE nuh, MAHR sih nuh *KJV, NAS, NIV, RSV, TEV*

Măr′thà MAHR thuh *KJV, NAS, NIV, RSV, TEV*

Mā′rÿ MAY rih *KJV, NAS, NIV, RSV, TEV*

Măs′chĭl MAHS keel *KJV*

Măsh MASH *KJV, NAS, RSV*

Mā′shăl MAY shal *KJV, NAS, NIV, RSV, TEV*

Măs′rĕ-kah MASS rih kuh, mass REE kuh *KJV, NAS, NIV, RSV, TEV*

Măs′sà MASS uh *KJV, NAS, NIV, RSV, TEV*

Măs′sah MASS uh *KJV, NAS, NIV, RSV, TEV*

Må-thū′så-là muh THYOO suh luh *KJV*

Mā′trĕd MAY tred *KJV, NAS, NIV, RSV, TEV*

Mā′trī MAY trigh *KJV, NIV, TEV*

Mā′trītes MAY trights *NAS, RSV*

Măt′tan MAT uhn *KJV, NAS, NIV, RSV, TEV*

Măt′tå-nah MAT uh nuh, ma TAY nuh *KJV, NAS, NIV, RSV, TEV*

Măt-tå-nī′ah mat uh NIGH uh *KJV, NAS, NIV, RSV, TEV*

Măt′tå-thà MAT uh thuh *KJV, NAS, NIV, RSV, TEV*

Măt-tå-thī′ås mat uh THIGH uhs *KJV, NAS, NIV, RSV, TEV*

Măt′tåt-tah MAT uh tuh, mat TAT tuh *NAS, NIV, RSV, TEV*

Măt′tĕ-nàï MAT ih nigh, mat ih NAY igh *KJV, NAS, NIV, RSV, TEV*

Măt′thăn MAT than *KJV, NAS, NIV, RSV, TEV*

Măt′thăt MAT that *KJV, NAS, NIV, RSV, TEV*

Măt′thew̄ MATH yoo *KJV, NAS, NIV, RSV, TEV*

Măt-thī′ås muh THIGH uhs *KJV, NAS, NIV, RSV, TEV*

Măt-tī-thī′ah mat uh THIGH uh *KJV, NAS, NIV, RSV, TEV*

Măz′zå-rŏth MAZ uh rahth *KJV, RSV*

Mē′ah MEE uh *KJV*

Mĕ-ā′rah mih AY ruh, mih AHR uh *KJV, NAS, RSV, TEV*

Mĕ-bŭn′naï mih BUHN igh *KJV, NAS, NIV, RSV, TEV*

Mĕ-chē′rå-thīte mih KEE rah thight *KJV, NAS, RSV*

Mĕ-cō′nah mih KOH nuh, mee KOH nuh *NAS, RSV, TEV*

Mē′dăd MEE dad *KJV, NAS, NIV, RSV, TEV*

Mē′dăn MEE dan *KJV, NAS, NIV, RSV,*

TEV
Mēde MEED *KJV, NAS, NIV, RSV, TEV*
Mĕd′ĕ·bà MED uh buh *KJV, NAS, NIV, RSV, TEV*
Mē′dī·à MEE dih uh *KJV, NAS, NIV, RSV, TEV*
Mē′dī·an MEE dih uhn *KJV, NAS, NIV, RSV, TEV*
Mĕd·ĭ·tēr·rā′nē·an mehd ih tuhr RAY nih uhn *TEV*
Mĕ·gĭd′dō mih GID oh *KJV, NAS, NIV, RSV, TEV*
Mĕ·gĭd′dŏn mih GID ahn *KJV*
Mĕ·hēt′å·bēel mih HET uh beel *KJV*
Mĕ·hēt′å·bĕl mih HET uh bel *KJV, NAS, NIV, RSV, TEV*
Mĕ·hī′dà mih HIGH duh *KJV, NAS, NIV, RSV, TEV*
Mē′hīr MEE hur *KJV, NAS, NIV, RSV, TEV*
Mĕ·hō′lah mih HOH luh *TEV*
Mĕ·hō′lå·thīte mih HOH luh thight *KJV, NAS, NIV, RSV*
Mĕ·hū′jā·ĕl mih HYOO jay el *KJV, NAS, NIV, RSV, TEV*
Mĕ·hū′mǎn mih HYOO man *KJV, NAS, NIV, RSV, TEV*
Mĕ·hū′nĭm mih HYOO nim *KJV*
Mē·jär′kon mee-JAHR kuhn *KJV, NAS, NIV, RSV, TEV*
Mĕ·kē′rå·thīte meh KEE ruh thight *NIV*
Mĕ·kō′nah mih KOH nuh *KJV*
Mē′lah MEE luh, MELL uh *TEV*
Mĕl·å·tī′ah mel uh TIGH uh *KJV, NAS, NIV, RSV, TEV*
Mĕl′chī MEL kigh *KJV, NAS, RSV, TEV*
Mĕl·chī′ah mel KIGH uh *KJV*
Mĕl·chīs′ĕ·dĕk mel KIZ uh dek *KJV, TEV*
Mĕl·chī·shū′à mel kigh SHOO uh *KJV*
Mĕl·chīz′ĕ·dĕk mel KIZ uh dek *KJV, NAS, NIV, RSV, TEV*
Mē′lē·à MEE lee uh *KJV, NAS, NIV, RSV, TEV*
Mē′lĕch MEE lek, MEL ek *KJV, NAS, NIV, RSV, TEV*
Mĕl′ĭ·cū MEL ih kyoo *KJV*
Mĕl′ĭ·tà MEL ih tuh, meh LEET uh *KJV*
Mē′nī MEE nigh *TEV*
Mĕl′zär MEL zahr *KJV*
Mĕl′kī MEL kigh *NIV*
Mĕm′phĭs MIM fiss *KJV, NAS, NIV,*

RSV, TEV
Mĕ·mū′cǎn mih MYOO kan *KJV, NAS, NIV, RSV, TEV*
Mĕn′å·hĕm MEN uh hem *KJV, NAS, NIV, RSV, TEV*
Mē′nǎn MEE nan *KJV*
Mē′nĕ MEE nih *KJV, NAS, NIV, RSV*
Mĕn′nà MEN uh *KJV, NAS, NIV, RSV, TEV*
Mĕn·ū′hŏth men YOO hahth *KJV, RSV, TEV*
Mĕn′ū·ĭm MEN yoo im *KJV*
Mĕ·ŏn′ĕ·nĭm mih AHN ih nim *KJV*
Mĕ·ŏn′ō·thaĭ mih AHN oh thigh, mee OH no thigh *KJV, NAS, NIV, RSV, TEV*
Mĕph·ā′ăth mef AY ath *KJV, NAS, NIV, RSV, TEV*
Mĕ·phĭb′ō·shĕth meh FIB oh sheth *KJV, NAS, NIV, RSV, TEV*
Mē′răb MEE rab *KJV, NAS, NIV, RSV, TEV*
Mĕ·raĭ′ah mih RIGH uh, mih RAY yuh *KJV, NAS, NIV, RSV, TEV*
Mĕ·rā′iŏth mih RAY yahth, mih RIGH yoth *KJV, NAS, NIV, RSV, TEV*
Mĕ·rā′rī mih RAY righ *KJV, NAS, NIV, RSV, TEV*
Mĕ·rā′rīte mih RAY right *KJV, NAS, NIV, RSV, TEV*
Mĕr·å·thā′ĭm mer uh THAY im *KJV, NAS, NIV, RSV, TEV*
Mĕr·cū′rĭ·ŭs mur KYOO rih uhs *KJV*
Mē′rĕd MEE red *KJV, NAS, NIV, RSV, TEV*
Mĕr′ĕ·mŏth MER ih mahth *KJV, NAS, NIV, RSV, TEV*
Mē′rĕs MEE ress, MEE reez *KJV, NAS, NIV, RSV, TEV*
Mĕr′ĭ·bäh MER ih bah *KJV, NAS, NIV, RSV, TEV*
Mĕr′ĭ·bah-Kā′dĕsh MER ih buh-KAY desh *NAS, NIV*
Mĕr′ĭ·bäth MER ih bath *KJV, NAS*
Mĕr′ĭ·bäth-kā′dĕsh MEHR ih bahth-KAY desh *NAS, RSV*
Mĕr′ĭb-bā′ăl MER ib-BAY uhl *KJV, NAS, NIV, RSV, TEV*
Mĕr′ĭ·bŏth MER ih bahth *KJV*
Mĕ·rō′dǎch mih ROH dak, MER oh dak *KJV, RSV*
Mĕ·rō′dǎch-bǎl′å·dǎn mih ROH dak-BAL uh dan *KJV, NAS, NIV, RSV, TEV*

Mē′rŏm   MEE rahm   *KJV, NAS, NIV,*
RSV, TEV
Mē·rŏn′oth   mih RAHN uth   *TEV*
Mē·rŏn′ō·thīte   mih RAHN oh thight
KJV, NAS, NIV, RSV, TEV
Mē′rŏz   MEE rahz   *KJV, NAS, NIV, RSV,*
TEV
Mē′sĕch   MEE sek   *KJV*
Mē′shà   MEE shuh   *KJV, NAS, NIV, RSV,*
TEV
Mē′shăch   MEE shak   *KJV, NAS, NIV,*
RSV, TEV
Mē′sĕch   MEE sek   *KJV*
Mē′shĕch   MEE shek   *KJV, NAS, NIV,*
RSV, TEV
Mē′shĕk   MEE shehk   *TEV*
Mē·shĕl′ĕ·mī′ah   mih SHEL uh MIGH
uh   *KJV, NAS, NIV, RSV, TEV*
Mē·shĕz′å·bēel   mih SHEZ uh beel   *KJV*
Mē·shĕz′å·bĕl   mih SHEZ uh behl, meh
SHEHZ uh behl   *NAS, NIV, RSV, TEV*
Mē·shĭl′lĕ·mĭth   mih SHIL uh mith   *KJV,*
NAS, NIV, RSV, TEV
Mē·shĭl′lĕ·mŏth   mih SHIL uh mahth
KJV, NAS, NIV, RSV, TEV
Mē·shō′băb   mih SHOH bab   *KJV, NAS,*
NIV, RSV, TEV
Mē·shŭl′lam   mih SHUHL uhm   *KJV,*
NAS, NIV, RSV, TEV
Mē·shŭl′lĕ·mĕth   mih SHUHL uh meth
KJV, NAS, NIV, RSV, TEV
Mē·sō′bå·īte   mih SOH buh ight   *KJV*
Mĕs′o·po·tā′mĭ·à   MESS uh puh TAY
mih uh   *KJV, NAS, NIV, RSV, TEV*
Mĕs·sī′ah   muh SIGH uh   *KJV, NAS, NIV,*
RSV, TEV
Mĕs·sī′às   muh SIGH uhs   *KJV*
Mĕth′ĕg·ăm′mah   METH eg-AM uh,
MEE theg-AM uh   *KJV, NIV, RSV*
Mē·thū′sā·ĕl   mih THYOO say el   *KJV*
Mē·thū′sĕ·lah   mih THYOO zuh luh
KJV, NAS, NIV, RSV, TEV
Mē·thū′shå·ĕl   mih THYOO shih ehl,
meh THOO shuh ehl   *KJV, NAS,*
NIV, RSV, TEV
Mē·ū′nĭm   mih YOO nim   *KJV, NAS,*
NIV, RSV, TEV
Mē·ū′nītes   mih YOO nights, mee OO
nights   *NAS, NIV, RSV, TEV*
Mĕz′å·hăb   MEZ uh hab   *KJV, NAS, RSV,*
TEV
Mē·zō′bå·īte   mih ZOH bay ight   *KJV,*
NAS, NIV, RSV
Mī′å·mĭn   MIGH uh min   *KJV*

Mĭb′här   MIB hahr   *KJV, NAS, NIV, RSV,*
TEV
Mĭb′săm   MIB sam   *KJV, NAS, NIV, RSV,*
TEV
Mĭb′zär   MIB zahr   *KJV, NAS, NIV, RSV,*
TEV
Mī′cà   MIGH kuh, MAIK uh   *NAS, NIV,*
RSV, TEV
Mī′cah   MIGH kuh (Mī′chah)   *KJV,*
NAS, NIV, RSV, TEV
Mī·cai′ah   migh KAY yuh   *KJV, NAS,*
NIV, RSV, TEV
Mī′chà (Mī′cà)   MIGH kuh   *KJV*
Mī′chåel   MIGH kuhl, MIGH kay uhl
KJV, NAS, NIV, RSV, TEV
Mī·chai′ah   migh KIGH uh, migh KAY
yuh   *KJV, TEV*
Mī′chàl   MIGH kuhl   *KJV, NAS, NIV,*
RSV, TEV
Mĭch′màs   MIK muhs   *KJV, NAS, RSV*
Mĭch′măsh   MIK mash   *KJV, NAS, RSV,*
TEV
Mĭch′mĕ·thah   MIK mih thuh   *KJV, RSV,*
TEV
Mĭch′mĕ·thäth   MIK mih thath   *NAS,*
NIV
Mĭc′măsh   MIK mash   *NIV*
Mĭch′rī   MIK righ   *KJV, NAS, RSV, TEV*
Mĭch′tàm   MIK tam   *KJV*
Mĭc′rī   MIK righ   *NIV*
Mĭd′dĭn   MID in   *KJV, NAS, NIV, RSV,*
TEV
Mĭd′ĭ·an   MID ih uhn   *KJV, NAS, NIV,*
RSV, TEV
Mĭd′ĭ·an·īte   MID ih uhn ight   *KJV, NAS,*
NIV, RSV, TEV
Mĭd′ĭ·an·īt′ish   MID ih uhn IGHT ish
KJV
Mĭg′dăl-Ē′dĕr   MIG dal-EE dihr   *NIV*
Mĭg̱′dăl-ĕl   MIG dal-el   *KJV, NAS, NIV,*
RSV, TEV
Mĭg̱′dăl-găd   MIG dal-gad   *KJV, NAS,*
RSV, TEV
Mĭg̱′dŏl   MIG dahl   *KJV, NAS, NIV, RSV,*
TEV
Mĭg̱′rŏn   MIG rahn   *KJV, NAS, NIV, RSV,*
TEV
Mĭj′å·mĭn   MIJ uh min   *KJV, NAS, NIV,*
RSV, TEV
Mĭk′lŏth   MIK lahth   *KJV, NAS, NIV,*
RSV, TEV
Mĭk·nei′ah   mik NIGH uh, mik NEE
yuh   *KJV, NAS, NIV, RSV, TEV*
Mĭl′å·lai   MIL uh ligh, mil uh LAY igh

KJV, NAS, NIV, RSV, TEV

Mĭl′cah   MIL kuh   KJV, NAS, NIV, RSV, TEV

Mĭl′cŏm   MIL kahm   KJV, NAS, RSV, TEV

Mĭ·lē′tŭm   migh LEE tuhm   KJV

Mĭ·lē′tŭs   migh LEE tuhs   KJV, NAS, NIV, RSV, TEV

Mĭl′lō   MIL oh   KJV, NAS, RSV

Mĭ·nī′å·mĭn   mih NIGH uh min, min IGH uh min   KJV, NAS, NIV, RSV, TEV

Mĭn′nī   MIN igh   KJV, NAS, NIV, RSV, TEV

Mĭn′nĭth   MIN ith   KJV, NAS, NIV, RSV, TEV

Mĭph′kăd   MIF kad   KJV, TEV

Mĭr′ĭ·am   MIR ih uhm   KJV, NAS, NIV, RSV, TEV

Mĭr′mà   MUR muh   KJV

Mĭr′mah   MUHR muh, MIHR muh   NAS, NIV, RSV, TEV

Mĭs′găb   MISS gab   KJV, NAS

Mĭsh′â·ĕl   MISH eh uhl, MIGH shih uhl, MISH ay ehl, MIGH shay el   KJV, NAS, NIV, RSV, TEV

Mī′shăl   MIGH shal   KJV, NAS, NIV, RSV, TEV

Mī′shăm   MIGH sham   KJV, NAS, NIV, RSV, TEV

Mī′shê·àl   MIGH shih uhl   KJV

Mĭsh′mà   MISH muh   KJV, NAS, NIV, RSV, TEV

Mĭsh·măn′nah   mish MAN uh   KJV, NAS, NIV, RSV, TEV

Mĭsh′rā·īte   MISH ray ight   KJV, NAS, NIV, RSV, TEV

Mĭs′pär   MISS pahr   NAS, NIV, RSV

Mĭs′pĕ·rĕth   MISS puh reth   KJV, NAS, NIV, RSV, TEV

Mĭs′rê·phŏth-mā′ĭm   MISS rih fahth-MAY im   KJV, NAS, NIV, RSV, TEV

Mĭth′an   MIHTH uhn   TEV

Mĭth′cah   MITH kuh   KJV, RSV

Mĭth′kah   MIHTH kuh   NAS, NIV, TEV

Mĭth′nĭte   MITH night   KJV, NAS, NIV, RSV

Mĭth′rê·dăth   MITH rih dath   KJV, NAS, NIV, RSV, TEV

Mĭt·ў·lē′nê   mit uh LEE nih   KJV, NAS, NIV, RSV, TEV

Mī′zär   MIGH zahr   KJV, NAS, NIV, RSV, TEV

Mĭz′päh   MIZ pah   KJV, NAS, NIV, RSV, TEV

TEV

Mĭz′pĕh   MIZ peh   KJV, NAS, RSV

Mĭz′pär (Mĭş′pär)   MIZ pahr   KJV

Mĭz′rā·ĭm   MIZ ray im   KJV, NAS, NIV

Mĭz′zah   MIZ uh   KJV, NAS, NIV, RSV, TEV

Mnā′son   NAY suhn, M'NAY suhn   KJV, NAS, NIV, RSV, TEV

Mō′ăb   MOH ab   KJV, NAS, NIV, RSV, TEV

Mō′å·bĭte   MOH uh bight   KJV, NAS, NIV, RSV, TEV

Mō·å·bĭt′ess   moh uh BIGHT ess   NAS, NIV, RSV

Mō·å·dī′ah   moh uh DIGH uh   KJV, NAS, RSV, TEV

Mō·lā′dah   moh LAY duh, MAHL uh duh   KJV, NAS, NIV, RSV, TEV

Mō′lĕch   MOH lek   KJV, NAS, NIV, RSV, TEV

Mō′lĭd   MOH lid   KJV, NAS, NIV, RSV, TEV

Mō′lŏch   MOH lahk   KJV, NAS, NIV, RSV

Mō·răsh′tīte   moh RASH tight   KJV

Mō·răs′thīte   moh RASS thight, MOH rass thight   KJV, TEV

Môr′dĕ·caì   MAWR dih kigh   KJV, NAS, NIV, RSV, TEV

Mō′rĕh   MOH reh   KJV, NAS, NIV, RSV, TEV

Mō′rĕ·shĕth   MOH rih sheth   NAS, NIV, RSV, TEV

Mō′rĕ·shĕth-găth   MOH rih sheth-gath, MAWR esh eth-gath   KJV, NAS, NIV, RSV, TEV

Mō·rī′ah   moh RIGH uh   KJV, NAS, NIV, RSV, TEV

Mō·sē′rà (Mō·sē′rah)   moh SEE ruh   KJV, TEV

Mō·sē′rah   moh SEE ruh   KJV, NIV, RSV

Mō·şē′rŏth   moh ZEE rahth, moh SEE ruhht   NAS, NIV, TEV

Mō′şĕs   MOH ziss   KJV, NAS, NIV, RSV, TEV

Mō′zà   MOH zuh   KJV, NAS, NIV, RSV, TEV

Mō′zah   MOH zuh   KJV, NAS, NIV, RSV, TEV

Mŭp′pĭm   MUHP im   KJV, NAS, NIV, RSV, TEV

Mū′shī   MYOO shigh   KJV, NAS, NIV, RSV, TEV

Mū′shīte   MYOO shight   KJV, NAS, NIV, RSV

Mŭs′rī MYOOS righ *TEV*
Mŭth-lăb′bĕn muhth-LAB en *KJV*
Mȳ′rà MIGH ruh *KJV, NAS, NIV, RSV, TEV*
Mȳs′ĭ·à MISS ih uh, MISH ih uh *KJV, NAS, NIV, RSV, TEV*

Nā′ăm NAY am *KJV, NAS, NIV, RSV, TEV*
Nā′à·mah NAY uh muh *KJV, NAS, NIV, RSV, TEV*
Nā′à·man NAY uh muhn, NAY muhn *KJV, NAS, NIV, RSV, TEV*
Nā′à·mà·thīte NAY uh muh thight *KJV, NAS, NIV, RSV*
Nā′à·mīte NAY uh might *KJV, NAS, NIV, RSV*
Nā′à·rah NAY uh ruh *KJV, NAS, NIV, RSV, TEV*
Nā′à·raì NAY uh righ *KJV, NAS, NIV, RSV, TEV*
Nā′à·răn NAY uh ran *KJV, NAS, NIV, RSV*
Nā′à·răth NAY uh rath *KJV*
Nā′ăsh·ŏn NAY ash ahn, nay ASH ahn *KJV*
Nā·ăs′on nay ASS uhn *KJV*
Nā′băl NAY bal *KJV, NAS, NIV, RSV, TEV*
Nā′bŏth NAY bahth *KJV, NAS, NIV, RSV, TEV*
Nā′chŏn (Nā′cŏn) NAY kahn *KJV*
Nā′chôr NAY kawr *KJV*
Nä′cŏn NAH cahn *KJV, NAS, NIV, RSV, TEV*
Nā′dăb NAY dab *KJV, NAS, NIV, RSV, TEV*
Năg′gaì NAG igh, NAG ay igh *KJV, NAS, NIV, RSV, TEV*
Năg′gē NAG eh *KJV*
Nà·hāl′àl nuh HAL uhl *NAS, NIV, RSV, TEV*
Nà·hā′li·ĕl nuh HAY li el, nuh HAL ih

el *KJV, NAS, NIV, RSV, TEV*
Nà·hăl′lăl nuh HAL al *KJV, TEV*
Nā′hà·lŏl NAY huh lahl *KJV, NAS, NIV, RSV*
Nā′hăm NAY ham *KJV, NAS, NIV, RSV, TEV*
Nā·hà·mā′nī nay huh MAY nigh *KJV, NAS, NIV, RSV, TEV*
Nā′hà·raì NAY huh righ *KJV, NAS, NIV, RSV, TEV*
Nā′hà·rī NAY huh rih *KJV*
Nā′hăsh NAY hash *KJV, NAS, NIV, RSV, TEV*
Nā′hăth NAY hath *KJV, NAS, NIV, RSV, TEV*
Năh′bī NA bigh *KJV, NAS, NIV, RSV, TEV*
Nā′hôr NAY hawr *KJV, NAS, NIV, RSV, TEV*
Năh′shŏn NA shahn *KJV, NAS, NIV, RSV, TEV*
Nā′hŭm NAY huhm *KJV, NAS, NIV, RSV, TEV*
Nain NAYN, NAY in *KJV, NAS, NIV, RSV, TEV*
Nai′ŏth NAY ahth *KJV, NAS, NIV, RSV, TEV*
Nā·ō′mī nay OH mih *KJV, NAS, NIV, RSV, TEV*
Nā′phăth NAY fath *RSV*
Nā′phăth·dôr NAY fath dawr *RSV*
Nā′phĕth NAY feth *NAS*
Nā′phĭsh NAY fish *KJV, NAS, NIV, RSV, TEV*
Nā′phŏth NAY fahth *NIV*
Nā′phŏth-Dôr′ NAY fahth DAWR *NIV, RSV*
Năph′tà·lī NAF tuh ligh *KJV, NAS, NIV, RSV, TEV*
Năph′tà·lītes NAF tuh lights *NIV*
Năph′tuh NAF tuh *NAS*
Năph′tū·hītes NAF tyoo hights *NIV*
Năph′tū·hĭm NAF tyoo him *KJV, NAS, RSV*
Năr·cĭs′sŭs nahr SIS uhs *KJV, NAS, NIV, RSV, TEV*
Nā′shĭm NAY shihm, nuh SHIHM *TEV*
Nā′than NAY thuhn *KJV, NAS, NIV, RSV, TEV*
Nà·thăn′à·ĕl nuh THAN ay uhl *KJV, NAS, NIV, RSV, TEV*
Năth·à·nī′ah nath uh NIGH uh *TEV*

Nā'than-mē'lĕch NAY thuhn-MEE lek
  KJV, NAS, NIV, RSV, TEV
Nā'ŭm NAY uhm *KJV, TEV*
Năz·â·rēne' naz uh REEN, NAZ uh
  reen *KJV, NAS, NIV, RSV, TEV*
Năz'â·rĕth NAZ uh reth *KJV, NAS, NIV,
  RSV, TEV*
Năz'â·rīte NAZ uh right *KJV, NIV, RSV,
  TEV*
Năz'ī·rīte NAZ uh right *NAS*
Nē'ah NEE uh *KJV, NAS, NIV, RSV, TEV*
Nē·ăp'o·lĭs nih AP uh lihs *KJV, NAS,
  NIV, RSV, TEV*
Nē·â·rī'ah nee uh RIGH uh *KJV, NAS,
  NIV, RSV, TEV*
Nē'baî NEE bigh, NEB ay igh *KJV,
  NAS, NIV, RSV, TEV*
Nē·bā'jŏth nih BAY jahth *KJV*
Nē·baî'ŏth nih BIGH ahth, nih BAY
  yahth *KJV, NAS, NIV, RSV, TEV*
Nē·băl'lāt nih BAL uht *KJV, NAS, NIV,
  RSV, TEV*
Nē'băt NEE bat *KJV, NAS, NIV, RSV,
  TEV*
Nē'bō NEE boh *KJV, NAS, NIV, RSV,
  TEV*
Nē'bō-Sär'sĕ·kĭm NEE boh-SAHR seh
  kihm *NIV*
Nĕb·ū·chăd·nĕz'zàr neb yoo kad NEZZ
  ur *KJV, NAS, NIV, RSV, TEV*
Nĕb·ū·chăd·rĕz'zàr neb yoo kad REZ
  ur *KJV, RSV*
Nĕb·ū·shăş'băn neb yoo SHAZ ban
  KJV
Nĕb'ū·shăz'băn NEHB yoo SHAZ ban
  NAS, NIV, TEV
Nĕb'ū·zär·ā'dăn NEB yoo zahr AY
  dan *KJV, NAS, NIV, RSV, TEV*
Nē'chō (Nē'cō) NEE koh *KJV*
Nē'cō NEE koh *KJV, NAS, NIV, RSV,
  TEV*
Nĕd·â·bī'ah ned uh BIGH uh *KJV, NAS,
  NIV, RSV, TEV*
Nĕg'ĕb NEG ehb, NEH gehv *RSV*
Nē'ĝĕv NEH gehv *NAS, NIV*
Nē·ĝî'nah ne GEE nah *KJV*
Nĕĝ'ĭ·nŏth NEG ih nahth *KJV, NAS*
Nē·hĕl'am neh HEHL uhm *RSV*
Nē·hĕl'â·mīte nih HEL uh might *KJV,
  NAS, NIV*
Nē·hē·mî'ah nee huh MIGH uh *KJV,
  NAS, NIV, RSV, TEV*
Nē'hī·lŏth NEE hih lahth *KJV*

Nē'hŭm NEE huhm *KJV, NAS, NIV,
  RSV, TEV*
Nē·hŭsh'tà nih HUHSH tuh *KJV, NAS,
  NIV, RSV, TEV*
Nē·hŭsh'tăn nih HUHSH tan *KJV,
  NAS, NIV, RSV, TEV*
Nē·ī'ĕl nih IGH el, NEH el *KJV, NAS,
  NIV, RSV, TEV*
Nē'kĕb NEE keb *KJV*
Nē·kō'dà nih KOH duh *KJV, NAS, NIV,
  RSV, TEV*
Nĕm·ū·ĕl NEM yoo el, nih MYOO uhl
  KJV, NAS, NIV, RSV, TEV
Nĕm'ū·ĕl·īte NEM yoo el ight *KJV,
  NAS, NIV, RSV, TEV*
Nē'phĕĝ NEE feg, NEF eg *KJV, NAS,
  NIV, RSV, TEV*
Nĕph'ī·lĭm NEF uh lim *KJV, NAS, NIV,
  RSV*
Nē'phĭsh NEE fish *KJV*
Nē·phĭsh'ē·sĭm nih FISH uh sim *KJV*
Nē·phī'sĭm neh FIGH sihm, nih PHIGH
  sihm *NAS, RSV, TEV*
Nĕph'thà·lĭm NEF thuh lim *KJV*
Nĕph·tō'ah nef TOH uh *KJV, NAS, NIV,
  RSV, TEV*
Nē·phüsh'ē·sĭm neh FOOSH ih sihm
  NAS, RSV, TEV
Nē·phü'sĭm nih FYOO sim *KJV*
Nĕp'thà·lĭm NEP thuh lim *KJV*
Nēr NUHR *KJV, NAS, NIV, RSV, TEV*
Nē·râi'ah neh RIGH uh, neh RAY uh
  NAS
Nē'rēus NEE roos, NEE rih uhs *KJV,
  NAS, NIV, RSV, TEV*
Nĕr'ĝăl NUHR gahl *KJV, NAS, NIV,
  RSV, TEV*
Nēr'ĝăl-sär-ē'zĕr NUHR gahl-sahr-EE
  zuhr *NAS, TEV*
Nĕr'ĝăl-shâ·rē'zĕr NUR gahl-shuh REE
  zur *KJV, NIV, RSV, TEV*
Nē'rī NEE righ *KJV, NAS, NIV, RSV,
  TEV*
Nē·rī'ah nih RIGH uh *KJV, NAS, NIV,
  RSV, TEV*
Nē·tā'îm nih TAY im, NEE tay im
  KJV, NAS, NIV, RSV, TEV
Nē·thăn'ē·ĕl nih THAN ih el, NETH uh
  neel *KJV*
Nē'thăn'ĕl nih THAN ehl, NETH uh
  nehl *NAS, NIV, RSV, TEV*
Nĕth·â·nī'ah neth uh NIGH uh *KJV,
  NAS, NIV, RSV, TEV*
Nĕth'ī·nĭms NETH uh nims *KJV, NAS*

Nĕ·tō′phah   nih TOH fuh   *KJV, NAS, NIV, RSV, TEV*
Nĕ·tŏph′å·thī   nih TAHF uh thigh   *KJV*
Nĕ·tŏph′å·thīte   nih TAHF uh thight   *KJV, NAS, NIV, RSV*
Nĕ·zī′ah   nih ZIGH ah   *KJV, NAS, NIV, RSV, TEV*
Nē′zīb   NEE zib   *KJV, NAS, NIV, RSV, TEV*
Nĭb′hăz   NIB haz   *KJV, NAS, NIV, RSV, TEV*
Nĭb′shăn   NIB shan   *KJV, NAS, NIV, RSV, TEV*
Nĭ·cā′nôr   nigh KAY nawr   *KJV, NAS, NIV, RSV, TEV*
Nĭ·co·dē′mŭs   nik uh DEE muhs   *KJV, NAS, NIV, RSV, TEV*
Nĭc·ō·lā′ĭ·tāne   nik oh LAY ih tayn   *KJV*
Nĭc·ō·lā′ĭ·tans   nik oh LAY ih tuhnz   *NAS, NIV, RSV, TEV*
Nĭc′ō·làs   NIK oh luhs   *KJV, NAS, NIV*
Nĭc·o·lā′us   nik uh LAY uhs   *RSV*
Nĭ·cŏp′ō·lis   nih KAHP oh liss   *KJV, NAS, NIV, RSV, TEV*
Nī′gêr   NIGH jur   *KJV, NAS, NIV, RSV*
Nīle   NIGHL   *NAS, NIV, RSV, TEV*
Nĭm′rah   NIM ruh   *KJV, NAS, NIV, RSV, TEV*
Nĭm′rĭm   NIM rim   *KJV, NAS, NIV, RSV, TEV*
Nĭm′rŏd   NIM rahd   *KJV, NAS, NIV, RSV, TEV*
Nĭm′shī   NIM shigh   *KIV, NAS, NIV, RSV, TEV*
Nĭn′ĕ·vĕ   NIN eh veh   *KJV*
Nĭn′ĕ·vēh   NIN uh vuh   *KJV, NAS, NIV, RSV, TEV*
Nĭn′ĕ·vīte   NIN uh vight   *KJV, NAS, NIV*
Nī′săn   NIGH san   *KJV, NAS, NIV, RSV, TEV*
Nĭs′rŏch   NIS rahk   *KJV, NAS, NIV, RSV, TEV*
Nō   NO   *KJV*
Nō·å·dī′ah   no uh DIGH uh   *KJV, NAS, NIV, RSV, TEV*
Nō′ah   NO uh   *KJV, NAS, NIV, RSV, TEV*
Nō·ā′mŏn   no-AY mahn   *KJV, NAS*
Nŏb   NAHB   *KJV, NAS, NIV, RSV, TEV*
Nō′bah   NO buh   *KJV, NAS, NIV, RSV, TEV*
Nō′baì   NO bigh, NAHB ay igh   *KJV*
Nŏd   NAHD   *KJV, NAS, NIV, RSV*
Nō′dăb   NO dab   *KJV, NAS, NIV, RSV, TEV*

No′e   NO eh   *KJV*
Nō′gah   NO guh   *KJV, NAS, NIV, RSV, TEV*
Nō′hăh   NO ha   *KJV, NAS, NIV, RSV, TEV*
Nŏn   NAHN   *KJV, NAS*
Nŏph   NAHF   *KJV*
Nō′phah   NO fuh   *KJV, NAS, NIV, TEV*
Nū′bĭ·ans   NYOO bih uhnz   *NIV*
Nŭn   NUHN   *KJV, NAS, NIV, RSV, TEV*
Nȳm′phà   NIHM fuh   *NAS, NIV, TEV*
Nȳm′phàs   NIM fuhs   *KJV, RSV*

Ō·bå·dī′ah   oh buh DIGH uh   *KJV, NAS, NIV, RSV, TEV*
Ō′bàl   OH buhl   *KJV, NAS, NIV, RSV, TEV*
Ō′bĕd   OH bed   *KJV, NAS, NIV, RSV, TEV*
Ō′bĕd-ē′dom   OH bed-EE duhm   *KJV, NAS, NIV, RSV, TEV*
Ō′bĭl   OH bill   *KJV, NAS, NIV, RSV, TEV*
Ō′bŏth   OH bahth, OH bohth   *KJV, NAS, NIV, RSV, TEV*
Ŏc′răn (Och′răn)   OCK ran   *KJV, NAS, NIV, RSV, TEV*
Ō′dĕd   OH ded   *KJV, NAS, NIV, RSV, TEV*
Ŏg   AHG   *KJV, NAS, NIV, RSV, TEV*
Ō′hăd   OH had   *KJV, NAS, NIV, RSV, TEV*
Ō′hĕl   OH hell   *KJV, NAS, NIV, RSV, TEV*
Ō·hō′lah   oh HOH luh   *KJV, NAS, NIV, RSV, TEV*
Ō·hō′lĭ·ab   oh HOH lih ab   *KJV, NAS, NIV, RSV, TEV*
Ō·hŏl′ĭ·bah   oh HAHL uh buh   *KJV, NAS, NIV, RSV, TEV*
Ō·hŏl·ĭ·bā′mah   oh HAHL ih BAY muh   *KJV, NAS, NIV, RSV, TEV*
Ŏl′īves   AHL ivz   *KJV, NAS, NIV, RSV, TEV*
Ŏl′ĭ·vĕt   AHL ih vet   *KJV, NAS, RSV*
Ō·lȳm′pàs   oh LIM puhs   *KJV, NAS, NIV, RSV, TEV*

Ō′màr   OH mur   *KJV, NAS, NIV, RSV, TEV*

Ō·mē′g̀à   oh MEE guh, oh MEG uh   *KJV, NAS, NIV, RSV*

Ŏm′rī   AHM righ   *KJV, NAS, NIV, RSV, TEV*

Ŏn   AHN   *KJV, NAS, NIV, RSV, TEV*

Ō′năm   OH nam   *KJV, NAS, NIV, RSV, TEV*

Ō′năn   OH nan   *KJV, NAS, NIV, RSV, TEV*

Ō·něs′ĭ·mŭs   oh NESS ih muhs   *KJV, NAS, NIV, RSV, TEV*

Ŏn·ė·sĭph′ō·rŭs   ahn ih SIF oh russ   *KJV, NAS, NIV, RSV, TEV*

Ō′nō   OH no   *KJV, NAS, NIV, RSV, TEV*

Ō′phĕl   OH fel   *KJV, NAS, NIV, RSV, TEV*

Ō′phīr   OH fur   *KJV, NAS, NIV, RSV, TEV*

Ŏph′nī   AHF nigh   *KJV, NAS, NIV, RSV, TEV*

Ŏph′rah   AHF ruh   *KJV, NAS, NIV, RSV, TEV*

Ō′rĕb   OH reb   *KJV, NAS, NIV, RSV, TEV*

Ō′rĕn   OH ren   *KJV, NAS, NIV, RSV, TEV*

Ō·rī′on   oh RIGH uhn   *KJV, NAS, NIV, RSV, TEV*

Ôr′năn   AWR nan   *KJV, NAS, RSV, TEV*

Ôr′pah   AWR puh   *KJV, NAS, NIV, RSV, TEV*

Ō′ṣēē   OH zee, OH see   *KJV*

Ō·shē′à   oh SHE uh   *KJV*

Ŏs·năp′pàr   ahs NAP ur   *KJV, NAS, RSV*

Ŏth′nī   AHTH nigh   *KJV, NAS, NIV, RSV, TEV*

Ŏth′nĭ·ĕl   AHTH nih el   *KJV, NAS, NIV, RSV, TEV*

Ō′zĕm   OH zem   *KJV, NAS, NIV, RSV, TEV*

Ō·zī′às   oh ZIGH uhs   *KJV*

Ŏz′nī   AHZ nigh   *KJV, NAS, NIV, RSV, TEV*

Ŏz′nīte   AHZ night   *KJV, NAS, NIV, RSV*

Pā·à·raî   PAY uh righ   *KJV, NAS, NIV, RSV, TEV*

Pād′an (Pād′dan)   PAY duhn   *KJV, NAS, NIV, RSV*

Pā′dan-ā′răm   PAY duhn-AY ram   *KJV*

Pād′dan   PAY duhn, PAD uhn   *NAS*

Pād′dan-ā′răm   PAY duhn-AY ram, PAD duhn-AR ruhm   *NAS, NIV, RSV*

Pā′dön   PAY dahn   *KJV, NAS, NIV, RSV, TEV*

Pā′g̀ĭ·ĕl   PAY gih el, PAY jih el   *KJV, NAS, NIV, RSV, TEV*

Pā′hăth-mō′ăb   PAY hath-MOH ab   *KJV, NAS, NIV, RSV, TEV*

Pā′ī   PAY igh   *KJV, NAS, RSV*

Pā′lăl   PAY lal   *KJV, NAS, NIV, RSV, TEV*

Păl·ēs·tī′nà   pal uhs TIGH nuh   *KJV*

Păl′ēs·tīne   PAL uhs tighn   *KJV*

Păl′lū   PAL yoo   *KJV, NAS, NIV, RSV, TEV*

Păl′lū·īte   PAL yoo ight   *KJV, NAS, NIV, RSV*

Păl′tī   PAL tigh   *KJV, NAS, NIV, RSV, TEV*

Păl′tĭ·ĕl   PAL tih el   *KJV, NAS, NIV, RSV, TEV*

Păl′tīte   PAL tight   *KJV, NAS, NIV, RSV*

Păm·phўl′ĭ·à   pam FIL ih uh   *KJV, NAS, NIV, RSV, TEV*

Păn′năg̀   PAN ag   *KJV*

Pā′phŏs   PAY fahs   *KJV, NAS, NIV, RSV, TEV*

Păr′à·dīse   PAR uh dighss   *TEV*

Pā′rah   PAY ruh, PAR uh   *KJV, NAS, NIV, RSV, TEV*

Pā′ran   PAY ruhn   *KJV, NAS, NIV, RSV, TEV*

Pär′bär   PAHR bahr   *KJV, NAS, RSV, TEV*

Pär·măsh′tà   pahr MASH tuh   *KJV, NAS, NIV, RSV, TEV*

Pär′mė·nàs   PAHR mih nuhs   *KJV, NAS, NIV, RSV, TEV*

Pär′năch   PAHR nak   *KJV, NAS, NIV, RSV, TEV*

Pā′rŏsh   PAY rahsh   *KJV, NAS, NIV, RSV, TEV*

Pär·shăn·dā′thà   pahr shan DAY thuh, pahr SHAN duh thuh   *KJV, NAS, NIV, RSV, TEV*

Pär′sĭn   PAHR sihn   *NIV, RSV*

Pär′thĭ′à   PAHR thih uh   *TEV*

Pär′thĭ·an   PAHR thih uhn   *KJV, NAS, NIV, RSV*

Pȧ·rū′ah   puh ROO uh   *KJV, NAS, NIV,*

RSV, TEV

Pär·vā'im   pahr VAY im   *KJV, NAS, NIV, RSV, TEV*

Pā'sǎch   PAY sak   *KJV, NAS, NIV, RSV, TEV*

Pǎs-dǎm'mǐm   pas-DAM im   *KJV, NAS, NIV, RSV, TEV*

Pǎ·sē'ah   puh SEE uh   *KJV, NAS, NIV, RSV, TEV*

Pǎsh'hǔr   PASH ur   *KJV, NAS, NIV, RSV, TEV*

Pǎsh'ǔr   PASH ur   *KJV*

Pǎss'ō·vēr   PASS oh vuhr, pass OH vuhr   *KJV, NAS, NIV, RSV, TEV*

Pǎt'á·rà   PAT uh ruh   *KJV, NAS, NIV, RSV, TEV*

Pǎth'rŏs   PATH rahs   *KJV, NAS, NIV, RSV, TEV*

Pǎth·rūs   PATH ruhs   *NAS, TEV*

Pǎth·rū'sīm   path ROO sim   *KJV, NAS, RSV*

Pǎth·rū'sītes   path ROO sights   *NIV*

Pǎt'mos   PAT muhs   *KJV, NAS, NIV, RSV, TEV*

Pǎt'rō·bàs   PAT roh buhs   *KJV, NAS, NIV, RSV, TEV*

Pā·ū   PAY oo   *KJV, NAS, RSV, TEV*

Paūl   PAWL   *KJV, NAS, NIV, RSV, TEV*

Paūl'ǔs   PAWL uhs   *KJV, NAS, RSV*

Pěd'á·hěl   PED uh hel, pih DAH el   *KJV, NAS, NIV, RSV, TEV*

Pě·dǎh'zūr   pih DA zur   *KJV, NAS, NIV, RSV, TEV*

Pě·daì'ah   pih DIGH uh, pih DAY yuh   *KJV, NAS, NIV, RSV, TEV*

Pě'kah   PEE kuh   *KJV, NAS, NIV, RSV, TEV*

Pěk'á·hī'ah   pek uh HIGH uh   *KJV, NAS, NIV, RSV, TEV*

Pě'kŏd   PEE kahd   *KJV, NAS, NIV, RSV, TEV*

Pě·lai'ah   pih LAY yuh, pih LIGH uh   *KJV, NAS, NIV, RSV, TEV*

Pěl·á·lī'ah   pel uh LIGH uh   *KJV, NAS, NIV*

Pěl·á·tī'ah   pel uh TIGH uh   *KJV, NAS, NIV, RSV, TEV*

Pě'lěg   PEE leg   *KJV, NAS, NIV, RSV, TEV*

Pě'lět   PEE let   *KJV, NAS, NIV, RSV, TEV*

Pě'lěth   PEE leth   *KJV, NAS, NIV, RSV, TEV*

Pě'lěth·ite   PEE leth ight, PEL uh thight   *KJV, NAS, NIV, RSV*

Pě'lon   PEHL uhn, PEE luhn, PIH

luhn   *TEV*

Pě'lō·nīte   PEE lo night, PEL oh night   *KJV, NAS, NIV, RSV*

Pě'lü'sī·ǔm   peh LOO sih uhm   *NIV, RSV*

Pě·nī'ěl   pih NIGH el, PEN ih uhl   *KJV, NAS, NIV, RSV, TEV*

Pě·nǐn'nah   pih NIN uh   *KJV, NAS, NIV, RSV, TEV*

Pěn'tě·côst   PEN tih kawst   *KJV, NAS, NIV, RSV, TEV*

Pě·nū'ěl   pi NYOO el, PEN yoo el   *KJV, NAS, NIV, RSV, TEV*

Pě'ôr   PEE awr   *KJV, NAS, NIV, RSV, TEV*

Pě'rǎth   PEE rath   *NIV*

Pěr'á·zǐm   PER uh zim, pih RAY zim   *KJV, NAS, NIV, RSV*

Pě'rěṣ   PEE rez   *KJV, NAS, NIV, RSV*

Pě'rěsh   PEE resh   *KJV, NAS, NIV, RSV, TEV*

Pě·rěz   PEE rez   *KJV, NAS, NIV, RSV, TEV*

Pě'rěz·ite   PEE rez ight   *KJV, NAS, NIV, RSV*

Pě'rěz-ǔz'zà   PEE rehz-UHZ uh   *NAS, RSV*

Pě'rěz-ǔz'zah   PEE rez-UHZ uh   *KJV, NAS, NIV, RSV, TEV*

Pēr'ġà   PUR guh   *KJV, NAS, NIV, RSV, TEV*

Pēr'ġà·mŏs   PUR guh mahs   *KJV*

Pēr'ġà·mǔm   PUR guh muhm   *KJV, NAS, NIV, RSV, TEV*

Pě·rī'dà   pih RIGH duh   *KJV, NAS, NIV, RSV, TEV*

Pěr'ǐz·zīte   PER ih zight   *KJV, NAS, NIV, RSV, TEV*

Pēr'ṣià   PUR zhuh   *KJV, NAS, NIV, RSV, TEV*

Pēr'ṣian   PUR zhuhn   *KJV, NAS, NIV, RSV, TEV*

Pēr'sǐs   PUR sis   *KJV, NAS, NIV, RSV, TEV*

Pě·rū'dà   pih ROO duh   *KJV, NAS, NIV, RSV, TEV*

Pě'tēr   PEE tur   *KJV, NAS, NIV, RSV, TEV*

Pěth·á·hī'ah   peth uh HIGH uh   *KJV, NAS, NIV, RSV, TEV*

Pě'thôr   PEE thawr   *KJV, NAS, NIV, RSV, TEV*

Pě·thū'ěl   pih THYOO el   *KJV, NAS, NIV, RSV, TEV*

Pě·ǔl'lē·thaì   pih UHL luh thigh   *NAS,*

Pĕ·ŭl′thaĭ pih UHL thigh *KJV*
Phă′lĕc FAY lek *KJV*
Phăl′lū FAL oo *KJV*
Phăl′tī FAL tigh *KJV*
Phăl′tĭ·ĕl FAL tih el *KJV*
Phå·nū′ĕl fuh NYOO uhl, FAN yoo el *KJV, NAS, NIV, RSV, TEV*
Phā′raōh FAY roh, FER oh *KJV, NAS, NIV, RSV*
Phā′raōh-hŏph′ra FAY roh-HAHF ruh *KJV*
Phā′raōh-nē′cho FAY roh-NEE koh *KJV*
Phā′raōh Nē′cō FAY roh-NEE koh *NAS, NIV, RSV, TEV*
Phā′rēṣ FAY reez, FAHR ess *KJV, NAS,*
Phā′rĕz FAY rez *KJV*
Phâr′ĭ·sä′ĭc fer ih SAY ihk *NAS*
Phâr′ĭ·sēē FER uh see *KJV, NAS, NIV, RSV, TEV*
Phā′rŏsh FAY rahsh, FAHR ahsh *KJV*
Phär′pär FAHR pahr *KJV, NAS, NIV, RSV, TEV*
Phär′zīte FAHR zight *KJV*
Phå·sē′ah fuh SEE uh *KJV*
Phē′bĕ FEE bih *KJV*
Phĕ·nī′cĕ fih NIGH sih *KJV*
Phĕ·nĭc′ĭ·à fuh NISH ih uh *KJV*
Phĭ′bĕ·sĕth FIGH bih seth, FIB uh seth *KJV*
Phĭ′chŏl (Phĭ′cŏl) FIGH kahl *KJV*
Phĭ′cŏl FIGH kahl *KJV, NAS, NIV, RSV, TEV*
Phĭl·å·dĕl′phĭ·à fil uh DEL fih uh *KJV, NAS, NIV, RSV, TEV*
Phĭ·lē′mon figh LEE muhn *KJV, NAS, NIV, RSV, TEV*
Phĭ·lē′tŭs fih LEE tuhs *KJV, NAS, NIV, RSV, TEV*
Phĭl′ĭp FILL ip *KJV, NAS, NIV, RSV, TEV*
Phĭl′ĭp·pī FILL ih pigh, fih LIP igh *KJV, NAS, NIV, RSV, TEV*
Phĭ·lĭp′pĭ·an fih LIP ih uhn *KJV, NAS, NIV, RSV, TEV*
Phĭ·lĭs′tĭ·à fih LIST ih uh *KJV, NAS, NIV, RSV, TEV*
Phĭ·lĭs′tĭm fih LISS tim *KJV*
Phĭl·ĭs′tīnes fih LISS teens *KJV, NAS, NIV, RSV, TEV*
Phĭ·lŏl′ō·ğŭs fih LAHL oh guhs, fuh LAHL uh guhs *KJV, NAS, NIV, RSV,*

Phĭn′ĕ·hàs FIN ih uhs *KJV, NAS, NIV, RSV, TEV*
Phlē′ğŏn FLEE gahn *KJV, NAS, NIV, RSV, TEV*
Phōē′bĕ FEE bih *KJV, NAS, NIV, RSV, TEV*
Phoe·nĭc′ĭ·à fuh NISH ih uh, fuh NISH uh *KJV, NAS, NIV, RSV, TEV*
Phōē′nĭx FEE nix *KJV, NAS, NIV, RSV, TEV*
Phrŷğ′ĭ·à FRIJ ih uh *KJV, NAS, NIV, RSV, TEV*
Phrŷ′ğĭ·an FRIH jih uhn *NAS*
Phū′rah FYOO ruh *KJV*
Phŭt FUHT *KJV*
Phū′vah FYOO vuh *KJV*
Phŷ′ğĕl′lŭs fih JEL uhs *KJV*
Phŷ·ğĕl′us fih JEHL uhs, FIGH gee luhs *NAS, NIV, RSV, TEV*
Pĭ·bē′sĕth pigh BEE seth *KJV, NAS, RSV*
Pĭ·hå·hī′rŏth pigh huh HIGH rahth *KJV, NAS, RSV, TEV*
Pī′làte PIGH luht *KJV, NAS, NIV, RSV, TEV*
Pĭl′däsh PILL dash *KJV, NAS, NIV, RSV, TEV*
Pĭl′ĕ·hä PILL ih ha, PIGH lih ha *KJV*
Pĭl′hà PIHL huh *NAS, NIV, RSV, TEV*
Pĭl′taĭ PILL tigh, pill TAY igh *KJV, NAS, NIV, RSV, TEV*
Pī′nŏn PIGH nahn *KJV, NAS, NIV, RSV, TEV*
Pī′răm PIGH ram *KJV, NAS, NIV, RSV, TEV*
Pī·rā′thŏn pigh RAY thahn *KJV, NAS, NIV, RSV, TEV*
Pī·rā′thŏn·ite pigh RAY thahn ight *KJV, NAS, NIV, RSV*
Pĭs′ğah PIZ guh *KJV, NAS, NIV, RSV, TEV*
Pī′shŏn PIGH shahn *NAS, NIV, RSV, TEV*
Pĭ·sĭd′ĭ·à pih SID ih uh *KJV, NAS, NIV, RSV, TEV*
Pĭ·sĭd′ĭ·an pih SID ih uhn *NAS*
Pĭ·sĭd′ĭ·an-Ăn′tĭ·ŏch pih SID ih uhn-AN tih ahk *NIV*
Pī′sŏn PIGH sahn *KJV*
Pĭs′pà PIHS puh *KJV, NAS, RSV, TEV*
Pĭs′pah PIHS puh *KJV, NIV*
Pī′thŏm PIGH thahm *KJV, NAS, NIV,*

RSV, TEV

Pī′thŏn PIGH thahn *KJV, NAS, NIV, RSV, TEV*

Pleı̆′å·dȩ̄s PLIGH uh deez, PLEE uh deez *KJV, NAS, NIV, RSV, TEV*

Pŏ̧ch′ĕ·rĕth PAHK uh reth, POH kuh reth *KJV, NAS, TEV*

Pŏ̧ch′ĕ·rĕth-hăz·zĕ·bā′ı̆m PAHK uh reth-haz uh BAY im *KJV, NAS, RSV, TEV*

Pŏ′kĕ·rĕth-Hăz·zĕ·bā′ı̆m POH kih reth-haz zih BAY ihm *NIV*

Pŏl′lŭx PAHL uhks *KJV, NIV*

Pŏn′tiŭs PAHN shuhs, PAHN tih uhs *KJV, NAS, NIV, RSV, TEV*

Pŏn′tŭs PAHN tuhs *KJV, NAS, NIV, RSV, TEV*

Pō·rā′thà poh RAY thuh, PAHR uh thuh, PAWR uh thuh *KJV, NAS, NIV, RSV, TEV*

Pôr′çiŭs PAWR shuhs, PAWR shih uhs *KJV, NAS, NIV, RSV, TEV*

Pôr′çı̆·ŭs-Fĕs′tŭs PAWR shih uhs-FEHS tuhs *NIV, TEV*

Pŏt′ı̆·phär POT ih fur *KJV, NAS, NIV, RSV, TEV*

Pō·tı̆′phĕ·rà poh TIH fih ruh, poh TIF uhr ruh *NAS, NIV, RSV, TEV*

Pō·tı̆ph′ĕr·ah poh TIF ur uh *KJV*

Prăĕ·tôr′ı̆·an prih TAWR ih uhn *NAS, RSV*

Prăĕ·tôr′ı̆·um prih TAWR ih uhm, prih TOH rih uhm *KJV, NAS, NIV, RSV*

Prı̆s′cà PRISS kuh *KJV, NAS, RSV*

Prı̆s·cı̆l′là prih SIL uh *KJV, NAS, NIV, RSV, TEV*

Prŏ̧ch′o·rŭs PRAHK uh ruhs *KJV, NAS, RSV, NIV*

Prŏc′o·rŭs PRAHK uh ruhs *NIV*

Psälms SAHLMS, SAHLMZ *KJV, NAS, NIV, RSV, TEV*

Ptŏl·ĕ·mā′ı̆s tahl uh MAY uhs *KJV, NAS, NIV, RSV, TEV*

Pū′à PYOO uh *KJV*

Pū′ah PYOO uh *KJV, NIV, RSV, TEV*

Pŭb′lı̆·ŭs PUHB lih uhs *KJV, NAS, NIV, RSV, TEV*

Pū′dĕņs PYOO denz *KJV, NAS, NIV, RSV, TEV*

Pū′hı̆te PYOO hight *KJV*

Pū′ı̄te PYOO ight *NIV*

Pŭl PUHL *KJV, NAS, NIV, RSV, TEV*

Pū′nı̆te PYOO night *KJV, NAS, RSV*

Pū′nŏn PYOO nahn *KJV, NAS, NIV,*

RSV, TEV

Pŭr PUHR *KJV, NAS, NIV, RSV*

Pū′rah PYOO uh *KJV, NAS, NIV, RSV, TEV*

Pū′rı̆m PYOO rim *KJV, NAS, NIV, RSV, TEV*

Pŭt PUHT *KJV, NAS, NIV, RSV*

Pū·tē′ō·lı̆ pyoo TEE oh ligh *KJV, NAS, NIV, RSV, TEV*

Pū′thı̄te PYOO thight *KJV, NAS, NIV, RSV, TEV*

Pū′tı̆·ĕl PYOO tih el *KJV, NAS, NIV, RSV, TEV*

Pū′vah PYOO vuh *NAS, RSV*

Pūv′vah PYOO vuh *NAS*

Pȳr′rhŭs PIR uhs *KJV, NAS, NIV, RSV, TEV*

Quar′tŭs KWAWR tuhs *KJV, NAS, NIV, RSV, TEV*

Quı̆·rı̆n′ı̆·ŭs kwi RIN ih uhs *KJV, NAS, NIV, RSV, TEV*

Rā′å·mà (Rā′å·mah) RAY uh muh *KJV, NAS, RSV, TEV*

Rā′å·mah RAY uh muh *KJV, NAS, NIV, RSV, TEV*

Rā·å·mī′ah ray uh MIGH uh *KJV, NIV, RSV, TEV*

Rā·ăm′sḝs ray AM seez *KJV, NAS, RSV*

Răb′bah RAB uh *KJV, NAS, NIV, RSV, TEV*

Răb′bàth RAB uhth *KJV*

Răb′bī RAB igh *KJV, NAS, NIV, RSV, TEV*

Răb′bīth RAB ith *KJV, NAS, NIV, RSV, TEV*

Răb·bō′nī ra BOH nigh *KJV, NAS, NIV, RSV, TEV*

Răb-măĝ RAB-mag *KJV, NAS, RSV*

Răb′-sà·rĭs RAB-suh riss *KJV, NAS, RSV*

Răb=shá′kĕh RAB-SHUH keh *KJV, NAS, RSV*

Rä′cà RAH kuh, RAY kuh *KJV, NAS, NIV*

Rä′chăb RAY kab *KJV*

Rä′cal (Ra′chàl) RAY kuhl *KJV, NAS, RSV, TEV*

Rä′chĕl RAY chuhl *KJV, NAS, NIV, RSV, TEV*

Răd′dā·ī RAD ay igh *KJV, NAS, NIV, RSV, TEV*

Rä′ĝău RAY gaw *KJV*

Rà·ĝū′ĕl (Răg′ū·ĕl) ruh GYOO el, RAG yoo el *KJV*

Rä′hăb RAY hab *KJV, NAS, NIV, RSV, TEV*

Rä′hăm RAY ham *KJV, NAS, NIV, RSV, TEV*

Rä′hĕl RAY hel *KJV*

Rä′kĕm RAY kem *KJV, NAS, NIV, RSV, TEV*

Răk′kàth RAK uhth *KJV, NAS, NIV, RSV, TEV*

Răk′kon RAK ahn *KJV, NAS, NIV, RSV, TEV*

Răm RAM *KJV, NAS, RSV, TEV*

Rä′mà RAY muh *KJV*

Rä′mah RAY muh *KJV, NAS, NIV, RSV, TEV*

Rä′măth RAY math *KJV*

Rä′măth-Mīz′pah RAY math-MIZ puh *NIV*

Rä·mà·thä′ĭm ray muh THAY ihm *NIV*

Rä·mà·thä′ĭm-zō′phĭm ray muh THAY ihm-ZOH fihm *KJV, NAS, RSV*

Rä′măth·īte RAY math ight *KJV, NAS, NIV, RSV*

Rä′măth-lĕ′hī RAY math-LEE high *KJV, NAS, NIV, RSV, TEV*

Rä′măth-mĭz′pĕh RAY math-MIZ peh *KJV, NAS, RSV, TEV*

Răm′ē·sĕş RAM uh seez *KJV, NAS, NIV, RSV, TEV*

Rà·mī′ah ruh MIGH uh *KJV, NAS, NIV, RSV, TEV*

Rä′mŏth RAY mahth *KJV, NAS, NIV, RSV, TEV*

Rä′mŏth-gĭl′ē·àd RAY mahth-GIL ih uhd *KJV, NAS, NIV, RSV, TEV*

Rä′mŏth-Nĕ′gĕv RAY mahth-NEH gehv *NIV*

Rä′phâ RAY fah *KJV, NAS, NIV, RSV, TEV*

Rä′phah RAY fuh *KJV, NAS, NIV, RSV, TEV*

Rä′phâ RAY phuh *KJV, NAS, NIV, RSV, TEV*

Rê·aî′ah rih IGH uh, rih AY yuh *KJV, NAS, NIV, RSV, TEV*

Rē′bà REE buh *KJV, NAS, NIV, RSV, TEV*

Rĕ·bĕc′cà reh BEK uh *KJV, NIV, RSV, TEV*

Rĕ·bĕk′ah reh BEK uh *KJV, NAS, NIV, RSV, TEV*

Rĕ′căb REE kab *NIV*

Rĕ′căb·īte REE kab ight *NIV*

Rĕ′cah REE kuh *NAS, NIV, RSV, TEV*

Rĕ′chăb REE kab *KJV, NAS, RSV, TEV*

Rĕ′chăb·īte REE kab ight, REK uh bight *KJV, NAS, RSV, TEV*

Rĕ′chah REE kuh *KJV*

Rĕd-Sēa REHD-SEE *KJV, NAS, NIV, RSV, TEV*

Rê·ĕl·aî′ah ree el IGH uh, ree el AY yuh *KJV, NAS, NIV, RSV, TEV*

Rē′ĝĕm REE ghem *KJV, NAS, NIV, RSV, TEV*

Rē′ĝĕm-mē′lĕch REE ghem-MEE lek REE ghem-MEL ek *KJV, NAS, NIV, RSV, TEV*

Rĕ·hà·bī′ah ree huh BIGH uh *KJV, NAS, NIV, RSV, TEV*

Rē′hŏb REE hahb *KJV, NAS, NIV, RSV, TEV*

Rĕ·hō·bō′am ree huh BOH uhm *KJV, NAS, NIV, RSV, TEV*

Rē′hō·bŏth REE hoh bahth, rih HOH bahth *KJV, NAS, NIV, RSV, TEV*

Rē′hō·bŏth-Îr REE hoh bahth-UR, ER *NAS, NIV, RSV*

Rē′hŭm REE huhm *KJV, NAS, NIV, RSV, TEV*

Rē′ī REE igh *KJV, NAS, NIV, RSV, TEV*

Rē′kĕm REE kem *KJV, NAS, NIV, RSV, TEV*

Rĕm·à·lī′ah rem uh LIGH uh *KJV, NAS, NIV, RSV, TEV*

Rē′mĕth   REE meth   *KJV, NAS, NIV, RSV, TEV*
Rĕm′mŏn   REM ahn   *KJV*
Rĕm′mŏn-mĕ·thō′är   REM ahn-meh THOH ahr, METH oh ahr   *KJV*
Rĕm′phăn   REM fan   *KJV*
Rĕph′ā·ĕl   REF ay el, REE fay el   *KJV, NAS, NIV, RSV, TEV*
Rē′phah   REE fuh   *KJV, NAS, NIV, RSV, TEV*
Rĕ·phaï′ah   rih FIGH uh, rih FAY yuh   *KJV, NAS, NIV, RSV, TEV*
Rĕph′ā·ĭm   REF ay im   *KJV, NAS, NIV, RSV, TEV*
Rĕph′ā′ītes   REF ay ights   *NIV*
Rē′phăn   REE fan   *KJV, NIV, RSV, TEV*
Rĕph′ĭ·dīm   REF ih dim   *KJV, NAS, NIV, RSV, TEV*
Rē′sĕn   REE sin   *KJV, NAS, NIV, RSV, TEV*
Rē′shĕph   REE shef   *KJV, NAS, NIV, RSV, TEV*
Rē′şĭn   REE zihn, REH zihn   *NIV*
Rē′ū   REE oo   *KJV, NAS, NIV, RSV, TEV*
Reū′bĕn   RHOO ben   *KJV, NAS, NIV, RSV, TEV*
Reū′bĕn·īte   RHOO ben ight   *KJV, NAS, NIV, RSV*
Reū′ĕl   RHOO el   *KJV, NAS, NIV, RSV, TEV*
Reū′mah   RHOO muh   *KJV, NAS, NIV, RSV, TEV*
Rē′zĕph   REE zef   *KJV, NAS, NIV, RSV, TEV*
Rē·zī′à   ree ZIGH uh, REE zih uh   *KJV*
Rē′zĭn   REE zin   *KJV, NAS, NIV, RSV, TEV*
Rē′zŏn   REE zahn   *KJV, NAS, NIV, RSV, TEV*
Rhē′ğĭ·um   REE jih uhm, REH jih uhm   *KJV, NAS, NIV, RSV, TEV*
Rhē′sà   REE suh   *KJV, NAS, NIV, RSV, TEV*
Rhō′dà   ROH duh   *KJV, NAS, NIV, RSV, TEV*
Rhōdes   ROHDZ   *KJV, NAS, NIV, RSV, TEV*
Rĭ′bā·ī   RIGH bay igh, rih BAY igh   *KJV, NAS, NIV, RSV, TEV*
Rĭb′lah   RIB luh   *KJV, NAS, NIV, RSV, TEV*
Rĭm′mon   RIM uhn   *KJV, NAS, NIV, RSV, TEV*
Rĭm·mō′nō   rih MOH no   *KJV, NAS, NIV, RSV, TEV*
Rĭm′mon-pā′rēz   RIM uhn-PAY reez   *KJV*
Rĭm′mon-pē′rĕz   RIM uhn-PEE rez   *KJV, NAS, NIV, RSV, TEV*
Rĭn′nah   RIN nuh   *KJV, NAS, NIV, RSV, TEV*
Rĭ′phăth   RIGH fath   *KJV, NAS, NIV, RSV, TEV*
Rĭsh·â·thā′ĭm   rish uh THAY ihm   *TEV*
Rĭs′sah   RISS uh   *KJV, NAS, RSV, TEV*
Rĭth′mah   RITH muh   *KJV, NAS, NIV, RSV, TEV*
Rĭz′ĭ·à   RIZ ih uh   *KJV, NAS, NIV, RSV, TEV*
Rĭz′pah   RIZ puh   *KJV, NAS, NIV, RSV, TEV*
Rō·bō′am   roh BOH uhm   *KJV*
Rŏd′â·nĭm   RAHD uh nim   *KJV, NAS, NIV, RSV*
Rō′ğĕ·lĭm   ROH guh lim, roh GHEE lim   *KJV, NAS, NIV, RSV, TEV*
Rŏh′ğah   ROH guh   *KJV, NAS, NIV, RSV, TEV*
Rō·măm′tī·ē′zĕr   roh MAM tigh EE zur   *KJV, NAS, NIV, RSV, TEV*
Rō′man   ROH muhn   *KJV, NAS, NIV, RSV, TEV*
Rōme   ROHM   *KJV, NAS, NIV, RSV, TEV*
Rŏm′phà   ROHM fuh   *NAS*
Rōsh   RAHSH   *KJV, NAS, NIV, RSV, TEV*
Rū′fŭs   ROO fuhs   *KJV, NAS, NIV, RSV, TEV*
Rū·hä′mah   roo HAH muh, roo HAY muh   *KJV, NAS*
Rū′mah   ROO muh   *KJV, NAS, NIV, RSV, TEV*
Rūth   ROOTH   *KJV, NAS, NIV, RSV, TEV*

Sä·bäch′thå·nī   sah BAHK thu nigh   *KJV, NAS, NIV, RSV, TEV*
Săb′a·ŏth   SAB ay ahth   *KJV, NAS*
Săb′bâth   SAB buhth   *NAS, NIV, RSV,*

TEV
Să·bē′an   suh BEE uhn   *KJV. NAS. NIV. RSV. TEV*
Săb′tà   SAB tuh   *KJV. NAS. NIV. RSV.*
Săb′tah   SAB tuh   *KJV. NAS. NIV. RSV. TEV*
Săb′tē·cà   SAB tee kuh, SAB tih kuh   *NAS. NIV. RSV. TEV*
Săb′tē·cah   SAB tee kuh, sab TEE kuh   *NIV*
Săb′tē·chah   SAB tee kuh   *KJV*
Să′cär   SAY kahr   *KJV. NAS. NIV*
Să′chär   SAY kawr   *RSV. TEV*
Să·chī′à   suh KIGH uh   *NAS. RSV. TEV*
Săd′dū·cēē   SAD joo see   *KJV, NAS, NIV, RSV, TEV*
Să′dŏc   SAY dahk   *KJV*
Să′här   SAY hahr, SAY huhr   *TEV*
Să·kī′à   suh KIGH uh   *NIV*
Săk′küth   SAK kooth   *RSV*
Să′là   SAY luh (Să′lah)   *KJV. RSV*
Săl′å·mīs   SAL uh miss   *KJV. NAS. NIV. RSV*
Să·lā′thĭ·ēl   suh LAY thih el   *KJV*
Săl′chah (Săl′cah)   SAL kuh   *KJV*
Săl′ê·cah   SAL ih kuh   *KJV. NAS. NIV. RSV. TEV*
Să′lēm   SAY luhm   *KJV. NAS. NIV. RSV. TEV*
Să′lĭm   SAY lim   *KJV. NAS. NIV. RSV. TEV*
Săl′lā·ī   SAL ay igh, sah LAY igh, SAL igh   *KJV. NAS. NIV. RSV. TEV*
Săl′lū   SAL yoo   *KJV. NAS. NIV. RSV. TEV*
Săl′mà   SAL muh   *KJV. NAS. NIV. RSV. TEV*
Săl′maì   SAL migh, SAL may igh   *KJV*
Săl′mŏn   SAL mahn   *KJV. NAS. NIV. RSV. TEV*
Săl·mō′nê   sal MOH nih   *KJV. NAS. NIV. RSV. TEV*
Să·lō′mê   suh LOH mih   *KJV. NAS. NIV. RSV. TEV*
Salt-Çï′tÿ   SAWLT-SIH tih   *TEV*
Să′lū   SAY lyoo   *KJV. NAS. NIV. RSV. TEV*
Să·mā′rĭ·à   suh MER ih uh, suh MAY rih uh   *KJV. NAS. NIV. RSV. TEV*
Să·mâr′ĭ·tan   suh MER ih tuhn   *KJV. NAS. NIV. RSV. TEV*
Săm′gär   SAM gahr   *NIV*
Săm′gär-nē′bō   SAM gahr-NEE boh   *KJV. RSV. TEV*

Săm′gär-nē′bu   SAM gahr-NEE buh   *NAS*
Săm′lah   SAM luh   *KJV. NAS. NIV. RSV. TEV*
Să′mŏs   SAY mahs   *KJV. NAS. NIV. RSV. TEV*
Săm·ō·thrāce′   sam oh THRAYS   *NAS. NIV. RSV*
Săm·ō·thrā′çĭ·à   sam oh THRAY shih uh   *KJV, TEV*
Săm′son   SAMP s′n   *KJV. NAS. NIV. RSV. TEV*
Săm′ū·ēl   SAM yoo el   *KJV. NAS. NIV. RSV. TEV*
Săn·băl′làt   san BAL uht   *KJV. NAS. NIV. RSV. TEV*
Săn′hē·drĭn   SAN he drihn, san HE drihn   *NIV*
Săn·săn′nah   san SAN nuh   *KJV. NAS. NIV. RSV. TEV*
Săph   SAF   *KJV. NAS. NIV. RSV. TEV*
Să′phĭr   SAY fur, SAF ur   *KJV*
Să′phŏn   SAY fahn   *TEV*
Săp·phī′rà   suh FIGH ruh   *KJV. NAS. NIV. RSV. TEV*
Să′rah (Să′rà)   SER uh   *KJV. NAS. NIV. RSV. TEV*
Să′raì   SAY righ, SER ay igh   *KJV. NAS. NIV. RSV. TEV*
Să′räph   SAY raf   *KJV. NAS. NIV. RSV. TEV*
Sär′dĭs   SAHR diss   *KJV. NAS. NIV. RSV. TEV*
Sär′dīte   SAHR dight   *KJV*
Să·rĕp′tà   suh REP tuh   *KJV*
Sär′gŏn   SAHR gahn   *KJV. NAS. NIV. RSV*
Să′rĭd   SAY rid   *KJV. NAS. NIV. RSV. TEV*
Să′rŏn   SAY rahn   *KJV*
Sär′sê·chĭm   SAHR sih kim, sahr SEE kim   *KJV. RSV. TEV*
Sär-sē′kĭm   SAHR-SEE kihm   *NAS*
Să′rŭch   SAY ruhk, SER uhk   *KJV. TEV*
Să′tan   SAY tuhn   *KJV. NAS. NIV. RSV. TEV*
Saūl   SAWL   *KJV. NAS. NIV. RSV. TEV*
Să′vĭ′·ôr   SAY vih awr, SAY vihawr   *NAS, NIV, RSV, TEV*
Scē′và   SEE vuh   *KJV. NAS. NIV. RSV. TEV*
Scÿth′ĭ·an   SITH ih uhn   *KJV. NAS. NIV. RSV*
Sē′bà   SEE buh   *KJV. NAS. NIV. RSV.*

TEV

Se′băm SEE bam *KJV, NAS, NIV, RSV*

Se′băt SEE bat *KJV, TEV*

Se·cā′cah sih KAY kuh, SEK uh huh *KJV, NAS, NIV, RSV, TEV*

Se′chū (Se′cū) SEE kyoo *KJV*

Se′cū SEE kyoo *KJV, NAS, NIV, RSV, TEV*

Se·cŭn′dŭs sih KUHN duhs *KJV, NAS, NIV, RSV, TEV*

Se′gŭb SEE guhb *KJV, NAS, NIV, RSV, TEV*

Se′ĭr SEE ur *KJV, NAS, NIV, RSV, TEV*

Se′ĭ·rah SEE ih ruh, see IGH ruh, *NAS, NIV, RSV, TEV*

Se·ĭ′răth sih IGH rath, SEE uh rath *KJV*

Se′là (Se′lah) SEE luh *KJV, NAS, NIV, RSV, TEV*

Se′là·hăm·măh′le·kŏth SEE luh-huh MAH lih kahth *KJV, NIV*

Se′lĕd SEE led *KJV, NAS, NIV, RSV, TEV*

Se·lĕū′cĭ·à sih LYOO shih uh *KJV, NAS, NIV, RSV, TEV*

Sĕm SEM *KJV*

Sĕm·à·chī′ah sem uh KIGH uh *KJV, NAS, RSV, TEV*

Sĕm′à·kī′ah sem uh KIGH uh *NIV*

Sĕm′ē·ī SEM ih igh *KJV*

Sĕm′ē·ĭn SEHM ee ihn *NAS, NIV, RSV*

Se·nā′ah sih NAY uh, SEN ay uh *KJV, NAS, NIV*

Se′nâte SIH net *NAS*

Se′nĕh SEE neh *KJV, NAS, NIV, RSV, TEV*

Se′nĭr SEE nir *KJV, NAS, NIV, RSV, TEV*

Sĕn·năch′er·ĭb suh NAK ur ib *KJV, NAS, NIV, RSV, TEV*

Se·nū′ah sih NYOO uh, SEN yoo uh *KJV*

Se·ō′rĭm see OH rim, see OWR im *KJV, NAS, NIV, RSV, TEV*

Se′phăr SEE far *KJV, NAS, NIV, RSV, TEV*

Se·phā′răd sih FAY rad, SEF uh rad *KJV, NAS, NIV, RSV*

Se·phär·vā′ĭm see far VAY im, sef ahr VAY im *KJV, NAS, NIV, RSV, TEV*

Se·phär′vīte see FAR vight, SEF ahr vight *KJV, NAS, NIV, RSV, TEV*

Se′rah SEE ruh *KJV, NAS, NIV, RSV, TEV*

Se·raĭ′ah sih RIGH uh *KJV, NAS, NIV,*

RSV, TEV

Sĕr′à·phĭm SER uh fim *KJV, NAS, RSV*

Se′rĕd SEE red *KJV, NAS, NIV, RSV, TEV*

Se′rĕ·dīte SEE rih dight, SEE ruh dight *NAS, NIV, RSV*

Sĕr′gĭ·ŭs SUHR jih uhs *KJV, NAS, RSV*

Sĕr′gĭ·us-Pāu′lŭs SUHR jih uhs-PAW luhs *NIV*

Se′rŭg SEE ruhg *KJV, NAS, NIV, RSV, TEV*

Sĕth SETH *KJV, NAS, NIV, RSV, TEV*

Se′thŭr SEE thur *KJV, NAS, NIV, RSV, TEV*

Se·vĕn′eh sih VEN eh, sih VEEN eh *KJV*

Shā·à·lăb′bĭn shay uh LAB in *KJV, NAS, NIV, RSV*

Shā·ăl′bĭm shay AL bim *KJV, NAS, NIV, RSV, TEV*

Shā·ăl′bon shay AL buhn *RSV, TEV*

Shā·ăl′bō·nīte shay AL boh night, shay al BOH night *KJV, NAS, NIV*

Shā′à·lĭm SHAY uh lihm *NAS, NIV, RSV, TEV*

Shā′ăph SHAY af *KJV, NAS, NIV, RSV, TEV*

Shā·à·rā′ĭm shay uh RAY im *KJV, NAS, NIV, RSV, TEV*

Shā·ăsh′găz shay ASH gahz *KJV, NAS, NIV, RSV, TEV*

Shăb′be·thaĭ SHAB ih thigh *KJV, NAS, NIV, RSV, TEV*

Shà·chī′à shuh KIGH uh, SHAK ih uh *KJV*

Shăd′daĭ SHAD igh, SHAD ay igh *KJV*

Shăd′răch SHAD rak, SHAY drak *KJV, NAS, NIV, RSV, TEV*

Shā′ge SHAY gih *KJV*

Shā′gee SHAY ghee *NIV, RSV, TEV*

Shā′gee SHAY gih, SHAY ghee *NAS*

Shā′här SHAY hahr *KJV, TEV*

Shā·hà·rā′ĭm shay huh RAY im *KJV, NAS, NIV, RSV, TEV*

Shā·hà·zī′mah shay huh ZIGH muh *KJV*

Shā′hà·zū′mah SHAY huh ZOO muh, shuh ha ZOO muh *NAS, NIV, RSV*

Shā′lĕm SHAY luhm *KJV*

Shā′lĭm SHAY lim *KJV*

Shăl·ī′shā SHAL uh shah *KJV, NIV, TEV*

Shăl′lĭ·shäh SHAL ih shah, shuh LIGH

shuh *NAS, RSV*
Shăl′lĕ·chĕth SHAL ih keth *KJV, NAS, RSV, TEV*
Shăl′lĕ·kĕth SHAL ih keth *NIV*
Shăl′lŭm SHAL uhm *KJV, NAS, NIV, RSV, TEV*
Shăl′lŭn SHAL uhn *KJV, NIV*
Shăl′mā·ī SHAL may igh, SHAL migh *KJV, NAS, NIV, RSV, TEV*
Shăl′măn SHAL man *KJV, NAS, NIV, RSV, TEV*
Shăl·man·ē′şēr shal muhn EE zur *KJV, NAS, NIV, RSV, TEV*
Shā′mà SHAY muh *KJV, NAS, NIV, RSV*
Shăm·ȧ·rī′ah sham uh RIGH uh *KJV*
Shā′mĕd SHAY med *KJV*
Shā′mēr SHAY muhr *KJV*
Shăm′gär SHAM gahr *KJV, NAS, NIV, RSV, TEV*
Shăm′hŭth SHAM huhth *KJV, NAS, NIV, RSV, TEV*
Shā′mĭr SHAY mur *KJV, NIV, RSV, TEV*
Shăm′laì SHAM ligh, SHAM lay igh *KJV, RSV, TEV*
Shăm′mà SHAM uh *KJV, NAS, NIV, RSV, TEV*
Shăm′mah SHAM uh *KJV, NAS, NIV, RSV, TEV*
Shăm′mā·ī SHAM ay igh *KJV, NAS, NIV, RSV, TEV*
Shăm′mŏth SHAM ahth *KJV, NAS, NIV, RSV, TEV*
Shăm′mū·à (Shăm′mū·ah) SHAM yoo uh *KJV, NAS, NIV, RSV, TEV*
Shăm′shĕ·raì SHAM shuh righ *KJV, NAS, NIV, RSV, TEV*
Shā′phăm SHAY fam *KJV, NAS, NIV, RSV*
Shā′phăn SHAY fan *KJV, NAS, NIV, RSV, TEV*
Shā′phăt SHAY fat *KJV, NAS, NIV, RSV, TEV*
Shā′phēr SHAY fur *KJV*
Shā′phĭr SHAY fur *KJV, NAS, NIV, RSV, TEV*
Shā′raì SHAY righ, shuh RAY igh *KJV, NAS, NIV, RSV, TEV*
Shȧ·rā′īm shuh RAY im *KJV*
Shā′ràr SHAY rur *KJV, NAS, NIV, RSV, TEV*
Shȧ·rē′zēr shuh REE zur *KJV, NAS, NIV, RSV, TEV*

Shăr′on SHER uhn *KJV, NAS, NIV, RSV, TEV*
Shâr′on·īte SHER uhn ight *KJV, NAS, NIV, RSV*
Shȧ·rū′hĕn shuh ROO hen *KJV, NAS, NIV, RSV, TEV*
Shā′shaì SHAY shigh *KJV, NAS, NIV, RSV, TEV*
Shā′shăk SHAY shak *KJV, NAS, NIV, RSV, TEV*
Shā′ŭl SHAY uhl *KJV, NAS, NIV, RSV, TEV*
Shā′ŭl·īte SHAY uhl ight *KJV, NAS, NIV, RSV*
Shā′vĕh SHAY veh *KJV, NAS, NIV, RSV, TEV*
Shā′vĕh-kir·ĭ·ȧ·thā′ĭm SHAY veh-kir ih uh THAY im *KJV, NAS, NIV, RSV*
Shăv′shà SHAV shuh *KJV, NAS, NIV, RSV*
Shē′ăl SHEE al *KJV, NAS, NIV, RSV, TEV*
Shē·ăl′tĭ·ĕl shih AL tih el *KJV, NAS, NIV, RSV, TEV*
Shē·ȧ·rī′ah shee uh RIGH uh *KJV, NAS, NIV, RSV, TEV*
Shē′är-jā′shŭb SHEE ahr-JAY shuhb *KJV, NAS, NIV, RSV, TEV*
Shē′bà SHEE bah *KJV, NAS, NIV, RSV, TEV*
Shē′băm SHEE bam *KJV*
Shĕb·ȧ·nī′ah sheb uh NIGH uh *KJV, NAS, NIV, RSV, TEV*
Shĕb′ȧ·rĭm SHEB uh rim *KJV, NAS, NIV, RSV*
Shē′băt SHE bat, shih BAT *NAS, NIV, RSV, TEV*
Shē′bēr SHEE bur *KJV, NAS, NIV, RSV, TEV*
Shĕb′nà (Shĕb′nah) SHEB nuh *KJV, NAS, NIV, RSV, TEV*
Shĕb′ŭ·ĕl SHEB yoo el, shi BYOO uhl *KJV, NAS, NIV, RSV, TEV*
Shĕc·ȧ·nī′ah (Shĕch·ȧ·nī′ah) shek uh NIGH uh *KJV, NAS, NIV, RSV, TEV*
Shĕch′ĕm SHEK uhm, SHEE kuhm *KJV, NAS, NIV, RSV, TEV*
Shĕch′ĕm·īte SHEK uhm ight, SHEE kuhm ight *KJV, NAS, NIV, RSV*
Shĕd′ĕ·ŭr SHED ih ur, shi DEE ur *KJV, NAS, NIV, RSV, TEV*
Shē′ē·rah SHEE uh ruh *KJV, NAS, NIV, RSV, TEV*
Shē·hȧ·rī′ah shee huh RIGH uh *KJV,*

NAS, NIV, RSV, TEV
Shē′lah   SHEE luh   *KJV, NAS, NIV, RSV, TEV*
Shē′lån·īte   SHEE luhn ight, shee LAY night   *KJV, NAS, NIV, RSV*
Shĕl·ĕ·mī′ah   shel uh MIGH uh   *KJV, NAS, NIV, RSV, TEV*
Shē′lĕph   SHEE lef   *KJV, NAS, NIV, RSV, TEV*
Shē′lésh   SHEE lesh   *KJV, NAS, NIV, RSV, TEV*
Shē·lō′mī   shih LOH migh, SHEL oh migh   *KJV, NAS, NIV, RSV, TEV*
Shē·lō′mith   shih LOH mith, SHEL oh mith   *KJV, NAS, NIV, RSV, TEV*
Shē·lō′mŏth   shih LOH mahth, SHEL oh moth   *KJV, NAS, NIV, RSV, TEV*
Shē·lū′mī·ĕl   shih LYOO mih el   *KJV, NAS, NIV, RSV, TEV*
Shĕm   SHEM   *KJV, NAS, NIV, RSV, TEV*
Shē′mä   SHEE mah, shuh MAH   *KJV, NAS, NIV, RSV, TEV*
Shē·mā′ah   shih MAY uh, SHEM ay uh   *KJV, NAS, NIV, RSV, TEV*
Shē·maī′ah   shih MAY yuh, shem uh IGH uh   *KJV, NAS, NIV, RSV, TEV*
Shĕm·å·rī′ah   shem uh RIGH uh   *KJV, NAS, NIV, RSV, TEV*
Shĕm·ē′bĕr   shem EE bur   *KJV, NAS, NIV, RSV, TEV*
Shē′mĕd   SHEE med   *KJV, NAS, NIV, RSV, TEV*
Shē′mĕr   SHEE mur   *KJV, NAS, NIV, RSV, TEV*
Shē·mī′da   shih MIGH duh   *KJV, NAS, NIV, RSV, TEV*
Shē·mī′dah   shih MIGH duh   *KJV*
Shē·mī′då·īte   shih MIGH duh ight   *KJV, NAS, NIV, RSV*
Shĕm′ī·nīth   SHEM uh nith   *KJV, NAS, NIV, RSV*
Shē·mir′å·mŏth   shih MIR uh mahth, shih MIGH ruh moth   *KJV, NAS, NIV, RSV, TEV*
Shē·mū′ĕl   shih MYOO el, SHEM yoo uhl   *KJV, NIV, RSV, TEV*
Shĕn   SHEN   *KJV, NAS, NIV, TEV*
Shē·nā′zär   shih NAY zahr, SHEN uh zahr   *KJV*
Shē·nāz′zär   shih NAY zahr, SHEN uh zahr, shen AZ zahr   *NAS, NIV, RSV, TEV*
Shē′nīr   SHEE nur   *KJV*
Shē′ōl   SHEE ohl   *NAS, RSV*

Shē′phăm   SHEE fam   *KJV, NAS, NIV, RSV, TEV*
Shĕph·å·tī′ah   shef uh TIGH uh   *KJV, NAS, NIV, RSV, TEV*
Shē′phē·läh   SHEH fih lah, sheh FEE luh   *NAS, RSV*
Shē′phĕr   SHEE fur   *KJV, NAS, NIV, RSV, TEV*
Shē′phī   SHEE figh   *KJV, NAS, RSV, TEV*
Shē′phō   SHEE foh   *KJV, NAS, NIV, RSV, TEV*
Shē·phū′phăm   shih FYOO fam, sheh FOO fuhm   *NAS, RSV, TEV*
Shē·phū′phăn   shih FYOO fan   *KJV, NAS, NIV, RSV, TEV*
Shē′rah   SHEE ruh   *KJV, TEV*
Shĕr·ē·bī′ah   sher uh BIGH uh   *KJV, NAS, NIV, RSV, TEV*
Shē′rĕsh   SHEE resh   *KJV, NAS, NIV, RSV, TEV*
Shē·rē′zĕr   shih REE zur, shahr EE zur   *KJV*
Shē′shăch   SHEE shak   *KJV, NAS, NIV*
Shē′shaī   SHEE shigh   *KJV, NAS, NIV, RSV, TEV*
Shē′shăk   SHE shak   *NAS*
Shē′shăn   SHEE shan   *KJV, NAS, NIV, RSV, TEV*
Shĕsh′băz′zär   shesh BAZ ur   *KJV, NAS, NIV, RSV, TEV*
Shĕth   SHETH   *KJV, NAS, NIV, RSV*
Shē′thär   SHEE thahr   *KJV, NAS, NIV, RSV, TEV*
Shē′thär-Bŏz′ē·naī   SHE thahr-BAHZ ih nigh   *NAS, NIV, RSV, TEV*
Shē′thär-bŏz′naī   SHEE thahr-BAHZ nigh   *KJV*
Shē′và   SHEE vuh   *KJV, NAS, NIV, RSV*
Shīb′ah   SHIHB uh, SHIHV uh   *KJV, NAS, NIV, RSV*
Shīb′bō·lĕth   SHIB oh leth   *KJV, NAS, NIV, RSV, TEV*
Shīb′mah   SHIB muh   *KJV*
Shīc′rŏn   SHIK rahn   *KJV*
Shig·ḡaī·ŏn   shih GAY ahn, shih GIGH yahn   *KJV*
Shiḡ·ī·ō′nŏth   shig ih OH nahth, shih GIGH uh nahth   *KJV, NAS, NIV, RSV*
Shī′hŏn (Shī′ŏn)   SHIGH hahn   *KJV*
Shī′hŏr   SHIGH hawr   *KJV, NAS, NIV, RSV, TEV*
Shī′hŏr-līb′năth   SHIGH hawr-LIB nath   *KJV, NAS, NIV, RSV, TEV*
Shīk′kĕr·ŏn   SHIK ur ahn   *KJV, NAS,*

NIV, RSV, TEV

Shĭl′hī   SHIL high   *KJV, NAS, NIV, RSV, TEV*

Shĭl′hĭm   SHIL him   *KJV, NAS, NIV, RSV, TEV*

Shĭl′lĕm   SHIL em   *KJV, NAS, NIV, RSV, TEV*

Shĭl′lĕm·īte   SHIL em ight   *KJV, NAS, NIV, RSV*

Shĭ·lō′ah   shigh LOH uh   *KJV, NAS, NIV, RSV, TEV*

Shĭ′lōh   SHIGH loh   *KJV, NAS, NIV, RSV, TEV*

Shĭ·lō′nī   shigh LOH nigh   *KJV*

Shĭ′lō·nīte   SHIGH loh night   *KJV, NAS, NIV, RSV*

Shĭl′shäh   SHIL shah   *KJV, NAS, NIV, RSV, TEV*

Shĭm′ė·à (Shĭm′ė·ah)   SHIM ih uh   *KJV, NAS, NIV, RSV, TEV*

Shĭm′ė·ăm   SHIM ih am   *KJV, NAS, NIV, RSV*

Shĭm′ė·ăth   SHIM ih ath   *KJV, NAS, NIV, RSV, TEV*

Shĭm′ė·ăth·īte   SHIM ih uhth ight   *KJV, NAS, NIV, RSV, TEV*

Shĭm′ė·ī   SHIM eh igh   *KJV, NAS, NIV, RSV, TEV*

Shĭm′ė·ītes   SHIM ee ights, SHIM ih ights   *NAS, NIV, RSV*

Shĭm′hī   SHIM high   *KJV*

Shĭm′ė·on   SHIM ih uhn   *KJV, NAS, NIV, RSV, TEV*

Shĭm′īte   SHIM ight   *KJV*

Shĭm′ma   SHIM uh   *KJV*

Shĭ′mŏn   SHIGH mahn   *KJV, NAS, NIV, RSV, TEV*

Shĭm′răthʹ   SHIM rath   *KJV, NAS, NIV, RSV, TEV*

Shĭm′rī   SHIM righ   *KJV, NAS, NIV, RSV, TEV*

Shĭm′rĭth   SHIM rith   *KJV, NAS, NIV, RSV, TEV*

Shĭm′rŏm   SHIM rahm   *KJV*

Shĭm′rŏn   SHIM rahn   *KJV, NAS, NIV, RSV, TEV*

Shĭm′rŏn′īte   SHIM rahn ight   *KJV, NAS, NIV, RSV, TEV*

Shĭm′rŏn-mē′rŏn   SHIM rahn-MEE rahn   *KJV, NAS, NIV, RSV, TEV*

Shĭm′shàì   SHIM shigh, SHIM shay igh   *KJV, NAS, NIV, RSV, TEV*

Shĭ′năb   SHIGH nab   *KJV, NAS, NIV, RSV, TEV*

Shĭ′när   SHIGH nahr   *KJV, NAS, NIV, RSV*

Shĭ′ŏn   SHIGH ahn   *KJV, NAS, NIV, RSV, TEV*

Shĭ′phī   SHIGH figh   *KJV, NAS, NIV, RSV, TEV*

Shĭph′mīte   SHIF might   *KJV, NAS, NIV, RSV*

Shĭph′rah   SHIF ruh   *KJV, NAS, NIV, RSV, TEV*

Shĭph′tan   SHIF tuhn   *KJV, NAS, NIV, RSV, TEV*

Shĭ′shà   SHIGH shuh   *KJV, NAS, NIV, RSV, TEV*

Shĭ′shăk   SHIGH shak   *KJV, NAS, NIV, RSV, TEV*

Shĭt·rā′ī   shit RAY igh, SHIT ray igh   *KJV, NAS, NIV, RSV, TEV*

Shĭt′tĭm   SHIT im   *KJV, NAS, NIV, RSV*

Shī′zà   SHIGH zuh   *KJV, NAS, NIV, RSV, TEV*

Shō′à   SHOH uh   *KJV, NAS, NIV, RSV, TEV*

Shō′băb   SHOH bab   *KJV*

Shō′băch   SHOH bak   *KJV, NAS, NIV, RSV*

Shō′bā·ī   SHOH bay igh   *KJV, NAS, NIV, RSV, TEV*

Shō′băl   SHOH bal   *KJV, NAS, NIV, RSV, TEV*

Shō′bĕk   SHOH bek   *KJV, NAS, NIV, RSV, TEV*

Shō′bī   SHOH bigh   *KJV, NAS, NIV, RSV, TEV*

Shō′cō (Shō′chō, Shō′choh)   SHOH koh   *KJV*

Shō′hăm   SHOH ham   *KJV, NAS, NIV, RSV, TEV*

Shō′mēr   SHOH mur   *KJV, NAS, NIV, RSV, TEV*

Shō′phăch   SHOH fak   *KJV, NAS, NIV, RSV*

Shō′phăn   SHOH fan   *KJV, NAS, NIV, RSV, TEV*

Shō·shăn′nĭm   shoh SHAN im   *KJV*

Shō·shăn′nĭm-ē′dŭth   shoh SHAN im-EE duhth   *KJV*

Shū′à (Shūah)   SHOO uh   *KJV, NAS, NIV, RSV*

Shū′ah   SHOO uh   *KJV, NAS, NIV, RSV, TEV*

Shū′ăl   SHOO al   *KJV, NAS, NIV, RSV, TEV*

Shū′bā·ĕl   SHOO bay el   *KJV, NAS, NIV,*

RSV

Shū′hăh SHOO ha *KJV, NAS, NIV, RSV, TEV*

Shū′hăm SHOO ham *KJV, NAS, NIV, RSV, TEV*

Shū′hăm·īte SHOO ham ight *KJV, NAS, NIV, RSV*

Shū′hīte SHOO hight *KJV, NAS, NIV, RSV, TEV*

Shū′lăm·īte (Shū′lăm·mīte) SHOO lam ight *KJV, NAS, NIV, RSV*

Shū′măth·īte SHOO math ight *KJV, NAS, NIV, RSV, TEV*

Shū′nam·mīte SHOO nuhm ight *KJV, NAS, NIV, RSV*

Shū′nĕm SHOO nem *KJV, NAS, NIV, RSV, TEV*

Shū′nī SHOO nigh *KJV, NAS, NIV, RSV, TEV*

Shū′nīte SHOO night *KJV, NAS, NIV, RSV*

Shū′phăm SHOO fam *KJV, NIV*

Shū′phăm·īte SHOO fam ight *KJV, NAS, NIV, RSV*

Shŭp′pĭm SHUHP im *KJV, NAS, NIV, RSV, TEV*

Shūr SHOOR *KJV, NAS, NIV, RSV, TEV*

Shū′shăn SHOO shan *KJV*

Shū′shăn·chītes SHOO shan kights *KJV*

Shū′shăn-ē′dŭth SHOO shan-EE duhth *KJV*

Shū·thăl′hīte shoo THAL hight *KJV*

Shū′thĕ·lah SHOO thih luh, shoo THEE luh *KJV, NAS, NIV, RSV, TEV*

Shū·thē′lă·hīte shoo THEE luh hight *KJV, NIV, RSV*

Shū·thē′lă·īte shoo THEE luh ight, shoo THUH luh ight *NAS*

Sī′à SIGH uh *KJV, NAS, NIV, RSV, TEV*

Sī′â·hà SIGH uh huh *KJV, NAS, NIV, RSV, TEV*

Sĭb′bĕ·caì (Sĭb′bĕ·chaì) SIB uh kigh *KJV, NAS, NIV, RSV, TEV*

Sĭb′bō·lĕth SIB oh leth *KJV, NAS, NIV, RSV*

Sĭb′mah SIB muh *KJV, NAS, NIV, RSV, TEV*

Sĭb′ră·im SIB ray im *KJV, NAS, NIV, RSV, TEV*

Sī′chĕm SIGH kem *KJV*

Sĭd′dĭm SID im *KJV, NAS, NIV, RSV, TEV*

Sī′don SIGH duhn *KJV, NAS, NIV, RSV, TEV*

Sī·dō′nĭ·an sigh DOH nih uhn *KJV, NAS, NIV, RSV, TEV*

Sī′hŏn SIGH hahn *KJV, NAS, NIV, RSV, TEV*

Sī′hôr SIGH hawr *KJV*

Sĭk′kūth SIHK uth *NAS*

Sī′làs SIGH luhs *KJV, NAS, NIV, RSV, TEV*

Sĭl′là SIL uh *KJV, NAS, NIV, RSV, TEV*

Sĭ·lō′ah sih LOH uh *KJV*

Sĭ·lō′am sih LOH uhm *KJV, NAS, NIV, RSV, TEV*

Sĭl·vā′nŭs sihl VAY nuhs *KJV, NAS, RSV*

Sĭm′ĕ·on SIM ih uhn *KJV, NAS, NIV, RSV, TEV*

Sĭm′ĕ·on·īte SIM ih uhn ight *KJV, NAS, NIV, RSV*

Sī′mon SIGH muhn *KJV, NAS, NIV, RSV, TEV*

Sī′mon-Pē′tĕr SIGH muhn-PEE tuhr *KJV, NAS, NIV, RSV, TEV*

Sĭm′rī SIM righ *KJV*

Sĭn SIN *KJV, NAS, NIV, RSV, TEV*

Sī′nà SIGH nuh *KJV*

Sī′nā·ī SIGH nay igh, SIGH nigh *KJV, NAS, NIV, RSV, TEV*

Sī′nĭm SIGH nim *KJV, NAS, NIV*

Sī′nīte SIGH night *KJV, NAS, NIV, RSV, TEV*

Sī′on SIGH`uhn *KJV*

Sĭph′mŏth SIF mahth *KIV, NAS, NIV, RSV, TEV*

Sĭp′pā′ī SIP ay igh, SIHP igh *KJV, NAS, NIV, RSV, TEV*

Sī′rah SIGH ruh *KJV, NAS, NIV, RSV, TEV*

Sĭr′ĭ·ŏn SIHR ih ahn *KJV, NAS, NIV, RSV, TEV*

Sĭs′â·maì SIS uh migh *KJV*

Sĭs′ĕr·à SIS ur uh *KJV, NAS, NIV, RSV, TEV*

Sĭs′maì SIHS migh, SIHS may igh *NAS, NIV, RSV, TEV*

Sĭth′rī SITH righ *KJV, NAS, NIV, RSV, TEV*

Sĭt′nah SIT nuh *KJV, NAS, NIV, RSV*

Sī′văn SIGH van, see VAHN *KJV, NAS, NIV, RSV, TEV*

Sī′yon SIGH yahn *NIV*

Smŷr′nà SMUR nuh *KJV, NAS, NIV, RSV, TEV*

Sō SOH *KJV, NAS*

Sō′chō (Sō′cōh, Sō′chōh) SOH koh

KJV, NAS, NIV, RSV, TEV
Sŏ′cō   SOH koh   NAS, NIV, RSV, TEV
Sŏ′dī   SOH digh   KJV, NAS, NIV, RSV, TEV
Sŏd′om   SAHD uhm   KJV, NAS, NIV, RSV, TEV
Sŏd′ŏ·mà   SAHD oh muh   KJV
Sŏd′om·īte   SAHD uhm ight   KJV, NAS, RSV
Sŏl′o·mon   SAHL uh muhn   KJV, NAS, NIV, RSV, TEV
Sŏp′à·tēr   SAHP uh tur, SOH puh tur   KJV, NAS, NIV, RSV, TEV
Sŏph′ě·rěth   SAHF uh reth, SOH fih reth   KJV, NAS, NIV, RSV, TEV
Sŏ′rěk   SOH rek   KJV, NAS, NIV, RSV, TEV
Sŏ·sĭp′à·tēr   so SIP uh tur   KJV, NAS, NIV, RSV, TEV
Sŏs′thĕ·nĕṣ   SAHS thih neez   KJV, NAS, NIV, RSV, TEV
Sŏ′tā·ī   SOH tay igh, soh TAY igh   KJV, NAS, NIV, TEV
Spain   SPAYN   KJV, NAS, NIV, RSV, TEV
Stā′chy̆s   STAY kiss   KJV, NAS, NIV, RSV, TEV
Stĕph′à·nàs   STEF uh nuhs   KJV, NAS, NIV, RSV, TEV
Stē′phĕn   STEE vuhn   KJV, NAS, NIV, RSV, TEV
Stō′ic   STOH ihk   NAS, NIV, RSV, TEV
Stō′icks   STOH iks   KJV
Sū′ah   SOO uh   KJV, NAS, NIV, RSV, TEV
Sū′cà·thīte   SOO kuh thight   NAS, RSV, TEV
Sŭc′cōth   SUHK ahth   KJV, NAS, NIV, RSV
Sŭc′cŏth-bē′nŏth   SUHK ahth-BEE nahth   KJV, NAS, NIV, RSV, TEV
Sū′chà·thīte   SOO kuh thight, SOO kath ight   KJV
Sū′dăn   SOO dan   TEV
Sū′da·nĕṣe   SOO duh neez   TEV
Sū′ĕz   SOO ehz   TEV
Sŭk′kī·ims   SUHK ih ims   KJV, NAS, RSV
Sŭk′kīte   SUHK kight   NIV, TEV
Sŭk′kŏth   SUHK ahth   TEV
Sŭph   SOOF   KJV, NAS, NIV, RSV, TEV
Sū′phah   SOO fuh   KJV, NAS, NIV, RSV, TEV
Sūr   SUR   KJV, NAS, NIV, RSV, TEV
Sū′sà   SOO suh   NAS, NIV, RSV, TEV
Sū′săn·chīte   SOO san kight   KJV, RSV,

TEV
Sū·ṣăn′nà   soo ZAN uh   KJV, NAS, NIV, RSV, TEV
Sū′sī   SOO sigh   KJV, NAS, NIV, RSV, TEV
Sy̆′chär   SIGH kahr   KJV, NAS, NIV, RSV, TEV
Sy̆′chĕm   SIGH kem   KJV
Sy̆·ē′nĕ   sigh EE nih   KJV, NAS, RSV
Sy̆m′ĕ·on   SIM ih uhn   KJV
Sy̆n′ty̆·chē   SIN tih kee   KJV, NAS, NIV, RSV, TEV
Sy̆r′à·cūṣe   SEER uh kyooz   KJV, NAS, NIV, RSV, TEV
Sy̆r′ĭ·à   SIHR ih uh   KJV, NAS, NIV, RSV, TEV
Sy̆r′ĭ·an   SIHR ih uhn   KJV, NAS, NIV, RSV, TEV
Sy̆·rō·phĕ·nīc′ian   sigh roh fih NISH uhn   KJV, RSV
Sy̆·rō·phoĕ·nī′cian   sigh roh fih NEE shuhn   NAS, NIV
Sy̆r′tīs   SUHR tihs, SIHR tihs   NIV, RSV

Tā′à·năch   TAY uh nak   KJV, NAS, NIV, RSV, TEV
Tā′à·näth-shī′lōh   TAY uh nath-SHIGH loh   KJV, NAS, NIV, RSV, TEV
Tăb′bā·ŏth   TAB ay oth, tuh BAY ahth   KJV, NAS, NIV, RSV, TEV
Tăb′bàth   TAB uhth   KJV, NAS, NIV, RSV, TEV
Tā′bĕ·al   TAY bih uhl   KJV, TEV
Tăb′ēĕl   TAB uhl, TAY bih el, TAB eel   KJV, NAS, NIV, RSV, TEV
Tăb′ĕ·rah   TAB uh ruh   KJV, NAS, NIV, RSV, TEV
Tăb′ī·thà   TAB ih thuh   KJV, NAS, NIV, RSV, TEV
Tā′bôr   TAY bawr   KJV, NAS, NIV, RSV, TEV
Tăb-rĭm′on   tab-RIM uhn   KJV

Tăb-rĭm′mon   tab-RIM uhn   *KJV, NAS, NIV, RSV, TEV*

Tăch′e·mon   TAK ee muhn   *TEV*

Tăch′mo·nīte   TAK muh night   *KJV, TEV*

Tăd′môr   TAD mawr   *KJV, NAS, NIV, RSV*

Tā′hăn   TAY han   *KJV, NAS, NIV, RSV, TEV*

Tā′hăn·īte   TAY han ight   *KJV, NAS, NIV, RSV, TEV*

Tă·hăp′ȧ·nĕṣ   tuh HAP uh neez   *KJV, NAS, TEV*

Tā′hăsh   TAY hash   *KJV, NAS, NIV, RSV, TEV*

Tā′hăth   TAY hath   *KJV, NAS, NIV, RSV, TEV*

Tăh·che′mo·nīte   tah KEE muh night   *NAS, RSV*

Tăh·ke′mo·nīte   tah KEE muh night   *NIV*

Tăh′pan·hĕṣ   TA puhn heez, ta PAN heez   *KJV, NAS, NIV, RSV, TEV*

Tăh′pĕ·nĕṣ   TA pih neez   *KJV, NAS, NIV, RSV*

Tăh·rē′ȧ   ta REE uh   *KJV, NAS, NIV, RSV*

Tăh′tĭm-hŏd′shĭ   TA tim-HAHD shih   *KJV, NAS, NIV*

Tăl′ĭ·thȧ   TAL ih thuh   *NAS, NIV, RSV*

Tăl′ĭ·thȧ-cū′mĭ   TAL ih thuh-KOO mih   *KJV*

Tăl′ĭ·thȧ-koüm   TAL ih thuh-koom   *TEV*

Tăl′maì   TAL migh   *KJV, NAS, NIV, RSV, TEV*

Tăl′mŏn   TAL mahn   *KJV, NAS, NIV, RSV, TEV*

Tā′mah   TAY muh   *KJV*

Tā′mär   TAY mahr   *KJV, NAS, NIV, RSV, TEV*

Tăm′mŭz   TAM uhz   *KJV, NAS, NIV, RSV, TEV*

Tā′năch   TAY nak   *KJV*

Tăn·hŭ′mĕth   tan HYOO meth   *KJV, NAS, NIV, RSV, TEV*

Tā′phăth   TAY fath   *KJV, NAS, NIV, RSV, TEV*

Tăp·pū′ah   ta PYOO uh, TAP yoo uh   *KJV, NAS, NIV, RSV, TEV*

Tā′rah   TAY ruh, TER uh   *KJV*

Tär′ȧ·lah   TAHR uh lah   *KJV, NAS, NIV, RSV, TEV*

Tā′rĕ·ȧ   TAY rih uh, tuh REE uh   *KJV, NAS, NIV, RSV, TEV*

Tär′pĕ·līte   TAR puh light   *KJV*

Tär′shĭsh   TAHR shish   *KJV, NAS, NIV, RSV, TEV*

Tär′sŭs   TAHR suhs   *KJV, NAS, NIV, RSV, TEV*

Tär′tăk   TAHR tak   *KJV, NAS, NIV, RSV, TEV*

Tär′tăn   TAHR tan   *KJV, NAS, RSV*

Tăt′naì   TAT nigh, TAT nay igh   *KJV*

Tăt′tĕ·naì   TAT tih nigh   *NAS, NIV, RSV, TEV*

Tē′bah   TEE buh   *KJV, NAS, NIV, RSV, TEV*

Tĕb·ȧ·lī′ah   teb uh LIGH uh   *KJV, NAS, RSV, TEV*

Tē′bĕth   TEE beth, tay VAYTH   *KJV, NAS, NIV, RSV, TEV*

Tē·hăph′nĕ·hĕṣ   tih HAF nuh heez   *KJV, NAS, RSV*

Tē·hĭn′nah   tih HIN nuh   *KJV, NAS, NIV, RSV, TEV*

Tē′kĕl   TEE k'l, TEK uhl   *KJV, NAS, NIV, RSV*

Tē·kō′ȧ (Tē·kō′ah)   tih KOH uh   *KJV, NAS, NIV, RSV, TEV*

Tē·kō′īte   tih KOH ight   *KJV, NAS, NIV, RSV*

Tĕl-ā′bĭb   tell-AY bib   *KJV, NAS, RSV, TEV*

Tē′lah   TEE luh   *KJV, NAS, NIV, RSV, TEV*

Tē·lā′ĭm   tih LAY im, TELL uh im   *KJV, NAS, NIV, RSV*

Tē·lăs′sȧr   tih LASS ur   *KJV, NAS, RSV, TEV*

Tĕl-Ạs′sȧr   TEHL-ASS suhr   *NIV*

Tĕl-Ȧ·vĭv′   TEHL-uh VEEV   *NIV*

Tē′lĕm   TEE lem   *KJV, NAS, NIV, RSV, TEV*

Tĕl-hȧ·rē′shȧ   tell-huh REE shuh   *KJV, TEV*

Tĕl-här′sȧ   tell-HAHR suh   *KJV*

Tĕl-här′shȧ   tell-HAHR shuh   *KJV, NAS, NIV, RSV, TEV*

Tĕl-mē′lah   tell-MEE luh   *KJV, NAS, NIV, RSV, TEV*

Tē′mà   TEE muh   *KJV, NAS, NIV*

Tē′mah   TEE muh   *KJV, NAS, NIV, RSV, TEV*

Tē′măn   TEE man   *KJV, NAS, NIV, RSV, TEV*

Tē′mȧ·nī   TEE muh nigh, TEM uh nigh   *KJV*

Tē′man·īte   TEE muhn ight   *KJV, NAS, NIV, RSV*

Tĕ′mĕ·nī　TEE muh nigh, TEM uh nih
KJV, NAS, NIV, RSV, TEV
Tĕ′rah　TEE ruh　*KJV, NAS, NIV, RSV, TEV*
Tĕr′à·phĭm　TER uh fim　*KJV, NAS, RSV*
Tĕ′rĕsh　TEE resh　*KJV, NAS, NIV, RSV, TEV*
Tĕr′ti·ŭs　TUR shih uhs　*KJV, NAS, RSV, TEV*
Tĕr·tŭl′lŭs　tur TUHL uhs　*KJV, NAS, RSV, TEV*
Thăd′dǎe·ŭs　THAD ih uhs　*NAS, NIV, RSV, TEV*
Thăd′dé·ŭs　THAD ih uhs　*KJV*
Thā′hăsh　THAY hash　*KJV*
Thā′mah　THAY muh　*KJV*
Thā′mär　THAY mahr　*KJV*
Thā′rà　THAY ruh　*KJV*
Thär′shĭsh　THAHR shish　*KJV*
Thēbeṣ　THEEBZ　*NAS, NIV, RSV*
Thē′bĕz　THEE bez　*KJV, NAS, NIV, RSV, TEV*
Thĕ·lā′sàr　thih LAY sur　*KJV*
Thĕ·ōph′ĭ·lŭs　thih AHF ih luhs　*KJV, NAS, NIV, RSV, TEV*
Thĕs·så·lō′nĭ·an　thess uh LOH nih uhn　*KJV, NAS, NIV, RSV*
Thĕs′så·lō·nī′cà　THESS uh loh NIGH kuh　*KJV, NAS, NIV, RSV, TEV*
Thēū·dàs　THYOO duhs　*KJV, NAS, NIV, RSV, TEV*
Thĭm′nå·thăh　THIM nuh tha　*KJV*
Thom′às　TAHM uhs　*KJV, NAS, NIV, RSV, TEV*
Thŭm′mĭm　THUHM im　*KJV, NAS, NIV, RSV, TEV*
Thy̆·å·tī′rà　thigh uh TIGH ruh　*KJV, NAS, NIV, RSV, TEV*
Tĭ·bĕr′ĭ·às　tigh BIR ih uhs　*KJV, NAS, NIV, RSV, TEV*
Tĭ·bĕr′ĭ·ŭs　tigh BIR ih uhs　*KJV, NAS, NIV, RSV, TEV*
Tĭb′hăth　TIB hath　*KJV, NAS, RSV, TEV*
Tĭb′nī　TIB nigh　*KJV, NAS, NIV, RSV, TEV*
Tī′con　TIGH kuhn　*TEV*
Tī′dăl　TIGH dal　*KJV, NAS, NIV, RSV, TEV*
Tĭg′lăth-pĭ·lē′ṣer　TIG lath-puh LEE zur　*KJV, NAS, NIV, RSV, TEV*
Tī′gris　TIGH griss, TAIG grihs　*NAS, NIV, RSV, TEV*
Tĭk′văh　TIK vah　*KJV, NAS, NIV, RSV, TEV*

Tĭk′văth　TIK vath　*KJV. TEV*
Tĭl′ğăth-pĭl·nĕ′ṣēr　TIL gath-pill NEE zur　*KJV, NAS. RSV*
Tī′lŏn　TIGH lahn　*KJV, NAS, NIV, RSV, TEV*
Tĭ·māē′ŭs　tigh MEE uhs　*KJV, NAS, NIV, RSV, TEV*
Tĭm′nà　TIM nuh　*KJV, NAS, NIV, RSV, TEV*
Tĭm′nah　TIM nuh　*KJV, NAS, NIV, RSV, TEV*
Tĭm′năth　TIM nath　*KJV, NIV*
Tĭm′năth-hē′rēṣ　TIM nath-HEE reez　*KJV, NAS, NIV, RSV*
Tĭm′năth-sē′rah　TIM nath-SEE ruh　*KJV, NAS, NIV, RSV, TEV*
Tĭm′nīte　TIM night　*KJV, NAS, NIV, RSV*
Tī′mŏn　TIGH mahn　*KJV, NAS, NIV, RSV, TEV*
Tĭ·mō′thĕ·ŭs　tih MOH thih uhs　*KJV*
Tĭm′o·thy̆　TIM uh thih　*KJV. NAS, NIV, RSV, TEV*
Tĭph′sah　TIF suh　*KJV, NAS, NIV, RSV, TEV*
Tī′răs　TIGH ras, TIGH ruhs　*KJV, NAS, NIV, RSV, TEV*
Tī′răth·īte　TIGH rath ight, TIGH ra thight　*KJV, NAS, NIV, RSV, TEV*
Tĭr·hā′kah　tur HAY kuh　*KJV, NAS, NIV, RSV, TEV*
Tĭr·hā′nah　tur HAY nuh　*KJV, NAS, NIV, RSV, TEV*
Tĭr′ĭ·à　TIR ih uh, TIGH rih uh　*KJV, NAS, NIV, RSV, TEV*
Tĭr·shā′thà　tur SHUH thuh, TUR shuh thuh　*KJV*
Tĭr′zah　TUR zuh　*KJV, NAS, NIV, RSV, TEV*
Tĭsh′bē　TISH bee　*NIV, RSV, TEV*
Tĭsh′bīte　TISH bight　*KJV, NAS, NIV, RSV*
Tĭt′ĭ·us　TIT ih uhs, TIH shuhs　*NAS, RSV*
Tĭt′ĭ·ŭs-Jŭst′ŭs　TIT ih uhs-JUST uhs　*NIV, TEV*
Tī′tŭs　TIGH tuhs　*KJV, NAS, NIV, RSV, TEV*
Tĭz　TIHZ　*TEV*
Tī′zīte　TIGH zight　*KJV, NAS, NIV, RSV*

Tō'ah   TOH uh   *KJV, NAS, NIV, RSV, TEV*

Tŏb   TAHB   *KJV, NAS, NIV, RSV, TEV*

Tŏb-ăd·o·nī'jah   tahb-ad uh NIGH juh
KJV, NAS, NIV, RSV, TEV

Tō·bī'ah   toh BIGH uh   *KJV, NAS, NIV, RSV, TEV*

Tō·bī'jah   toh BIGH juh   *KJV, NAS, NIV, RSV, TEV*

Tō'chĕn   TOH ken   *KJV, NAS, RSV, TEV*

Tō·gär'mah   toh GAHR muh   *KJV, NAS, NIV, RSV, TEV*

Tō'hū   TOH hyoo   *KJV, NAS, NIV, RSV, TEV*

Tō'ī   TOH igh   *KJV, NAS, RSV, TEV*

Tŏk'hăth   TAHK hath   *KJV, NAS, NIV, RSV*

Tō'lä   TOH luh   *KJV, NAS, NIV, RSV, TEV*

Tō'lăd   TOH lad   *KJV, NAS, NIV, RSV, TEV*

Tō'lä·ite   TOH lay ight   *KJV, NAS, NIV, RSV*

Tō'phĕl   TOH fel   *KJV, NAS, NIV, RSV, TEV*

Tō'phĕt   TOH fet   *KJV*

Tō'phĕth   TOH feth   *KJV, NAS, NIV, RSV, TEV*

Tō'ū   TOH oo   *KJV, NAS, NIV, RSV*

Trăch·o·nī'tĭs   trak uh NIGH tihs   *KJV, NAS, RSV, TEV*

Trĭ'po·lĭs   TRIH puh lihs   *NIV*

Trō'ăs   TROH az   *KJV, NAS, NIV, RSV, TEV*

Trō·gȳl'lǐ·ŭm   troh JIL ih uhm, troh GIL ih uhm   *KJV*

Trŏph'ǐ·mŭs   TRAHF ih muhs   *KJV, NAS, NIV, RSV, TEV*

Trȳ·phae'nà   trigh FEE nuh   *NAS, RSV*

Trȳ·phē'nà   trigh FEE nuh   *KJV, NIV*

Trȳ·phō'sà   trigh FOH suh   *KJV, NAS, NIV, RSV, TEV*

Tū'băl   TYOO buhl   *KJV, NAS, NIV, RSV, TEV*

Tū'băl-cain   TYOO buhl-kayn   *KJV, NAS, NIV, RSV, TEV*

Tȳch'ǐ·cŭs   TIK ih kuhs   *KJV, NAS, NIV, RSV, TEV*

Tȳ·răn'nŭs   tigh RAN uhs   *KJV, NAS, NIV, RSV, TEV*

Tȳre   TIGHR   *KJV, NAS, NIV, RSV, TEV*

Tȳr'ǐ·an   TIHR ih uhn, TIGH rih uhn   *NAS, NIV, RSV*

Tȳ'rŭs   TIGH ruhs   *KJV*

Ū'căl   YOO kal   *KJV, NAS, NIV, RSV*

Ū'ĕl   YOO el   *KJV, NAS, NIV, RSV, TEV*

Ū'lai   YOO ligh, YOO lay igh   *KJV, NAS, NIV, RSV, TEV*

Ū'lăm   YOO lam   *KJV, NAS, NIV, RSV, TEV*

Ŭl'là   UHL uh   *KJV, NAS, NIV, RSV, TEV*

Ŭm'mah   UHM uh   *KJV, NAS, NIV, RSV, TEV*

Ŭn'nī   UHN igh   *KJV, NAS, NIV, RSV, TEV*

Ŭn'nō   UHN oh   *KJV, RSV, TEV*

Ū·phär'sĭn   yoo FAR sin   *KJV, NAS*

Ū'phăz   YOO faz   *KJV, NAS, NIV, RSV, TEV*

Ŭr   UR   *KJV, NAS, NIV, RSV, TEV*

Ŭr'băne   UR bayn   *KJV*

Ŭr·bā'nŭs   ur BAY nuhs   *KJV, NAS, NIV, RSV, TEV*

Ū'rī   YOO righ   *KJV, NAS, NIV, RSV, TEV*

Ū·rī'ah   yoo RIGH uh   *KJV, NAS, NIV, RSV, TEV*

Ū·rī'às   yoo RIGH uhs   *KJV*

Ū'rī·ĕl   YOO rih el   *KJV, NAS, NIV, RSV, TEV*

Ū·rī'jah   yoo RIGH juh   *KJV, NAS*

Ū'rĭm   YOO rim   *KJV, NAS, NIV, RSV, TEV*

Ū'thai   YOO thigh, YOO thay igh   *KJV, NAS, NIV, RSV, TEV*

Ŭz   UHZ   *KJV, NAS, NIV, RSV, TEV*

Ū'zai   YOO zigh, YOO zay igh   *KJV, NAS, NIV, RSV, TEV*

Ū'zăl   YOO zal   *KJV, NAS, NIV, RSV, TEV*

Ŭz'zà   UHZ uh   *KJV, NAS, NIV, RSV, TEV*

Ŭz'zah   UHZ zuh   *KJV, NAS, NIV, RSV, TEV*

Ŭz'zĕn-shē'ė·rah   UHZ zihn-SHEE ih ruh   *NAS, NIV, RSV, TEV*

Ŭz′zĕn-shē′rah   UHZ uhn-SHEE ruh
KJV

Ŭz′zī   UHZ zigh   *KJV, NAS, NIV, RSV, TEV*

Ŭz·zī′à (Ŭz·zī′ah)   uh ZIGH uh   *KJV, NAS, NIV, RSV, TEV*

Ŭz′zĭ·ĕl   UHZ ih uhl   *KJV, NAS, NIV, RSV, TEV*

Ŭz·zĭ-ē′līte   uhz ih EE light   *KJV, NAS, NIV, RSV, TEV*

Xĕr′xēş   ZURK seez   *NIV, TEV*

Vā′hĕb   VAY heb   *KJV*

Vaî′zå·thà   VIGH zuh thuh   *NAS, NIV, RSV, TEV*

Vå·jĕz′å·thà   vuh JEZ uh thuh, vaj uh ZAY thuh   *KJV*

Vå·nī′ah   vuh NIGH uh   *KJV, NAS, NIV, RSV, TEV*

Văsh′nī   VASH nigh   *KJV*

Văsh′tī   VASH tigh   *KJV, NAS, NIV, RSV, TEV*

Vē′dan   VEE duhn   *NAS*

Vŏph′sī   VAHF sigh   *KJV, NAS, NIV, RSV, TEV*

Yäh′wĕh   YAH weh, (AD oh nigh)   *NIV*

Yau′dī   YAW dih (Judah)   *NIV*

Yī′ron   YIGH ruhn   *NAS, RSV, TEV*

Zā′å·nā′ĭm   ZAY uh NAY im   *KJV, TEV*

Zā′å·năn   ZAY uh nan   *KJV, NAS, NIV, RSV, TEV*

Zā′å·năn′nĭm   ZAY uh NAN im   *KJV, NAS, NIV, RSV, TEV*

Zā′å·văn   ZAY uh van   *KJV, NAS, NIV, RSV, TEV*

Zā′băd   ZAY bad   *KJV, NAS, NIV, RSV, TEV*

Zăb′baì   ZAB igh, ZAB ay igh   *KJV, NAS, NIV, RSV, TEV*

Zăb′bŭd   ZAB uhd   *KJV, NAS, TEV*

Zăb′dī   ZAB digh   *KJV, NAS, NIV, RSV, TEV*

Wä′dī   WAH dih   *NAS, NIV*

Wä′hĕb   WA heb   *NAS, NIV, RSV, TEV*

Zăb′dĭ·ĕl   ZAB dih el   *KJV, NAS, NIV, RSV, TEV*

Zā′bŭd   ZAY buhd   *KJV, NAS, NIV, RSV, TEV*

Zăb′ū·lŏn   ZAB yoo lahn   *KJV*

Zăc′cā·ī   ZAK ay igh, zak AY igh   *KJV, NAS, NIV, RSV, TEV*

Zăc·chāē′ŭs   za KEE uhs   *KJV, NIV, RSV, TEV*

Zăc·chē′ŭs   za KEE uhs   *NAS*

Zăc′cŭr (Zăc′chŭr)   ZAK ur   *KJV, NAS, NIV, RSV, TEV*

Zăch·â·rī′ah   zak uh RIGH uh   *KJV*

Zăch·â·rī′ăs   zak uh RIGH uhs   *KJV, NAS*

Zā′chēr   ZAY kur   *KJV*

Zā′dŏk   ZAY dahk   *KJV, NAS, NIV, RSV, TEV*

Zā′dŏk·ītes   ZAY dahk ights   *NIV*

Zā′hăm   ZAY ham   *KJV, NAS, NIV, RSV, TEV*

Zā′här   ZAY hahr   *NIV*

Zā′ĭr   ZAY ir   *KJV, NAS, NIV, RSV, TEV*

Zā′lăph   ZAY laf   *KJV, NAS, NIV, RSV, TEV*

Zăl′mon   ZAL muhn   *KJV, NAS, NIV, RSV, TEV*

Zăl·mō′nah   zal MOH nuh   *KJV, NAS, NIV, RSV, TEV*

Zăl·mŭn′nà   zal MUHN uh   *KJV, NAS, NIV, RSV, TEV*

Zăm·zŭm′mĭm   zam ZUM im   *KJV, NAS, RSV, TEV*

Zăm·zŭm′mītes   zam ZUHM mights   *NIV*

Za·năn′nim   zuh NAN ihm, za NAN ihm   *TEV*

Ză·nō′ah   za NO uh   *KJV, NAS, NIV, RSV, TEV*

Zăph′năth-păn·ē′ah   zaf EE nath-pan EE uh   *KJV, NAS, NIV, RSV, TEV*

Zăph′năth-pā·â·nē′ah   ZAF nath-pay uh NEE uh   *KJV, TEV*

Zā′phŏn   ZAY fahn   *KJV, NAS, NIV, RSV, TEV*

Zā′rà   ZAY ruh (Zā′rah)   *KJV*

Zā′rĕ·ah   ZAY rih uh, zuh REE uh   *KJV*

Zā′rĕ·âth·īte   ZAY rih uhth ight, zuh REE uh thight   *KJV*

Zā′rĕd   ZAY red   *KJV*

Zăr′ĕ·phăth   ZAR ih fath   *KJV, NAS, NIV, RSV, TEV*

Zâr′ĕ·tăn   ZER uh tan   *KJV*

Zăr′ĕ·thăn   ZAR ih than, ZER ih than   *KJV, NAS, NIV, RSV, TEV*

Zā′rĕth-shā′här   ZAY reth-SHAY hahr   *KJV*

Zär′hīte   ZAHR hight   *KJV*

Zăr′tà·nah   ZAR tuh nuh, zahr TAY nuh   *KJV*

Zär′thăn   ZAHR than   *KJV*

Zăt′thū   ZAT thoo   *KJV*

Zăt′tū   ZAT yoo   *KJV, NAS, NIV, RSV, TEV*

Zā′văn   ZAY van   *KJV*

Zā′zà   ZAY zuh   *KJV, NAS, NIV, RSV, TEV*

Zĕ′al·ot   ZEHL uht   *NAS, NIV, RSV*

Zĕb·â·dī′ah   zeb uh DIGH uh   *KJV, NAS, NIV, RSV, TEV*

Zē′bah   ZEE buh   *KJV, NAS, NIV, RSV, TEV*

Zĕ·bā′im   zih BAY im   *KJV*

Zĕb′e·dēē   ZEB uh dee   *KJV, NAS, NIV, RSV, TEV*

Zĕ·bī′dah   zih BIGH duh, ZEB ih duh   *KJV, NAS, NIV, RSV, TEV*

Zĕ·bī′nà   zih BIGH nuh   *KJV, NAS, NIV, RSV, TEV*

Zĕ·boì′ĭm   zih BOY im   *KJV, NAS, NIV, RSV, TEV*

Zĕ·bō′ĭm   zih BOH im   *KJV, NAS, NIV, RSV*

Zĕ·bū′dah   zih BYOO duh   *KJV*

Zē′bŭl   ZEE buhl   *KJV, NAS, NIV, RSV, TEV*

Zĕb′ū·lŏn·īte   ZEB yoo lahn ight   *KJV*

Zĕb′ū·lŭn   ZEB yoo luhn   *KJV, NAS, NIV, RSV, TEV*

Zĕb′ū·lŭn·īte   ZEB yoo luhn ight   *KJV, NAS, NIV, RSV*

Zĕch·â·rī′ah   zek uh RIGH uh   *KJV, NAS, NIV, RSV, TEV*

Zē′chēr   ZEE kur   *KJV, NAS, RSV, TEV*

Zē′dăd   ZEE dad   *KJV, NAS, NIV, RSV, TEV*

Zĕd·ē·kī′ah   zed uh KIGH uh   *KJV, NAS, NIV, RSV, TEV*

Zē′ĕb   ZEE eb   *KJV, NAS, NIV, RSV, TEV*

Zē′kēr   ZEE kuhr   *NIV*

Zē′lah (Zē′là)   ZEE luh   *KJV, NAS, NIV, RSV, TEV*

Zē′lĕk   ZEE lek   *KJV, NAS, NIV, RSV, TEV*

Zĕ·lō′phĕ·hăd   zih LOH fih had   *KJV, NAS, NIV, RSV, TEV*

Zĕ·lō·tĕş   zih LOH teez   *KJV*

Zĕl′zah   ZEL zuh   *KJV, NAS, NIV, RSV,*

TEV

Zĕm′a̍·rā′ĭm   zem uh RAY im   *KJV,*
NAS, NIV, RSV, TEV

Zĕm′a̍·rīte   ZEM uh right   *KJV, NAS,*
NIV, RSV, TEV

Zē′mȇr   ZEE mihr   *RSV*

Zĕ·mī′ra̍   zih MIGH ruh   *KJV*

Zĕ·mī′rah   zih MIGH ruh   *NAS, NIV,*
RSV, TEV

Zē′năn   ZEE nan   *KJV, NAS, NIV, RSV,*
TEV

Zē′na̍s   ZEE nuhs   *KJV, NAS, NIV, RSV,*
TEV

Zĕph·a̍·nī′ah   zef uh NIGH uh   *KJV,*
NAS, NIV, RSV, TEV

Zē′phăth   ZEE fath   *KJV, NAS, NIV, RSV,*
TEV

Zĕph′a̍·thah   ZEF uh thuh   *KJV, NAS,*
NIV, RSV, TEV

Zē′phī   ZEE figh   *KJV, NAS, RSV, TEV*

Zē′phō   ZEE foh   *KJV, NAS, NIV, RSV,*
TEV

Zē′phŏn   ZEE fahn   *KJV, NAS, NIV, RSV,*
TEV

Zē′phŏn·īte   ZEE fahn ight   *KJV, NAS,*
NIV, RSV

Zēr   ZUR   *KJV, NAS, NIV, RSV, TEV*

Zē′rah   ZEE ruh   *KJV, NAS, NIV, RSV,*
TEV

Zĕr·a̍·hī′ah   zer uh HIGH uh   *KJV, NAS,*
NIV, RSV, TEV

Zē′ra̍·hīte   ZEE ruh hight   *KJV, NAS,*
NIV, RSV

Zē′rĕd   ZEE red   *KJV, NAS, NIV, RSV,*
TEV

Zĕr′ĕ·dà(h)   ZER ih duh, ze REE duh
KJV, NAS, NIV, RSV, TEV

Zĕr·ĕ·dā′thah   zer uh DAY thuh, zih
RED uh thuh   *KJV*

Zĕr′ĕ·rah   ZER uh ruh   *NAS, NIV, RSV*

Zĕr′ĕ·răth   ZER ih rath   *KJV*

Zē′rĕsh   ZEE resh   *KJV, NAS, NIV, RSV,*
TEV

Zē′rĕth   ZEE reth   *KJV, NAS, NIV, RSV,*
TEV

Zē′rĕth-shā′här   ZEE reth-SHAY hahr,
ZER eth-SHAY hahr   *KJV, NAS,*
NIV, RSV, TEV

Zē′rī   ZEE righ   *KJV, NAS, NIV, RSV,*
TEV

Zē′rôr   ZEE rawr   *KJV, NAS, NIV, RSV,*
TEV

Zĕ·rū′ah   ze ROO uh   *KJV, NAS, NIV,*
RSV, TEV

Zĕ·rŭb′ba̍·bĕl   zuh RUHB uh buhl   *KJV,*
NAS, NIV, RSV, TEV

Zĕr·u̍·ī′ah   zer uh IGH uh   *KJV, NAS,*
NIV, RSV, TEV

Zē′thăm   ZEE tham   *KJV, NAS, NIV,*
RSV, TEV

Zē′thăn   ZEE than   *KJV, NAS, NIV, RSV,*
TEV

Zē′thär   ZEE thahr   *KJV, NAS, NIV, RSV,*
TEV

Zeūs   ZOOS   *NAS, NIV, RSV, TEV*

Zī′à   ZIGH uh   *KJV, NAS, NIV, RSV, TEV*

Zī′bà   ZIGH buh   *KJV, NAS, NIV, RSV,*
TEV

Zĭb′ĕ·on   ZIB ih uhn   *KJV, NAS, NIV,*
RSV, TEV

Zĭb′ĭ·à(h)   ZIB ih uh, ZIGH bih uh   *KJV,*
NAS, NIV, RSV, TEV

Zĭch′rī   ZIK righ   *KJV, NAS, RSV, TEV*

Zĭc′rī   ZIK righ   *NIV*

Zĭd′dĭm   ZID im   *KJV, NAS, NIV, RSV,*
TEV

Zĭd·kī′jah   zid KIGH juh   *KJV*

Zī′don   ZIGH duhn   *KJV*

Zī·dō′nĭ·an   zigh DOH nih uhn   *KJV*

Zĭf   ZIF   *KJV*

Zī′hà   ZIGH huh   *KJV, NAS, NIV, RSV,*
TEV

Zĭk′lăg̱   ZIK lag   *KJV, NAS, NIV, RSV,*
TEV

Zĭl′lah   ZIL uh   *KJV, NAS, NIV, RSV, TEV*

Zĭl′lĕ·thaı̍   ZIHL lih thigh   *KJV, NAS,*
NIV, RSV, TEV

Zĭl′pah   ZIL puh   *KJV, NAS, NIV, RSV,*
TEV

Zĭl′thaı̍   ZIL thigh   *KJV*

Zĭm′mah   ZIM uh   *KJV, NAS, NIV, RSV,*
TEV

Zĭm′nah   ZIHM nuh   *TEV*

Zĭm′răn   ZIM ran   *KJV, NAS, NIV, RSV,*
TEV

Zĭm′rī   ZIM righ   *KJV, NAS, NIV, RSV,*
TEV

Zĭn   ZIN   *KJV, NAS, NIV, RSV, TEV*

Zī′nà   ZIGH nuh   *KJV, NAS, RSV, TEV*

Zī′on   ZIGH uhn   *KJV, NAS, NIV, RSV,*
TEV

Zī′ôr   ZIGH awr   *KJV, NAS, NIV, RSV,*
TEV

Zĭph   ZIF   *KJV, NAS, NIV, RSV, TEV*

Zī′phah   ZIGH fuh   *KJV, NAS, NIV, RSV,*
TEV

Zĭph′ĭms   ZIF ims   *KJV*

Zĭph′ĭ·ŏn   ZIF ih ahn   *KJV, NAS, RSV*
Zĭph′ītes   ZIF ights   *KJV, NAS, NIV, RSV*
Zĭph′rŏn   ZIF rahn   *KJV, NAS, NIV, RSV, TEV*
Zĭp′pôr   ZIP pawr   *KJV, NAS, NIV, RSV, TEV*
Zĭp·pō′rah   zip POH ruh, ZIP oh ruh   *KJV, NAS, NIV, RSV, TEV*
Zĭth′rī   ZITH righ   *KJV*
Zĭv   ZIV   *KJV, NAS, NIV, RSV, TEV*
Zĭz   ZIZ   *KJV, NAS, NIV, RSV, TEV*
Zī′zà (Zī′zah)   ZIGH zuh   *KJV, NAS, NIV, RSV, TEV*
Zō′ăn   ZOH an   *KJV, NAS, NIV, RSV, TEV*
Zō′àr   ZOH ur   *KJV, NAS, NIV, RSV, TEV*
Zō′bà (Zō′bah)   ZOH buh   *KJV, NAS, NIV, RSV, TEV*
Zō·bē′bah   zoh BEE buh   *KJV, NAS, RSV, TEV*
Zō′här   ZOH hahr   *KJV, NAS, NIV, RSV, TEV*
Zō′hē·lĕth   ZOH huh leth   *KJV, NAS, NIV*
Zō′hĕth   ZOH heth   *KJV, NAS, NIV, RSV, TEV*
Zō′phah   ZOH fuh   *KJV, NAS, NIV, RSV, TEV*

Zō′phaì   ZOH figh   *KJV, NAS, NIV, RSV, TEV*
Zō′phär   ZOH fahr   *KJV, NAS, NIV, RSV, TEV*
Zō′phĭm   ZOH fim   *KJV, NAS, NIV, RSV, TEV*
Zō′rah   ZOH ruh   *KJV, NAS, NIV, RSV, TEV*
Zō′răth′īte   ZOH rath ight   *KJV, NAS, NIV, RSV*
Zō′rīte   ZOH right   *KJV, NAS, NIV, RSV, TEV*
Zō·rŏb′à·bĕl   zoh RAHB uh buhl   *KJV*
Zū′àr   ZYOO ur   *KJV, NAS, NIV, RSV, TEV*
Zŭph   ZUHF   *KJV, NAS, NIV, RSV, TEV*
Zū′phīte   ZOO fight   *NIV*
Zŭr   ZUR   *KJV, NAS, NIV, RSV, TEV*
Zū′rĭ·ĕl   ZOO rih el   *KJV, NAS, NIV, RSV, TEV*
Zū′rĭ-shăd′dā·ī   ZOO rih-SHAD ay igh   *KJV, NAS, NIV, RSV, TEV*
Zū′zims (Zū′zĭm)   ZOO zims   *KJV, NAS, RSV, TEV*
Zū′zītes   ZOO zights   *NIV*

287

Distinctives
of
Versions and Translations

The following paragraphs on each of the versions included in this handbook seek only to define or indicate distinctives. In no way are these descriptions intended to be exhaustive or persuasive. Each version has been chosen for this book because of its continued or expected popularity among students of the Bible.

King James Version

When Queen Elizabeth of England died in 1603, the crown passed to a Scottish king, James I. Shortly after arriving in England, he called together a conference of churchmen and theologians for the purpose of "hearing and determining things pretended to be amiss in the Church." Only one notable resolution came: "That a translation be made of the whole Bible, as consonant as can be to the original Hebrew and Greek, and this to be set out and printed, without any marginal notes, and only to be used in all churches of England in time of divine service."

King James remarked, "I wish some special pains were taken from an uniform translation, which should be done by the best-learned men in both Universities, then reviewed by the Bishops, presented to the Privy Council, lastly ratified by Royal authority, to be read in the whole Church, and none other."

Six panels of translators, forty-seven scholars in all, had the work divided among them with rather strict guidelines concerning ecclesiastical words, common usage of proper names, chapter and verse divisions, and other matters. After proceeding on the course laid out by King James, the version which we now know with his name attached was published in 1611. It is commonly called the Authorized Version. The new version bore the title:

> "The Holy Bible, conteyning the Old Testament and the New: Newly Translated out of the Originall tongues, with the former Translations diligently compared and revised, by his Majesties speciall commandement. Appointed to be read in Churches. Imprinted in London by Robert Barker, Printer to the Kings most Excellent Majestie, Anno Domini 1611." [1]

New American Standard Bible

The producers of the NASB were imbued with the conviction that interest in the American Standard Version, first published in 1901, should

[1] *The English Bible,* A History of Translations, by F. F. Bruce. Oxford University Press, New York, 1961, pages 93-96.

be renewed and increased. They labored with prayerful seriousness to this end. They cited the following reasons why this new translation project should be undertaken:

- The American Standard Version of 1901 has been in a very real sense the standard for many translations.

- It is a monumental product of applied scholarship, assiduous labor and thorough procedure.

- It has enjoyed universal endorsement as a trustworthy translation of the original text.

- The British and American organizations were governed by rules of procedure which assured accuracy in the completed work.

- The American Standard Version, itself a revision of the 1881-1885 edition, is the product of international collaboration, invaluable for perspective, accuracy, and finesse.

- Unlike many modern translations of the Scriptures, the American Standard Version retains its acceptability for pulpit reading and for personal memorization.

Perhaps the most important reason for this undertaking was a disturbing awareness that the American Standard Version of 1901 was fast disappearing from the scene. A generation unacquainted with this great work had come into being. Recognizing its responsibility, The Lockman Foundation felt an urgency to preserve this noble translation as a heritage for coming generations. The complete text of this translation was released and published in 1971.

New International Version

The New International Version is a completely new translation of the Holy Bible made by more than one hundred scholars working directly from the best available Hebrew, Aramaic, and Greek texts. It had its beginning after several years of exploratory study by committees from the Christian Reformed Church and the National Association of Evangelicals. Finally, a group of scholars met at Palos Heights, Illinois, in 1965 and concurred in the need for a new translation of the Bible in contemporary English. This group, though not made up of official church representatives, was transdenominational. Its recommendation for a new translation was endorsed by a large number of leaders from many denominations who met in Chicago the next year.

Responsibility for the new version was delegated to a self-governing body of fifteen, the Committee on Bible Translation, composed mainly of

292

biblical scholars. In 1967 the New York Bible Society undertook the financial sponsorship of the project. This made it possible to enlist the help of many distinguished scholars. They were drawn from many denominations to help safeguard the translation from sectarian bias.

From the beginning of the project, the Committee on Bible Translation held to certain goals for the New International Version: It was projected as an accurate translation, one that would have clarity and literary quality and so prove suitable for public and private reading, teaching, preaching, memorizing, and liturgical use. The Committee also sought to preserve some measure of continuity with the long tradition of translating the Scriptures into English.

In working toward these goals, the translators were united in their commitment to the authority and infallibility of the Bible as God's Word in written form. They worked under the conviction that the Bible contains the divine answer to the deepest needs of humanity, that it sheds unique light on our path in a dark world, and that it sets forth the way to our eternal well-being.

Revised Standard Version

The Revised Standard Version of the Bible is an authorized revision of the American Standard Version, published in 1901, which was a revision of the King James Version, published in 1611. In the early 1930s the International Council of Religious Education appointed a committee to investigate whether further revision of the 1901 text was necessary. For more than two years the Committee worked on the problem. They decided there was a need for a thorough revision which would stay as close as possible to the Tyndale King James tradition, in light of present knowledge of Hebrew and Greek texts.

In 1937 the revision was authorized by vote of the Council, which directed that the resulting version should "embody the best results of modern scholarship as to the meaning of the Scriptures, and express this meaning in English diction which is designed for use in public and private worship and preserves those qualities which have given to the King James Version a supreme place in English literature."

Thirty-two scholars served as members of the committee charged with making the revision. They secured the review and counsel of an advisory board of fifty representatives of the cooperating denominations. The committee worked in two sections, one dealing with the Old Testament and one with the New Testament. Each section submitted its work for scrutiny by members of the other section. All changes had to be agreed upon by a two-thirds vote of the total membership of the committee. The New Testament in this version was published in 1946. The publication of the entire Revised

Standard Version of the Bible was authorized by vote of the National Council of the Churches of Christ in the U.S.A. in 1951.

Today's English Version

The Bible in Today's English Version is a new translation which seeks to state clearly and accurately the meaning of the original texts in words and forms that are widely accepted by people who speak English. This translation, published in 1966 (N.T.) and 1976 (O.T. & N.T.), does not follow the traditional vocabulary and style found in the historic English Bible versions. It attempts to express the Bible's content and message in a standard, everyday, natural form of English.

The Bible in Today's English Version (Good News Bible) was translated and published by the United States Bible Societies for use throughout the world. The primary concern of the translators was to provide a faithful translation which expresses the meaning of the Hebrew, Aramaic, and Greek texts. They tried to avoid words and forms not in current or widespread use. Every effort was made to use language that was natural, clear, simple, and unambiguous. Such biblical terms as hours of the day, weights and measures, distances, and area are rendered in their modern English equivalents. When a person or place is called by two or more different names in the original, this translation normally uses only the more familiar name.

The Bible Societies trust that English-speaking people everywhere will find increased understanding of the Bible through reading and studying this translation.

Notes